The Principle of Complementarity in International Criminal Law

Mohamed M. El Zeidy
Biography

Mohamed M. El Zeidy holds a Ph.D. in International Law (2007) and an LL.M. in International Human Rights Law (2001) from the Irish Centre for Human Rights, National University of Ireland, Galway. He also holds an LL.M. in Public Law (1999) from Cairo University, a Licence en Droit and Bachelor of Police Sciences (1993) from the Police College in Cairo. He served as a Judge, Senior Public Prosecutor and Public Prosecutor at the Egyptian Ministry of Justice (1997-2007). He is a member of the Egyptian Society of Criminal Law and the International Association of Penal Law. He has published widely in the area of International Criminal Law. He is currently a Legal Officer at the Pre-Trial Division of the International Criminal Court. This work was finalised prior to the current employment at the ICC. The views expressed in it do not necessarily reflect those of the International Criminal Court or the Egyptian Ministry of Justice.

The Principle of Complementarity in International Criminal Law: Origin, Development and Practice

by

Mohamed M. El Zeidy

MARTINUS NIJHOFF PUBLISHERS

LEIDEN • BOSTON
2008

This book is printed on acid-free paper.

ISBN: 978 90 04 16693 6

Koninklijke Brill NV incorporates the imprints Brill, Hotei Publishers, IDC Publishers, Martinus Nijhoff Publishers and VSP.

http://www.brill.nl

Typeset by *jules guldenmund layout & text,* The Hague

PRINTED IN THE NETHERLANDS.

Table of Contents

Table of Cases

The *Ad hoc* Tribunals

Prosecutor v. Duško Tadić, Case No. (IT-94-1-AR72), Decision on the Defence Motion for Interlocutory Appeal on Jurisdiction, 2/10/1995

Prosecutor v. Duško Tadić , Case No. (IT-94-1-T), Decision on the Defence Motion on the Principle of *Non Bis In Idem,* 14/11/1995

Prosecutor v. Duško Tadić A/K/A "Dule", Case No. (IT-94-1-T), Decision on the Defence Motion on Jurisdiction, 10/08/1995

Prosecutor v. Duško Tadić, Case No. (IT-94-1-T), Sentencing Judgment, 14/07/1997

Prosecutor v. Duško Tadić, Case No. (IT-94-1-T*bis*-R117), Sentencing Judgment, 11/11/1999

Prosecutor v. Duško Tadić, Case No. (IT-94-1-A and IT-94-1-A*bis*), Judgment in Sentencing Appeal, 26/01/2000

Prosecutor v. Duško Tadić, Case No. (94-1-A-R77), Judgment on Allegations of Contempt Against Prior Counsel, Milan Vujin, 31/01/2000

Prosecutor v. Alfred Musema, Case No. (ICTR-96-5-D), Decision on the Formal Request for Deferral Presented by the Prosecutor, 12/03/1996

Prosecutor v. André Rwamakuba, Case No. (ICTR-98-44C-PT), Decision on Defence Motion for Stay of Proceedings *Article 20 of the Statute,* 3/06/2005

Prosecutor v. Anto Furundžija, Case No. (IT-95-17/1-A), Judgment 21/07/ 2000

Prosecutor v. Bernard Ntuyahaga, Case No. (ICTR-98-40-T), Decision on the Prosecutor's Motion to Withdraw the Indictment, 18/03/1999

Prosecutor v. Milošević, Case No. (IT-02-54), *Decision on Preliminary Motions*, 8/11/2001

Prosecutor v. Dragan Nikolić, Case No. (IT-94-2-A), Sentencing Judgment, 18/12/2003

Prosecutor v. Dragan Nikolić, Case No. (IT-94-2-A), Judgment on Sentencing Appeal, 4/02/2005

Prosecutor v. Enver Hadžihasanović Amir Kubura, Case No. (IT-01-47-T), Judgment, 15/03/2006

Prosecutor v. Gojko Jankovic, Case No. (IT-96-23/2-PT), Decision on Referral of Case Under Rule 11 *Bis*, 22/07/2005

Prosecutor v. Gojko Jankovic, Case No. (IT-96-23/2-*AR11bis*.2), Appeals Decision on Rule *11 bis*, 15/11/2005

Prosecutor v. Ivica Rajić, a.k.a. Viktor Andrić, Case No. (IT-95-12-S), Sentencing Judgment, 8/05/2006

Prosecutor v. Joseph Kanyabashi, Case No. (ICTR-96-15-T), Decision on the Defence Motion on Jurisdiction, 18 /06/1997

Prosecutor v. Théoneste Bagosora, Case No. (ICTR-96-7-D), Decision on the Application by the Prosecutor for a Formal Request for Deferral, 17/05/1996

Prosecutor v. Michel Bagaragaza, Case No. (ICTR-2005-86-R11bis), Decision on the Prosecution Motion for Referral to the Kingdom of Norway, *Rule 11* bis *of the Rules of Procedure and Evidence*, 19/05/2006

Prosecutor v. Prosper Mugiraneza, Case No. (ICTR-99-50-AR73), Decision on Prosper Mugiraneza's Interlocutory Appeal from Trial Chamber II Decision of 2 October 2003 Denying the Motion to Dismiss the Indictment, Demand Speedy Trial and for Appropriate Relief, 27/02/2004

Prosecutor v. Michel Bagaragaza, Case No. (ICTR-05-86-*AR11*bis), Decision on Rule 11 *bis* Appeal, 30/08/2006

Prosecutor v. Mrkšić, Šlijvančanin and Radić, Case No. (IT-95-13-R61), 10/12/1998

Prosecutor v. Mucic et al. "Celebici" Case No. (IT-96-21-T*bis*-R117), Sentencing Judgment, 9/10/2001

Prosecutor v. Mucic et al. "Celebici" Case No. (IT-96-21-T), Judgment, 16/11/1998

Prosecutor v. Radio Television Libre des Mille Collines SARL, Case No. (ICTR-96-6-D), Decision on the Formal Request for Deferral Presented by the Prosecutor, 12/03/1996

Prosecutor v. Radislav Krstic, Case No. (IT-98-33-T), Judgment, 02/08/2001

Prosecutor v. Radovan Stankovic, Case No. (IT-96-23/2-PT), Decision on Referral of Case Under Rule 11 *bis* Partly Confidential and *Ex Parte*, 17/05/2005

Prosecutor v. Rahim Ademi and Mirko Norac, Case No. (IT-04-78-PT), Decision for Referral to the Authorities of the Republic of Croatia Pursuant to Rule *11 bis*, 14/09/2005

Prosecutor v. Re: Republic Of Macedonia, Case No. (IT-02-55-MISC.6), Decision on the *Prosecutor's Request* for Deferral and Motion for Order to the Former Yugoslav Republic of Macedonia, 4/10/2002

Prosecutor v. Moinina Fofana et al., Case No. (SCSL-04-14-PT), Decision on the Preliminary Defence Motion on the Lack of Personal Jurisdiction filed on Behalf of Accused Fofana, 3/03/2004

Prosecutor v. Sam Hinga Norman, Case No. (SCSL-2004-14-AR72 (E)), Decision on Preliminary Motion Based on Lack of Jurisdiction (Judicial Independence), 13/03/2004

Prosecutor v. Sam Hinga Norman, Case No. (SCSL-2004-14-AR72 (E)), Decision on Preliminary Motion Based on Lack of Jurisdiction (Judicial Independence), Separate Opinion of Justice Geoffrey Robertson, 13/03/2004

Prosecutor v. Sam Hinga Norman, Case No. (SCSL-2004-14-AR72 (E)), Decision on Preliminary Motion Based on Lack of Jurisdiction (Child Recruitment), (Dissenting Opinion of Justice Robertson), 31/05/2004

Prosecutor v. Samuel Hinga Norman, Case No. (SCSL-2003-08-PT), Decision on the Defence Preliminary Motion on Lack of Jurisdiction: Command Responsibility, 15/10/ 2003

Prosecutor v. Tihomir Blaskic, Case No. (IT-95-14-AR108*bis*), Judgment on the Request of the Republic of Croatia for Review of the Decision of Trial Chamber II of 18 July 1997, 29/10/1997

Prosecutor v. Vladimir Kovačević, Case No. (IT-01-42/2-I), Decision on Referral of Case Pursuant to Rule 11 *Bis With Confidential and Partly Ex Parte Annexes*, 17/11/2006

Prosecutor v. Zeljko Mejakic, Momcilo Gruban, Dusan Fustar, Dusko Knezevic, Case No. (IT-02-65-PT), Decision on Prosecutor's Motion for Referral of a Case pursuant to Rule 11 *Bis*, 20/07/2005

Prosecutor v. Zlatko Aleksovski, Case No. (IT-95-14/1-AR77), Judgment on Appeal by Anto Nobilo Against Finding of Contempt, 30/05/2001

The European Court of Human Rights

Abdoella v. The Netherlands, Application No. 12728/87, Eur. Ct. H.R., Judgment (Merits and Just Satisfaction) of 25/11/1992

Akkoc v. Turkey, Application Nos. 22947/93, 22948/93, Eur. Ct. H.R., Judgment (Merits and Just Satisfaction) of 10/10/2000

Aksoy v. Turkey (1), Application No. 21987/93, Eur. Ct. H.R., Judgment (Merits and Just Satisfaction) of 18/12/1996

Angelucci v. Italy, Application No. 12666/87, Eur. Ct. H.R., Judgment (Merits and Just Satisfaction) of 19/02/1991

Anguelova v. Bulgaria, Application No. 38361/97, Eur. Ct. H.R., Judgment (Merits and Just Satisfaction) of 13/06/2002

Ashingdane v. The United Kingdom, Eur. Ct. H.R., Judgment (Merits and Just Satisfaction) of 28/05/1985

Avsar v. Turkey, Application No. 25657/94, Eur. Ct. H.R., Judgment (Merits and Just Satisfaction) of 10/07/2001

Baischer v. Austria, Application No. 32381/96, Eur. Ct. H.R., Judgment (Merits and Just Satisfaction) of 20/12/2001

Barberà, Messegué and Jabardo v. Spain, Application No. 10590/83, Eur. Ct. H.R., Judgment (Merits) of 06/12/1988

Brannigan and McBride v. The United Kingdom, Application No. 4553/89; 14554/89, Eur. Ct. H.R., Judgment (Merits) of 25/05/1993

Buchholz v. Germany, Application No. 7759/77, Eur. Ct. H.R., Judgment (Merits) of 6/05/1981

Buscemi v. Italy, Application No. 29569/95, Eur. Ct. H.R., Judgment (Merits and just Satisfaction) of 16/09/1999

Calleja v. Malta, Application No. 75274/01, Eur. Ct. H.R., Judgment (Merits and Just Satisfaction) of 7/04/2005

Campbell and Fell v. The United Kingdom, Application No. 7819/77; 7878/77, Eur. Ct. H.R., Judgment (Merits and Just Satisfaction) of 28/06/1984

Castillo Algar v. Spain, Application No. 28194/95, Eur. Ct. H.R., Judgment (Merits) of 28/10/1998

Chyb v. Poland, Application No. 20838/02, Eur. Ct. H.R., Judgment (Merits and Just Satisfaction) of 22/08/2006

Corigliano v. Italy, Application No. 8304/78, Eur. Ct. H.R., Judgment (Merits and Just Satisfaction) of 10/12/1982

De Cubber v. Belgium, Application No. 9186/80, Eur. Ct. H.R., Judgment (Merits) of 26/10/1984

Demicoli v. Malta, Application No. 13057/87, Eur. Ct. H.R., Judgment (Merits and Just Satisfaction) of 27/08/1991

Depiets v. France, Application No. 53971/00, Eur. Ct. H.R., Judgment (Merits) of 10/02/2004

Deweer v. Belgium, Application No. 6903/75, Eur. Ct. H.R., Judgment (Merits and Just Satisfaction) of 27/02/1980

Di Pede v. Italy, Application No. 15797/89, Eur. Ct. H.R., Judgment (Merits and Just Satisfaction) of 26/09/1996

Eckle v. Germany, Application No. (8130/78), Eur. Ct. H.R., Judgment (Merits) of 15/07/1982

Engel and Others v. The Netherlands, Application Nos. 5100/71; 5101/71; 5102/71; 5354/72; 5370/72, Eur. Ct. H.R., Judgment (Merits) of 8/06/1976

Ergi v. Turkey Application No. 23818/94, Eur. Ct. H.R., Judgment (Merits and just Satisfaction) of 28/07/1998

Fehr v. Austria, Application No. 19247/02, Eur. Ct. H.R., Judgment (Merits and just Satisfaction) of 3/02/2005

Ferarantelliand Santangelo v. Italy, Application No. 19874/92, Eur. Ct. H.R., Judgment (Merits and Just Satisfaction) of 07/08/1996

Finucane v. The United Kingdom, Application No. 29178/95, Eur. Ct. H.R., Judgment (Merits and Just Satisfaction) of 1/07/2003

G.W. v. The United Kingdom Application No. 34155/96, Eur. Ct. H.R., Judgment (Merits and Just Satisfaction) of 15/06/2004

Grieves v. The United Kingdom, Application No. 57067/00, Eur. Ct. H.R., Judgment (Merits and just Satisfaction) of 16/12/2003

H. v. France, Application No. 10073/82, Eur. Ct. H.R., Judgment (Merits and Just Satisfaction) of 24/10/1989

Hagert v. Finland , Application No. 14724/02, Eur. Ct. H.R., Judgment (Merits and Just Satisfaction) of 17/01/2006

Hauschildt v. Denmark, Application No. 10486/83, Eur. Ct. H.R., Judgment (Merits and Just Satisfaction) of 24/05/1989

Hornsby v. Greece (1), Application No. 18357/91, Eur. Ct. H.R., Judgment (Merits) of 19/03/1997

Hugh Jordan v. The United Kingdom, Application No. 24746/94, Eur. Ct. H.R., Judgment (Merits and Just Satisfaction) of 4/05/2001

Ireland v. The United Kingdom, Application No. 5310/71, Eur. Ct. H.R., Judgment (Merits and Just Satisfaction) of 18/01/1978

Khashiyev and Akayeva v. Russia, Application Nos. 57942/00 and 57945/00, Eur. Ct. H.R., Judgment (Merits and Just satisfaction) of 24/02/2005

Kismir v. Turkey, Application No. 27306/95, Eur. Ct. H.R., Judgment (Merits and Just Satisfaction) of 31/05/2005

Klamecki v. Poland , Application No. 25415/94, Eur. Ct. H.R., Judgment (Merits) of 28/03/2002

König v. Germany, Application No. 6232/73, Eur. Ct. H.R., Judgment (Merits) of 28/06/1978

Kuznetsov v. Ukraine, Application No. 39042/97, Eur. Ct. H.R., Judgment (Merits and Just Satisfaction) of 29/04/2003

Kyprianou v. Cyprus, Application No. 73797/01, Eur. Ct. H.R., Judgment (Merits and Just Satisfaction) of 15/12/2005

Labita v. Italy Application No. 26772/95, Eur. Ct. H.R., Judgment (Merits and Just Satisfaction) of 6/04/2000

Langborger v. Sweden, Application No. 11179/84, Eur. Ct. H.R., Judgment (Merits and Just Satisfaction) of 22/06/1989

Lavents v. Latvia, Application No. 58442/00, Eur. Ct. H.R., Judgment (Merits and Just Satisfaction) of 28/11/2002)

Majewski v. Poland, Application No. 52690/99, Eur. Ct. H.R., Judgment (Merits and Just Satisfaction) of 11/10/2005

Makaratzis v. Greece, Application No. 50385/99, Eur. Ct. H.R., Judgment (Merits and Just Satisfaction) of 20/12/2004

Matwiejczuk v. Poland, Application No. 37641/97, Eur. Ct. H.R., Judgment (Merits and Just Satisfaction) of 2/12/2003

Matznetter v. Austria, Application No. 2178/64, Eur. Ct. H.R., Judgment (Merits) of 10/11/1969

McCann and Others v. The United kingdom, Application No. 18984/91, Eur. Ct. H.R., Judgment (Merits and Just Satisfaction) of 27/09/1995

McKerr v. The United Kingdom, Application No. 28883/95, Eur. Ct. H.R., Judgment

(Merits and Just Satisfaction) of 04/05/2001

McShane v. The United Kingdom, Application No. 43290/98, Eur. Ct. H.R., Judgment (Merits and Just Satisfaction) of 28/05/2002

Mladen Naletilić v. Croatia, App. No. 51891/99, Eur. Ct. H.R., Decision as to the Admissibility of the Application No. 51891/99, 4 May 2000

Morel v. France, Application No. 34130/96, Eur. Ct.H.R., Judgment (Merits) of 06/06/2000

Multiplex v. Croatia, Application No. 58112/00, Eur. Ct. H.R., Judgment (Merits and Just Satisfaction) of 10/07/2003

Nachova and others v. Bulgaria, Applications Nos. 43577/98 and 43579/98, Eur. Ct. H.R., Judgment of 6/07/2005

Neumeister v. Austria, Application No. 1936/63, Eur. Ct. H.R., Judgment (Merits) of 27/06/1968, para. 19

Öcalan v. Turkey Application No. 46221/99, Eur. Ct. H.R., Judgment (Merits and Just Satisfaction) of 12/03/2003

Palka v. Poland, Application No. 49176/99, Eur. Ct. H.R., Judgment (Merits and Just Satisfaction) of 11/10/2005

Papachelas v. Greece, Application No. 31423/96, Eur. Ct. H.R., Judgment (Merits and Just Satisfaction) of 25/03/1999

Pélissier and Sassi v. France, Application No. 25444/94, Eur. Ct. H.R., Judgment (Merits and Just Satisfaction) of 25/03/1999

Philis v. Greece (no. 2) (1), Application No. 19773/92, Eur. Ct. H.R., Judgment (Merits and Just Satisfaction) of 27/06/1997

Piersack v. Belgium, Application No. 8692/79, Eur. Ct. H.R., Judgment (Merits) of 01/10/1982

Poltoratskiy v. Ukraine, Application No. 38812/97, Eur. Ct. H.R., Judgment (Merits and Just Satisfaction) of 29/04/2003

Puglies v. Italy (No. 1), Application No. 11840/85, Eur. Ct. H.R., Judgment (Merits and Just Satisfaction) of 19/02/1991

Ringeisen v. Austria, Application No. 2614/65, Eur. Ct. H.R., Judgment (Merits) of 16/07/1971

Rylski v. Poland, Application No. 24706/02, Eur. Ct. H.R., Judgment (Merits) of 4/07/2006

Schwarzenberger v. Germany, Application No. 75737/01, Eur. Ct. H.R., Judgment (Merits) of 10/08/2006

Shanaghan v. The United Kingdom, Application No. 37715/97, Eur. Ct. H.R., Judgment (Merits and Just Satisfaction) of 4/05/2001

Slobodan Milošević v. The Netherlands, App. No. 77631/01, Eur. Ct. H.R., Decision as to the Admissibility of the Application No. 77631/01, 19 March 2002

Sramek v. Austria, Application No. 8790/79, Eur. Ct. H.R., Judgment (Merits and Just Satisfaction) of 22/10/1984

Steck –Risch and Others v. Liechtenstein, Application No. 63151/00, Eur. Ct. H.R., Judgment (Merits and Just Satisfaction) of 19/05/2005

Stögmüller v. Austria, Application No. 1602/62, Eur. Ct. H.R., Judgment (Merits) of 10/11/1969

Sürek v. Turkey (No. 3), Application No. 24735/94, Eur. Ct. H.R., Judgment (Merits and Just Satisfaction) of 8/07/1999

Tanis and Others v. Turkey, Application No. 65899/01, Eur. Ct. H.R., Judgment (Merits and Just Satisfaction) of 02/08/2005

Tepe v. Turkey, Application No. 27244/95, Eur. Ct. H.R., Judgment (Merits and Just Satisfaction) of 9/05/2003

Thorgeir Thorgeirson v. Iceland, Application No. 13778/88, Eur. Ct. H.R., Judgment (Merits and Just Satisfaction) of 25/06/1992

Timurtas v. Turkey, Application No. 23531/94, Eur. Ct. H.R., Judgment (Merits and Just Satisfaction) of 13/06/2000

Krasuki v. Poland, Application No. 61444/00, Eur. Ct. H.R., Judgment (Merits) of 14/06/2005

Warsicka v. Poland, Application No. 2065/03, Eur. Ct. H.R., Judgment (Merits) of 16/01/2007

Wemhoff v. Germany , Application No. 2122/64, Eur. Ct. H.R., Judgment (Merits and Just Satisfaction) of 27/06/1968

Wettstein v. Switzerland, Application No. 33958/96, Eur. Ct. H.R., Judgment (Merits and Just Satisfaction) of 21/12/2000

Zappia v. Italy (1), Application No. 24295/94, Eur. Ct. H.R., Judgment (Merits and Just satisfaction) of 26/09/1996

Akdivar and Others v. Turkey (1), Application No. 21893/93, Eur. Ct. H.R., (Preliminary objection) of16/09/1996

Van Oosterwijck v. Belgium, Application No. 7654/76, Eur. Ct. H.R., (Preliminary Objection) of 06/11/1980

European Commission of Human Rights

X v. The Federal Republic of Germany, Application No. 6946/75, Eur. Comm. H.R., Decision of 6/07/1976 on the Admissibility of the Application

X v. The Netherlands, Application No. 9433/81, Eur. Comm. H.R., Decision of 11/12/1981 on the Admissibility of the Application

Crociani, Palmiotti, Tanassi, Lefebvre D'ovidio v. Italy, Application Nos. 8603/79; 8722/79; 8723/79, Eur. Comm. H.R., Decision of 18/12/1980 on the Admissibility of the Applications

Thomas Eccles and others v. Ireland, Application No. 12839/87, Eur. Comm. H.R., Decision of 09/12/1988 on the Admissibility of the Application

The Inter-American Court of Human Rights

Baena-Ricardo et al (270 Workers v. Panamá) Case, Judgment of 2/02/2001, Inter-Am Ct. H.R. (Ser. C) No. 72 (2001)

Bámaca- Velásquez v. Guatemala Case, Judgment of 25/11/2000, Inter-Am Ct. H.R. (Ser. C) No. 70 (2000)

Benjamin et al v. Trinidad and Tobago, Preliminary Objections, Judgment of 1/09/2001, Inter-Am.Ct.H.R. (Ser.C) No. 80 (2001)

Benjamin et al. Case, *Preliminary Objections*, Judgment of 1/09/2001, Inter-Am Ct. H.R. (Ser. C) No. 81 (2001)

Cantoral- Benavides v. Perú, Judgment of 18/08/2000, Inter-Am Ct. H.R. (Ser. C) No. 69 (2000)

Cantos v. Argentina, Judgment of 28/11/2002, Inter-Am Ct. H.R. (Ser. C) No. 97 (2002)

Cayara v. Perú Case, Preliminary Objections, Judgment of 3/02/1993, Inter-Am Ct. H.R. (Ser. C) No. 14 (1993)

Constantine et al. v. Trinidad and Tobago Case, Preliminary Objections, Judgment of 1 September 2001, Inter-Am.Ct.H.R. (Ser.C) No.82

Durand-Ugarte v. Perú, Judgment of 16/08/2000, Inter-Am Ct. H.R. (Ser. C) No. 68 (2000)

Fairen Garbi and Solis Corrales, Preliminary Objections, Judgment of 26/06/1987, Inter-Am.Ct.H.R. (Ser.C) No. 2(1987)

Fairén-Garbi and Solís-Corrales v. Honduras, Judgment of 15/03/1989, Inter-Am Ct. H.R. (Ser. C) No. 6 (1989)

Gangaram-Panday v. Suriname, Judgment of 21/01/1994, Inter-Am Ct. H.R. (Ser. C) No. 16 (1994)

Garrido and Baigorria v. Argentina Case, Reparations (Art. 63(1) American Convention on Human Rights), Judgment of 27/08/1998, Inter-Am Ct. H.R. (Ser. C) No. 39 (1998)

Genie- Lacayo v. Nicaragua, Judgment of 29/01/1997, Inter-Am Ct. H.R. (Ser. C) No. 30 (1997)

Godinez- Cruz v. Honduras, Judgment of 20/01/1989, Inter-Am Ct. H.R. (Ser. C) No. 5 (1989)

Hilaire Case, *Preliminary Objections*, Judgment of 1/09/2001, Inter-Am Ct. H.R. (Ser. C) No. 80 (2001)

Hilaire, Constantine and Benjamin et al. v. Trinidad and Tobago, Judgment of 21/06/2002, Inter-Am Ct. H.R. (Ser. C) No. 94 (2002)

Maritza Urrutia v. Guatemala Case, Judgment of 27/11/2003, Inter-Am Ct. H.R. (Ser. C) No. 103 (2003

Myrna Mack Chang v. Guatemala Case, Judgment of 25/11/2003, Inter-Am Ct. H.R. (Ser. C) No. 101 (2003)

Paniagua Morales et al. ("Panel Blanca") Case, Judgment of 8/03/1998, Inter-Am Ct. H.R. (Ser. C) No. 37 (1998)

Suárez- Rosero v. Ecuador, Judgment of 12/ 11/1997, Inter-Am Ct. H.R. (Ser. C) No. 35 (1997)

Velasquez Rodriguez v. Honduras, Judgment of 29/07/1988, Inter-Am Ct. H.R. (Ser. C) No. 4 (1988)

Velásquez Rodriguez, Preliminary Objections, Judgment of 26/06/1987, Inter-Am Ct. H.R. (Series C) No. 1(1987)

Villagran Morales et al. case (The "Street Children" Case) *v. Guatemala*, Judgment of 19/11/1999, Inter-Am Ct. H.R. (Ser. C) No. 63 (1999)

Judicial Guarantees in States of Emergency (Arts. 27(2), 25 and (8) American Convention on Human Rights), Advisory Opinion OC-9/87 of 6/10/1987, Inter-Am Ct. H.R. (Series A) No. 9

Exceptions to the Exhaustion of Domestic Remedies (Arts. 46(1), 46(2) (a) and 46(2) (b) of the American Convention on Human Rights), Advisory Opinion OC-11/90 of 10 August 1990, Inter-Am Ct. H.R. (Series A) No. 11, (1990)

The Human Rights Committee

Sahadeo v. Guyana, HRC, Communication No. 728/1996, UN Doc. CCPR/C/73/D/728/1996, 100/11/1996

Ratiani v. Georgia, HRC, Communication No. 975/2001, UN Doc. CCPR/C/84/D/975/2001, 04/08/2005

Rajapakse et al. v. Sri Lanka, HRC, Communication No. 1250/2004, UN Doc. CCPR/C/87/D/1250/2004, 5/09/2006

Muñoz v. Spain, HRC, Communication No. 1006/2001, UN Doc. CCPR/C/79/D/1006/2001, 4/02/2004

Pratt and Morgan v. Jamaica, HRC, Communication Nos. 210/1986 and 225/1987, UN Doc. CCPR/C/35/D/210/1986, 7/04/1989

A.P. v. Italy, HRC, Communication No. 204/1986, 2/11/1987, UN. Doc. CCPR/C/OP/1

Committee Against Torture

Hajrizi Dzemajl et al. v. Yugoslavia, CAT, Communication No. 161/2000, UN Doc. CAT/C29/D/161/2000, 02/12/2002

The Permanent Court of International Justice

Advisory Opinion, International Labour Organization – Competence to Regulate Conditions of Agricultural Labor, Etc., 1922 P.C.I.J. (Ser. B) Nos. 2&3

Free Zones of Upper Savoy and The District of Gex, Judgment of 7/06/1932, P.C.I.J. , Series A./B., No. 46

The International Court of Justice

Military and Paramilitary Activities in and Against Nicaragua (Nicaragua v. United States of America), 1986 I.C.J., Judgment (Merits), 27/06/1986

Case Concerning the Application of the Convention on the Prevention and Punishment of the Crime of Genocide (Bosnia and Herzegovina v. Serbia and Montenegro), 2007 I.C.J., Judgment (Merits), 26/02/2007

Military and Paramilitary Activities in and Against Nicaragua (Nicaragua v. United States of America), 1984 I.C.J., Jurisdiction of the Court and Admissibility of the Application, 26/11/1984

Fisheries Jurisdiction Case (Spain v. Canada), 1998 I.C.J., Jurisdiction of the Court, 4/12/1998

Border and Transborder Armed Actions (Nicaragua v. *Honduras)*, Jurisdiction and Admissibility, Judgment, I.C.J. Reports 1988

Nuclear Tests Case (Australia v. France), 1974 I.C.J., 20/12/1974

Nuclear Tests Case (New Zealand v. France), 1974 I.C.J., 20/12/1974

Case Concerning the Temple of Preah Vihear Case (Cambodia v. Thailand), Preliminary Objections, 1961 I.C.J., 26/05/1961

Interpretation of Peace Treaties with Bulgaria, Hungary, and Romania (First Phase), Advisory Opinion of 30/03/1950, I.C.J. Reports 1950

Case Concerning Armed Activities on the Territory of the Congo (Democratic Republic of the Congo v. Uganda), I.C.J.,19/12/2005

Case Concerning Avena and Other Mexican Nationals (Mexico v. United States of America), Request for the Indication of Provisional Measures, 2003 I.C.J., 5/02/2003

Case Concerning Armed Activities on the Territory of the Congo (Democratic Republic of Congo v. Rwanda), Request for the Indication of Provisional Measures, 2002 I.C.J., 10/07/2002

Legal Consequences for States of the Continued Presence of South Africa in Namibia (South-West Africa), Advisory Opinion of 21/06/ 1971, I.C.J. Reports 1971

Conditions of Admission of a State to Membership in the United Nations (Article 4 of Charter), Advisory Opinion of 28/05/1948, I.C.J. Reports 1947 – 1948

The European Court of Justice

Case C-499/99 *Commission v. Kingdom of Spain* [2002] ECR I-6031

Case C-105/02 *Commission v. Federal Republic of Germany* [2006]

Case C-275/04 *Commission v. Kingdom of Belgium* [2006]

The International Criminal Court

Prosecutor v. Joseph Kony, Vincent Otti, Raska Lukwiya, Okot Odhiambo, and Dominic Ongwen, Prosecution's Request that the Warrant of Arrest for Raska Lukwiya Be Withdrawn and Rendered Without Effect Because of His Death, No.: ICC-02/04-01/05-271, 29/02/2008

Prosecutor v. Mathieu Ngudjolo Chui, Decision on the Evidence and Information provided by the Prosecution for the Issuance of a Warrant of Arrest for Mathieu Ngudjolo Chui, No.: ICC-01/04-02/07-3, reclassified as public pursuant to Oral Decision dated 12/02/2008

Prosecutor v. Mathieu Ngudjolo Chui, Warrant of Arrest for Mathieu Ngudjolo Chui, No.: ICC-01/04-02/07-1-tENG, unsealed pursuant to Decision ICC-01/04-02/07-10 dated 7/02/2008

Prosecutor v. Thomas Lubanga Dyilo, Decision on Victims' Participation, No.: ICC-01/04-01/06-1119, 18/01/2008

Prosecutor v. Joseph Kony, Vincent Otti, Raska Lukwiya, Okot Odhiambo, and Dominic Ongwen, Decision to terminate the Proceedings Against Raska Lukwiya, No.: ICC-02/04-01/05-248, 11/07/2007

Prosecutor v. Ahmad Muhammad Harun ("Ahmad Harun") and Ali Muhammad Ali Abd-Al-Rahman ("Ali Kushayb"), Decision on the Prosecution Application under Article 58(7) of the Statute, No.: ICC-02/05-01/07-1-Corr, 27/04/2007

Situation in Darfur, Prosecutor's Application under Article 58 (7), No.: ICC-02/05-56, 27/02/ 2007

Decision on the Applications for Participation in the Proceedings of VPRS1, VPRS2, VPRS3, VPRS4, VPRS5, and VPRS6, No.: ICC-01/04, 17 January 2006, (public redacted), No:.ICC-01/04-101-etEN-Corr., 17/02/ 2007

Prosecution's Reply under Rule 89 (1) to the Applications for Participation of Applicants a/0010/06, a/0064/06 to a/0070/06, a/0081/06 and a/0111/06 to a/0127/06 in the Uganda Situation, No.: ICC-02/04-85, 28/02/2007

Prosecutor v. Thomas Lubanga Dyilo, Decision on the Prosecutor's Application for a Warrant of Arrest, Art. 58, No.: ICC-01/04-01/06-8-US-Corr, 10/02/ 2006, unsealed pursuant to Decision ICC-01/04-01/06-37 dated 17/03/2006

Prosecutor v. Thomas Lubanga Dyilo, Judgment on the Appeal of Mr. Thomas Lubanga Dyilo against the Decision on the Defence Challenge to the Jurisdiction of the

Warrant of Arrest for Dominic Ongwen Issued on 8 July 2005, No.: ICC-02/04-01/05-57, 8/07/2005

Situation in the Democratic Republic of the Congo, Judgment on the Prosecutor's Application for Extraordinary Review of Pre-Trial Chamber I's 31 March 2006 Decision Denying Leave to Appeal, No.: ICC-01/04-168, 13/07/2006

Situation in Darfur, Conclusions aux fins d'exception d'incompétence et d'irrecevabilité, No.: ICC-01/05-20-Corr., 13/10/2006

Situation in Darfur, Décision relative aux conclusions aux fins d'exception d'incompétence et d' irrecevabilité, No.:ICC-02/05-34, 22/11/ 2006

Décision relative au système définitif de divulgation et à l'établissment d'un échéancier, Annexe I, Analyse de la décisions relative au système définitif de divulgation, No. : ICC-01/04-01/06-102, 15/05/2006

World War I Cases

Supreme Court at Leipzig, *Judgment in the Case of Karl Heynen*, 26/05/1921, *in* 16 *American Journal of International Law* 674 (1922)

Supreme Court at Leipzig, *Judgment in the Case of Emil Müller*, 30/05/921, *in* 16 *American Journal of International Law* 684 (1922)

Supreme Court at Leipzig, *Judgment in the Case of Robert Neumann*, 2/06/ 921, in 16 *American Journal of International Law* 696 (1922)

Supreme Court at Leipzig, *Judgment in the Case of Lieutenants Dithmar and Boldt Hostpital Ship* "Landovery Castle", 16/07/1921, in 16 *American Journal of International Law* 708 (1922)

Supreme Court at Leipzig, *Judgment in the Case of Commander Karl Neumann Hospital Ship* "Dover Castle", 4/06/1921, in 16 *American Journal of International Law* 704 (1922)

World War II Cases

International Military Tribunal (Nuremberg), Judgment and Sentences, 1/10/ 1946, *reprinted in* 41 *American Journal of International Law* 172 (1947)

Trials of War Criminals Before the Neurnberg Military Tribunals under Control Council Law No. 10 (Ministries case), Vol. XIII

Trials of War Criminals Before the Neurnberg Military Tribunals under Control Council Law No. 10 (The High Command case), Vol. XI

Trials of War Criminals Before the Nuernberg Military Tribunals Under Control Council Law No. 10 (Flick Case), Vol. VI

Trials of War Criminals Before the Nuernberg Military Tribunals under Control Council Law No. 10 (Justice Case), Vol. III

National Courts

Preiss/Breismeister Architects, Respondent, v. *Westin Hotel Company-Plaza Hotel Division*, Supreme Court of New York, Appellate Division, First Department, 86 A.D.2d 844; 448 N.Y.S.2d 651, 25/02/1982, (Dissenting Opinion of Judge JJ. Silverman)

Bernard Zuber, Respondent v. *Commodore Pharmacy, Inc.*, Supreme Court of New York, Appellate Division, Second Department, 24 A.D.2d 649; 262 N.Y.S.2d 155, 19/07/1965, (Judges Beldock et al. Dissenting Opinion)

Gaddafi, France, Court of Appeal of Paris (Chambre d'accusation), 20/10/ 2000, 125 I.L.R., 490, 497 (2004)

Gaddafi, France, Court of Cassation, 13/03/2001, 125 I.L.R., 508 (2004)

Public Prosecutor v. Djajić, No. 20/96 , Supreme Court of Bavaria, 3d Strafsenat, May 23, 1997, in 92 *American Journal of International Law* 528 (1998)

Re G, Military Tribunal, Division 1, Lausanne Switzerland, 18/04/1997, in 92 *American Journal of International Law* 78 (1998)

United States v. Benitez, 28 F. Supp. 2d 1361 (S.D. Fla. 1988)

Ministére Public v. Karamira, Jugement du 14/02/1997 du tribunal de 1 è instance de Kigali, available at. http://www.icrc.org

Egyptian Court of Cassation, Criminal Appeal No. 61, Judicial Year 9, 12/12/1938

Egyptian Court of Cassation, Criminal Appeal No 4117, Judicial Year 56, 11/12/1986

List of Abbreviations

FO	Records created and inherited by the Foreign Office
TS	Records created or inherited by the Treasury Solicitor and HM Procurator General's Department
LCO	Records of the Lord Chancellor's Office and various legal commissions and committees
CAB	Records of the Cabinet Office
UN GAOR	United Nations General Assembly Official Records
UN Doc.	United Nations Document
Supp.	Supplement
GA Res.	General Assembly Resolution
UNTS	United Nations Treaty Series
ECHR	European Court of Human Rights
ERCHR	European Convention on Human Rights
Inter-Am.Ct.H.R.	Inter-American Court of Human Rights
ACHR	American Convention on Human Rights
HRC	Human Rights Committee
ICCPR	International Covenant on Civil and Political Rights

I.C.J.	International Court of Justice
P.C.I.J.	Permanent Court of International Justice
ILC	International Law Commission
YILC	Yearbook of the International Law Commission
ILR	International Law Reports

Foreword

When Mohamed El Zeidy asked me to write a brief foreword to his book entitled "The Principle of Complementarity in International Criminal Law: Origin, Development and Practice", I accepted without hesitation. I had known Dr. El Zeidy for some time and often discussed with him, in particular, various aspects of the International Criminal Court (ICC). I was immediately impressed by his intellectual skills and personal attitude. His previous involvement in the research and study of international criminal law had already led him to publish extensively on matters such as *The Principle of Complementarity in International Criminal Law...* 23 *Michigan JIL* (2002); *The Ugandan Government Triggers the First Test of the Complementarity Principle...* 5 *ICLR* (2005); *The International Criminal Court's Ad hoc Jurisdiction Revisited* 99 *AJIL* (2005) – with Stahn and Olasolo); *Egypt and Current Efforts to Criminalise International Crimes* 5 *ICLR* (2005); *Some Remarks on the Question of the Admissibility of a Case during Arrest Warrant Proceedings before the International Criminal Court* 19 *Leiden JIL* (2006); *The Gravity Threshold under the Statute of the International Criminal Court* 19 *Criminal LF* (2008). This book on the doctrine of complementarity undoubtedly represents a major undertaking so far and deserves to be fully praised for reasons of both depth of analysis of a complex matter and originality of contribution.

It is largely accepted that the "complementarity" of the ICC *vis-à-vis* national jurisdictions constitutes one of the key features (if not *the* key feature) of the Court. Since the beginning of the *travaux préparatoires*, delegations agreed that, unlike in the system of the *ad hoc* Tribunals (based on the "primacy" of their jurisdiction over domestic courts) the ICC should intervene only when national jurisdictions are "unavailable" or "ineffective" (to use the terminology of the original International Law Commission draft statute) Naturally, the real problem was to shape concretely the way in which the principle of complementarity would operate, and to find the right balance between respect for State sovereignty and effectiveness of the Court's action. The final compromise, mainly reflected in Articles 17 to 20 of the Rome Statute, achieved some important results in seeking this balance. At the same time, it raises a number of substantive and procedural issues that the Court will be called to address through its jurisprudence (and, to some extent, has already been facing). Many scholars have stressed that, in the end, the manner in which the principle of complementarity is applied in the Court's case-law will have a bearing effect on the role and authority of the ICC as a judicial institution capable of filling possible gaps in the fight against impunity for the most heinous crimes.

The idea of making the ICC "complementary" to national jurisdictions was not brought up and developed in a vacuum of legal experiences and debates. When dealing with complementarity, the meaning, and value as precedents, of the mechanisms set out in the Nuremberg Charter and in the 1948 Genocide Convention were discussed at length during the *travaux préparatoires*. Even the concept of "subsidiarity" in the relationships between European institutions and member States of the European Union was often evoked as an example to be considered in the same respect. The prevailing sense was, however, that the complementarity of the ICC represented a true novelty in modern international criminal law rather than a refinement of previous notions and legal frameworks.

Dr. El Zeidy's book intends to correct this latter perception. At the outset, it contains a careful review of the history of the notion of complementarity as it evolved prior to the Rome Statute: from the proposals submitted by official and non-official bodies in the aftermath of WWI, to the 1937 League of Nations Convention for the creation of an international criminal court, from the Nuremberg Charter to the Genocide Convention and the 1951-1953 draft statutes of the Committees on International Criminal Jurisdiction. The book contains the most thorough and comprehensive analysis so far of the historical development of the doctrine of complementarity. Dr. El Zeidy concludes that at least two models of complementarity emerge from the pre-ICC experiences: first, the model of "optional complementarity", based on State consent and voluntary relinquishment of jurisdiction; second, the model of a clear division of competence and responsibilities between national and international jurisdictions, based on the different categories of perpetrators to be prosecuted and punished.

Another section of Dr. El Zeidy's book is devoted to the work of the International Law Commission in preparing the draft codes of offences against the peace and security of mankind and the statute for an international criminal court (1983-1994).

A third model of complementarity is derived from the study of this work. It is described as "a combination of the consensual system introduced in the first major model coupled with an admissibility mechanism that acted as safety valve to frame a new version of complementarity". The author highlights the fact that the core idea was to limit the exercise of the Court's jurisdiction to the most serious crimes of international concern with which the national courts could not deal. With the introduction of the system of admissibility, complementarity materialized in a different form, representing a modified model of its own. The 1994 complementarity model was taken as the main basis for future developments, which finally led to the idea found in the Rome Statute

The bulk of Dr. El Zeidy's discussion is contained in a second part of the book, dealing with the "Principle of Complementarity in the Statute of the International Criminal Court". In particular, the content of Article 17 of the Rome Statute is dissected in each of its components (unwillingness and inability of States as conditions for the admissibility of the case) and examined thoroughly, together with the issues raised by the emerging practice of self-referrals, which has characterized the activity of the ICC so far. Special attention is also devoted to the other provisions of the Statute (articles 18 to 20) and the related problems of interpretation. The author concludes that the system envisaged by the Rome Statute combines two regimes: a regime of mandatory complementarity, according to which if a State is unwilling or unable to deal with a situation or a case within its domestic courts, the Court can proceed without any further consent of that State; and a regime of optional complementarity, which applies when, as a result of a self-referral, a State consents to relinquish its jurisdiction in favour of the Court's. At the same time, Dr. El Zeidy submits that a new dimension to the principle of complementarity (indicated as "positive" complementarity and regarded as consistent with the Statute) has resulted from the prosecutorial policy to encourage States to carry out their own investigations with the support of the ICC.

At the time when the ICC is fully engaged in its judicial activities and is confronted with major questions of interpretation and application of the Statute, including the crucial aspect of the relationships with national jurisdictions, Dr. El Zeidy's book represents a commendable (and successful) effort to provide a comprehensive analysis of the regime of complementarity on which the ICC is based, together with sound and original solutions for the most delicate issues arising from it. It is easy to predict that this study not only may be seen as a cornerstone in the academic debate over complementarity, but could also benefit the future developments of judicial practice in the areas concerned.

Judge Mauro Politi
The International Criminal Court
The Hague

Introduction

1. As the International Criminal Court is gathering momentum and facing a growing case-load, it appears necessary to revisit the fundamental concept underpinning the Rome Statute: complementarity. Despite its apparent simplicity, this notion is extremely complex and the Court is now faced with pressing questions regarding its interpretation. Yet, no comprehensive study has hitherto been undertaken regarding the multiple facets, historical and contemporary, legal, philosophical and practical of the notion of complementarity. This book proposes to fill that gap in the literature and thereby hopes to provide a contribution to the field of international criminal law. It examines the letter of the law as well as the available jurisprudence, and draws on various bodies of literature, with primary emphasis on legal scholarship.

In the English language, the term "complementarity" means "a complementary relationship or situation",[1] or "a state or system that involves complementary components".[2] Components are complementary if they complete each other.[3] The word "complementary" is the adjective of the verb "to complement". For anything to complement another, it has to "add (something) in a way that...completes it",[4] and make it perfect;[5] "one of two parts that make up a whole or complete each other".[6]

In the field of science, the notion of "complementarity" is applied in physics, psychology, biology and economics. The foundation of complementarity in philosophy of science is attributed to the Danish Physicist Niels Bohr.[7] Some commentators, however, believe that the idea of complementarity has eastern origins that go back

1 *The Oxford English Reference Dictionary*, 2nd edn. (Oxford, New York: Oxford University Press, 1996), p. 296 [hereinafter Oxford Reference Dictionary].

2 *Collins English Dictionary: 21st Century Edition*, 5th ed. (London: Harper Collins Publishers, 2001), p. 327 [hereinafter Collins English Dictionary].

3 *Oxford Reference Dictionary*, *supra* note 1, p. 296.

4 *The New Oxford Thesaurus of English*, (Oxford: Oxford University Press, 2000), p. 170. The word is derived from the Latin *complere* "to fill up, fulfill, or complete", *ibid.*

5 *Webster's Third New International Dictionary of The English Language Unabridged*,(Germany: Ursula Schumer, 1993), p. 464.

6 *Collins English Dictionary*, *supra* note 2, p. 327.

7 Jeffrey Bub, "Complementarity", in Rita G. Lerner et al. (eds.), *Encyclopedia of Physics* (London. Amsterdam: Addison-Wesley Publishing, 1981), p. 138.

to ancient Chinese thinking 2,500 years ago. The belief was based on the fact that opposite concepts form a "complementary" relationship. This was represented by the archetypal poles *yin* and *yang*. In 1947 Bohr was awarded the "Danish order of the Elephant" for his outstanding achievements in physics and he chose a design for a coat of arms to be placed in the church of the Frederiksborg Castle at Hillerød. The design was the symbol representing complementarity (*yin* and *yang*) inscribed with the words *Contraria sunt Complementa* (opposites are complementary or complements).[8]

In Bohr's opinion, the notion referred to a "complementary relationship between spatio-temporal descriptions and the application of casual principles".[9] Subsequently faced with the question of wave-particle duality[10] caused by the different experimental results,[11] Niels Bohr invoked the idea of "complementarity" in the interpretation of quantum mechanics.[12] According to some experimental evidence, "light", for example, emerged as a wave-like phenomenon for certain measurements.[13] Based on different experimental results under different conditions of observation, light displayed a particle-like nature.[14] Since the concepts of wave and particle are mutually exclusive and based on different idealizations,[15] light could not be understood as both simultaneously.[16] In Bohr's opinion, analysis of nature requires encountering "mutually exclu-

8 Fritjof Capra, *The Tao of Physics: An Explanation of the Parallels Between Modern Physics and Eastern Mysticism*, 3rd. edn. (Great Britain: Flamingo, 1992), pp. 173 – 174; Izhak Englard, *infra* note 15, p. 190; Gerald Holton, *infra* note 20, pp. 105 – 106.

9 Edward MacKinnon, 'Niels Bohrs on the Unity of Science: PSA: Proceedings of the Biennial Meeting of the Philosophy of Science Association', 2 *PSA* 224, 229 (1980).

10 *Ibid.*, p. 230.

11 Robert Eisberg and Robert Resnick, *Quantum Physics of Atoms, Molecules, Solids, Nuclei, and Particles* (New York, London: John Wiley and Sons, 1974), p. 70.

12 But see Holcomb's different opinion; he argues that according to Bohr the wave and particle duality is an extension of Complementarity and "not the core of [his] view". To him Complementarity in Bohr's sense is about "micro-system properties such as position and momentum rather than their natures or natural kinds": Harmon R. Holcomb III, 'Latency Versus Complementarity: Margenau and Bohr on Quantum Mechanics', 37 *The British Journal for the Philosophy of Science* 193, 195 (1986).

13 Thomas R. Blackburn, 'Sensuous-Intellectual Complementarity in Science', 172 *Science* 1003, 1004 (1971); Jay Tidmarsh, 'A Process Theory of Torts', 51 *Washington & Lee Law Review* 1313, 1428 n. 83 (1994).

14 *Ibid.*

15 Izhak Englard, "The Idea of Complementarity as a Philosophical Basis for Pluralism in Tort Law," in David G. Owen (ed.), *Philosophical Foundations of Tort Law* (New York, Oxford: Clarendon Press, 1995), p. 188.

16 Avner Levin, 'Discussion: Quantum Physics in Private Law', 14 *Canadian Journal of Law & Jurisprudence* 249, 250 (2001); Raymond B. Marcin, 'Schopenhauer's Theory of Justice', 43 *Catholic University Law Review* 813, 834 (1994) (noting that particle and wave are mutually exclusive concepts and still certain subatomic entities can be rightly represented as a particle and as a wave, however not at the same time).

sive modes of description" and treating them instead as "complementary".[17] Quoting Bohr, one commentator stated, "[a] description of the whole of a system in one picture is impossible; there are complementary images which do not apply simultaneously but nevertheless are not contradictory and exhaust the whole only together".[18] Bohr described the relationship between the wave and particle as complementary, because they together provide a complete explanation of the physical reality.[19]

Bohr believed that complementarity may apply analogously to other fields of science such as biology, sociology and psychology. Arguing in favour of this hypothesis he stated:

> It is significant that... in other fields of knowledge, we are confronted with situations reminding us of the situation in quantum physics. Thus, the integrity of living organisms, and the characteristics of conscious individuals and human cultures present features of wholeness, the account of which implies a typical complementarity of mode of description....We are not dealing with more or less vague analogies, but with clear examples of logical relations which, in different contexts, are met with in wider fields.[20]

Elsewhere he said:

> The epistemological lesson we have received from the new development in physical science, where the problems enable a comparatively concise formulation of principles, may also suggest lines of approach in other domains of knowledge where the situation is of essentially less accessible character. An example is offered in biology, where mechanistic and vitalistic arguments are used in a typically complementary manner. In sociology, too, such dialectics may often be useful, particularly in problems confronting us in the study and comparison of human cultures, where we have to cope with the element of complacency inherent in every national culture and manifesting itself in prejudices which obviously cannot be appreciated from the stand point of other nations.[21]

An interesting application of Bohr's idea is to be found in the field of psychology. Bohr, influenced by personal experience, thought of the relationship of concepts such as love and justice, thoughts and sentiments. He concluded that they are complementary. Elaborating on this idea, he stated:

---

17 R. B. Lindsay, 'Where is Physics Going?', 38 *The Scientific Monthly* 240, 244 (1934).

18 M. Born, 'Physics and Metaphysics', 82 *The Scientific Monthly* 229, 235 (1956). Earlier, Albert Einstein recognized the paradox of the wave - particle explanation of light but did not find or set up a relationship between them like Bohr did. In April 1924 Einstein expressed this view when he said: "We now have two theories of light, both indispensable, but, it must be admitted, without any logical connection between them, despite twenty years of colossal effort by theoretical physicists".

19 Levin, *supra* note 16, p. 255.

20 Gerald Holton, *Thematic Origins of Scientific Thought: Kepler to Einstein*, rev. edn. (Cambridge, Massachusetts: Harvard University Press, 1988), p. 118 (quoting Neils Bohr).

21 Niels Bohr, 'On the Notions of Causality and Complementarity', 111 *Science* 51, 54 (1950).

> We only have to reflect by way of complementarity, as we do in using such terms as 'thoughts' and 'sentiments', in order to describe the situation in which each human being is actually placed. These terms point towards those aspects of our inner experiences which are equally essential, but which are mutually exclusive in the sense that even our warmest feelings completely lose their nature when we try to express them by way of clear logical reasoning. Similar situations emerge in our living together with other human beings, where neither of the terms 'justice' and 'love' can be dispensed with…we must make clear to ourselves that the use of the notion of justice in its extreme consequence, excludes love, to which we are called upon in relation to our parents, brothers and sisters, and friends.[22]

Although Bohr believed that the concept of complementarity (*Contraria sunt Complementa*) may apply by analogy to different fields of science, such understanding of complementarity does not seem to have been applied to the sphere of international criminal law. Complementarity is perceived in international criminal law as a principle that defines and organizes the relationship between domestic courts and the permanent International Criminal Court (ICC). The principle of complementarity provides national courts with primacy to exercise jurisdiction over the core crimes defined under the ICC Statute. Only when national courts manifest "unwillingness" or "inability" to adjudicate on an alleged crime may the International Criminal Court step in to remedy the deficiencies resulting from the failure of one or more States to fulfill their duties.

Bearing this in mind, although domestic and international prosecution of international crimes seem "equally essential", to use to Bohr's words, they do not seem mutually to exclude one another. The application of the principle of complementarity in international criminal law requires the exclusion of neither domestic courts nor the International Criminal Court. On the contrary, the core idea is *fundamentally* based on the existence of the two jurisdictions simultaneously completing each other's work. It follows that the idea of complementarity in international criminal law is distinct from the one applied in physics and the other fields of science. Perhaps, the only similarity between these concepts lies in the fact that both represent the feature of wholeness. In the case of physics, "exhausting the whole" is what makes a "wave" and a "particle" complementary descriptions of light. They are both essential to the description and complete each other. In the case of international criminal law, the International Criminal Court completes the tasks of national courts when they fail in performing their job. Thus, they are both necessary for achieving punishment, prevention and deterrence. From this perspective they satisfy the idea of "completeness" or "wholeness".

One commentator argues that "the term 'complementarity' in international criminal law may be somewhat of a misnomer", because the "two systems function in opposition and to some extent with hostility with respect to each other".[23] This view raises

22 Englard, *supra* note 15, pp. 191 – 192.

23 William A. Schabas, *An Introduction to the International Criminal Court*, 2nd edn. (Cambridge: Cambridge University Press, 2004), p. 85.

an interesting question whether the author's understanding of the notion would tie in with the idea of complementarity in physics.

While the complementarity-related provisions under the Rome Statute certainly reflect a sort of unfriendly relationship between the Court and States, as discussed later in this study, this does not necessarily lead to the conclusion that the relationship could not be seen as complementary from a different angle. Since the International Criminal Court and national courts play an active role in achieving a common goal aimed at ending impunity for the core crimes,[24] one fails to see a reason for not considering such a relationship as also complementary.

2. When we speak of "complementarity" in international criminal law, many, if not all, scholars think of the 1998 Rome Statute of the International Criminal Court.[25] Academic discussions on the subject often start from the 1994 International Law Commission's Draft Statute for an International Criminal Court as though believing that the roots of the idea go back only to 1994.[26] Others researched further and

24 See in the same vein the statement made by the Finnish delegate during the plenary meetings of the Rome Conference supporting this view: *Summary Record of the 6 th Plenary Meeting*, 17 June 1998, UN Doc. A/CONF.183/SR.6, para. 31 (noting that the "exercise of jurisdiction of of the International Criminal Court was limited by the principle of complementarity, based on the acknowledgment that the Court and national courts served the same objective…").

25 John T. Holmes, "The Principle of Complementarity", in R. S. Lee (ed.), *The International Criminal Court: The Making of the Rome Statute, Issues Negotiations Results* (The Hague, London, Boston: Kluwer Law International, 1999), p. 41; John T. Holmes, "Jurisdiction and Admissibility", in Roy S. Lee et al. (eds.), *The International Criminal Court: Elements of Crimes and Rules of Procedure and Evidence* (Ardsley: Transnational Publishers, 2001), p. 321; J. T. Holmes, "Complementarity: National Courts *Versus* the ICC", in Antonio Cassese et al. (eds.), *The Rome Statute of the International Criminal Court*, Vol. I (Oxford: Oxford University Press, 2002), p. 667; Antonio Cassese, *International Criminal Law* (Oxford: Oxford University Press, 2003), p. 351; Brian Concannon, 'Beyond Complementarity: The International Criminal Court and National Prosecutions, A View From Haiti', 32 *Columbia Human Rights Law Review* 201 (2000); Sharon A. Williams, "Issues of Admissibility", in O. Triffterer (ed.), *Commentary on the Rome Statute: Observers' Notes, Article by Article* (Baden-Baden, Nomos Verlagsgesellschaft: 1999), p. 390; André Klip, 'Complementarity and Concurrent Jurisdiction', 19 *Nouvelles études pénals* 173 (2004); Michael A. Newton, 'Comparative Complementarity: Domestic Jurisdiction Consistent with the Rome Statute of the International Criminal Court, 167 *Military Law Review* 20 (2001); Katherine L. Doherty and Timothy L.H. McCormak, ' "Complementarity" as a Catalyst for Comprehensive Domestic Penal Legislation', 5 *University of California Davis International Law & Policy* 147 (1999); Bartram S. Brown, 'Primacy or Complementarity: Reconciling the Jurisdiction of National Courts and International Criminal Tribunals', 23 *Yale Journal of International Law* 383 (1998).

26 Flavia Lattanzi, "The Complementarity Character of the Jurisdiction of the Court with Respect to National Jurisdictions", in Flavia Lattanzi (ed.), *The International Criminal Court: Comments on the Draft Statute* (Naples: Editoriale Scientifica, 1998), p. 9; Kai Ambos, 'Establishing an International Criminal Court and an International Criminal Code

concluded that while the "first reference to the adjective 'complementary' is to be found as late as in the 1994 Report of the International Law Commission containing the final Draft Statute", its "evolution" can be traced to the working group of 1992.[27] A slightly different conclusion was reached by another scholar who argued that the 1991 Commission's discussion envisaged the mechanism, "without expressly referring to the concept of complementary jurisdiction".[28]

These are misconceptions, and this work aims to correct such assertions. In Part A, I will defend two basic claims:

First, that the notion of complementarity is manifestly not the product of the 1994 International Law Commission's work. Nor is it the sole outcome of any recent work on the subject during the 21st century. It is an idea that developed over a long period of time until it was inserted into the 1998 Rome Statute. For the purpose of this analysis, Chapters I and II track and discuss in detail all the major proposals regarding the idea of complementarity prepared by the official and non-official bodies from World War I until 1998. Such a lengthy survey covering a period of almost 75 years provides a systematic analysis of what influenced the ideas of legal scholars when it came to studying the question of the relationship between national courts and the proposed international criminal court at the time.

Secondly, and correlatively to the first claim, the book argues that the concept of complementarity has been re-shaped and has emerged in different guises. Each model introduced at a particular time was grounded on different legal and – often overlapping – philosophical theories. The study will demonstrate that there are at least four major models of complementarity. Each of these models embodies a set of comparable models.

The first major complementarity model is mainly the outcome of the 1937 Convention for the Creation of an International Criminal Court and the 1951 and 1953 Draft Statutes of the Committees on International Criminal Jurisdiction. The book calls this model *optional complementarity* since it was based on the ideas of State consent and voluntary relinquishment of jurisdiction.

The second major complementarity model resulted from the Nuremberg experience. This is a slightly different model since it was based neither on the ideas of States' unwillingness or inability, nor on the system of voluntary submission of cases. Rather, it was merely based on the division of responsibilities between national and international jurisdictions. Each of the national and international jurisdictions had its own different mandate, thus avoiding conflicts of jurisdiction.

The third major model was a modified scheme of complementarity adopted by the 1994 Working Group of the International Law Commission. This model was based on

– Observations from an International Criminal Law Viewpoint', 7 *European Journal of International Law* 519 (1996).

27 Immi Tallgren, 'Completing the "International Criminal Order": The Rhetoric of International Repression and the Notion of Complementarity in the Draft Statute for an International Criminal Court' 67 *Nordic Journal of International Law* 107, 120 (1998).

28 Oscar Solera, 'Complementary Jurisdiction and International Criminal Justice', 84 *International Review of the Red Cross* 145, 151 (2002).

a combination of the consensual system introduced in the first major model coupled with an admissibility mechanism that acted as a safety valve to frame a new version of complementarity.

The fourth major model is the traditional complementarity reflected in the 1998 Rome Statute. This model is based on a reverse approach, yet it was still inspired by the theories underpinning the first and third models with technical modifications in relation to its application. This model lies between the categories of *optional* and *mandatory* complementarity. It follows from this analysis that "complementarity" should not be conceived as an "absolute" principle. Rather, it is a flexible idea that is subject to variations depending on the time and context of its emergence.

3. Part B of the book will shift the focus from this theoretical hypothesis to a practical level – taking the Rome Statute complementarity model as the framework of application. The practical application of this model encompasses a two-level approach: one at the Statute's level, that is studying the Statute's procedural regime, and the other at the domestic level, namely examining national implementing legislation. This book is mainly concerned with the first approach, leaving the second for other pieces of research.

The application of the Rome Statute complementarity model in the context of the Statute is a question that requires a detailed examination of the main provisions governing its application – namely Articles 17 to 20 of the Statute. These provisions are far from being perfectly drafted, leaving their full understanding and interpretation to the assessment of the Court.

So far, the Court has neither fully dealt with these provisions nor provided interpretations for significant questions arising from their application. With this in mind, Chapter III focuses the analysis on Article 17 of the Rome Statute. This chapter attempts to identify the gaps and offer interpretative guidelines to be taken into consideration by the Court in its assessment of the questions involving the application of the principle of complementarity. It also explores the direct implications arising from the application of this provision in light of the current jurisprudence of the International Criminal Court. This involves studying questions such as self-referrals and waivers of complementarity. The analysis will take into account the relevant jurisprudence of the different human rights bodies. Support for some claims will also be drawn from the jurisprudence of the Permanent Court of International Justice (PCIJ), the International Court of Justice (ICJ), and the European Court of Justice (ECJ).

Chapter IV builds on Chapter III to present a detailed examination of the complementarity-related provisions under the Statute (Articles 18 to 20). As with Chapter III, the aim is to highlight the procedural problems of interpretation, and propose suitable solutions that could serve future applications. This Chapter also looks at issues that have a direct effect on the procedural regime of Articles 18 and 19 of the Statute. This entails an examination of the impact of waivers of complementarity on the application of Articles 18 and 19 of the Statute.

Chapter IV concludes by challenging the classical idea of complementarity studied throughout Chapters III and IV of the book, and instead, it shows that complementarity has a positive dimension that was not really contemplated by the drafters of the Statute. Indeed, the Office of the Prosecutor of the International Criminal Court deems positive complementarity to be one of the cardinal strategies to re-shape the practice of complementarity for years to come. The Chapter tests the legality of the practice, its compatibility with the different provisions of the Statute, particularly those regulating the entire complementarity regime, and its likely influence on the Court's future activities. In so doing, the examination will also consider the relevant international case-law to be applicable. Chapter V presents the general conclusions of this study.

Part A

Chapter I: Development of the Law on Complementarity between 1919 and 1937

1. Peace Treaties during the 20th Century: The Treaty of Versailles

At the close of World War I there were international calls for the prosecution and punishment of those responsible for war crimes. At the Preliminary Peace Conference the Allies decided to create a "Commission on the Responsibility of the Authors of the War and on Enforcement of Penalties" (Commission) tasked with *inter alia*, investigating and reporting on the facts and evidence necessary to determine who was responsible for "the World War". This required trying the ex-Kaiser of Germany and determining the guilt of certain individuals involved in criminal acts that took place during hostilities and whether prosecutions could be initiated against them.[29] What was a suitable forum for prosecutions was another question to be examined by the Commission. Sub-Commission III was created to report to the Commission on this. The Sub-Commission supported the position that war criminals (those who were directly responsible for ordering the commission of illegal acts of war and those who failed in the prevention of such acts) belonging to enemy countries be brought before a "High Tribunal" (of international character) composed of 22 judges from the United States, the British Empire, France, Italy, Japan, Belgium, Greece, Poland, Portugal, Romania, Serbia and Czechoslovakia.[30] However, both the United States and Japan objected. The former saw the creation of an international criminal tribunal as "unprecedented" and felt that it was better to find recourse in an existing system.[31] The Japanese agreed that it was unprecedented to establish an international tribunal

29 Carnegie Endowment For International Peace (Division of International Law), *Reports of Majority and Dissenting Reports of American and Japanese Members of the Commission of Responsibilities: Conference of Paris 1919* (Oxford: Clarendon Press, 1919), pp. 1 – 3 [hereinafter Commission of Responsibilities Report]. On the proceedings of the Paris Conference, see generally further Geo A. Finch, 'The Peace Conference of Paris, 1919: Its Organization and Method of Work', 13 *American Journal of International Law* 159 (1919).

30 Commission of Responsibilities Report, *supra* note 29, pp. 24 – 26, 59.

31 *Ibid.*, pp. 58 – 60, 74; *Cf.* Robert Lansing, ' Some Legal Questions of the Peace Conference', 13 *American Journal of International Law* 631, 646 – 647 (1919).

to try enemies after the war ended.[32] Despite the American opposition the Commission was persuaded by the idea of establishing a "High Tribunal" with jurisdiction over Heads of State such as the former Kaiser. A provision was added to that effect in the clause dealing with the jurisdiction of the tribunal.[33]

When it came to drafting the original treaty the Allied Powers, despite relying on the essence of the penalty clauses initially prepared by the Commission,[34] included somewhat different "penalty provisions" in the final text of the Treaty of Versailles.[35] Indeed, the six "penalty provisions" initially proposed were separated, and the main ideas accepted were combined into Articles 228-230 of the final version of the treaty.[36]

---

32 Commission of Responsibilities, *supra* note 29, p. 80; *Cf.* Sheldon Glueck, 'By What Tribunal Shall War Offenders be Tried?', 56 *Harvard Law Review* 1059, 1079 (1943).

33 Commission of Responsibilities, *supra* note 29, p. 77.

34 On March 29, 1919, the Commission was asked to consider any other relevant matters that might be useful, and thus considered preparing a draft of penalty provisions to be inserted in the Preliminaries of Peace, *ibid.*, p. 27. Although the Commission's Draft of 29 March lacked a provision regarding trying the Kaiser, the final text of the treaty included a provision to this effect at the Allies' insistence (art. 227). For further discussion regarding the Trial of the ex-Kaiser, see Quincy Wright, 'The Legal Liability of the Kaiser', 13 *The American Political Science Review* 120 (1919); W. Garner, 'Punishment of Offenders Against the Laws and Customs of War', 14 *American Journal of International Law* 70, 90 – 94(1920); John Fischer Williams, "International Criminal Law", in John Fischer Williams (ed.), *Chapters on Current Law and the League of Nations*, (London. New York. Toronto: Longmans, Green and Co., 1929), pp. 242 – 243.

35 Treaty of Peace Between the Allied and Associated Powers and Germany, signed at Versailles , June 28, 1919, entered into force January 10, 1920, Arts. 228 – 230, *reprinted in* Hugh J. Schonfield, *The Treaty of Versailles: The Essential Text and* Amendments, (London: Peace Book Company, 1940), p. 74 [hereinafter Treaty of Versailles]; see also Howard S. Levie, *Terrorism in War-The Law of War Crimes*, (Oceana Publications, 1993), p. 26. Thus, for example the Commission's proposal of creating a high tribunal of international character was rejected. Alternatively, the essence of an American proposal that called for the creation of military tribunals was adopted. On the American proposal see Commission of Responsibilities, *supra* note 29, p. 75.

36 The proposed provisions stipulated:

> Article I,
>
> The *Enemy* Government admits that even after the conclusion of peace, every Allied and Associated State may exercise, in respect of any enemy or former enemy, the right which it would have had during the war to try and punish any enemy who fell within its power and who had been guilty of a violation of the principles of the law of nations as these result from the usages established among civilized peoples, from the laws of humanity and from the dictates of public conscience.
>
> Article II,
>
> The *Enemy* Government recognises the right of the Allied and Associated States, after the conclusion of peace, to constitute a High tribunal composed of members named by the Allied and Associated States in such numbers and in such proportions as they may think proper, and admits the jurisdiction of such tribunal to try and punish enemies or former enemies guilty during the war of violations of the principles of the law of nations as these

Despite German objections to the inclusion of the penalty provisions or the so-called "points of honour" the Allies insisted on the unconditional signature of the treaty.[37] The failure to convince the Allies to omit the "points of honour" caused a

result from the usages established among civilized peoples , from the laws of humanity and from the dictates of public conscience. It agrees that no trial or sentence by any of its own courts shall bar trial and sentence by the High Tribunal or by a national court belonging to one of the Allied or Associated States.

Article III,

The *Enemy* Government recognises the right of the High Tribunal to impose upon any person found guilty the punishment or punishments which may be imposed for such an offence or offences by any court in any country represented on the High Tribunal or in the country of the convicted person. The *Enemy* Government will not object to such punishment or punishments being carried out.

Article IV,

The *Enemy* Government agrees, on the demand of any of the Allied or Associated States, to take all possible measures for the purpose of the delivery to the designated authority, for trial by the High Tribunal or, at its instance, by a national court of one of such Allied or Associated States, of any person alleged to be guilty of an offence against the laws and customs of war or the laws of humanity who may be in its territory or otherwise under its direction or control. No such person shall in any event be included in any amnesty or pardon.

Article V,

The *Enemy* Government agrees, on the demand of any of the Allied and associated States, to furnish to it the name of any person at any time in its service who may be described by reference to his duties or station during the war or by reference to any other description which may make his identification possible and further agrees to furnish such other information as may appear likely to be useful for the purpose of designating the persons who may be tried before the High Tribunal or before one of the national courts of an Allied or associated State for a crime against the laws and customs of war or the laws of humanity.

Article VI,

The *Enemy* Government agrees to furnish, upon the demand of any Allied or Associated State, all General Staff plans of campaign, orders, instructions, reports, logs, charts, correspondence, proceedings of courts, tribunals or investigating bodies, or such other documents or classes of documents as any Allied or Associated State may request as being likely to be useful for the purpose of identifying or as evidence for or against any person, and upon demand as aforesaid to furnish copies of any such documents, Commission *of Responsibilities, supra* note 11, pp. 81-82. As mentioned by the U.S. Secretary of State at the time, "The report of the Commission on Responsibilities, with the reservations annexed, was laid before the Conference and received the immediate consideration of the Council of Four...The decision reached is [reflected] in Articles 227-230 of the Peace Treaty": Lansing, *supra* note 31, p. 647.

37 Alma Maria Luckau, *The German Delegation At the Paris Peace Conference: A Documentary Study of Germany's Acceptance of the Treaty of Versailles* (New York: Columbia University Press, 1941), pp. 100 –112. Gustav Bauer, who headed the government just 24 hours before the Allied ultimatum for the signing of the treaty expired, was of the view that "The Government of German Republic is ready to sign the Peace Treaty, without thereby acknowledging that the German people are the responsible authors of the World War, and without accepting Articles 227 to 231": *ibid.*, p. 109. However, the Allied refusal caused the opposite effect – namely an unconditional signature.

clear division between political parties in Germany.[38] Faced with the threat of political "chaos" and "economic disaster", and to save the German people from further suffering, the German National Assembly finally authorized the government to sign the treaty unconditionally.[39]

According to Articles 228-230 of the Versailles Treaty, Germany agreed to turn over suspected war criminals to the Allies for trial by Allied National Military Tribunals. In cases of violations that affected the nationals of more than one power, Germany agreed to turn suspects over to a Mixed (Inter-Allied) Military Tribunal composed of judges from the affected Powers.[40] A list of 895 alleged war criminals was completed by the Commission and passed to the German Government on February 3, 1920.[41] However, Baron Kurt von Lersner, President of the German Peace

38 *Ibid.*, pp. 109 – 112.

39 *Ibid.*, pp. 104, 110, 112; Ruth Henig, *Versailles and After1919-1933*, 2nd edn. (London, New York: Routledge, 1995), p. 50.

40 Treaty of Versailles, Arts. 228-229; *Cf.* Lansing, *supra* note 31, p. 648 (noting that the Tribunal is of international military character).

Article 228 states:

> The German Government recognizes the right of the Allied and Associated Powers to bring before military Tribunals persons accused of having committed acts in violation of the laws and customs of war. Such persons shall, if found guilty, be sentenced to punishments laid down by law. This provision will apply notwithstanding any proceedings or prosecution before a Tribunal in Germany or in the territory of her allies. The German Government shall hand over to the Allied and Associated Powers, or to such one of them as shall so request, all persons accused of having an act in violation of the laws and customs of war, who are specified either by name or by rank, office or employment which they held under the German authorities.

Article 229 states:

> Persons guilty of criminal acts against the nationals of one of the Allied and Associate Powers will be brought before the military Tribunals of that Power. Persons guilty of criminal acts against the nationals of more than one of the Allied and Associated Powers will be brought before military Tribunals composed of members of the military Tribunals of the Powers concerned. In every case the accused will be entitled to name his own counsel.

Article 230 states:

> The German Government undertakes to furnish all documents and information of every kind, the production of which may be considered necessary to ensure the full knowledge of the incriminating acts, the discovery of offenders, and the just appreciation of responsibility.

41 M. Cherif Bassiouni, *Al Mahkama Al Genaia Al Dewaliah: Nashatoha Wa Nezameha Al Asasy Maa Derasah Ltarikh Legan Al Tahkik Al Dewaliah Wa Al Mahakem Al Genaia Al Dewaliah Al Sabekah* (*The International Criminal Court: Its Establishment and Its Statute with a Study of the History of the International Investigative Commissions & The Former International Criminal Tribunals)* (Cairo: Nadi Al Koudah, 2001), p. 12 [hereinafter The ICC]; See also M. Cherif Bassiouni, "International Criminal Investigations and Prosecutions: From Versailles to Rwanda", in M. Cherif Bassiouni (ed.), *International Criminal Law: Enforcement*, 2nd edn., Vol. II (Ardsley, New York: Transnational Publishers, Inc, 1999), pp. 33 – 34 [hereinafter From Versailles to Rwanda]. However, there is a conflict between sources as to the number of alleged war criminals listed for prosecution.

Delegation in Paris, refused to accept this extradition list, demanded by France, England, Belgium, Italy, Poland, Rumania and Serbia, as it contained military leaders such as Hindenburg, General von Mackensen and Ludendorff.[42] Moreover, Lersner said, it was unacceptable for the German government to surrender its citizens to a foreign tribunal. Germany should be allowed to try the alleged war criminals before its national courts.[43] Following some debate, the Allies accepted a German offer to try a selected number of offenders before its Reichsgericht (Supreme Court), sitting at Leipzig.[44] A list of 45 people was prepared by an Inter-Allied Commission instead of the original list and forwarded to the German Government on May 7 1920.[45] The Allies maintained that even though they allowed Germany to exercise its criminal jurisdiction and try the accused in German courts, they reserved their right under Article 228 of the Versailles Treaty to set aside the German verdicts in case of unsatisfactory

See, Telford Taylor, *The Anatomy of the Nuremberg Trials* (New York, 1992), p. 17 (noting that the Allies produced a list of 854 individuals, including political and military figures); also Aron Naumovich Trainin, *Hitlerite Responsibility under Criminal Law* (London: New York, Hutchinson & Co., 1945), p. 22 (noting that the list included 890 people); Manfred Lachs, *War Crimes: An Attempt to Define the* Issues (London: Stevens & Sons, 1945), p. 79 (noting that the list embodied 896 alleged war criminals); Garner, *supra* note 34, p.77 n. 18 (1920) agreed (noting that the number of requested people were 896).

42 M. Cherif Bassiouni, Sharon A. Williams et al., *International Criminal Law: Cases and Materials* (Durham, North Carolina: Carolina Academic Press, 1996), p. 709 [hereinafter ICL Cases and Materials]; M. Cherif Bassiouni, *Crimes Against Humanity in International Criminal Law* (Dordrecht/Boston/London: Martinus Nijhoff Publishers, 1992), pp. 199 – 200; M. Cherif Bassiouni, 'World War I: "The War To End All Wars" and the Birth of a Handicapped International Criminal Justice System', 30 *Denver Journal of International Law and Policy* 244, 281 – 282 (2002) [hereinafter World War I]; Trainin, *supra* note 41, p. 22; Garner, *supra* note 34, p. 77.

43 James F. Willis, *Prologue To Nuremberg: The Politics and Diplomacy of Punishing War Criminals of the First World War* (Westport,. Conn: Greenwood Press, 1982), p. 118.

44 William A. Schabas, "International Sentencing: From Leipzig (1923) to Arusha (1996)", in M. Cherif Bassiouni (ed.), *International Criminal Law: Enforcement, supra* note 41, p. 172; Bassiouni, *The ICC, supra* note 41, p. 17; Bassiouni, Sharon Williams, *ICL Cases and Materials, supra* note 42, p. 709; Trainin, *supra* note 41, p. 22.

45 *German War Trials : Report of the Proceedings Before the Supreme Court in Leipzig* (London, 1921), p. 4 [hereinafter Leipzig Report]; During the meetings of the Council of Heads of Delegations there was an agreement to meet the German demands in terms of reducing the number of alleged war criminals. Fewer to be selected for trials was seen as sufficient to satisfy the Allies' demands – that is "to make an example" or "a symbol" of those who violated the laws of humanity, see *The Council of Heads of Delegations: Minutes of Meeting September 15: Notes of A Meeting of the Heads of Delegations of the Five Great Powers Held in M. Clemenceau's Room at the War Office*, Paris, on Monday, 15 September, 1919, at 10:30 a.m. (HD–53), *reprinted in, Papers Relating to the Foreign Relations of the United States: The Paris Peace Conference 1919*, Vol. VIII (Washington, DC: Government Printing Office, 1946), p. 214 [hereinafter PRFRUS Vol. VIII].

results.[46] Faced with this threat, Germany passed new legislation and assumed jurisdiction in order to be able to prosecute the selected offenders under national laws.[47]

Germany sought to maintain respect for its sovereignty by exercising its criminal jurisdiction in its own national courts. The notion of complementarity can be recognized in the Treaty's commitment to try and punish offenders if Germany failed to do so. Although, strictly speaking, the language of Article 228 of the Versailles Treaty echoes the notion of primacy and seems to emphasize the supremacy of the Allied Tribunals (national and mixed on an international level) over German national courts, the fact that the Allies subsequently agreed to defer to the German courts, rather than enforce their rights to prosecute the alleged war criminals, denotes a shift from the notion of primacy to the more restrained notion of complementarity. Indeed, based on the Commission's examination, the Allied Governments decided that:

> [T]he offer of the German Government was compatible with the execution of Article 228 of the Treaty of Peace, and the Allied Governments accordingly decided that without taking any part in the Trials, so as to leave full and complete responsibility with the German Government, they would leave to that Government the duty of proceeding with the prosecution and judgment upon the understanding that the Allies would thereafter consider the results of these prosecutions and whether the German Government were sincerely resolved to administer justice in good faith. If it should be shown that the procedure proposed by Germany did not result in just punishment being awarded to the guilty, the Allied Powers reserved in the most express manner the right of bringing the accused before their own tribunals.[48]

Since the Inter-Allied Commission concluded that the German offer was compatible with the execution of Article 228 of the Versailles Treaty, it is clear that the Allies finally intended a different interpretation of this Article – that is, one premised upon complementarity rather than upon primacy, as an initial reading of the provision might suggest.[49] Actually, the requirement of this provision was never fully

46 Leipzig Report, *supra* note 45, pp. 4, 17; Bassiouni, *World War I*, *supra* note 42, p. 282.

47 Bassiouni, *The ICC*, *supra* note 41, p. 18.

48 Leipzig Report, *supra* note 45, pp. 4, 17 – 18. However, see the opposite opinion of the United Nations War Crimes Commission regarding the interpretation of Articles 228 and 229 of the Treaty of Versailles, when it said: "[W]hen one reads Articles 228 and 229 of the Versailles Treaty it is obvious that the German offer to try the war criminals before their own courts was in complete opposition with the letter and with the spirit of the Treaty", *History of the United Nations War Crimes Commission and the Development of the Laws of War*, (London: HMSO, 1948), p. 51.

49 It is interesting to note that a complementarity proposal was initially tabled in May 1919 even before that referred to in the text above. This proposal appeared as Article 2 among a series of penalty clauses drafted by the Drafting Committee of the Peace Conference. Article 2 reads: "The German Government not having ensured the punishment of the persons accused of having committed acts in violation of the laws and customs of war, such persons will be brought before military tribunals by the Allied and Associated Powers, and if found guilty , sentenced to the punishments laid down by military law..." It is

implemented. Although the German trials proved unsatisfactory,[50] the Allies failed to exercise the right they had reserved under Articles 228 and 229 to take up the proceedings.[51]

The idea of complementarity as set out in the Peace Treaty crystallized when the Allies demanded the surrender of the large number of alleged German war criminals and the Germans refused due to what they claimed was the impossibility of executing this request. The political conditions in Germany had at the time deteriorated to such an extent that the government itself might have been overthrown if Article 228 had been interpreted strictly, and the surrender of the requested people complied with.[52] Lloyd George of Britain warned of the disastrous consequences if the treaty provisions were to be interpreted "literally".

A liberal interpretation of the penalty provisions was the best solution to avoid the destruction of the German government and to comply with the developments of and changes in "public sentiments" which demanded a return to the "ordinary business of life".[53] Furthermore, the differences in the Allies' judicial systems, which showed the impediments that might arise in conducting the proceedings, contributed to the decision that the trials would be better held before the Supreme Court in Leipzig.[54]

---

clear from the language of the Article that it gives Germany priority in trying the alleged war criminals and if this resulted in impunity, the Allies' Tribunals would interfere. Britain's Mr. Lloyd George mentioned at the time that this provision had been criticized on the ground that trial before German courts might amount either to immunity for people who violated the laws and customs of war or to "nominal sentence", see *The Council of Four: Minutes of Meeting May 1:Notes of A Meeting Held at President Wilson's House in the Place des Etats-Unis,* Paris, on Thursday, May 1, 1919, at 11 a.m.(IC–178D), *reprinted in* PRFRUS Vol. V., pp. 389 – 399; also *ibid., Draft Clauses Prepared By the Drafting Committee of the Peace Conference, on Instructions Received from the Council of the First Delegates of the Powers With General Interests After Consideration of Report of the Commission,* Appendix IV to (IC–178D), pp. 401 – 402. Thus, by that time in 1919 the Allies had rejected the complementarity idea and favoured complete control by the Allied Tribunals over the situation. Not until 1920 did the Allies reverse their position by giving Article 228 a liberal interpretation that favoured a complementarity scheme as explained in the text above.

50 Meher Grigorian, "The Role of Impunity in Genocide: An Analysis of War Crimes Trials Within the Context of International Criminal Law", in Colin Tatz et al., (eds.), *Genocide Perspectives II: Essays on Holocaust and Genocide,* (Sydney: Brandl & Schlesinger, 2003), p. 138 [hereinafter Genocide Perspectives]; Charles Cheney Hyde, 'Punishment of war Criminals', 37 *American Society of International Law Proceedings* 39, 41 (1943); L.C. Green, 'Is There An International Criminal Law', 21 *Alberta Law Review* 251, 254 (1983); Glueck, *supra* note 32, p. 1074.

51 Remigiusz Bierzanek, "War Crimes: History and Definition", in M. Cherif Bassiouni (ed.), *International Criminal Law: Enforcement,* Vol. III (Dobbs Ferry, New York: Transnational Publishers, 1987), p. 36.

52 Claud Mullins, *The Leipzig Trials: An Account of the War Criminals Trials and a Study of German Mentality* (London: H. F. & G. Witherby, 1921), pp. 9, 24, 26.

53 Willis, *supra* note 43, p. 124.

54 Mullins, *supra* note 52, p. 26.

The main factor that prompted the use of complementarity seemed to be the preservation of German sovereignty, reflected in her right to exercise her own criminal jurisdiction. The Versailles Treaty did not address this issue directly. The idea of handing Germans over to the Allies to be prosecuted before a foreign tribunal countered considerable opposition. Generals and admirals of the German army such as Tirpitz and Lundendorff issued a declaration noting that they would refuse to stand trial before a foreign tribunal since "it would not be compatible with [German] soldiers' honour and [their] sense of personal dignity".[55] Moreover, as mentioned previously, Von Lersner of Germany announced that no German government would agree to surrender its citizens to a foreign tribunal.[56]

That the Allies were aware of these facts and finally agreed to accept the complementarity compromise which required that they yield to the German demand to exercise its national criminal jurisdiction was a *de facto* result of respect for German sovereignty. It follows that Article 228 of the Versailles Treaty could be regarded as a precedent for the application of the principle of complementarity.

Despite this conclusion the complementarity provision in the Versailles Treaty lacked the criteria that helped in assessing the validity of the German trials – namely admissibility requirements. This, in a sense, did not change the essence of the principle. Rather it showed that the principle was crystallizing and has developed through time.

2. Other Peace Treaties: St Germain-En-Laye, Trianon, Neuilly-Sur-Seine, and Sèvres

At the time the Treaty of Versailles was being negotiated the Allies were preparing other peace treaties with other enemy governments. Another four peace treaties were drafted for negotiation with Austria,[57] Bulgaria,[58] Hungary,[59] and Turkey.[60] The final

55 Willis, *supra* note 43, p. 121.

56 *Ibid.*, p. 118.

57 Treaty of Peace between the Allied and Associated Powers and Austria, Signed at Saint-Germain-En-Laye, September 10, 1919, *reprinted in*, Carnegie Endowment for International Peace, *The Treaties of Peace 1919-1923*, Vol. I (New York: Carnegie Endowment for International Peace, 1924), pp. 265 *ff.* [hereinafter Carnegie, and Treaty of St. Germain].

58 Treaty of Peace Between the Allied and Associated Powers and Bulgaria, and Protocol, Signed at Neuilly-sur-Seine, November 27, 1919, *reprinted in* 14 *American Journal of International Law* 185 *ff.* (supp. 1920) [hereinafter Treaty of Neuilly].

59 Treaty of Peace Between the Allied Associated Powers and Hungary and Protocol and Declaration, Signed at Trianon, June 4, 1920, *reprinted in* Carnegie, *supra* note 39, pp. 457 *ff.* [hereinafter Treaty of Trianon]. Although the Hungarian Treaty was almost drafted by July 1919, the deteriorating situation in Hungary continued and led to the postponement of some of the negotiations and the signature of the treaty until 1920, see Alan Sharp, *The Versailles Settlement: Peace Making in Paris*, (Hampshire: Palgrave, 1991), p. 148.

60 Treaty of Peace Between the Allied Powers and Turkey, Signed at Sèvres, August 10, 1920, *reprinted in* 15 *American Journal of International Law* 179*ff.* (supp. 1921)[hereinafter Treaty of Sèvres].

texts of the penalty clauses in those treaties are very similar to those found in the Versailles Treaty.[61] Articles 173 of the Treaty of St. Germain, 157 of the Treaty of Trianon, 118 of the Treaty of Neuilly, and 226 of the Treaty of Sèvres copied the wording of Article 228 of the Versailles Treaty.[62] The negotiations surrounding those treaties reveal that the Allied Powers intended to insert identical provisions that corresponded to Article 228 of the Versailles Treaty. Indeed, on May 9, 1919 during a meeting of the Council of Four it was agreed that "Articles 228...of the Conditions of Peace handed to the German Delegates should be taken by the Drafting Committee as the basis for the preparation of corresponding articles in the Treaties of Peace with Austria and with Hungary."[63] The same view was expressed by the Council of Five at its meeting in August 12, 1919. It agreed to a resolution proposed by the Commission on the Responsibility of the Authors of War, upon instructions from the Supreme Council, to follow the "solutions" already adopted regarding other enemy Powers. It was stated that the Commission's "liberty of decision is restricted by [those] solutions [regarding] penalties in the Treaty with Germany...[and thus] Articles relating to penalties to be inserted in the Treaty of Peace with Hungary probably cannot differ...."[64]

The question remains, therefore, whether the conclusion reached in relation to the interpretation of Article 228 of the Versailles Treaty may be applied to the other peace treaties. To put it differently, could it be argued that the corresponding provisions under the other peace treaties also mirror a complementarity scheme?

The Inter-Allied Commission concluded that the German offer to try war criminals before its domestic courts subject to the Allies' subsequent intervention in case of failure (which reflects a complementarity scenario) was "compatible with the execution of Article 228" of the Versailles Treaty. The wording of the corresponding penalty provisions is identical to that of Article 228, thus, arguably, those common Articles were meant to be understood in similar terms. Accordingly, the idea of complementarity could be seen in those provisions as well.

61 Treaty of St. Germain, arts. 173-176; Treaty of Neuilly, arts. 118-120; Treaty of Trianon, arts. 157-160; Treaty of Sèvres, Arts. 226-230.

62 Treaty of St. Germain, Art. 173; Treaty of Trianon, Art. 157; Treaty of Neuilly, Art. 118; and Treaty of Sèvres, Art. 226.

63 *The Council of Four: Minutes of Meeting May 9: Notes of A Meeting Held at President Wilson's House in the Place des Etats-Unis,* Paris, on Friday, May 9, 1919, at 4 p.m.(CF–4), *reprinted in* PRFRUS Vol. V., p. 530. It should be noted that the original Articles prepared by the Commission of Responsibilities intended to be applied to Germany, Austria, Hungary, Bulgaria and Turkey. Given that the Supreme Council prepared Articles 228 – 230 of the Versailles Treaty and mentioned that the language should equally be drafted in the Austrian and Hungarian Treaties does not mean that they do not apply to the other peace treaties. The mention was restricted to those countries since the discussion at that time was focusing on the preparation of the peace treaties with Austria and Hungary, see *ibid.*

64 *The Council of Heads of Delegations: Minutes of Meeting August 12: Notes of a Meeting of the Heads of Delegations of the Five Great Powers Held in M. Pichon's Room at the Quai d'Orsay,* Paris, on Tuesday, 12 August, 1919, at 3:30 p.m.(HD–29), *reprinted in,* PRFRUS Vol. VII., p. 673.

James Willis, who wrote one of the most authoritative works on this subject, argued that the penalty clauses of all other peace treaties, such as the Austro-Hungarian, appeared in almost identical terms to that of the Versailles Treaty to reduce the chance of the German government "complain[ing] of discrimination."[65] If this is true, then it is safe to argue that the Allies might have intended to apply or give effect to the penalty clauses in the other peace treaties in the same manner as applied in Article 228 of the Versailles Treaty to avoid any complaint to that effect. Indeed, with regard to Austria, Hungary, and Bulgaria for example, while the Allies officially requested the surrender of alleged war criminals belonging to those countries, it does not appear that genuine steps were taken by those governments to comply with this demand. Instead they asked to be treated in the same way as the Germans. In a brief note dated February 18, 1920, the Hungarians objected to the Allies' request for the surrender of alleged war criminals to be tried before Allied Military Tribunals. They considered that the penalty provisions were "so humiliating that they could not be imposed, even on a conquered state, except by force."[66] Alternatively, they urged the Allies to accept an offer to allow all belligerents to try their own nationals accused of violating the laws and customs of war in their own courts.[67]

Similarly, the Bulgarians opposed the inclusion of Articles 118-120 which govern the penalty clauses in the Treaty of Neuilly. Such objection did not initially find support from the Allies during their meetings in 1919. They mentioned that:

> Articles 118 to 120, concerning penalties, cannot be altered in accordance with the Bulgarian request without endangering the very principle of justice on which they are based... [moreover they] cannot agree that any weight be attached to legal proceedings, prosecutions or sentences instituted or pronounced by Bulgarian tribunals since Article 118 is only a necessary result of the system of legal proceedings which they desire to organise, failing which such proceedings would be absolutely without effect.[68]

Although these statements reflect the difficulty in reversing the Allied position regarding the punishment of alleged Bulgarian war criminals, and it looked as though it would be even more difficult to arrive at any sort of compromise as had happened with Germany, the flow of events showed the opposite. In a meeting of the War

65 Willis, *supra* note 43, p. 149.

66 Francis Deák, *Hungary at the Paris Peace Conference: The Diplomatic History of the Treaty of Trianon* (New York: Morningside Heights: Columbia University Press, 1942), p. 235.

67 *Ibid*; Willis, *supra* note 43, p. 150 (noting that the Allies accepted the idea that the Hungarians try the cases before their own courts. However, no steps were taken by the Hungarians.)

68 *The Council of Heads of Delegations: Minutes of Meeting November 1:Notes of A Meeting of the Heads of Delegations of the Five Great Powers Held in M. Pichon's Room, Quai d'Orsay*, Paris, on Saturday, November 1, 1919, at 3:30 p.m. (Reply of the Allied and Associated Powers to the Observations of the Bulgarian Delegation on the Conditions of Peace, Appendix A to HD–81), *reprinted in* , PRFRUS Vol. VIII., pp. 888-889.

Criminals Committee held on August 6, 1920, it was agreed to reduce the number of alleged war criminals which appeared in the original lists, and were required to be surrendered to the Allied Tribunals.[69]

Jules Cambon, the President of the meeting, asked Greece to reduce the numbers in its list, which included 176 names, and urged the Serbo-Croat – Slovenes to take this into account before submitting their list.[70] Upon receipt of the lists, the Bulgarian government not only objected and filed an urgent appeal to the Allied and Associated Powers,[71] but also requested permission to try the alleged war criminals before its own courts.[72] The Allied Powers gave full consideration to the matter, but initially did not consent. The Serbian representative opposed the idea on the ground that the offences committed were so grave and that public opinion might not allow such a proposal to be accepted.[73] However, the Greeks were ready to consent provided that the execution of the sentences was guaranteed.[74] The Romanians agreed as well, but with a different proviso – that is to increase the numbers of alleged war criminals included in the list.[75] After some debate, having been influenced by the opinions of the other representatives, the Serbian representative reversed his opinion and said that "he would recommend to his Government that permission should be accorded to Bulgaria to try her own criminals as an experiment, reserving full rights under the Treaty if such trials were not satisfactory."[76] It was finally agreed that the President and the Secretary should draft a reply to the Bulgarian Government first to be submitted to the Supreme Council "in the same terms, mutatis mutandis, as that sent to Germany, and that a test list should be selected by the Serbian, Greek, and Rumanian Governments".[77]

69 George Grahame to Earl Curzon, FO 371/4715 (C3398), 6 August 1920. This meeting was attended by the Allied Governments (of Great Britain, Italy, Japan, Czecho-Slovakia/The Serb-Croat-Slovene State, Romania, Poland and Greece).

70 *Ibid.*

71 Hewart Dering to Earl Curzon, FO 371/4671 (C8608), 2 October 1920.

72 Report of the Inter-Allied Committee, FO 371/4732 (C12778).

73 *Ibid.*

74 *Ibid.*

75 *Ibid.*

76 *Ibid.*

77 *Ibid*; for an account of the views represented apart from in this meeting, see Law Officers Department to Earl Curzon, FO 371/4671 (C9192), 20 October 1920; Attorney General(on behalf of Earl Curzon) to Hewart, FO 371/4671 (C8608), 18 October 1920 (among the reasons for accepting this offer as mentioned by the Attorney General on behalf of Earl Curzon is that if Bulgarian war criminals were tried before Greek or Yugoslav courts this might "perpetuate the tension existing between these countries and Bulgaria". In addition, the Allies would be "relieved of the responsibility of trying these criminals in their own courts…Bulgarian courts should [therefore] have the responsibility of these trials"). *ibid.*

With the Austrians, the Allied and Associated Powers followed the same path and thus agreed to reduce the initial lists of war criminals.[78] The Serbo – Croat – Slovenes for example, presented a list of 302 names,[79] but it was agreed to drop some, and the final list forwarded to the Austrian Government contained only 200.[80] It was acknowledged that the alleged crimes were not of the "first magnitude",[81] and "[t]he object of the prosecution of war criminals – in itself a new procedure – was to condemn the new theory of 'frightfulness' in war as applied by the Germans and their Allies by condemning the most flagrant crimes caused by it."[82] Furthermore, while rejecting the Austrian demand for the insertion of an amnesty clause in the Treaty of St. Germain,[83] the Allied and Associated Powers agreed to treat the Austrians on an equal footing with the Germans, Hungarians and Bulgarians. Therefore, the Austrians were allowed to try alleged war criminals before their own courts.[84]

The Austrians and the Bulgarians did try some of the alleged war criminals. The Austrians established a Commission of Inquiry into the Military Breaches of Duty which court-martialled Generals Ljubičić and Lütgendorff for ordering the murder of Russian and Serbian prisoners of war. The Bulgarian government headed by Alexander Stamboliski categorized the trials and divided them into two stages. The first stage sought the trial of Radoslavov's Cabinet and ex-high officials for their responsibility for the war. The second was dedicated to trying minor war criminals, and it was reported that 534 people were court- martialled for violating the laws of war.[85]

The Turkish situation was different and very significant as the Allied and Associated Powers were more concerned with punishing Turkish officials for the massive killings and deportations of Armenians, which took place in Turkey in 1915, and the

78 Derby to Earl Curzon, FO 371/4715 (C4544), 21 August 1920.

79 George Grahame to Earl Curzon, FO 371/4715 (C3398), 6 August 1920.

80 Derby to Earl Curzon, FO 371/4715 (C6161), 7 September 1920.

81 George Grahame to Earl Curzon, FO 371/4715 (C3398), 6 August 1920. The same view was expressed earlier by the Italian Minister of Foreign Affairs during a meeting of the Council of Four in 1919, when he said that "there were certain number of personal cases [by Austrians and Hungarians], although the question was less serious than in the case of Germany", see *The Council of Four: Minutes of Meeting May 8: Notes of A Meeting Held at President Wilson's House in the Place des Etats-Unis,* Paris, on Thursday, May 8, 1919, at 11 a.m. (CF–1), *reprinted in*, PRFRUS Vol. V., p. 517.

82 George Grahame to Earl Curzon, FO 371/4715 (C3398), 6 August 1920.

83 Renner to President of the Peace Conference, Georges Clemenceau, *Note Accompanying Certain Austrian Counter Proposals to the June 2 Draft of the Treaty*, July 12, 1919, *reprinted in* Nina Almond, Ralph Haswell Lutz (eds.), *The Treaty of St. Germain: A Documentary History of Its Territorial and Political Clauses: With A Survey of the Documents of the Supreme Council of the Paris Peace Conference* (California: Stanford University Press, 1935), pp. 210-211.

84 Willis, *supra* note 43, p. 150.

85 *Ibid*., pp. 151-153.

mistreatment of prisoners of war during World War I.[86] Before signing the Treaty of Sèvres and in order to save the peace negotiations from failing, the Cabinet of Grand Vizier Ahmet Izzet Pasha passed a resolution to the effect that the leaders of the Young Turk movement and the members of the "Committee of the *Ittihad ve Terakki* Party" (the Committee of Union and Progress) should be put on trial for bringing the Ottoman Empire into World War I, and for the massacres and deportation of Turkish Armenians.[87]

On April 28, 1919 the Courts-Martial initiated trials in Constantinople (Istanbul) and convicted popular figures.[88] Accordingly, national demonstrations took place in a massive manner in Istanbul on May 20-23, 1919. This prompted the government to release 41 prisoners, 26 of whom were ordered to be released by the Court-Martial.[89] Moreover, the police authorities were ordered to suspend all arrests.[90] As a result, the British took effective steps to transfer the detainees to British custody to face trial, and actually arrested 68 Turks,[91] despite the Turkish Government's objection. The Turkish Foreign Minister initially objected to surrendering the offenders on the ground that the trial before the Allied Tribunals would diminish Turkey's sovereign right to try its own subjects. He went on to say:

> [T]he compliance with the British request] would be in direct contradiction with its sovereign rights in view of the fact that by international law each State has [the] right to try its subjects for crimes or misdemeanours committed by in its own territory by its own

86 Egon Schwelb, 'Crimes Against Humanity', 23 *British Yearbook of International Law* 178, 181 – 182 (1946); Grigorian, *Genocide Perspectives, supra* note 50, p. 135; Bassiouni, *From Versailles to Rwanda, supra* note 41, p. 35.

87 Grigorian, *Genocide Perspectives, supra* note 50, p. 135. Historians confirm that the Committee of Union and Progress leaded by Talaat Pasha, Minister of the Interior, and Enver Pasha, Minister of War, were responsible for the Armenian genocide, see Frank Chalk and Kurt Jonassohn, *The History And Sociology of Genocide: Analysis and Case Studies* (New Haven & London: Yale University Press, 1999), p. 267.

88 Grigorian, *Genocide Perspectives, supra* note 50, p. 135. Britain which at the time had around 320,000 soldiers occupying Turkey, pressed for the trial of the Turkish suspects, and thus, the Tribunal was set up in Constantinople: see Samantha Power, *A Problem From Hell: America and the Age of Genocide* (New York: Basic Books, 2002), p. 14.

89 Vahakn N. Dadrian, 'Genocide as a Problem of National and International Law: The World War I Armenian Case and Its Contemporary Legal Ramifications', 14 *Yale Journal of International Law* 221, 284 (1989) [hereinafter Genocide as a Problem]; Power, *supra* note 88, p. 15.

90 Dadrian, *Genocide as a Problem, supra* note 89, pp. 284 – 285.

91 Gary Jonathan Bass, *Stay the Hand of Vengeance: The Politics of War Crimes Tribunals* (Princeton and Oxford: Princeton University Press, 2000), p. 128; Vahakn N. Dadrian, "Armenian Genocide, Court-Martial of Perpetrators", in Israel W. Charny (ed.), *Encyclopedia of Genocide*, Vol. I (Denver, Colorado, Oxford, England: ABC-CLIO, 1999), p. 88 (noting that most of the detainees were *Ittihadist* ministers and were transferred to Malta); *Cf.* Dadrian, *Genocide as a Problem, supra* note 89, p. 285 (noting that the number was sixty-seven).

> tribunals. Moreover, His Britannic Majesty having by conclusion of an armistice with the Ottoman Empire recognized [the] latter as a *de facto* and *de jure* Sovereign State, it is incontestably evident that the Imperial Government possesses all the prerogatives for freely exercising [the] principles inherent in its sovereignty.[92]

The British, however, thought that "it was undesirable to leave it to the Turkish authorities to try to punish such offenders as could not be competently tried by Military Courts."[93]

Despite the Turkish efforts to try the Young Turk leaders, the Council of Ten did not appreciate these initiatives and thus refused the Turkish Government's demand to be exempted from including the penalty clauses to be imposed by virtue of the Peace Treaty (Sèvres).[94] The Commission on Responsibilities, therefore, inserted Articles 226-230 into the Treaty of Sèvres. Article 226, like Articles 228 of the Versailles Treaty, 173 of the St. Germain Treaty, 157 of the Trianon Treaty, and 118 of the Neuilly Treaty, recognized the right of the Allied Powers to prosecute individuals accused of violating the laws and customs of war before domestic or mixed domestic tribunals, "notwithstanding any proceedings or prosecutions before a tribunal in Turkey."[95]

Further, Article 230 of the Treaty of Sèvres obliged Turkey to surrender those responsible for the massacres committed during the continuance of the state of war on territory forming part of the Turkish Empire on August 1, 1914. In addition, the Allied Powers reserved the right to designate a tribunal, including a court created by the League of Nations, to try those responsible.[96] Had the Turkish Government not objected, the Allied Powers would have formally requested a list of 142 people alleged to have mistreated prisoners of war.[97]. On June 11, 1921 it informed the British that when the Turkish detainees held in Malta were released, "those accused of crimes would be put on impartial trial at Ankara in the same way as German prisoners were being tried in Germany".[98] A concurring view was expressed by Yusuf Kemal, the Turkish foreign minister when he said to Curzon that Turkey's "national pride" required equal treatment to that granted to German alleged war criminals.[99] Thus, Turkey should exercise its national jurisdiction over those responsible for the alleged violations. Indeed, when Yusuf Kemal pressed for an "all-for all release", the British complied and

92 FO 608/244/3749 (folio 315).

93 FO 608/244/3700 (folio 311-312).

94 Willis, *supra* note 43, p. 156.

95 Treaty of Sèvres, Art. 226 (1).

96 *Ibid.*, Art. 230. As Lippman has rightly noted, the inclusion of a provision such as Article 230 was "unprecedented": Matthew Lippman, 'The Convention on the Prevention and Punishment of the Crime of Genocide: Fifty Years Later', 15 *Arizona Journal of International & Comparative Law* 415, 420 (1998).

97 Willis, *supra* note 43, p. 158.

98 FO 371/6509 (folio 47).

99 Vahakn N. Dadrian, 'The Armenian Genocide and the Legal and Political Issues in the Failure to Prevent or To Punish the Crime', 29 *The University of West Los Angeles Law Review* 43, 62 (1998) [hereinafter Armenian Genocide]; Willis, *supra* note 43, p. 161.

on 23 October 1921 released all the Turks suspects, with the exception of some who were released on 1 November 1921.[100]

The British were expecting the Turks to satisfy the need for justice and try those released before Turkish courts. Unfortunately, internal pressure caused by the nationalist movement greatly influenced the proceedings and the government's powers to ensure justice.[101] The Allies' respect for Turkey's sovereign rights was another factor that resulted in the failure of the Istanbul Trials.[102] Furthermore, the French and Italian hesitancy in designating an international tribunal in accordance with the letter of Article 230 of the Treaty of Sèvres weakened even the British desire to pursue Turkish criminals.[103] These factors played a major role in scrapping the unratified Treaty of Sèvres and replacing it with the Treaty of Lausanne which did not include any provision that dealt with the punishment of war criminals or the Armenian massacres.[104] Instead, the Treaty of Lausanne came with an "unpublicized annex" which granted amnesty to Turkish officials.[105]

The Turkish situation before the signing of the Treaty of Sèvres *de facto* mirrors a complementarity scenario. The fact that the Turkish Government was permitted to initiate proceedings against the Young Turks before its domestic courts denotes respect for Turkey's national sovereignty, which represents the first element that the idea of complementarity requires. The subsequent British intervention after the release of some prisoners reflects the second element of complementarity. When Turkey failed to take proper action the Allies intervened and deported prisoners to Malta to face international trials, despite their release in 1921 in exchange for other British prisoners, as mentioned previously.[106]

As to the interpretation of Article 226 of the Sèvres Treaty, subsequent events and negotiations reversed its initial literal meaning. On March 16, 1921, in an attempt to revise the Treaty of Sèvres, Curzon and Bekir Sami, the Turkish Foreign Minister (of the Angora government), signed an agreement to the effect that all British prisoners should be released in exchange for the Turks held in Malta with the exception of war

100 Jackson Nyamuya Maogoto, *War Crimes and RealPolitik: International Justice from World War I to the 21st Century* (Boulder, London: Lynne Rienner Publishers, 2004), p. 60; Power, *supra* note 88, p. 16.

101 *Ibid.*, p. 61; Dadrian, *Armenian Genocide, supra* note 99, pp. 57 – 58.

102 Dadrian, *Genocide as a Problem, supra* note 89, p. 314.

103 *Ibid.*

104 Treaty With Turkey and Other Instruments Signed at Lausanne, July 24, 1923, *reprinted in* 18 *American Journal of International Law* 1 *ff.* (Supp. 1924).

105 Bassiouni, *The ICC, supra* note 41, pp. 14 – 15; Lachs, *supra* note 41, p. 81.

106 See *supra* notes 89 – 91 and text above; see also Power, *supra* note 88, p. 16 (noting that "[t]he British had grown frustrated by the incompetence and politicization of what they called the "farcical" Turkish judicial system. Fearing none of the suspects in Turkish custody would ever be tried, the British…shipped many of the arrested to Malta for eventual international trials").

criminals and those accused of the massacres.[107] Later on June 28, 1921, Yusuf Kemal, the new foreign minister, refused to ratify this agreement on the ground that it would violate Turkish sovereignty if the Allies asserted jurisdiction over the Turkish prisoners as explained previously.[108] The British thought that at least the eight people accused of mistreatment of British prisoners of war should be tried.[109]

Yet, realizing the difficulty of initiating proceedings and the pressure imposed by the Turkish Nationalists, Curzon accepted the "all for all exchange" of prisoners. This resulted in dropping the idea of trying Turkish war criminals before the Allied Tribunals. It was agreed therefore, to leave this task to the Turks based on their promise to do it.[110] Thus, the final outcome reflects the Allied deferral to the Turkish government, recognizing its right to exercise its national jurisdiction over alleged war criminals.

The Allied powers failed however to intervene with the Turkish government when the latter failed to fulfil its promise. The change in the political atmosphere prompted the Allies to conclude the Treaty of Lausanne, which ruled out any hope of pursuing war criminals.[111] As one commentator stated, it was a "triumph of the principle of impunity over the principle of retributive justice."[112] Although the Peace Treaties failed to reach the expected results in terms of trying war criminals effectively, this does not lead to the conclusion that the complementarity mechanism tested for the first time in the twentieth century was also a failure. Perhaps, the introduction of the principle was not appropriate at a time when political imperatives were of great significance and prevailed over the rule of law.

3. The 1920 Advisory Committee of Jurists

After the conclusion of the Treaty of Versailles, and while the Allied and Associated Powers were still concerned with the matter of negotiating peace treaties with Turkey and Hungary, the Council of the League of Nations decided to put into effect Article 14 of the Treaty of Versailles (Covenant of the League of Nations). By virtue of Article 14, the "Council shall formulate and submit to the Members of the League for adoption plans for the establishment of a Permanent Court of International Justice..."[113] In February 1920, the Council of the League of Nations decided to appoint a Committee of experts known as the Advisory Committee of Jurists to prepare a plan for

107 *Negotiations With the Turkish Nationalists for the Mutual Release of Prisoners of War*, Memorandum by the Secretary of State for War, 29 August 1921, Appendix D : Agreement for the Immediate Release of Prisoners, FO/371/6504 (E10117/132/44) (C.P. 3269).

108 Willis, *supra* note 43, p. 161; Dadrian, *Armenian Genocide, supra* note 99, p. 62.

109 Power, *supra* note 88, p. 16.

110 See *supra* notes 98 – 102 and text above.

111 M. Cherif Bassiouni, 'Combating Impunity for International Crimes,' 71 *University of Colorado Law Review* 409, 413 – 414 (2000).

112 Vahakn N. Dadrian, 'The Historical and Legal Interconnections Between the Armenian Genocide and the Jewish Holocaust: From Impunity to Retributive Justice,' 23 *Yale Journal of International Law* 503, 511 (1998).

113 Treaty of Versailles (Covenant of the League of Nations), Art. 14.

establishing the court.[114] The aim, as stated by the Minister of Foreign Affairs for the Netherlands, M M. le Jonkheer van Karnebeek, was to introduce into "international relations" a permanent tribunal "with a purely judicial basis, and empowered to resolve by rules of law disputes which might arise between States."[115]

However, the demand of Baron Descamps, the President of the Committee, went even further. He thought that an integral solution to the problem of international jurisdictions required more than a permanent tribunal of international justice.[116] A high court of international justice should be established alongside the permanent tribunal of international justice and composed of one judge from each State selected by representatives of the states at the Court of Arbitration.[117] It should have jurisdiction over specific cases that affected "international public order [such as] crimes against the universal law of nations", which were referred to it by the Council or the Assembly of the League of Nations.[118] Moreover, the court would be of a preventive or deterrent nature – that is, to "prevent the perpetration of [future] crimes against the law of nations."[119]

The proposal apparently gained majority support, but actually there were several objections from the members,[120] with the exception of M. De Lapradelle who backed and clarified Descamps' idea. He noted that:

114 'Second Public Meeting of the Council of the League of Nations, Held in London at St. James's Palace, on Friday, 13 February, 1920', 2 *League of Nations Official Journal* 32, 33, 36-37 (March 1920).

115 *Procès-Verbaux of the Proceedings of the Advisory Committee of Jurists*, June 16th – July 24th 1920, Vol. III, p. 3 [hereinafter Procès-Verbaux Vol. III]. For an account of the significant meetings studying the possibility of creating the court, see Second Public Meeting, *supra*, pp. 32-38; Report presented by the French Representative, M. Léon Bourgeois, and adopted by the Council of the League of Nations, 6 *League of Nations Official Journal* 318, 318-321(September 1920); Report presented by the French Representative, M. Léon Bourgeois, and adopted by the Council of the League of Nations, 8 *League of Nations Official Journal* 12, 12-21; *Procès Verbaux of the First Assembly of the League of Nations*, Third Committee, First Meeting, Held on Monday, November 22, 1920, pp. 3-7; *Procès Verbaux of the First Assembly of the League of Nations*, Third Committee, Second Meeting , held on November 24, 1920, pp. 7-11; *Procès Verbaux of the First Assembly of the League of Nations*, Third Committee, Fifth Meeting , Held on December 9, 1920, pp. 6-11; *Procès Verbal of the Tenth Session of the Council of the League of Nations*, Held in Brussles, 20 October, 1920 – 28 October, 1920, pp. 161-179 [hereinafter Procès Verbal of the Council of the League].

116 *Procès-Verbaux Vol. III*, p. 48.

117 *Ibid.*, pp. 49, 111.

118 *Ibid*; also 'Closing Session of the Advisory Committee of Jurists, 24 th July 1920', 5 *League of Nations Official Journal* 238, 240 (July-August 1920).

119 *Procès-Verbaux Vol. III*, p. 500.

120 See also Manley O. Hudson, 'The Proposed International Criminal Court', 32 *American Journal of International Law* 549, 550 (1938); George Manner, 'The Legal Nature and Punishment of Criminal Acts of Violence Contrary to the Laws of War', 37 *American Journal of International Law* 407, 429 (1943).

> It was now a question of building up the future and not ranking up the past. There was no longer any question of particular crimes; no one knew who would be the perpetrators of the crimes in the future, and therefore a Court could be constructed *in abstracto*...A stable judicial organization was required which could take action against those guilty of crimes against international justice, no matter what nation they belonged to.[121]

A similar statement was made by M. Adatchi, who thought that since the proposed court would not deal with crimes defined *ex post facto*, he could agree to it. Yet, given the limited time and mandate the Committee had been entrusted with, it was not practical to pursue the proposal.[122] Also M. Altamira feared that the President's proposal might be seen as exceeding the Committee's mandate, unless he succeeded in showing the "ties [that] might exist between the Permanent Court of Justice and the High Court of [Justice]".[123] Other members, M. Loder, and M. Fernandes, saw a different problem – the need to establish a court before defining the applicable law or without defining the crimes to be tried, and setting the penalties for them.[124] On the other hand, M. Ricci-Busatti objected on the ground that he did not know exactly what was meant by "a crime against the universal law of nations".[125] More important is the fact that individuals could not in his opinion commit "infractions of International Law, as it was law between states".[126] The latter opinion was also shared by Elihu Root, who added that if it was necessary to establish such a court, it would be imperative to impose an obligation upon all States to extradite accused persons, since neither the court nor any other State is allowed to arrest an accused within the territory of another State.[127]

Descamps' proposal failed also to explain the nature or extent of the jurisdiction of the proposed court. Lapradelle argued that, "it would be better if these cases [crimes of international character] were dealt with by an international tribunal, considering the uncertainties attaching to national jurisdictions." Thus, the main aim was to establish "a uniform jurisdiction on this subject".[128] This suggests that the intention was to establish a court with exclusive jurisdiction over specific crimes.

Nevertheless, in his draft proposal, Descamps mentioned that the high court of international justice "will be competent to judge certain cases which the Assembly

121 *Procès-Verbaux Vol. III*, pp. 500-501.

122 *Ibid.*, p. 502.

123 *Ibid.*, pp. 501-502.

124 *Ibid.*, pp. 503-505.

125 *Ibid.*, p. 503.

126 *Ibid.* As one commentator rightly observed, "The presupposition that direct powers over individuals were reserved for the sovereign State and its national law remained a key axiom of much legal argument in the twentieth century": Ole Spiermann, "'Who Attempts Too Much Does Nothing well': The 1920 Advisory Committee of Jurists and The Statute of the Permanent Court of International Justice", 73 *British Yearbook of International Law* 187, 229 (2002).

127 *Procès-Verbaux Vol. III*, p. 506.

128 *Ibid.*, p. 510.

or Council of the League of Nations will submit to it by reason of their exceptional gravity…"[129]. Thus, it could be argued that the language used in the draft proposal suggests that only a selected number of cases based on their gravity were to be referred to the high court, and presumably there would remain cases of lesser magnitude. Most likely dealing with these would be the task of national courts. Thus, jurisdiction would not be exclusive, and might be seen from a different perspective as concurrent and complementary on the basis of the division of labour between the two jurisdictions. In this context, the concurrent and complementary jurisdiction proposed differs from the idea set out in the World War I Peace Treaties. The idea of complementarity embedded in the penalty provisions presupposed the failure of the German government to conduct genuine proceedings before the Allied Powers had intervened. Descamp's proposal represented a different model of complementarity based on the single idea of division of labour, something that appears later at Nuremberg.[130]

Yet, not all types of crimes "against the universal law of nations", even of exceptional gravity, were to be tried before the high court. Lord Phillimore, a member of the Committee, advanced this thesis, and classified "crimes against the universal law of nations" into three categories. First, "acts committed during time of peace; second, crimes of war; finally, the crime of having made war (nowadays known as aggression)".[131] As for crimes committed in time of peace, Lord Phillimore thought that national jurisdiction should suffice. The defendant could be tried either before the courts of his own country or in other jurisdictions where he might be found.[132] This would ensure the speedy and effective administration of justice.[133] Where there was a declaration of an "unjust war", and if "such a court were established …, it might be well, if only as deterrent, to confer upon it jurisdiction…, but it is hardly likely that such a jurisdiction would often be exercised".[134]

By contrast, crimes perpetrated during the course of war by the subjects of an enemy State against those of other State or States should be dealt with by an "international court of criminal justice".[135] In Lord Phillimore's opinion, if the accused were tried before either side's courts, the trial would be seen as unjust and might result in reprisals if the state of war continued.[136] In this regard, Phillimore explicitly called for a court with exclusive jurisdiction over crimes committed during war, while preserv-

129 *Ibid.*, p. 49. The original draft suggested the establishment of a "High Court, placed at the summit of International Justice and called upon to take cognisance of crimes committed against international good order and the universal law of nations". See F. B. Schick, 'International Criminal Law – Facts and Illusions', 11 *Modern Law Review* 290, 292 (1948).

130 See Chapter II, *infra*.

131 *Procès-Verbaux Vol. III*, p. 507.

132 *Ibid.*

133 *Ibid.*

134 Lord Phillmore, 'An International Criminal Court and the Resolutions of the Jurists', 3 *British Yearbook of International Law* 79, 82 (1922-1923).

135 *Procès-Verbaux Vol. III*, pp. 507 – 508; Phillimore, *supra* note 134, p. 82.

136 Phillimore, *supra* note 134, p. 83.

ing domestic fora only for crimes committed during peacetime. It follows that both Descamps' and Phillimore's ideas were not inspired by the jurisdictional mechanism (complementary mechanism) set out in the Versailles and other peace treaties. Lord Phillimore thought that the Versailles precedent demonstrated that, despite the impartial proceedings taken by the German court in trying German alleged war criminals, the final outcome was unsatisfactory from the Allies' perspective.[137] Thus, an international criminal jurisdiction was a workable solution in these circumstances.

On the other hand, scholars such as Professor Brierly thought that trials before the offender's national courts, such as had occurred at Leipzig, should not be allowed, not because their outcome would appear unsatisfactory, but because they were *de facto* unsatisfactory. Instead, he argued that the least objectionable solution would be, "while leaving a right of trial to the courts of the territory where the crime was committed, to give a collateral jurisdiction to those of the Power against whose nationals it was committed, perhaps with a right of appeal on points of international law to the Hague Court."[138] This solution preserved the role of national courts, but reduced that of the proposed international court.

While Descamps' proposal was open to two different interpretations, as explained above, it in any event ruled out the jurisdictional mechanism found in the application of Article 228 of the Versailles Treaty – namely giving priority to national courts while saving the intervention of a higher forum for cases of failure of the national jurisdiction to act properly. Unfortunately, Descamps' and Phillimore's ideas were officially killed when the second resolution adopted by the Committee concerning the establishment of a high court was rejected by the Third Committee of the Assembly of the League on the ground that:

> [T]here is not yet any international penal law recognized by all nations and that, if it were possible to refer certain crimes to any jurisdiction, it would be more practical to establish a special chamber in the Court of International Justice. The Committee therefore considers that there is no occasion for the Assembly of the League of Nations to adopt any resolution on this subject.[139]

137 *Ibid.*, p. 82.

138 J. L. Brierly, 'Do We Need An International Criminal Court?',8 *British Yearbook of International Law* 81, 83 (1927).

139 *Records of the First Assembly of the League of Nations*, Tenth Meeting of the Third Committee, 1920, p. 764; *Historical Survey of the Question of International Criminal Jurisdiction*, U.N. Doc., A/CN.4/7/Rev.1, p. 11 [hereinafter Historical Survey U.N.Doc., A/CN.4/7Rev.1]. The deliberations of the Committee resulted in the adoption of three resolutions to be submitted to the Council of the League of Nations, the second of which concerned the creation of a high court of international justice. The resolution contained 4 Articles on the creation of high court of justice as follows. Article 1: "A High Court of International Justice is hereby established; Article 2: This Court shall be composed of one Member for each State, to be chosen by the group of Delegates of each State on the Court of Arbitration; Article 3: The High Court of International Justice shall be competent to try crimes constituting a breach of international public order or against the universal law of nations, referred to it by the Assembly or by the Council of the League of Nations; Arti-

Later, on 18 December 1920 at the thirty-first plenary meeting of the Assembly of the League, the Rapporteur of the Third Committee concluded that:

> The Committee is of the opinion that it would be useless to establish side by side with the Court of International Justice another Criminal Court, and it is best to entrust criminal cases to the ordinary tribunals as is at present the custom in international procedure. If crimes of this kind should in the future be brought within the scope of an international penal law, a criminal department might be set up in the Court of International Justice. In any case, consideration of this problem is, at the moment, premature.[140]

This unfortunate conclusion was reached not only because of the conclusions reached by the Third Committee but also due to the main fact that States were not yet prepared to give up any part of their sovereign rights.[141]

4. The 1922 – 1924 Conferences of the International Law Association

The International Law Association is a scientific body that was originally called "The Association for the Reform and Codification of the Law of Nations", and was founded in October 1873.[142]At its thirty-first conference held at Buenos Aires in 1922, its members convened to discuss the desirability of establishing an international criminal court to prosecute violations of the laws and customs of war and those offences perpetrated in violation of the laws of humanity.

In a paper presented at the conference, Professor Hugh H. L. Bellot said that there was a "crying need for the creation of a Permanent International Criminal Court or a Permanent International High Court of Justice",[143] and after some discussion the conference resolved that "the creation of an International Criminal Court is essential

cle 4: The Court shall have the power to define the nature of the crime, to fix the penalty and to decide the appropriate means of carrying out the sentence. It shall formulate its own rules of procedure", *Procès-Verbaux Vol. III*, pp. 747 – 748. In its report adopted on October 27, 1920, the Council of the League of Nations decided to submit the resolutions of the Committee of Jurists to the Assembly of the League, where the Third Committee reached the above mentioned result, *see Procès-Verbal of the Council of the League*, pp. 181, 183; *Ibid.*, 8 *League of Nations Official Journal* 20, 20 – 21 (November – December 1920).

140 *Historical Survey*, U.N.Doc., A/CN.4/7Rev.1, p. 12; see also H. Donnedieu De Vabres, 'La Cour Permanente De Justice Internationale et Sa Vocation en Matière Criminelle', 1 *Revue Internationale de Droit Pénal* 175, 175 (1924).

141 Indeed such a fear was reflected in Descamps's statement to the members of the Committee that "There is no need whatever to imagine that the institution of a High Court would amount to the creation of a super-State, and would involve an unjustified abdication of sovereign powers", *Procès-Verbaux Vol. III*, p. 512.

142 *The International Law Association: Its Object, Origin, and Work* (London: Temple, 1910), pp. 1-2.

143 *Report of the Thirty-First Conference*, Held at Buenos Aires, 24 August – 30 August, 1922, p. 63 [hereinafter Report of the Thirty-First conference].

in the interests of justice, and... that the matter is one of urgency".[144] Professor Bellot was accordingly instructed to draft a statute for consideration by a committee of the International Law Association.

At the thirty-third meeting in Stockholm, Professor Bellot set out the difficulty of appointing such a committee and finally submitted the prepared draft statute to the conference for examination and approval.[145] The draft consisted of 47 provisions. Articles 24 to 26, which are the main concern of this study, deal with the jurisdictional powers of the court. Yet, they lack an explicit explanation of the nature or extent of the jurisdiction of the court. Article 24 states:

> The Court shall be open to the subjects or citizens of every State, whether belligerent or neutral, and whether during a war or after its conclusion. Provided always, that no complaint or charge shall be entertained by the Court unless the complainant has first obtained the *fiat* or formal consent of the Law Officers, Public Prosecutor, or Minister of Justice, as the case may be, of his own State.[146]

Arguably, the requirement that the complaint should not be "entertained by the Court unless the complainant has first obtained consent" suggests that the court would not have exclusive jurisdiction at all times; rather there was sometimes the possibility of concurrent jurisdiction.[147] The State would choose either to try the case if it had jurisdiction or refer it to the court after obtaining formal consent. Indeed, in presenting the main outlines of the draft statute at the Buenos Aires conference in 1922, Profes-

144 *Report of the Thirty-Third Conference*, Held at Stockholm, 8 September – 13 September, 1924, p. 75[hereinafter Report of the Thirty-Third Conference].

145 *Ibid*; see also Hugh H-L. Bellot, 'La Cour Permanente Internationale Criminelle', 3 *Revue Internationale de Droit Pénal* 333, 335 (1926).

146 *ILA Draft Statute for the Permanent International Criminal Court*, Art. 24; see also Art. 25, which stated: "The jurisdiction of the Court embraces all complaints or charges of violation of the laws and customs of generally accepted as binding or contained in International Conventions or in Treaties in force between States of which the complainants and defendants are subjects or citizens respectively. The Court shall also have jurisdiction over all offences committed contrary to the laws of humanity and the dictates of public conscience".

147 Indeed, since putting the idea of consent into practice means that the triggering mechanism would lie within the power of the State and not the international court, and there was a chance that the international court would not deal exclusively with all cases. For further clarification of this point, see *Report of the Thirty-First Conference*, pp. 75 – 77. It is not clear from the wording of draft Article 24 whether Professor Bellot intended to leave the triggering mechanism of the court subject to State control or whether this was accidental. However, see Judge Caloyanni's opinion where he mentioned that Professor Bellot "makes it a condition *sine quâ non* that the complaint should obtain the *fiat* of the competent authority of his country, because there may be cases which, although just, would not be sufficient evidence to substantiate them": M. Mégalos A. Caloyanni, 'The Permanent International Court of Criminal Justice', 2 *Revue Internationale de Droit Pénal* 326, 339-340 (1925).

sor Bellot made a similar argument when he explained his ideas on the extent of the jurisdiction of the court. He proposed two different scenarios for the competence of the court.

First, in time of war, war criminals would normally be tried before their own military courts unless the belligerent "choose to send them for trial to the International Court [and therefore] there seems to be no valid objection to giving concurrent jurisdiction to the latter".[148] This statement is in line with the argument raised above and seems to be the key to the intended interpretation of Article 24 of the draft if applied in time of war. Some members, such as Hammarskjöuch and Brunet, developed this thesis during the 1924 Stockholm Conference and thought that the court should function like a court of appeal to which cases would be brought after having been tried by national tribunals.[149]

In clarifying the proposal, Charles Henry Butler of the United States argued that the appeal to the court would determine "whether the national Court had properly executed justice in such a way as to satisfy the nation which claimed that the offence had been committed against its national".[150] The provisions on competence, which appeared in the 1924 draft, did not address this move forward.[151] At a first glance, Butler's proposal appears to be calling for a court of appeal on points of law. Yet, the phrase, "whether the national Court had properly executed justice" supports a finding that the idea of sham proceedings underlies the proposal and serves as an exception for the proposed court to exercise jurisdiction.[152] If this is so, then it may be argued that Butler's proposal reflects the underlying notion of the principle of complementarity reflected in the Treaty of Versailles. Nonetheless, the proposal seems to suggest that an appeal to the court would be with the State's consent. This means that the court had no power to determine that proceedings were sham before the case was referred to it. Thus, the complementarity idea reflected here functions in a different manner from that found under the penalty provisions of the Peace Treaties.

Secondly, where war crimes were being tried after the conclusion of peace, the situation appears different, as the international criminal court would deal exclusively with all war crimes, said Professor Bellot.[153] He mentioned that the reason was:

148 *Report of the Thirty- First Conference*, p. 77.

149 *Report of the Thirty-Third Conference*, pp. 92-93.

150 *Ibid.*, p. 103.

151 Even the discussions of the 1926 conference did not mention Bellot's vision of the nature of jurisdiction between national courts and the international court as discussed in 1922, nor the advance made by Hammarskjöuch, and Gaston Brunet during the Stockholm conference: see *Report of the Thirty-Fourth Conference*, held at Vienna, August 5 to August 11, 1926, pp. 118, 169-225, 279-309. On the 34th conference see generally M. Emeric Vadasz, 'Jurisdcition Criminelle Internationale', 5 *Revue de Droit International de Sciences Diplomatiques et Politiques* 274, 274-275 (1927).

152 According to this argument, the term "court of appeal" is not intened to include the technical meaning of appeal.

153 *Report of the Thirty- First Conference*, pp. 76-77.

> [U]pon the conclusion of peace [military] courts cease to possess any jurisdiction; and as the civil courts of belligerents usually have no jurisdiction, unless the offence has been committed within their national territory and the offender is actually within the area of their jurisdiction, there is no possibility of bringing offenders to justice. Unless, therefore, the Treaty of Peace includes provisions for the surrender of war criminals for trial and punishment, no court of one belligerent possesses any power to try the nationals of another belligerent.[154]

Although it was Professor Bellot's intention, and the understanding of the members, that where peace had been concluded the court should have exclusive jurisdiction over all war crimes,[155] his statement implies that occasionally the court would also have concurrent jurisdiction – for instance when civil (non-military) courts had jurisdiction based on the fact that the crime had been perpetrated within the belligerent's territory where the offender was to be found. Accordingly, an international criminal court would act as a supplementary jurisdiction triggered only when national courts lacked competence. In this respect, it may be argued that the required nature of the jurisdiction of the proposed court is supplementary or complementary.

However, according to a different interpretation, his language might be understood to mean that civil (national) courts would be granted primary jurisdiction (perhaps exclusive), and thus it is not clear in this case whether there would be a concurrent role for the international criminal court. Moreover, reading Bellot's quotation in the light of Article 24 as well as his statement during the Buenos Aires conference makes it clear that there might also be the possibility of situations arising during peace time, where the State had jurisdiction, yet State officials preferred to refer the case to the court. Arguably, the optional jurisdiction proposed by Professor Bellot in the Buenos Aires conference is not limited in application to cases dealt with during wartime.

These early proposals serve as examples of how the idea of complementarity was in the process of being crystallized. Unfortunately, these proposals were dead letters as some states were still reluctant to give up part of their sovereign rights to a foreign tribunal. As one commentator put it, some states "have not besides lost view of the difficulties that the principle of the sovereignty of each State would raise when there would be a question of surrendering a national to be tried by another tribunal than the national".[156]

5. 1925 Inter-Parliamentary Union Conference

A year later, in 1925, the Inter-Parliamentary Union met for its 23rd conference in Washington, D.C. and Ottawa to study a report prepared by Professor Vespasian V.

154 *Ibid.*, p. 63.

155 *Ibid.*, p. 86, where Mr Bewes a member of the Association said that he understood Mr. Bellot's proposal in the sense that "When war is over ...the International Court should be the Court of first instance and of final instance...". Indeed, the proposal was carried by 31 votes to 22.

156 Caloyanni, *supra* note 147, p. 337.

Pella (acting on behalf of the Permanent Committee to study questions of the Union) on the "Criminality of Wars of Aggression and the Organization of International Repressive Measures."[157] The subject of criminalizing wars of aggression and their description as international crimes was initially considered in the 22nd Inter-Parliamentary Conference. During the general debate at Berne in 1924, Professor Pella proposed to the "Juridical and Executive Committees" that this question be placed on the agenda of the 1925 Washington Conference for detailed consideration and suggestions.[158]

In the 1925 report, Professor Pella examined the question from various angles and under several headings. Under the first heading, "International Criminality", he posed the problem of establishing an international penal code and the idea of international repression. Such examination covered not only the crime of aggression, but also all international offences committed by individuals. One of the major problems was to reconcile the notion of State sovereignty[159] with international repression. In so doing, Professor Pella argued that there was a distinction between exterior sovereignty and interior sovereignty.[160] The former is not absolute due to the "very nature of the relations between nations and the necessity of international harmony by the sovereignty of other States".[161] It is therefore settled that every nation must regulate its activity and avoid violent action against "innocent and inoffensive States".[162] Thus, "absolute independence of sovereignties" should be replaced by the theory of the "limitation of exterior sovereignties to the extent required for the maintenance of order and of international justice".[163] However, in the case of interior sovereignty, States are free to act within their own territories – "one of the essential conditions of the existence of the independence of nations".[164] Yet, this does not apply where States use their territories in a manner inconsistent with the most "elementary precepts of humanity

157 See *Report of the 1925 Inter-Parliamentary Union, XXIII Conference, Washington and Ottawa*, 1-13 October 1925, p. 94 [hereinafter Report of the 1925 Inter-Parliamentary Union].

158 *Ibid.*

159 On the concept of sovereignty and its origins see Jean Bodin, *Les Six Livres de la République* (A Paris: chez Jacques du Puys, 1577) [VIII]; L. Oppenheim, *International Law: A Treatise*, Vol. I. – Peace , 6th edn. (London. New York. Toronto: Longmans & Co., 1947), pp. 116-120; J. L. Brierly, *The Law of Nations: An Introduction to the International Law of Peace*, 6th edn. (Oxford: Clarendon Press, 1963), pp. 6 – 49; F. H. Hinsley, *Sovereignty*, 2nd edn. (Cambridge: Cambridge University Press, 1986), 1 – 45, 214 – 235.

160 *Report of the 1925 Inter-Parliamentary Union*, p. 100. On the distinction *see Report of the International Commission on Intervention and State Sovereignty*, 2001, para. 1.35, available at http://www.iciss.ca/pdf/Commission-Report.pdf.

161 *Report of the 1925 Inter-Parliamentary Union*, p. 100.

162 *Ibid.*

163 *Ibid.*

164 *Ibid.*, p. 101.

and to the customs unanimously recognized by the civilized world". The notion of international repression is, therefore, permissible.[165]

Under the title "International Crimes and Offences committed by Individuals", Professor Pella studied the question of repressive measures for acts committed by individuals, and considered those acts to be "contrary in their nature to the law of nations and international morality".[166] Thus in order to "insure energetic repressive measures and also to avoid both excessive severity and culpable leniency, those actions partaking of the nature of an offence must not come within the competence of the States involved but must come before an international juridical body whose impartiality can be guaranteed".[167]

This statement reflects Professor Pella's understanding of the nature of jurisdiction in the case of international offences committed by individuals. According to one reading, the phrase "States involved" might refer to States with a direct link to the crimes in question. Thus, based on this interpretation, the courts of those States should be denied the competence to try those cases. It follows from this reading that States which have no direct link with the crimes are still competent to assert jurisdiction concurrently with the international criminal court. This interpretation is problematic, because it is not consistent with Professor Pella's statement, which speaks of a court with exclusive jurisdiction.

It is doubtful whether this was the intended interpretation. This is because there was no provision that regulated the conflict of jurisdiction that arose between national courts and the international court. It cannot be said that Professor Pella intended to deny the belligerent states in the case of war crimes, for example, the competence to try crimes committed by their nationals or the enemy power while still granting it to other states with no direct link with the crimes committed. The main aim was to ensure that these cases were tried before an international tribunal whose "impartiality can be guaranteed". Thus, national courts were to be denied competence to deal with those offences. An international criminal court should, therefore, exclusively enjoy the primacy to try cases involving international crimes. This interpretation is in line with Professor Pella's statement, cited above, and finds support in different parts of this report as seen below.

Under the heading "International Public Proceedings", Professor Pella explained the procedure to be followed when filing complaints concerning international offences committed by individuals. He argued that in the case of offences such as international military offences and all others committed in time of war that amounted to a violation of the "rules and customs of international law", common law offences committed on occupied territory (such as massacres, pillage, and rape) and serious infractions committed by diplomatic representatives in the exercise of their duties,

165 *Ibid.* This view became evident through time and the writings of scholars: see Henry Schermers, "Different Aspects of Sovereignty", in Gerard Kreijen et al. (eds.), *State, Sovereignty, and International Governance* (Oxford: Oxford University Press, 2002), pp. 187-188.

166 *Report of the 1925 Inter-Parliamentary Union*, p. 106.

167 *Ibid.*

any State might "bring complaints or accusations with a view to the institution of public proceedings directly" before the "public international prosecution office".[168]

After hearing the report, the Inter-Parliamentary conference passed a resolution calling for a permanent sub-committee to study the causes of wars of aggression and to prepare a preliminary draft of an international legal code. In doing so, the conference requested the sub-committee to take into account the principles found in Professor Pella's report and summarized in an annex to the resolution.[169] Some of these principles referred to the question of international criminal jurisdiction.

The Permanent Court of International Justice "must have power to adjudicate upon all international crimes and offences".[170] In cases where individuals are guilty of committing international offences, a special criminal chamber should be set up in accordance with Article 26 of the Statute of the Court.[171] This chamber "would have jurisdiction" over all international offences committed by individuals, and those by their nature "would not come within the jurisdiction of the national courts".[172]

This sentence entails at least three different interpretations. The first supports the above conclusion – that the criminal chamber would enjoy exclusivity to try all international offences. A second interpretation may be that the criminal chamber would enjoy exclusive jurisdiction "over all international offences", and other offences of "international" character, which would normally not fall within the jurisdiction of national courts. Presumably, Pella intended to refer to the crime of waging aggressive war, which was considered to be a crime committed by a State. This interpretation also suggests that the competence of the proposed court was intended to be exclusive. A final interpretation is merely based on the meaning of the phrase "would have jurisdiction" over all international offences. "Would have" does not mean *per se* that the criminal chamber should try all international offences at all times; rather it means that it enjoys jurisdiction over all types of international offences and may exercise it whenever the situation allows. There is a difference between to "have jurisdiction" and the exercise of this jurisdiction. Having jurisdiction does not mean that the criminal chamber will exercise it exclusively. Although the language used by the drafters is confusing as to the nature of the proposed court's jurisdiction, Professor Pella's early statements suggest that the drafters' intention was to establish a criminal chamber with exclusive jurisdiction. The idea behind Pella's conclusion tends to deprive do-

168 *Ibid.*, pp. 107, 116-117. Professor Pella presumed that a public international prosecution office should first be established in connection with the League of Nations.

169 See *Resolution of the Inter-Parliamentary Union on the Criminality of Wars of Aggression and the Organization of International Repressive Measures, reprinted in* U.N.Doc., A/CN.4/7Rev.1, pp. 70-71.

170 See *Fundamental Principles of An International Legal Code for the Repression of International Crimes*, Annex to the Resolution, *reprinted in* U.N.Doc., A/CN.4/7Rev.1, p. 73 [hereinafter Fundamental Principles].

171 Statute of the Permanent Court of International Justice, Art. 26; see also Vespasian V. Pella, 'Towards an International Criminal Court', 44 *American Journal of International Law* 37, 37 – 38 (1950).

172 *Fundamental Principles, supra* note 170, p. 73.

mestic courts "involved" of the ability to deal with international offences in order to ensure the impartiality of the proceedings – a prevailing idea that most international law scholars adopted after the experience of the Leipzig trials.

6. 1926 International Congress of Penal Law

After the Inter-Parliamentary Union stopped meeting, discussions on the subject of establishing an international criminal court continued at an unofficial level. In 1926, the *Association Internationale de Droit Pénal* (International Association of Penal Law) held its first International Congress of Penal Law in Brussels. Twenty-four delegations from Europe, asia and America, participated in the congress.[173] Around 350 individuals of 40 different nationalities were registered as members.[174] The congress discussed several questions including the legislative development of penal law in the twentieth century, punishment and security measures, and the desirability of establishing an international penal jurisdiction, and the manner of its organization.[175]

As to the question of international penal jurisdiction, the delegations discussed the desirability of establishing an international penal jurisdiction and the manner of its organisation. It was clear that the majority of the delegates favoured the idea,[176] yet they held different views as to the competence and organization of the proposed court. Some delegates, such as M. Erasmo Boudet, the Cuban representative, thought that there was an "urgent necessity" to establish an international penal jurisdiction through the preparation of an international convention that defines the crimes that would fall under its jurisdiction.[177] This international penal code would cover crimes such as (but not limited to) prostitution, drug trafficking, counterfeiting of currency, and crimes of national security.[178] Others, like M. Fernando Segura of Bogota, while admitting the significance of establishing such an international penal jurisdiction, raised a major problem, namely that States would be reluctant to submit their sovereign rights to a foreign jurisdiction.[179]

As to the nature of the competence of the court, the majority of the delegates who favoured the idea argued that there was a major role the court should play in solving the problem of conflict of jurisdiction between States (positive and negative).

173 *Premier Congrès Intenrationale de Droit Pénal: Actes du Congrès*, Bruxelles, 26 – 29 Juillet 1926, p. 6 [hereinafter 1926 *Actes du Congrès*].

174 *Ibid.*

175 M. Enrico Ferri, 'The Italian Criminology at the International Congresses of Brussels and Vienna', 4 *Revue Internationale de Droit Pénal* 156, 158, 160,168 (1927).

176 However, a minority such as Professor Jaroslav Kallab of Cheqoslovacia thought that there was no urgent need to establish an international penal jurisdiction, because the Permanent Court of International Justice could take up its role by virtue of the summary proceedings as set out in Articles 29, and 30 of its Statute: see *1926 Actes du Congrés*, p. 471.

177 *Ibid.*, pp. 373-374.

178 *Ibid.*, pp. 375-376.

179 *Ibid.*, pp. 75-76.

Professor Donnedieu de Vabres of France pointed out the danger resulting from cases of negative conflict of jurisdiction, namely denial of justice and the increase in the impunity gap.[180] Thus, it was indispensable to have a unified law to be applied by the new court in order to avoid this dilemma.[181] This court, like the Permanent Court of International Justice, would be competent to provide an opinion on which national court had jurisdiction over a case in a situation where a conflict of jurisdiction arose.[182]

M. N. Politis of Greece supported the core of this proposal and added that the repression of piracy as a crime committed in time of peace was an example that might lead to conflict of jurisdiction. National courts might have concurrent jurisdiction over this crime, and yet exceptionally sometimes none of the States' courts might be competent to judge.[183] What we now call an "impunity gap" might, therefore, result in a case of lack of jurisdiction. The problem of positive conflict of jurisdiction might appear however, in the case of different States seeking to assert jurisdiction. Thus, a criminal chamber composed of five Judges could be set up within the Permanent Court of International Justice. This chamber would decide on questions of conflict of jurisdiction and determine which national court should proceed with a particular case.[184] Furthermore, there was an additional role in a case of negative conflict of jurisdiction where the place in which the crime was committed was unknown or contested; in such cases it would be for the criminal chamber to judge the case.[185]

However, the situation would be different in cases of the repression of felonies and misdemeanours committed in time of war, such as violations of the laws and customs of war, or the crime of waging war. Mr. Politis suggested that despite objections that might arise from belligerent States regarding the surrender of their nationals, it is very useful to rely exclusively on an international penal jurisdiction that will assure the impartiality of proceedings and effective sanctions.[186]

Yet, a court with exclusive jurisdiction was not the only option for other delegates such as Professor Saldana of Spain. In his report, Professor Saldana argued that the Permanent Court of International Justice should be given supreme penal jurisdiction. The penal jurisdiction of the Permanent Court of International Justice would be triggered in time of peace or war in the following cases:

1. The case where the national criminal jurisdiction is doubtful, the discussion of which on the international realm is always disappointing, and its penal result is without any 'utility';

180 *Ibid.*, p. 398.

181 *Ibid.*

182 *Ibid.*, p. 399.

183 A similar statement was made by Senator M.R. Garofalo of Italy: see *1926 Actes du Congrés*, p. 428.

184 *Ibid.*, p. 414.

185 *Ibid.*, p. 415; M.R. Garofalo shared the same view, *ibid.*, p. 428.

186 *Ibid.*, pp. 415 – 416.

2. All extra national penal cases: a) concerning the subject, each time when the perpetrator or the victim is born in a non civilized country, savage or barbarian country;
3. Common international Crimes. Prepared and perpetrated either on the territory of different countries or by criminals hiding behind a nationality – they habitually prepared or aided or committed again those crimes;
4. International political crimes;
5. International Military Crimes. Acts committed in violation of the laws and customs of war or committed against persons carrying the nationality of several nations or countries;
6. All the crimes against international law, that is, against "droit des gens". Also the crimes committed against the international public order;
7. National Crimes, or collective social crimes that are not punished by a state, or its gravity exceeds the material or moral repressive power of a state (such as trade slavery, piracy, savagery such as great political or racial massacres).[187]

At first glance, one may observe that if any of the paragraphs listed above had been met, this would be sufficient to trigger the jurisdiction of the penal chamber of the Permanent Court of International Justice. In particular, paragraphs 1, 2, 3, 5 (second part), and 7 may each be read on their own to trigger the jurisdiction of the penal chamber of the Permanent Court of International Justice. However, reading paragraphs 1, 4, 5 (first part) and 6 separately may be misleading. If for example, an international political crime (para. 4) or any other international crime (para.6) had been committed on the territory of State X the penal chamber would always conduct the proceedings. This reading is problematic because it means that the proposal calls for a court with exclusive jurisdiction over all international crimes, which is not accurate if one reads the language of paragraph 1.

Paragraph 1 requires the existence of *sham* proceedings before the penal jurisdiction of the Permanent Court of International Justice can arise. Paragraph 6 on the other hand allows the Permanent Court of International Justice to exercise penal jurisdiction over all international crimes without any restrictions. If the two paragraphs were read separately, this would lead to inconsistency and render paragraph 1 inoperative. This is because the first paragraph implies that the court cannot exercise jurisdiction without the national criminal jurisdiction failing first. However, paragraph 6 empowers the Permanent Court of International Justice to exercise jurisdiction over any international crime without any limitation or reference to paragraph 1. Thus, whether the nature of the jurisdiction proposed by Saldana is exclusive or complementary remains unclear.

If one reads paragraph 1 as applying only to ordinary domestic crimes, then it could be argued that the jurisdiction of the proposed penal chamber is complementary to that of national courts in situations of ordinary crimes, and exclusive in connection with all international crimes.

According to a different interpretation, paragraph 1 may be treated as an operative paragraph that needs to be read together with paragraphs 2, 4, and 6 in order to be

187 *Ibid.*, p. 385.

consistent. Thus, the penal jurisdiction of the Permanent Court of International Justice may, therefore, exercise jurisdiction over any international crime including violations of the law and customs of war, and political crimes in cases where the "national proceeding is doubtful...and its penal result is without any utility".[188] This seems to be a logical interpretation and neatly presents a mechanism of complementary, rather than exclusive, jurisdiction over international crimes. This is similar in *principle* to the notions introduced during the Peace Treaties of World War I, and at the 1924 International Law Association Stockholm conference.

After all reports had been presented, the congress adopted a *vœu* listing of several recommendations that would result in the Permanent Court of International Justice being entrusted with repressive powers in penal matters. The Court would be competent to judge both individuals and states. It would impose penal sanctions and take "security measures" against a State that was accused of violating international law, including performing acts of aggression against another state. Penal sanctions also apply to individuals who have committed any crime in violation of international law in time of peace or war, or crimes that constitute a threat to world peace. An international convention will define the crimes and prescribe the appropriate penal sanctions.[189]

The nature or extent of jurisdiction is not easy to determine because the provisions governing the jurisdiction of the penal chamber are open to different interpretations. The language is similar to that of the principles adopted by the 1925 Inter-Parliamentary Union. Indeed, recommendation 3 states that the Permanent Court "be competent to judge any penal liability incurred by a State...or any violation of international law". Recommendation 4 proceeds by saying that "in addition the Permanent Court be competent to judge individual liabilities incurred...and any violation of international law committed in time of peace or war...".[190]

In one sense, the phrase "be competent to judge any penal liability...or any violation of international law" in recommendations 3 and 4 may be understood as meaning that the Court would enjoy exclusive competence over all international crimes in time of peace as well as war. However, according to a different line of argument similar to that set out in the previous section, to "be competent" does not mean that the Court would exercise such competence at all times. Rather, the jurisdiction of the Court would be exercised whenever there was a chance. Accordingly, there would be a role for national courts alongside the penal chamber of the Permanent Court of International Justice. The problem with this conclusion is that the recommendations neither indicate the role of national courts nor specify the relationship between national courts and the proposed penal chamber – leaving the nature of the competence of the penal chamber vague. This conclusion clearly rejects the complementa-

188 Paragraphs 2, 3, 5(second part), and 7 are open to two different interpretations; the first targets an exclusive penal jurisdiction; while the second interpretation might be read in light of operative paragraph one like paras. 2, 4, and 6.

189 An English translation of the *vœu* is *reprinted in Historical Survey*, U.N.Doc., A/CN.4/7Rev.1, pp. 15, 74 – 75.

190 *Ibid.*, p. 74.

rity proposal tabled by Professor Saldana.[191] The congress however, recommended that in the case of accused individuals who cannot be brought before national courts either because the territory where the crime was committed is not known or sovereignty over that territory is "in dispute", they would be "amenable" to the jurisdiction of the Court;[192] thus, occasionally creating a sort of subsidiary or complementary jurisdiction between the penal chamber and national courts though different from Professor Saldana's idea.

The implementation of these recommendations required the governing Council of the *Association Internationale de Droit Pénal* to appoint a commission to draft the statute for the penal chamber, in accordance with the above recommendations.[193] The commission first met in Paris on January 8, 1927, and appointed Professor Pella to draft the statute.[194] In January 1928, the commission adopted Professor Pella's draft and distributed it to all States represented at the congress and to the League of Nations.[195] The statute did not strictly follow the recommendations adopted by the congress. However, it took into consideration some of the main ideas listed in these recommendations, for example, the establishment of a criminal chamber of the Permanent Court of International Justice instead of the creation of an independent judicial organ, and providing this chamber with repressive powers over international offences committed by States and individuals during time of either war or peace, and solving the conflict of jurisdiction arising between the courts of different States. Apart from this role, the nature of the jurisdiction of the criminal chamber was clearer than that proposed in the recommendations of the congress. Article 36 of the draft statute states:

> In addition to offences committed by States and to international offences committed by individuals which by their nature are incapable of being declared crimes or of being made punishable by national criminal codes, the Criminal Chamber shall have jurisdiction over such offences committed by individuals in respect of which jurisdiction may be renounced by individual States by international convention. These shall include in particular:

191 The proposal also differed from one tabled by Professor De Vabres. As a long term plan, De Vabres proposed the intervention of a superior jurisdiction after a procedure conducted before the State courts and that it would plays the part a of supreme court of cassation which would be a court of law and not of fact. Yet Professor De Vabres did not explain the procedure governing the functioning of this court in relation to national courts: see *1926 Actes du Congrés*, p. 399.

192 Recommendation 5, in *Historical Survey*, U.N.Doc., A/CN.4/7Rev.1, pp. 74 – 75. The requirement that the criminal chamber may exercise jurisdiction when the territory where the crime was committed was not known establishes a complementary relationship through the sharing of the burden between national and international criminal jurisdictions – like that exercised by the International Military Tribunal at Nuremberg. See chapter II *infra*.

193 Recommendation 11, in *Historical Survey*, U.N.Doc., A/CN.4/7Rev.1, p. 75; see also p. 15.

194 Vespasien V. Pella, *La Guerre-Crime et les Criminels de Guerre*, (Geneva, 1964), p. 129.

195 V.V. Pella, 'Draft for a Statute Establishing a Criminal Chamber in the Permanent Court of International Justice', 17 *Revue Internationale de Droit Penal* 230, 230 (1946).

a. Crimes and offences committed in time of peace and likely to endanger the peaceful relations of States or which ought, by reason of the circumstances in which they are committed, to be made subject to international criminal jurisdiction for their effective repression.
b. Crimes and offences committed during war, especially international military offences and offences *communis juris* committed by military persons in occupied territories.[196]

One aspect of the extent of the competence of the criminal chamber may be understood from reading the second part of the chapeau. This states that "the Criminal Chamber shall have jurisdiction over such offences [set out in paragraphs A and B] committed by individuals with respect to which jurisdiction may be renounced by individual States".[197] A literal reading supports the conclusion that only if States "renounced" or relinquished their jurisdiction to the criminal chamber in relation to any of the crimes committed in time of peace that endangered the "peaceful relations" or offences committed during war, the criminal chamber could exercise its jurisdiction. Using the verb "may" in the phrase "may be renounced" makes it evident that renunciation of jurisdiction was optional, and therefore Article 36 intended to preserve the role of national courts in adjudicating on cases where States preferred to retain jurisdiction.

7. 1937 League of Nations Convention for the Creation of an International Criminal Court

The 1937 League of Nations Convention was the first official and genuine attempt to establish an international criminal court since the Peace Treaties following World War I. Unlike the informal attempts made during the 1920s, which were influenced to a great extent by the atrocities committed during World War I, the 1937 convention emerged in a different atmosphere.

Between the years 1931 and 1934 tensions and political crises grew within the Balkans, and Central and Southern Europe, which led to a flow of terrorism supported by Hitler and Mussolini.[198] Yugoslavia specifically was faced with an "Ustaša campaign" of terrorist attacks backed by Italy and Hungary.[199] In December 1933, Ustaša failed to carry out a plan to assassinate King Alexander of Yugoslavia in Zagreb.[200]

196 *Historical Survey*, U.N.Doc., A/CN.4/7Rev.1, p. 83. The French version can be found in Pella, *supra* note 195, p. 138.

197 See chapeau of Article 36.

198 For an account of the political situation that intensified terrorism at the time see Martin David Dubin, *International Terrorism: Two League of Nations Conventions, 1934-1937* (Millwood, New York: Kraus Microform, 1991), pp. 7-10; see generally Thomas M. Franck, and Bert B. Lockwood, 'Preliminary Thoughts Towards an International Convention on Terrorism', 68 *American Journal of International Law* 69, 69 (1974).

199 Dubin, *supra* note 198, p. 7.

200 *Ibid.*

A successful attempt, however, took place on October 9, 1934.[201] Veličko Kerin, a veteran Bulgarian assassin operating from Bulgaria and some others from Ustaša operating from Italy and Hungary, killed King Alexander and the French Foreign Minister Jean Louis Barthou, during the King's visit to Marseilles.[202] The assassination was been planned in Rome in August 1934 by Ante Pavelić, head of the Ustaša. He was assisted by others including an Austrian national, Georges Perčević, a former Austro-Hungarian military officer.[203]

The French Government unsuccessfully requested their extradition from Italy and Austria.[204] In response to the refusal to extradite, the French Government addressed a letter to the Secretary General of the League of Nations emphasizing the significance of fighting international political crimes and calling for the negotiation of an international convention for the suppression of terrorism, and the establishment of an international criminal court to try individuals accused of acts of terrorism as defined in the convention.[205]

In a resolution adopted by the Council of the League of Nations on December 10, 1934, the Council decided to set up a committee of experts for the international repression of terrorism (committee of experts) to study the question of the repression of terrorism with a view to drawing up a preliminary draft of an international convention to "assure the repression of conspiracies or crimes committed with a political

201 Péter Kovác, 'La Société des Nations et son Action Aprés L'attentat Contre Alexandre, roi de Yugoslavie', 6 *Revue d'Histoire du Droit International* 65 (2004) (narrating the detailed events of the assassination and the reactions taken afterwards); For a summary see Roberta Arnold, *The ICC as a New Instrument for Repressing Terrorism* (Ardsley, New York: Transnational Publishers, 2004), p. 7; Arthur K. Kuhn, 'The Complaint of Yugoslavia against Hungary with Reference to the Assassination of King Alexander', 29 *American Journal of International Law* 87, 87 (1935); Leo Gross, 'International Terrorism and International Criminal Jurisdiction', 67 *American Journal of International Law* 508, 508 (1973).

202 Dubin, *supra* note 198, pp. 10 – 11; see generally Philip Marshal Brown, 'International Criminal Justice', 35 *American Journal of International Law* 118, 119 (1941); John W. Bridge, 'The Case for an International Criminal Court of Criminal Justice and the Formulation of International Criminal Law', 13 *International & Comparative Law Quarterly* 1255, 1267 – 1268 (1964); But see M. Cherif Bassiouni, *International Terrorism: Multilateral Conventions (1937-2001)* (Ardsley, New York: Transnational Publishers, 2001), p. 47 (noting that King Alexander and Barthou were assassinated by means of a plan executed by a Croatian nationalist).

203 Dubin, *supra* note 198, p. 11.

204 *Ibid.*, p. 12; *Cf.* Elizabeth Chadwick, 'A Tale of Two Courts: The 'Creation' of a Jurisdiction?', 9 *Journal of Conflict & Security Law* 71, 86 (2004); Valerie J. Munson, Note, 'The Case Concerning United States Diplomatic and Consular Staff in Tehran', 11 *California Western International Law Journal* 543, 547(1981).

205 *Historical Survey*, U.N.Doc., A/CN.4/7Rev.1, p. 16; see also Antoine Sottile, *The Problem of the Creation of a Permanent International Criminal Court* (Nendeln. Liechtenstein: Kraus Reprint LTD., 1966), pp. 18 – 19.

and terrorist purpose".[206] At its first session in Geneva from April 30 to May 8, 1935, the committee examined the French suggestions initially presented to the Council of the League of Nations on December 9, 1934.[207] Furthermore, it examined the observations and proposals of several Governments at the suggestion of the French.

The French suggestions were no more than thoughts and explanations of the "sole object" of the future convention. The main aim, as explained by the French Government, was to facilitate the repression of political terrorist acts.[208] In reaching this target, the proposal adopted the idea of setting up an international criminal court to function concurrently with national courts, and only when specified criteria have been met. The chapeau of Part B of the proposal stated that the international criminal court "would have to try individuals" accused of any of the acts mentioned above in the following cases:

> a. Where the accused has taken refuge in a country other than that which desires to prosecute him, and the country of refuge prefers to bring up the accused for judgment before the International Criminal Court rather than grant extradition to the State applying it;
> b. Where the State on whose territory the act was committed prefers to waive prosecution before its own courts in the particular case concerned.[209]

A literal reading of the chapeau of part B in the light of paragraphs (a) and (b) suggests that the proposed international criminal court would not enjoy primary jurisdiction; rather it was intended to be a default jurisdiction that was triggered only when any of the criteria listed above in paragraph (a) or (b) is satisfied. This conclusion finds support in the statement made by the French Government when it said that "[t]he suppression of the acts above referred to [in part A of the proposal] will rest with the courts of each State. Nevertheless, an international criminal court would be set up at the same time."[210] Moreover, in commenting on the French proposal Professor Vespasian V. Pella, the delegate of the Romanian Government, said that his Government

> [F]ully recognises that, in present circumstances, the system advocated by the French Government would be the one most easily realisable in practice. Though maintaining the basic principle of *priority of jurisdiction for national courts*, the French proposals do not exclude the possibility of investing an international court with certain powers. Exercise of jurisdiction by an international court would therefore only be conceivable if the State which held the accused in custody *voluntarily* renounced its right to exact punishment. It might even

206 The committee was composed of 11 members from Belgium, United Kingdom, Chile, France, Hungary, Italy, Poland, Roumania, the USSR, Spain and Switzerland. For the text of this resolution see *Report to the Council on the First Session of the Committee,* Held from April 30 to May 8, 1935, League of Nations document C.184.M.102.1935V., p. 2 [hereinafter League of Nations document C.184.M.102.1935V].

207 League of Nations document C.542.M.249.1934.VII.

208 *Ibid*; see also League of Nations document C.184.M.102.1935V, p. 22.

209 *Ibid.*

210 *Ibid.*

be said that this conception resembles to a certain extent the idea of *jurisdiction by delegation*.[211]

The proposal certainly called for a court with a sort of subsidiary or complementary jurisdiction. The French suggestion discussed above regarding the competence of the proposed international criminal court appeared to be the main framework for further drafts. The committee found it essential to "express" the ideas in the form of a series of provisions, and thus adopted 17 Articles to be considered as the first part of the convention on terrorism.[212] The Belgian, French, Romanian and Spanish delegates tabled a draft scheme and introductory note regarding an international criminal court just to enable "the practical aspects of the matter to be examined".[213] The draft scheme contained Articles 18 to 62 and it was considered the second part of the convention.[214]

A preliminary provision on the nature of the jurisdiction of the proposed international criminal court did not appear with those in the second part of the convention that address the issue of an international criminal court. Instead, it was positioned as Article 9 of the first part of the convention which covers acts of terrorism. There was no obvious reason except that the committee inserted Article 9 "solely to show the system contemplated by some members of the committee in the eventuality of an international criminal court's being set up".[215] After the committee had exchanged views on the matter, it decided to reserve the second session for all decisions regarding the establishment of an international criminal court.[216]

At the second session held in Geneva from January 7 – 15, 1936, the committee of experts for the international repression of terrorism, having examined the provisions of the texts concerning the prevention and punishment of terrorism and of an international criminal court which were submitted by the Belgian, French, Romanian and Spanish delegations during the first session, considered that "it would be preferable to submit two draft conventions to States for their appreciation".[217] One convention would be on the prevention and punishment of terrorism, while the other was to be addressed to the establishment of an international criminal court. The delegates were divided as to the desirability of creating a court in principle and also the "timelines" for its creation. Moreover, according to this idea, States would be free to become con-

211 League of Nations document C.184.M.102.1935V, p. 19.

212 League of Nations document C.184.M.102.1935V, Appendix I, pp. 3-6.

213 *Ibid.*, p. 3.

214 *Ibid.*, Appendix II, pp. 7-11. These drafts were submitted to the Council of the League of Nations in the form of report C.184.M.102.1935V mentioned above, and circulated to all of its Members.

215 *Ibid.*, p. 3, and Appendix I, art. 9, p. 5.

216 *Ibid.*, p. 3.

217 *Report to the Council Adopted by the Committee for the International Repression of Terrorism on January 15th, 1936*, League of Nations document A.7.1936.V.[C.36(I).1936.V], p. 2.

tracting parties only to the convention on terrorism where they felt unable for whatever reason to surrender an accused person to the international criminal court.[218]

Article 3 of the draft convention for the creation of an international criminal court covers the question of the competence of the proposed court and states that:

1. In the cases referred to in Article 10 of the Convention for Prevention and Punishment of Terrorism, each High Contracting Party to the present Convention shall be entitled, instead of prosecuting before his own tribunal, to send the accused for trial before the Court.
2. A High contracting Party shall further be entitled, instead of extraditing, to send the accused for trial before the Court if the State demanding extradition is also a party to the present Convention.[219]

---

218 *Ibid.*

219 See Article 3, Appendix II, p. 8. Article 10 of the Draft Convention for Prevention and Punishment of Terrorism reads: "Where in virtue of the present Convention a High Contracting Party has to bring to trial a person accused of one of the offences provided for by Articles 2 and 3, the law of that High Contracting Party shall determine what court shall have jurisdiction to try such person." Moreover, Article 2 of the same draft reads: "With this object, each High Contracting Party should make the following acts criminal offences, whether they affect his own interests or those of another High Contracting Party, in all cases where they are directed to the overthrow of a Government or an interruption in the working of public services or a disturbance in international relations, by the use of violence or by the creation of a state of terror – viz. :

(I) Any act intended to cause death or grievous bodily harm or loss of liberty to:
  (a) Heads of States; persons exercising the prerogatives of the head of the State; their heredity or designated successors;
  (b) The wives or husbands of the above-mentioned persons;
  (c) Members, officers or servants of Governments;
  (d) Members of the constitutional or legislative bodies;
  (e) Persons holding judicial office;
  (f) Diplomatic representatives or consuls;
  (g) Members of the armed forces of the State;

(2) Willful destruction of, or damage to:
  (a) Public buildings or other public property;
  (b) Means of communication and transport or installations belonging thereto;
  (c) Property belonging to public utility undertakings;
  (d) Any willful act calculated to endanger the lives of members of the public, and in particular interference with the working of means of communication, the use of explosives or incendiary materials, the propagation of contagious diseases, or the poisoning of drinking water or food;
  (e) Manufacture, possession, export, import, transport, sale, transfer or distribution of any material or object with a view to the commission of an act falling within the present Article;

A close reading of Article 3 suggests that the provision is in essence a mere reiteration of the French suggestions. The difference, however, lies in paragraph (1), which does not limit the case of waiver of prosecution before a State's own courts to the territorial State. Instead, paragraph (1) makes it accessible to any contracting party which is unwilling or unable to try the case before its domestic courts for whatever reason to leave prosecution to the international criminal court.

On January 15, 1936 the committee of experts adopted a report including the draft convention for an international criminal court, and a draft concerning the convention on terrorism. This report was presented to the Council of the League of Nations for consideration and, "should it deem it desirable and opportune..., to forward the ... report...to the Governments for their consideration".[220]

Indeed, the Council submitted the committee of experts' drafts to the governments requesting their observations.[221] The main problem of the majority of States was not limited to a specific provision such as Article 3 of the proposed draft, which governed the competence of the proposed court. The system contemplated by the drafters in Article 3 was not opposed in principle. The problem lay in the principal idea of establishing an international criminal court. The Indian delegate argued that acts of terrorism should not be brought to an international *forum* because the "Government of India have adequate legal powers to deal with it".[222] Consequently, India would be "unlikely ever [to] wish to resort to the proposed Court".[223] Moreover, because the jurisdiction of the proposed court was optional in the sense that there was no obligation "upon any party to the Convention to remit any person to the Court,

(f) Willfully giving assistance by any means whatever to a person or an accomplice of a person who does any of the acts set out above."

Article 3 of the same draft states:

"(1) Each High contracting Party should also make criminal offences:
   (I) Any attempt to commit any of the acts set out in Article 2;
   (II) Any conspiracy, and any direct incitement, whether successful or not, to commit any of the acts set out in Article 2, any willful complicity and any help given towards the commission of such an act, whether the conspiracy, incitement, complicity or help takes place or is given in the country where the act is, or is to be, committed or in another country.

(2) Acts of participation in the offences dealt with in the present Convention will be treated as separate offences when the persons committing them can only be brought to trial in different countries.

(3) The as to obligation incitement shall be without prejudice to any rules of domestic law as to treating incitement which has not taken place in public and has not been successful as a criminal offence."

220 *Ibid.*, p. 3.

221 See *Historical Survey*, U.N.Doc., A/CN.4/7Rev.1, p. 17.

222 *Observations by Governments on the Draft Convention for the Prevention and Punishment of Terrorism, and Draft Convention for the Creation of an International Criminal Court, Series I*, League of Nations document A. 24.1936. V., p. 8.

223 *Ibid.*

they feel doubtful whether this organisation would serve any practical purpose."[224] A similar view was held by the United Kingdom delegate when he said that his government would not agree to participate in a scheme that favoured repression of terrorism by an international criminal court – a job that could be "done with more efficiency by national courts".[225] After his government had carefully and sympathetically examined the drafts prepared by the committee of experts "they are of the opinion that the time has not yet arrived for the creation of the proposed Court,... [and therefore] the proposal should, for the time being at any rate, be abandoned".[226] Similar comments came from Hungary,[227] Norway,[228] Venezuela[229] and Poland.[230] Others such as Czechoslovakia, while accepting in principle the idea of concluding an international convention for an international criminal court, thought that because of the many States that had adopted a negative attitude towards the proposed draft convention,

224 *Ibid.*

225 *Ibid.*, p. 4

226 *Ibid.*

227 "With reference to the draft Convention for the Creation of an International Criminal Court, the Hungarian Government wishes to recall that...it was not in favour of the creation of an International Criminal Court...The Hungarian Government, while emphasising once again that it cannot see its way to accept the draft Convention for the Creation of an International Criminal Court and maintaining its general standpoint unaltered, is nevertheless anxious to reply to the request made to it on behalf of the Council and to submit some observations on certain provisions of the draft in question, on the understanding that these observations do not in any way imply that it considers the creation of an International Criminal Court and the conclusion of a Convention on this matter necessary or even desirable." For the full text of the observations see *ibid.*, pp. 5 – 8 (but the observations did not include any discussion regarding Article 3 of the proposed Convention).

228 "The Norwegian Government regrets that, for reasons of principle, it is unable to support this draft", see *ibid.*, p. 10. (This was the only observation made regarding the proposed international criminal court).

229 "[T]he opinion of the Department for Foreign Affairs of Venezuela, after examining the draft Convention for the Prevention and Punishment of Terrorism and the draft Convention for the Creation of an International Criminal Court , is favourable in the former and unfavorable in the latter case." On the full text see *ibid.*, p. 12 (Similarly the observations fell short of a discussion regarding the competence of the court as set out in Article 3 of the proposed draft).

230 "The Polish Government sees no need for the creation of an International Criminal Court. Though it does not wish to prevent in any way other countries from setting up such a Court, it thinks that the existence of the Criminal Court would have no effect, *de facto* or *de jure*, on those signatories to the Convention for the Repression of Terrorism who did not recognize the Criminal Court. The signatories to the said Convention who recognize the Court could never cite the existence of the latter in reply to requests from the other signatories which were warranted by the actual terms of the Convention." For the full text *see Observations by Governments on the Draft Convention for the Prevention and Punishment of Terrorism, and Draft Convention for the Creation of an International Criminal Court, Series II,* League of Nations document A. 24 (a).1936.V., pp. 1-3.

"it is opposed to any discussion of this draft which would delay the successful conclusion of the first Convention [on terrorism]".[231]

At the Seventh meeting of the Seventeenth Ordinary Session of the Assembly of the League of Nations, the First Committee opened a "general discussion" on the proposed draft convention. Disagreements about the necessity of establishing the proposed court came from the same countries which referred to their original observations. Yet, countries such as the United Kingdom and Australia thought that governments which opposed the idea should not place any obstacles in the way of the adoption of the proposed convention by States which wanted it.[232] M. Paul-Boncour, the French delegate, backed the United Kingdom's proposal, suggesting further that the convention for the proposed court "should, like the first, be revised by the experts and then submitted to a diplomatic conference". The reason for this call was explained by the French delegate

> [I]f it was decided that the Committee of Experts should not revise the Convention on the creation of an International Criminal Court, the States which were in favour of its creation would be unable, at the diplomatic conference, to decide to set it up as between themselves. It was therefore very desirable that, as for the first Convention, and since the stage of accessions had not been reached, the Convention on the International Criminal Court should also be revised by the Committee of Experts in the sense that certain points should be defined and a greater measure of agreement sought.[233]

Belgium and Romania likewise pushed for a revision by the committee of experts of the second draft.[234]

The question of the competence of the proposed court received little attention, because none of the delegates "desired" to make observations on any of the Articles of the draft. Instead, few countries, apart from Romania, made general non-technical statements regarding the jurisdiction of the proposed court – namely Article 3 of the proposed draft. Two statements out of a total of three were favourable to the subsidiary or complementary system contemplated by Article 3. Dr. Leitmaier, the Austrian delegate, said that the Austrian Government "would be glad, if necessary, to be able to hand over an accused person to an international criminal jurisdiction for punishment or for a decision regarding his extradition".[235] Likewise, V. V. Pella, the

231 *Observations by Governments on the Draft Convention for the Prevention and Punishment of Terrorism, and Draft Convention for the Creation of an International Criminal Court, Series III*, League of Nations document A. 24 (b). 1936.V. (C.194.M.139.1937.V.), p. 6.

232 See 'Records of the Seventeenth Ordinary Session of the Assembly: Minutes of the First Committee', *League of Nations Official Journal* 47, 50 (1936) (Special Supplement No. 156) [hereinafter Minutes of the First Committee].

233 *Ibid.*

234 *Ibid.*, p. 51.

235 *Ibid.*, p. 50.

Romanian delegate, favoured the mechanism embodied in Article 3 of the draft, and presented a detailed explanation supporting his argument:

> Supposing that a crime coming within the scope of the first Convention had been committed in a certain country and its author had taken refuge in Roumania. There might be in Roumania at the time a strong current of public opinion favourable to the concepts which had led that individual to commit his crime; and that current of opinion might not view sympathetically the extradition of the offender to the applicant country. On the other hand, Roumania might say: I will not extradite, but I will cause this person to be judged by my courts. Under the Roumanian Constitution, crimes must be tried by jury, and popular juries were the most prone to feel the influence of public opinion. They might therefore acquit the perpetrator of the crime. States were not exempt from international responsibility, even in respect of the decisions of their own courts. Consequently, if Roumania accorded extradition, the Government would come into conflict with its own public opinion, which might think that it was committing an act of injustice by delivering up the individual to a jurisdiction by which he might be judged without objectivity, or where he might become a victim of a sort of vengeance. If, on the other hand, the person in question were acquitted by the Roumanian courts, the Roumanian Government would not be exempt from its international responsibility.[236]

By contrast, M. Undén of Sweden thought that although the "jurisdiction" of the proposed court was "restricted", "very considerable difficulties would certainly arise in connection with the competence of the proposed Court".[237] Following these observations, a draft resolution was submitted by V. V. Pella and M. Rolin to the committee.[238] The principle of the resolution was adopted at the same meeting.[239] However, at the eighth meeting, the discussion continued on a paragraph-by-paragraph basis, and after some amendments the whole resolution was adopted.[240] The resolution noted the

236 *Ibid.*, p. 51.

237 *Ibid.*, p. 50.

238 The text of the resolution concerning an international criminal court reads: "[the Assembly] Feels that the trial of persons guilty of such[terrorist] attacks by an International Criminal Court is considered by some Governments to constitute an alternative which in certain cases would be preferable to extradition or to prosecution, and that on this ground the second Convention has for the Governments a value, even if not capable of securing general acceptance; Recommends that the Committee revise its conclusions in light of the observations to be found in the Government replies or formulated in the course of the debates, in order that the Council may convene a diplomatic conference in 1937, if possible before the next ordinary session of the Assembly": see *ibid.*, p. 52.

239 *Ibid.*, p. 56.

240 The text of the final resolution concerning the international criminal court reads: "Notes that certain Governments have disputed the advisability of creating an international criminal court, but that the trial of persons guilty of such attacks by such a court is felt by other Governments to constitute an alternative which, in certain cases, would be preferable to extradition or to prosecution, and that on this ground the second convention has been regarded by the latter Governments as valuable, even if it is not capable of securing

significance for some delegates of an international criminal court, the jurisdiction of which was occasionally to be preferred to that of prosecution before national courts or extradition to another State. It also recommended that the committee of experts revise the two draft conventions in light of the observations of governments in order to ensure that a diplomatic conference be convened in 1937.[241]

At the third session, having considered the adopted report and resolution submitted by the First Committee to the Assembly of the League of Nations on October 10, 1936, the committee of experts "proceeded" with a final review of its two draft conventions prepared at the second session.[242] As to the second convention on the establishment of an international criminal court, the committee was "influenced" by the idea that changes should be made to the effect that States parties to the convention on the international criminal court "cannot rely on the Court in their relations" with those States that would accept only the convention on the prevention and punishment of terrorism.[243] This idea was actually taken from an observation made by Czechoslovakia on March 13, 1937.[244]

The provision on competence of the proposed court stayed as Article 3, but with some modifications. The important innovation in Article 3[245] lay in making reference

general acceptance; Recommends that the Committee revise its conclusions regarding its two drafts in the light of the observations to be found in the Governments' replies or formulated in the course of the debates, in order that the Council may convene a diplomatic conference in 1937": *see* League of Nations document A.72.1936.V. *in ibid.*, Annex 7, p. 85.

241 *Ibid.*

242 *Report Adopted by the Committee for the International Repression of Terrorism on April 26th, 1937*, League of Nations document C.222.M.162.1937.V., p. 2.

243 *Ibid.*, p. 3.

244 League of Nations document A. 24 (b). 1936. V. (C.194.M.139.1937.V.), pp. 5-6.

245 Article 3 of the new draft reads:

"1. In the cases referred to in Articles 2, 3, 8, and 9 of the Convention for Prevention and Punishment of Terrorism, each High contracting Party to the present Convention shall be entitled, instead of prosecuting before his own tribunal, to send the accused for trial before the Court.

2. A High Contracting Party shall further be entitled in the cases mentioned in Article 7 of the said Convention, instead of extraditing, to send the accused for trial before the Court if the State demanding extradition is also a Party to the present Convention.

3. The provisions of the present Article shall be applicable only if the accused is a national of a State which is a Party to the present Convention and if the offence is directed against the interests of a High Contracting Party to the present Convention."

to Articles 7,[246] 8,[247] and 9[248] of the terrorism convention. A general reading of Article 3(1) suggests that the provision was attempting to limit the option of sending a case to the proposed international criminal court to the satisfaction of any of the criteria set out in Articles 2, 3, 8, and 9 of the convention for the prevention and punishment of terrorism.

Article 8(1) of the proposed terrorism convention suggests that a State would be obliged to prosecute the accused only if he or she were a national of that State, had returned to its territory after committing his crime, and extradition of nationals was not recognized. Once more, reading Article 3(1) together with Article 8(1), suggests that only the State of nationality of the accused enjoyed the option of either prosecuting before its own courts or committing the accused for trial before the proposed international criminal court. Only after the requirements of Article 8(1) are fulfilled, the State of nationality would have the option of sending its national to the proposed international criminal court. The same holds true with regard to Article 9 which obliges the *forum deprehensionis* (that is, the State where the person is arrested) to prosecute the accused before its national courts once he or she has been found on its

246 Article 7 reads:

1. Without prejudice to the provisions of paragraph 4 below, the acts set out in Articles 2 and 3 shall be deemed to be included as extradition crimes in any extradition treaty which has been, or may hereafter be, concluded between any of the High Contracting Parties.
2. The High Contracting Parties who do not make extradition conditional on the existence of a treaty shall henceforward, without prejudice to the provisions of paragraph 4 below and subject to reciprocity, recognise the acts set out in Articles 2 and 3 as extradition crimes as between themselves.
3. For the purposes of the present Article, any act specified in Articles 2 and 3, if committed in the territory of the High Contracting Party against whom it is directed, shall also be deemed to be an extradition crime.
4. The obligation to grant extradition under the present Article shall be subject to any limitations recognised by the law of the country to which application is made.

247 Article 8(1) states: "When the principle of the extradition of nationals is not recognised by a High Contracting Party, nationals who have returned to the territory of their own country after the commission abroad of an offence mentioned in Articles 2 or 3 should be prosecuted and punished in the same manner as if the offence had been committed in their own country..."

248 Article 9 further reads:

Foreigners who are on the territory of a High Contracting Party and who have committed abroad any of the acts set out in Articles 2 and 3 should be prosecuted and punished as though the act had been committed in the territory of that High Contracting Party, if the following conditions are fulfilled – namely, that:

a. Extradition has been demanded and could not be granted for a reason not connected with the act itself;
b. The law of the country of refuge recognises the jurisdiction of its own courts in respect of offences committed abroad by foreigners;
c. The foreigner is a national of a country which recognises the jurisdiction of its own courts in respect of offences committed abroad by foreigners.

territory, provided that paragraphs (a), (b) and (c) are satisfied. When reading Article 9 in the light of Article 3(1) of the proposed draft of the international criminal court, one may safely argue that the *forum deprehensionis* would no longer be limited to prosecution before its own courts. Instead, it would enjoy the same right of either surrendering the accused to the international criminal court or prosecution before its domestic courts, should it wish to do so. Yet, should none of these criteria be satisfied, the chapeau of Article 9 seems implicitly to suggest that a "High Contracting Party" would have no choice other than to send the case directly to the proposed international criminal court. The reference to Articles 7, 8, and 9 in Article 3 of the proposed international criminal court statute makes the provision complicated from a practical perspective.[249]

The reasons for the modifications of Article 3 do not appear in the direct discussions on Article 3 of the previous draft. Instead, they were tackled in the course of the general debate concerning the desirability of establishing an international criminal court and the discussion of the convention on terrorism. One reason may be found in the observation made by Czechoslovakia on March 13, 1937.[250] Some governments made comments showing their concern about the possibility of acting contrary to the existing rules of extradition, such as the prohibition of extradition of nationals and for political offences. Apart from that, Article 3 preserved the original scheme proposed by the French government in 1934, namely the system establishing and organizing the complementary relationship between national courts of the "High Contracting" States and the proposed international criminal court.

After revising the two draft conventions, the committee of experts on April 26, 1937 adopted its report, which was communicated to the governments, so that the two draft conventions would be a useful basis for convening a diplomatic conference in 1937.[251] On May 27, 1937, the Council of the League of Nations adopted a resolution directing the Secretary General to invite all the members of the League and some non-member States to participate in the diplomatic conference. The conference took place in Geneva from November 1 – 16, 1937.[252]

At the second, third, fourth and twelfth meetings held on November 1, 2, and 8, 1937, delegations from the United Kingdom, Norway, Yugoslavia, India, Netherlands, Hungary, Haiti, Poland, France, Czechoslovakia, Union of Soviet Socialist Republics, Switzerland, Belgium, Spain, Venezuela, Argentine Republic, Romania and Greece

249 See also *Observations by Governments on the Draft Convention for the Prevention and Punishment of Terrorism, and Draft Convention for the Creation of an International Criminal Court, Series II (Poland),* League of Nations document A. 24 (a).1936.V., pp. 2-3.

250 *Observations by Governments on the Draft Convention for the Prevention and Punishment of Terrorism, and Draft Convention for the Creation of an International Criminal Court, Series III,* League of Nations document A. 24 (b). 1936. V. (C.194.M.139.1937.V.), pp. 4-6.

251 *Report Adopted by the Committee for the International Repression of Terrorism on April 26th, 1937,* League of Nations document C.222.M.162.1937.V., p. 3.

252 *Historical Survey,* U.N.Doc., A/CN.4/7Rev.1, p. 17.

engaged in a general discussion on the proposed court – some of the delegates making similar observations to those raised during the drafting process prior to the conference.[253]

During the twelfth meeting, Belgium's Carton De Wiart, the President of the conference, proposed to start examining "at a first reading", Article by Article, the draft convention for the proposed court. The Czechoslovak delegation proposed amendments to Article 3(3) of the convention,[254] while the Greek delegation thought that Article 3 needed to be clearer in the sense that it should state, where a contracting party has preferred to send the accused person to the international criminal court instead of extraditing him or her or prosecuting him before its own courts, that no other State may raise objections to the competence of that State to exercise that right.[255] After extensive debate on the issue, Article 3 was referred to the drafting committee for reconsideration.

At the seventeenth meeting, delegations were invited to look again at the draft convention taking into account the observations made hitherto. The numbering of the Articles had been changed and Article 3 became Article 2 in order to make the order more logical.[256] Article 3(3) of the former draft was deleted and substituted by language that accommodated the Greek concerns. Article 3(2) was slightly modified. Yet, the scope of the provision remained unchanged. The phrase "in cases where he is able to grant extradition in accordance with Article 8 [then Article 7] of the said Convention" was added to the text.[257] The reason, as explained by the delegation of the Netherlands, was to make the text clearer in the sense that a "State would only send the accused before the [international criminal court] if it were able to grant his extradition".[258] The scope of Article 3(1) stayed as it was with the exception that the word "tribunal" was replaced by the word "courts", and the numerical order of Articles 2, 3, 8, 9 of the convention on terrorism, which appeared in Article 3(1), was changed. Instead, those Articles appeared as 2, 3, 9, and 10, respectively.[259] There was no substantial difference in relation to those provisions; rather the slight amendments made to those provisions were purely stylistic.[260] Of paramount importance is the fact that the drafters preserved the original scope of Article 3 (currently Article 2), which, as

253 See *Proceedings of the International Conference on the Repression of Terrorism*, Geneva, November 1 to 16, 1937, League of Nations document C.94.M.47.1938.V., pp. 52-69, 117-118.[hereinafter Proceedings of the International Conference].

254 For the full text see *ibid.*, pp. 119-120.

255 *Ibid.*, pp. 117-118.

256 *Ibid.*, p. 162.

257 *Ibid.*

258 *Ibid.*

259 See the text of paragraph 2 in *ibid* for the changes made.

260 These provisions were adopted and appear in the final text of the convention for the prevention and punishment of terrorism, opened for signature at Geneva, November 16, 1937, Arts. 2, 3, 9, and 10, *reprinted in* Manley Hudson, 7 *International Legislation* 862, 865 – 866, 868 (1941).

mentioned previously, was originally introduced by France in 1934 on the basis of the principle *aut dedere aut punire/judicare*.

A State had the option of either trying the accused before its own national courts, or extraditing him or her to another contracting party to the convention or the international criminal court, or committing him or her for trial before the international criminal court should it wish to do so.[261] Despite the enormous work put into drafting the convention, no State had ratified it except India.[262] But, as Professor Pella puts it, the convention "marked a decisive turning-point in the history of...public law...The dogma of sovereignty [that renders] cases belong exclusively to national courts, [has been] abandoned".[263]

Concluding Observations

The penalty provisions found in the Peace Treaties concluded after World War I reflected the real origins of the notion of complementarity in the modern era. Domestic prosecutions in Leipzig were deemed unsatisfactory, especially after a Commission established to enquire about its effectiveness recommended that the Allies should not send further cases to Leipzig. Instead, the German Government had been requested to surrender alleged war criminals in accordance with the Allies' reservation under Article 228 of the Treaty of Versailles. Similarly, neither the Hungarians nor the Turks took genuine steps to bring war criminals before their domestic courts. Nor did the Allies succeed in enforcing the letter of the penalty provisions as a result of these countries' failure to prosecute effectively before their own courts. Yet, it might still be argued that the failure of post-World War I prosecutions should not be attributed to the application of the theory of complementarity. Rather, the lack of will of the Allied governments as well as political pressure prompted them to drop the idea of prosecution.

The unsatisfactory results, especially those emanating from the Leipzig trials, influenced to a great extent the thoughts and work of legal scholars during the period following World War I. Thus, the result of the discussions was that the proposals tabled by the different unofficial bodies favoured the establishment of an international

261 Convention for the Creation of an International Criminal Court, opened for signature at Geneva, November 16, 1937, Art. 2, *in* Hudson, *supra* note 262, p. 880; J. G. Starke, 'The Convention for the Creation of an International Criminal Court', 19 *British Yearbook of International Law* 216, 216 (1938). For a critique regarding Article 2, see I. Blishchenko, N. Shdanov, 'The Problem of International Criminal Jurisdiction', 14 *Canadian Yearbook of International Law* 283, 285(1976).

262 The Convention was signed by 13 States. India was the only State that had ratified the Convention for the Prevention and Punishment of Terrorism on January 1, 1941. See L.C. Green, 'International Crimes and the Legal Process', 29 *International and Comparative Law Quarterly* 567, 572 (1980); *Cf.* John F. Murphy, 'Defining International Terrorism: A Way Out of the Quagmire', 19 *Israel Yearbook on Human Rights* 13, 15 (1989); John Dugard, 'Towards the Definition of International Terrorism', 67 *American Society of International Law Proceedings* 94, 95 (1973); Hudson, *supra* note 262, p. 862.

263 Pella, *supra* note 171, p. 39.

criminal court having exclusive jurisdiction over international offences. This does not deny the fact that few proposals called for the establishment of an international criminal court with a sort of concurrent and complementary jurisdiction. These proposals failed to gain support at the time also because of the Leipzig experience. The negotiation of the 1937 draft statute prepared under the auspices of the League of Nations for the establishment of an international criminal court mirrored a change of direction. The drafters stressed the significant role of national courts, and thus proposed a complementarity system based on the principle of *aut dedere aut judicare,* whereby a State had the choice of prosecuting before its own courts, extraditing to another State or referring the case to the proposed international criminal court. The introduction of this provision was the beginning for future proposals favouring a mechanism of complementarity.

Chapter II: The Development of the Law of Complementarity between 1941 – 1998

During World War II, the problem of dealing with atrocities committed during the course of war was more compelling. The idea of establishing an international judicial organ to try war criminals was the focus of activities of several bodies. Problems relating to the establishment of this organ remained to be resolved through the studies prepared by un- and semi-official bodies. One of the issues under discussion was the question of the nature of the competence of the proposed court. Unlike the majority of the proposals that were tabled post-World War I, which inclined toward an international criminal court with exclusive competence over certain categories of crimes, discussions during and after World War II considered the role of national courts significant in the repression of international crimes. Accordingly, on several occasions, the discussions surrounding this question favoured a system of sharing the burden between national courts and the proposed international criminal court. This chapter examines two main questions. First, what was the nature of jurisdiction proposed for the future court? Secondly, what was the philosophy behind choosing any of these mechanisms? In answering these questions, this chapter starts by examining the major draft proposals and discussions surrounding the question of competence from 1941 to 1994.

1. London International Assembly

The London International Assembly was the first to propose a clear complementary relationship between domestic courts and a future international criminal court. In 1941, the Assembly was created under the auspices of the League of Nations Union.[1] This body was not official, but the Allied governments chose the members to make recommendations in relation to the question of war crimes committed during the

1 *Historical Survey of the Question of International Criminal Jurisdiction*, U.N. Doc., A/CN.4/7/Rev.1, p. 11 [hereinafter Historical Survey U.N.Doc., A/CN.4/7Rev.1], p. 18; Jonathan A. Bush, "'The Supreme...Crime" and its Origins: The Lost Legislative History of the Crime of Aggressive War", 102 *Columbia Law Review* 2324, 2342 (2002).

course of World War II[2] and in relation to finding suitable solutions to ensure effective punishment for those who were responsible for those deeds.

The question of the punishment of war criminals and the possibility of establishing an international mechanism to deal with war crimes were the subject of ample discussions before commissions I and II of the London International Assembly. During the debates that took place before the commissions, several problems were raised surrounding the establishment of an international judicial organ to deal with the atrocities committed during the war. Among the major problems was the question of the competence of the proposed court.

In examining the question of competence during a meeting of commission II which took place in 10 July 1942, M. de Baer of Belgium argued that, although the establishment of an international criminal court was necessary, such a court could not be expected to try all war crimes.[3] The number of cases would be too large for an international court. Accordingly, national courts should continue to contribute to such a task whenever they had jurisdiction (with the exception of Germany's national courts), leaving the "most serious crimes" to come under the jurisdiction of the international criminal court.[4] With the exception of certain situations,[5] as a general rule, "[e]verything that can be judged by National Courts shall be judged by them in their own way without any interference."[6] These ideas were further developed and modified in a note presented to commission I during its meeting on September 1943, when

2 *Ibid* ; John W. Bridge, 'The Case for an International Court of Criminal Justice and the Formulation of International Criminal Law', 13 *International & Comparative Law Quarterly* 1255, 1268 (1964).

3 *London International Assembly – Commission II on the Trial of War Criminals*, TS 26/873, p. 232.

4 *Ibid.*

5 These situations include: "(a) criminals in respect of whom no Allied Court has jurisdiction; (b) criminals in respect of whom, although an Allied Court has jurisdiction, it is impossible for such Court to exercise it; (c) criminals in respect of whom two or more Allied Courts have jurisdiction." Moreover, it is vital that "any national Court would be given the faculty of waiving its right to try any criminal when for any reason whatever such trial is not desirable and in this case the criminal would be judged by the International Criminal Court": *ibid.*, p. 234.

6 *Ibid.* A similar view was espoused by Lord Maugham during the debates in the House of Lords concerning the question of war crimes. He argued that there were some instances where national courts could not try certain cases. These situations included: "(a) crimes against persons deprived of their nationality; (b) cases of mass murder as the consequences of an order, such as the drastic removal of food stuffs ordered by a German officer or by some sort of German tribunal, resulting in widespread starvation of the population; (c) similar acts causing death by exposure; (d) orders for the removal of young women to unknown destinations, obviously for the purpose of prostitution; (e) cases where two or more courts of different Allied States have jurisdiction; (f) cases where it is uncertain which of two or more such courts have the necessary jurisdiction, and finally, (g) cases where, owning to political unrest in the country where the crime was committed, it might be difficult to hold a proper trial". See *History of the United Nations War Crimes Commission and the Development of the Laws of War* (London: HMSO,

M de Baer said that "[i]t is only when a trial by a national court is impossible or inconvenient, that the case should be tried by an International or United Nations' Court."[7] He used the terms "impossible" or "inconvenient" as criteria to be fulfilled before the international criminal court could adopt the proceedings instead of national courts. In order to meet any of the requirements of "impossibility" or "inconvenience", it had to be shown that the case concerned:

1. crimes in respect of which no Allied court has jurisdiction;
2. crimes in respect of which, although an Allied court has jurisdiction, the trial is for some reason inconvenient, and the country concerned decides that the case shall be tried by an International(United Nations') Court.[8]

Under the first requirement, lack of competence was considered as an admissibility test needing to be fulfilled so that the international criminal court could exercise its jurisdiction.[9] In addition, the idea in the final phrase of paragraph 2 seemed to be borrowed from the 1937 League of Nations Draft Statute for an International Criminal Court[10] and clearly established optional concurrent and complementary jurisdiction between national courts and the proposed international criminal court, which provided the State with the choice of the forum to try the case. A State for some reason might prefer to waive jurisdiction in favour of the international criminal court instead of bringing a case before its own domestic courts.

Similar conclusions were highlighted in the preliminary report prepared by the sub-committee headed by J. M. de Moor of the Netherlands. In a meeting of commission II which took place in 19 January 1943, J. M. de Moor, concurring with M. de

1948), p. 442 (The debates in the House of Lords 7 October, 1942) [hereinafter History of the UNWCC].

7 *London International Assembly – Commission I for Questions Concerned with the Liquidation of the War*, TS 26/873, p. 282.

8 M de Baer identified five cases that might meet the second paragraph as follows: (1) "In the case of criminals who have committed crimes in several Allied countries. In respect of these criminals it would be impractical to try them successively in each of the countries where they have committed their crimes; (2) In the case of criminals who have committed crimes of an international nature, the effect of which was to be obtained in several countries or who have given orders to commit crimes to be carried out in several countries (e.g. Goering, Himmler, etc..); (3) In the case of heads of State; (4) In cases where a national court would be unable to obtain evidence, because the witnesses are residing in an Axis country and cannot be compelled to leave that country, and where such evidence could be obtained by an International Court functioning in the Axis country where the witnesses are residing; (5) In the case where on account of the unsettledness of the post-war situation a trial in the country concerned might cause disturbances, and where a trial elsewhere would be more convenient or remove any suspicion of vindictiveness": *ibid.*, pp. 282 – 283.

9 This also applies to M. de Baer's initial proposal tabled on 10 July 1942. See *supra* note 5 and accompanying text.

10 *See* Chapter I, *supra*.

Baer's opinion, thought that establishing an international criminal court with exclusive jurisdiction was not a valid option.[11] Instead, the obligatory competence of the proposed court would be limited to specific cases where national courts (military or civilian) were not in a position to try a case.[12]

The philosophy behind opting for a court with a complementary jurisdiction as proposed by the London International Assembly may be deduced from the discussions of the members of commissions I and II. One main reason was to avoid flooding the international criminal court with cases that it could not accommodate.[13] Moreover, national courts were the *forum conveniens* – best equipped with the evidence, witnesses and the machinery to act promptly toward crimes committed on their territory.[14] But, at the same time, they demanded that the rest of the cases be dealt with so that war criminals would not escape justice. Thus, the only solution was to divide labour between the proposed international court and already-established national courts. Yet, there were some situations where national courts lacked the jurisdiction to try certain cases. This was clear in cases where the crimes were committed by the Axis powers on their own territory against Allied nationals. Such crimes included the torture and killing of prisoners of war, as well as crimes committed against Jews and stateless people in Germany.[15] Meanwhile, still influenced by the experience of the Leipzig trials, the London International Assembly was against the idea of leaving these cases to German courts.[16]

The outcome of the discussions of the London International Assembly finally appeared in a draft vonvention for the vreation of an international criminal court, in November 1943.[17] The nature or scope of the jurisdiction of the proposed court ap-

11 *London International Assembly – Commission II on the Trial of War Criminals*, TS 26/873, pp. 228 – 229.

12 J. M. de Moor mentioned thee situations where the international criminal court might adopt the proceedings: 1) "The group of cases, which by their special international character and nature as for instance those of Hitler, Himmler etc. are indicated for an International Court. 2) Those cases in which two or more States would be competent and for which those States have note made a special arrangement about preference in the same case as there is a regulation of preference between the courts of one State. 3) Those cases in which no State is competent": *ibid.*, p. 229.

13 *Ibid*; *London International Assembly – Commission I for Questions Concerned with the Liquidation of the War*, TS 26/873, p. 284; *London International Assembly – Commission II on the Trial of War Criminals*, TS 26/873, p. 232.

14 *London International Assembly – Commission I for Questions Concerned with the Liquidation of the War*, TS 26/873, p. 282.

15 *Ibid.*, pp. 281-282. Support was given to the proposal that crimes committed against the Jews in Germany and stateless should not go unpunished: see Egon Schwelb, 'Crimes Against Humanity', 23 *British Yearbook of International Law* 178, 184 (1946); and *generally* John Hagan, Scott Greer, 'Making War Criminal', 40 *Criminology* 231, 235 (2002).

16 See, e.g., the Report prepared by Sheldon Glueck, *London International Assembly – Commission I for Questions Concerned with the Liquidation of the War*, TS 26/873, p. 236.

17 The draft was prepared by M. de Baer and amended by Commission I before being published: *London International Assembly – Commission I for Questions Concerned with the Liquidation of the War*, TS 26/873, pp. 324 – 325.

peared in Articles 3 and 4(1) of the draft.[18] Although the final provisions differed to some extent from those proposed during the meetings of the Assembly, the core idea remained untouched. Article 3(1) of the draft stipulated that "[a]s a rule, no case shall be brought before the Court when a domestic Court of any one of the United Nations has jurisdiction to try the accused and it is in a position and willing to exercise such jurisdiction."[19] This represented the main idea intended by the drafters: to provide national courts with primary jurisdiction and save the international criminal court for exceptional situations, thereby preserving the sovereign rights of States. Those exceptional situations appearing in the form of an exhaustive list in the earlier proposals were absent from the text of Article 3.[20] Instead, the last sentence of Article 3(1) ("it is in a position and willing to exercise such jurisdiction") suggests that it is a catch-all clause capturing all situations that would prevent a domestic court from exercising jurisdiction.

Using the phrase "it is in a position" represents the *ability* of the State, while the previous phrase is a test of the *willingness* of the State to take up the proceedings. Yet, the provision is not clear as to who will assess the "position" or the "willingness" of the State if it wishes to refer a case to the international criminal court. Is it the court? Or it is left to the discretion of the State? Reading Article 3(1) in the light of Article 4(1) suggests that the intended procedure is for the State to have the option of sending a case to the international criminal court if it is neither willing nor able to deal with the case before its domestic courts in the territory where the accused is residing or present.

Article 4(1) was borrowed directly from M. de Baer's proposal, which permitted the custodial State to waive its jurisdiction in favour of the international criminal

---

18 See draft convention for the creation of an international criminal court, Arts. 3, 4 (1) [hereinafter LIA Draft]. Article 3 states: 1) "As a rule, no case shall be brought before the Court when a domestic Court of any one of the United Nations has jurisdiction to try the accused and it is in a position and willing to exercise such jurisdiction. 2) Accused persons in respect of whom the domestic Courts of two or more United Nations have jurisdiction, may however, by mutual agreement of the High Contracting Parties concerned, be brought before the Court. 3) Provided that the Court consents, any crime as defined in Article 2 may be brought before the International Criminal Court, either by national legislation of the State concerned, or by mutual agreement of the High Contracting Parties concerned in the trial." Further Article 4 (1) states: 1) "Each H.C.P. shall be entitled, instead of prosecuting before his own Courts a person residing or present in his territory who is accused of a war crime, to commit such accused for trial to the I.C.C."

19 LIA Draft, Art. 3(1).

20 See the criteria proposed by M. de Baer and J. M. de Moor, *London International Assembly – Commission I for Questions Concerned with the Liquidation of the War*, TS 26/873, pp. 282-283; *London International Assembly – Commission II on the Trial of War Criminals*, TS 26/873, p. 229.

court,[21] a mechanism that gained support in legal doctrine at the time.[22] Again, a reading of Article 4(1) suggests that the person who is "residing or present" on the territory of the State that would prefer not to deal with the case might also be a national of that State or might have committed his or her crime on the territory of that State. According to this reading, Article 4(1) permits the mechanism of a waiver of complementarity to be discussed later in chapter III.

2. International Commission for Penal Reconstruction and Development

In a conference held in Cambridge on 14 November 1941, at the request of M. de Vleeschouwer, the Belgian Minister of Justice, it was agreed that a Permanent Commission for Penal Reconstruction and Development should be established.[23] The Commission was a semi-official body composed of scholars from the United Kingdom and other Allied countries.[24] At the conference, a resolution was passed unanimously that mandated the Commission to "establish a Committee to consider the Rules and Procedure to Govern the case of Crimes against International Public Order, in collaboration with other bodies working on the same subject, and to report thereon to the International Commission for Penal Reconstruction and Development".[25] This committee was chaired by Sir Arnold McNair who on 28 April 1942 framed a questionnaire composed of 14 questions to be distributed to the members of the committee for their observations.[26]

One issue that was raised concerned the type of tribunal that should punish the war criminals of World War II.[27] In this context, Sir Arnold McNair tabled two questions. First, if it were desired "to resort to existing tribunals so far as they have jurisdiction; for instance, would the ordinary military courts and the ordinary municipal criminal courts of the Allied Powers have adequate jurisdiction to deal with the ma-

21 *London International Assembly – Commission II on the Trial of War Criminals*, TS 26/873, p. 234; *London International Assembly – Commission I for Questions Concerned with the Liquidation of the War*, TS 26/873, p. 282.

22 See, e.g., Vespasian V. Pella, 'Towards an International Criminal Court', 44 *American Journal of International Law* 56, 56 n. 49 (1950) (supporting the proposal of an international criminal court provided with optional jurisdiction as proposed by the LIA).

23 See *International Commission for Penal Reconstruction and Development: Proceedings of the Conference held in Cambridge on the 14th November, 1941, Between Representatives of Nine Allied Countries and of the Department of Criminal Science in the University of Cambridge*, p. 11 [hereinafter Proceedings of the Cambridge Conference].

24 Historical Survey U.N.Doc., A/CN.4/7Rev.1, p. 19; Antoine Sottile, 'The Creation of a Permanent International Criminal Court', 29 *Revue de Droit International de Sciences Diplomatiques et Politiques* 267, 284 (1951).

25 *Proceedings of the Cambridge Conference*, pp. 33 – 34.

26 *Confidential Report of the International Commission for Penal Reconstruction and Development: Questionnaire of 28 April, 1942*, W.2., pp. 1 – 4.

27 *Ibid.*, p. 2.

jority of crimes committed by enemy persons and their adherents?"[28] Second, "is it desirable to create a special court to deal with the residue of crimes over which the above-mentioned courts would not have jurisdiction?"[29]

Sir Arnold McNair was testing the possibility of establishing an international criminal court with a limited jurisdiction that functioned in a complementary manner with national courts when dealing with the "residue of crimes" that did not come under the jurisdiction of any of the Allied courts – the exact idea of the London International Assembly. In principle, the idea gained the majority's support with the exception of clear opposition from Yugoslavia.[30] Yet, the proposed situations that were to come under the jurisdiction of the international criminal court varied.

Professor Stranský of Czechoslovakia argued that one of the most significant "conditions of the success of any attempt to punish war criminals will be the greatest possible limitation of international criminal jurisdiction".[31] This was because "it can hardly be expected that any State would – in the realm of criminal law – give up its right to jurisdiction over its own citizens for crimes committed against their own legal government and their duties of loyal citizens".[32] Accordingly, it is significant to have recourse to national courts as long as they have jurisdiction.[33] An international criminal court, therefore, would adopt proceedings only in "specified situations".[34]

Similarly, Professors Glaser and Winiarski of Poland thought that, in "principle", national jurisdictions should conduct prosecutions and "produce the evidence" as long as they enjoyed competence.[35] International jurisdiction "should be established for special cases where justified by exceptional circumstances,...[such as] crimes committed by the same person in different countries, when extradition is needed/ from a neutral country/, etc".[36] Members such as Mr. Bodson of Luxembourg took a similar view, yet without spelling out completely the type of cases where, in his opinion, national courts might lack jurisdiction.[37]

28 *Ibid.*

29 *Ibid.*

30 *Ibid.*, p. 7. (Bozidar Vlajić of Yugoslavia arguing that trials "should be left to the exclusive competence of the respective countries").

31 *Confidential Report of the International Commission for Penal Reconstruction and Development: Answers to the Questionnaire of 28 April, 1942*, D.1a, p. 3.

32 *Ibid.*

33 *Confidential Report of the International Commission for Penal Reconstruction and Development: Questionnaire of 28 April, 1942*, W.2., p. 20.

34 1) "Cases where victims belong to two or more Allied States; 2) Crimes of an international character which exceed the limits of the individual states; 3) Cases which do not come under national jurisdiction." *Ibid.*, p. 21.

35 *Ibid.*, pp. 24, 31.

36 *Ibid.*, p. 24. Another example was mentioned in this context "persons responsible for the behaviour of the occupying forces, authoritative bodies or their members": *ibid.*

37 *Ibid.*, p. 23. With the exception of one scenario that he proposed, namely where crimes were committed in Germany. In this situation, the international criminal court should step in: *ibid.*, p. 17.

Mr Wold of Norway thought that the majority of war crimes should be dealt with by the national courts of the territorial State or the State whose nationals were victims of the crimes.[38] Thus, "only exceptional cases would have to be committed for trial by international courts".[39] Where nationals of several countries were victims of crimes committed by one person, the perpetrator should be tried before an international criminal court instead of the courts of different countries, thus ensuring expediency and coherent sentencing.[40] Some crimes that had "taken effect in several countries as a result of a centralized plan relating to the conquest or occupation of Allied countries" should even be dealt with by an international criminal court.[41] In any event, it would be the responsibility of an "international authority" to select certain cases that warranted being tried by the international criminal court.[42]

Other members, such as Mr. Stavropoulos of Greece, agreed in principle that national courts (whether civilian or military) should try "all cases over which they would ordinarily have jurisdiction" but rejected the idea of establishing an international criminal court.[43] Instead, he proposed a "special Inter-Allied Court"[44] similar to the one introduced in Article 228 of the Treaty of Versailles[45] – vested with subsidiary jurisdiction over certain situations: 1) where national courts lacked jurisdiction; 2) and where the "accused might have committed crimes on territories of two or more Allied States".[46] The reasons were twofold. For a court to be "substantially" international, Stavropoulos said that the judges should not be limited to those of the Allied States. The court should be composed of judges from neutral and enemy countries.[47] Moreover, establishing such a court would require a great deal of time, which would result in justice delayed.[48] Comparable conclusions were reached by J. M. de Moor of Holland who adopted a similar approach to that followed during the meetings of the London International Assembly.[49] Judging the thousands of war criminals before

38 *Ibid.*, p. 10.

39 *Ibid.*

40 *Ibid.*, pp. 17 – 18.

41 *Ibid.*, p. 18.

42 *Ibid.*

43 *Ibid.*, p. 22.

44 *Ibid.*

45 *Cf.* Chapter I, *supra.*

46 *Confidential Report of the International Commission for Penal Reconstruction and Development: Questionnaire of 28 April, 1942*, W.2., p. 22.

47 *Ibid.*

48 *Ibid.*, p. 23.

49 *Confidential Report of the International Commission for Penal Reconstruction and Development: Comments on the Chairman's Note*, G.2., pp. 6-7. J. M. de Moor identified four situations in which the International Criminal Court might adopt proceedings. "(a) Crimes in respect of which no United Nations' Court has jurisdiction(e.g. crimes committed in Germany against Jews and stateless persons and possibly against Allied nationals); (b) crimes in respect of which a United Nations' Court has jurisdiction but which the State concerned elects not to try in its own Courts(for reasons such as the following:

an international criminal court was an impractical solution.[50] Domestic courts were competent and in a better position to try the large number of war crimes committed on the Allies' territories.[51] Yet, several States were "already occupied in meeting a serious objection" relating to the punishment of war crimes committed outside their territories, such as those committed in German concentration camps.[52] Thus, in a situation such as this and others, the establishment of an international criminal court seemed to be the practical solution.

Belgium's De Baer was the first to introduce a scheme for an international criminal court vested with complementary jurisdiction.[53] He thought that, as a matter of practicality, it was more plausible to opt for a court tied with a system that did not interfere with the jurisdiction of national courts.[54] This was because the existing hurdle of national sovereignty would make it difficult to request the territorial States to renounce domestic jurisdiction in favour of an international judicial organ.[55] Accordingly, States should have the option of either choosing to send a case to the international criminal court or dealing with it before its own courts[56] – an element which was clearly overlooked by the members of the International Commission for Penal Reconstruction and Development when responding to the questionnaire. The proposed scheme ensured that States voluntarily curtailed their national sovereignty and were not compelled to do so.[57]

At a later meeting held at the Polish Institute on 15 July 1942, H. Lauterpacht presented a memorandum on the matter. Unlike the majority view which supported the establishment of an international criminal court with a sort of complementary or subsidiary jurisdiction, H. Lauterpacht thought that there were some practical obstacles that mitigated against the establishment of such an institution in general.[58] Instead, he argued that military and civil courts composed of judges of high standing

(a) where a trial in the country concerned might lead to disturbances; (b) where a Municipal Court would find it difficult to obtain evidence); (c) crimes which have been committed or which have taken effect in several countries or against nationals of different countries; (d) crimes committed by Heads of States".

Cf. London International Assembly – Commission II on the Trial of War Criminals, TS 26/873, p. 229.

50 *Ibid.*, p. 4.

51 *Ibid.*

52 *Ibid.*, p. 5.

53 See *London International Assembly – Commission II on the Trial of War Criminals*, TS 26/873, pp. 228-229, 232, 234, 282-283.

54 *Confidential Report of the International Commission for Penal Reconstruction and Development: Answers to the Questionnaire of 28 April, 1942*, D.1b., p. 6.

55 *Ibid.*, pp. 6-7.

56 *Ibid.*, p. 7.

57 *Ibid.*

58 *International Commission for Penal Reconstruction and Development: Memorandum by Professor H. Lauterpacht*, D.3., pp. 24-25.

would suffice to guarantee a speedy and impartial trial.[59] Alongside these courts, there should be established quasi-international courts of appeal composed of judges from several member States of the United Nations, supplemented by enemy and neutral "assessors" sitting in each of these States.[60] This might be a "satisfactory substitute" for an international criminal court.[61] It was finally resolved to set up a sub-committee composed of M. de Baer as Chair and Mr. Jean Burnay of France, Professor Stephan Glaser of Poland, and Professor Hersch Lauterpacht, who attended the meetings by invitation.[62] The sub-committee was to examine the extent to which the punishment of war crimes could be achieved by means of national jurisdictions, both military and civilian[63] – a question that was almost identical to that studied in the questionnaire of 28 April 1942.

On 24 August 1942, M. de Baer, the Chairman of the sub-committee, prepared a questionnaire concerning the issue under consideration and passed it to the members of the sub-committee for their comments.[64] The majority's replies were tied, in principle, to the view that an international criminal court was feasible as a supplementary jurisdiction to that of national courts. In his reply to the questionnaire, Professor Glaser thought that the role of national courts was indispensable in the punishment of war crimes. National courts were, for many practical reasons, the *forum conveniens*.[65] The machinery of international tribunals was very complicated and slow, and thus should be "established only for special cases where justified by exceptional circumstances", where national laws fell short of criminalizing some crimes committed by the enemy.[66]

M. de Baer, an advocate of a system of complementary jurisdiction, applied a similar line of reasoning to that followed during the meetings of the London International Assembly.[67] An international criminal court should be set up with jurisdiction over

59 *Ibid.*, p. 25.

60 *Ibid.*, p. 26. Lauterpacht expressed a similar view in an article published in 1944 based on the memoranda submitted to the ICFPRC. See H. Lauterpacht, 'The Law of Nations and the Punishment of War Crimes', 21 *British Yearbook of International Law* 58, 82 – 83 (1944).

61 *Ibid.*, pp. 26 – 27.

62 *International Commission for Penal Reconstruction and Development: Introductory Note by the Secretary General*, D. I., p. 2.

63 *Ibid.*

64 *Confidential Report of the International Commission for Penal Reconstruction and Development: Note to Members of the Sub-Committee*,W.5., pp. 1-2.

65 *Confidential Report of the International Commission for Penal Reconstruction and Development: Answers to Questionnaire of Dr de Baer's Note to Members of the Sub-Committee*, D.6., pp. 14 – 15.

66 *Ibid.*

67 *Confidential Report of the International Commission for Penal Reconstruction and Development: Answers to Questionnaire of Dr de Baer's Note to Members of the Sub-Committee*, D. 5., pp. 6 – 7; *Cf. London International Assembly – Commission II on the Trial of War Criminals*, TS 26/873, pp. 228-229, 232, 234, 282 – 283.

the "residue of crimes",[68] similar in principle to those mentioned in his proposals to the London International Assembly.[69] A system like the one proposed ensured that, 1) all war crimes would not go unpunished; 2) the jurisdiction of national courts was not "curtailed", thus respecting States' national sovereignty; and 3) cases involving crimes committed on German soil would not be judged by German courts[70] – a situation that was unwarranted following the Leipzig experience. Professor Lauterpacht opposed the entire system of complementarity proposed by M. de Baer and the majority of the members.[71]

Yet, if the sub-committee and the International Commission for Penal Reconstruction and Development recommended the establishment of an international criminal court with a "residuary segment of cases", it would be more reasonable to apply the system of complementarity differently. The machinery proposed by M. de Baer and others was based on the assumption that cases that could not be brought before national courts on the basis of the principle of territoriality should go before the international criminal court. These cases "probably" included those against some "prominent war criminals" who deserved "speedy and exemplary punishment" that could not be subjected to the delays connected with the establishment of an international criminal court.[72] Thus, it was proposed that the triggering of the jurisdiction of the international criminal court should not depend on the territoriality principle as explained above.

68 *Confidential Report of the International Commission for Penal Reconstruction and Development: Answers to Questionnaire of Dr de Baer's Note to Members of the Sub-Committee*, D. 5., p. 7. (M. de Baer mentioned the following cases where an international criminal court might step in: "(i) crimes in respect of which no Allied Court had jurisdiction, (ii) specifically international crimes as to which two or more Allied Courts have jurisdiction, (iii) crimes in respect of which, although an Allied Court has jurisdiction the nation concerned prefers not to try it in its own courts, (iv) crimes committed in Axis countries against the "heimatlose", persons who cannot prove their nationality or who have been deprived from their nationality": *ibid.*

69 Although there were slight differences between the two proposals, they shared an important common element – that was that national courts would always enjoy primacy over war crimes as long as they were competent. *Cf.* the similarities and differences between the two proposals. *London International Assembly – Commission I for Questions Concerned with the Liquidation of the War*, TS 26/873, p. 282-283.

70 *Confidential Report of the International Commission for Penal Reconstruction and Development: Answers to Questionnaire of Dr de Baer's Note to Members of the Sub-Committee*, D. 5., pp. 7-8.

71 *Confidential Report of the International Commission for Penal Reconstruction and Development: Answers to Questionnaire of Dr de Baer's Note to Members of the Sub-Committee*, D. 7., pp. 19-21; see also his earlier views presented at the Polish Institute on 15 July 1942, *International Commission for Penal Reconstruction and Development: Memorandum by Professor H. Lauterpacht*, D.3., pp. 24-27.

72 *Confidential Report of the International Commission for Penal Reconstruction and Development: Answers to Questionnaire of Dr de Baer's Note to Members of the Sub-Committee*, D. 7., p. 20.

Instead, the standard should be that all cases of high magnitude should be judged by national courts,[73] while cases which were "less grave" should be dealt with by an international criminal court.[74] In instances where States lacked jurisdiction over certain crimes committed outside their territorial reach, legislation could easily be passed to "circumvent" this obstacle.[75] This proposal did not curtail the proposed system of "residuary jurisdiction", yet it ensured that cases involving high level war criminals were dealt with effectively and speedily. The materials discussed above and others were included in a Report prepared by Sir Arnold McNair, the Chairman of the committee. On 29 July 1943, this Report was submitted to a full meeting of the International Commission for Penal Reconstruction and Development.[76] The Commission unanimously agreed to submit the Report to the "appropriate authority" of each of the Allied Governments.[77]

3. Draft Convention for the Establishment of a United Nations War Crimes Court prepared by the United Nations War Crimes Commission

The United Nations War Crimes Commission was an official body established on 20 October 1943 upon a recommendation of Lord Chancellor of the United Kingdom, to investigate war crimes committed by the Axis powers during World War II.[78] The Commission's task also extended to examining the available evidence and reporting to the Allied governments for the purpose of requesting the alleged perpetrators

---

73 Professor Lauterpacht mentioned 18 acts that fell into this category. Some examples may be mentioned here: "1. Grave crimes against person and property committed without any pretence of legal authority or order, i.e., crimes of private lust. These include murder, manslaughter, infliction of grievous bodily harm, torture, false imprisonment, blackmail, rape, theft and pillage on a large scale." For the rest of the list see *ibid.*, pp. 17 – 18.

74 *Ibid.* Crimes of lesser magnitude may include for example: "arbitrary destruction of property, unlawful requisitions, removal of private and public property, confiscation of property, etc." For the rest of the list see *ibid.*, p. 19.

75 *Ibid*; see also Lauterpacht, *supra* note 60, p. 67. (noting that "[t]he law of Great Britain, of the United States, and of many other States, does not, as a rule, recognize the competence of national courts in respect of criminal acts committed by aliens abroad. But there would be not question of any retroactivity, contrary to justice and to established principles of law, if Great Britain were to alter her law so as to enable her tribunals, civil or military, whether functioning in Great Britain or abroad, to assume jurisdiction over German nationals who committed in Germany criminal offences against British prisoners of war or British civilians in circumstances not authorized by international law": *ibid.*

76 *International Commission for Penal Reconstruction and Development: Introductory Note by the Secretary General*, D. I., p. 3.

77 *Ibid.*

78 *United Nations War Crimes Commission Progress Report*, C.48, 12 September, 1944, p. 1.

to surrender the moment fighting ceased.[79] From the outset, the Commission was concerned with the question of establishing a war crimes court or an inter-Allied tribunal to try major war criminals in accordance with the letter of the Moscow Declaration of 1943.[80]

On 22 February 1944, the American and Australian delegates led a campaign favouring the establishment of such a court. The Commission authorized committee II (on enforcement) to start discussing the matter promptly.[81] On 14 April 1944, the United States presented a draft convention for the creation of an inter-Allied court taking into consideration the draft convention of the London International Assembly.[82] The draft convention retained the jurisdiction of national courts. The idea was that the "bulk of the cases" were to be dealt with before these courts. The inter-Allied court was designed to deal with cases where national courts lacked jurisdiction under international law or as a result of a gap in domestic legislation. Also, where for any "sufficient reason" the country concerned preferred to refrain from exercising domestic jurisdiction.[83] This draft was taken as the basis of committee II's future discussions.[84]

On 29 June 1944, a sub-committee was appointed to redraft the jurisdictional provision and make several recommendations. Central to these recommendations was an idea which stressed the primacy of national courts in exercising jurisdiction over their nationals. Should a State with jurisdiction over the crime prefer to cede its primacy to the international court, it was at liberty to do so.[85] These recommendations tied in with the main purposes of the United States draft.

In its progress report adopted by the Commission on 19 September 1944, committee II showed satisfaction that an inter-Allied tribunal or an international court competent to exercise jurisdiction in any case of a violation of the laws of war was to be established.[86] Thus, another draft convention prepared by committee II appeared on 30 September 1944,[87] later followed by an accompanying explanatory memoran-

79 *Ibid; also United Nations War Crimes Commission,* Memorandum by Sir Cecil Hurst, LCO 2/2976.

80 The Triparte Conference at Moscow, Oct. 19 – 30, 1943, *reprinted in* International Conciliation, No. 395, pp. 599 – 605 (1943)[hereinafter Moscow Declaration].

81 History of the UNWCC, *supra* note 6, p. 443,

82 *United Nations War Crimes Commission,* Draft Convention on the Trial and Punishment of War Criminals, II/II, 14 April 1944.

83 *Ibid.*, art. 27; Foreign Office to Sir Donald Somervell, S,W,1, 15 April, 1944.

84 History of the UNWCC, *supra* note 6, p. 443.

85 *Questions as to the Jurisdiction of the Proposed Court Prepared by the Sub-Committee,* II/23, 29 June 1944.

86 *United Nations War Crimes Commission Progress Report,* [C 12588/14/62], 19 September, 1944, p. 3.

87 *United Nations War Crimes Commission,* Draft Convention for the Establishment of a United Nations War Crimes Court, C.50(1), 30 September, 1944.

dum.[88] The preamble to this convention reflected the essence of the United States' draft and the sub-committee's recommendations regarding the nature of the proposed court's jurisdiction. Preamble paragraph 4 of the convention stated that having "decided to set up an Inter-Allied Court before which the Governments of the United Nations may at their discretion bring the trial persons accused of an offence to which the Convention applies in preference to bringing them before a national court..."[89] The preamble established a complementarity mechanism,[90] consistent with that created under the United States' draft and the sub-committee's recommendations. The system also ties in with that found under Article 2 of the 1937 League of Nations Convention and Articles 3(1) and 4(1) of the London International Assembly's draft.[91]

As a general rule, national courts had the primary jurisdiction to try the crimes under consideration.[92] A State, however, had the freedom to decide whether it was unwilling to deal with a certain case before its national courts and to refer the case to the inter-Allied court.[93] This conclusion was mirrored in the language of preamble paragraph 3 of the draft convention, which provided that "[m]indful of the possibility that cases may occur in which such crimes cannot be *conveniently or effectively* punished by a national court" (emphasis added).[94]

Although the system of complementarity embodied in the draft for the war crimes court was clearly inspired by that of the London International Assembly, there is no direct evidence to suggest that it was intended to base it on the 1937 League of Nations provision. The reasons for favouring a system of complementarity in the draft of the war crimes court were the same as for thinking of establishing it. Some of those reasons appeared in documents that were issued after the drafting of the convention.

The Moscow Declaration stated that the perpetrators of the German atrocities were to be judged before the national courts of the Allied countries in which the crimes took place.[95] The United Nations War Crimes Commission acknowledged

88 *United Nations War Crimes Commission*, Explanatory Memorandum To Accompany the Draft Convention for the Establishment of a United Nations War Crimes Court, C.58, 6 October, 1944.

89 *United Nations War Crimes Commission*, Draft Convention for the Establishment of a United Nations War Crimes Court, C.50 (1), 30 September, 1944, preamble para. 4.

90 Preamble paragraph 4 was also inspired by the jurisdictional provision proposed by the sub-committee on 29 June 1944. See *Questions as to the Jurisdiction of the Proposed Court Prepared by the Sub-Committee*, II/23, 29 June 1944.

91 *London International Assembly – Commission I for Questions Concerned with the Liquidation of the War*, TS 26/873, pp. 324-325, Arts. 3(1), 4(1).

92 *United Nations War Crimes Commission*, Draft Convention for the Establishment of a United Nations War Crimes Court, C.50 (1), 30 September 1944, preamble para. 2. Paragraph 2 states: "[r]ecognising that in general the appropriate tribunals for the trial and punishment of such crimes will be national courts of the United Nations".

93 *Ibid.*, preamble paras. 3 – 4.

94 *Ibid.* preamble para. 3.

95 Moscow Declaration, *supra* note 80.

that the majority of cases submitted to the Commission for investigation should be brought to trial before the national courts of the Allied powers. Yet, it acknowledged the differences between the Anglo-American and the continental legal systems, which would have led to some of these cases going unpunished as a result of the courts' lack of jurisdiction.[96] Some Allied countries felt that "for constitutional and other reasons it would [have been] difficult for them to ensure in a satisfactory manner the trial of at any rate all cases in which they were concerned in their national courts, as contemplated in the Moscow Declaration".[97] There was fear that some acts which constituted a serious violation of the laws of war would be tried under the ordinary criminal law of some continental law countries. This would have resulted in the imposition of inadequate penalties.[98] Also there were cases where "the authors of some of the atrocities committed by enemy were not committed in any one particular country" .[99] On several occasions, the question was raised of the atrocities committed against the Jews in Germany. Because Allied courts lacked jurisdiction over crimes committed by Germans on German soil, some raised the question whether the establishment of an inter-Allied court would have solved the problem.[100]

The idea of establishing a United Nations war crimes court by means of a treaty to be signed in a diplomatic conference vanished. The British vigorously opposed it on several grounds, including the time factor.[101] Instead, it was seen to be more plausible to establish mixed military tribunals to speed up the proceedings once hostilities had ceased.[102] Later efforts were directed towards establishing the Nuremberg International Military Tribunal to try the major war criminals in accordance with the Moscow Declaration.

96 *United Nations War Crimes Commission Progress Report,* [C 12588/14/62], 19 September, 1944, pp. 3 – 4.

97 From Foreign Office to Lord Chancellor (C 13600/14/62), 14 October 1944; From the Secretary of State to Sir C. Hurst, LCO 2/2976, December 1944.

98 *United Nations War Crimes Commission Progress Report,* C.48, 12 September 1944, p. 4.

99 *Ibid.*

100 *United Nations War Crimes Commission,* Memorandum by The Lord Chancellor, LCO 2/2976, 30 March 1944, p. 4; W.P. (44) 294, 2 June 1944, pp. 2 – 3; Foreign Office to F. Mayell (C 7347/14/62), 5 June 1944; *United Nations War Crimes Commission,* Memorandum by Sir Cecil Hurst; Donald Somerwell to Lord Chancellor, SW.1, LCO 2/2976, 3 May 1994; Donald Somerwell to Sir William Malkin, LCO 2/2976, 28 February 1944.

101 Foreign Office to Lord Chancellor (C 13600/14/62), 14 October 1944. It was stated even earlier than the conclusion of the convention that the establishment of such a court would have violated the Moscow Declaration, which called for the trial of mid-level German perpetrators before national courts.

102 *United Nations War Crimes Commission,* Suggestions to Accompany the Recommendation for the Establishment of Mixed Military Tribunals, C.59, 6 October 1944; Foreign Office to Washington, No. 9342, LCO 2.2976, 26 October 1944.

4. The Nuremberg International Military Tribunal

The International Military Tribunal, established at the end of World War II, reflected another form of the complementarity principle and the significance of cooperation with national criminal jurisdictions.[103] The International Military Tribunal was set up to try only the major war criminals,[104] while the bulk of the task of prosecution was left to internal criminal jurisdictions. This was done in a subsidiary manner. In the Moscow Declaration of 1943,[105] the three main Allied powers declared that German war criminals should be judged and punished in the countries in which their crimes were committed (that is, according to the principle of territorial jurisdiction). Only "the major criminals, whose offenses have no particular geographical localization," would be punished "by joint decision of the Governments of the Allies."[106] This declaration was referred to in the London Agreement of August 8, 1945[107] establishing the Nuremberg Tribunal. Thus, the fact that the International Military Tribunal judged only 22 accused, of whom 19 were found guilty and three were acquitted,[108] was due

103 But see Georg Schwarzenberger, 'The Problem of an International Criminal Law,' 3 *Current Legal Problems* 263, 290 – 291(1950) (noting that neither the IMTFE nor the IMT was international in character).

104 See generally on the Nuremberg trials Robert K. Woetzel, *The Nuremberg Trials in International Law* (London: Stevens & Sons, 1960); Roger S. Clark, "Nuremberg and Tokyo in Contemporary Perspective" in Timothy L.H. McCormack et al. (eds.), *The Law of War Crimes: National and International Approaches* (The Hague/London/Boston: Kluwer Law International, 1997), p. 171.

105 Moscow Declaration, *supra* note 80.

106 *Ibid.*, p. 601; see also Paolo Benvenuti, "Complementarity of the International Criminal Court to National Criminal Jurisdictions, in Flavia Lattanzi et al. (eds.), *Essays on the Rome Statute of the International Criminal Court*, Vol. I (Il Sirente, 1999), p. 24; see generally George Schwarzenberger, 'The Judgment of Nuremberg,' 21 *Tulane Law Review* 329 (1946 – 1947).

107 London Agreement of Aug. 8, 1945, *reprinted in* 1 Trial of Major War Criminals Before the International Military Tribunal 8, pp. 8 – 9 (1947) [hereinafter London Agreement].

108 International Military Tribunal (Nuremberg), Judgment and Sentences, October 1, 1946, *reprinted in* 41 *American Journal of International Law* 172, 333 (1947). Although Hjalmar Schacht, Franz Von Papen and Hans Fritzsche were acquitted by the IMT, they were eventually retried before the Spruchkammer (Denazification Court) in Nuremberg. See Telford Taylor, *The Anatomy of the Nuremberg Trials* (New York, 1992), pp. 611-614; see also William A. Schabas, *Genocide in International Law: The Crimes of Crimes* (Cambridge: Cambridge University Press, 2000), p. 278;Roger S. Clark and Madelein Sann, 'Coping with Ultimate Evil through the Criminal Law,' 7 *Criminal Law Forum* 1, 3 – 4(1996). It might be argued that such a practice reflected Germany's insistence on exercising its national criminal jurisdiction. Thus, this demonstrates that States deem it important to ensure that their role in exercising their criminal jurisdiction in the repression of such crimes, which derives from their sovereignty, is not hindered by International Tribunals. Unlike Germany, where those accused and convicted of war crimes became, for the most part, pariahs in their society, Japan did not view such persons convicted by the International Military Tribunal for the Far East (IMTFE) as criminals, but as victims. Shigemitsu

to the recognition of the role of national criminal jurisdictions. The others would "be sent back to the countries in which their abominable deeds were done in order that they may be judged and punished according to the laws of these liberated countries and of free governments".[109]

> [G]ermans who take part in wholesale shooting of [Polish] officers or in the execution of French, Dutch ... or have shared in slaughters inflicted on the people of Poland or in territories of the Soviet Union ... will be brought back to the scene of their crimes and judged on the spot by the peoples whom they have outraged.[110]

The International Military Tribunal represented a different approach from that adopted at the end of World War I. The Treaty of Versailles and other peace treaties outlined the concept of the deferral of jurisdiction, which reflected the direct application of complementarity. The inter-Allied tribunals of the Peace Treaties had a direct relationship with the German national courts and deferred to them on the condition that the inter-Allied tribunals would intervene if the German courts failed to act. The doctrine of "state sovereignty" played a major role in shaping the settlement.

In contrast, the International Military Tribunal reflected the principle of primacy, or the supremacy of international law over national law, with regard to trying major war criminals for core crimes. Although there was no explicit discussion concerning this issue during the judgment of the International Military Tribunal, there was a supremacy element to the Tribunal itself.[111] However, due to the lack of a direct relationship between the International Military Tribunal and national courts – since

Mamoru, a career diplomat who was Foreign Minister in Tojo Midelki's Wartime Cabinet, was sentenced by the IMTFE to 7 years' imprisonment. He was released on parole on 21 Nov. 1950, and in Nov. 1951 he was given clemency. Later, in 1954 he became Foreign Minister.

109 Moscow Declaration, *supra* note 80; Preamble to the London Agreement, *supra* note 107(affirming the trials of minor war criminals on the national level, where their crimes had occurred); also Article 4 of the London Agreement, which affirms the trials of minor war criminals on the national level, where their crimes took place. Article 4 states: "Nothing in this agreement shall prejudice the provisions established by the Moscow Declaration concerning the return of war criminals to the countries where they committed their crimes": *ibid.*, p. 9.

110 Moscow Declaration, *supra* note 80. By 1948, European countries and the United States had brought a total of 969 cases in their respective courts, involving 3,470 accused, of whom 952 were sentenced to death, 1,905 were imprisoned and 613 were acquitted. See M. Cherif Bassiouni, *Al Mahakamah Al Genaiah Al Dowaliah: Nashaatoha wa Nezamiha Alaasasi Maa Derasah Letarikh Legan Al Tahkik Al Dowaliah wa Al Mahakem Al Genaiah Al Dowaliah Al Sabikah* (*The International Criminal Court: Its Establishment, Its Statute, and A Study of the History of the International Investigative Commissions and the Former International Criminal Tribunals*) (Cairo: Nadi Al Koudah, 2001), p. 23.

111 See also Leila Sadat Wexler, 'Panel Discussion: Association of American Law Schools Panel on the International Criminal Court', 36 *American Criminal Law Review* 223, 249 (1999).

both had different jurisdictions and tried different categories of war criminals – the complementarity principle emerged in a different form. The Tribunal tried only major criminals, whose offences were not associated with any particular geographical location, leaving the minor criminals to national criminal jurisdictions. This task was undertaken by the national courts established by governments with competence to adjudicate on war crimes at the places where they were committed as well as by the occupying powers themselves, each within its own zone, with its own set of courts, applying its own scheme of law.[112]

In order to establish a minimum common basis for the trials to be conducted in the four zones of occupation, in December 1945, the Allied Control Council, acting as a legislative body for all of Germany, enacted Law No. 10 entitled "Punishment of Persons Guilty of War Crimes, Crimes against Peace, Crimes against Humanity". Consequently, it was the responsibility of each zone commander to implement Law No. 10 in his zone.[113] This serves as a good example for effective cooperation in the sense of complementarity between national and international criminal jurisdictions.[114]

5. The Principle of Complementarity in the Drafting History of the Genocide Convention

Pursuant to General Assembly Resolution 96(I) of 11 December 1946, the Economic and Social Council (ECOSOC) was requested to "undertake the necessary studies with a view to drawing up a draft convention on the crime of genocide."[115] In acting upon this request, the ECOSOC adopted Resolution 47(IV) instructing the Secretary General to draw up a draft convention on genocide with the assistance of some ex-

112 Antonio Cassese, "From Nuremberg to Rome: International Military Tribunals to the International Criminal Court", in Antonio Cassese et al. (eds.), *The Rome Statute of the International Criminal Court*, Vol. I (Oxford: Oxford University Press, 2002), p. 7 [hereinafter Cassese Commentary]; M. Cherif Bassiouni, 'The Time Has Come for an International Criminal Court', 1 *Indiana International & Comparative Law Review* 1, 5 (1991).

113 See Allied Control Council Law No. 10, Punishment of Persons Guilty of War Crimes, Crimes against Peace and Crimes against Humanity, 20 December 1945, Official Gazette of the Control Council for Germany, No. 3, 31 January 1946; Benvenuti, *supra* note 106, p. 24.

114 As one commentator has rightly argued , "[t]he agreement between the Four Major Powers fighting at that time against Germany, and those nineteen States, which in addition signed the Nuremberg Statute, was based on *mutual trust*. Accordingly, there was no need to centralize the prosecution so as to guarantee uniformity with an international court beside Nuremberg and Tokyo. Rather a far-reaching complementarity existed. On both levels the prosecution and sentencing were based on a practical division of labour": Otto Triffterer, "Preliminary Remarks: The Permanent International Criminal Court – Ideal and Reality", in Otto Triffterer (ed.), *Commentary on the Rome Statute of the International Criminal Court: Observers' Notes, Article by Article* (Baden – Baden: Nomos Verlagsgesellschaft, 1999), p. 38 [hereinafter Triffterer Commentary].

115 G.A.Res., 96 (I), 1st Session, Fifty-fifth plenary meeting.

perts in the field for consideration at a later session.[116] The draft was considered by the Sixth Committee during several meetings and, upon its recommendation, the General Assembly adopted Resolution 180(II) of 21 November 1947 requesting the ECOSOC to study further the draft prepared by the Secretariat, and to "proceed with the completion of a convention".[117] In doing so, by virtue of Resolution 117(VI) of 3 March 1948, the ECOSOC established an *Ad hoc* Committee to prepare a draft convention on genocide, taking into account the draft convention prepared by the Secretariat. The draft convention prepared by the *Ad hoc* Committee was the subject of discussions at the Sixth Committee;[118] the General Assembly, using the committee's report, passed Resolution 260(III) of 9 December 1948 approving the Convention on the Prevention and Punishment of the Crime of Genocide.[119]

The final text of Article VI of the Convention states that an act of genocide may be tried by a "competent" domestic tribunal as well as by such "international penal tribunal as may have jurisdiction".[120] Article VI makes no such reference to the nature of the relationship between these tribunals. The drafting history of the Genocide Convention, however, reveals the complexity and diversity of opinions on the reconciliation of the ideas of national and international repression of international crimes such as genocide. Some delegations thought that national repression of acts of genocide was sufficient, while others argued to the contrary: international repression was the only viable solution. A third group of states proposed a functioning relationship between national and international jurisdictions, where international repression would function as a last resort in cases where national repression fails to fulfil the task. This proposal respected national sovereignty and became known as the principle of complementary jurisdiction.

In its initial proposals on the Genocide Convention, the Secretariat, which acted with the assistance and advice of Donnedieu de Vabres, Vespasian Pella and Raphael Lemkin, clearly favoured establishing an international tribunal with optional jurisdiction in some cases and compulsory in others, based mainly on the 1937 League of Nations Draft Statute for an International Criminal Court. Two alternative models were considered for the organization of the tribunal: the first was an international tribunal with jurisdiction over all international crimes;[121] the second, a "special" international

116 ECOSOC.Res., 47(IV), 4th Session, *in* Historical Survey UN Doc., A/CN.4/7Rev.1, p. 30.

117 *Ibid.*, pp. 30-31; G.A.Res., 180(II), 2 nd. Session, 123rd plenary meeting.

118 Historical Survey UN Doc., A/CN.4/7Rev.1, p. 31.

119 G.A.Res., 260 (III), 3 rd Session, 179th plenary meeting, 9 December 1948, pp. 174-177. On the origins of genocide see Raphael Lemkin, *Axis Rule in Occupied Europe* (Carnegie Endowment for International Peace, 1944).

120 Convention on the Prevention and Punishment of the Crime of Genocide, adopted 9 Dec. 1948, entered into force 12 Jan. 1951, 78 UNTS 277, Art 6. For a contemporary application of Article VI before domestic courts see e.g., *Munyeshyaka*, French Court of Cassation (Criminal Chamber), 6 January, 1998, 127 ILR, p. 137.

121 UN Doc. E/447. Article IX of the Secretariat Draft which deals with all matters concerning international crimes reads: "The High Contracting Parties pledge themselves to

tribunal, was to have limited jurisdiction over genocide.[122] The two models were appended to the Secretariat's draft.[123] The international court or tribunal would have complementary or subsidiary jurisdiction to hear a case if a State was "unwilling" to try or extradite offenders, or where genocide had been committed "with the support or toleration of the State".[124] This proposal tied in to some extent with a proposal introduced by de Vabres during a meeting of the Committee on the Progressive Development of International Law and its Codification on 15 May 1947.[125]

---

commit all persons guilty of genocide under this Convention for trial to an international court in the following cases: 1. When they are unwilling to try such offenders themselves under Article VII or to grant their extradition under Article VIII. 2. If the acts of genocide have been committed by individuals acting as organs of the State or with the support or toleration of the State"; see also Schabas, *supra* note 108, pp. 369 – 370.

122 Two draft proposals were also submitted dealing only with the crime of genocide. One was a draft for a permanent court, while the other was for an *ad hoc* court. For example, Article 2(1) of the draft for a permanent court concerning the nature of the competence reads: "1. In cases of acts of genocide committed by individuals acting as organs of the State or having been supported or tolerated by the State, each High Contracting Party and any other State which arrested such individuals on its territory may, if unwilling to extradite or punish the said individuals, request…to commit them for trial to the Court": UN Doc. E/447; Historical Survey U.N.Doc., A/CN.4/7Rev.1, pp. 123-124, 131. The provision concerning the nature of competence in the two drafts is almost identical.

123 UN Doc. E/447, Article X ; Historical Survey UN Doc., A/CN.4/7Rev.1, pp. 122 – 123.

124 UN Doc. E/447, Article IX ; Historical Survey UN Doc., A/CN.4/7Rev.1, p. 121; see also Lawrence J. LeBlanc, *The United States and the Genocide Convention* (Durham, London: Duke University Press, 1991), p. 154; Schabas, *supra* note 108, p. 369.

125 By virtue of General Assembly resolutions 94(I), and 95(I) of 11 December 1946, a Committee on the Progressive Development of International Law and its Codification was created, and directed to "treat as a matter of primary importance plans for the formulation, in the context of a general codification of offences against the peace and security of mankind, or of an International Criminal Code, of the principles recognized in the charter of the Nürnberg Tribunal and in the judgment of the Tribunal." The Committee consisted of 17 Members of the United Nations appointed by the General Assembly on the basis of a recommendation of the President. See G.A.Res., 94(I), 1st Session, Fifty-fifth plenary meeting; G.A.Res., 95(I), 1st Session, Fifty-fifth plenary meeting. For a thorough discussion of the work of the Committee see Yuen-Li Liang, 'The General Assembly and the Progressive Development and Codification of International Law', 42 *American Journal of International Law* 66 (1948). At its second meeting on 13 May 1947, the French representative Donnedieu de Vabres brought up the question of establishing an international criminal court. On 15 May 1947 he submitted a memorandum containing his vision of the future Court. The proposed court was envisaged to have two distinct "fields" of jurisdiction: (I) jurisdiction to be conferred on a criminal chamber to be established in the International Court of Justice to deal with issues such as: "conflicts regarding judicial and legislative competence". (II) Jurisdiction conferred on an International Court of Justice to deal with issue such as all international infringements committed in time of peace, including offences against the law of nations, war crimes and all common law offences connected with crime against humanity committed by State rulers. De Vabres proposed that the scope of competence be complementary or subsidiary based on the

Raphael Lemkin, another expert consulted, disagreed with the complementarity mechanism introduced by de Vabres and Pella. Instead, he argued in favour of the deletion of paragraph 1 of Article IX of the Secretariat draft and proposed a different complementarity scheme. According to Lemkin, only rulers and leaders of criminal organizations responsible for acts of genocide should be tried before the international tribunal,[126] while other cases of lesser magnitude should either be dealt with before national courts of the territorial State or be extradited to another State for trial.[127]

In the *Ad hoc* Committee, there were opinions on the question of national and international repression. Mr. Morozov of the USSR, stressed that no exception should be created, even in the case of genocide, to the principle of respecting national sovereignty by preserving a state's territorial jurisdiction.[128] He vigorously opposed creating an international tribunal to try the crime of genocide.[129] Instead, he proposed the following new language for Article IX of the draft submitted by his delegation:

> The Convention should provide that persons guilty of genocide shall be prosecuted as being guilty of a criminal offence; that crimes thus committed within the territory coming under the law of a State shall be referred to the national courts for trial in accordance with the internal legislation of that [S]tate.[130]

Thus, the Soviet Union held the view that only national courts should carry out such a duty. Mr. Perez-Perozo of Venezuela[131] and Mr. Rudzinski of Poland supported the

1937 League of Nations Convention in the sense that the "State holding the offender having the option, according to the case, of trying him in its own tribunals, to extradite him (if its jurisdiction is subsidiary) or, on the contrary, to hand him over to the international tribunal." See *The Charter and Judgment of the Nürnberg Tribunal: History and Analysis (Memorandum submitted by the Secretary-General)*, 1949, UN Doc., A/CN.4/5, pp. 23-29. This proposal and others were included in a report of the Committee, which was submitted to the second Session of the General Assembly and then referred to the Sixth Committee for consideration. Although the Sixth Committee discussed the report, the part on the question of international criminal jurisdiction was completely left out. See Historical Survey UN Doc., A/CN.4/7Rev.1, pp. 29 – 30.

126 Lemkin introduced a similar opinion in an early work on genocide when he stated: "The liability for genocide should rest…[as well on] members of governments and political bodies which organized or tolerated genocide…The enforcement should be planned very carefully, and should not be left solely to the courts of the countries where the crime was committed". See Raphael Lemkin, 'Genocide A New International Crime Punishment and Prevention', 17 *Revue Internationale de Droit Penal* 360, 367 (1946).

127 UN Doc. E/447, Comments on Article (IX), p. 41; Historical Survey UN Doc. A/CN.4/7Rev.1, p. 122.

128 UN Doc. E/AC.25/7; UN Doc. E/AC.25/SR.7, p. 4.

129 UN Doc. E/AC.25/SR.7, pp. 4-5; See also Schabas, *supra* note 108, p. 356.

130 UN Doc. E/AC.25/7; UN Doc. E/AC.25/SR.7, p. 3.

131 UN Doc. E/AC.25/SR.7, p. 5. Venezuela feared that the establishment of such a judicial body might wound national pride. It claimed the whole idea was inconsistent with the

same view.[132] By contrast, France conceived of an international tribunal with exclusive competence because it had no confidence in national justice systems to assume responsibility for genocide prosecutions.[133]

John Maktos of the United States, who was in favour of establishing an international penal tribunal to try those perpetrating genocide, tabled a moderate proposal.[134] He proposed a tribunal with minimal powers,[135] based upon a rule of complementarity by which an international court would have jurisdiction only if the State with territorial jurisdiction could not or had failed to act.[136] The proposal dispelled any fears on the part of states "lest the international court, with its powers as yet undefined, infringed their sovereign rights".[137] Thus, a significant number of ratifications of the convention were to be secured.[138] The *Ad hoc* Committee adopted the principle of complementarity by four votes to none with three abstentions.[139]

In the Sixth Committee, Mr. Messina of the Dominican Republic, supporting the view of the USSR,[140] in essence arguing that the Constitution of the country "recog-

principle of respect for national sovereignty laid down in Article 2(7) of the Charter of the United Nations.

132 *Ibid.*, p. 11. Poland claimed that it would be premature to establish an international court. Although Poland's delegate's wording does not clearly reflect opposition to the idea of an International Tribunal, nonetheless, one may deduce that such wording implies indirect opposition to this idea, because of the prevailing notion of State sovereignty.

133 UN Doc. E/AC.25/SR.7, p. 9. "No State would commit its governing authorities to its own courts", said the delegate of France. *Ibid.* Nevertheless, this idea reflects only the minority's opinion.

134 UN Doc. E/AC.25/SR.7, p. 12.

135 UN Doc. E/AC.25/SR.8, pp. 13 – 15.

136 *Ibid.*, pp. 13, 15. The chair proposed the following: "the jurisdiction of the international court would be exercised in cases where it has found that the State in which the crime was committed, had not taken adequate measures for its punishment"; Schabas, *supra* note 108 p. 371; and also Pella, *supra* note 22, p. 55, 55n.45 (who thought that the establishment of an international tribunal with a sort of complementary jurisdiction similar to that proposed by the United States Delegation could resolve some cases where "offenses against the law of nations" were committed by "individuals acting as instrumentalities of states, or with the incitement or abetment of states".

137 UN Doc. E/AC.25/SR.8, pp. 13, 15.

138 *Ibid.*

139 UN Doc. E/AC.25/SR.8, p. 15. However, the inclusion of the principle of complementarity in the convention was finally rejected by five votes to one (United States) with one abstention (USSR) on the basis that the inclusion of a paragraph to that effect might prejudice the question of the jurisdiction of the court. See *Official Records of the Second Session of the General Assembly*, Sixth Committee, 42 nd meeting; *and* UN Doc. A/C.6/SR.98, p. 379.

140 UN Doc. A/C.6/SR.98, p. 379. Mr. Morozov of the USSR argued vigorosly against the idea of establishing an International Penal Tribunal when he said:"The Committee would be taking a wrong course by seeking a solution of the problem of punishing genocide by the establishment of an international tribunal. International jurisdiction was a violation

nized the jurisdiction of national tribunals alone with respect to crimes committed in the territory of the [State], [and thus] was consequently opposed to the very principle of sharing that jurisdiction with an international tribunal."[141] Similarly, Mr. Perozo of Venezuela thought that it would have been more plausible "to leave the punishment of genocide to national courts", as the time was not ripe for the establishment of an international tribunal.[142] One of the main reasons for such opposition, as explained by other representatives, was the existing hurdle of national sovereignty. Mr. Abdoh of Iran recalled that "States were jealous of their national sovereignty and that they had readily recognized the jurisdiction of the International Court of Justice only because recourse to that court was optional."[143] A similar conclusion was drawn by the representatives of Czechoslovakia[144] and USSR.[145]

Those views did not find support in the opinion of the representative of Chile, who argued that the principle of national sovereignty was not absolute, and as a result of evolution, the principle of "international solidarity" should replace the old dictum.[146] On a parallel line of argument, Mr. Demesmin of Haiti concluded that the constitutional provisions of certain countries or the principle of "national sovereignty" of states could not be used as an argument against the principle of the international punishment of genocide.[147] In the same vein, Mr. Dihigo, the representative of Cuba backing Mr. Chaumont of France,[148] thought that, as far as State responsibility was concerned, the punishment of genocide on the national level "could only be inadequate or ineffective".[149]

---

of the sovereign right of every State to judge crimes committed in its territory; and the sovereignty of States was the very basis of the United Nations. There was no exception to that rule in the case of genocide ": *ibid.*

141 UN Doc. A/C.6/SR.97, p. 367.

142 UN Doc. A/C.6/SR.98, p. 378.

143 UN Doc. A/C.6/SR.97, p. 368. However, interestingly the representative of Iran later reversed his opinion on the question of sovereignty. See UN Doc. A/C.6/SR.100, p. 395 (stating that "[t]he *Ad Hoc* Committee on Genocide had constantly borne in mind the principle of the sovereignty of States. That principle was in no way inconsistent with the principle of subsidiary universal punishment").

144 UN Doc. A/C.6/SR.98, p. 376.

145 UN Doc. A/C.6/SR.100, p. 403.

146 UN Doc. A/C.6/SR.97, p. 372.

147 *Ibid.*, p. 369.

148 *Ibid.*, p. 373; UN Doc. A/C.6/SR.98, pp. 380 – 382; see also the statement made by Mr. Chaumont at the 64th meeting: "genocide was an international crime; its punishment should therefore be on an international scale. Genocide implied, in fact, the complicity, or at least the toleration of Governments. It would not therefore be sufficient to provide for its punishment in domestic legislation, because such measures might not be carried out. It might therefore be desirable to set up an international penal court to punish the crime". UN Doc. A/C.6/SR.64.

149 UN Doc. A/C.6/SR.97, p. 368.

Other representatives, such as Mr. Khan of Pakistan, proposed a system of complementary relationships between the intended international tribunal and national courts, differing from the one proposed during the meetings of the *Ad hoc* Committee. Mr. Khan suggested that national courts should deal with crimes committed by private individuals while the international tribunal should be saved for cases involving government officials,[150] which was originally found in the Secretariat Draft.[151] Mr. Iksel, the representative of Turkey,[152] favoured this proposal, while India had some reservations.[153]

The United States re-introduced its initial proposal tabled during the work of the *Ad hoc* Committee. John Maktos, the representative of the United States, proposed that:

> Jurisdiction of the International Tribunal in any case shall be subject to a finding by the Tribunal that the State in which the crime was committed had failed to take appropriate measures to bring to trial persons who, in the judgment of the court, should have been brought to trial or had failed to impose suitable punishment upon the convicted of the crime.[154]

The delegate of Uruguay backed this proposal and argued that the convention could not be "effective unless it provided for an international tribunal to remedy any failure on the part of national courts to take punitive measures".[155] Thus, national courts of the territorial State should enjoy primary jurisdiction over persons charged with any of the acts enumerated in Article IV. Should the competent authorities of the State in question "fail to proceed to such punishment effectively", any of the Parties to the Convention could refer the case to the International Court of Justice, which would be competent to rule on any such failure on the part of the State. If the State's failure was proved, the latter "shall deal with and pronounce judgment on the crime of genocide".[156]

150 *Ibid.*, p. 367.

151 See Article IX (2) of the Secretariat Draft, UN Doc. E/447; Historical Survey U.N.Doc., A/CN.4/7Rev.1, p. 121.

152 UN Doc. A/C.6/SR.97, p. 370.

153 *Ibid.*, p. 372. Mr. Sundaram of India stated: "[H]is delegation did not reject *a priori* the jurisdiction of an international court in cases an act of genocide was committed or tolerated by Governments; he observed, however, that if two kinds of courts for the repression of the crime of genocide were envisaged, the cases when over which national courts would have jurisdiction and the cases which would have to be submitted to the international court must be clearly determined in advance": *ibid.*

154 UN Doc. A/C.6/235; UN Doc. A/C.6/SR.98, p. 378; UN Doc. A/C.6/SR.100, p. 399; Schabas, *supra* note 108, p. 373.

155 UN Doc. A/C.6/SR.97, p. 365.

156 UN Doc.A/C.6/209; see also Schabas, *supra* note 18, p. 373. This proposal ties in with the above conclusion. However, the difference was that Uruguay intended that a criminal chamber of the ICJ was to be the competent tribunal that would deal with cases in question. Uruguay withdrew its amendment later after the resolution on the international pe-

Although the United States and Uruguayan proposals, similarly, called for an international penal tribunal with complementary jurisdiction, the complementarity mechanism differed in *substance* from those introduced during the meetings of the London International Assembly, International Commission for Penal Reconstruction and Development, United Nations War Crimes Commission and the Committee on the Progressive Development of International Law and its Codification.

The United States and Uruguayan proposals were based on the assumption that some measures would have been initiated already in relation to a specific case, yet were not deemed adequate. The proposals tabled by the other bodies did not require any proceedings to be initiated or even be evaluated in order to trigger the competence of the international penal tribunal.[157] The State could have elected, for some reason, not to deal with the case from the outset and preferred to send it to the international tribunal without even being judged as having failed to handle the case, which was clearly based on the 1937 League of Nations model.[158] Accordingly, a State's inaction would suffice to trigger the jurisdiction of the tribunal. Nevertheless, the two systems contemplated by the drafters were similar in *essence*, since they proposed an international penal tribunal that would do what national courts were not capable of doing. Unfortunately, due to the divergences regarding the idea of international repression in general, the system of complementarity *proper* did not find its way into the final text of Article VI of the Genocide Convention.

6. The Role of the International Law Commission in the Development of the Principle of Complementarity (1950 – 1994)

The issue of the formulation of the principles recognized in the Charter of the Nuremberg Tribunal and its judgment prompted the General Assembly to adopt Resolution 177(II) of 21 November 1947. The Resolution directed the International Law Commission to prepare a "draft code of offences against the peace and security of man kind".[159]

The discussion of the 1948 Genocide Convention also generated the idea of considering a plan to study the question of international criminal jurisdiction. By virtue of Resolution 260 (III) A of 9 December 1948, the General Assembly adopted the

nal tribunal was adopted. See e.g., UN Doc. A/C.6/SR.99, p. 391; UN Doc./A/C.6/SR.100, p. 398.

157 But these proposals do not address the situation where a State has initiated proceedings and either failed properly to handle the case or preferred for any reasons to send the case to the tribunal. Would the tribunal still be competent to take up the proceedings?

158 This does not deny the fact that beside the case of optional jurisdiction found in these proposals, there are other cases of compulsory jurisdiction that were introduced in these proposals, yet different from that proposed by Pella, de Vabres, the United States, and Uruguay, as their language, do not require a *determination* of States' failure or any measures to be initiated before the international tribunal can interfere.

159 G.A.Res., 177(II), Second Session, Hundred and twenty-third plenary meeting, 21 November 1947.

Genocide Convention.[160] At the same meeting, having in mind the increasing need for an international judicial organ for the trial of certain crimes under international law including genocide, it passed Resolution 260(III) B, inviting the International Law Commission to study the "desirability" and "possibility" of executing this plan.[161] Acting upon these resolutions, the International Law Commission began studying the two questions in parallel.

6.1 The 1951 Draft Code of Offences against the Peace & Security of Mankind

The 1951 Draft Code of Offences against the Peace and Security of Mankind (draft code) lacks any reference to the type of tribunal being considered for the punishment of the crimes set out in the draft. Consequently, it does not mirror any relationship between domestic and international tribunals. This is simply because the initial mandate of the International Law Commission was restricted to the preparation of a draft code of international offences that threaten peace and security. Nonetheless, the question of the implementation of the provisions of the code through either a mechanism of international or national repression was brought up on several occasions in relation to other issues that were under consideration by the International Law Commission.

At its first session, the International Law Commission appointed Mr. Jean Spiropoulos to be the Special Rapporteur on the subject of the draft code and invited him to prepare a working paper to be submitted to the Commission at its second session.[162] This he did.[163] The final part of the report had the text of a draft code appended to it, including seven provisions appearing under the title "basis of discussion". It was taken as the main basis of the Commission's discussion.[164] In July 1950, the Commission examined the basis of discussion of Mr. Spiropoulos's report. These discussions imposed an obligation upon the parties to the code to enact the necessary legislation to give effect to the code.[165] They further referred to the trial of people who had committed any of the acts punishable under the code by a "competent tribunal",

160 G.A.Res., 260(III) A, Third Session, 179th plenary meeting, 9 December 1948.

161 G.A.Res., 260(III) B, Third Session, 179th plenary meeting, 9 December 1948.

162 *Report of the International Law Commission on its Second Session*, 5 June to 29 July 1950, Official Records of the General Assembly, Fifth Session, Supplement No. 12 (A/1316), 1950 *YILC*, Vol. II, p. 379 [hereinafter 1950 *ILC Report*].

163 UN.Doc. A/CN.4/25, 1950 *YILC*, Vol. II, pp. 253 – 278. For further details on the Commission's first meeting concerning the preparation of a draft code see *Summary Record of the Thirteenth meeting*, 31 May 1949, UN Doc. A/CN.4/SR 30, pp. 6 – 14.

164 1950 *YILC*, Vol. II., pp. 277 – 278.

165 *Ibid.*, p. 278. Basis of discussion number 4 reads: "The parties to the code undertake to enact the necessary legislation giving effect to the provisions of the present code and, in particular, to provide effective penalties for persons guilty of any of the acts declared punishable by the code": *ibid.*

presumably international, yet without infringing the "penal jurisdiction possessed by States under their municipal law".[166]

The proposals made it clear that national courts alongside an international tribunal should try crimes proscribed under the code. But how such a relationship between national and international tribunals should be organized in practice was not explained. Mr. Spiropoulos, the report's author, argued that since no international tribunal was yet established, the Commission should adopt a provision similar to that found in the Genocide Convention. In his opinion, since "all crimes were of a political nature, no State would be willing for its officials to be tried by its own courts",[167] thus, arguably favouring the engagement of an international tribunal, once it has been created.

Mr. Alfaro thought that national courts or tribunals should deal with crimes under the code until an international tribunal had been established.[168] He proposed the insertion of the words, "[p]ending the establishment of an international tribunal competent to try these crimes".[169] Similarly, Mr. Scelle, the Chairman, supported a view to the same effect.[170]

In considering the questions of political crimes, extradition and the non-extradition of nationals, other members, such as Mr. El-Khoury, reached a slightly different conclusion. He argued that as long as no international tribunal existed, the "application of the Code would necessarily be confined to domestic courts or to special courts set up for each case".[171] Yet, "there would still be cases which would have to be tried before domestic courts", even despite the setting up of an international tribunal.[172] Thus, Mr. El-Koury's idea of implementing the code called for a sort of complementary relationship between national courts and the future international court.

The Commission set up a drafting sub-committee, composed of Messrs. Alfaro, Hudson and Spiropoulos, to prepare a provisional text.[173] Article IV of the provisional text still endorsed the original idea that prevailed during the Commission's discussion that national courts should not deal with the crimes defined in the code once an

166 *Ibid.* Basis of discussion number 5 reads: "1. The parties to the code undertake to try by a competent tribunal persons having committed on their territory any of the acts declared punishable by the present code. 2. The foregoing provision does not affect the penal jurisdiction possessed by States under their municipal law": *ibid.*

167 1950 *YILC*, Vol. I, p. 170.

168 *Ibid.*

169 *Ibid.*

170 *Ibid.*

171 *Ibid.*, pp. 175 – 176.

172 *Ibid.*, p. 176. But he did not specify what these cases were. It is not clear though whether he meant certain acts referred to in the code or crimes other than those mentioned in the code. In either situation, it may be argued that El-Koury imagined an international tribunal that divided the responsibilities with national courts.

173 1950 *ILC Report*, 1950 *YILC*, Vol. II, p. 380.

international tribunal had been set up.[174] Mr. Spiropoulos, on the other hand, was requested to prepare another draft on the basis of the drafting committee's provisional text to be presented at the Commission's third session.[175]

During the examination of Mr. Spiropoulos' second draft, the question of national versus international penal jurisdiction was raised. One member reiterated that an international penal tribunal should enjoy exclusive competence over the crimes under the code.[176] Another member tabled a proposal to amend the first line of the text of Article 5.[177] Article 5 was based on the text of Article IV of the provisional text. It was construed as follows: the future international penal tribunal would enjoy exclusive competence over crimes under the code.[178] A suggestion was made to delete the reference to an international criminal court, even though, at the time of this comment, none such existed.[179] Yet another view suggested that "all reference to the possibility of an international criminal jurisdiction being established in the future should not be deleted", because it was impossible to adopt a code "based exclusively" on the jurisdiction of national courts.[180] If the present text of Article 5 was deemed unsatisfactory, the Commission would consider a different formulation, based on the text of Article VI of the Genocide Convention.[181] According to this proposal, states would undertake to bring the perpetrators of the offences in question to trial "before their national courts..., and subsequently, to bring the guilty persons before the international court, when the latter was established".[182]

Arguably, the interpretation given by one member to Article VI of the Genocide Convention did not seem to change the original scheme introduced in Article 5 of the draft code – namely that the future international penal tribunal would still have exclusive jurisdiction over the defined crimes. Other members, such as Mr. Alfaro, believed that the "activities" of national courts had not been satisfactory since the Leipzig experience and, therefore, international crimes should "in any case" be tried

174 UN Doc. A/CN.4/R.6. Article IV of the provisional text reads: "Pending the establishment of a competent international criminal court, the States adopting this Code undertake to enact the necessary legislation for the trial and punishment of persons accused of committing any of the crimes under international law as defined in the Code."

175 *Report of the International Law Commission on its Third Session*, 16 May to 27 July, Official Records of the General Assembly, Sixth Session, Supplement No. 9 (A/1858), 1951 *YILC*, Vol. II, p. 134.

176 1951 *YILC*, Vol. I, p. 84.

177 *Ibid.*, p. 242.

178 Article 5 reads: "Pending the establishment of a competent international criminal court, the States which adopt this Code undertake to enact the necessary legislation for the trial and punishment of persons accused of committing any of the offences defined in this Code": *ibid.*, p. 242 n. 15.

179 *Ibid.*, p. 242.

180 *Ibid.*, pp. 242 – 243.

181 *Ibid.*, p. 242.

182 *Ibid.*

by an international tribunal.[183] Similar conclusions, yet based on a different line of reasoning, were reached by Mr. Francois[184] and Mr. Scelle.[185] The discussions on these issues were conclusive, and the 1951 Code contained no provision reflecting them.[186]

6.2 The 1954 Draft Code of Offences against the Peace & Security of Mankind

Although the 1951 draft made no reference to the type of tribunal that was supposed to deal with the crimes defined in the code, the question of inserting a provision to that effect re-emerged in the course of the discussion of the changes proposed to that draft, which later led to the adoption of the 1954 draft code. The consideration of the 1951 draft code was initially included in the provisional agenda of the sixth session of the General Assembly.[187]

In November 1951, the General Assembly postponed its consideration of the subject to the seventh session.[188] At that session, the United Kingdom representative argued that "it was not ripe" for the General Assembly to consider the draft code, "that the comments received by governments should be submitted to the Interna-

183 *Ibid.*, p. 243. But see the interesting observation made by the Dutch Government in reply to the ILC's Questionnaires concerning the preparation of a draft code. The Dutch Government said: "With respect to the implementation, in its most appropriate form, distinction should be made between that which is the final objective in view in this respect and that which might be accepted at the present moment. The final objective should be the establishment of an international tribunal, before which tribunal persons who have committed indictable offences according to the code shall be tried, and the obligation of the States to give up the accused residing within their territory for trial and possible punishment, and, failing this, the possibility to force the States thereto. With regard to the question as to what may be achieved at the present moment,...States as a whole haven not yet reached such a degree of solidarity that they would entrust an international tribunal with these trials. Hereby the question of compulsory inclusion of the offences of the code in domestic penal law is a matter of foremost consideration while it is also assumed that, upon agreement, smaller groups of States may already be willing to accept jurisdiction of an international tribunal at the present moment": UN Doc. A/CN.4/19 Add. 1, 1950 *YILC*, Vol. II, pp. 252 – 253.

184 1951 *YILC*, Vol. I, p. 243.

185 *Ibid.*, p. 244.

186 1951 *YILC*, Vol. II, pp. 134 – 137 (with 5 Articles adopted). Article 1 of the code only stated that crimes under the code are punishable, without spelling out by what means the individuals responsible should be tried. Moreover, Article 5 of the code stipulated that the penalties should be "determined by the tribunal exercising jurisdiction" over the accused. Thus, it dud not refer to whether such intended tribunal was domestic or international or both.

187 1953 *YILC*, Vol. I, p. 352. On the 1954 draft Code, see D.H.N. Johnson, 'The Draft Code of Offences against the Peace and Security of Mankind', 4 *International and Comparative Law Quarterly* 445(1955); M. Cherif Bassiouni, 'International Law and the Holocaust', 9 *California Western International Law Journal* 202, 254 – 257 (1979).

188 1954 *YILC*, Vol. II, p. 149.

tional Law Commission; and that only after having considered the comments could the Commission present to the General Assembly its final recommendations in the matter".[189] The General Assembly dropped the item from the final agenda of the seventh session on the basis that the International Law Commission would continue to consider the matter.[190] The Commission, in turn, was seised with the matter at its fifth session in 1953.[191] It requested the Special Rapporteur to prepare a "Third Report" concerning the draft code for submission at the Commission's sixth session.[192] The Report generally "retained" the 1951 draft with slight departures based on the governments' comments and proposals introduced by the Special Rapporteur.[193]

In considering the modified draft text of Article 1,[194] some members proposed a reference to the mechanism by which an offender would be punished. Article 1 of the modified text, like Article 1 of the 1951 draft, did not specify the type of tribunal that should deal with offences in the code. Mr Codrova thought it was significant to specify whether offenders "would be punished under national law or by an international tribunal".[195] One member proposed that offenders should be punished "by each State until such time as an international criminal court is set up".[196] Others opposed any tendency to make the drafting of the code "contingent" on the establishment of an international tribunal.[197] A different group preferred the second proposal, subject to the Commission's finding that "the establishment of an international tribunal was a very remote possibility".[198] It was believed that a reference to the future international tribunal should be added to the text of Article 1, since entrusting "that function to individual governments" would be very dangerous.[199]

Although this proposal ensured that an international tribunal enjoyed exclusive competence over the crimes defined under the code, the lack of reference to the role of national courts during the transitional period could have been interpreted to mean that the provision deprived national courts of their powers to adjudicate upon these cases prior to the establishment of an international tribunal. But, when the two proposals were put to the vote, Mr. Codrova's proposal was adopted by six votes to

189 1953 *YILC*, Vol. I, p. 352.

190 1954 *YILC*, Vol. II, p. 149.

191 *Ibid.*

192 UN Doc. A/CN.4/85, *ibid.*, pp. 112-122.

193 1954 *YILC*, Vol. I, p. 123.

194 The text of Article 1 had been modified by the Special Rapporteur and read as follows: "The offences against the peace and security of mankind defined in this Code are crimes under international law, for which the responsible individuals shall be liable to punishment": UN Doc. A/CN.4/85, 1954 *YILC*, Vol. II, pp. 114-115.

195 1954 *YILC*, Vol. I, p. 124.

196 *Ibid.*

197 *Ibid.*

198 *Ibid.*

199 *Ibid.*

three with four abstentions,[200] while the other proposal was rejected by six votes to two with five abstentions.[201]

Mr. Cordova's proposal did not survive to the end. Later, it was decided to reconsider the text of Article 1.[202] Some members argued against the exclusive competence given to the future international tribunal as proposed by Mr. Cordova in the previous meeting. In their view, crimes such as violation of the laws and customs of war, "by tradition", should be punished by the State apprehending the offender.[203] Because it was difficult to specify in the draft code which tribunal would be competent, it was more plausible to revert to the original draft of Article 1.[204] National courts could not be deprived of the jurisdiction which "they in any case possessed", and thus it was reasonable to revert to the text of Article 1 of the 1951 draft.[205] One member even went a step further and argued that the establishment of an international criminal court would affect States' sovereign powers and should not be referred to at all.[206]

Mr. Cordova explained that his proposal was not intended to interfere with the role of national courts. Instead, national courts would continue to function until an international tribunal was established. Only then would the international tribunal have exclusive jurisdiction.[207] Although it was deemed significant expressly to state that in the text of Article 1,[208] the question of deletion of the words "by an international court" was decided by eight votes to none with two abstentions.[209] After considerable discussion regarding the different Articles under the draft code, the Commission adopted the 1954 draft code as a whole by six votes to none with five abstentions.[210] The draft, together with commentaries, was submitted to the General Assembly for consideration. The General Assembly, considering that the draft code "raises problems closely related to that of the definition of aggression", decided to postpone consideration of the draft code "until the Special Committee on the question of defining aggression has submitted its report".[211]

200 *Ibid.*

201 *Ibid.*

202 *Ibid.*, p. 133.

203 *Ibid.*

204 *Ibid.*

205 *Ibid.*, p. 134.

206 *Ibid.*

207 *Ibid.*, p. 133.

208 *Ibid.*, p. 134.

209 *Ibid.*

210 *Ibid.*, p. 195.

211 G.A. Res., 897(IX), Ninth Session, 504th plenary meeting, 4 December 1954; see also Benjamin B. Ferencz, 'An International Criminal Code and Court: Where they Stand and Where they're Going', 30 *Columbia Journal of Transnational Law* 375, 384, 377 (1992).

Although the final text of the 1954 draft code,[212] like the 1951 draft, lacked any reference to the tribunals responsible for punishment, it was clear during the discussions surrounding the two drafts that there was a trend towards organizing the relationship between national courts and the proposed international court in such a manner that would provide national courts with a role only during a transitional period, pending the establishment of an international tribunal that would later exercise exclusive jurisdiction over the crimes defined in the code.

The discussions also revealed that members who did not support such an exclusive role for the international tribunal were inclined towards absolute domestic jurisdiction. There was little or no support for the idea of organizing the relationship between national and international jurisdiction through a mechanism of complementarity, similar to what was proposed during the work of the London International Assembly, the International Commission for Penal Reconstruction and Development, the United Nations War Crimes Commission and the drafting of the Genocide Convention.

6.3 The 1949 – 1950 Meetings of the International Law Commission Concerning the Question of International Criminal Jurisdiction

The meetings of the International Law Commission studying the question of international criminal jurisdiction and the competence of the future court reflected fundamental differences in treating the same question that was initially under consideration by the Commission when it studied the 1951 and 1954 draft codes. The Members of the Commission who supported the establishment of an international criminal court were inclined towards one enjoying exclusive competence over the crimes in the code. The Commission's trend proved changeable in relation to this issue when it studied the question of international criminal jurisdiction. Some members instead called for an international court with a complementary jurisdiction – a proposal that was completely overlooked when the codes were drafted.[213]

When General Assembly Resolution 260 (III) B came into effect, the International Law Commission considered the question of international criminal jurisdiction at its first session held on 3 June 1949. At that session, the Commission decided to appoint Mr. Ricardo J. Alfaro and Mr. Emil Sandström as Special Rapporteurs and charged them to prepare reports to be presented at the Commission's second session.[214] In doing so, the Special Rapporteurs presented two reports to the session which opened at Geneva on 5 June 1950.[215] The Commission took these reports as the basis of its

212 *Report of the International Law Commission covering the work of its sixth session*, 3 June – 28 July 1954, 1954 *YILC*, Vol. II, pp. 151 – 152.

213 With the exception of a proposal tabled by Mr. El-Koury that called for an international court that shares the burden with national courts. See 1950 *YILC*, Vol. I, p. 176.

214 *Summary Record of the Thirtieth Meeting*, First Session, UN Doc. A/CN.4/SR.30, pp. 15-18; UN Doc. A/CN.4/15, p. 2 and A/CN.4/20, p. 19, 1950 *YILC*, Vol. II.

215 UN Doc. A/CN.4/15, pp. 1-17and A/CN.4/20, pp. 18-23, 1950 *YILC*, Vol. II.

discussion during the several meetings held in 1950.[216] The reports focused on two central questions. The first was the desirability and the second the possibility of establishing an international judicial organ as requested in General Assembly Resolution 260 (III) B.[217]

Initially, the organization of the court and its competence were not the focus of the Commission's work at this stage. But, members such as Mr. Hudson argued in favour of a system of complementarity based on the 1937 League of Nations Convention. It was "where national jurisdiction was inadequate, that it could be said an international jurisdiction was called for, and therefore desirable," he said.[218] Another member agreed with the proposal on the ground that States might try the "experiment on a small scale" by bringing before the international criminal court a person guilty of crimes against the peace in cases where, for political reasons, they preferred not to try them in their own courts.[219] The Chairman argued that there was a need for the setting up of an international organ that "would be competent to judge all war criminals, to whichever side they belonged". A situation such as the assassination of the King of Yugoslavia was a good indication of the need for an international criminal jurisdiction enabling States to "have cases difficult and even dangerous for themselves settled by a non-national organ". The punishment of the crime of genocide also required an international criminal court.[220]

Mr. Brierly, while acknowledging the usefulness of opting for an international court with "strictly voluntary jurisdiction" like the one based on the 1937 model, warned of the implications that might arise in the selection of this option. In his opinion, it was implicit that the complementarity scheme envisaged might risk the court being useless, because it would not have a deterrent effect in preventing the type of crimes condemned by the Nuremberg Tribunal.[221] Thus, the Commission should be concerned with the establishment of an international criminal jurisdiction that would be binding in nature.[222]

No vote was taken on these proposals because, as mentioned previously, the question of competence was not at the heart of the discussions. Yet the debates on the competence of the proposed court were significant. The discussions concerning the question of the competence of the future international criminal court in the drafting process of the 1951 and 1954 draft codes inclined towards exclusivity of jurisdiction over the crimes defined in the Code.

216 See e.g., *Summary Record of the Forty-First Meeting*, Second Session, UN Doc. A/CN.4/SR.41 [hereinafter UN Doc. A/CN.4/SR.41].

217 *Ibid*; *Summary Record of the Forty-Second Meeting*, Second Session, UN Doc. A/CN.4/SR.42 [hereinafter UN Doc. A/CN.4/SR.42]; *Summary Record of the Forty-Third Meeting*, Second Session, UN Doc. A/CN.4/SR.43[hereinafter UN Doc. A/CN.4/SR.43]; UN Doc. A/CN.4/15, pp. 1 – 17 and A/CN.4/20, pp. 18 – 23, 1950 *YILC*, Vol. II.

218 UN Doc. A/CN.4/SR.42, pp. 7 – 8, 10.

219 UN Doc. A/CN.4/SR.43, p. 7.

220 *Ibid.*, p. 12.

221 UN Doc. A/CN.4/SR.42, p. 11.

222 *Ibid.*

Members who were not in support of an international criminal jurisdiction yet favoured absolute domestic repression. Thus, there were no discussions concerning the idea of an international criminal court with complementary jurisdiction. When it came to studying the question of international criminal jurisdiction, more or less, at the same intervals, this view had partially changed with the introduction of proposals that favoured an international criminal court with complementary jurisdiction based on the 1937 League of Nations Convention, for almost the same crimes as those mentioned in the 1951 and 1954 draft codes. It was as if the International Law Commission drew a distinction between repression of the crimes under the code and those to be under the international criminal jurisdiction. After consideration of the whole matter of establishing an international criminal court, the Chairman put the two central questions to the vote. By eight votes to one with two abstentions, the Commission decided that it was desirable to establish an international judicial organ.[223] By seven votes to three with one abstention, the Commission decided that the establishment of an international judicial organ was possible.[224]

6.4 The 1951 Committee on International Criminal Jurisdiction

A report on the International Law Commission's work during its second session was submitted to the General Assembly.[225] Having given "preliminary consideration to part IV of the report of the [ILC] on the work of its second session,"[226] the General Assembly decided, by Resolution 489(V) of 12 December 1950, to convene a Committee – separate from the International Law Commission – composed of the representatives of 17 United Nations' Member States.[227]

The Committee met in Geneva on 1 August 1951 for the purpose of "preparing one or more preliminary draft conventions and proposals relating to the establishment and the statute of an international criminal court".[228] In 1952, the Report of the Committee on International Criminal Jurisdiction was published.[229] The Committee proceeded with its work on the understanding that the task to be performed, including participation in the deliberations and voting on any draft texts, by no means "commit[ted]" any government "to any of the decisions which the Committee might eventually adopt".[230] It was on the basis of this understanding that the Committee prepared a draft statute for a future international criminal court consisting of 55 Ar-

223 UN Doc. A/CN.4/SR.43, p. 14.

224 *Ibid.*, p. 15.

225 1950 *ILC Report*, 1950 *YILC*, Vol. II, pp. 378 – 379.

226 G.A.Res., 489 (V) , Fifth Session, 320th plenary meeting, 12 December 1950.

227 *Ibid.*

228 *Ibid.*

229 *Report of the Committee on International Criminal Jurisdiction on its Session Held from 1 to 31 August 1951*, G.A. Official Records, Seventh Session, Supplement No. 11 (A/2136) [hereinafter 1951Geneva Report].

230 *Ibid.*, p. 2.

ticles. The Committee confined two provisions of the statute to organizing the competence of the proposed court.

Article 26 of the draft stipulated that "[j]urisdiction may be conferred upon the Court by States parties to the Statute, by convention or, with respect to a particular case, by special agreement or by unilateral declaration".[231] Article 27 imposed a limitation on Article 26,[232] specifying that no person would be tried by the court unless both the territorial State and the State of nationality of the accused had conferred jurisdiction upon the court in accordance with Article 26.[233] These provisions did not explicitly spell out the nature of competence between the international criminal court and domestic courts. It was clear from their wording that the competence of the proposed court was based on the principle of *consent*. Consent of the State of nationality and the territorial State was obtained either through a convention covering future cases to be later concluded between two or more States, separate from that establishing the court, or on an *ad hoc* basis in relation to a specific case or crime that had already been committed by virtue of a special agreement between two or more States, or by a unilateral declaration made by a State "renouncing jurisdiction in favour of the international criminal court". Conferring jurisdiction by any of these methods should be subject to the approval of the General Assembly.[234]

The system contemplated by the drafters reflects a complementary mechanism comparable to that found in the 1937 League of Nations Convention, despite the absence of an explicit reference to it during the Committee's discussions. According to this system, it was implicit that a State should have the option of either dealing with the specific case or crime in question before its own domestic courts or waive its primary jurisdiction in favour of the court if it was *unwilling* to deal with that case. When compared to the mechanism embodied in the 1937 Convention, the apparent difference was that Article 26 of the 1951 draft did not explicitly require the State to extradite the accused person as an alternative to prosecution before its domestic

231 *Ibid.*, annex Article 26, p. 23.

232 In commenting on the limitation provided in Article 27 of the Committee's draft, the Dutch government has stated: "it [is]advisable to not to recommend deletion of article 27 because in that case there is a great chance that the court will not come into being at all." See *Comments Received from Governments Regarding the Report of the Committee on International Criminal Jurisdiction, Official Records of the General Assembly, Seventh Session*. Agenda Item 52, UN Doc. A/2186 and Add. 1., p. 9 [hereinafter UN Doc. A/2186 and Add. 1]; But see Quincy Wright, 'Proposal for an International Criminal Court', 46 *American Journal of International Law* 60, 68 (1952) (noting that the provision "permits a government, by refusing to extend jurisdiction, to exempt its officials or nationals accused of international crimes from trial and thus does away with the principle, accepted in the Nuremberg Charter, that international criminal law is superior to national legislation").

233 *1951 Geneva Report.*, annex Article 27, p. 23. On account of the drafting history of Article 27, see, *inter alia*, *Summary Record of the Fifth Meeting, First session*, UN Doc. A/AC.48/SR.5, pp. 20 – 21 [hereinafter UN Doc. A/AC.48/SR.5; *Summary Record of the Sixth Meeting, First session*, UN Doc. A/AC.48/SR.6, pp. 3 – 17 [hereinafter A/AC.48/SR.6].

234 *1951 Geneva Report.*, annex Article 28, p. 23.

courts or the international criminal court in accordance with the principle of *aut dedere aut judicare.* Yet this did not deny the fact that the mechanism enshrined in Article 26 shared with the 1937 League of Nations Convention the idea of *voluntary* submission to the jurisdiction of the international criminal court where the State was *unwilling* to initiate proceedings before its domestic courts. Support for this analysis is found in a memorandum submitted by the Secretary General on 2 July 1951,[235] and the Committee's discussion of the subject.[236]

The Secretary General stated in his memorandum that the jurisdiction of the court "would in principle be optional" in the sense that governments would be under no obligation "in any circumstances" to commit accused persons for trial to the court.[237] The system considered avoided states being under an obligation to "disseise" their national courts in favour of the court – a situation that was unlikely to gain a state's agreement.[238] There might be a situation where a crime committed against a national of one state had not been dealt with by the courts of another. In that event, the latter could, "if wished", "divest itself of its responsibility" by relinquishing jurisdiction to the international criminal court.[239]

Members of the Committee made similar statements in the course of the discussion of Article 24 of the draft statute annexed to the Secretariat draft.[240] The French delegate said that for the time being it would be "sufficient to indicate that the jurisdiction of the court would be determined by conventions or whenever a State, in order to relieve itself of its international responsibility, decided to waive its own jurisdiction in favour of that of the court".[241] The Danish representative believed that

235 UN Doc. A/AC.48/1; see also the memorandum prepared by Professor Vespasien V. Pella and submitted to the Committee on 17 July 1951. Professor Pella argued that, while States were entitled to prosecute international crimes such as crimes against the peace before their domestic courts, "there [was] nothing to prevent [them] from bringing [cases] before an International Criminal Court". UN Doc. A/AC.48/3, pp. 104 – 105.

236 See *Summary Record of the Third Meeting, First session*, UN Doc. A/AC.48/SR.3 [hereinafter A/AC.48/SR.3]; *Summary Record of the Seventh Meeting, First session*, UN Doc. A/AC.48/SR.7 [hereinafter U.N. Doc. A/AC.48/SR.7]; UN Doc. A/AC.48/SR.6.

237 UN Doc. A/AC.48/1, p. 25.

238 *Ibid.*, p. 26.

239 *Ibid.* p. 54.

240 The Secretariat prepared two preliminary drafts. The first was based on the assumption that the Court was established by General Assembly resolution, and the second on the assumption that the Court was established by an international convention. Members of the Committee had chosen the second draft as the main basis for their discussions. Article 24 of the second draft states: "The Court shall have jurisdiction to judge: (1) Crimes under international law; (2) Crimes under common law involving the responsibly of one State party to this Convention towards other States parties; (3) Crimes under common law, for the judgment of which the Court has been given jurisdiction by conventions to which the States acceding to this Convention are likewise parties": *ibid.*, annex II, p. 98.

241 UN Doc. A/AC.48/SR.3, p. 17. At that meeting the discussions had taken crimes under national law which were of international concern, such as drug trafficking and terrorism, as examples of the types of crimes that the international criminal court might deal with in

some consideration should be given to the "advisability of making the court accessible to States which in certain circumstances might agree to bring specific cases before it".[242] He imagined the possibility of "extending the functions of the court in such a way that States whose national courts proved inadequate or less appropriate in given cases could bring such cases" before the proposed international criminal court.[243] The Secretary to the Committee thought that the point "might be one for consideration at some later stage".[244]

At the sixth meeting, the Danish representative, elaborating on this point, stated that because several crimes were on "the borderline between political and the non-political", states might be reluctant to extradite accused persons to other domestic courts.[245] In this case, it was more plausible to send such cases to the international criminal court by virtue of "special agreements". The French delegate thought that in some instances, for "political reasons", a state which had not conferred jurisdiction on the court by virtue of a prior convention might "wish" to "delegate" jurisdiction to the Court.[246] He referred to a statement made by the Chairman of the Drafting Sub-Committee in support of that view. He also mentioned that "jurists" would like to observe the way such a Court operated before "placing full confidence in it". Some States might have been hesitant to be bound from the start by "broad prior conventions". "In a particular instance such States, while not already bound by a convention on the jurisdiction of the court, might be tempted to test that institution either by an agreement or by a unilateral declaration of renunciation".[247]

The methods of conferring jurisdiction on the court in relation to crimes under international law through a "special agreement" or a "unilateral declaration" were approved by nine votes to none with four abstentions.[248] The 1951 Geneva Report, which included a survey of these opinions and others expressed by the Committee's

exceptional cases. Yet this does not deny the fact that the principle of relinquishment of jurisdiction or *voluntary* submission was intended to apply equally to all crimes that fall under the jurisdiction of the international criminal court. Thus, it could be argued that these were only examples of exceptional situations that might extend to apply to all other crimes under the draft statute.

242 *Ibid.*, p. 15.

243 *Ibid.*

244 *Ibid.*, pp. 15 – 16.

245 UN Doc. A/AC.48/SR.6, pp. 26 – 27.

246 *Ibid.*, p. 28; see also the statement made by the French representative during the fifth meeting, UN Doc. AC.48/SR.5, pp. 16 – 17.

247 UN Doc. A/AC.48/SR.7, pp. 5 – 6. A similar statement was made by the French delegate during the Committee's eighth meeting. "In the experimental period through which the court would pass in its early stages, States must be free to test the court. That was particularly true in the case of crimes under international law. States which would hesitate to confer general jurisdiction on the court in respect of, for example, the crime of genocide, might nonetheless desire to bring cases of genocide before it": *Summary Record of the Eighth Meeting, First session*, U.N. Doc. A/AC.48/SR.8, p. 11.

248 *Ibid.*, p. 6.

members, was transmitted to the governments with a request for their comments to be made no later than 1 June 1952.

Article 26 of the 1951 Geneva draft was not subject to technical re-examination until the 1953 Committee on International Criminal Jurisdiction set to work. Nonetheless, in the course of its general debate whether an international criminal court should be established at this "juncture", or whether further study was "required", the Sixth Committee[249] touched on this issue, but only from a political viewpoint (*i.e.*, without literally examining the text of Article 26). Some members favoured the system of a state's *consent* and the *voluntary* relinquishment of jurisdiction to the court, as embodied in Articles 26, and 27 of the 1951 Geneva draft, while others vigorously criticized it on the ground of the practical difficulty of bringing an accused to the court.

The French representative, favouring the scheme of *voluntary* submission of cases to the international criminal court, stated that, at the end of a war, the conquered State might be compelled to yield to the jurisdiction of the Court and hand over its former leaders.[250] Also, those leaders could be handed over after an internal revolution or a change of government.[251] Furthermore, it was not impossible to imagine cases such as the assassination of a statesman or a foreign personality, where a State would agree to "relinquish its judicial competence in favour of international jurisdiction".[252]

The Dutch representative, while supporting the French view in principle, disagreed with the types of cases to be referred to the court. He thought that it was possible that "internal changes brought about by normal democratic processes, which would not be catastrophic, might lead certain governments to bring before an international court, rather than before their own domestic courts, members of a previous majority accused of war propaganda or other crimes".[253] Yet, the court should not deal with crimes such as those committed against foreign personalities, since it was not intended to "try all international criminals".[254] In the same vein, the Greek representa-

249 In doing so, the Sixth Committee during the General Assembly's seventh session also discussed the Committee's report and the observations received by the governments. See René Marius Reeder, *The Establishment of an International Criminal Court: Some General Problems* (Amsterdam: Nuss, 1962), p. 20.

250 *Official Records of the General Assembly*, Seventh Session, Sixth Committee, 321 st Meeting, U.N. Doc. A/C.6/321, p. 96 [hereinafter U.N.Doc. A/C.6/SR.321].

251 *Ibid.*

252 *Ibid.*

253 *Official Records of the General Assembly*, Seventh Session, Sixth Committee, 323 rd. Meeting, U.N. Doc. A/C.6/SR. 323, p. 106 [hereinafterU.N.Doc. A/C.6/SR.323].

254 *Ibid.* This view was shared by Mr. Robinson, the Israeli delegate who argued that "[T]he French representative, had thought that the competence of the court should not be limited to international crimes but should be extended to lesser crimes involving the responsibility of States and to so-called crimes of international concern...If the competence of the court was broadened to that extent, there would surely be a risk that all the crimes which caused States any embarrassment might be brought before it. It would then be

tive thought that there might be situations where acts of genocide were committed on the territory of a certain State. In order to avoid "being held responsible" against its will, that State might agree to hand the offenders over to the international criminal court.[255] Other members believed that the system of State *consent* and *voluntary* submission of cases was useless and impracticable.

The British representative vigorously argued that the 1951 draft statute imposed no obligations on governments in relation to bringing cases before the court. Nor did it require any "compulsory action" on the State to make it work. He cited the 1937 League of Nations Convention, which shared with the draft a corresponding clause regarding the competence of the court, to serve as a "warning" of failure in the future.[256] In his opinion, because the proposed court was to have no "direct compulsory powers", the government's consent was the "cardinal issue".[257] Crimes against peace, or humanity, and genocide were not committed by individuals in their personal capacity, but rather as representatives of the State in pursuance of a government policy or "at any rate with the connivance" of the government. It was "extremely doubtful", therefore, that governments would be willing "in practice" to provide assistance or "subsequently impose those obligations on themselves by means of particular conventions".[258] Only under abnormal or exceptional situations illustrated by the French representative could accused persons be brought before the court.[259]

Criticizing the system of competence embodied in Articles 26 and 27 of the 1951 draft statute, the Belgian representative said, as a "direct result" of the proposed limited competence and conditions of exercising such competence, that the court "would be incapable of administering justice uniformly and equally; its dispensation of justice would be *ad hoc*, haphazard and sporadic".[260] The competence of the court had apparently been modelled on the principles which governed the "establishment of arbitral tribunals to settle disputes between States". These principles should not have applied to criminal justice relating to the liability of individuals. It followed that

necessary to consider how to protect the court against an undue influx of cases..." See *Official Records of the General Assembly*, Seventh Session, Sixth Committee, 325 th Meeting, pp. 119-120 [hereinafterU.N.Doc. A/C.6/SR.325].

255 *Ibid.*, p. 118.

256 U.N.Doc. A/C.6/SR.321, pp. 97 – 98.

257 *Ibid.*, p. 97.

258 *Ibid.*, pp. 98 – 99. The Union of South Africa has taken a similar view in its comments regarding the Committee's draft statute. See U.N.Doc. A/2186 and Add. 1, p. 12.

259 U.N. Doc. A/C.6/SR. 321, p. 99. A similar view was voiced by Mr. Cortina, the Cuban representative, who stated that "while war criminals were individuals, their crimes were committed in a certain political atmosphere from which it was hard to detach them, and it would be difficult to bring them before an international court before the collapse of the regime that had fostered them." See *Official Records of the General Assembly*, Seventh Session, Sixth Committee, 326 st Meeting, p. 127 [hereinafter UN Doc. A/C.6/SR.326].

260 *Official Records of the General Assembly*, Seventh Session, Sixth Committee, 328 th Meeting, p. 136 [hereinafter UN Doc. A/C.6/SR.328].

the draft statute marked a "retrograde step, which was its fundamental flaw".[261] As the Chinese representative put it, the "Committee's choice of method inevitably result[s] in weakening the powers and functions of the court".[262] This choice might have even resulted in a court being recognized by "only a limited number of States".[263]

The British representative, although he disagreed with the system of competence proposed by the Committee, acknowledged that the Committee was prompted to opt for the type of competence envisaged. It was "quite obviously believed that, if any such obligations were imposed on governments under the statute, hardly any government would be willing to sign the statute and the court would never be set up".[264] Thus, the "Committee was perfectly justified in postulating the consent of States as necessary to the jurisdiction and functioning of the court".[265]

But if this were so, how could it ever be possible for states to accept a court with compulsory powers, as demanded by the British representative? If states were not willing to render assistance or submit cases to the court on the basis of *voluntary* submission, as argued earlier by the British representative, then it was obvious that it would be more difficult to adhere to a court with compulsory powers. This suggests that the problem was not one of rejecting the system of complementary jurisdiction based on *voluntary* relinquishment of jurisdiction, as asserted by the British, Belgian, Chinese, Cuban and Indian delegates, but rather that states were not generally willing, at the time, to submit any part of their sovereignty to an international criminal court,[266] whether with optional or compulsory powers. Support for this conclusion was found in statements made by a number of states.

The Venezuelan delegate argued that many states found it difficult to "accept any restrictions on sovereignty which would be incompatible with their legal traditions".[267] The Ukrainian representative said that the establishment of an international

261 *Ibid.*

262 *Official Records of the General Assembly*, Seventh Session, Sixth Committee, 322 nd. Meeting, p. 102 [hereinafter UN Doc. A/C.6/SR.322].

263 *Ibid*; see also the concurring statement made by Mr. Banerjee, the Indian representative who argued that "[t]he complete absence of compulsory powers to enable the court to exercise its jurisdiction effectively over all States was one of the difficulties made manifest in the Committee's report...The establishment of an ineffective international institution would not only add to world problems but would also adversely affect the prestige of the United Nations..." See UN Doc. A/C.6/SR.326, p. 126.

264 UN Doc. A/C.6/SR.321, p. 98.

265 This statement is to be found in the comments received from the British government regarding the Committee's draft statute. *See* U.N.Doc. A/2186 and Add. 1, p. 12.

266 In the same vein see H. Donnedieu de Vabres, 'Some Observations on the Scheme for the Establishment of a Permanent International Criminal Court', 30 *Revue de Droit International de Sciences Diplomatiques et Politiques* 227, 228 (1952); M. Cherif Bassiouni, A Draft International Criminal Code and Draft Statute for an International Criminal Tribunal, (Dordrecht/Boston/Lancaster: Martinus Nijhoff Publishers, 1987), pp. 5,7; Paul D. Marquardt, 'Law Without Borders: The Constitutionality of an International Criminal Court', 33 *Columbia Journal of Transnational Law* 73, 85 (1995).

267 UN Doc.A/C.6/SR.323, p. 107.

criminal court was indeed "incompatible with the principle of non-intervention and respect for the sovereignty of States", because it denied states their territorial right to exercise jurisdiction over acts committed on their soil.[268] Thus, there "seemed little enthusiasm on the part of States to give up some of their national sovereignty in favour of an international court," added the Egyptian delegation.[269] The representatives of Poland,[270] the Byelorussian Soviet Socialist Republic,[271] the USSR,[272]Iraq,[273] Yugoslavia[274] and Czechoslovakia[275] made statements to the same effect. The 1951 Geneva Report, which included a survey of the opinions expressed by the Committee's members, was transmitted to the governments of Member States with a request for their comments.[276]

6.5 The 1953 Committee on International Criminal Jurisdiction

In 1952, the General Assembly decided to appoint a different Committee to explore the implications and consequences of establishing an international criminal court and of the various methods by which this might be done, to study the relationship between such a court and the United Nations and its organs, to re-examine the draft statute prepared by the 1951 Geneva Committee and submit a report to be considered by the General Assembly at its ninth session.[277] It made some amendments to Article 26 of the 1951 draft, so as not only to provide for the method of conferring jurisdiction, but also "explicitly" to define the "meaning" and the "effect" of such conferment. Article 26 of the 1953 revised draft provided that:

1. Jurisdiction of the Court is not to be presumed;
2. A State may confer jurisdiction upon the Court by convention, by special agreement or by unilateral declaration;

268 UN Doc.A/C.6/SR.324, p. 111.

269 UN Doc.A/C.6/SR.326, p. 124.

270 UN Doc.A/C.6/SR.327, pp. 129 – 130.

271 UN Doc.A/C.6/SR.328, p. 136.

272 UN Doc.A/C.6/SR.327, p. 133.

273 UN Doc.A/C.6/SR.328, p. 137.

274 UN Doc.A/C.6/SR.326, p. 125.

275 UN Doc.A/C.6/SR.327, p. 133.

276 UN Doc.A/2186 and Add. 1, p. 2.

277 *Ibid.*, para. 3(a), (b), p. 63. Generally on the 1951 Draft, Ivan Kerno, 'Le Projet De Statut De La Cour Criminelle Internationale', 29 *Revue de Droit International de Sciences Diplomatiques et Politiques* 363 (1951). But according to one scholar the main reason for revising the 1951 draft statute was that the major powers did not wish to "assume political responsibility for the demise of a permanent international criminal court within only five and six years, respectively, of the IMTFE's and IMT's judgments". See M. Cherif Bassiouni, 'From Versailles to Rwanda in Seventy-Five Years: The Need to Establish a Permanent International Criminal Court', 10 *Harvard Human Rights Journal* 11, 53 (1997).

3. Conferral of jurisdiction signifies the right to seize the Court, and the duty to accept its jurisdiction subject to such provisions as the State or States have specified;
4. Unless otherwise provided for in the instrument conferring jurisdiction upon the Court, the laws of a State determining national criminal jurisdiction shall not be affected by that conferral.[278]

This was the idea of complementarity mirrored in the principle of *voluntary* submission or waiver of the state's primacy to the jurisdiction of the international criminal court in the case of the state's unwillingness to act.

Members in favour of establishing such an institution were aware of the "intricacy" of the situation and, thus, were willing to proceed only with the "utmost caution".[279] For them, it was better to establish a court with "imperfect powers" and "limited competence" than to create nothing.[280]

At the Committee's second meeting, the French delegate stressed the significance of respecting the principle of the "voluntary accession" of States, which promoted "the development of an international criminal jurisdiction".[281] Similar examples to those mentioned during the meetings of the 1951 Committee were rehearsed.[282] A state might deem it appropriate in some case of political and legal complexity to submit to the jurisdiction of the international criminal court.[283] Moreover, the court should try cases which "could not better be brought before national courts".[284]

Yet, the drafters were keen that paragraph 2 of Article 26, which mirrored the principle of *voluntary* submissions, should not be drafted in a manner that would divest domestic courts of their primary jurisdiction. It was their intention to stress the role of domestic courts alongside that of the international criminal court. Thus, paragraph 2 was drafted in positive language in order to avoid "any implication" or misunderstanding that if a "State conferred jurisdiction on the court, that jurisdiction would have to be exclusive rather than concurrent".[285] This process entailed two dif-

278 *Ibid.*, annex Article 26, pp. 24 – 25.

279 *1953 Committee's Report*, p. 4.

280 *Ibid* ; see also *Summary Record of the Fourth Meeting* , UN Doc. A/AC.65/SR.4, p. 7 (Mr. Röling, the Dutch representative, acknowledged that the jurisdiction of the proposed court would not be perfect when he said, "the jurisdiction thus created would be elastic in nature and in extent, allowing for variations in the relations between States, as a convention, aiming to set up a fully-fledged jurisdiction, could not do": *ibid*; and also *Summary Record of the Fifth Meeting* UN Doc. A/AC.65/SR.5, p. 8 (Mr. Dautricourt of Belgium confirmed that the Court should be established with "limited competence").

281 *Summary Record of the Second Meeting*, UN Doc. A/AC.65/SR.2, p. 3.

282 See e.g., UN Doc. A/AC.48/SR.6, pp. 26 – 28.

283 *1953 Committee's Report*, p. 9. Again the example was brought up in the context of crimes under national law of international concern.

284 *Ibid.*

285 *Ibid.*, p. 14. Also, unlike Article 26 of the 1951 draft statute, which covered cases *post factum*, paragraph 2 of the revised draft was intended to be limited to future conventions, special agreements and unilateral declarations – namely dealing with cases or specific

ferent stages that required attention. The first stage began when the State conferred jurisdiction upon the court. After such conferment, the second stage would come into play when the State in question was still considering the *forum conveniens* for the case to be tried. During this interval, domestic courts as well as the international criminal court were to enjoy *concurrent,* as opposed to *exclusive,* jurisdiction over the case. In this context, it would be within the State's powers and not those of the international criminal court to solve the problem of conflict of jurisdiction. The State, therefore, could opt for a court of its choosing (either domestic courts or the international criminal court). Thus, the plain conferment of jurisdiction on the court would not have the effect of providing the latter with exclusive powers over a certain crime or case, prompting the State to yield to the court.[286] Paragraph 4 of Article 26 of the revised draft statute was adopted to support that meaning in the sense that the jurisdiction of national courts would remain "intact" and would be *concurrent* with that of the court,[287] unless otherwise provided in the instruments conferring jurisdiction on the court.[288] Paragraph 3 clarified further that the mere conferment of jurisdiction upon the court did not, by any means, impose obligations on the State to submit the case to the court.[289] On the contrary, it merely "passively" permitted the accused to be tried by the court,[290] if the state decided so, after the requirements of Article 27

crimes *ante factum: ibid.* This idea was also presented by the French and Australian representatives. See generally Yuen-Li Liang, 'Notes on Legal Questions Concerning the United Nations: The Establishment of an International Criminal Court – the Second Phase', 47 *American Journal of International Law* 638, 648 (1953).

286 One can draw an analogy with the system of the current ICC Statute studied in chapters III and IV. Conferment of jurisdiction in the 1953 draft may be comparable with a situation where a State ratifies the Rome Statute. In the latter situation, the mere ratification of the Statute does not trigger the activities of the Court unless, *inter alia*, the State refers a situation to it (considered to be a self-referral if the State has a direct link with the crime) etc. In the 1953 draft conferment of jurisdiction by a convention or special agreement or a unilateral declaration might be analogous in the sense that it did not trigger the activities of the court unless the State decided to waive its primacy in favour of the international criminal court.

287 This was an Israeli proposal, which was adopted by 10 votes to none, with 4 abstentions. *See* UN Doc. A/AC.65/SR.18, p. 11; see also *1953 Committee's Report,* p. 14.

288 *Summary Record of the Eighteenth Meeting,* UN Doc. A/AC.65/SR.18, pp. 9 – 11 [hereinafter UN Doc. A/AC.65/SR.18]. It was argued that, by inserting a special provision in the instrument conferring jurisdiction, the court might be provided with exclusive competence over a particular crime, if the State so desired. See *1953 Committee's Report,* p. 14.

289 *Summary Record of the Seventeenth Meeting,* UN Doc. A/AC.65/SR.17, p. 9. The insertion of the text of paragraph 3 was another safeguard. It was based on an earlier draft proposal submitted by the drafting sub-committee. For an account of the text drafted by the sub-committee see UN Doc. A/AC.6/L.7, Art. 26 (2).

290 *1953 Committee's Report,* p. 14. Article 27 of the revised draft set out the requirements that jurisdiction had to be conferred upon the court by the "State or States" of nationality of the accused and by the "State or States in which the crime is alleged to have been committed": *1953 Committee's Report,* annex Article 27, p. 25.

had been fulfilled.[291] Consequently, after the conferment of jurisdiction, the State in question might still have chosen to bring a specific case before the court or before its own domestic courts in accordance with paragraph 4.[292] The system contemplated in Article 26 retained the idea of complementarity that was initially found in the 1937 League of Nations Convention.

The drafting history of the 1951 and 1953 draft statutes[293] reveals that it was the intention to establish an international criminal court with very limited powers, based on a system that respected States' sovereignty. The complementarity mechanism reflected in the system of *voluntary* submission of jurisdiction as provided for in Article 26 was the maximum that could be achieved at the time. The report of the 1953 Committee on International Criminal Jurisdiction, to which the revised draft statute was annexed, was submitted to the General Assembly for consideration. The expected "domino effect" occurred. The General Assembly, seeing the connection between the question of defining aggression, the Draft Code of Offences against the Peace and Security of Mankind and the question of an international criminal jurisdiction, decided temporarily to postpone consideration of the question of international criminal jurisdiction.[294] As a result, both the 1953 revised draft statute and the 1954 draft Code were laid on the table until the General Assembly received the report of the Special Committee on the definition of aggression.[295]

6.6 Draft Code of Offences against the Peace & Security of Mankind (Resumed- First Phase 1983 – 1989)

The International Law Commission did not return to the question of implementation until the 1980s. The Commission appointed Mr. Doudou Thiam as a Special Rap-

291 For the drafting history of Article 27 of the revised draft *see Summary Record of the Eleventh Meeting*, UN Doc. A/AC.65/SR.11, pp. 15 – 17; *Summary Record of the Twelfth Meeting*, UN Doc. A/AC.65/SR.12, pp. 3 – 11; UN Doc. A/AC.65/SR.18, pp. 4 – 8.

292 *1953 Committee's Report*, p. 14 (the Committee adopted the text of paragraph 3 by 11 votes to none, with two abstentions).

293 For a brief summary of the draft statutes see William N. Gianaris, 'The New World Order and the Need for an International Criminal Court', 16 *Fordham International Law Journal* 88, 94 – 95 (1992 – 1993).

294 G.A. Res., 898(IX), Ninth Session, 512th plenary meeting.

295 *Ibid*; see also J. Y. Dautricourt, "The International Criminal Court: The Concept of International Criminal Jurisdiction – Definition and Limitation of the Subject", in M. Cherif Bassiouni et al. (eds.), *A Treatise on International Criminal Law: Crimes and Punishment*, Vol. I, (Springfield.Illiniois: Charles C Thomas Publisher, 1973), p. 650; Michael P. Scharf, 'The Jury Is Still Out on the Need for an International Criminal Court', 1 *Duke Journal of International and Comparative Law* 135, 139 (1991).

porteur for the subject in 1982[296] and resumed its work on the draft code in 1983.[297] During the first phase, the Special Rapporteur prepared seven different reports for the Commission's examination.[298] Not every report necessarily tackled the question of implementation and the type of jurisdiction applying the code. The question of implementation, however, raised concerns among the majority of the Commission's members. Consequently, the issue was brought up frequently in relation to other questions being examined by the Commission. The first report presented by the Special Rapporteur at the Commission's thirty-fifth session in 1983 sparked the discussion on the question of international criminal jurisdiction.

Mr. Doudou Thiam, recognizing the problem of having a code without machinery to implement it, realized the significance of raising the issue in his report for future discussions. One main aspect relating to the implementation of the code was the type of jurisdiction that should deal with the crimes in the code. A possible solution was to retain the view adopted during the Commission's meetings in the 1950s – namely that the code could be applied by national courts until an international criminal court was established to deal with the crimes defined in it.[299] The essence of this idea gained some support during the Commission's discussions in 1983. Some members argued

296 *Report of the International Law Commission on the Work of its Thirty-Fourth Session*, 3 May – 23 July 1982, *Official Records of the General Assembly*, Thirty-Seventh Session, Supplement No. 10 (A/37/10), 1982 *YILC*, Vol. II, Part Two, p. 121.

297 See Benjamin B. Ferencz, 'The Draft Code of Offences Against the Peace and Security of Mankind', 75 *American Journal of International Law* 674 (1981); Timothy L.H.McCormak and Gerry J. Simpson, 'The International Law Commission's Draft Code of Crimes against the Peace and Security of Mankind: An Appraisal of the Substantive Provisions', 5 *Criminal Law Forum* 1 (1994); Rosemary Rayfuse, 'The Draft Code of Crimes against the Peace and Security of Mankind: Eating Disorders at the International Law Commission', 8 *Criminal Law Forum* 43 (1997).

298 *First Report on the Draft Code of Offences against the Peace and Security of Mankind*, UN.Doc. A/CN.4/364, 1983 *YILC*, Vol. II, Part One, pp. 137 – 152; *Second Report on the Draft Code of Offences against the Peace and Security of Mankind*, UN.Doc. A/CN.4/377, 1984 *YILC*, Vol. II, Part One, pp. 89 – 100 [hereinafter Second Report, 1984 *YILC*, Vol. II, Part One]; *Third Report on the Draft Code of Offences against the Peace and Security of Mankind*, UN.Doc. A/CN.4/387, 1985 *YILC*, Vol. II, Part One, pp. 63 – 83 [hereinafter Third Report,1985 *YILC*, Vol. II, Part One]; *Fourth Report on the Draft Code of Offences against the Peace and Security of Mankind*, UN.Doc. A/CN.4/398, 1986 *YILC*, Vol. II, Part One, pp. 53 – 86 [hereinafter Fourth Report, 1986 *YILC*, Vol. II, Part One]; *Fifth Report on the Draft Code of Offences against the Peace and Security of Mankind*, UN.Doc. A/CN.4/404, 1987 *YILC*, Vol. II, Part One, pp. 1 – 10 [hereinafter Fifth Report, 1987 *YILC*, Vol. II, Part One]; *Sixth Report on the Draft Code of Offences against the Peace and Security of Mankind*, UN.Doc. A/CN.4/411, 1988 *YILC*, Vol. II, Part One, pp. 197 – 204 [hereinafter Sixth Report, 1988 *YILC*, Vol. II, Part One]; *Seventh Report on the Draft Code of Offences against the Peace and Security of Mankind*, UN.Doc. A/CN.4/419, 1989 *YILC*, Vol. II, Part One, pp. 81 – 90 [hereinafter Seventh Report, 1989 *YILC*, Vol. II, Part One].

299 *Summary Records of the Meetings of the Thirty – Fifth Session* (3 May – 22 July 1983), 1983 *YILC*, Vol. I, p. 151 [hereinafter 1983 *YILC*, Vol. I].

that crimes under the code fell exclusively within the competence of an international criminal court to be established for that purpose.

In 1983, one member thought that it would be "highly imprudent and dangerous to leave it to national courts to enforce that code...No matter how objective the national court might be in seeking to apply the code, it would inevitably be argued that justice had not been done...Implementation of the code should therefore be ensured by an international criminal court".[300] Another member stated that "[s]ince it was the conflict between independent Powers which gave rise to most offences against the peace and security of mankind, the normal process of national administration of justice could hardly be adequate."[301] This was not the case in relation to other offences against the international order, such as trafficking in people and narcotic drugs which could "very well be tried by national courts, with some international co-operation".[302] It was believed that the draft code should "be administered by an impartial [international] tribunal" in order to be accepted, instead of being applied by any "State into whose hands a hapless foreign official might fall. The State could indict, try and punish, according to its unilateral interpretation and findings".[303] This process would be "more harmful to international peace and security".[304]

Other members thought of a different mechanism that provided neither the future international court nor national courts with exclusive competence over the crimes under the code. One member believed that "if the Commission reached the conclusion that States could commit such offences, it would be inconceivable that the punishment of such crimes should be a matter exclusively for national jurisdiction."[305] This language suggested that the future international criminal court should play a role alongside that of national courts. Yet, the conditions under which the two jurisdictions may function were not addressed any further.

Another member advanced this idea when he stated that there was no reason to avoid the jurisdiction of national courts to "exist side by side" with that of the international criminal court.[306] A system of complementary jurisdiction, based on the principle of *aut dedere aut judicare* as embodied in the 1937 League of Nations Convention, was considered to be an option.[307] According to this proposal, national

300 *Ibid.*, p. 15.

301 *Ibid.*, p. 24.

302 *Ibid.*

303 *Ibid.*, p. 39.

304 *Ibid.*, pp. 38 – 39.

305 *Ibid.*, p. 25.

306 *Ibid.*, p. 275.

307 Mr. Njenga did not use these exact words; rather, this conclusion could be deduced from the statement he made: "The code could impose an obligation on each State to extradite offenders or to prosecute them, even when they were not citizens of that State and even when the crime in question was not committed in its territory": *ibid.* Thus, if the jurisdiction of national courts were to "exist side by side" with that of the international court in the light of a system of extradition or prosecution, then we are talking about the complementarity mechanism embodied in the 1937 League of Nations Convention.

courts and the international criminal court would enjoy concurrent jurisdiction over the crimes in question to be exercised by any of them, depending on each individual situation.

In 1985, one view acknowledged that the "maximum system" to be achieved at the time would be one based on the maxim *aut dedere aut judicare,* as proposed in the 1983 meetings.[308] But, in cases involving international crimes committed by State agents, the Commission would be faced with a "formidable obstacle" if required to impose the obligation to judge or to extradite. "Some very old countries which had suffered from excessive centralization, and were now faced with violent manifestations of unsatisfied regionalism, would not easily agree to bind themselves too absolutely and rigorously by obligations as strict as the obligation to punish or extradite…", said one member.[309]

Other members criticized domestic punishment of crimes under the code because a "revolutionary Government which had overthrown an established Government" could accuse former leaders of being criminals and punish them with all the "rigour of internal law".[310] Accordingly, "international machinery" for the implementation of the code was an "absolute necessity".[311] Another proposal favoured domestic repression through the transitional system. According to this view, it was difficult to set up a permanent international criminal court "immediately"; thus, "some transitional mechanism could possibly be devised with a view to guaranteeing the necessary objectivity".[312] This mechanism required States to enact the necessary legislation to enable them to deal with crimes under the code, "pending the establishment of such [an international criminal] court".[313]

In 1986, the Special Rapporteur, recognizing the political sensitivity and difficulty of the question of an international criminal jurisdiction, included a provision restricting the implementation of the code to national courts.[314] Article 4 (1) of the draft Articles prepared by the Special Rapporteur imposed an obligation on the custodial State to try or extradite the alleged perpetrator (*aut dedere aut judicare*) of an offence had been committed against the peace and security of mankind on the basis of inter-State cooperation.[315] Paragraph 2 apparently did no more than ensure that paragraph 1 "does not prejudge the establishment of [a future] international criminal jurisdiction".[316] Thus, the system contemplated seemed to exclude the international machinery from being part of the *aut dedere aut judicare* as originally reflected in the

308 *Summary Records of the Meetings of the Thirty- Seventh Session* (6 May – 26 July 1985), 1985 *YILC*, Vol. I, p. 11 [hereinafter 1985 *YILC*, Vol. I].

309 *Ibid.*

310 *Ibid.*, p. 74.

311 *Ibid.*

312 *Ibid.*, p. 43.

313 *Ibid.*

314 Fourth Report, 1986 *YILC*, Vol. II, Part One, pp. 53 – 86.

315 Fourth Report, 1986 *YILC*, Vol. II, Part One, Art. 4(1), p. 82.

316 Fourth Report, 1986 *YILC*, Vol. II, Part One, Art. 4(2), p. 82.

1937 League of Nations Convention, at least until such machinery had been set up. This left the proposed system depending exclusively on domestic courts. This view did not find support in the opinion of several members who favoured the existence of an international court to apply the code. None of them, though, referred to the nature of the relationship between national courts and the proposed international court.[317]

Again, pushing for an international court with exclusive jurisdiction, one member said, "[e]ven if, in a particular set of circumstances involving application of the code, justice was done by a national court in a trial of an alien for an offence against the peace and security of mankind committed outside its territory, justice would not be seen to be done".[318] It was, therefore, indispensable to have an international criminal court enjoying "exclusive or quasi-exclusive jurisdiction" to try offences under the code.[319] Other members, however, favoured the system of a transitional period introduced earlier in 1951, 1954 and in the Special Rapporteur's first report, whereby crimes under the code were to be prosecuted by national courts until an international criminal court had been established.[320]

The Commission's view seemed to change during the Commission's thirty-ninth session in 1987. The Special Rapporteur retained Article 4 of his previous report,[321] proving that relying on national courts was the maximum to be achieved at the time in the absence of an international judicial organ. Proposals such as those that generally called for an international criminal jurisdiction with exclusive competence over the crimes in the code vanished during this session.[322] Several members of the Commission were instead inclined to accept the mechanism contemplated in Article 4(1) – namely implementing the code through having recourse to domestic courts on the basis of the Latin maxim *aut dedere aut judicare*.[323] Mr. Thiam, the Special Rapporteur, argued that the philosophy behind drafting Article 4 was not to treat the issue as

317 *Summary Records of the Meetings of the Thirty – Eighth Session* (5 May – 11 July 1986), 1986 *YILC*, Vol. I, pp. 118, 124, 133, 152 [hereinafter 1986 *YILC*, Vol. I] (statements by McCaffrey, Gonzalez, Balanda, and Arangio Ruiz). Mr. Tomuschat backed this idea during the 1966th meeting when said: "Acceptance of an international jurisdiction would be a test of whether the draft code was taken seriously...": *ibid.*, p. 153.

318 *Ibid.*, p. 142.

319 *Ibid.*

320 *Ibid.*, p. 139. "Until such time as there was an international criminal court, it was entirely reasonable to propound the principle of universal jurisdiction".: *ibid.*

321 Art. 4 of the fifth Report reads: "1.Every State has the duty to try or extradite any perpetrator of an offence against the peace and security of mankind arrested in its territory. 2. The provision is paragraph 1 above does not prejudge the establishment of an international criminal jurisdiction": Fifth Report, 1987 *YILC*, Vol. II, Part One, Art. 4(1), p. 3.

322 But *see* the observation by the State of Qatar that it was of the view that "an international criminal jurisdiction is the option most suited to the particular nature of offences against the peace and security of mankind": *Observations of Member States received pursuant to General Assembly Resolution 41/75*, UN Doc. A/CN.4/407and Add.1and 2, 1987 *YILC*, Vol. II, Part One, p. 12.

323 See e.g., the statements made by Mr. Barsegov, *Summary Records of the Meetings of the Thirty – Ninth Session* (4 May – 17 July 1987), 1987 *YILC*,Vol. I, p. 13 [hereinafter 1987

a matter of choice between national and international jurisdiction, as stated by some members earlier,[324] but rather to combine the jurisdiction of national courts with that of the international criminal court. [325] Thus, a "flexible system" was chosen "in which the rule of extradition, while making it possible to give preference to territorial jurisdiction, did not exclude international jurisdiction".[326]

The Special Rapporteur's statement in light of the language of Article 4 suggests that he intended to rely exclusively on domestic courts only for a transitional period until an international criminal court could be established that would function side by side with national courts. This interpretation was supported by an earlier statement made by the Special Rapporteur when he said "[t]he most logical solution of the problem would be an international criminal jurisdiction; but in the absence of such an institution, and pending a decision on the advisability of establishing it,...the best solution in the present circumstances was still reliance on the principle of universal jurisdiction".[327] Although the Special Rapporteur failed to mention the conditions governing the relationship between the two jurisdictions, one possibility was that an international criminal court, once established, would be part of the system contemplated in Article 4 (*aut dedere aut judicare*) – reflecting a complementary regime corresponding to that found in the 1937 League of Nations Convention.[328]

In 1988, the Special Rapporteur's idea of having a "combined system" of national and international jurisdictions gained little attention. Several members rejected the idea of providing national courts with the role of repressing international crimes. They thought that there was lack of evidence that States would try their officials for crimes of this magnitude, such as genocide, and "still less to extradite [them]... and allow another State to try them".[329] International machinery with compulsory juris-

YILC, Vol. I] , Mr. Rodrigues, *ibid.*, p. 15, Mr. Rao, *ibid.*, p. 16, Mr. Illueca, *ibid.*, p. 53, and Al-Khasawneh, *ibid.*, p. 54.

324 1987 *YILC*, Vol. I, pp. 60 – 61.

325 Such an understanding ties with the only statement of its kind made by Mr. Francis. His statement clearly supports a sort of complementary jurisdiction that is based on the division of labour between national and international jurisdictions. He "would favour a parallel jurisdiction under the code, rather than an exclusively national or international jurisdiction. In that way, both institutions – a national tribunal and some kind of international tribunal – would bear the burden of enforcing the code": *ibid.*, p. 17.

326 *Ibid.*, p. 61.

327 *Ibid.*, p. 6.

328 Yet the apparent difference between the system introduced by the Special Rapporteur and that found in the 1937 League of Nations Convention was the obligatory language used in the text of Article 4 of the draft Articles. While Article 4 used the obligatory clause "Every State has the duty to try or extradite", the provision under the 1937 Convention used the optional language "each High contracting Party to the present Convention shall be entitled, instead of prosecuting before his own tribunal, to send the accused for trial before the Court".

329 *Summary Records of the Meetings of the Fortieth Session* (9 May – 29 July 1988), 1988 *YILC*, Vol. I, pp. 67, 100, 275 [hereinafter 1988 *YILC*, Vol. I].

diction guaranteeing the necessary degree of impartiality was therefore necessary.[330] Other members including the Special Rapporteur favoured the idea of applying the code by way of domestic courts for a transitional period.[331]

One member believed that not all crimes under the code should fall within the exclusive competence of an international criminal jurisdiction. He introduced a proposal that forged a sort of complementary relationship between national and international jurisdictions on the basis of the division of responsibilities, in the sense that some crimes could be tried before national courts and others before an international judicial organ.[332] The crime of aggression should be tried only through international machinery.

In 1989, the question of national *versus* international jurisdiction in relation to the suppression of the crime of aggression or threat of aggression was at the heart of the discussions. The small group that initially supported the view that implementation of the code should take place through domestic courts, on the basis of the mechanism enshrined in Article 4(1), began to change its view. This group argued, not without good reason, that the crime of aggression or the threat of aggression could not be left to the jurisdiction of national courts, thus apparently excluding this category from being subject to the system of repression contemplated by the Commission – a mechanism that they supported earlier.

One member argued that the crime of the threat of aggression "should be entrusted to an international criminal court, since the difficulties would begin as soon as a national court had to determine whether there had been a threat of aggression".[333] Another member said that the crime of the threat of aggression was one that "could not be applied by national courts. It was therefore comforting to note an emerging consensus on the idea of establishing an international criminal court".[334] These statements indirectly called for the same complementary system introduced in 1988.[335] An international criminal jurisdiction should deal exclusively with crimes such as

330 *Ibid.*, p. 68.

331 *Ibid.*, pp. 114, 281 – 282; see also the views expressed in the Sixth Committee concerning Article 4, *Topical Summary of the Discussion held in the Sixth Committee of the General Assembly during its Forty – Third Session, prepared by the Secretariat*, UN Doc. A/CN.4/L.431, pp. 53 – 60.

332 1988 *YILC*, Vol. I., p. 105. The possibility of having a combined system of national courts and an international criminal court was also mentioned in the commentary on Article 4 of the new text provisionally adopted by the Drafting Committee. Yet, the commentary fell short of any explanation as to the role each jurisdiction should play in relation to the other. *Report of the International Law Commission on the Work of its Fortieth Session* (9 May – 29 July 1988), UN.Doc. A/43/10, 1988 *YILC*, Vol. II, Part Two, p. 67 [hereinafter 1988 ILC Report].

333 *Summary Records of the Meetings of the Forty – First Session* (2 May – 21 July 1989), 1989 *YILC*,Vol. I, p. 294 [hereinafter 1989 *YILC*, Vol. I].

334 *Ibid.*, p. 295.

335 1988 *YILC*, Vol. I., p. 105.

aggression and the threat of aggression, while other crimes under the code, such as war crimes, could be dealt with in national courts.[336]

Mr. Graefrath instead tabled two different schemes. The first called for a complementarity mechanism that was based on Article 26 of the 1953 revised draft statute for an international criminal court, as well as Article 23 of the statute for an international criminal court[337] adopted by the International Law Association in 1984.[338]

A State had the option of either dealing with a specific case before its own courts or, if unwilling, submitting it to the jurisdiction of the international criminal court[339] – a mechanism that was comparable to that found in the 1937 League of Nations Convention. Because this mechanism introduced "an element of insecurity by giving the State concerned a choice in the matter", he preferred a second – more effective – mechanism that provided an international criminal court with review powers over the final judgments of national courts whenever the State considered that a trial abroad "had not been in conformity with the code".[340] This solution had the advantage of relying on the existing domestic machinery, making the idea of establishing an international criminal court more accessible to States.[341]

6.7 Second Phase (1990 – 1994)

The determination of the appropriate relationship between national and international jurisdictions and its organization remained one of the puzzling issues the Commission had to face even during the second phase of its work (1990 – 1994). Unlike in the first phase, which saw general views being expressed on the subject, the Commission went into an in-depth examination at the second stage, aiming to reach concrete proposals. This change of approach was the result of General Assembly Resolutions

336 See also similar statements made by Messieurs. Tomuschat and Arangio-Ruiz. 1989 *YILC*,Vol. I, pp. 295 – 296.

337 1989 *YILC*, Vol. I, p. 38.

338 *Report of the Sixty-First Conference*, held in Paris, 1984, p. 257.

339 When comparing the complementarity scheme proposed at this meeting and the one proposed at the 2060th meeting, one might notice a technical difference. Although both proposals are based on the idea of division of tasks between national and international jurisdictions, the scheme proposed during the 2060th meeting provides national courts with exclusive jurisdiction over some crimes, and the international criminal court with exclusive jurisdiction over others such as aggression. This is very different from the proposal tabled above, because the latter creates a concurrent rather than a mutually exclusive jurisdiction between national and international jurisdiction.

340 1989 *YILC*, Vol. I, p. 38. Mr. Graefrath limited the access to the Court to the complaining State "whose national had been tried by a foreign court, and the State on whose territory or against which the offence had been committed when the offender had been tried by another State".

341 *Ibid.* A corresponding proposal was tabled in the Sixth Committee during its meetings in 1989, see *Topical Summary of the Discussion Held in the Sixth Committee of the General Assembly during its Forty – Fourth Session, prepared by the Secretariat*, UN Doc. A/CN.4/L.443, pp. 39 – 40. For the other alternative proposals, see *ibid* ., pp. 38 – 40.

43/164 (1988),[342] 44/32(1989),[343] and 44/39 (1989),[344] which requested the Commission to address the question of an international criminal court or other international criminal trial mechanism. Acting upon the resolutions, the Special Rapporteur prepared his eighth report,[345] dedicating part III to exploring alternative proposals in relation to the organization of the future international criminal court.[346] The question of the nature or extent of the competence of such a future court in relation to national courts was not directly addressed in this report. The issue was brought up, however, in the course of the discussion of part III of the report during the Commission's meetings.

One of the main obstacles in the face of accepting the involvement of an international jurisdiction in the process of prosecuting international crimes was the question of sovereignty. This matter was not explicitly addressed during the Commission's work from 1983 – 1989. Nor was it raised during the 1950s discussions. Yet, it was clear that States were often reluctant to surrender any part of their sovereign rights to a foreign tribunal. Faced with such a threat, the Commission demanded a solution that reconciled States' concerns on the one hand and the right of the international community to repress those crimes covered by the code on the other hand. A system that preserved the right of national courts to exercise their criminal jurisdiction in the presence of the international machinery was a conceivable compromise. This was the main underlying philosophy for treating the subject during the Commission's work in 1990 and onward. It was on the basis of this background that some of the proposals tabled during the Commission's meetings in 1990 were heading, to a certain extent, towards a system of complementarity comparable to that enshrined in the current Statute of the International Criminal Court.

In 1990, Mr. Graefrath sparked off the discussions on the issue when he argued that, because the question of an international criminal court was so closely connected with the principle of State sovereignty, "extreme care and circumspection had to be applied in approaching the issue".[347] The extent to which State sovereignty might be

342 G.A.Res. 43/164, 76th plenary meeting.

343 G.A.Res. 44/32, 72nd plenary meeting.

344 G.A.Res. 44/39, 72nd plenary meeting.

345 *Eighth Report on the Draft Code of Crimes Against the Peace and Security of Mankind*, UN.Doc. A/CN.4/430 and Add.1, 1990 *YILC*, Vol. II, Part One, pp. 27 – 39.

346 *Ibid.*, pp. 36 – 39.

347 *Summary Records of the Meetings of the Forty-Second Session* (1 May – 20 July 1990), 1990 *YILC*,Vol. I, p. 31 [hereinafter 1990 *YILC*, Vol. I]. Mr. Graefrath further explored the idea of sovereignty as an obstacle in the face of an international criminal jurisdiction in academic forums, see Bernhard Graefrath, 'Universal Criminal Jurisdiction and an International Criminal Court', 1 *European Journal of International Law* 67, 72 – 75, 78 (1990). The Chairman, Mr. Jiuyong Shi, expressed a similar view, yet in a different context when said: "[T]he very principle of the establishment of an international criminal court gave rise to a number of problems...One of those problems, and perhaps the most important one, was the result of the current state o international relations. Very few States would be prepared to surrender even a small part of their sovereignty in respect of jurisdiction..., the Com-

affected depended on whether the future international criminal court was intended to "replace, compete with or *complement* national jurisdiction"[348] (emphasis added). This might have taken the form of a court exercising "exclusive jurisdiction, or only concurrent jurisdiction with national courts; whether it functioned as a court of first instance or as a court of reviewing final national judgments with a view to guaranteeing objective and uniform jurisprudence".[349] Currently, it would be more plausible to establish one that acted as a "review court"[350] – a proposal he had introduced earlier.[351]

In what circumstances it may have acted as a "review court" was not really addressed. Recognizing that the system proposed by Mr. Graefrath was missing an indispensable element – that is, the conditions under which such a court may review decisions emanating from national courts. Several members later tackled the issue. One view presented assumed that States were "willing to accept an international mechanism, in addition to national courts, [but] under what conditions would each jurisdiction be exercised..."[352] A different proposal tabled in an earlier meeting suggested that "some kind of exhaustion of domestic remedies be envisaged" to organize such a relationship.[353]

Other members suggested that the international criminal court should use its review powers of appeal or cassation in the event of a State's failure "to bring to justice certain individuals who had committed serious crimes" because of not "being strong

mission should therefore be more imaginative, bearing in mind the reality of international relations. Idealism rarely helped to solve problems of a practical nature": *ibid.*, p. 53.

348 *Ibid.*, p. 32. This was the first time the term "complement" was invoked to sketch the relationship between domestic and international jurisdictions. Moreover, the word "complement" is the verb and its adjective is "complementary", as reflected in the language of the current Rome Statute.

349 *Ibid.*, p. 31. Although Mr. Graefrath stated that the correspondent meaning of the terms "replace, compete with, or complement" was to have either a court with exclusive jurisdiction, concurrent with national courts, a court of first instance or a review court, he failed to mention which term precisely matched what system. It is not easy therefore to make such a speculative determination, since this would very much depend on the angle at which the term is viewed.

350 *Ibid.*, p. 32. Yet, other members such as Mr. Illueca thought about the question differently. Reiterating a view which had gained some support in earlier sessions, they thought that the best solution would be an international criminal court enjoying exclusive jurisdiction. As Mr. McCaffrey put it, opting for a different mechanism would frustrate "the objectives of uniformity of interpretation and application": *ibid.*, pp. 23, 41 – 42.

351 1989 *YILC*, Vol. I, p. 38.

352 1990 *YILC* Vol. I., p. 57. As Article 4 (*aut dedere aut judicare*) was provisionally adopted during an earlier session, and part of a separate parallel question under discussion by the Commission, namely Articles of the draft code, it did not necessarily come up during the discussions of this session. But it was a common understanding that the reference to the exercise of jurisdiction by national courts implied the possibility of application of the system contemplated in Article 4.

353 *Ibid.*, p. 43.

enough to do so; judges were intimidated; witnesses refused to speak for fear of reprisals".[354] Perhaps, it might act as a court of "second instance" if there were grounds to believe that "a judgment of a national court violated international rules or was founded on an erroneous basis". This might have taken different forms, such as an act of genocide that had been tried as an ordinary crime; and if a national court refused to hear a case, despite the fact that there were reasonable grounds "for instituting proceedings".[355] These ideas of having an international criminal court with review competence were viewed as a possible option in the report of the Working Group.[356] The Working Group arrived at the conclusion that there were three possible options concerning the nature of the international criminal court's jurisdiction.

One possibility was to opt for a court with exclusive jurisdiction where States would "refrain from exercising jurisdiction over crimes falling under the competence of the specified court". A second possibility was to support a system of concurrent jurisdiction where a State would have the option of choosing between initiating proceedings before a national court or before the international criminal court; and a final possibility was to provide the international criminal court with "review competence" to re-examine decisions of national courts when that "became necessary".[357]

The system of concurrent jurisdiction contemplated by the Working Group seemed to be based on the 1953 revised draft statute for an international criminal court as well as the draft statute of the 1984 International Law Association.[358] Since the mechanism

354 *Ibid.*, p. 40.

355 *Ibid.*, p. 60. As Mr. Barsegov argued, "[t]hat was not mere speculation, for experience showed that national courts were reluctant to convict nationals of their State who were accused of having committed the crime of genocide in the territory and with the apparatus of that State": *ibid.* But *see* Mr. Razafindralambo's opinion in which he expressed concerns about this proposals, and doubted the practicality of an international criminal court with powers to review cases on appeal decided by national courts. In practice, it was unlikely that a State which had chosen to bring a case before a national court would later agree to have the decision reviewed by the international criminal court: *ibid.*, p. 55.

356 *Ibid.*, pp. 71 – 72. Members of the Working Group were: Mr. Al-Baharna, Mr. Beesley, Mr. Bennouna, Mr. Diaz Gonalez, Mr. Graefrath, Mr. Illueca, Mr. Koroma, Mr. Pawlak, Mr. Sreenivasa Rao, Mr. Roucounas, the *ex officio* Special Rapporteur and the Rapporteur of the Commission.

357 *Draft Code of Offences Against the Peace and Security of Mankind: Report of the Working Group Established by the Commission Pursuant to the Request from the General Assembly in Paragraph 1 of its Resolution 44/39*, UN.Doc. A/CN.4/L.454 [and Corr.1], 1990 *YILC* Vol. II, Part Two, p. 23.

358 Indeed this might be deduced from the statement made by Mr. Graefrath at the 2154th meeting who was also a member of the Working Group when he asked: "[W]ould the court have exclusive jurisdiction, or would the competence of national courts continue to exist concurrently? The 1953 draft statute had favoured concurrent jurisdiction, as did the very recent drafts of the International Law Association...such a solution had been proposed because States were not prepared to give up their jurisdiction over criminal offences committed in their territory or against their very existence." 1990 *YILC* Vol. I , p. 32.

enshrined in the 1953 draft reflected a sort of complementary relationship between national and international jurisdiction, the system proposed by the Working Group was, therefore, not only concurrent but also complementary. The Working Group had failed to mention the sort of situations where the international criminal court could exercise its "review competence" if such an option were selected.

In 1991, the Special Rapporteur omitted the system of "review competence" from his ninth report.[359] The Special Rapporteur had, in the alternative, drafted a provision regarding the future court's jurisdiction inspired, to some extent, by the system of State consent to confer jurisdiction as embedded in the 1953 revised draft statute for an international criminal court.[360] The provision implicitly established a concurrent and complementary relationship between national courts and the international criminal court, similar to that found in the 1953 draft, in the sense that a State may try a case before its own courts or voluntarily submit it to the international criminal court.

This system differed technically from that embodied in Article 4 (*aut dedere aut judicare*) which was provisionally adopted by the Commission, since it neither imposed an obligation on States to try or extradite the alleged perpetrator, nor did it provide States with complete freedom to decide on the sort of action to be taken.[361]

359 *Ninth Report on the Draft Code of Crimes Against the Peace and Security of Mankind*, UN.Doc. A/CN.4/435 and Add.1, 1991 *YILC* Vol. II, Part One, pp. 37 – 44 [hereinafter Ninth Report, 1991 *YILC* Vol. II, Part One]. The Special Rapporteur thought that opting for a system of review would create "hierarchical scale" where the international criminal court would occupy a "higher position" than national courts.

360 *Ibid.*, p. 41. Paragraphs 1 and 2 of the draft provision proposed state: "1. The Court shall try individuals accused of the crimes defined in the code of crimes against the peace and security of mankind [accused of crimes defined in the annex to the present statute] in respect of which the State or States in which the crime is alleged to have been committed has or have conferred jurisdiction upon it. 2. Conferral of jurisdiction by the State or States of which the perpetrator is a national, or by the victim State or the State against which the crime was directed, or by the State whose nationals have been the victims of the crime shall be required only if such States also have jurisdiction, under their domestic legislation, over such individuals": *ibid.*, p. 41. Thus, it is clear that the provision relies merely on the idea of the consent of the State to choose either to confer jurisdiction upon the international criminal court or to leave the case to be tried before its domestic courts.

361 Mr. Razafindralambo shared similar fears when he stated that there remained the possibility of "no conferral of jurisdiction" and that a case "would not be referred to any court, whether national or international". This would be more in the "nature of denial of justice..." *Summary Records of the Meetings of the Forty – Third Session* 29 April – 19 July 1991, 1991 *YILC* Vol. I, p. 30 [hereinafter 1991 *YILC* Vol. I]. Similarly, Mr. Francis took the situation of the Gulf War as an example when said: "it was conceivable that an offender might be found in another State and protected by a regime which supported the offender's position. Such a State would be unlikely to consent to the jurisdiction of the international court. The Commission must [therefore] be realistic and send the General Assembly draft proposals including a 'drag net' which would be effective in bringing all offenders against the Code to trial": *ibid.*, p. 36.

As the Special Rapporteur put it, although the system contemplated had its drawbacks it "is a makeshift solution, a necessary concession to State sovereignty"...,[362] which "reflected the present realities of international criminal law".[363] Some members, although acknowledging the sort of problem facing the Special Rapporteur, could not agree with the system contemplated in the draft provision under consideration.[364]

Again, pushing for a system of review, Mr. Graefrath argued that an international criminal court acting as "a review body to complement national jurisdiction"[365] was a method that avoided "the surrender of national criminal jurisdiction".[366] Such a mechanism had even been supported by several representatives in the Sixth Committee[367] and some members of the Commission.[368] Other members instead tabled a compromise proposal. The international criminal court should have exclusive jurisdiction over crimes that were dealt with at the Nuremberg and Tokyo military trials (waging aggressive war and crimes against humanity),[369] but only a review or complementary function in the case of war crimes and crimes relating to illicit traffic in narcotic drugs, that were supposed to fall under the primary jurisdiction of national courts.[370]

---

362 Ninth Report, 1991 *YILC* Vol. II, Part One, p. 43.

363 1991 *YILC* Vol. I, p. 6.

364 Mr. Graefrath feared that the entire system proposed by the Special Rapporteur would "neither contribute to the establishment of a meaningful international jurisdiction nor provide for the effective implementation mechanism that the Code required": *ibid.*, p. 11. Given the "natural tendency" of States to refuse to relinquish their jurisdiction, the [international criminal court's] competence "would be reduced considerably", said Mr. Barboza: *ibid.*, p. 17. A parallel line of argument was set out by Mr. Razafindralambo when he argued that "the drawback of the proposed system [of the principle of concurrent jurisdiction] was that it would bring into play simultaneously jurisdiction *ratione materiae* and jurisdiction *ratione personae*, when clarity dictated that they should be dealt with separately": *ibid.*, p. 31. Moreover, paragraph 2 of the draft provision, which referred to a requirement that consent to confer jurisdiction should be given "by the State of nationality of the perpetrator, the victim State or the State whose nationals had been the victims of the crime, would contradict the whole purpose of the establishment of criminal jurisdiction, opening a Pandora's box by allowing many States to deny such jurisdiction", Mr. Njenga added: *ibid.*, p. 26.

365 *Ibid.*, p. 11. This was the first time the word "complement" was introduced as the corresponding meaning of the term "review function". Thus, arguably the underlying meaning behind the idea of "review function" was to have international machinery that "complement[ed]" national criminal jurisdiction.

366 *Ibid.* But see the statement made by Mr. Barsegov who argued that the question of the international criminal court "having review competence in its capacity as a higher court was particularly delicate...[and] was likely to encounter objections from individual States": *ibid.*, p. 39.

367 *Ibid.*, p. 11.

368 *Ibid.*, pp. 28 – 29. These members were Tomuschat and Al-Khasawneh.

369 By contrast, other members such as Mr. Mahiou and Mr. Razafindralambo were more inclined towards a system of exclusive jurisdiction for all crimes:. *ibid.*, pp. 18, 30.

370 *Ibid.*, pp. 22 – 23, 30.

A slightly different view suggested that, in addition to the exclusive jurisdiction and review function to be provided to the international criminal court, the latter would also enjoy the sort of concurrent jurisdiction – reflected in the Special Rapporteur's draft provision – that granted a State the choice of sending any of the less serious crimes to the international court if it wished to do so.[371]

Mr. Barsegov proposed for the first time a complementary scheme based on a mandatory *aut dedere aut judicare*. In cases where national courts "refused to institute proceedings", the international criminal court should be empowered to step in as a court of "first instance", the jurisdiction of which "was not founded on the State's discretionary powers of referral of individual cases".[372] Thus, a State's failure to act would "automatically" trigger the jurisdiction of the international criminal court without necessarily obtaining the State's consent.[373]

In the Sixth Committee, opinions were divided between an international court with exclusive jurisdiction, a system of concurrent or complementary jurisdiction based on the 1953 draft statute, a mechanism of review competence and a system based on the nature of the crime, whereby the international criminal court would have exclusive jurisdiction over one category of crimes and concurrent jurisdiction over the other.[374] Some reservations were expressed in relation to each system, especially that of review competence.[375]

The Special Rapporteur thought that the system of exclusive jurisdiction over certain crimes coupled with concurrent and optional jurisdiction with national courts over the other type of crimes was the one that met with the fewest objections in the Sixth Committee. He believed that this proposal was a "midway solution between the demand for exclusive jurisdiction, and the demand for systematic and general

371 *Ibid.*, p. 41.

372 *Ibid.*, p. 39.

373 *Ibid.*

374 *Topical Summary of the Discussion Held in the Sixth Committee of the General Assembly during its Forty-Sixth Session, prepared by the Secretariat,* UN.Doc. A/CN.4/L.469, pp. 63 – 64 [hereinafter Sixth Committee Discussion, UN.Doc. A/CN.4/L.469].

375 *Ibid.* Members expressed reservations concerning the possibility of endowing the international criminal court with review competence over decisions of national courts. One view was pointed out that "it was extremely doubtful that States would be prepared to agree that decisions of their courts, including their Supreme Courts, could be subject to revision outside their own judicial systems. Another representative, taking note of some of the arguments in favour of the system of review competence mentioned in paragraph 116 of the 1991 Commission's report, such as the practice of human rights bodies in relation to national courts, ruled out the possibility of drawing an analogy between these bodies and the international criminal court. He pointed out that while the role of a human rights body is limited to determining whether a State was in breach of a human right, the international criminal court has a far larger role in assessing the "weight of evidence" over cases from national courts. Owing to that limited role in relation to that of the international criminal court, Governments were less likely to "disfavour" the former than the latter: *ibid.*

application of the conferral-of-jurisdiction".[376] The new provision concerning the extent of jurisdiction for the future international court was drafted in his tenth report on the basis of this idea. This proposal was not unanimously accepted by members of the Commission. Aside from the drafting changes proposed – by many members – in relation to this provision, the members found different reasons for feeling either satisfied or dissatisfied with the Special Rapporteur's proposal.

Some members saw the Special Rapporteur's proposal as impractical; especially as it favoured a regime of exclusive jurisdiction. One member argued – not without good reason – that unless the special circumstances in which the "Nürnberg and Tokyo Tribunals had been established obtained, it would be impractical to demand that a State should hand over the allegedly responsible individual for trial by the international criminal court...[w]hat was more, with exclusive jurisdiction as envisaged..., many States would be reluctant to become parties to the statute of the court."[377]

Another member shared the exact same view when he said it was unimaginable that a government involved in the commission of aggression, genocide, or apartheid would "take part in proceedings against itself by handing over its nationals or by requesting that they should be brought to trial. It was only if the aggressor State was defeated...that an international court could take effective action."[378] The proposal was not "feasible" at the present time because it would have been a limitation that made matters worse. A regime of optional and concurrent jurisdiction, as contained in the Special Rapporteur's ninth report, would be preferable.[379] This would be the system with the best chance of gaining wide acceptance,[380] for States continued to be jealous of their sovereignty.[381]

Other members, while accepting in principle the system envisaged by the Special Rapporteur, objected to the list of crimes adopted. They thought that crimes such as illicit international trafficking in drugs or the kidnapping of diplomats should not fall under the system of exclusive jurisdiction. States were not "prepared to give up the exercise of their sovereignty [since those crimes are originally tried before domestic courts],...[thus] the international criminal court should have only subsidiary jurisdiction".[382] Weaker States might perhaps accept exclusive jurisdiction for illicit international trafficking in drugs. Where a crime was dealt with effectively, the "State would like to retain its national jurisdiction and would be hesitant to recognize the exclu-

376 *Tenth Report on the Draft Code of Crimes against the Peace and Security of Mankind*, UN. Doc. A/CN.4/442, 1992 *YILC*, Vol. II, Part One, p. 56 [hereinafter Tenth Report, 1992 *YILC* Vol. II, Part One].

377 *Ibid.*, p. 35. Mr Shi intended that precisely in cases of genocide, systematic mass violations of human rights and apartheid.

378 *Ibid.*, p. 17.

379 *Ibid.*, p. 20.

380 *Ibid.*, p. 37. Yet a court with that system was not his preference.

381 *Ibid.*, p. 12. Also Mr. Bowett thought that optional jurisdiction had the benefit of leaving States free to decide: *ibid.*, p. 33. Similarly, Mr Koroma thought that if the jurisdiction of the court became optional, this would entice States to become parties: *ibid.* p. 49.

382 *Ibid.*

sive and compulsory jurisdiction of the international court."[383] These crimes were not matters "that could properly be dealt with by the exclusive jurisdiction of the court". Only when States were implicated in crimes such as aggression, threat of aggression or intervention, where it was unimaginable that the State would try itself, the jurisdiction of the court should be exclusive and compulsory.[384]

The views expressed on the matter were clearly contradictory. The Special Rapporteur recognized that his proposal for just optional jurisdiction,[385] which had been rejected at the ninth session, gained support in the current session.[386] The proposed intermediate solution, which provided for exclusive jurisdiction in the current session, had also been criticized.[387] Discussion of the subject-matter was a very complex task to achieve. Thus, it was decided to establish a Working Group to propose "flexible and viable solutions" on the basis of the debates during which opposing points of view had been expressed.[388]

The 1992 Working Group recognized that, hitherto, the Commission had not expressed any preference for any version of the three different models of criminal jurisdiction proposed by the Working Group established in 1990.[389] Nor did any clear preference emerge in the debates of the Sixth Committee in 1991 concerning this matter.[390] General Assembly Resolution 46/54 of 1991 also set out this position, as it *invited* the Commission further to analyse and consider the matter.[391]

During the meetings held by the Working Group in 1992, it was a common understanding that any attempt to establish a "workable international trial system must start from a modest and realistic base".[392] Thus, the Working Group agreed that a

383 *Ibid.*, p. 39.

384 *Ibid.*, p. 25.

385 Ninth Report, 1991 *YILC* Vol. II, Part One, p. 41.

386 See Mr. Thiam's statement on this point: 1992 *YILC* Vol. I , p. 60.

387 *Ibid.*

388 *Ibid.*, p. 62. The Working Group was chaired by Mr. Koroma, and composed of Mr. Al-Baharna, Mr. Arangio-Ruiz, Mr. Crawford, Mr. Idris, Mr. Jacovides, Mr. Mikulka, Mr. Pellet, Mr. Robinson, Mr. Rosenstock, Mr. de Saram, Mr. Vereshchetin and Mr. Villagran Kramer, with Mr. Thiam in his capacity as Special Rapporteur, participating *ex officio*.

389 *Report of the International Law Commission on the Work of its Forty-Fourth Session* (4 May – 24 July 1992), Annex *Report of the Working Group on the Question of an International Criminal Jurisdiction*, UN.Doc. A/47/10, 1992 *YILC*, Vol. II, Part Two, p. 60 [hereinafter 1992 ILC Report].

390 *Sixth Committee Discussion*, UN.Doc. A/CN.4/L.469, pp. 63 – 66.

391 G.A.Res. 44/39, 67th plenary meeting. "*The General Assembly,...3. Invites* the International Law Commission, within the framework of the of the draft Code of Crimes against the Peace and Security of Mankind, to consider further and analyse the issues raised in its report on the work of its forty-second session concerning the question of an international criminal jurisdiction, including proposals for the establishment of an international criminal court or other international criminal trial mechanism in order to enable the General Assembly to provide guidance on the matter": *ibid.*

392 1992 *ILC Report, supra* note 389, p. 64.

court would be, essentially, a facility for the States parties to its statute, available in case of need.[393] The effective choice, therefore, lay between either a court that was a supplementary facility for States or no court at all.[394] It followed that the future international criminal court should have neither compulsory nor exclusive jurisdiction.[395] The international criminal court, instead, might prove useful and act in the following identified situations: among other things, cases where the State's custody of the accused was under threat of further acts of terrorism, for example, if it proceeded with the trial, or where the criminal justice system of a small State was overwhelmed by the magnitude of a particular offence; or cases where alleged criminals, who were formerly members of the government of a particular State committed their crimes in that capacity, and the "successor Government is *unwilling* or *unable* to try them, for whatever reason, or would prefer an international trial because of its greater legitimacy in the circumstances"[396] (emphasis added).

The Working Group had also suggested a system of conferment of jurisdiction similar to that proposed by the Special Rapporteur in his ninth report. A state party to the Statute was required to confer jurisdiction upon the international criminal court by a process of *ad hoc* acceptance or unilateral declaration in relation to particular offences before the international criminal court might exercise jurisdiction.[397] Yet the Working Group did not address the question whether there was a relationship between the situations defined above and the system of conferment of jurisdiction proposed.

Arguably, the two ideas might not be mutually exclusive and could be reconciled into one system. If a State party was "unwilling" or "unable" to try a case, it had the option to relinquish jurisdiction in favour of the international criminal court. As the Working Group put it, this approach established a system whereby "the international criminal court would be *complementary* to the existing system of national courts"[398] (emphasis added). It certainly acknowledged that the system of conferment of ju-

393 *Ibid.*

394 *Ibid.*

395 *Ibid.* In commenting on the report of the Working Group, some States supported in principle the approach taken by the Working Group hitherto. These members were Australia, Italy and Spain. Yet this approach failed to convince on the basis of different reasons in the opinion of States such as Belarus, Panama and the USA. *See Comments of Governments on the Report of the Working Group on the Question of an International Criminal Jurisdiction*, UN Doc. A/CN.4/452 and Add.1-3, 1993 *YILC*, Vol. II, Part One, pp. 127 – 143. Members such as Mexico went as far as rejecting the entire idea of an international criminal court, because the delivery and administration of justice within [a State's] territory was a basic function of the State and an obligation from which it could not escape. Transferring that obligation to a supranational body not only had direct effects in the area of territorial sovereignty, but also conflicted with the constitutional basis of some States": *ibid.*, pp. 137 – 139.

396 1992 *ILC Report, supra* note 389 p. 62.

397 *Ibid.*, pp. 65 – 66.

398 *Ibid.*, p. 77.

risdiction, which was originally based on the 1953 revised draft, created not only a concurrent jurisdiction with national courts, but also a complementary relationship, as argued earlier.

The Working Group's report was an effort to end the deadlock and suggested a middle way of responding affirmatively to the problem.[399] This approach was understandable to many representatives of the Sixth Committee who envisaged that the court should have neither compulsory nor exclusive jurisdiction.[400] Nor should it be an appeal court reviewing decisions of national courts.[401] The prevailing trend was mainly inclined towards a system that did not prejudice the role of domestic courts. In the opinion of many delegations, the nature of the jurisdiction of the proposed court should rather be optional and concurrent with that of national courts.[402] Different terms were used by some delegations to express such an idea.

One representative said that the jurisdiction of the future court should be "subsidiary to, or at the most concurrent with, that of national courts", in order to avoid the disruption of national jurisdictions, which were primarily responsible for punishing international crimes.[403] Another representative argued that if the main reason for establishing an international criminal court was the lack of sufficient enforcement at the national level, then it would "suffice to set up an optional and concurrent international jurisdiction which would supplement national jurisdiction without superseding it".[404] A different suggestion favoured a system of "preferential jurisdiction", whereby the international criminal court would give judgment at first and sole instance, if the case was brought before it. Otherwise, national courts "would be, or would again be competent" to try the accused.[405]

Although many of the delegations to the Sixth Committee supported the Working Group's scheme, none of them reintroduced the terms "unwilling" and "unable" as criteria supporting the application of the system proposed. Nor had the Sixth Committee's discussions resulted in the selection of a precise relationship between national and international jurisdictions. Yet, the meetings showed that the systems of exclusive jurisdiction and review competence were not valid options. A workable system of combining international and national jurisdictions was the most favourable.

In 1993, the Special Rapporteur followed the majority view favouring the combination of national and international jurisdictions in one system. In his eleventh report, he retained the system initially introduced in the ninth report, which called

399 *Ibid.*

400 *Topical Summary of the Discussion Held in the Sixth Committee of the General Assembly during its Forty-Seventh Session, prepared by the Secretariat*, UN Doc. A/CN.4/446, p. 15.

401 *Ibid.*, p. 18.

402 *Ibid.*, p. 15.

403 *Ibid.*, p. 16.

404 *Ibid.*

405 *Ibid.*, p. 18.

for a mechanism of optional, concurrent and complementary jurisdiction.[406] Article 5(1) and[407] (2),[408] in conjunction with Article 23(2) of the Special Rapporteur's eleventh report,[409] endorsed the same system, but in an explicit manner. Article 5(1) and (2) retained the ideas of consent and conferment of jurisdiction, and made them prerequisites for the international criminal court to exercise such jurisdiction, while Article 23(2) explicitly made it clear that any State, whether or not a party to the Statute of the international court, might, "instead of having an accused person tried under its own jurisdiction, refer him to the Court".[410] Such an option, in the words of the Special Rapporteur, "seems to have won the support of the majority in the Commission".[411]

The Special Rapporteur's eleventh report had been carefully studied by the 1993 Working Group which was re-established at that session.[412] The Working Group's mandate was obtained from paragraph 6 of General Assembly Resolution 47/33, which *requested* the Commission to continue its work for the elaboration of a draft statute for an international criminal court as a "matter of priority" by having recourse to the 1992 Working Group's report, debates that took place in the Sixth Committee, and any "written comments" received from States.[413] The 1993 Working Group had drafted a set of complex, detailed provisions that dealt with issues of the jurisdiction of the court (Articles 22 – 26).[414] The details of these articles are not relevant in this

406 *Eleventh Report on the Draft Code of Crimes Against the Peace and Security of Mankind: Draft Statute for an International Criminal Court*, UN. Doc. A/CN.4/449, 1993 *YILC*, Vol. II, Part One, pp. 111 – 124 [hereinafter Eleventh Report, 1993 *YILC* Vol. II, Part One].

407 Article 5(1) of the proposed draft provision reads: "The jurisdiction of the Court shall not be presumed": *ibid.*, p. 115.

408 Article 5(2) stipulates: "The Court shall have jurisdiction over every individual, provided that the State of which he is a national, and the State in whose territory the crime is presumed to have been committed, have accepted its jurisdiction": *ibid.*

409 Article 23(2) stipulates: "2. (a) Any State, whether or not it be a party to the Statute of the Court, may, instead of having an accused person tried under its own jurisdiction, refer him to the Court": *ibid.*, p. 120.

410 *Ibid.* Reading Article 5(1) and (2) together with Article 23(2), one could understand that the State has first to confer jurisdiction, then decide whether to submit the case either to the international court or to national courts. If it decides to defer to the international criminal court, the territorial State and State of nationality have to accept the exercise of such jurisdiction.

411 *Ibid.*, p. 114.

412 *Summary Records of the Meetings of the Forty-Fifth Session* 3 May – 23 July 1993, 1993 *YILC* Vol. I, p. 10 [hereinafter 1993 *YILC* Vol. I]. The Working Group was chaired by Mr. Koroma and consisted of: Messrs, Al-Baharan, Arangio-Ruiz, Crawford, de Saram, Guney, Pellet, Razfindralambo, Robinson, Rosenstock, Thiam, Tomuschat, Vereshchetin, Villagran Kramer and Yankov.

413 G.A. Res. 47/33, Forty-Seventh Session, Agenda item 129, 4 February 1992, para. 6.

414 *Report of the International Law Commission on the Work of its Forty-Fifth Session* (3 May – 23 July 1993), UN Doc. A/48/10, 1993 *YILC* Vol. II, Part Two, pp. 106 – 111.

context. What matters is the determination of the intended nature of competence of the proposed international criminal court in relation to national courts.

Under Article 23, the Working Group drafted three alternative proposals (A, B, and C). In alternatives "A"[415] and "C",[416] the Working Group chose an "opting in" system whereby the international criminal court could not exercise jurisdiction unless a special declaration was lodged to that effect.[417] By contrast, alternative "B"[418] supported a system of "opting out" in the sense that a State, by becoming a party to the Statute, "would automatically confer jurisdiction to the Court"[419] over the crimes listed in Article 22. These alternatives were proposed to satisfy two different opinions expressed during the discussion. While some members thought that the system set out in alternative "A" was the one which "best reflected the consensual basis of the Court's jurisdiction", as recommended by the 1992 Working Group, others did not believe that the consensual basis or the recommendations of the 1992 Working Group "led to a system like the one laid down in alternative 'A'."[420] Instead, they favoured an opting out system, as set out in alternative "B".

The relationship between national courts and the proposed international court was not directly addressed in the text of Article 23. Yet, Article 24 seemed to make the connection and clarified the intended approach. Article 24(1)(a) made it clear that any State party that conferred jurisdiction on the international criminal court in relation to any of the crimes listed under Article 22 also had jurisdiction under the relevant treaty criminalizing the conduct to try the suspect before its own courts.[421]

415 *Ibid.*, pp. 107 – 108. Paragraph 1 of alternative "A" reads: "A State Party to this Statute may, by declaration lodged with the Registrar, accept at any time the jurisdiction of the Court over one or more of the crimes referred to in article 22": *ibid.* p. 107.

416 *Ibid.*, p. 108. Paragraphs 1 and 2 of alternative "C" read: "1. A State Party to this Statute may, by a declaration lodged with the Registry, accept at any time the jurisdiction of the Court. 2. Unless otherwise specified,, a declaration of acceptance under paragraph 1 shall be deemed to confer jurisdiction on the Court with regard to all of the crimes listed in article 22": *ibid.*

417 *Ibid.* Yet, alternative "C" differs from alternative "A" in the sense that a State party, by lodging a declaration of acceptance of the jurisdiction of the court, shall be deemed to confer jurisdiction over all the crimes listed under Article 22 as opposed to one or more of those crimes, unless otherwise specified. By contrast, in alternative "A" the conferment of jurisdiction with regard to all crimes listed in Article 22 is not to be presumed unless clearly stated in the declaration. Thus, despite this difference, the two provisions are considered as part of an "opting in" system.

418 *Ibid.* Paragraphs 1 and 2 of alternative "B" read: "1. Unless it makes the declaration provided for in paragraph 2, a State becoming a Party to this Statute is deemed to have accepted the jurisdiction of the Court over any crime refereed to in article 22, if it is a Party to the treaty which defines that crime. 2. A State Party to the present Statute may, by declaration lodged with the Registrar, indicate that it does not accept the jurisdiction of the Court over one or more of the crimes referred to in paragraph 1": *ibid.*

419 *Ibid.*

420 *Ibid.*, p. 108.

421 Art. 24(1) (a). See also commentary on Article 24: *ibid.*, p. 109.

If that State, nevertheless, preferred to initiate proceedings before the international criminal court, and the suspect was not in the territory of any State with jurisdiction under the relevant treaty, yet present on the territory of the State of nationality or the territorial State, the consent of either of those two States was also required in order for the international criminal court to have jurisdiction.[422] Reading Articles 23 and 24 together suggests that they established a system of optional, concurrent and complementary jurisdiction between the proposed international criminal court and national courts, whereby a State has the option of either its domestic courts dealing with a crime, or, if unwilling to proceed, voluntarily relinquishing jurisdiction to the international criminal court, an idea that had been circulating since it was first proposed in 1951 and later revised by the Committee on International Criminal Jurisdiction.

The 1993 Working Group's report included the jurisdictional provisions and received an in-depth examination from members of the Commission[423] as well as from the re-established 1994 Working Group on a draft statute for an international criminal court.[424] The views concerning the provisions on jurisdiction (Articles 22 – 26) differed,[425] yet it was a common understanding that the jurisdictional clauses contemplated were complex. In its revised draft statute, the 1994 Working Group simplified those provisions and notably retained the original idea of establishing an optional, concurrent and complementary jurisdiction between the international criminal court and national courts on the basis of an "opting in" system as per Articles 21[426]

422 Art. 24 (2). See also commentary on Article 24: *ibid.*

423 The Commission examined the 1993 Working Group report at its 2329th to 2334th meetings, held from 3 to 9 May 1994. *See Summary Records of the Meetings of the Forty-Sixth Session* 2 May – 22 July 1994, 1994 *YILC* Vol. I, pp. 2 – 38 [hereinafter1994 *YILC* Vol. I].

424 *Report of the International Law Commission on the Work of its Forty-Sixth Session* (2 May – 22 July 1994), with Annex Draft Statute for an International Criminal Court, UN Doc. A/49/10, 1994 *YILC* Vol. II, Part Two, p. 20 [hereinafter 1994 ILC Report or 1994 ILC Draft Statute]. Also, observations received from 25 governments were taken into account. See *Observations of Governments on the Report of the Working Group on a Draft Statute for an International Criminal Court*, UN Doc. A/CN.4/458 and Add.1 – 8, 1994 *YILC* Vol. II Part One, pp. 24 – 96 [hereinafter Observations of Governments]. Generally on the 1994 Draft see P. Sreenivasa Rao, 'Trends in International Criminal Jurisdiction', 35 *Indian Journal of International Law* 17, 21 – 27 (1995); and generally on the development of the Commission's work on the subject since 1991 see Mathew D. Peter, 'The Proposed International Criminal Court: A Commentary on the Legal and Political Debates Regarding Jurisdiction that Threaten the Establishment of an Effective Court', 24 *Syracuse Journal of International Law and Commerce* 177, 185 – 197 (1997).

425 See generally *Summary Records of the 2329th. – 2334th. Meetings*, 1994 *YILC* Vol. I, pp. 2 – 38; *Observations of Governments*, pp. 24 – 96 ; *Topical Summary of the Discussion Held in the Sixth Committee of the General Assembly during its Forty-Eighth Session prepared by the Secretariat*, UN.Doc. A/CN.4/457, pp. 22 – 28 [hereinafter Sixth Committee Discussion, UN.Doc. A/CN.4/457].

426 1994 *ILC Draft Statute, supra* note 424, Art. 2.

and 22,[427] whereby a State party to the Statute could accept the jurisdiction of the court only after a declaration had been lodged with the Registrar.

The real innovation was the introduction of the term "complementary" in the preamble as well as a provision concerning the admissibility of a case, for the first time in a draft statute since the Commission began its early work on the subject. Preamble paragraph 3 *emphasized* that the international criminal court "is intended to be complementary to national criminal justice systems in cases where such trial procedures may not be available or may be ineffective".[428] The situations of "unavailability" or "ineffectiveness" of the trial procedures were described in Article 35 of the draft statute.[429] According to this provision, the court could decline to exercise its jurisdiction over a specific case on the ground that the crime:

a. Has been duly investigated by a State with jurisdiction over it, and the decision of that State not to proceed to a prosecution is apparently well-founded;
b. Is under investigation by a State which has or may have jurisdiction over it, and there is no reason for the Court to take any further action for the time being with respect to the crime; or
c. Is not of such gravity to justify further action by the Court.[430]

Article 35 was drafted in the negative by setting out the situations where the court might decline, as opposed to exercising, jurisdiction. Arguably, this was to ensure that having recourse to the international criminal court was the exception and not

427 *Ibid.*, Art. 22. For example., Article 22(1) states: "A State Party to this Statute may: (a) at any time it expresses its consent to be bound by the Statute, by declaration lodged with the depositary; or (b) At a later time, by declaration lodged with the Registrar; accept the jurisdiction of the Court with respect to such of the crimes referred to in article 20 as it specifies in the declaration".

428 *Ibid.*, preamble para. 3.

429 These terms were proposed by Mr. Robinson when commenting on an earlier version of the 1994 draft at the Commission's 2357th meeting p. 195. However, the reasons for not using the terms "unwilling" and "unable" proposed earlier by the 1992 Working Group in the 1994 ILC Draft Statute instead of "unavailability" or "ineffectiveness" are unclear. These terms appeared twice during the 1994 work. First, Mr. Rao argued that: "Jurisdiction should be based on cooperation among the States concerned, which would mean that the court could not act if the States concerned were willing and able to exercise their own jurisdiction over the offence". See 1994 *YILC* Vol. I, p. 23. Secondly, although I have found no further reference to these terms in the summary records of the meetings held in 1994, in the final report of the ILC to the General Assembly, these terms appeared as if had been raised during the discussions: "There were different views as to whether the nature of the court in terms of its relationship to national courts was adequately addressed in the present draft...others envisaged [the court]as an option for prosecution when the States concerned were unwilling or unable to do so, subject to the necessary safeguards against misuse of the court for political purposes": 1994 *ILC Report, supra* note 424, p. 21.

430 1994 *ILC Draft Statute, supra* note 424, Art. 35.

the rule. Failing to meet the conditions listed under Article 35 definitely would have established a presumption in favour of a decision that domestic procedures were neither available nor effective. Thus, the Court could have stepped in on the basis of its "complementary" function, reflected in the preamble, to remedy the deficiency resulting from the domestic proceedings. As the 1994 Working Group stated in its commentary, the court was intended to function in cases where there "is no prospect of those persons being duly tried in national courts. The emphasis is thus on the court as a body which will complement existing national jurisdictions…and which is not intended to exclude the existing jurisdiction of national courts".[431]

The term "complementary" had been introduced for the first time by the 1992 Working Group.[432] Its verb, "complement", was proposed even earlier by Mr. Graefrath during the Commission's meetings in 1990.[433] The verb and its adjective were both used at the time to describe the possible relationship between domestic courts and the future international criminal court. However, the inclusion of the term "complementary" in the preamble to the 1994 draft statute was an entirely new idea proposed by New Zealand in that year.

In its observations on the 1993 Working Group's report, New Zealand stated that several provisions of the draft statute touched on the "interrelationship" between national courts and "national processes" on the one hand and the "international criminal court" on the other, in respect of the crimes at issue. "Consideration should be given to making a suitable reference, perhaps in the preamble to the statute, to this relationship and to the respective roles and complementarity of the national and international processes".[434] Similarly, Article 35, which mirrored the 1994 Working Group's approach towards the concept of complementarity, was the outcome of a proposal tabled by Mr. James Crawford during the Commission's meetings in 1994.[435]

Recognizing that the proposed court might have been "swamped by peripheral complaints" involving minor offenders – a concern that was raised by some delegations during the meetings of the Sixth Committee[436] – Mr. Crawford thought of a

431 1994 *ILC Report, supra* note 424, p. 27.

432 1992 *ILC Report, supra* note 389, p. 77.

433 1990 *YILC* Vol. I, p. 32.

434 *Observations of Governments, supra* note 424, p. 61. The term "complementary" was also used by Japan in its written observations received later on 13 May 1994 when it said: "[t]he court should be a realistic and flexible organ complementary to the existing system":*Ibid.*, p. 48. Members such as Mr. He also invoked the term at the Commission's meetings. See 1994 *YILC* Vol. I, pp. 38, 115.

435 1994 *YILC* Vol. I, p. 9.

436 See *Sixth Committee Discussion*, UN.Doc. A/CN.4/457, p. 23 ("Some representatives insisted on the importance of the criterion of the seriousness of the crimes. One of them said that the court's jurisdiction should be limited to the most serious crimes, those which most deeply offended the conscience of the international community. Another representative pointed out that the court should clearly not deal with petty offences. It should be activated only in cases of such gravity as to require the involvement of the international community as a whole. Accordingly …the tribunal should be empowered

procedural mechanism that filtered the sorts of cases going before the court from the limitations arising out of the consent requirements set out in Articles 21 – 22. The international criminal court "should have power to stay a prosecution on specified grounds…The grounds might include, say, the existence of an adequate national tribunal with jurisdiction over the offence[437] or the fact that the acts alleged were not of sufficient gravity to warrant trial at the international level".[438] A provision to that effect adapted the court's case load to the resources available and ensured that national sovereignty was respected, said Mr. Eiriksson.[439] This also emphasized the idea that the international criminal court was intended to "supplement, rather than replace, existing national criminal jurisdictions" as well as reduce the possibility of being used as a "political tool", Mr. Crawford added.[440]

The idea of introducing Article 35 as a limitation on the exercise of the court's jurisdiction found full support from Messrs. Rosenstock,[441] Eiriksson[442] and Ro-

to make that distinction in individual cases"). See also in the same vein a statement made by the Czech Republic in its observations on the 1993 Working Group report: "I would not be appropriate to overburden the tribunal with cases which can be effectively punished by States themselves. A certain degree of seriousness of the breach should therefore also be a precondition for the jurisdiction of the tribunal. The mechanism of the tribunal should be reserved for the most serious international crimes, especially in the event when prosecution before domestic courts cannot be guaranteed": *Observations of Governments, supra* note 424, p. 39. The same concern was raised by Mr. Crawford. *See* 1994 *YILC* Vol. I, p. 193.

437 1994 *YILC* Vol. I, p. 9. According to Mr. Crawford, this meant that the court could not act if the "States concerned were willing and able to exercise their own jurisdiction over the offence": *ibid.*, p. 23. Similarly, in its observations on the 1993 Working Group draft statute, Chile argued in similar terms that the competence of the tribunal "should be subsidiary to that exercise by national courts". International criminal jurisdiction should, therefore, as a general rule, come into play only in the absence of national jurisdiction: *Observations of Governments, supra* note 424, p. 36.

438 *Ibid.*, p. 9.

439 *Ibid.*, p. 33. This was also one of the main concerns that the United States had raised in its observation on the 1993 Working Group draft. The United States urged the Commission to take into account that the "budgetary and administrative requirements of the tribunal must be handled with great care. The tribunal could be an extraordinarily expensive undertaking, especially if it is used at any one time for extensive investigation or more than a limited number of cases": *Observations of Governments, supra* note 424, p. 80.

440 1994 *YILC* Vol. I, pp. 9, 191. As might be inferred from the report of the 1994 Working Group, the "clear requirements of acceptance of jurisdiction" and "principled controls on the exercise of that jurisdiction" explained the exact purpose of having an international criminal court that would be *complementary* to national criminal jurisdictions as reflected in the preamble. See 1994 *ILC Report, supra* note 424, p. 37.

441 1994 *YILC* Vol. I, p. 27.

442 *Ibid.*, p. 33.

drigues.[443] Yet some members disagreed with the drafting,[444] while others thought the provision was ambiguous because it was not clear whether it was concerned with jurisdiction, admissibility or the appropriateness of prosecution.[445] The Special Rapporteur thought that the entire provision was "inappropriate" because "no court could have 'discretionary powers', except in respect of its own internal functioning".[446] In assessing the entire jurisdictional system, one view believed that "[w]hy create an international criminal court if, at the same time, every thing was being done to ensure that no cases were ever brought before it?"[447] Mr. Crawford, by contrast, thought that the provision was "essential" because, after "two years work, the conclusion was reached "that it was impossible to confine the court's jurisdiction merely by defining the crimes it would have to try. In point of fact, the crimes in question covered a wide range of situations, some of them rather minor; and that was why the court must be vested with the additional power".[448] Article 35 was adopted, despite some requests for its deletion.[449] The Commission's forty-sixth session showed how the notion of complementarity was rapidly evolving from the mere jurisdictional provisions based on an early idea presented in 1951 and 1953 to a functional system that balanced and organized the relationship between domestic courts and the proposed international criminal court.

6.8 The Final Phase for the Adoption of the Principle of Complementarity (1995 – 1998)

The 1994 complementarity model was taken as the basis for future work, which led to the adoption of the complementarity principle found in the 1998 Rome Statute. The concept of complementarity as it exists today finally crystallized with the adoption of an *Ad hoc* Committee on the Establishment of an International Criminal Court (*Ad hoc* Committee) to study and develop the 1994 International Law Commission's draft statute.

In the *Ad hoc* Committee, some delegations, while supporting the establishment of an international criminal court, were unwilling to create a body that could "impinge on national sovereignty".[450] It was stressed that complementarity should establish a "strong presumption in favour of national jurisdiction". This was justified on account

443 *Ibid.*, p. 210.

444 *Ibid.*, p. 226.

445 *Ibid.*, p. 227.

446 *Ibid.*, p. 228.

447 *Ibid.*, p. 212.

448 *Ibid.*, p. 230.

449 *Ibid.*, p. 300.

450 *Report of the Ad hoc Committee on the Establishment of an International Criminal Court*, UN GAOR, 50th Sess., Supp. No. 22, UN Doc. A/50/22 (1995), paras. 29 – 51 [hereinafter 1995 *Ad hoc Committee Report*].

of the advantages of domestic systems.[451] It was also stated that, in treating the principle of complementarity, "a balanced approach was necessary".[452] While preserving the primacy of national jurisdictions was important, it was also significant to avoid any attempt that rendered the jurisdiction of the proposed court "merely residual to national jurisdiction".[453]

The drafters recognized that the question of complementarity and the relationship between the proposed court and national courts would have to be studied in a number of other interconnected areas, for example, in regard to international judicial cooperation and issues involving surrender, among others.[454] Generally, the main target was to achieve consensus on the relationship, since States were hesitant to accept any compromise proposal touching on a fundamental issue without having a clear sense "of how the final, complete picture" would be. Once the legal relationship between national jurisdictions and the proposed court was established, it was easier "to make progress on other major issues".[455]

One of the main questions was whether the principle of complementarity should be reflected in the preamble or embodied in an article of the 1994 draft statute. Two views were expressed. According to one view, given the significance of the principle of complementarity, a simple reference in the preamble was deemed insufficient. The principle should be either defined or referred to in an article of the statute, preferably in its "opening part". A definition of that kind would mirror the importance of considering the principle of complementarity in the interpretation of subsequent provisions.[456] According to the other view, the principle could be developed in the preamble. The drafters made reference to Article 31 of the Vienna Convention on the Law of Treaties, according to which the preamble to a treaty was considered part of the context within which a treaty should be interpreted. A statement on complementarity in the preamble would shape part of the context in which "the Statute as a whole was to be interpreted and applied".[457]

Many delegations believed that defining the principle in an abstract manner would not serve the purpose. Thus, the practical implications of the principle had to be studied carefully.[458] The *Ad hoc* Committee also discussed how far the court's

451 1995 *Ad hoc Committee Report, supra* note 450, para. 31.

452 *Ibid.*, para. 33.

453 *Ibid.*

454 *Ibid.*, para. 34.

455 J. T. Holmes, "The Principle of Complementarity", in R. S. Lee (ed.), *The International Criminal Court: The Making of the Rome Statute, Issues. Negotiations. Results* (The Hague. London. Boston: Kluwer Law International, 1999), p. 43.

456 1995 *Ad hoc Committee Report, supra* note 450, paras. 35-36.

457 *Ibid.*, para. 37; see also Vienna Convention on the Law of Treaties, May 23, 1969, Art. 31, 1155 U.N.T.S. 331, 340 (entered into force Jan. 27, 1980) [hereinafter Vienna Convention]. Article 31 states: "a treaty shall be interpreted in good faith in accordance with the ordinary meaning to be given to the terms of the treaty in their context and in the light of its object and purpose ... ": *ibid.*

458 1995 *Ad hoc Committee Report, supra* note 450, para. 30.

jurisdiction should extend in regard to national jurisdiction. It realized that, unlike the jurisdiction of the two *ad hoc* tribunals, which was provided for and exercised independently of "the unavailability or effectiveness of local authorities to prosecute" the alleged criminals, the jurisdiction of the proposed international criminal court was limited only to those cases where national proceedings were "unavailable" or "ineffective".[459]

The reference to the phrase "or may be ineffective" in the 1994 draft statute preamble made it evident that the International Law Commission had believed that the court's jurisdiction "should extend beyond those situations where the national jurisdiction simply did not function".[460] Yet, the draft was silent with respect to the term "unavailable", presumably satisfied that the court could exercise jurisdiction if the national system failed to proceed as described in Article 35 of the Commission's draft.[461] Many delegations pointed out that the terms "available" or "ineffective" were ambiguous, lacking standards of assessment.[462] The *Ad hoc* Committee made the observation that the commentary to the preamble clearly "envisaged a very high threshold for exceptions to national jurisdiction" and that the International Law Commission expected the proposed court to step in only where there was "no prospect" that the alleged perpetrators of serious crimes would be "duly tried in national courts".[463]

In late 1995, the *Ad hoc* Committee was replaced by a Preparatory Committee. The 1996 Preparatory Committee adopted an identical approach when it discussed the issue of complementarity for the first time in March 1996.[464] The vague definitions of "unavailability or ineffectiveness" of national judicial systems were also criticized during the 1996 Session of the Preparatory Committee. Some delegations believed that the words "unavailable" or "ineffective" required a definition. Others thought that the words "should be omitted altogether".[465]

It was pointed out that besides the third paragraph of the preamble, the principle of complementarity involved a number of other provisions. Article 35 on admissibility was central among them. States criticized the formulation of Article 35 because the criteria referred to in that article, on the basis of which the court decided whether the case before it would be inadmissible, were "too narrow".[466] They covered only those cases being investigated and did not cover cases that had been or were being pros-

459 Flavia Lattanzi, "The Complementarity Character of the Jurisdiction of the Court with Respect to National Jurisdictions", in Flavia Lattanzi et al. (eds.), *supra* note 106, p. 9.

460 Holmes, *supra* note 455, p. 44.

461 *Ibid.*

462 1995 *Ad hoc Committee Report, supra* note 450, para. 41.

463 *Ibid.*, para. 42.

464 *Report of the Preparatory Committee on the Establishment of an International Criminal Court*, UN GAOR, 51st Sess., Vol. 1, Supp. No. 22, UN Doc. A/51/22 (1996), para. 154 [hereinafter 1996 *Preparatory Committee Report*, Vol. I].

465 1996 *Preparatory Committee Report*, Vol. I, *supra* note 464, para. 161.

466 *Ibid.*, para. 164.

ecuted at the time.[467] Past or current legal proceedings should be subject to qualifications such as "impartiality" and "diligent prosecution".[468] Grounds for inadmissibility, such as those found in Article 42 *ne bis in idem*, could also be included in Article 35, making it the main article on complementarity in the operative part of the statute.[469]

Other delegations pointed to the complexity of determining "ineffective" procedures and criticized the "subjective character" of the proposed standards. They called for more "stringent and objective criteria" that would better serve security and clarity.[470] Although some delegations believed that notions such as "absence of good faith" and "unconscionable delay" in the conduct of national proceedings were necessary tools for the clarification of this matter, yet others thought they were "vague" and "confusing".[471] Realizing this fact was a first step in adding new criteria in order to achieve a clearer and more objective standard.[472]

At the commencement of the sittings of the Preparatory Committee in the August 1997 session, the Chairman requested the head of the Canadian delegation, Mr. John Holmes, to "coordinate informal consultations" on the issue.[473] The coordinator produced a draft provision on complementarity, which was later approved by the Committee at the end of the August session.[474] In order to attain consensus, a text box was placed at the beginning of the draft article to explain its origins.[475] Also several footnotes were added to clarify the intended approach. The inclusion of the footnotes made it clear that the final version of the draft article depended on the results of discussions on other matters in the statute.[476] The terms "unwilling" or

467 *Ibid.*

468 *Ibid.*

469 *Ibid.*

470 *Ibid.*, para. 166.

471 *Ibid.*

472 *Report of the Preparatory Committee on the Establishment of an International Criminal Court*, 51st Sess., Vol. 2, Supp. No. 22, UN Doc. A/51/22 (1996) [hereinafter 1996 Preparatory Committee Report, Vol. II], p. 3. See for instance the new proposal for the preamble to the International Law Commission Draft: "Emphasizing further that the international criminal court shall complement national criminal justice systems when they are unable or unwilling to fulfill their obligations to bring to trial such persons": *ibid.*, p. 2.

473 See *Decisions Taken by the Preparatory Committee at Its Session Held 4 to 15 August 1997*, UN GAOR, 52nd mtg., UN Doc. A/AC.249/1997/L.8/Rev.1 (1997) [hereinafter 1997 Preparatory Committee Decisions]. The Preparatory Committee did not discuss the issue of complementarity again until the August 1997 session.

474 Holmes, *supra* note 455, p. 46.

475 1997 *Preparatory Committee Decisions*, *supra* note 473, p. 10. The text box reads: "The following draft text represents the results of informal consultations on Article 35 and is intended to facilitate the work towards the elaboration of the Statute of the Court. The content of the text represents a possible way to address the issue of complementarity and is without prejudice to the views of any delegation. The text does not represent agreement on the eventual content or approach to be included in this article": *ibid.*

476 *Ibid.*, pp. 11 – 12 ; *also* Holmes, *supra* note 455, p. 46.

"unable" genuinely appeared in draft Article 35,[477] for the first time since its initial appearance in the report of the 1992 Working Group.[478] Moreover, a set of conditions for determining a State's "unwillingness" or "inability" was also explored in the same provision.[479] This progress continued, and similar draft Articles emerged during the Inter-Sessional Meeting in Zutphen[480] and in the Draft Final Act.[481] Most delegations accepted the view that the compromise on complementarity had been agreed upon. They also believed that the "text box and the alternative approach would disappear over time".[482] Yet a number of delegations still raised the issue of sovereignty in relation to the definition of "unwillingness".

477 1997 *Preparatory Committee Decisions, supra* note 473, pp. 10 – 11. Article 35(2) of the Draft reads: "Having regard to paragraph 3 of the preamble, the Court shall determine that a case is inadmissible where: a) the case is being investigated or prosecuted by a State which has jurisdiction over it, unless the State is unwilling or unable genuinely to carry out the investigation or prosecution; b) the case has been investigated by a State which has jurisdiction over it and the State has decided not to prosecute the person concerned, unless the decision resulted from the unwillingness or inability of the State genuinely to prosecute": *ibid.*, Art. 35(2).

478 1992 *ILC Report, supra* note 389, p. 62. The difference lies in the fact that the 1992 Working Group did not use the term "genuinely".

479 1997 *Preparatory Committee Decisions, supra* note 473, pp. 11 – 12. Article 35(3) states: "In order to determine unwillingness in a particular case, the Court shall consider whether one or more of the following exist, as applicable: a) the proceedings were or are being undertaken or the national decision was made for the purpose of shielding the person concerned from criminal responsibility for crimes within the jurisdiction of the Court as set out in article 20; b) there has been an undue delay in the proceedings which in the circumstances is inconsistent with an intent to bring the person concerned to justice; c) the proceedings were not or are not being conducted independently or impartially and they were or are being conducted in a manner which, in the circumstances, is inconsistent with an intent to bring the person concerned to justice": *ibid.*, Art. 35(3). Article 35(4) states: "In order to determine inability in a particular case, the Court shall consider whether, due to a total or partial collapse or unavailability of its national judicial system, the State is unable to obtain the accused or the necessary evidence and testimony or otherwise unable to carry out its proceedings": *ibid.*, Art. 35(4). However, see the statement made by the Preparatory Committee in relation to an alternative approach to be considered, which reads: "An alternative approach, which needs further discussion, is that the Court shall not have the power to intervene when a national decision has been taken in a particular case. That approach could be reflected as follows: The Court has no jurisdiction where the case in question is being investigated or prosecuted, or has been prosecuted, by a State which has jurisdiction over it". See 1997 *Preparatory Committee Decisions, supra* note 473, p. 12.

480 See *Report of the Inter-Sessional Meeting From 19 to 30 January 1998 in Zutphen, the Netherlands*, Art. 11, pp. 42 – 43, UN Doc. A/AC.249/1998/L.13 (1998).

481 *Report of the Preparatory Committee on the Establishment of an International Criminal Court, Draft Statute & Draft Final Act*, Art. 15, UN Doc. A/Conf.183/2/Add.1 (1998) [hereinafter 1998 Draft Final Act].

482 Holmes, *supra* note 455, p. 48.

In Rome,[483] the question of complementarity was discussed in general terms during the plenary meetings. Many delegations supported in principle the scheme of "unwillingness" and "inability" reflected in Article 15 of draft submitted by the Preparatory Committee to the Rome Conference.[484] Later, the question of complementarity was assigned to the Committee of the Whole. It was agreed from the outset that discussions on complementarity should be as limited as possible.[485] The coordinator, recognizing the sensitivity of opening the door to major discussions on complementarity, decided not to hold informal consultations on the subject.[486] Some delegations were still unhappy with the complementarity compromise reached during the work of the Preparatory Committee. In order to accommodate these concerns, the coordinator, instead, carried out bilateral meetings aiming to reach consensus.[487] The significant part of the debate focused on three major problems concerning the interpretation of the principle of complementarity.

One concern was that Article 15(2) of the draft report of the Preparatory Committee submitted to the Rome Conference generally lacked objective criteria in determining a State's "unwillingness". Mr. John Holmes, the coordinator, attempted to

483 See generally on the Rome Conference, Philippe Kirsch and Robinson Darryl, "Reaching Agreement at the Rome Conference", *Cassese, Commentary, supra* note 112, pp. 81 – 82, 90; M. Cherif Bassiouni, 'Negotiating the Treaty of Rome on the Establishment of an International Criminal Court', 32 *Cornell International Law Journal* 443 (1999).

484 *Report of the Preparatory Committee on the Establishment of an International Criminal Court*, 14 April 1998, UN Doc., A/CONF.183/2, Art. 15; for an account of the views of delegations supporting the scheme, see *Summary Record of the 2 nd Plenary Meeting*, 15 June 1998, UN Doc., A/CONF.183/SR.2, para. 70; *Summary Record of the 3 rd Plenary Meeting*, 16 June 1998, UN Doc. A/CONF.183/SR.3, paras. 48, 88; *Summary Record of the 4th Plenary Meeting*, 16 June 1998, UN Doc. A/CONF.183/SR.4, paras. 27, 42; *Summary Record of the 5th Plenary Meeting*, 17 June 1998, UN Doc. A/CONF.183/SR.5, paras. 21, 39; *Summary Record of the 6th Plenary Meeting*, 17 June 1998, UN Doc. A/CONF.183/SR.6, paras. 31, 100; *Summary Record of the 7th Plenary Meeting*, 18 June 1998, UN Doc. A/CONF.183/SR.7, para. 101; *Summary Record of the 8th Plenary Meeting*, 18 June 1998, UN Doc. A/CONF.183/SR.8, paras. 1, 77.

485 See Sharon Williams, "Issues of Admissibility", *Triffterer Commentary, supra* note 114, p. 390. "Article 17 could not be opened up for substantial change or the package based on compromise would have folded. This was made clear in the general debate in the Committee of the Whole by the coordinator. Not all States were completely satisfied, but saw the article as a delicately balanced compromise. However, some delegations including China, Egypt, Mexico, Indonesia, India, and Uruguay wanted to reopen the negotiations. Thus, the intention of the coordinator who had continued with his role at the request of the Bureau of the Committee of the Whole in Rome was to 'resist holding informal consultations for as long as possible' for two reasons. First, this would have led to unending consultations and proposals, and accordingly impede adopting a strengthened complementarity Article. Second, the coordinator was of the view that bilateral contacts with delegations would afford him a better opportunity for gauging concerns of States opposed to the Draft Statute's text."

486 Holmes, *supra* note 455, p. 52.

487 *Ibid.*

clarify that the underlying purpose of using the terms "unwilling" and "unable" was not that the "Court should serve as an appellate body or a court of last resort for national legal systems. Where States assumed their obligations, the Court had no role; only where there was a failure due to inability or unwillingness was the Court engaged".[488] Yet, the Chinese delegate argued that the "the criteria for determining the unwillingness of a State to carry out an investigation listed in [Article 15 (2)] were highly subjective, and gave the Court unduly high powers".[489] A similar concern was raised by the Indian delegate.[490] Others, such as the Pakistani delegate, suggested retaining the idea of inability, yet the deletion of the term "unwillingness" and the conditions defining it set out in Article 15(2).[491] The Iraqi delegate pushed further for the redrafting of Article 15 as a whole. In his view, "[a]rticle 15 must be drafted so as to make it consistent with the principle of complementarity between the Court and national jurisdictions". Thus, Article 15(2) and (3) should be deleted *in toto.*[492]

Second and third concerns focused on the criterion of delay under Article 15(2)(b) and the terms used for testing inability under Article 15(3).[493] As will be discussed in more detail under the relevant parts of chapter III, these problems were actually technical ones which required slight amendments to Article 15. The negotiations finally succeeded in accommodating these concerns, and the final solutions are reflected in the current text of Article 17 of the Rome Statute.[494]

6.9 *The 1919 – 1994 Complementarity Models* vis-à-vis *the Rome Statute Model*

"Complementarity" is no more than a term that describes the relationship between national and international jurisdictions. It helps to solve the conflict of jurisdiction that arose over certain cases by the organization of the *exercise* of such jurisdiction through either the domestic or international forum at any given time. To the extent that international jurisdiction played a role alongside domestic jurisdictions, "complementarity" emerged in various shapes depending on the scope, degree and nature of such contribution granted to the international jurisdiction. It follows that "complementarity" is not an absolute principle so much as a flexible idea subject to variations, which results in models being slightly different from the traditional type reflected in

488 *Summary Record of the 11th Meeting,* 22 June 1998, UN Doc. A/CONF.183/C.1/SR.11, para. 19.

489 *Summary Record of the 12th Meeting,* 23 June 1998, UN Doc. A/CONF.183/C.1/SR.12, para. 9.

490 *Ibid.*, para. 10.

491 *Summary Record of the 35th Meeting,* 13 July 1998, UN Doc. A/CONF.183/C.1/SR.35, para. 56.

492 *Ibid.*, para. 65.

493 Holmes, *supra* note 455, pp. 52 – 53.

494 Rome Statute of the International Criminal Court, Adopted by the United Nations Diplomatic Conference of Plenipotentiaries on the Establishment of an International Criminal Court, 17 July 1998, UN Doc. A/CONF.183/9, Art. 17.

Article 17 of the Rome Statute. This section will limit the examination to the major drafts studied in order to serve as examples demonstrating such an assertion.

The first noticeable model – apart from that mirrored in the penalty provisions of World War I – is the one that emerged from the 1937 League of Nations Convention. According to this model, which was based on the principle of *aut dedere aut judicare*, a State Party to the convention was "entitled" to refer a case to the international criminal court if it was unwilling or unable for whatever reason to prosecute the case before its own domestic courts or to extradite to another State. The main feature of this model lies in the fact that it created an optional and consensual basis to the exercise of jurisdiction by the international criminal court – a significant feature introduced at the time to satisfy States' demands to preserve their national sovereignty.

The idea of granting an international criminal court a sort of optional "complementary" jurisdiction, in the event of a State's unwillingness to act, influenced to a great extent the preceding draft statutes prepared by United Nations official bodies and other non-official bodies. The jurisdictional mechanism proposed by the London International Assembly during World War II, the International Commission for Penal Reconstruction and Development and the United Nations War Crimes Commission (1942 – 1943) established a system of optional concurrent and complementary jurisdiction that mainly corresponded to the 1937 model. Similarly, the proposal tabled by de Vabres during the meeting of the 1947 Committee on the Progressive Development of International Law and its Codification and the initial draft proposal for the Genocide Convention prepared by the Secretariat relied on the 1937 model as well. Occasional references pointed towards the 1937 complementarity model during the 1949 – 1950 International Law Commission meetings on the question of international criminal jurisdiction.

The 1951 and 1953 draft statutes, prepared by the two Committees on International Criminal Jurisdiction, established a system of *voluntary* submission of cases to the international criminal court through a mechanism of conferment of jurisdiction ("opting in system"), which created the same regime with slight technical differences – rendering this model, in principle, similar to the 1937, 1942 – 1943, and 1947 models. Yet, the problem common to these models lay in the fact that, in practice, if the unwilling State decided neither to prosecute nor to refer the case to the international criminal court, the latter had no power to request deferment to its jurisdiction, which rendered these models toothless.

The 1953 model was taken as the main ground for the future work of the International Law Commission. The 1990 and 1992 – 1993 Working Groups and the Special Rapporteur's ninth and eleventh reports also proposed an optional concurrent and complementary regime inspired by the 1953 model. The system of complementarity established by these draft statutes and proposals fits under the umbrella of one major model that may be defined as *optional complementarity.*

The second major model was reflected in the Nuremberg experience, where there was a clear complementary relationship between the Nuremberg International Military Tribunal and national courts. Yet, each jurisdiction focused on different types of offenders. The International Military Tribunal dealt with the major war criminals, while the mid- to lower rank criminals were dealt with by national courts. The main feature of this model lies in the fact that it does not rely on the idea of a State's failure to act for triggering the jurisdiction of an international tribunal. Rather, the complementary relationship was exercised in a friendly manner on the basis of a division of responsibilities between the two levels of jurisdiction. This is certainly due to the lack of possible conflicts of jurisdiction.

In 1988 and 1989, the International Law Commission proposed a mechanism of complementary jurisdiction which seemed to have been inspired by the Nuremberg experience. National courts were to deal with minor crimes, such as war crimes, while the international criminal court should focus on other types of crimes such as aggression. This proposal was also based on the idea of division of labour and the symmetry in exercising the two-tier jurisdiction. The only difference was that the Nuremberg model distributed the powers between national and international jurisdictions on the basis of the level or degree of responsibility of the perpetrators. By contrast, the model proposed by the International Law Commission relied on the nature of the crimes. However, both ideas represent one major model that may be defined as *friendly* or *amicable* complementarity.

The third major model was a modified scheme of complementarity adopted by the 1994 International Law Commission's Working Group. This model was based on a combination of the consensual system introduced in the first model and, as lately reflected in the 1993 Working Group's draft, was coupled with an admissibility mechanism that acted as a safety valve to frame a new version of complementarity. Although the system contemplated by the drafters shared with the first model the mechanism of optional, concurrent and complementary jurisdiction that provided States with the freedom of choice of the *forum conveniens*, this modified version had a higher threshold that was not triggered by just meeting the regular jurisdictional requirements that were set out in Articles 21 – 22 and 25 of the 1994 draft statute, as in the previous mentioned drafts. Thus, if, for example, the custodial State, a party to the statute which accepted the jurisdiction of the court, chose to lodge a complaint with the Prosecutor[495] and refer a certain case to the international criminal court, due to its unwillingness to try a case before its national courts, that case had to pass an admissibility test before the court. This last requirement was lacking in all of the preceding draft statutes proposed by the Commission. Yet, this model shared with the first model the lack of enforcement powers on the part of the court in the event of a State's inaction, resulting from the latter's unwillingness or inability to act.

The fourth major model was the traditional one mirrored in the current 1998 Rome Statute. This model was based on a reverse approach, yet it was still inspired by the theories underpinning the first two models with technical modifications in relation to its application. Under the current regime, the jurisdiction of the ICC is *compulsory*, and thus, once the State has ratified the Statute, it is automatically subjected to its jurisdiction, provided that certain requirements have been met. In order for this jurisdiction to be activated – as in the 1994 International Law Commission Draft – preconditions to the exercise of jurisdiction (accompanied by a referral by

495 1994 *ILC Draft Statute*, *supra* note 424, Art. 25 (2).

a State Party or the Security Council) as well as admissibility conditions have to be satisfied.

The technical difference, however, lies in the fact that the Rome Statute model created a dual regime of *mandatory* and *optional complementarity* that functioned alongside each other. According to the *mandatory* structure, the question of the determination of *inadmissibility* seems obligatory according to a literal reading of the chapeau of Article 17, which states that the "Court *shall* determine that a case is *inadmissible* where..." Such determination is *mandatory*, at least during the situation phase.[496] The 1994 model did not even provide a distinction between situations and cases and, thus, there was no question of determining the admissibility of a situation *versus* a case.[497]

According to the Rome Statute model, if the State was unwilling or unable to deal with a situation or case before its own domestic courts, the Court could proceed following this situation or case without any State's further consent. This was not the case in terms of the 1994 Draft, which left the State free to decide whether it would defer jurisdiction to the court in the event of its unwillingness to act. According to the jurisdictional mechanism vested in the 1994 draft, a State's failure to investigate, prosecute or try a case before its domestic courts did not automatically trigger the jurisdiction of the international criminal court by requesting the situation or case to be transferred to its jurisdiction.[498] If the custodial State Party, which accepts the

496 See Arts. 18, 53(1)(b), ICC Rule 55(2). Such a determination is optional during the stage of a case when the Court is acting *proprio motu* as as in the 1994 International Law Commission Draft. See Rome Statute, Art. 19(1). For further elaboration on these points see section..., chapter III *infra*; and also see Mohamed M. El Zeidy, 'Some Remarks on the Question of Admissibility of a Case During Arrest Warrant Proceedings before the International Criminal Court', 19 *Leiden Journal of International Law* 741, 746 – 748 (2006).

497 There are few noticeable references in the literature that recognize the distinction between the question of admissibility of situations and cases. See Héctor Olásolo, *The Triggering Procedure of the International Criminal Court* (Leiden. Boston: Martinus Nijhoff Publishers, 2005), pp. 164 – 166; Héctor Olásolo, 'The Lack of Attention to the Distinction between Situations and Cases in National Laws on Co-operation with the International Criminal Court with Particular Reference to the Spanish Case', 20 *Leiden Journal of International Law* 193 (2007); Mohamed M. El Zeidy, 'Critical Thoughts on Article 59(2) of the ICC Statute', 4 *Journal of International Criminal Justice* 448, 464 (2006); Mohamed M. El Zeidy, 'The Ugandan Government Triggers the First Test of the Complementarity Principle: An Assessment of the First State's Party Referral to the ICC', 5 *International Criminal Law Review* 83, 110 (2005).

498 This understanding might find support in the view of a member of the ILC when he commented on the 1993 draft prepared by the 1993 Working Group on the basis of which the jurisdictional clauses of the 1994 draft were prepared: "It should not be forgotten that the court's jurisdiction was not only a conferred, but also a concurrent, jurisdiction...it did not mean that a case must automatically be judged by the court. A case that might be under the jurisdiction of the international criminal court could well remain in the national courts. If a State decided to put a case before the international criminal court, by so doing it renounced the jurisdiction of the national courts..." See 1994 *YILC* Vol. I, p. 29.

jurisdiction of the court under Article 22,[499] lodges a complaint under Article 25 (2)[500] against another State where the crimes were alleged to have been committed, and the latter territorial State refuses to accept the jurisdiction of the court in accordance with Article 21(1)(b)(ii),[501] the court has no power to exercise jurisdiction over the case and, by implication, the question of admissibility will not arise.

Arguably, the 1994 model pointed in the direction of the Rome Statute model when discussions in the 1995 *Ad hoc* Committee began in relation to an independent prosecutor.[502] The Rome Statute model empowered the Prosecutor to "initiate" an investigation *proprio motu*,[503] and, if satisfied that there was a "reasonable basis to proceed",[504] to request the Pre-Trial Chamber to authorize the commencement of the investigation after having evaluated the supporting materials, including, *inter alia*, the question of the admissibility of the situation.[505] It follows that the 1998 model enables the International Criminal Court to pursue a situation/case and request deferment to its jurisdiction in the event of a State's failure to act upon a certain situation – a system that is in a sense the reverse of what is found in the 1994 International Law Commission's draft, which left the decision to refer a case to the court within the complete freedom of the State. Moreover, having a Pre-Trial Chamber that plays a role during the stages of the admissibility of the situation or case, in order to balance the powers of the independent Prosecutor, was a novelty of the Rome Statute model.

When compared to earlier draft proposals, the Rome Statute model *in essence* seemed to have roots in the mechanisms established by the penalty provisions found in the peace treaties of World War I, as well as in a United States proposal tabled in the *Ad hoc* and Sixth Committee during the drafting of the 1948 Genocide Convention. According to the interpretation given to the penalty provisions in the Treaty of Versailles, in the event that the German trials were unsatisfactory, the Inter-Al-

499 1994 *ILC Draft*, *supra* note 424, Art. 22.

500 *Ibid.*, Art. 25(2).

501 *Ibid.*, Art. 21(1)(b)(ii). Article 21(b) required both the custodial State and the territorial State to accept the jurisdiction of the court before the latter might exercise its competence over a case.

502 Although the idea of having an independent prosecutor with *proprio motu* powers to "initiate an investigation in the absence of a complaint if it appears that a crime apparently within the jurisdiction of the court would otherwise not be duly investigated" was suggested in 1994 by one member of the Commission, it failed to gain support on the basis that the "investigation and prosecution of the crimes covered by the statute should not be undertaken in the absence of the support of a State or the Security Council, at least not at the present stage of development of the international legal system." 1994 *ILC Report*, *supra* note 424, p. 46.

503 Rome Statute, Arts. 15, 18, 53. See Salvatore Zappalà, *Human Rights in International Criminal Proceedings* (Oxford: Oxford University Press, 2003), p. 34 (noting that the *proprio motu* powers of the Prosecutor was one of the issues that caused "highest tension" between the delegations at the Rome Conference).

504 Rome Statute, Arts. 15(3) and 53(1).

505 *Ibid.*

lied Tribunals stepped in to adopt the proceedings, which deprived national courts of the sovereignty to decide. The United States proposal during the drafting of the Genocide Convention similarly provided the proposed international penal tribunal with the competence to make a finding to the effect that the State had either failed to take appropriate measures to bring the accused person to justice or had failed to impose an appropriate punishment. Based on this finding, the tribunal would exercise jurisdiction in lieu of the national court. Despite these similarities, there was no documented evidence that these ideas inspired the International Law Commission or members of the Committees that followed that path until the Rome Conference. Instead, during the International Law Commission's work, the reference was often to the 1953 revised draft statute.

As to *optional complementarity*, it clearly applied to a situation of self-referral. The admissibility system seemed to accept a situation whereby a State Party, from the outset, decided to waive its primary jurisdiction in favour of that of the International Criminal Court (State inaction) without even being deemed by the Court to be unwilling or unable to proceed. A self-referral was always followed by a waiver of complementarity. This was the reverse of the regime of *mandatory complementarity*; it was not because the Court determined that the State was unwilling or unable to proceed that the situation came before the Court, but rather because the State itself consented to relinquish jurisdiction in favour of the Court. This feature was not clear-cut in the 1994 model. Article 25 talked about a State "lodging a complaint" as opposed to "refer[ring] a situation", which apparently meant that a State was not expected to lodge "a complaint" against itself.[506] Yet, there was no evidence in the *travaux préparatoires* that supported either assumption. But the fact that the 1994 jurisdictional model established a system of *optional* concurrent jurisdiction made it strange to assume that the State with a direct link to the crimes might not think of choosing the proposed international criminal court as an alternative venue for the trial. The ideas of self-referrals and waivers of complementarity were also not seriously contemplated by the drafters of the 1998 Statute. Yet, recent practice shows its acceptance as an implicit form embodied in the text of Article 17.

7. The Primacy of the *Ad hoc* Tribunals

In this section, the chronology may not be strictly accurate, since it discusses the *ad hoc* tribunals created before 1998, and Rule 11*bis*, which is more contemporary. Yet, due to the fact that the discussion of the *ad hoc* tribunals, their primacy and the idea of completion strategy is a distinct question that requires separate treatment following a complete understanding of the idea of complementarity, this section will depart slightly from the correct chronology.

The International Criminal Tribunal for the Former Yugoslavia (ICTY) was created *ad hoc* by a decision of the United Nations Security Council to deal with the unique situation in the former Yugoslavia.[507] Another *ad hoc* Tribunal, the International Criminal

506 See chapter IV *infra*.

507 S.C. Res. 827(1993), adopted 25 May 1993 [hereinafter ICTY].

Tribunal for Rwanda (ICTR), was created to deal with a similarly disturbing situation in that country.[508] Article 9 of the ICTY Statute[509] and Article 8[510] of the ICTR Statute prescribe the relationship between the Tribunals and national courts. The establishment of the Tribunals was based on the principle of concurrent jurisdiction.

However, since both Tribunals had a special mission, that of contributing to the restoration and maintenance of peace in the Former Yugoslavia and Rwanda, they needed more than simple concurrent jurisdiction. Hence, the statutes granted them primacy over the jurisdiction of national courts.[511] The extraordinary jurisdictional priority granted to the *ad hoc* Tribunals is justified by the "compelling international humanitarian interests involved",[512] and by the Security Council's determination that both situations constituted a threat to international peace and security.[513] But, invoking such primacy is subject to the satisfaction of one or more of the situations defined under Rule 9 of the Rules of Procedure and Evidence of the ICTY and ICTR.[514] Ac-

---

508 S.C. Res. 955(1994), S/RES/955 (1994), adopted 8 Nov. 1994 [hereinafter ICTR].

509 Statute Of the International Tribunal for the Prosecution of Persons Responsible for Serious Violations of International Humanitarian Law Committed in the Territory of the Former Yugoslavia Since 1991, SC Res. 827/1993, reprinted in: I.L.M. 1192(1993), Art. 9.

Article 9 of the ICTY Statute states:

1. The International Tribunal and national courts shall have concurrent jurisdiction to prosecute persons for serious violations of international humanitarian law committed in the territory of the former Yugoslavia since 1 January 1991.
2. The International Tribunal shall have primacy over national courts. At any stage of the procedure, the International Tribunal may formally request national courts to defer to the competence of the International Tribunal in accordance with the present Statute and the Rules of Procedure and Evidence of the International Tribunals.

510 Statute of the International Tribunal for the Prosecution of Persons Responsible for Serious Violations of International Humanitarian Law Committed in Rwanda, SC Res. 955/1994, reprinted in: I.L.M. 1598 (1994), Art. 8.

Article 8 of the ICTR Statute states:

1. The International Tribunal for Rwanda and national courts shall have concurrent jurisdiction to prosecute persons for serious violations of international humanitarian law committed in the territory of Rwanda and Rwandan citizens for such violations committed in the territory of neighboring States, between 1 January 1994 and 31 December 1994.
2. The International Tribunal for Rwanda shall have primacy over the national courts of all States. At any stage of the procedure, the International Tribunal for Rwanda may formally request national courts to defer to its competence in accordance with the present Statute and the Rules of Procedure and Evidence of the International Tribunal for Rwanda.

511 For a thorough overview see Adolphus G. Karibi-White, 'The Twin *Ad hoc* Tribunals and Primacy Over National Courts', 9 *Criminal Law Forum* 55 (1999).

512 Bartram S. Brown, 'Primacy or Complementarity: Reconciling the Jurisdiction of National Courts and International Criminal Tribunals', 23 *Yale Journal of International Law* 383, 394 – 395 (1998).

513 Charter of the United Nations, adopted 26 June 1945, entered into force 24 October 1945, as amended by G.A. Res. 1991 (XVIII) 17 Dec. 1963, entered into force 31 Aug. 1965 (557 UNTS 119), Art. 39 [hereinafter UN Charter].

514 See ICTY, Rule 9; ICTR Rule 9.

cordingly, at any stage of the procedure, the International Tribunals may formally request the national courts to defer to their competence in accordance with the terms of the Statute and its Rules.[515] This stands in contradistinction to the complementarity regime chosen for the ICC Statute (Rome Statute complementarity model), which provides domestic courts with the priority to act, unless a State shows unwillingness or inability to proceed.[516]

Nonetheless, the two regimes established by these different institutions are based on a common ground – namely concurrence with the jurisdiction of national courts. While the mechanism established by the *ad hoc* Tribunals is based on *vertical* concurrent jurisdiction strengthened by primacy, the ICC's is based on the inverse *vertical* concurrent jurisdiction that provides national courts *vis-à-vis* the ICC with primacy to investigate situations, prosecute and try cases, known as complementarity.[517] Complementarity as embodied in the current ICC Statute also reflects the "jurisdictional relationship" between the ICC and domestic courts.[518] It organizes the exercise of such "jurisdictional relationship" through a system of admissibility of situations or cases.[519] Situations or cases that are deemed inadmissible are, therefore, the primary responsibility of national courts.[520] It follows that the Rome Statute complementarity model is based on the idea of division of labour between national and international jurisdictions. This section explores a new dimension to the exercise of traditional primacy and complementarity explained above.

515 ICTY Statute, Art. 9(2); ICTR Statute, Art. 8(2); See also *Report of the Secretary-General Pursuant to Paragraph 2 of Security Council Resolution 808(1993)*, UN SCOR, 48 th Sess., UN Doc. S/25704 (1993) [hereinafter Secretary –General's Report on the Former Yugoslavia], paras. 64- 5. In this respect the Secretary General emphasized that it was not the intention of the Security Council to preclude or prevent the exercise of jurisdiction by national courts with respect to the acts committed. For further discussion about concurrent jurisdiction see M. Cherif Bassiouni, *The Law of the International Criminal Tribunal for the Former Yugoslavia* (Irvington-on-Hudson, New York: Transnational Publishers, 1996), pp. 306-20; Virginia Morris, Michael P. Scharf, *An Insider's Guide to the International Criminal Tribunal for the Former Yugoslavia* , Vol. I (Irvington-on-Hudson, New York: Transnational Publishers, 1995), pp. 136-44.

516 Rome Statute, Art. 17.

517 While complementarity can never exist without concurrent jurisdiction, the opposite is not true. The existence of concurrent jurisdiction does not always mean that the relationship is complementary. On this observation *see* André Klip, 'Complementarity and Concurrent Jurisdiction', 19 *Nouvelles études pénals* 173(2004).

518 1996 *Preparatory Committee Report*, Vol. I, *supra* note 464, para. 153.

519 Rome Statute, Art. 17.

520 E.g., Rome Statute, preamble para. 6. "Recalling that it is the duty of every State to exercise its criminal jurisdiction": *ibid.* See also the decision of the Paris Court of Appeals in the *Kadhafi* case where the Court invoked ICC preambular paragraph 6 as a legal basis that justified a trial before French courts. Cour D'appel de Paris, chamber d'accusation, 2ème section, Arrêt du 20/10/2000, *in* Florence Poirat, 'Immunité de Jurisdiction pénale du chef d'Eatat étranger en exercise et régle coutumiére devant le Juge Judiciare', 105 *Revue Générale de Droit International Public* 473, 476 (2001).

7.1 *From Primacy to Complementarity*

Primacy as traditionally understood seeks to give the Tribunal the upper hand over any case that is under its jurisdiction. As argued above, the Prosecutor of the Tribunal may request that a case be ceded to it at any stage of the proceedings. But practice has proved that in some instances, although the Tribunal could have invoked its primacy *proper* to solve the conflict of jurisdiction over a specific case, it has sometimes chosen a different path, namely deferring to the jurisdiction of national courts on the basis of a division of labour. This has been exercised within the framework of the prosecutorial discretionary powers. While such a practice is not strictly primacy, it may create a relationship between national courts and the Tribunal that is closer to complementarity. This complementary relationship stands alongside the existing mechanism of primacy. Although the complementarity scheme established under the umbrella of prosecutorial discretionary powers shares with the Rome Statute complementarity model the idea of the division of tasks, the technicalities underlying the application of both systems are different – rendering each of them a distinct model of complementarity.

The existence of a plan for a "completion strategy" and the amendment of Rule 11*bis* of the Rules of Procedure and Evidence reflect a new angle in the understanding of primacy and complementarity. Rule 11*bis* as it currently stands permits the Tribunals to refer mid- and lower level cases that are already before them back to national courts, thereby entrusting them with the primary responsibility to investigate, prosecute and try a referred case. This decision to refer may be revoked by the Referral Bench if the State fails to conduct proper proceedings. While the initial decision to bring the case before the Tribunal is clearly one of primacy, the subsequent decision to send the case back to the national authorities providing them with the primary jurisdiction to proceed is closer to a practice of complementarity based on co-operation and the distribution of tasks – similar in idea to the model created in the exercise of prosecutorial discretion, but different in terms of application as well as the philosophical foundations, thus forming another model of its own. This model seems to be inspired to some extent by an earlier one created by the Nuremberg International Military Tribunal (IMT).

A fourth model appears in the decision to revoke an order referring a case to a State due to its failure "diligently [to] prosecute" or to provide a "fair trial". Like the Rome Statute complementarity model, the third model provides national courts *as opposed to* the Tribunals with primary jurisdiction over referred cases. Such primacy of domestic courts is subject to a test of genuine proceedings. Failing this test would still trigger the jurisdiction of the Tribunal to adopt the proceedings. This model, although different, is the closest to the current Rome Statute complementarity model as it seems to apply "diligent prosecution" and "fair trial" as criteria that act to restrict the exercise of the Tribunal's jurisdiction over a case that has already been referred to a national court. As the philosophical foundations underlying all these models and the technicalities of their application are different, as discussed later in this chapter, complementarity may emerge in different forms, creating various overlapping models. Yet, all these models are based on a common idea – the distribution of powers between national and international jurisdictions.

7.2 *The Legal Foundation of the Arising Complementarity Models*

Some scholars argue that the reason for entrusting the *ad hoc* Tribunals with "primacy" was mainly to remedy the apparent lack of will and ability to conduct fair trials before domestic courts,[521] in a sense resolving "conflicts with national jurisdictions that might shelter an offender from genuine prosecution".[522] In *Tadić*, the ICTY Appeals Chamber affirmed this:

> [W]hen an international tribunal such as the present one is created, it must be endowed with primacy over national courts. Otherwise, human nature being what it is, there would be a perennial danger of international crimes being characterized as 'ordinary crimes'..., or proceedings being 'designed to shield the accused', or cases not being diligently prosecuted. If not effectively countered by the principle of primacy, any one of those strategies might be used to defeat the very purpose of the creation of an international criminal jurisdiction, to the benefit of the very people whom it has been designed to prosecute (emphasis added).[523]

In practice, "primacy" seemed to have been applied for a different purpose. Neither in *Tadić*,[524] *Mrkšić and others*,[525] and *Re: The Republic of Macedonia*[526] before the

521 Antonio Cassese, *International Criminal Law* (Oxford: Oxford University Press, 2003), p. 349; Daphna Shraga and Ralph Zacklin, 'The International Criminal Tribunal for the Former Yugoslavia', 5 *European Journal of International Law* 360, 371 (1994).

522 William A. Schabas, *The UN International Criminal Tribunal, The Former Yugoslavia, Rwanda and Sierra Leone* (Cambridge: Cambridge University Press, 2006), p. 126.

523 *Prosecutor v. Duško Tadić*, Case No. (IT-94-1-AR72), *Decision on the Defence Motion for Interlocutory Appeal on Jurisdiction*, 2/10/1995, para. 58.

524 *Ibid.*, para. 52.

525 *Prosecutor v. Mrkšić, Šlijvančanin and Radić*, Case No. (IT-95-13-R61), *Decision on the Proposal of the Prosecutor for a Request to the Federal Republic of Yugoslavia (Serbia and Montenegro) to Defer the Pending Investigations and Criminal Proceedings to the Tribunal*, 10/12/1998. Although the Prosecutor relied not only on Rule 9(iii) but also on Rule 9(ii), the fact that he invoked Rule 9(ii) before even proving that the actual proceedings initiated were deemed biassed or not independent makes it clear that the request for deferral was mainly based on other reasons. On this point see the statement made by the Prosecutor, which supports this assertion: "[T]he continuing refusal of the Federal Republic of Yugoslavia (Serbia and Montenegro) to surrender the said accused indicates that the proceedings initiated in its territory would be neither impartial not independent and would be designed to shield the accused from his international criminal responsibility": *ibid.*, p. 3. Based on this statement it is clear that the proceedings were not neither impartial nor independent as asserted rather than that the Prosecutor mistakenly considered the State's refusal to surrender equivalent to a failure to act properly before domestic courts.

526 *Prosecutor v. Republic Of Macedonia*, Case No. (IT-02-55-MISC.6), *Decision on the Prosecutor's Request for Deferral and Motion for Order to the Former Yugoslav Republic of Macedonia*, 4/10/2002.

ICTY nor in *Musema*,[527] *Bagosora*[528] or in *Radio Television Libre des Mille Collins SARL*[529] before the ICTR, did the Prosecutors request adoption on the basis that the proceedings before national courts were *sham*. Instead, in all of these cases, the Prosecutor invoked Rule 9(iii) of the Rules of Procedure and Evidence of the ICTY and ICTR, which states that the investigations or criminal proceedings undertaken by the national authorities of the State are "closely related and otherwise involve factual or legal questions which may have implications for the Prosecutor's investigations or prosecutions". But, in *Tadić*, it was a common understanding that the Tribunal at the time was anxious for a case to try. As one commentator put it, at this early stage in the Tribunal's activities the Prosecutor was "desperate" for a case to prosecute. "Were Tadić to have been arrested ten years later, when the Tribunal was suffering under a crushing caseload as well as intense pressure from the Security Council to conclude its operations, it is highly unlikely that the Prosecutor would have meddled with German attempts to bring him to justice".[530]

While in these cases the ICTY and ICTR Prosecutors exercised *absolute* primacy, in other cases they refrained from doing so. In these other cases, the Prosecutors acted under the umbrella of their discretionary powers and entrusted national courts with the primary responsibility to act through a decision to defer to their jurisdiction. This practice reflects a sort of concurrence and complementarity that functioned alongside the existing system of primacy, and resulted in the division of labour on the basis of co-operation between the Tribunals and domestic courts.

Although in *Karamira* Prosecutor Goldstone deferred to the Rwandese courts *only* after a squabble with the government,[531] certainly nothing would have stopped him from insisting upon a trial before the ICTR on the basis of primacy,[532] if he still favoured doing so. Indeed, when Colonel Théoneste Bagosora was arrested in Cameroon on 11 March 1996, Prosecutor Goldstone insisted that he stand trial before the ICTR, despite the extradition requests from Rwanda and Belgium.[533] In the *Djaajić* and *Jorgić* cases investigated by the German authorities, the ICTY Prosecutor also

527 *Prosecutor v. Alfred Musema*, Case No. (ICTR-96-5-D), *Decision on the Formal Request for Deferral Presented by the Prosecutor*, 12 March 1996.

528 *Prosecutor v. Théoneste Bagosora*, Case No. (ICTR-96-7-D), *Decision on the Application by the Prosecutor for a Formal Request for Deferral*, 17/05/1996.

529 *Prosecutor v. Radio Television Libre des Mille Collines SARL*, (Case No. ICTR-96-6-D), *Decision on the Formal Request for Deferral Presented by the Prosecutor*, 12/03/1996.

530 William A. Schabas, *An Introduction to the International Criminal Court*, 2nd ed. (Cambridge: Cambridge University Press, 2004), pp. 125 – 126.

531 Madeline H. Morris, 'The Trials of Concurrent Jurisdiction: The Case of Rwanda', 7 *Duke Journal of Comparative and International Law* 349, 365n.91 (1997).

532 Froduald Karamira was tried before Rwandan courts, convicted and executed. See *Ministére Public v. Karamira*, Jugement du 14 février 1997 du tribunal de 1ère instance de Kigali, available at. http://www.icrc.org.

533 Payam Akhavan, 'The International Criminal Tribunal for Rwanda: The Politics and Pragmatic of Punishment', 90 *American Journal of International Law* 501, 509(1996).

deferred to the jurisdiction of national courts,[534] on the basis of mutual agreement and division of responsibilities. Explaining the underlying philosophy, the Prosecutor said:

> The Djajic and Jorgic cases were initiated and investigated by the German authorities, who consulted with the Office of the Prosecutor of the International Tribunal. The Prosecutor assessed that it was not appropriate to seek a deferral of these cases, and the decision was made that they continue to be prosecuted by the German authorities. There is on-going co-operation between the Prosecutor and the German authorities on these and other cases.[535]

Thus, the practice of the *ad hoc* Tribunals was not confined to the application of *strict* primacy; rather, occasionally a clear complementarity approach has been followed based on co-operation – extending the nature of jurisdiction underpinning the *ad hoc* Tribunals and reframing a new model of complementarity. Although the complementarity scheme established under this practice shares with the Rome Statute complementarity model the idea of distribution of responsibilities, the two systems are slightly different. The main difference lies in the fact that the Rome Statute complementarity model relies in its application on a system of admissibility that filters the type of situations or cases that can come before the ICC. By contrast, the system created under the practice of the *ad hoc* Tribunals does not embody such a mechanism for the selection of cases. Instead, the system contemplated is part of the policy of Prosecutor to use their discretionary powers in selecting the sort of cases that warrant trial before the Tribunals.

This trend has been reinforced in the Tribunals' "completion strategies".[536] According to Judge Jorda, President of the ICTY at the time, the strategy encompassed two

534 There are also some cases that were tried before national courts, although they could have been dealt with by the ICTY. See e.g., *Public Prosecutor v. Djajić*, No. 20/96 , Supreme Court of Bavaria, 3d Strafsenat, 23/05/1997 (summarized in Cristoph J. M. Safferling, 92 *American Journal of International Law* 528(1998)); *In Re G*, Military Tribunal, Division 1, Lausanne Switzerland, 18/04/ 1997 (summarized in Andreas R. Ziegler, *ibid*, p. 78). While these cases show a clear exercise of the concurrent jurisdiction given by the ICTY Statute to national courts, it also reflects the fact that there is a sort of complementary relationship between the two jurisdictions based on mutual cooperation and division of tasks. In the *Re G* case, although the accused was acquitted as the Military Tribunal failed to prove beyond reasonable doubt that he was in Keraterm and Omarska at the "time of the crimes", there is no evidence that the ICTY Prosecutor requested deferral to the jurisdiction of the ICTY. This acknowledges the exercise of another form of complementarity based on the distribution of responsibilities.

535 Sean D. Murphy, 'Progress and Jurisprudence of the International Criminal Tribunal for the Former Yugoslavia', 93 *American Journal of International Law* 57, 65 (1999) (citing Mr Justice Arbour's Statement Regarding War Crimes Related Trials Currently Underway in Germany, ICTY Doc. CC/PIO/171-E, 19 March 1997).

536 For more on the "completion strategies" see Daryl A. Mundis, 'Completing the Mandates of the Ad hoc International Criminal Tribunals: Lessons from the Nuremberg Process?

major components, namely to prosecute before the Tribunal "those presumed responsible for crimes which most seriously violate international public order and to give cases of lesser significance to the national courts."[537] The strategies, as referred to in SC Resolutions 1503 (2003),[538] 1534 (2004)[539] had as their target the completion of trial activities at first instance by the end of December 2008 and of appeals by the end of 2010. This process entailed some amendments to the Rules of Procedure and Evidence (Rules).[540]

As regards the ICTY, Rule 11*bis* has been amended four times since its adoption in 1997.[541] According to these amendments, Rule 11*bis* (A) permits the Tribunal to refer a case to the "national authorities" of either the territorial State,[542] the State where the accused was arrested,[543] or a State "having jurisdiction and being willing and ad-

28 *Fordham International Law Journal* 591(2004); Daryl A. Mundis, 'The Judicial Effects of the "Completion Strategies" on the Ad hoc International Criminal Tribunals,' 99 *American Journal of International Law* 142 (2005); Dominic Raab, 'Evaluating the ICTY and its Completion Strategy: Efforts to Achieve Accountability for War Crimes and their Tribunal,' 3 *Journal of International Criminal Justice* 82 (2005).

537 Address by HE Judge Claude Jorda, President of the International Criminal Tribunal for the Former Yugoslavia, to the United Nations Security Council on 23 July 2002, Press Release, The Hague, 26 July 2002 (JDH/P.I.S./690-e, available at. http://www.un.org/icty/pressreal/p690-e.htm. As one commentator mentioned, "The experience of the ICTY and ICTR has shown that international tribunals are only able to try a very small fraction of the perpetrators. Moreover, they are often too detached from local communities to respond effectively to the needs and expectations of victims' group and local societies. These limitations have encouraged the search for alternative and additional frameworks of justice, such as the transfer of cases involving mid-level perpetrators to domestic courts": Carsten Stahn, 'The Geometry of Transitional Justice; Choices of Institutional Design,' 18 *Leiden Journal of International Law* 425, 449 (2005).

538 S.C. Res. 1503, UN Doc. S/RES/1503(2003).

539 S.C. Res. 1534, UN Doc. S/RES/1534(2004).

540 See also Theodor Meron, 'Reflection on the Prosecution of War Crimes by International Tribunals,' 100 *American Journal of International Law* 551, 563 (2006).

541 ICTY RPE, Rule 11*bis* adopted 12 November 1997, revised 30 September 2002, Amended 10 June, 28 July 2004, and 11 February 2005. The last three amendments that took place in 10 June 2004, 28 July 2004, and 11 February 2005 respectively are of great significance to implementation of the completion strategy. For an account of the circumstances for such amendments see Michael Bohlander, 'Referring an Indictment from the ICTY and ICTR to another Court – Rule 11 *Bis* and the Consequences for the Law of Extradition,' 55 *International and Comparative Law Quarterly* 219, 220 – 222 (2006).

542 ICTY RPE, Rule 11 *bis* (A) (i).

543 ICTY RPE, Rule 11 *bis* (A) (ii).

equately prepared to accept such a case".[544] The Tribunal may order the referral, acting under its *proprio motu* powers or at the request of the Prosecutor.[545]

In reaching any such decision to refer a case pursuant to paragraph (A), the Referral Bench shall also "consider the gravity of the crimes" as well as the "level of responsibility of the accused"[546]; thus, ensuring that only those bearing the greatest responsibility shall stand trial before the Tribunal in accordance with paragraphs 4 and 5 of Security council resolution 1534.[547] This decision may be revoked by the Referral Bench at the Prosecutor's request, "at any time before the accused is found guilty or acquitted by a national court".[548] With an apparent technical exception,[549] the ICTR has a corresponding provision that sets out the exact requirements found in Rule 11*bis* of the ICTY Rules.[550]

---

544 ICTY RPE, Rule 11 *bis* (A) (iii). Here the reference to "jurisdiction" entails the meaning in the widest sense. As the ICTR Appeals Chamber in the recent Bagaragaza case stated: "The interpretation of Rule 11 *bis* (A) (iii) should rely on that definition which requires *ratione materiae, ratione personae, ratione loci, ratione temporis.* When confirming an indictment, the Confirming Judge must find that each of those requirements is satisfied in order for the Tribunal to have jurisdiction. In this case, the universal jurisdiction referred to in the submissions of the Kingdom of Norway will permit the prosecution of the Accused (*ratione personae*) for his acts allegedly committed in Rwanda (*ratione loci*) in 1994 (*ratione temporis*). The only aspect of jurisdiction which would not be covered by Norwegian law is the *ratione materiae*. The submission that Norwegian criminal law does not provide for the crime of genocide directly affects the finding of jurisdiction *ratione materiae*, where the legal qualification of the facts alleged in the confirmed Indictment is made": *Prosecutor v. Michel Bagaragaza*, Case No. (ICTR-2005-86-R11bis), *Decision on the Prosecution Motion for Referral to the Kingdom of Norway, Rule 11 bis of the Rules of Procedure and Evidence*, 19/05/2006, paras. 12 – 13.

545 ICTY RPE, Rule 11 *bis* (B).

546 ICTY RPE, Rule 11 *bis* (C). Here, the meaning tends to limit the examination of the gravity of the crime and level of responsibility to the specific case against the accused. As the Appeals Chamber in the *Jankovic* case concluded, "Nothing in Rule *11bis* of the Rules indicates that the Referral Bench is obliged to consider the gravity of the crimes charged and the level of responsibility of accused in other cases in order to make its referral decision. Although the Referral Bench may be guided by a comparison with an indictment in another case, it does not commit an error of law if it bases its decision on referral merely on the individual circumstances of the case before it". See *Prosecutor v. Gojko Jankovic*, Case No. (IT-96-23/2-*AR11bis*.2), Decision on Rule *11 bis* Referral, 15/11/2005, para. 26.

547 S.C. Res. 1534, UN Doc. S/Res/1534(2004) paras. 4 – 5.

548 ICTY RPE, Rule 11 *bis* (F).

549 This language is lacking in the corresponding provision under the ICTR Rules. Yet, from the beginning of its work, unlike the ICTY, the ICTR was focused on the senior leaders who bore the greatest responsibility for the atrocities committed in Rwanda. Thus, the idea of a completion strategy and the call to try only the senior leaders before the Tribunals, as reflected in Security Council Resolutions 1503 and 1534, was no more than a reiteration of a job that had been done for years. In the same vein see Erik Møse, 'Main Achievements of the ICTR', 3 *Journal of International Criminal Justice* 920, 932 (2005).

550 ICTR RPE, Rule 11 *bis*.

The *absolute* primacy of the *ad hoc* Tribunals experienced a noticeable change with the amendment of Rule 11*bis* on 10 June 2004. As it currently stands it represents a reverse approach to the practice of primacy. The Tribunals only deal with the most serious cases that involve those who bear the greatest responsibility, while the remaining cases of lesser magnitude are to be sent back to the national courts to be their primary responsibility, a system that reminds us of the complementary relationship established between the Nuremberg International Military Tribunal (IMT) and national courts following World War II.[551] The IMT was to try only the "major war criminals, whose offences have no particular geographical localization". The remainder would "be sent back to the countries in which their abominable deeds were done in order that they may be judged and punished according to the laws of these librated countries and of free governments".[552] This created a clear system of complementarity that relied on effective co-operation[553] on the basis of the distribution of functions and the level of responsibility of the accused.[554]

But there are substantial differences in terms of application as well as the underlying philosophical foundations between the IMT and the *ad hoc* Tribunals. As to the application, in the complementarity model created within the ambit of the prosecutorial discretionary powers, complementarity is backed up by primacy. At any stage of the proceedings, even after the Prosecutor's deferment to the jurisdiction of national courts, he or she may still use his or her discretion and invoke primacy to assert jurisdiction over the case in question. Under Rule 11*bis*, the idea of complementarity is not the outcome of the prosecutorial discretion to leave cases already before domestic courts to be judged by them. Instead, it emerges from the decision to share

551 For more on the theory of complementarity between the IMT and domestic courts see Chapter II, *supra*; and Mohamed M. El Zeidy, 'The Principle of Complementarity: A New Machinery to Implement International Criminal Law', 23 *Michigan Journal of International Law* 869, 874 – 876 (2002).

552 Moscow Declaration, *supra* note 80; *also* London Agreement, *supra* note 107. "[G]ermans who take part in wholesale shooting of [Polish] officers or in the execution of French, Dutch...or have shared in slaughters inflicted on the people of Poland or in territories of the Soviet Union...will be brought back to the scene of their crimes and judged on the spot by the peoples whom they have outraged." See Moscow Declaration, *supra* note 80.

553 For similar conclusions concerning the system of complementarity established by the IMT see Otto Triffterer, "Preliminary Remarks: The Permanent International Criminal Court – Ideal and Reality", Triffterer *Commentary*, *supra* note 114, p. 38. In this context, "the agreement between the four major powers fighting at that time against Germany, and those nineteen States, which in addition signed the Nuremberg Statute, to guarantee uniformity with an international court besides Nuremberg and Tokyo. Rather, a far-reaching complementarity existed. On both levels, the prosecution and sentencing were based on a practical division of labour": *ibid.*

554 Although it is not clear whether those major war criminals would still have to stand trial before the IMT if their crimes had been geographically determined. In other words, it is not clear whether the major war criminals stood trial before the IMT also on the basis of their level of criminal responsibility or merely, because their crimes had no "geographical localization".

the burden with national courts through the referral of some cases that were already before the Tribunals. Complementarity under this model is also backed by primacy to revoke an order of referral in certain situations, as discussed below.

By contrast, in the case of the IMT, there was no need to provide the Tribunal with powers of this kind since the trials both at the international and the national level were conducted under the control of the Allies.[555] Thus, the system established was no more than a mere division of labour to achieve a common goal; that is, prosecuting the enemy powers through a two-level system. There are also differences in the philosophical foundations. In a system predicated on prosecutorial discretion, it is clear that any decision either to defer jurisdiction to a national court or to refrain from invoking primacy relates to the interests of justice within its broader meaning. Although this might be the same in the case of Rule 11*bis* of the Rules of Procedure and Evidence of the *ad hoc* Tribunals, the philosophy underlying this is much broader. It should not be forgotten that Rule 11*bis* was amended precisely to serve a broader goal – that is to assist the Tribunals to meet their mandates through a plan for a "completion strategy".

On the contrary, in the case of the IMT, the idea of dealing with certain offenders internationally while dealing with others domestically was apparently come up with for a different reason. Quoting the language used in the Moscow declaration that "[G]ermans who take part in the wholesale shooting of [Polish] officers or in the execution of French, Dutch...will be brought back to the scene of their crimes and judged on the spot by the peoples whom they outraged" gives an impression that the choice was rooted in moral and political, rather than legal, grounds.[556]

Hence, the practice of the Prosecutors of the *ad hoc* Tribunals as well as the IMT establishes two overlapping yet distinct models of complementarity. Although in the case of Rule 11*bis* there is also a political dimension involved, the fact that the final purpose is different renders the complementarity idea created under it still distinct from that reflected in the system of the IMT. Although the various models share the idea of distribution of responsibilities, the Rome Statute complementarity model remains different.

In terms of application, the Rome Statute model uses the "unwilling" and "unable" tests coupled with detailed criteria that act as a restriction on admissibility, thus ensuring that only a limited number of situations or cases of certain gravity may be tried before the ICC. On the contrary, neither the models established under Rule 11*bis* and the discretionary powers of the Prosecutors of the *ad hoc* Tribunals nor that reflected by the system of the IMT require such conditions. Even the underlying philosophy is

555 In the same vein see Quincy Wright, 'The Law of the Nuremberg Trial', 41 *American Journal of International Law* 38, 39, 45 (1947). Generally on the Nuremberg Trials see Telford Taylor, *The Anatomy of the Nuremberg Trials: A Personal Memoir* (New York: Knopf, 1992); Robert K. Woetzel, *The Nuremberg Trials in International Law* (London: Stevens & Sons, 1960).

556 This does not deny the fact that sending Germans to the "scene of their crimes" implies that the well-established principle of territorial jurisdiction was a legal foundation for the establishment of competence *ratione loci.*

different. The Rome Statute complementarity model was mainly introduced to preserve States' sovereignty as well as to restrict the ICC's action to very well-defined exceptional situations.

While Rule 11*bis* (F) *apparently* retains the *absolute* primacy of the Tribunal through a decision to "revoke" the order and request "deferral" of the case, a close look at Rule 11*bis* (A)(iii) suggests an additional conclusion, namely the emergence of a mechanism that is more than just one of *absolute* primacy. It is apparent that, once the State which has received the case on the basis that it was "willing and adequately prepared to accept" it responsibly shows that it has failed properly to proceed with the case, the Tribunal may step in to remove the case from the jurisdiction of domestic courts in accordance with Rule 11*bis* (F). Although this provision does not mention the phrase "*failure* to proceed", it is implicit from reading the two Rules together that the Trial Chamber or the Referral Bench would not step in pursuant to Rule 11*bis* (F), unless there was a clear deficiency in the proceedings conducted before domestic courts. Any different interpretation given to these provisions would render "inoperative" the system intended for the purpose of the completion strategy.[557]

The conditions which permit the Tribunal's interference with domestic proceedings in a case of *failure* are not mentioned in Rule 11*bis* (F). Yet, the jurisprudence of the ICTY and ICTR is instructive in relation to this matter. In the *Stankovic* case, the ICTY Referral Bench stated that "Rules 11 *bis* (D)(iv) and 11 *bis* (F) serve as remedies against a failure of the relevant state to diligently prosecute a referred case or conduct a fair trial of the accused in a referred case."[558] This finding was upheld by the ICTY Referral Bench in the *Norac et al*,[559] *Mejakic et al*,[560] *Jankovic*[561] and *Kovačević*,[562] and

557 As the Inter-American Court of Human Right stated that the object and purpose of the American Convention "is the effective protection of human rights...[it] must, therefore, be interpreted so as to give it its full meaning and to enable the system...to attain its 'appropriate effects'". See *Fairén Garbi and Solís Corrales* Case, *Preliminary Objections*, Judgment of 26/06/1987, Inter-Am.Ct.H.R. (Ser.C) No. 2, para. 35. It is of vital importance to prevent any restrictions of interpretation that would render the system in question "inoperative". See *Constantine et al. v. Trinidad and Tobago* Case, *Preliminary Objections*, Judgment of 1/09/ 2001, Inter-Am.Ct.H.R. (Ser.C) No. 82, para. 73.

558 *Prosecutor v. Radovan Stankovic*, Case No. (IT-96-23/2-PT), *Decision on Referral of Case Under Rule 11 bis Partly Confidential and Ex Parte*, 17/05/2005, para. 93.

559 *Prosecutor v. Rahim Ademi and Mirko Norac*, Case No. (IT-04-78-PT), *Decision For Referral to the Authorities of the Republic of Croatia Pursuant to Rule 11 bis*, 14/09/2005, para. 57.

560 *Prosecutor v. Zeljko Mejakic, Momcilo Gruban, Dusan Fustar, Dusko Knezevic*, Case No. (IT-02-65-PT), *Decision on Prosecutor's Motion for Referral of a Case pursuant to Rule 11 Bis*, 20/07/2005, para. 134.

561 *Prosecutor v. Gojko Jankovic*, Case No. (IT-96-23/2-PT), *Decision on Referral of Case under Rule 11 Bis*, 22/07/2005, paras. 102 – 103.

562 *Prosecutor v. Vladimir Kovačević*, Case No. (IT-01-42/2-I), *Decision on Referral of Case pursuant to Rule 11 Bis With Confidential and Partly Ex Parte Annexes*, 17/11/2006, paras. 80 – 81(noting that non-compliance with the requirements of a fair trial would also trigger the power of the Tribunal to revoke an order of referral).

Trbić decisions.[563] When the *Jankovic* decision was appealed, the Chamber reached the same conclusion, stating that "the Referral Bench did not err in its finding that 'Rules *11bis* (D) (iv) and *11bis* (F) serve as precautions against a failure to diligently prosecute a referred case or conduct a fair trial.'"[564] Thus, it could be argued that the lack of *diligent prosecution*[565] and *a fair trial* are the main conditions that trigger the Tribunals powers to 'revoke the order and make a formal request of deferral'. Yet, neither the Rules nor the jurisprudence of the *ad hoc* Tribunals clearly define 'diligent prosecution', or spell out the criteria for its satisfaction.[566]

Rule 11*bis* (A)(iii) and (F), in light of the jurisprudence of the Tribunals, create a fourth model of complementarity comparable in *principle* to the Rome Statute model. Once the Tribunal determines that a case has not been "diligently prosecuted" before domestic courts, it is competent to proceed with its trial. This scenario corresponds to some extent to the system contemplated in the Rome Statute complementarity model, whereby, if a State manifests unwillingness or inability to proceed with a situation or case, the International Criminal Court is empowered to step in and itself proceed with that situation or case.

While the two systems overlap in terms of the general triggering method,[567] and may share some of the philosophical foundations such as entrusting the primary responsibility for investigation, prosecution and trial to the State,[568] drawing the

563 *Prosecutor v. Milorad Trbić*, Case No. (IT-05-88/1-PT), *Decision on Referral of Case under Rule 11 Bis with Confidential Annex*, 27/04/2007, para. 44.

564 *Prosecutor v. Gojko Jankovic*, Case No. (IT-96-23/2-*AR11bis.2*), *Appeals Decision on Rule 11 bis*, 15/11/2005, para. 56.

565 The term "diligent prosecution" was proposed during the 1996 Preparatory Committee negotiations concerning the establishment of an international criminal court. In the context of discussion of the admissibility provision proposed earlier by the 1994 ILC draft statute (Article 35), some delegations thought that the term should be used as a "qualification" for the quality of the national proceedings. Yet, the inclusion of the term was finally rejected, as some delegations thought that the term was "too subjective". See *1996 Preparatory Committee Report*, Vol. I, *supra* note 464, para. 164. However, the term was not adopted, as it was considered "too subjective". See John T. Holmes, "Complementarity: National Courts *Versus* the ICC", *Cassese Commentary*, *supra* note 112, p. 674.

566 Although the jurisprudence of the ICTY for example has restricted its suggestion in relation to revoking an order of referral to a failure of the State to conduct a "diligent prosecution" or a "fair trial", by reading the conditions set out in Rule 9, one could argue that these conditions could be reconciled within the entire system in question. In determining whether a referred case has been "diligently prosecuted", the Prosecutor may therefore take these conditions listed under Rule 9 into consideration as part of the mechanism established.

567 Arguably, the phrase "diligently prosecute a referred case or conduct a fair trial of the accused" used by the ICTY is a catch-all clause that captures any sort of *failure* to proceed on the part of the State. Accordingly, it may cover even admissibility situations such as those mentioned in the text of Article 17 of the current ICC Statute.

568 In the *Stankovic* decision, the ICTY Referral Bench supported this conclusion when it stated: "[R]referral of a case implies that the proceedings against an accused become the

balance between the cases to be tried internationally with the limited resources at hand,[569] and ensuring that only cases of extreme gravity are being dealt with at the international level, while those of lesser magnitude are the responsibility of domestic courts, finally have two different objectives.

Save for the similarities, complementarity *proper* as reflected in the 1998 Rome Statute was not introduced for the purpose of a "completion strategy" that aimed to send away cases already before the Court. The aim was, *inter alia*, to encourage States to enact domestic legislations in order to comply with their duty to exercise domestic jurisdiction.[570] The system of complementarity was also created to ensure that the International Criminal Court was only a facility for States to be used when needed,[571] thus respecting States' sovereign rights.[572] Thus, the complementarity schemes established by the practice of the *ad hoc* Tribunals might stand as distinct models of their own alongside the traditional Rome Statute complementarity model.

For more than a decade, the classical view has been that the *ad hoc* Tribunals are vested only with primacy *proper*. This is a misconception, as practice has demonstrated that the Tribunals occasionally have had to set aside the idea of invoking *strict* primacy in the face of national courts. Instead, the Prosecutors of these Tribunals found it practical to exercise a sort of complementarity in order to create a dialogue of understanding and cooperation that serves the main goal of narrowing, if not closing, the impunity gap.

The completion strategy plan backed by Security Council Resolutions 1503 (2003) and 1534 (2004) has even strengthened this idea, since the core of the practice merely relied on the idea of national courts complementing the Tribunals' mandate. National courts will do what the Tribunals would not have been able to do by 2008, if the entire case load had remained their primary responsibility. Rule 11*bis* has been

primary responsibility of the authorities, including the investigative, prosecutorial, and judicial organs, of the state concerned. [Once the State proves] failure to diligently prosecute a referred case or conduct a fair trial... Rule 11 *bis* (F) enables the Referral Bench, at the request of the Prosecutor, to revoke a referral order at any time before an accused is found guilty or acquitted by a national court, in which event Rule 11 *bis* (G) makes provision to enable the re-transfer of an accused to the seat of this Tribunal": *Prosecutor v. Radovan Stankovic*, Case No. (IT-96-23/2-PT), *Decision on Referral of Case under Rule 11 bis Partly Confidential and Ex Parte*, 17/05/2005, para. 93. The Referral Bench used identical words in the *Jankovic* decision. See *Prosecutor v. Gojko Jankovic*, Case No. (IT-96-23/2-PT), *Decision on Referral of Case under Rule 11 Bis*, 22/07/2005, para. 102.

569 In the same vein see William Burke-White, 'A Community of Courts: Toward a System of International Criminal law Enforcement', 24 *Michigan Journal of International Law* 1, 10 (2003).

570 See generally William W. Burke-White, 'Complementarity in Practice: The International Criminal Court as Part of a System of Multi-level Global Governance in the Democratic Republic of Congo', 18 *Leiden Journal of International Law* 557, 568 – 569 (2005); Jann J. Kleffner, 'The Impact of Complementarity on National Implementation of Substantive International Criminal Law', 1 *Journal of International Criminal Justice* 86, 87 (2003).

571 1992 *ILC Report, supra* note 389, p. 64; 1994 *ILC Report, supra* note 424, p. 21.

572 1995 *Ad hoc Committee Report, supra* note 450, paras. 29 – 51.

amended in this direction. The experience of the *ad hoc* Tribunals also shows that the notions of primacy and complementarity are not mutually exclusive; rather, they may be reconciled to function alongside each another. This is mirrored in Rule 11*bis*, which, although it creates a system of complementarity, does not rule out the Tribunals' existing primacy.[573] A similar conclusion, yet in a different context, was reached by ICTR Trial Chamber I in the *Ntuyahaga* decision on the Prosecutor's motion to withdraw the indictment:

> [A]lthough it accepts the submissions of the Prosecutor and the Belgian Government inasmuch as the Tribunal does not have exclusive jurisdiction over crimes included in its mandate and that its criminal proceedings are complementary to those of national jurisdictions, it wishes to underscore that, in its opinion, and as submitted by the Defence, the principle of concurrent jurisdiction as provided in paragraph (1) of Article 8 of the Statute, which recognizes the complementary nature of the judicial work performed by the Tribunal and national courts, must be read together with the provisions of paragraph 2 of said Article 8, which confers upon the Tribunal primacy over the national courts of all States.[574]

Early on in its activities, the ICTR realized and acknowledged that the system created by Article 8 of its Statute not only embodies *absolute* primacy, but also implied complementarity.

Although different models reflecting the complementary relationship between domestic and international jurisdictions have been invoked during the practice of the *ad hoc* Tribunals, these notions of complementarity are slightly different from the traditional complementarity model reflected in the current ICC Statute. It follows that there are many models of complementarity that may stand alongside one another.

Concluding Observations

During World War II, the main concern was to ensure that war criminals who committed atrocities would not escape punishment. As a corollary, the question of which forum should deal with the cases of war criminals was prominent. From 1941 to 1943, unofficial bodies, such as the London International Assembly and the International Commission for Penal Reconstruction and Development, studied the matter in great detail. One of the major problems facing these bodies was how to deal with the crimes committed by the Axis powers on their territory against Allied nationals. Crimes such as those committed against the Jews and stateless people in Germany

573 See ICTY Rule 11 *bis* (F), which provides that when the Referral Bench decides to revoke "an order and make formal request of deferral", this will be in accordance with Rule 10. Rule 10 refers to Rule 9. Thus, Rule 11*bis* (F) makes it clear that Rules 9 and 10, which govern the exercise of the traditional primacy of the Tribunal, are still applicable.

574 *Prosecutor v. Bernard Ntuyahaga*, Case No. (ICTR-98-40-T), *Decision on the Prosecutor's Motion to Withdraw the Indictment*, 18/03/1999.

were problematic, since the Allied tribunals lacked extraterritorial jurisdiction over them, and the demand was to avoid leaving their prosecution to German courts.

The London International Assembly recommended the establishment of an international criminal court with limited exercise of jurisdiction. It was understood that, in practice, the international court could not try all the cases of war criminals. On the other hand, the idea was that such an international jurisdiction should not curtail the role of domestic courts (whether civil or military) in order to safeguard their sovereign rights. The idea of having an international criminal court with a sort of complementary jurisdiction seemed to be the most plausible solution. Save for the technical differences, the London International Assembly introduced a complementary mechanism in Article 3(1) of its draft statute, comparable in principle to that eventually found in the Rome Statute.

By contrast, the International Commission for Penal Reconstruction and Development prepared not a draft statute, but rather a report which was submitted to governments for consideration. Nonetheless, from among the proposals tabled during its work, several members favoured a system of complementary jurisdiction similar to that proposed in the London International Assembly draft statute. These proposals failed to find their way into the Statute of the Nuremberg International Military Tribunal (IMT), which tried the Nazi war criminals after World War II. The idea of complementarity emerged, however, in a different form. The IMT tried only the major criminals whose offences had no particular geographical connection and left the minor criminals to national criminal courts. This task was undertaken by the national courts, established by governments with competence to adjudicate on war crimes at the places where they were committed, as well as by the occupying powers themselves, each within its own zone, with its own set of courts, applying its own scheme of law.

Article VI of the 1948 Genocide Convention did define a relationship between the national courts and the proposed international penal tribunal. Although it spoke of an "international penal tribunal as may have jurisdiction", the Convention was clearly based on the principle of territoriality. However, the drafting history of the Convention witnessed several proposals that forged a complementary relationship between the two aspects of jurisdiction. In the *Ad hoc* and Sixth Committees, the United States delegation, backed by the Uruguayan delegation, tabled proposals that corresponded, in essence, to the principle of complementarity found in the current ICC Statute.

The 1951 – 1953 Committees on International Criminal Jurisdiction drafted jurisdictional clauses that created an optional concurrent and complementary jurisdiction similar to that proposed during the work of the London International Assembly and the International Commission for Penal Reconstruction and Development, yet were technically different from the scheme mirrored in the Rome Statute complementarity model. When drafting the 1951 and 1954 Draft Codes of Offences against the Peace and Security of Mankind, the International Law Commission took a different approach. A number of the Commission's members favoured the establishment of an international criminal court with exclusive competence over the crimes defined in the codes. The idea of exclusivity of jurisdiction inspired the work of the International Law Commission when it resumed its work on the draft code in 1983. Only in the early 1990s did members of the Commission start seriously to realize that establishing an international criminal court with exclusive jurisdiction was not viable.

The trend shifted towards finding a way to reconcile the idea of an international criminal jurisdiction with national criminal jurisdictions. It was a common understanding that it was impossible to have an international criminal court that dealt with all cases. The court would be only a "facility" for States parties that would be available in case of need.

The reports prepared by the Special Rapporteur in the 1990s, as well as those of the Working Groups in 1990s reflected these ideas. The result was draft jurisdictional provisions that established a sort of concurrent and complementary relationship between national courts and the proposed international criminal court. Complementarity was conceived of as being both consensual and optional, ideas borrowed from the 1953 revised draft statute as well as Article 36 of the Statute of the International Court of Justice. As the Commission progressed with its work on the subject, ideas on the mechanism establishing the relationship between national and international jurisdictions became clearer.

The 1994 Working Group retained the regime of concurrent and complementary jurisdiction, but with some modifications. Apart from the limitations on the court's competence reflected in the general jurisdictional clauses, the 1994 Working Group introduced, for the first time, an admissibility system that acted as a second layer in filtering the types of cases that should or should not go before the court. The underlying idea was to restrict the exercise of the court's jurisdiction to those most serious crimes of international concern with which the national courts could not deal. With the introduction of the system of admissibility, complementarity emerged in a different form, representing a modified model of its own. The 1994 complementarity scheme was taken as the main basis for future work, which finally led to the idea found in the current ICC Statute. Despite the similarities with the 1994 model, the Rome Statute version of complementarity stood as a unique model that delivered a reverse system of *mandatory* complementarity.

In contrast to the idea of complementarity was the system of primacy that was endorsed by the two *ad hoc* Tribunals established by the Security Council during the 1990s. At the beginning of their work, the Tribunals exercised strict primacy in relation to several cases, thus requesting transfer of proceedings currently before national courts. But this did not deny the fact that, on other occasions, the *ad hoc* Tribunals exercised a sort of complementarity with national courts, based on the division of labour, which was implicitly created by the system envisaged in Articles 8 and 9 of the ICTR and ICTY Statutes. This view was even acknowledged by the ICTR Trial Chamber in the *Ntuyahaga* case. Under the completion strategies of the Tribunals, the Rules of Procedure and Evidence were amended to accommodate the referral of some cases that were already before the Tribunals. The idea found much support in Security Council Resolutions 1503 and 1534. Rule 11*bis,* common to the two Tribunals as it currently stood, was modified to implement this concept. Technically, whether inadvertently or intentionally, the ideas behind this Rule established two models of complementarity.

The first model seemed to be inspired by the system established between the IMT and domestic courts acting under Control Council Law No. 10 after World War II. It relied on the distribution of cases between the international criminal jurisdiction and national jurisdictions, depending on the gravity of the crime and level of responsibility of the accused. The second model overlapped with the first, yet created a *mandatory* system of complementarity, which shared some underlying philosophies with the system of complementarity found under the Rome Statute complementarity model. Save for the similarities, the two models established by Rule 11*bis* had different goals and thus stood as models of their own. Although chapters I and II of the book argue that complementarity can take different forms, each of which was introduced during a certain period for some distinct and overlapping reasons, all these models share one common philosophical denominator: the idea of *doing what the other could or would not do* through a division of tasks.

Part B

Chapter III The Principle of Complementarity in the International Criminal Court's Statute

In chapters I and II, the study was confined to the development of the concept of complementarity as part of the broader problem of establishing an international criminal jurisdiction, a process that took almost 75 years. These chapters concluded that complementarity is not an absolute principle, but rather one subject to variations depending on the circumstances of its application. Each model was introduced during a certain period of time for overlapping philosophical reasons. The notion of complementarity embedded in the current International Criminal Court's Statute (ICC)[1] appears among those models – it is known as the Rome Statute model. Chapter III will shift the focus from this theoretical hypothesis to a practical level, taking the Rome Statute model as its framework. This requires a detailed examination of the main provision governing its application – namely Article 17 of the Statute. The provision is far from being perfectly drafted, leaving its full understanding and interpretation to the assessment of the Court. Hitherto, the Court has neither fully dealt with this provision nor provided interpretations for some of the significant questions arising from its application. With this in mind, the chapter points to the gaps as well as offering interpretative guidelines to be taken into consideration by the Court in its assessment of these matters.

1. The Rome Statute Complementarity Model

To attain the goal of international justice, Article 1 of the ICC Statute states in simple language that the Court shall "be a permanent institution and shall have the power to exercise its jurisdiction over persons for the most serious crimes of international concern ... and shall be complementary to national criminal jurisdictions". The ICC Statute does not define the term "complementarity" anywhere. But, the plain texts of paragraph 10 of the preamble[2] and of Article 1 compel the conclusion that the ICC is intended to supplement the domestic punishment of international violations, rather

1 Rome Statute of the International Criminal Court, Adopted by the United Nations Diplomatic Conference of Plenipotentiaries on the Establishment of an International Criminal Court, 17 July 1998, UN Doc., A/CONF.183/9 [hereinafter ICC/ Rome Statute].

2 This text reads, "the International Criminal Court established under this Statute shall be complementary to national criminal jurisdictions". Rome Statute, preamble para. 10.

than supplant domestic enforcement of international norms. The complementarity principle is intended to preserve the ICC's power over irresponsible States that refuse to prosecute those who commit heinous international crimes. It balances that supranational power against the sovereign right of States to prosecute their own nationals without external interference.[3] The reference to the principle of complementarity in both the preamble and Article 1 is duplicative, but was done to stress the significant and central role it will play in the future.[4] The principle of complementarity is elaborated in Articles 17 – 20 of the Statute.

1.1 The Determination of Complementarity under Article 17

Under the "rubric of admissibility" in Article 17,[5] the ICC Statute reflects the balance and the complex relationship between national legal systems and the ICC.[6] In order to implement the complementarity principle, the Prosecutor and the Chambers of

3 See also Oscar Solera, 'Complementary Jurisdiction and International Criminal Justice', 84 *International Review of the Red Cross*, 145, 147 (2002).

4 *Report of the Ad hoc Committee on the Establishment of an International Criminal Court*, UN GAOR, 50th Sess., Supp. No. 22, UN Doc. A/50/22 (1995), paras. 36 – 37 [hereinafter 1995 *Ad hoc* Committee Report]; also John T. Holmes, "The Principle of Complementarity", in Roy S. Lee (ed.), *The International Criminal Court: The Making of the Rome Statute, Issues. Negotiations. Results*, (The Hague. London. Boston: Kluwer Law International, 1999), p. 56.

5 Article 17(1) reads: "Having regard to paragraph 10 of the Preamble and article 1, the Court shall determine that a case is inadmissible where: a) The case is being investigated or prosecuted by a State which has jurisdiction over it, unless the State is unwilling or unable genuinely to carry out the investigation or prosecution; b) The case has been investigated by a State which has jurisdiction over it and the State has decided not to prosecute the person concerned, unless the decision resulted from the unwillingness or inability of the State genuinely to prosecute; c) The person concerned has already been tried for conduct which is the subject of the complaint, and a trial by the Court is not permitted under article 20, paragraph 3". Article 17(2) reads: "In order to determine unwillingness in a particular case, the Court shall consider, having regard to the principles of due process recognized by international law, whether one or more of the following exist, as applicable: a) The proceedings were or are being undertaken or the national decision was made for the purpose of shielding the person concerned from criminal responsibility for crimes within the jurisdiction of the Court referred to in article 5; b) There has been an unjustified delay in the proceedings which in the circumstances is inconsistent with an intent to bring the person concerned to justice; c) The proceedings were not or are not being conducted independently or impartially, and they were or are being conducted in a manner which, in the circumstances, is inconsistent with an intent to bring the person concerned to justice. Article 17(3) reads: "In order to determine inability in a particular case, the Court shall consider whether, due to a total or substantial collapse or unavailability of its national judicial system, the State is unable to obtain the accused or the necessary evidence and testimony or otherwise unable to carry out its proceedings".

6 William A. Schabas, *An Introduction to the International Criminal Court*, 2nd ed., (Cambridge: Cambridge University Press, 2004), p. 85.

the Court should respect and adhere to the Statute's admissibility criteria. The admissibility scheme under the Rome Statute is analogous to the system adopted by the international human rights bodies. The international body shall not proceed with a case unless a petinioner exhaust domestic remedies. Domestic jurisdictions enjoy primacy to deal with their own alleged human rights violations, and only if remedies were deemed "inadequate or ineffective", the international body could proceed.[7]

Article 17 of the Rome Statute represents the most direct mechanism for allocating responsibility for a prosecution between the ICC on the one hand, and one or more States that may have jurisdiction, on the other hand. If, according to the criteria listed in Article 17, a situation or case is deemed "inadmissible", the ICC Statute blocks the powers of the Prosecutor as well as the judicial Chambers from proceeding. These admissibility criteria, therefore, establish the "critical bulwark" that protects States' sovereign rights to deal with these situations or cases before their domestic jurisdictions rather than before the ICC.[8] Providing the ICC with the authority to decide on the *forum* was the outcome of the negotiations that took place in the 1995 *Ad hoc Committee*.[9] There was a common agreement that for "practical reasons",[10] the "burden of proof as to the appropriateness of an exception to the exercise of national jurisdiction should be on the international criminal court".[11]

The chapeau of Article 17 is drafted in negative form, "a case is *inadmissible* were...", certain conditions set out in its paragraph 1(a) – (c) are fullfiled. Failure to meet any of these conditions makes it clear that a situation or case is *de facto* admissible.[12] As one commentator puts it, the drafting of the provision in a negative form "does not *per se* create a presumption, in the technical sense of the word, in favour of inadmissibility".[13] Yet there remains a lack of clarity as to the reasons for drafting this provision in

7 *Akdivar and Others v. Turkey (1)*, Application No. 21893/93, Eur. Ct. H.R., (Preliminary objection) of16/09/1996, paras. 67 – 68; *Van Oosterwijck v. Belgium*, Application No. 7654/76, Eur. Ct. H.R., (Preliminary Objection) of 06/11/1980, paras. 36 – 40; *Velásquez Rodriguez*, Preliminary Objections, Judgment of 26/06/1987, Inter-Am Ct. H.R. (Series C) No. 1(1987), paras. 87 – 88; *Exceptions to the Exhaustion of Domestic Remedies* (Arts. 46(1), 46(2) (a) and 46(2) (b) of the American Convention on Human Rights), Advisory Opinion OC-11/90 of 10 August 1990, Inter-Am Ct. H.R. (Series A) No. 11, (1990), paras. 40 – 41.

8 See also Michael A. Newton, 'Comparative Complementarity: Domestic Jurisdiction Consistent with the Rome Statute of the International Criminal Court', 167 *Military Law Review* 20, 47 – 48 (2001); Kai Ambos, 'The International Criminal Court and the Traditional Principles of International Cooperation in Criminal Matters', 9 *Finnish Yearbook of International Law* 413, 418 (1998).

9 1995 *Ad hoc Committee Report, supra* note 4, paras. 48 – 49.

10 The report fell short of any explanation of those "practical reasons" mentioned.

11 1995 *Ad hoc Committee Report, supra* note 4, para. 49.

12 For a similar conclusion see Carsten Stahn, 'Complementarity, Amnesties and Alternative Forms of Justice: Some Interpretative Guidelines for the International Criminal Court', 3 *Journal of International Criminal Justice* 695, 709 (2005).

13 Markus Benzing, 'The Complementarity Regime of the International Criminal Court: International Criminal Justice Between State Sovereignty and the Fight Against Impunity', 7 *Max Planck Yearbook of United Nations Law* 591, 600 – 601 (2003).

the negative. The first reflection on the idea of *inadmissibility* of cases is to be found in Article 35 of the 1994 International Law Commission Draft Statute.[14] However, the commentary did not tackle the legal justification behind such formulation.[15] Nor have the subsequent negotiations on the subject directly explored the issue.[16] Yet, obviously the drafters created a strong presumption in favour of domestic prosecution. The International Criminal Court is the exception to the presumption.[17]

The hardest part of the complementarity test lies in the exceptions to the conditions for *inadmissibility* set out in Article 17. Paragraph (1) suggests that there are four main situations that require close examination in order to determine the question of admissibility. Firstly, whether the case is being investigated or prosecuted by a State having jurisdiction; secondly, whether a State has investigated and concluded that there is no basis on which to prosecute; thirdly, whether the person has already been tried for this conduct; and, finally, whether the case is of insufficient gravity to be brought before the Court.[18] In the *Lubanga* decision,[19] Pre-Trial Chamber I treated the admissibility test as involving two main parts. Firstly, the criteria set out in Article 17(1) (a) – (c) (complementarity) and, secondly, the gravity threshorld under Article 17(1) (d), which is beyond the scope of this study.[20]

14 *Report of the International Law Commission on the Work of its Forty – Sixth Session* (2 May – 22 July 1994), with Annex Draft Statute for an International Criminal Court, UN Doc. A/49/10, 1994 *YILC* Vol. II, Part Two, Art. 35, p. 52 [hereinafter 1994 ILC Draft Statute].

15 *Ibid.*

16 1995 *Ad hoc Committee Report, supra* note 4, paras. 29 – 51; *Report of the Preparatory Committee on the Establishment of an International Criminal Court,* UN GAOR, 51st Sess., Vol. 1, Supp. No. 22, UN Doc. A/51/22 (1996), paras. 153 – 169 [hereinafter 1996 Preparatory Committee Report, Vol. I].

17 See e.g., 1996 *Preparatory Committee Report,* Vol. I, *supra* note 16, para. 154 (where some delegations argued that complementarity "is not a question of the Court having primary jurisdiction or even concurrent jurisdiction. Rather, its jurisdiction should be understood as having an exceptional character").

18 Rome Statute, Art. 17(1).

19 *Prosecutor v. Thomas Lubanga Dyilo, Decision on the Prosecutor's Application for a Warrant of Arrest, Art. 58,* No. ICC-01/04-01/06-8-US-Corr, 10/02/2006, para. 29, unsealed pursuant to Decision ICC-01/04-01/06-37 dated 17/03/2006.

20 For a discussion on the question of gravity and the International Criminal Court see Mohamed M. El Zeidy, 'The Gravity Threshold Under the Statute of the International Criminal Court', 19 *Criminal Law Forum* (forthcoming 2008); Ray Murphy, 'Gravity Issues and the International Criminal Court', 17 *Criminal Law Forum* 281 (2006). On the treatment of gravity by the Court see *Prosecutor v. Thomas Lubanga Dyilo, Decision on the Prosecutor's Application for a Warrant of Arrest, Art. 58,* No. ICC-01/04-01/06-8-US-Corr, 10/02/2006, paras. 41 – 75, unsealed pursuant to Decision ICC-01/04-01/06-37 dated 17/03/2006; *Report on the Activities Performed during the First Three Years (June 2003 – June 2006),* pp. 5 – 6; *Third Report of the Prosecutor of the International Criminal Court to the UN Security Council Pursuant to UNSCR 1593(2005),* 14 June 2006, p. 2; *Fourth*

Also, the admissibility assesment under Article 17 (1) (a) – (c) is twofold. Firstly, there is a requirement to check, as mentioned above, whether the State has taken action in relation to a certain situation or case that satisfies Article 17(1) (a) – (c). Within the context of a "case" phase, not every investigation carried out by a State would satisfy this first requirement. As Pre-Trial Chamber I stated in the *Lubanga* and *Darfur* decisions, that "it is *a conditio sine qua non* for a case arising from the investigation of a situation to be inadmissible that national proceedings encompass both the person and the conduct which is the subject of the case before the Court".[21] If the answer to any of the requirements that fall under Article 17 (1) (a) – (c) is in the affirmative, the language of the chapeau to Article 17(1) imposes an obligation upon the Court to find a situation or case inadmissible,[22] provided that the gravity threshold has been also met. By contrast, a negative answer will render the situation or case admissible under the plain meaning of Article 17[23] as none of the criteria set out in sub-paragraphs (a)–(c) has been met.[24] Accordingly, there is no need to delve into an examination of a State's "unwillingness" or "inability" under Article 17(2) and (3). Secondly, a further test comes into play when there are already proceedings on foot and there is a need to test the quality of such proceedings. In this context only, the "unwillingness" or "inability" determination applies.

Although a State with jurisdiction over a case may have been investigating or prosecuting, the case may still be deemed *admissible* before the ICC if it has been proven that the State is "unwilling" or "unable" to carry out "genuine" domestic proceedings in relation to its investigation, prosecution or trial.[25] This understanding finds support in the recent decision of ICC Pre-Trial Chamber I in the *Lubanga* case:

Report of the Prosecutor of the International Criminal Court, Mr. Luis Moreno Ocampo, To the UN Security Council Pursuant to UNSCR 1593 (2005), 14 December 2006, p. 3.

21 *Prosecutor v. Thomas Lubanga Dyilo, Decision on the Prosecutor's Application for a Warrant of Arrest, Art. 58*, No. ICC-01/04-01/06-8-US-Corr, 10/02/2006, paras. 31,37, unsealed pursuant to Decision ICC-01/04-01/06-37 dated 17/03/2006; *Prosecutor v. Ahmad Muhammad Harun ("AHMAD HARUN")and Ali Muhammad Ali-Abd-Al-Rahman ("ALI KUSHAYB"), Decision on the Prosecution Application under Article 58(7) of the Statute*, No.: ICC-02/05-01/07-1-Corr, 27/04/2007, paras. 24 – 25.

22 See the chapeau of Article 17, which reads: "[T]he Court shall determine that a case is inadmissible were..." For the same observation see John T. Holmes, "Complementarity: National Courts *Versus* the ICC", in Antonio Cassese et al., (eds.), *The Rome Statute of the International Criminal Court*, Vol. I (Oxford: Oxford University Press, 2002), p. 673 [hereinafter Cassese Commentary] (noting that if any of the criteria of Article 17(1) has been met, and in order to avoid a possible conflict of jurisdiction, "it was decided that Article 17 should obligate the Court to declare the case inadmissible").

23 Provided that the gravity test has been met pursuant to Article 17(1) (d).

24 In the same vein see Bruce Broomhall, *International Justice & The International Criminal Court*, (Oxford: Oxford University Press, 2003), p. 89.

25 Rome Statute, Art. 17(1) (a); See also in support of this reading *Summary Record of the 11th Meeting*, 22 June 1998, UN Doc. A/CONF.183/C.1/SR.11, para. 19 (statement by Mr. John Holmes during the meetings of the Committee of the whole at Rome, noting that Article 15(1) (a) and (b), currently 17(1) (a) and (b), "contained the exceptions where the

> The Chamber also notes that when a State with jurisdiction over a case is investigating, prosecuting or trying it, or has done so, it is not sufficient to declare such a case inadmissible. The Chamber observes on the contrary that a declaration of inadmissibility is subject to a finding that the relevant State is not unwilling or unable to genuinely conduct its national proceedings in relation to that case within the meaning of article 17(1)(a) to (c), (2) and (3) of the Statute.[26]

Not every investigation will meet the test of Article 17. A State's investigation should extend to cases falling within the jurisdiction of the Court and those that are likely to be the focus of the Office of the Prosecutor. In his first report to the Security Council concerning the situation in Darfur, the ICC Prosecutor revealed the techniques used by his Office to test admissibility. He stated:

> [T]he OTP has studied the Sudanese institutions, laws and procedures. In this context, the Government of Sudan has provided information relating to the Sudanese justice system, the administration of criminal justice in various parts of Darfur, traditional systems for alternative dispute resolution,...The Office has also interviewed more than a dozen individuals and sought information on national proceedings that may have been undertaken in relation to crimes within the jurisdiction of the Court allegedly committed in Darfur, including mechanisms provided to allow individuals to report crimes and have access to justice. The Office has also gathered information regarding multiple ad hoc mechanisms that have been created by the Sudanese authorities in the context of the conflict in Darfur, such as...the Special Courts created under the Special Courts Act in 2004, the Specialized Courts that replaced them...In light of the information reviewed, the Prosecutor determined, on 1 June 2005, the existence of sufficient information to believe that there are cases that would be admissible in relation to the Darfur situation...this decision does not represent a determination on the Sudanese legal system as such, but is essentially a result of the absence of criminal proceedings relating to the cases on which the OTP is likely to focus.[27]

Blocking the International Criminal Court requires the State to take *bona fide* action.[28] The key element in determining the decentralization of investigations and the distribution of tasks between national courts and the ICC is the "willingness" or "abil-

---

Court could declare a case admissible, that is, if the State was unwilling or unable to carry out the investigation or its decision not to prosecute was based on its unwillingness or inability to prosecute").

26 *Prosecutor v. Thomas Lubanga Dyilo, Decision on the Prosecutor's Application for a Warrant of Arrest, Art. 58*, No. ICC-01/04-01/06-8-US-Corr, 10/02/2006, para. 32, unsealed pursuant to Decision ICC-01/04-01/06-37 dated 17/03/2006.

27 *First Report of the Prosecutor of the International Criminal Court, Mr. Luis Moreno Ocampo, To the Security Council Pursuant to UNSCR 1593(2005)*, 29 June 2005, pp. 3 – 4.

28 Morten Bergsmo, 'Occasional Remarks on Certain State Concerns about the Jurisdictional Reach of the International Criminal Court, and Their Possible Implications for the

ity" "genuinely" to carry out the domestic proceedings. The burden of proof in the main rests on the ICC Prosecutor. This does not deny the fact that for the purpose of reaching conclusions on States' unwillingness under Article 17(2), part of the burden of proof would logically be transferred to the State. This may be inferred from the language of Rules 51 and 55(2).[29] The nature of the "unwillingness" and "inability" tests, as argued by one scholar, will often mean that the Prosecutor expends more resources in the preparation of the admissibility argument than in proving guilt of an alleged perpetrator.[30] These terms seem to endow both the Prosecutor and the Court with wide discretionary powers of assessment and, thus, the drafters considered definition of these terms to be essential.

1.2 The Criterion of Unwillingness

Defining "unwillingness" was difficult, especially as some delegations were opposed to any inclusion of the concept. They thought that providing the Court with the power to judge States' capacity would impinge on State sovereignty, as well as placing the State in an "embarrassing" situation, depriving the Court of the State's cooperation.[31] Difficulties also centred on how "subjective or objective" the test for determining "unwillingness" should be.[32] The intention was to reduce the number of terms that included subjective elements.[33] Determining the intention of the State not to proceed with a prosecution by relying on a criterion such as "apparently well founded" as referred to in Article 35(1) of the 1994 International Law Commission Draft was perceived as subjective.[34] Also the idea of testing the validity of domestic proceedings by using terms such as "ineffective" trial procedures was rejected for the same reasons.[35] Yet, it was clear that the Court has to maintain some subjectivity in order to have some "latitude" when deciding on States' unwillingness.[36] Consequently, the

Relationship Between the Court and the Security Council', 69 *Nordic Journal of International Law* 87, 96 (2000).

29 *Report of the Preparatory Commission for the International Criminal Court*, UN Doc. PCNICC/2000/1/Add. 1 (2000), ICC Rules, 51, 55(2) [hereinafter ICC Rule]; also for a detailed discussion regarding Rule 51, see section 1.2.4.3 *infra*. For a detailed discussion of the question of burden of proof before the ICC see Megan A. Fairlie, 'Establishing Admissibility at the International Criminal Court: Does the Buck Stop with the Prosecutor, Full Stop?', 39 *International Lawyer* 817 (2005).

30 Morten Bergsmo, 'The Jurisdictional Regime of the International Criminal Court (Part II, Articles 11-19)', 6 *European Journal of Crime, Criminal Law and Criminal Justice* 29, 43 (1998).

31 1996 *Preparatory Committee Report*, Vol. I, *supra* note 16, para. 161.

32 Holmes, *supra* note 4, p. 49.

33 *Ibid.*

34 1994 *ILC Draft Statute*, *supra* note 14, Art. 35(1); Holmes, *supra* note 4, p. 49.

35 1994 *ILC Draft Statute*, *supra* note 14, preamble para. 3; 1996 *Preparatory Committee Report*, Vol. I, *supra* note 16, para. 161.

36 Holmes, *supra* note 4, p. 50.

drafters compromised by adding the word "genuinely" as the least disagreeable and most objective term.[37]

Contrary to the opinion of one commentator,[38] the term "genuinely" actually appeared for the first time in the work of the Working Group on Complementarity in the August 1997 session.[39] It was adopted to achieve "broad consensus", despite the opposition of some delegations who still considered it vague.[40] One scholar argues that "genuinely" in the context of Article 17 "compels States to carry out investigations and prosecutions and to make decisions about whether to prosecute in a manner consistent with the aims of the Rome Statute".[41] Such an observation is true, but does not add much to the interpretation of Article 17, as it is evident that the main idea behind the entire system of complementarity is to ensure that States carry out their duties of investigation, prosecution and trial, in a manner that achieves the goals behind the Rome Statute.

Neither the Statute nor the Rules or the Regulations of the Court define the term "genuine". The Court has not tackled this question in its jurisprudence so far. Plainly, "genuine" means "authentic or real – something that has the quality of what it is purported to be or to have".[42] The *travaux préparatoires* provide no particular guidance "for the utilization" of this term.[43] However, it has been argued that the most "resemblance to genuineness is perhaps the concept of good faith".[44] Indeed, on several occasions the European Court of Justice has used these terms, although in a different

---

37 *Ibid* ; see also Sharon Williams, "Issues of Admissibility", in Otto Triffterer (ed.), *Commentary on the Rome Statute: Observers' Notes, Article by Article*, (Nomos Verlagsgesellschaft: Baden-Baden, 1999), p. 392 [hereinafter Triffterer Commentary].

38 Leila Nadya Sadat, *The International Criminal Court and the Transformation of International Law: Justice for the New Millennium*, (Ardsley, New York: Transnational Publishers, 2002), p. 124 (noting that the "term 'genuinely' was drawn in 1998 from the Zutphen Intersessional Draft").

39 See *Decisions Taken By the Preparatory Committee at its Session Held from 4 to 15 August 1997*, (A/AC.249/1997/L.8/Rev. 1, 1997), Art. 35(2) (a), (b), p. 10 [1997 Preparatory Committee Decisions]. Article 35(2)(a) states: "Having regard to paragraph 3 of the preamble, the Court shall determine that case is inadmissible where: (a) the case is being investigated or prosecuted by a State which has jurisdiction over it, unless the State is unwilling or unable genuinely to carry out the investigation or prosecution; (b) the case has been investigated by a State which has jurisdiction over it and the State has decided not to prosecute the person concerned, unless the decision resulted from the unwillingness or inability of the State genuinely to prosecute…".

40 Holmes, *supra* note 4, p. 50.

41 Rod Jensen, "Complementarity, 'Genuinely' and Article 17: Assessing the Boundaries of an Effective ICC", in Jann K. Kleffner et al., (eds.), *Complementary Views on Complementarity: Proceedings of the International Roundtable on the Complementary Nature of the International Criminal Court*, Amsterdam, 25/26 June 2004, (The Hague: T.M.C. Asser Press, 2006), p. 160.

42 *Black's Law Dictionary*, Seventh Edition, (St. Paul, Minn.: West Group, 1999), p. 695.

43 Holmes, *Cassese Commentary*, *supra* note 22, p. 674.

44 For a similar observation, see *ibid.*

context. In *Commission v. Spain*, the Sixth Chamber seemed to have used the terms "genuine" and "good faith" interchangeably, leading to the same meaning.[45] The same standard was applied by the First Chamber in *Commission v. Federal Republic of Germany*[46] and *Commission v. Kingdom of Belgium*.[47]

Reading the word "genuinely" in its context ("unless the State is unwilling or unable *genuinely* to carry out the investigation or prosecution") suggests two different interpretations. First, the term may qualify the State's "unwillingness" or "inability" to investigate or prosecute.[48] According to this interpretation, it is not enough for the State to be merely unwilling or unable to carry out the investigation or prosecution. Rather it has to be proved that there is an element of *genuineness* accompanying such unwillingness or inability. Secondly, according to a different construction, the term "genuinely" might apply to the last part of the sentence – that is, to qualify the phrase "to carry out the investigation or prosecution". Based on this interpretation, the Court should be satisfied that the investigation or prosecution carried out by the State in question is "genuine" before deferring to domestic jurisdiction. Otherwise any national proceedings, even if inadequate, would be a stumbling block in the face of the ICC's jurisdiction.[49] Although the provision is drafted in a manner that might seem to support the first interpretation, the prevailing view is that the second reading is the appropriate one.[50] Be that as it may, the inclusion of the term "genuinely" clearly raises the threshold of *objective* scrutiny in testing the quality of States' national proceedings. The International Court of Justice (ICJ) has applied a parallel standard in determining whether to exercise its jurisdiction in contentious proceedings.

In the *Nuclear Tests* cases, the ICJ stated that the "Court can exercise jurisdiction in contentious proceedings only when a dispute genuinely exists between the parties".[51] In order to establish the existence of such an international dispute, the Court

45 Case C-499/99 *Commission v. Kingdom of Spain* [2002] ECR I-6031, para. 24.

46 Case C-105/02 *Commission v. Federal Republic of Germany* [2006], paras. 93 – 94 (where the Court seemed to have used the phrase "cooperate in good faith" as reflecting "genuine cooperation"). *Ibid.*

47 Case C-275/04 *Commission v. Kingdom of Belgium* [2006], paras. 82 – 83(noticeably the Court used the exact wording found in the *Commission v. Federal Republic of Germany*).

48 Some scholars have also raised the possibility of interpreting the provision in such a manner. See Leila Nadya Sadat and S. Richard Carden, 'The New International Criminal Court: An Uneasy Revolution', 88 *Georgetown Law Journal* 381, 418 (2000) (arguing whether the term "genuinely" refers to situations where the "State's motives are not genuine or to situations where the State is really unable or unwilling to prosecute").

49 *Informal Expert Paper: The Principle of Complementarity in Practice*, p. 8 [hereinafter Informal Expert Paper].

50 *Ibid.* See specifically fns. 8 – 9. "Earlier drafts ("to genuinely carry out", "to genuinely prosecute") were adjusted on purely technical grounds to avoid splitting the infinitive. It is also confirmed by the purpose of including the term "genuinely", *i.e.* to restrict the class of national proceedings warranting deference from the ICC…". *Ibid.*, n. 8.

51 *Nuclear Tests Case (Australia v. France)*, 1974 I.C.J., 20/12/1974, para. 57; *Nuclear Tests Case (New Zealand v. France)*, 1974 I.C.J., 20/12/1974, para. 60.

argued elsewhere in the judgment that this is "a matter for objective determination by the Court".[52] This suggests that the *genuineness* of a dispute may be determined only through an "objective" assessment by the Court. It follows that, as a matter of *principle*, the *genuineness* of an act cannot be determined without an "objective" assessment. The determination of the *genuineness* of the proceedings carried out by the State may also require an "objective" evaluation.

What may constitute an objective evaluation of the genuineness of proceedings is not an easy question to answer, as it depends on the circumstances of each case. Yet one cannot support an argument that a domestic investigation or prosecution "qualifies as genuine only if it provides the defendant with due process".[53] While securing "due process" rights for the defendant is an important aspect of any civilized criminal process, a "genuine" investigation or prosecution within the meaning of Article 17(1) requires a broader assessment, which may include, *but is not limited to*, the rights of the accused.

From a practical point of view, the evaluation of the genuineness of any proceedings necessitates the scrutiny of the domestic judicial proceedings in relation to a specific case as a whole from the moment it starts until the stage where the assessment commences.[54] If for example, the criminal proceedings have resulted in acquittal, then there is a need to inquire into police reports concerning investigations, prosecution evidence, forensic reports and the trial records to check whether the quality of the procedure met the required international standards. Similarly, where a conviction resulted in the imposition of a light sentence, the same process should apply.

One commentator has argued that appreciating the quality of domestic proceedings, reflected in the willingness of the State to investigate, requires more than the mere opening of an investigation into a "general" situation. The investigation should be "in fact directed toward the persons truly responsible".[55] While this is true, one has

---

52 *Interpretation of Peace Treaties with Bulgaria, Hungary, and Romania (First Phase), Advisory Opinion of 30/03/1950*, I.C.J. Reports 1950, p. 74; *Nuclear Tests Case (Australia v. France)*, 1974 I.C.J., 20/12/1974, para. 55; *Nuclear Tests Case (New Zealand v. France)*, 1974 I.C.J., 20/12/1974, para. 58.

53 Kevin Jon Heller, 'The Shadow Side of Complementarity: The Effect of Article 17 of the Rome Statute on National Due Process', 17 *Criminal Law Forum* 255, 259 (2006).

54 For a similar observation see *Villagran Morales et al. v. Guatemala* (The "Street Children" Case), Judgment of 19/11/1999, Inter-Am Ct. H.R. (Ser. C) No. 63 (1999), para. 222 ("In order to clarify whether the State has violated its international obligations owing to the acts of its judicial organs, the Court may have to examine the respective domestic proceedings". In this context, the ECHR pointed out that the domestic proceedings, including the decisions of the Courts of Appeal, should be considered "as a whole". See *Delta v. France*, Application No. 11444/85, Eur. Ct. H.R., Judgment (Merits and Just Satisfaction) of 19/12/1990, para. 35; *Vidal v. Belgium*, Application No. 12351/86, Eur. Ct. H.R., Judgment (Merits) of 22/04/1992, para. 33; *Edwards v. The United Kingdom*, Application No. 13071/87, Eur. Ct. H.R., Judgment (Merits) of 16/12/1992, para. 34.

55 Mireille Delmas-Marty, 'Interactions between National and International Criminal Law in the Preliminary Phase of Trial at the ICC', 4 *Journal of International Criminal Justice* 2, 4 – 5 (2006).

to be careful with the distinction between the different phases of the proceedings. It is doubtful whether a State, at the very initial stages of a large-scale complex investigation into a situation, would be able *strictly* to determine the "persons truly responsible" for the purpose of a prosecution. Instead, at this stage the investigation should target the leaders of all the groups involved that may prove to be most responsible. Selecting identified persons for the purpose of a prosecution in relation to a select number of specified incidents does not take place before the proceedings enter into a "case" stage in accordance with Article 19 of the Statute.

In *Paniagua Morales et al*, the Inter-American Court of Human Rights (IACHR) considered that Guatemala had failed to carry out a "*genuine* and effective investigation", although an investigation was already underway in relation to some of the acts perpetrated. A "genuine investigation" requires the State to use "all the legal means at its disposal" in the conduct of a serious criminal process that identifies the suspects involved and leads to actual trial and appropriate punishment if necessary.[56]A similar view was also voiced by the IACHR in *Urrutia*,[57] and in other cases to be discussed in detail later under the notion of "shielding the person form criminal responsibility" in accordance with Article 17(2) (a).

The Rome Statute does not leave the term "unwilling" in the abstract. Rather it defines the situations that may assist the Court in making a determination of a State's unwillingness. The chapeau of Article 17(2) stipulates that for the purpose of determining "unwillingness" in a certain case, the "Court shall consider,...whether one or more of the following exist, as applicable". Paragraph 2 provides for three scenarios; if any of them has taken place, this is a clear indication of the State's "unwillingness".

A number of scholars have argued that the conditions set out in paragraph (2) are "illustrative" rather than exhaustive,[58] because the phrase "shall *consider* whether"

56 *Paniagua Morales et al.* ("Panel Blanca"), Judgment of 8/03/ 1998, Inter-Am Ct. H.R. (Ser. C) No. 37 (1998), in particular paras. 94, 139, 160, 169, 171, 178; See also *Garrido and Baigorria v. Argentina*, Reparations (Art. 63(1) American Convention on Human Rights), Judgment of 27/ 08/1998, Inter-Am Ct. H.R. (Ser. C) No. 39 (1998) para. 73; *Myrna Mack Chang v. Guatemala*, Judgment of 25/11/ 2003, Inter-Am Ct. H.R. (Ser. C) No. 101 (2003), in particular paras. 13, 134.86, 139, 155, 159, 203, 217.

57 *Maritza Urrutia v. Guatemala*, Judgment of 27/11/2003, Inter-Am Ct. H.R. (Ser. C) No. 103 (2003), paras. 104, 119, 124 – 126.

58 Darryl Robinson, 'Serving the Interests of Justice: Amnesties, Truth Commissions and the International Criminal Court', 14 *European Journal of International Law* 481, 500 (2003); Christopher Keith Hall, 'Suggestions Concerning International Criminal Court Prosecutorial Policy and Strategy and External Relations', [Expert Consultation Process on General Issues Relevant to the ICC Office of the Prosecutor:], 28 March 2003, p. 16. On the opposite view Claudia Cárdenas Aravena, "The Admissibility Test Before the International Criminal Court under Special Consideration of Amnesties and Truth Commissions", in Jann K. Kleffner et al. (eds.), *supra* note 41, p. 121 ("Paragraphs 2 and 3 of Article 17 contain exhaustive legal definitions of both terms, adopted as those best reflecting the complementary function of the ICC"); Holmes, *Cassese Commentary, supra* note 22, p. 675 (stating that the "drafting of this provision" would not support an interpretation that the Court could "make an admissibility determination related to a State's

does not "impose a fixed requirement".[59] But the words "shall *consider*" do not necessarily imply that the list is merely "illustrative". Reading the phrase "shall *consider*" together with the last phrase "whether one or more of the *following* exist" supports the presumption that the list is exhaustive rather than "illustrative". The drafters could have used the words "such as", "for example" or "including but not limited to" as in Article 90(6), "*inter alia*" as found in the chapeau of Article 97, or explicitly said that the list was open-ended, if this was the intended meaning. Moreover, Article 17 is drafted in the negative in favour of inadmissibility. "Unwillingness" is the exception to this rule and, thus, the provision should be given a narrow interpretation – treating the list under paragraph (2) as exhaustive.[60]

Since "unwillingness" as elaborated in Article 17(2) is in effect a test of the good faith of national authorities, the Statute ensures the effectiveness of this test through the conditions set out in paragraph (2). The first criterion requires the Court to establish that the proceedings (a) "were or are being undertaken or the national decision was made for the purpose of shielding the person concerned from criminal responsibility";[61] or (b) that there "has been an unjustified delay in the proceedings which in the circumstances is inconsistent with an intent to bring the person concerned to justice"; or (c) that "the proceedings were not or are not being conducted independently or impartially, and they were or are being conducted in a manner which, in the circumstances, is inconsistent with an intent to bring the person concerned to justice".

The first criterion still embodies an element of subjectivity when it comes to the assessment of the quality of justice in the light of States' actual intentions. Thus, it requires meticulous examination. As one commentator puts it, this condition requires the Prosecutor to prove "a devious intent on the part of the State, contrary to its apparent actions".[62] By contrast, the second and third criteria incline more towards objectivity than subjectivity of assessment. The reference to the key issues "unjustified" justice "delay" and the lack of "independence or impartially" in carrying out the domestic proceedings draws *some sort of objective boundaries* to the assessment – making the test less subjective.[63] Such objectivity is enhanced by the additional

unwillingness based on criteria not included in Article 17"); and Williams, *supra* note 37, p. 393 (noting that it "is an exhaustive list").

59 Robinson, *supra* note 58, p. 500.

60 In the same vein see Benzing, *supra* note 13, p. 606; and generally Stahn, *supra* note 12, p. 709.

61 Rome Statute, Art. 17(2) (a).

62 Louise Arbour and Morten Bergsmo, "Conspicuous Absence of Jurisdictional Overreach", in Herman A. M. von Hebel et al. (eds.), *Reflections on the International Criminal Court* (The Hague: T.M.C. Asser Press, 1999), p. 131.

63 This does not deny the fact that even in applying international standards to determine the quality of domestic proceedings a subjective element will often be involved as the assessment will vary from one case to another depending on the circumstances of each case.

phrase "the Court shall consider, having regard to the principles of due process recognized by international law", reflected in the chapeau of Article 17(2).[64]

Arguably, the phrase requires that the assessment of the quality of justice, as reflected in sub-paragraphs (a) – (c), takes into consideration "procedural" as well as "substantive" due process rights[65] (which cover the entire judicial process including the rights of the accused) enshrined in human rights instruments[66] and developed in the jurisprudence of international judicial bodies. This conclusion finds support in the language of Article 21(3) of the Statute, which requires that the "application" and interpretation of the law of the Statute "must be consistent with internationally recognized human rights".[67] The Appeals Chamber in *Lubanga* confirmed such understanding when it stated that Article 21(3):

> [R]equires the exercise of jurisdiction of the Court in accordance with the internationally recognized human rights norms...Human rights underpin the Statute; every aspect of it... first and foremost in the context of the Statute, the right to a fair trial, a concept broadly perceived and applied, embracing the judicial process in its entirety.[68]

The phrase "having regard to the principles of due process recognized by international law" was originally intended to be added to the paragraph that dealt with the

64 Rome Statute, Chapeau of Art. 17 (2). On the origins of the principle of "Due process" see Rodney L. Mott, *Due Process of Law: A Historical and Analytical Treaties of the Principles and Methods Followed by the Courts in the Application of the Concept of the "Law of the Land"* (Indianapolis, 1926); Warren M. Billings, 'Pleading, Procedure, and Practice: The Meaning of Due Process of Law in Seventeenth-Century Virginia', 47 *The Journal of Southern History* 569 (1981) (noting that "due process" is a "venerable Anglo-American Tenet").

65 See e.g., *Baena-Ricardo et al (270 Workers v. Panamá)*, Judgment of February 2, 2001, Inter-Am Ct. H.R. (Ser. C) No. 72 (2001), para. 137 (where the Court defined the term "due process" as consisting of "the right of all persons to a hearing, with due guarantees and within a reasonable time, by a competent, independent, and impartial judge or tribunal, previously established by law, in the substantiation of any accusation of a criminal nature made against him or her or for the determination of her or his rights") ; also Schabas, *supra* note 6, p. 86 ; But see Newton, *supra* note 8, p. 66 (noting that since the Statute does not define this phrase, the Prosecutor would have a wide margin of discretion to meet the objective admissibility criteria).

66 For a similar observation in relation to the human rights instruments existing at the time see William J. Brennan, "International Due Process and the Law", 48 *Virginia Law Review* 1258, 1259 (1962).

67 Rome Statute, Art. 21(3).

68 *Prosecutor v. Thomas Lubanga Dyilo, Judgment on the Appeal of Mr. Thomas Lubanga Dyilo against the Decision on the Defence Challenge to the Jurisdiction of the Court pursuant to article 19(2) (a) of the Statute of 3 October 2006*, No.: ICC-01/04-01/06-772, 14/12/2006, paras. 36 – 39; See also the recent decision rendered by Trial Chamber I, which refers to the obligation of interpreting the Statute in the light of internationally recognized human rights as set out in Article 21(3) of the Statute: *Prosecutor v. Thomas Lubanga Dyilo, Decision on Victims' Participation*, No.: ICC-01/04-01/06-1119, 18/01/2008, paras. 34 – 35.

independence and impartiality of the national proceedings in order to ensure greater objectivity. In advancing the negotiations on part 2 of the Statute, the Bureau of the Committee of the Whole, embraced this idea in both its Discussion Paper and its Proposal.[69] As the bilateral negotiations continued, several delegations favoured the idea, yet indicated their concern that this still left other criteria relating to unwillingness less objective. Accordingly, it was agreed to add to the chapeau the phrase "unwillingness" to serve all the sub-paragraphs.[70] That said, Article 17(2) as a whole is still associated with some subjectivity and there is a high threshold to be met, especially in proving States' hidden intent to bring the alleged perpetrators to justice.[71]

1.2.1 Shielding a Person from Criminal Responsibility

The language of Article 17(2) (a) suggests that that the notion of "shielding the person from criminal responsibility" is broad enough to cover the situations explored in sub-paragraphs (b)–(c). An "unjustified delay" accompanied by an intent not to bring the person to justice is *indeed* a scenario that reflects the idea of "shielding the person from criminal responsibility". Similarly, the lack of independent or impartial proceedings, with the intention that the accused escapes justice, is another scenario that falls under the umbrella of "shielding from the criminal responsibility". Thus, these abnormalities in conducting domestic proceedings for the purpose of escaping justice are clearly part of the general scheme of *shielding* people from criminal responsibility. If any of these scenarios take place, by implication there is a lack of "genuine" domestic proceedings as required under Article 17(1) (a) – (b). It follows that there is a clear overlap between these criteria, yet it is not clear why the drafters provided for separate conditions. Sub-paragraphs (b) – (c) are contributing factors to the determination that domestic proceedings are *sham,* aiming to shield the accused from criminal responsibility, in accordance with sub-paragraph (a).[72]

The first reference to the idea of "shielding" an accused from criminal responsibility appears in Article 10(2) (b) of the ICTY Statute[73] as well as in Rule 9(ii) of the Rules of Procedure and Evidence of the Tribunal.[74] In *Tadic*, the Appeals Chamber briefly

69 Bureau Discussion Paper on Part 2 (Jurisdiction, Admissibility and Applicable Law), UN Diplomatic Conference of Plenipotentiaries on the Establishment of an International Criminal Court, Committee of the Whole, Art. 15 (2) (c), U.N. Doc. A/CONF. 183/C.1/L.53, 6 July 1998 [hereinafter Bureau Discussion Paper UN Doc. A/CONF. 183/C.1/L.53]. Article 15(2) (c) states: "The proceedings were not or are not being conducted independently or impartially *in accordance with the norms of due process recognized by international law...*" ; see also Holmes, *supra* note 4, p. 53.

70 Williams, *supra* note 37, pp. 390 – 391. However, see Rome Statute, Art. 20 (3), (b) where the term "due process" remained attached to the terms "independently" or "impartially".

71 In the same vein see Theo Van Boven, "The Principle of Complementarity: The International Criminal Court and National Laws", in Jan Wouters et al. (eds.), *De Genocidewet in Internationaal Perspectief* (Brussel: Larcier, 2002), p. 67.

72 But see the opening of section 1.2.5 *infra.*

73 ICTY Statute, Art. 10(2) (b).

74 ICTY Rule 9(ii).

referred to these provisions in the context of defending the Tribunal's own primacy over national courts. The Tribunal stated:

> [W]hen an international tribunal such as the present one is created, it must be endowed with primacy over national courts. Otherwise, human nature being what it is, there would be a perennial danger of ..., or proceedings being "designed to shield the accused"...If not effectively countered by the principle of primacy, any one of those stratagems might be used to defeat the very purpose of the creation of an international criminal jurisdiction, to the benefit of the very people whom it has been designed to prosecute.[75]

Reference was made to the same provisions in the Trial Chamber's decision concerning the defence motion on the principle of *non bis in idem.*[76] Neither of these decisions really elaborated on the notion of "proceedings being designed to shield the accused from international criminal responsibility". Nor has the ICTR Trial Chamber explicitly referred to the notion of "shielding" in its equivalent decision on jurisdiction and primacy of the Tribunal.[77] The question has not arisen because there do not appear to have been any such sham proceedings. During these periods the Rome Statute was in the process of being drafted. The idea of "shielding" re-emerged at the discussions of the 1995 *Ad hoc Committee.* It was pointed out that:

> [W]hile the jurisdiction of an international criminal court was compelling where there was no functioning judicial system, the intervention of the court in situations where an operating national judicial system was being used as a shield required very careful consideration.[78]

During the discussions of the Preparatory Committee in 1996, it was made clear that there is a need for more "stringent and objective criteria" for the sake of "greater clarity and security" in assessing the effectiveness of domestic proceedings.[79] The intention to "shield" the accused was one such criterion.[80] The concept of shielding an accused from criminal responsibility appeared for the first time among the texts of articles recommended by the Working Group on Complementarity in the August 1997 session.[81] The proposed text apparently remained without any substantial change, finding its way in the current text of Article 17(2) (a).

---

75 *Prosecutor v. Duško Tadić,* Case No. IT-94-1-AR72, Decision on the Defence Motion for Interlocutory Appeal on Jurisdiction, 2/10/1995, para. 58.

76 *Prosecutor v. Duško Tadić,* Case No. IT-94-1-T, Decision on the Defence Motion on the Principle of *non bis in idem,* 14/11/1995.

77 *Prosecutor v. Joseph Kanyabashi,* Case No. ICTR-96-15-T, Decision on the Defence Motion on Jurisdiction, 18/06/1997, paras. 30 – 32.

78 1995 *Ad hoc Committee Report, supra* note 4, para. 45.

79 1996 *Preparatory Committee Report,* Vol. I, *supra* note 16, para. 166.

80 *Ibid.* In the context of *ne bis in idem* see *ibid.,* para. 173.

81 1997 *Preparatory Committee Decisions, supra* note 39, Art. 35(3)(a), p. 11. Paragraph 3(a) states: "the proceedings were or are being undertaken or the national decision was made

1.2.2 The Leipzig Precedent

In an early historical context, a relevant precedent that may perhaps be close to the idea of shielding the "person concerned from criminal responsibility" is the *Leipzig* trials of Germans after the First World War before the *Reichsgericht*.[82] Out of the original list of more than 850 names, only a handful were found guilty and given light sentences.[83] Karl Heynen, who was charged with the ill-treatment of prisoners of war, was "ultimately" sentenced to 10 months' imprisonment.[84] Also Emil Muller[85] and Robert Neumann, who were charged with similar counts, received six months' imprisonment.[86]

Relatively heavier sentences were passed on Cruscius, charged by the French with shooting several prisoners of war, who was given two years',[87] and Lieutenants Dithmar and Boldt, in the "Landovery Castle" case, where both were found guilty of "intermediate degree of killing" or "second-degree murder" and were sentenced to four years' imprisonment.[88] Dithmar was dismissed from the service,[89] while Boldt was

---

for the purpose of shielding the person concerned from criminal responsibility for crimes within the jurisdiction of the Court as set out in article 20". When it is compared to the current text of Article 17(2) (a), one may observe that the slight change in the language of the last sentence of the provision was only stylistic.

82 For a detailed analysis see chapter I, *supra.*

83 M. Cherif Bassiouni, "International Criminal Investigations and Prosecutions: From Versailles to Rwanda", in M. Cherif Bassiouni (ed.), *International Criminal Law: Enforcement*, 2nd ed. (Ardsley, New York, Transnational Publishers, 1999), p. 38.

84 Supreme Court at Leipzig, *Judgment in the Case of Karl Heynen*, 26/05/1921, *in* 16 *American Journal of International Law* 674 (1922). For a summary of the judgment and sentence see *German War Trials: Report of the Proceedings before the Supreme Court in Leipzig* (London, 1921), pp. 8 – 9 [hereinafter Leipzig Report].

85 Supreme Court at Leipzig, *Judgment in the Case of Emil Müller*, 30/05/1921, *in* 16 *American Journal of International Law* 684 (1922). For a summary see *Leipzig Report, supra* note 84, pp. 9 – 11.

86 Supreme Court at Leipzig, *Judgment in the Case of Robert Neumann*, 2/06/1921, *in* 16 *American Journal of International Law* 696 (1922). For a summary see *Leipzig Report, supra* note 84, p. 12.

87 The United Nations War Crimes Commission, *History of the United Nations War Crimes Commission and the Development of the Laws of War* (London: H.M. Stationery Office, 1948), p. 47 [UNWCC].

88 Supreme Court at Leipzig, *Judgment in the Case of Lieutenants Dithmar and Boldt Hostpital Ship* "Landovery Castle", 16/07/1921, *in* 16 *American Journal of International Law* 708 (1922) [hereinafter Landovery Castle case]. For a summary see *Leipzig Report, supra* note 84, pp.13 – 15. Because the German government could not find Patzig, it ordered the German Public Prosecutor to charge Dithmar and Boldt whose names were never on the lists, UNWCC, *supra* note 87, p. 47.

89 *Landovery Castle* case, *supra* note 88, p. 723.

deprived of the right to wear a uniform.[90] Lieutenant-commander Karl Neumann was acquitted on the defence of superior orders in the "Dover Castle" case.[91]

Similar acquittal verdicts were delivered in relation to Krushka and von Schack, accused by the French, while no action was taken in relation to the Italian cases.[92] These results triggered the Allies' anger, and an Inter-Allied Commission appointed to assess the quality of the Leipzig trials concluded that "in almost all the cases the court has given no satisfaction in that certain accused have been acquitted when they should have been condemned, and that even in those case where the accused have been judged guilty the penalty applied has not been sufficient".[93] As Alexander Cadogan of the British Foreign Office put it, the Leipzig "experiment has been pronounced a failure".[94] Out of the total number of cases brought before the Supreme Court at Leipzig, hundreds of accused persons "were acquitted or summarily dismissed".[95]

Those who were convicted "were not even made to serve their sentence[s]", as several escaped with the help of their prison warders, who were "publicly congratulated".[96] The war criminals were "treated as heroes". A recommendation was made to the effect that the Allies should act under the terms of Articles 228 – 229 of the Treaty of Versailles – securing a re-trial before their military tribunals.[97] Condemnation of the Leipzig failure has been shared by many scholars.[98] When one puts this precedent in the context of Article 17(2)(a), the findings reached by the Inter-Allied Commission, as well as Germany's failure to fulfil its obligations in relation to the accused serving their sentences, imply that the "national decision" might have been made for

90 *Ibid.*

91 Supreme Court at Leipzig, *Judgment in the Case of Commander Karl Neumann Hospital Ship* "Dover Castle", 4/06/1921, *in* 16 *American Journal of International Law* 704 (1922).

92 UNWCC, *supra* note 87, p. 47.

93 FO 371/7529/C17096, Allied-German Negotiations in War Criminals, 7 January 1992, *quoted in* Gary Jonathan Bass, *Stay the Hand of Vengeance: The Politics of War Crimes Tribunals* (Princeton and Oxford: Princeton University Press, 2000), p. 81.

94 FO 371/7529/C17096, 9 December 1922, *quoted in ibid.*

95 UNWCC, *supra* note 87, p. 48.

96 *Ibid.*

97 James F. Willis, *Prologue to Nuremberg: The Politics and Diplomacy of Punishing War Criminals of the First World War* (Westport. Connecticut: Greenwood Press, 1982), p. 140. The political atmosphere and the demand not to humiliate the Germans any further contributed to the dropping of the idea of imposing the terms of Articles 228 – 229 of the Versailles Treaty.

98 J. L. Brierly, 'Do We Need an International Criminal Court?', 8 *British Yearbook of International Law* 81, 83 (1927); 'The Trial of Axis War Criminals: The Question of Procedure', 13 *Fortnightly Law Journal* 119, 120 – 121 (1943) (calling the German trials "German Trickery"); Mahmoud Nagib Hosney, *Deroose Fee Al Kanoon Al Genaie Al Dowaly* (Lessons in International Criminal Law) (Cairo: Dar Al- Nahda Al-Arabia, 1959 – 1960), pp. 28 – 29.

the "purpose of shielding" the accused persons from criminal responsibility.[99] Had these cases been tried before an international tribunal, clearly the sentences would have been greater and carried out effectively.

A group of commentators has argued that a scenario that relies on the outcome of a trial – like the one mentioned above – would not qualify for the purpose of determining a case admissible before the ICC, since this "would undermine the accused's right to be presumed innocent at trial once before the ICC. Therefore, the admissibility assessment should be based on *procedural* and *institutional* factors, not the substantive outcome."[100]

Although this is true and compatible with the "principles of due process recognized by international law", as reflected in the chapeau of Article 17(2),[101] one should not overlook the fact that Article 17(1) (c) in conjunction with Article 20(3) exists to cover a situation where trial proceedings, which lead to its outcome, reflect a State's intention to "shield the person from criminal responsibility".[102] If such a "purpose" has been proved, the situation or case should be deemed admissible according to the terms of Article 17(1) (c). The test requires the "outcome" of the trial to be looked at as

99 See also Rome Statute, Art. 20 (3) (a), which permits a second trial before the ICC if the domestic proceedings "were for the purpose of shielding" the person from criminal responsibility. Since the Inter-Allied Commission ordered a re-trial as a result of the failure of domestic efforts, it could be argued that the Leipzig trials may serve as a good example for the application of Article 20(3)(a). However, this was not the view of Claud Mullins who has written one of the most authoritative monographs on the trials and attended all of the British trials. To him, although the trials may be criticized as being "inadequate from the point of view of jurisprudence, the trials were not a farce and the seven German judges endeavored throughout to be true to the traditions of fairness and impartiality which are the pride of all judicial courts". See Claud Mullins, *The Leipzig Trials: An Account of the War Criminals Trials and a Study of German Mentality* (London: H. F. & G. Witherby, 1921), p. 35. There were difficulties surrounding the gathering of evidence and calling of witnesses as well as the difference in the procedural systems applied in each of the Allied countries when compared with the German system. This might have led to unsatisfactory results. *Ibid.*, pp. 35 – 43, 209 – 234. He proceeded by saying "I am convinced that the War Trials produced results of great political and ethical value, both at the time and for posterity. From this point of view I am convinced that the trials were successful...If the object of the trials is held to have been revenge and the punishment of individuals, then the trials may have failed. If the object was to convince the Germany of 1921 of its crimes during the war, then again there was little success". *Ibid.*, p. 226. But reading his last statement suggests that he admitted that the trials "have failed" from the legal point of view adequately to punish the German war criminals. But see the recent work of David Hunt, 'The International Criminal Court: High Hopes, 'Creative Ambiguity' and an Unfortunate Mistrust in International Judges', 2 *Journal of International Criminal Justice* 56, 63 (2004) (noting that no "mention seems to have been made during the discussions in Rome of the very relevant trials of German war criminals in Leipzig in 1921, which the German government took every opportunity to evade...".

100 *Informal Expert Paper*, *supra* note 49, p. 14.

101 Rome Statute, Art. 17(2).

102 *Ibid.*, Arts., 17(1) (c), 20 (3).

a point of *fact*; in order for the ICC to challenge this outcome an assessment of all the procedural aspects that led to the outcome also seems indispensable. Thus, the test by no means excludes the possibility of addressing the "procedural factors".

This is not to deny that the accused's rights might perhaps be at stake, if a Pre-Trial Chamber determined admissibility by merely relying on substantial evidence at a preliminary stage of assessment that led to the acquittal of an accused at the domestic level.[103] Rather there is a problem with Articles 17(1) (c) and 20(3) to the extent that they favour the assumption that a disappointing trial outcome is a result of *sham* proceedings; lenient sentences incompatible with the gravity of the crimes or perhaps the failure of a State *deliberately* to execute a sentence on an accused might render a case admissible for re-trial before the ICC.[104]

1.2.3 Some Guidelines Reflecting the Notion of Shielding

Drawing up an exhaustive list of situations that reflect a State's intention to "shield a person from criminal responsibility" is impossible, since this is dependent on the factual circumstances of each case. What is possible, though, is the provision of some guidelines on the basis of legal analysis extracted from the practice of other international judicial bodies. Sometimes the national decision reflects a straightforward case of a State that is acting in bad faith. A national decision that passes an amnesty law or some instruction to that effect, which exempts alleged perpetrators from facing justice, is a clear-cut example of allowing the "person concerned" to avoid criminal responsibility. An order such as the Barbarossa, issued by the German High Command in May 1941, is another example. According to this order, prosecution for "crimes committed against inhabitants by the Wehrmacht and its auxiliaries... [was] not obligatory and would take place only if necessary for the maintenance of discipline or the security of Forces".[105] But this is not always the case; therefore, an attempt to pinpoint some examples seems necessary.

Since Article 17(2)(a) is all about testing the effectiveness of domestic proceedings, any *intentional* deficiency or serious negligence in carrying out domestic proceedings that lead to negative results, through certain acts or omissions, might reflect the State's intention to "shield a person from criminal responsibly". Thus an ineffective or non-"genuine" investigation might be considered inversely proportionate to the concept of shielding from criminal responsibility. That is, the more accurate and thorough the domestic proceedings are, the more difficult to find is proof of an "intent to shield a person from criminal responsibility" and *vice versa*.

On several occasions, especially in the context of examining violations of the right to life and the prohibition of torture, the European Court of Human Rights (ECHR) implicitly adopted this standard of assessment. The Court made it clear that a crimi-

103 *Informal Expert Paper*, *supra* note 49, p. 14.

104 There are conflicting views on whether Article 20(3) is confined to the irregularities of the proceedings that take place before trial, or extends to those actions that take place after the trial, which in a sense reflect the original States' intention not to hold an accused person responsible. See chapter IV *infra*.

105 *German High Command Trial, Law Reports of Trials of War Criminals*, pp. 29 – 31.

nal investigation has to be serious and effective. For an investigation to be considered effective certain conditions have to be met. Failing to meet these conditions without adequate justification favours a presumption that the State is shielding the person concerned from criminal responsibility.

In *McCann and others v. United Kingdom*, the ECHR stated that "[t]he obligation to protect the right to life under this provision (art. 2), read in conjunction with the State's general duty under Article 1 (art. 2+1) of the Convention to 'secure to everyone within their jurisdiction the rights and freedoms defined in [the] Convention', requires by implication that there should be some form of effective official investigation…".[106] Effective investigation as understood from the prevailing trend in ECHR jurisprudence necessitates a twofold test. The first test, which is commonly applied to cases of violations of Articles 2 and 3 of the Convention, requires that the investigation be "capable of leading to the identification and punishment of those responsible".[107] It is an obligation of "means" rather than "result".[108] The second test, while it varies from case to case depending on the factual circumstances of each, tends to show what the national authorities should or should not do in order to achieve the main goal set out in the first test. Analysis of the relevant ECHR case law reveals that

106 *McCann and Others v. The United kingdom*, Application No. 18984/91, Eur. Ct. H.R., Judgment (Merits and Just Satisfaction) of 27/09/1995, para. 161; *Makaratzis v. Greece*, Application No. 50385/99, Eur. Ct. H.R., Judgment (Merits and Just Satisfaction) of 20/12/2004, para. 73.

107 *Tanis and Others v. Turkey*, Application No. 65899/01, Eur. Ct. H.R., Judgment (Merits and Just Satisfaction) of 02/08/2005, para. 203; *Khashiyev and Akayeva v. Russia*, Application Nos. 57942/00 and 57945/00, Eur. Ct. H.R., Judgment (Merits and Just satisfaction) of 24/02/2005, para. 121; *McKerr v. The United Kingdom*, Application No. 28883/95, Eur. Ct. H.R., Judgment (Merits and Just Satisfaction) of 04/05/2001, para. 113; see also in the context of the application of the 1984 UN Convention Against Torture, *Hajrizi Dzemajl et al. v. Yugoslavia*, CAT, Communication No. 161/2000, UN Doc. CAT/C29/D/161/2000, 02/12/2002, para. 9.4(noting that "a criminal investigation must seek both to determine the nature and circumstances of the alleged acts and to establish the identity of any person who might have been involved therein").

108 *McShane v. The United Kingdom*, Application No. 43290/98, Eur. Ct. H.R., Judgment (Merits and Just Satisfaction) of 28/05/2002, para. 96; *Anguelova v. Bulgaria*, Application No. 38361/97, Eur. Ct. H.R., Judgment (Merits and Just Satisfaction) of 13/06/2002, para. 139; *Avsar v. Turkey*, Application No. 25657/94, Eur. Ct. H.R., Judgment (Merits and Just Satisfaction) of 10/07/2001, para. 394. But see *Villagran Morales et al. v. Guatemala* (The "Street Children" Case), Judgment of 19/11/1999, Inter-Am Ct. H.R. (Ser. C) No. 63 (1999), para. 228 (where the Court seems to have taken a stricter approach than that of the ECHR in terms of interpreting "effective investigation". The Court thus stated, "[i]f we confront the facts in this case with the foregoing, we can observe that Guatemala conducted various judicial proceedings on the facts. However, it is clear that those responsible have not been punished, because they have not been identified or penalized by judicial decisions that have been executed. This consideration alone is enough to conclude that the State has violated Article 1.1 of the Convention, since it has not punished the perpetrators of the corresponding crimes". Thus, it seems that for the IACHR the test is one of means as well as of result.

the Court was always guided by a sort of common element in determining the effectiveness of domestic proceedings.

In the recent *Nachova et al. v. Bulgaria* case, the ECHR Grand Chamber spelt out several conditions on the basis of which domestic criminal proceedings may be deemed effective. These conditions may be summarized as follows:

1. The authorities must take all reasonable steps available to secure the evidence concerning the incident, including eyewitness testimony and forensic evidence.
2. The conclusions of the investigation must be based on thorough, objective and impartial analysis of all the relevant elements.
3. Any deficiency in the investigation which undermines its ability to establish the circumstances of the case or the person responsible is liable to fall foul of the required measure of effectiveness.[109]

When the Court applied these conditions to the circumstances of the case it found that:

1. The investigating authorities ignored some relevant facts including highly technical ones.
2. There was a lack of strict examination of all the material circumstances.
3. The authorities conducted the investigation in an excessively narrow legal framework, ignoring indispensable and obvious investigative steps.[110]

The first three conditions spell out the *standard* positive obligations on the State to secure "genuine" and "effective" proceedings, while the next three criteria are the negative obligations or the omissions that the State should refrain from committing in order to avoid its proceedings from being declared "ineffective". The latter may be subject to change depending on the circumstances of each case. Having applied these rules, the Court concluded that the "authorities ignored those significant facts and, without seeking any proper explanation, merely...terminated the investigation. The investigator and the Prosecutors thus *shielded* Major G. from prosecution"[111] (emphasis added). Reading the last phrase, "without seeking any proper explanation", together with the next sentence, the "investigator and the Prosecutors thus shielded major G. from prosecution", in the light of the overall conditions set out by the Court suggests that the failure of the State to meet any of these conditions or criteria renders domestic proceedings ineffective. When these deficiencies in proceedings are accompanied by a lack of "proper explanation" on the part of the State, they emphasize the indication that the State is acting in bad faith for the purpose of shielding the accused, as the decision suggests. It follows that a lack of "proper explanation" seems to be a significant element in the determination of a State's negative intentions.

Nonetheless, in other decisions, while the element of lack of explanation for the State's actions was applied, the Court did not use the phrase "shield from prosecu-

109 *Nachova and others v. Bulgaria*, Applications Nos. 43577/98 and 43579/98, Eur. Ct. H.R., Judgment of 6/07/2005, para. 113.

110 *Ibid.*, paras. 114 – 117.

111 *Ibid.* para. 116.

tion". Instead it stated that the investigations "had been perfunctory and superficial".[112] Arguably, this is a matter of terminology that leads to the same conclusion. Although in these other decisions the Court relied on the same set of conditions explored above in testing the seriousness of domestic proceedings, the Court listed additional factors reflecting the ineffectiveness of domestic proceedings.

In *Poltoratskiy v. Ukraine*,[113] and *Kuznetsov v. Ukraine*,[114] the ECHR considered that the lack of "any contemporaneous records which could demonstrate step by step the nature of the investigation carried out into the allegations" is another factor which determines the State's bad faith in carrying out a serious investigation. Another factor may be extracted from *Tepe v. Turkey*, where the ECHR found that the failure to involve a "forensic specialist" in cases that involved unnatural death and the decision of the prosecutor to refrain from carrying out a "full medico-legal autopsy", which would have provided valuable information, is another "striking omission", which contributed, *inter alia*, to the view that the investigation was ineffective,[115] and by implication inferred that the State intended to carry out improper proceedings.

Similar standards were applied by the IACHR in its landmark *Velasquez Rodriguez* decision, in the context of the crime of enforced disappearance and the violation of the right to life. In *Velasquez Rodriguez v. Honduras*, as well as in other cases that showed the same trend, the IACHR, like the ECHR, stated that according to Article 1(1) of the Convention the State is "obliged to investigate every situation involving a violation of the rights protected under the Convention".[116] Investigations must be carried out in a "serious manner and not as mere formality preordained to be ineffective".[117] They must have an "objective and be assumed by the State as its own

112 See e.g., *Timurtas v. Turkey*, Application No. 23531/94, Eur. Ct. H.R., Judgment (Merits and Just Satisfaction) of 13/06/2000, paras. 88, 110.

113 *Poltoratskiy v. Ukraine*, Application No. 38812/97, Eur. Ct. H.R., Judgment (Merits and Just Satisfaction) of 29/04/2003, para. 126.

114 *Kuznetsov v. Ukraine*, Application No. 39042/97, Eur. Ct. H.R., Judgment (Merits and Just Satisfaction) of 29/04/2003, para. 106 and also (Partly Dissenting Opinion of Judge Sir Nicolas Bratza) (noting that the majority concluded that the investigation was not effective and did not reflect any serious effort, largely on the basis that the national decision dismissed the complaint as well as on the "lack of any contemporaneous record to demonstrate, step by step, the nature of the investigation carried out by those authorities").

115 *Tepe v. Turkey*, Application No. 27244/95, Eur. Ct. H.R., Judgment (Merits and Just Satisfaction) of 9/05/2003, paras. 181 – 182; See also Section 12 of the United Nations Economic and Social Council Resolution 1989/65 of 24 May 1989 on the Principles on the Effective Prevention and Investigation of Extra-Legal, Arbitrary and Summary Executions).

116 *Velasquez Rodriguez v. Honduras*, Judgment of 29/07/1988, Inter-Am Ct. H.R. (Ser. C) No. 4 (1988), para. 176; *Fairén-Garbi and Solís-Corrales v. Honduras*, Judgment of 15/03/1989, Inter-Am Ct. H.R. (Ser. C) No. 6 (1989), para. 152.

117 *Velasquez Rodriguez v. Honduras*, Judgment of 29/07/1988, Inter-Am Ct. H.R. (Ser. C) No. 4 (1988), para. 177; *Villagran Morales et al. v. Guatemala* (The "Street Children" Case), Judgment of 19/11/1999, Inter-Am Ct. H.R. (Ser. C) No. 63 (1999), para. 226.

legal duty" aiming at an "effective search for the truth" by the government.[118] Thus, the State must "use the means at its disposal...to identify those responsible, [and] to impose the appropriate punishment...".[119] When applying these standards, the Court concluded that domestic proceedings were ineffective, in violation of Article 1(1) of the Convention, for mainly the following reasons:

1. Failure of the organs of Executive Branch to carry out a serious investigation, as there was no investigation of public allegations of a series of disappearances.
2. The investigation carried out in accordance with the Commission's decision was done by the armed forces, the body accused of being involved in the practice.
3. No proceedings were initiated under national law to establish the responsibility of the perpetrators and punish them.
4. Ignoring the Commission's request for information; this was interpreted by the Commission as evidence for the accuracy of the allegations against the State.[120]

Although the Court failed explicitly or directly to state that the deficiency in carrying out effective investigation was the result of the State's intention to "shield" the alleged perpetrators from prosecution, this conclusion may be deduced from the Court's legal reasoning in reaching its decision. In one section of the judgment the Court stated that it was "convinced, and has so found, that the disappearance...was carried out by agents who acted under the cover of public authority".[121] In another section, the Court concluded that "it must be presumed that the [victim's] fate was decided by the authorities who systematically executed detainees without trial and concealed their bodies in order to avoid punishment".[122] Thus, if the perpetrators were public authorities or agents acting under cover of those authorities, it is clear that the State avoided conducting a serious, effective investigation, as explored in the five points above, because the State demanded the "shield[ing]" of those responsible from prosecution. The Court did not seem to make this link, but the argument finds support in the Court's statement that the perpetrators "concealed" the victims' bodies to "avoid punishment". Thus it is evident that the deficiency in investigation was for the purpose of allowing State officials to avoid criminal responsibility.

The same factual circumstances occurred in *Godinez Cruz v. Honduras*, where the IACHR applied identical standards of proof in concluding that domestic proceedings were ineffective.[123] The Court concluded that the State was acting in such a manner for the purpose of shielding the perpetrators from prosecution and punishment, as argued

118 *Ibid.*

119 *Velasquez Rodriguez v. Honduras*, Judgment of 29/07/1988, Inter-Am Ct. H.R. (Ser. C) No. 4 (1988), para. 181 ; *Bámaca- Velásquez v. Guatemala*, Judgment of 25/11/2000, Inter-Am Ct. H.R. (Ser. C) No. 70 (2000), para. 211.

120 *Velasquez Rodriguez v. Honduras*, Judgment of 29/07/1988, Inter-Am Ct. H.R. (Ser. C) No. 4 (1988), paras. 179 – 180.

121 *Ibid.*, para. 182.

122 *Ibid.*, para. 188.

123 *Godinez- Cruz v. Honduras*, Judgment of 20/01/1989, Inter-Am Ct. H.R. (Ser. C) No. 5 (1989), paras. 189 – 190.

previously.[124] It follows that the standards applied in the *Rodriguez* decision and reiterated in the *Cruz* case may also assist in the determination of whether a State is intending seriously to pursue justice or "shield the person from criminal responsibility", in the form of conducting *sham* proceedings. This argument finds support in the language used by the IACHR in *Gangaram-Panday v. Suriname,* where the Court stated:

> [I]n the exercise of its judicial functions and when ascertaining and weighing the evidence necessary to decide the cases before it, the Court may, in certain circumstances, make use of both circumstantial evidence and indications or presumptions on which to base its pronouncements when they lead to consistent conclusions as regards the facts of the case...[125]

Although in *Velasquez Rodriguez* and *Godinez Cruz,* the State's negative intention to shield the perpetrators was not directly declared by the Court and, thus, it was proved through legal analysis, as shown above, this was not the situation in *Myrna Mack Chang,* where the Court pointed out other significant omissions in the domestic criminal process that led it *explicitly* to conclude that the aim was to shield the accused from criminal responsibility. Aside from failing "adequately [to] protect the scene of the crime",[126] the Court determined that acts such as "altering or hiding" the report of the police investigations by substituting the original with another under orders from a State's authority,[127] as proved by the circumstances of this case, "demonstrates that there was an attempt to cover-up those responsible...and this constitutes an obstruction of justice and an inducement for those responsible of the facts to remain in situation of impunity".[128] The Court reached the same conclusion in relation to acts such as the manipulation of the evidence requested by the authorities in charge of the investigation by another organ of the State (Ministry of National Defence).[129]

While these cases are meant to serve as guidelines for the Court's assessment, they are not meant to be exhaustive,[130] as additional standards of proof may arise in other cases depending on the factual circumstances surrounding each. This is precisely mirrored in the variety of scenarios of omissions arising in each case cited above, which led the human rights bodies to rule on each occasion that domestic proceedings were deficient. Yet, the examples set out above tend to show that there are some standards in any criminal investigation that need to be complied with, the absence of which may establish an assumption in favour of States' bad faith.

124 *Ibid.*, paras. 192, 198.

125 *Gangaram-Panday v. Suriname,* Judgment of 21/01/1994, Inter-Am Ct. H.R. (Ser. C) No. 16 (1994), para. 49.

126 *Myrna Mack Chang v. Guatemala,* Judgment of 25/11/2003, Inter-Am Ct. H.R. (Ser. C) No. 101 (2003), paras. 166 – 167.

127 *Ibid.*, paras. 168 – 171.

128 *Ibid.*, paras. 172, 174

129 *Ibid.*, para. 173.

130 See e.g., *Informal Expert Paper, supra* note 49, p. 14, and Annex 4, pp. 28 – 31 (providing with examples, some of which tie in with the above conclusions).

1.2.4 The Criterion of Unjustified Delay

Notwithstanding the above examples, the purpose of "shielding the person from criminal responsibility" may sometimes be difficult for the Prosecutor or the Court to prove. The drafters agreed to add a second criterion, "undue delay", to facilitate the application of the complementarity test.[131] This phrase was originally attached to the intention of the State to bring the accused to justice.[132] As the term was subject to criticism in the Committee of the Whole for "being too low a threshold",[133] it was replaced, upon a proposal from Mexico, by "unjustified delay", as it currently appears under Article 17(2) (b).[134] The word "unjustified" provides the State with the opportunity to explain the reason, if any, for the delay before the Court makes a determination on admissibility, rendering this test more objective.[135] Nonetheless, it cannot be denied that the change has its shortcomings as it increases the burden of proof on the Prosecutor, leaving room for a State acting in bad faith to invoke various invented justifications, rendering the admissibility assessment more difficult to achieve. Such difficulty is exacerbated because the test requires the Court to determine further whether the delay, in the circumstances of the specific case, "is inconsistent with an intent to bring the person concerned to justice".[136]

In order to check whether Article 17(2)(b) has been complied with, three questions have to be answered. First, whether there has been a delay in the proceedings; secondly, whether such a delay was "unjustified"; and, thirdly, whether such an "unjustified delay" was, in the circumstances of the situation or case, accompanied by the intention not "to bring the person concerned to justice". Arguably, the answer to the second question may occasionally be sufficient to answer the third question. If, for instance, the Prosecutor succeeded in proving that there was a delay in the process which was *deliberate or intentional,* and therefore "unjustified", would this not create a presumption that the State did not intend to "bring the person concerned to justice"? This might sometimes be the case, but in some other occasions, an "unjusti-

131 Holmes, *supra* note 4, p. 50. Other terms such as "unconscionable delay" emerged in the 1996 Preparatory Committee discussions. 1996 *Preparatory Committee Report,* Vol. I, *supra* note 16, para. 166.

132 Holmes, *supra* note 4, p. 50.

133 Williams, *supra* note 37, pp. 390 – 391.

134 See Mexico: Revised Proposals Regarding Articles 12 bis, 15, and 108, UN Doc. A/CONF.183/C.1/L.14/REV.1, 24 June 1998. The change proposed by Mexico appeared in Article 15(2) (b) of the Bureau Discussion paper regarding part 2, as well as in the Bureau proposal regarding part 2. See UN Doc. A/CONF.183/C.1/L.53, Art. 15(2) (b), 6 July 1998; UN Doc. A/CONF.183/C.1/L.59, Art. 15(2) (b), 10 July 1998.

135 Holmes, *supra* note 4, p. 54; see also ICC Rule 51. It should be noted, however, that Article 14(3) (c) of the ICCPR talks of "undue delay"; yet, the HRC still requires the State to provide it with explanation of any sort of unwarranted delay. See, *inter alia, Sahadeo v. Guyana,* HRC, Communication No. 728/1996, UN Doc. CCPR/C/73/D/728/1996, 10/11/1996.

136 Rome Statute, Art. 17(2) (b).

fied delay" might take place for different reasons, not necessarily for the purpose of shielding the accused from criminal responsibility.

For example, poor administration of justice or slight negligence or carelessness on the part of the State may be a factor that causes "unjustified delay", while not necessarily reflecting bad faith, unless proven otherwise. To prove that any of these scenarios embodies an element of bad faith, the wording, "which in the circumstances is inconsistent with intent to bring the person concerned to justice", would help. The phrase presumably obliges the Court to inquire into the circumstances of each situation or case separately, in order to determine whether, according to the facts of a given case, the intention was to avoid the accused facing justice. Thus, the underlying meaning of "unjustified delay" under Article 17(2)(b) does not target or cover any sort of delay that has no link or connection with the idea of shielding an accused from facing justice; rather it *directly* affects the domestic proceedings leading to the punishment of the alleged perpetrators. In making an overall evaluation of compliance with Article 17(2) (b), the Court is to be guided by "the principles of due process recognized by international law". The Court "must" also make sure that its conclusions are "consistent with internationally recognized human rights".[137]

Neither the Statute nor the Rules or Regulations of the Court state what may constitute a delay within the meaning of Article 17(2) (b). Nor do they spell out what may constitute a "justified" or "unjustified" delay. Even the main literature on the subject falls short of any feasible explanation.[138] Major human rights instruments tend to guarantee a trial within a "reasonable time"[139] and without "undue delay".[140] This "underlines the importance of rendering justice without delays which might jeopardise

137 Rome Statute, Art. 21 (3).

138 See *inter alia*, Antonio Cassese, *International Criminal Law* (Oxford: Oxford University Press, 2003), p. 352 [hereinafter ICL]; M. Cherif Bassiouni, *Introduction to International Criminal Law* (Ardsley, New York: Transnational Publishers, 2003), p. 518 ; Williams, *supra* note 37, pp. 393 – 394; Sadat, *supra* note 38, p. 123; Schabas, *supra* note 6, pp. 85 – 89; Arbour, Bergsmo, *supra* note 62, p. 131; Solera, *supra* note 3, p. 166.

139 European Convention for the Protection of Human Rights and Fundamental Freedoms (ERCHR), signed 4 Nov. 1950, entered into force 3 Sept. 1953, 213 UNTS 221, ETS 5, Arts. 5(3), 6 (1); American Convention on Human Rights (Pact of San José) (ACHR), signed 22 Nov. 1969, entered into force 18 July 1978, OASTS 36, O.A.S. Off. Rec. OEA/Ser.L/V/11.23, doc.21, rev. 6 (1979), Arts. 7(5), 8 (1). This term appears in Article 5(3) as well as Article 6(1). Although the periods may overlap, Article 6(1) is broader in scope as it covers delays in the entire proceedings in relation to all parties. Thus, this section is confined to looking at issues relating to Article 6(1). For the distinction between the protection of Articles 5(3) and 6 (1) see *Matznetter v. Austria*, Application No. 2178/64, Eur. Ct. H.R., Judgment (Merits) of 10/11/1969, para. 12; *Stögmüller v. Austria*, Application No. 1602/62, Eur. Ct. H.R., Judgment (Merits) of 10/11/1969, para. 5.

140 International Covenant on Civil and Political Rights (ICCPR), adopted 16 Dec. 1966, entered into force 23 March 1976, G.A. Res. 2200A (XXI), UN Doc. A/6316 (1966), 999UNTS 171, Arts. 9(3), 14(3) (c). While Article 14(3) (c) talks about trial "without undue delay". Article 9(3) says "trial within a reasonable time".

its effectiveness and credibility".[141] They are also designed to ensure that an accused does not have to "lie under a charge for too long"[142] in a "state of uncertainty about his fate".[143] When reading the cases decided by the bodies monitoring the application of these instruments, one may observe that the protection underlying the right is not triggered until "an individual is subject to a 'charge'".

When compared to the language found in Article 17(2) (b) of the ICC Statute, it seems clear that the provision of the Statute is broader in application and reach. Under the ICC Statute, an investigation evolves into a *situation vis-à-vis* a *case*, which means that there are no identifiable suspects for the purpose of prosecution for a certain phase and period of the investigation. It follows that the evaluation of the speed or delay resulting from the domestic process would begin during the situation phase, which is earlier than is required under the human rights instruments, namely to have an identified person who is "subject to a charge", or arrest, or being officially notified that he will be prosecuted.[144] Moreover, Article 17(2) (b) is concerned with a broader pattern of events, in the sense that it is not designed to address delays that touch upon the rights of the accused *stricto sensu*, but rather to address delays relating to the *entire* criminal process within the general scheme of events; that is, a delay which directly impacts on the idea of bringing an accused to justice.

Yet, in theory, an unjustified delay caused by the relevant authorities for the purpose of sheltering an accused from responsibility might still, from a human rights law perspective, violate the rights of the accused, despite such delay working in his or her favour. The reference to the "principles of due process" in the chapeau of Article 17(2) clearly directs the Prosecutor to take into account in his overall assessment the element of the rights of the accused. But this could not be the decisive factor in determining admissibility, for the reasons explained above.

In any event, the above argument does not lead to a conclusion that the standards designed by the human rights bodies explored below are not applicable by analogy to the ICC process. Rather, it tends to show that the criterion of "unjustified delay",

141 *H. v. France*, Application No. 10073/82, Eur. Ct. H.R., Judgment (Merits and Just Satisfaction) of 24/10/1989, para. 58.

142 *Wemhoff v. Germany*, Application No. 2122/64, Eur. Ct. H.R., Judgment (Merits and Just Satisfaction) of 27/06/1968, para. 18.

143 *Stögmüller v. Austria*, Application No. 1602/62, Eur. Ct. H.R., Judgment (Merits) of 10/11/1969, para. 5.

144 *Eckle v. Germany*, Application No. 8130/78, Eur. Ct. H.R., Judgment (Merits) of 15/07/1982, para. 73; *Deweer v. Belgium*, Application No. 6903/75, Eur. Ct. H.R., Judgment (Merits and Just Satisfaction) of 27/02/1980, para. 42; *Wemhoff v. Germany*, Application No. 2122/64, Eur. Ct. H.R., Judgment (Merits and Just Satisfaction) of 27/06/1968, para. 19. The IACHR considers the starting point for examining domestic proceedings is the arrest of the accused. See *Suárez –Rosero v. Ecuador*, Judgment of 12/11/1997, Inter-Am Ct. H.R. (Ser. C) No. 35 (1997), para. 70. This is the period that begins in the application of Article 6(1) proceedings. Yet, the period in relation to Article 5(3) of the Convention and its counterparts in the other human rights instruments begins on the day the accused is taken into custody or detention. See, *inter alia*, *Labita v. Italy* Application No. 26772/95, Eur. Ct. H.R., Judgment (Merits and Just Satisfaction) of 6/04/2000, paras. 145, 147.

in the context of the ICC, serves a wider goal. It also follows that there are phases in the criminal process that require assessment, which might have been outside the scope of the jurisprudence of these human rights bodies when they examined delays in domestic proceedings. Yet, the standards applied by these bodies may still serve as guidelines for the ICC in assessing an entire criminal process.

The question of what may constitute a "delay" is not an issue that can be determined according to strict time limits.[145] As will be seen in the next few pages, a violation of the principle of reasonableness of time varies from one case to another, depending on the circumstances of each case. Indeed, in the early *König v. Germany* case, an authority on the issue at hand, the ECHR explicitly stated that "the reasonableness of the duration of proceedings covered by Article 6 para. 1 (art. 6-1) of the Convention [in civil as well as in criminal matters] must be assessed in each case according to its circumstances".[146] The Court has continued to follow the same approach even in its most recent decisions.[147]

This approach is also consistent with the practice of the Human Rights Committee (HRC). In the recent *Ratiani v. Georgia* case, the HRC declared that "what constitutes "undue delay" depends on the circumstances of each case".[148] This cannot be "translated into a fixed number of days, months or years", stated ICTR Trial Chamber III in *Prosecutor v. Rwamakuba*.[149] Still the assessment of the duration of a criminal process was always done within certain parameters, according to a combined set of conditions initially elaborated on by the human rights bodies.

Again in *König v. Germany*, the ECHR stated when inquiring into the "reasonableness" of time spent in a criminal process that due regard should be given to three main criteria: 1) the complexity of the case; 2) the applicant's conduct; and 3) the manner "in which the matter was dealt with by the judicial authorities".[150] In drafting these conditions, the Court was guided by the factual circumstances of the earlier

145 DJ Harris, M O'Boyle and C Warbrick, *Law of the European Convention on Human Rights* (London, Dublin, Edinburgh: Butterworths, 1995), p. 223.

146 *König v. Germany*, Application No. 6232/73, Eur. Ct. H.R., Judgment (Merits) of 28/06/1978, para. 99.

147 See, *inter alia*, *Chyb v. Poland*, Application No. 20838/02, Eur. Ct. H.R., Judgment (Merits and Just Satisfaction) of 22/08/2006, para. 35; *Palka v. Poland*, Application No. 49176/99, Eur. Ct. H.R., Judgment (Merits and Just Satisfaction) of 11/10/2005, para. 28.

148 *Ratiani v. Georgia*, HRC, Communication No. 975/2001, UN Doc. CCPR/C/84/D/975/2001, 04/08/2005, para. 10.7.

149 *Prosecutor v. André Rwamakuba*, Case No. ICTR-98-44C-PT, *Decision on Defence Motion for Stay of Proceedings Article 20 of the Statute*, 3/06/ 2005, para. 26.

150 *König v. Germany*, Application No. 6232/73, Eur. Ct. H.R., Judgment (Merits) of 28/06/1978, para. 99.

Neuimeister[151] and *Ringeisen v. Austria* [152] cases, decided in 1968 and 1971 respectively. Currently these are still the standard conditions applied by the ECHR.[153]

The IACHR applies the same criteria in determining whether delays were justified or unjustified in accordance with Article 8(1) of the American Convention on Human Rights. In *Genie Lacayo*, the Court, admitting the difficulty in defining the notion of "reasonable time", reflected in Article 8(1) of the Convention, argued that since the term corresponds to that found in Article 6(1) of the European Convention on Human Rights, the conditions applied by the ECHR are similarly applicable.[154] Similarly, in the recent case of *Prosecutor v. Mugiraneza*, the ICTR Appeals Chamber seems to have followed the same path as the ECHR, without explicitly acknowledging the fact, when it concluded that in determining whether there has been a violation of the right to be tried without undue delay, "it is necessary to consider", *inter alia*, certain factors that are *in fact* almost identical to those applied by the ECHR. These factors are: "1) The length of the delay; 2) The complexity of the proceedings, such as the number of charges, the number of accused, the number of witnesses, the volume of evidence, the complexity of facts and law; 3) The conduct of the parties; 4) The conduct of the relevant authorities; and 5) The prejudice to the accused if any".[155]

But, in *X v. The Federal Republic of Germany*, a unique decision dating back to 1976, the government initiated criminal proceedings against the applicant on suspicion of him having been involved in committing war crimes on a large scale against the Jews during the Nazi regime. The applicant complained of the length of the proceedings,

151 *Neumeister v. Austria*, Application No. 1936/63, Eur. Ct. H.R., Judgment (Merits) of 27/06/1968.

152 *Ringeisen v. Austria*, Application No. 2614/65, Eur. Ct. H.R., Judgment (Merits) of 16/07/1971.

153 With the exception that the phrase "judicial authorities" appearing in the third condition was replaced by the broader term "relevant authorities" to cover acts or omissions attributed to any responsible organ of the State. Also in some decisions a related element was added – namely "the importance of what is at stake for the applicant in litigation". See, *inter alia*, *Majewski v. Poland*, Eur. Ct. H.R., Judgment (Merits and Just Satisfaction) of 11/10/2005, para. 38. But this element has no significant application in the context of this study, as it is confined to civil rights before administrative courts. On this point see *Buchholz v. Germany*, Application No. 7759/77, Eur. Ct. H.R., Judgment (Merits) of 6/05/1981, para. 49.

154 *Genie- Lacayo v. Nicaragua*, Judgment of 29/ 01/1997, Inter-Am Ct. H.R. (Ser. C) No. 30 (1997), para. 77; and the view in *Suárez –Rosero v. Ecuador*, Judgment of 12/11/1997, Inter-Am Ct. H.R. (Ser. C) No. 35 (1997), para. 72.

155 *Prosecutor v. Prosper Mugiraneza*, Case No. ICTR-99-50-AR73, *Decision on Prosper Mugiraneza's Interlocutory Appeal from Trial Chamber II Decision of 2 October 2003 Denying the Motion to Dismiss the Indictment, Demand Speedy Trial and for Appropriate Relief*, 27/02/2004. As will be seen in the following pages the additional factors invoked by the Tribunal are also part of the assessment. Perhaps the factor of the "prejudice to the accused if any", which is equivalent to the factor of "the importance of what at stake", is not applied in the context of the European Court of Human Rights except in civil applications. See *supra* note 151.

which began in April 1965 and lasted for a period of more than 11 years. The European Commission of Human Rights concluded that, having regard to the exceptional nature of these crimes as well as the fact that the international community "requires the competent authorities to investigate and prosecute" them, regardless of the lapse of time since the commission of the acts, the "criteria determining the reasonableness of the length of the ordinary criminal proceedings are not applicable". Accordingly, there was no violation of Article 6(1) of the Convention.[156]

The Commission did not seem to completely rule out such a possibility, as it proceeded by saying "assuming, however, that the criteria developed in the case-law of the Commission and the Court in relation to the length of ordinary criminal proceedings were to be applied, the Commission's finding would be no different".[157] The decision suggests that the Commission was willing to compromise fair trial rights for the sake of the effective prosecution of war crimes. It also suggests that the Commission had not clearly determined, as stated above, whether the ordinary conditions should/should not apply as asserted, since it finally applied them. As some scholars have correctly argued, "it is hard to understand why special criteria should apply".[158] Assuming that the Commission's opinion at the time was interpreted strictly, as excluding the application of the ordinary rules, this was a single decision with no *precedential* value.

Indeed when the Commission was faced with a similar application later in *X. v. The Netherlands*, where the applicant was charged with crimes against humanity and complained of the length of proceedings, which lasted for five years, the Commission applied the three ordinary criteria, and yet found that the delay was not excessive, given all the circumstances of the case.[159] Moreover, the fact that the Appeals Chamber of the ICTR invoked the same standards as applied by the ECHR in cases similar in nature and magnitude to those dealt with before the ICC reinforces the argument that those conditions qualify to be applied in the context of the ICC.[160] The chapeau of Article 17(2), read in light of Article 21(3) of the Rome Statute, compels the Court to deliver decisions that are consonant with international human rights standards

156 *X v. The Federal Republic of Germany*, Application No. 6946/75, Eur. Comm. H.R., Decision of 6/07/1976 on the Admissibility of the Application, pp. 114 – 116.

157 *Ibid.*, p. 116.

158 P. van Dijk and G.J.H. van Hoof, *Theory and Practice of the European Convention on Human Rights*, Third Edition (The Hague-London-Boston: Kluwer Law International, 1998), p. 450.

159 *X v. The Netherlands*, Application No. 9433/81, Eur. Comm. H.R., Decision of 11/12/1981 on the Admissibility of the Application, pp. 233 – 242.

160 One may note also that the Statute requires that a hearing to confirm the charges must be held within a "reasonable time". Also, in its Court Capacity Model, there are assessments of the length of trial, projecting an average trial to last slightly less than three years from arrest until final judgment, apportioning 3 months for the confirmation of charges, 6 months for disclosure and preparation for trial, 15 months for the trial itself and finally 9 months for the appeal. Actually, the Court never met such deadlines in the *Lubanga* case. See *Report on the Court Capacity Model*, Document ICC-ASP/5/10, para. 23.

elaborated pursuant to the jurisprudence of the relevant human rights institutions. Should these standards develop, the Court's assessment of these issues should also change to ensure full harmony.

1.2.4.1 Complexity of the Case

Several reasons may render a case complex for the purposes of such a determination, yet, depending on the other two criteria and the overall factual circumstances, the Court may/may not deem the delay justified.[161] These may include, *inter alia,* a large amount of documentary evidence,[162] the number of suspects involved,[163] the size and complexity of the acts committed[164] or the nature of the charges,[165] the number of witnesses,[166] the possibility of reaching these witnesses[167] in cases relying on mutual legal assistance requesting investigative steps to be carried out abroad or in differ-

---

161 See e.g., *Ferrantelli and Santangelo v. Italy* (1), Application No. 19874/92, Eur. Ct. H.R., Judgment (Merits and Just Satisfaction) of 7/08/1996, para. 42 (where the Court, despite thinking the case complex when "examined as a whole", reached the conclusion that the time requirement in Article 6(1) had not been complied with because, "and this is the decisive consideration, the applicants were not convicted with final effect until sixteen years after the events"); *Hagert v. Finland,* Application No. 14724/02, Eur. Ct. H.R., Judgment (Merits and Just Satisfaction) of 17/01/2006, paras. 29, 36 (where the Court admitted that despite the complexity of the case the delays were unreasonable when weighed with other circumstances).

162 See e.g., the recent *Hagert v. Finland* , Application No. 14724/02, Eur. Ct. H.R., Judgment (Merits and Just Satisfaction) of 17/01/2006, para. 29. But see the early case of *Eckle v. Germany,* Application No. (8130/78), Eur. Ct. H.R., Judgment (Merits) of 15/07/1982, paras. 81, 85 – 87 (where the Court found that in the circumstances of the case as a whole, the delay was excessive and unjustified, despite the large amount of evidentiary material); and in the context of the IACHR *Genie- Lacayo v. Nicaragua,* Judgment of 29/01/1997, Inter-Am Ct. H.R. (Ser. C) No. 30 (1997), paras. 69, 78 (noting that although the case was complex, due to "very extensive" investigations and "evidence copious" when weighed in light of the entire circumstances, a period of 5 years since the date when an order to initiate proceedings was issued was deemed lengthy and violated Article 8(1) of the Convention; *Suárez –Rosero v. Ecuador,* Judgment of 12/11/1997, Inter-Am Ct. H.R. (Ser. C) No. 35 (1997), para. 73(having regard to the three conditions lead down by the ECHR in light of the circumstances of the case, the Court still found that a period of more than 50 months "far exceeds the reasonable time contemplated in the American Convention").

163 *Neumeister v. Austria,* Application No. 1936/63, Eur. Ct. H.R., Judgment (Merits) of 27/06/1968, para. 20.

164 *Ibid.*

165 *Calleja v. Malta,* Application No. 75274/01, Eur. Ct. H.R., Judgment (Merits and Just Satisfaction) of 7/04/2005, para. 128.

166 *Wemhoff v. Germany,* Application No. 2122/64, Eur. Ct. H.R., Judgment (Merits and Just Satisfaction) of 27/06/1968, para. 20 (opinion of the Commission shared by the Court).

167 *Neumeister v. Austria,* Application No. 1936/63, Eur. Ct. H.R., Judgment (Merits) of 27/06/1968, para. 20.

ent countries,[168] the need to obtain expert evidence,[169] and technical difficulties in general.[170]

1.2.4.2 The Conduct of the Applicant

Sometimes delay in proceedings may be attributable to the conduct of the applicant or the victim. If this is so, the State takes no responsibility. Delays such as those resulting in failure to appear in court when summoned, adjournment of hearings upon the applicant's request,[171] refusing to appoint a defence lawyer,[172] or filing a number of preliminary pleas requesting the examination of a large number of witnesses[173] are all acts that fall within the responsibility of the applicant when determining the length of the delay in the proceedings. Such behaviour may contribute to delay in domestic proceedings, and, thus, it is not "capable of being attributed to the respondent State", which is to be considered when determining whether the "proceedings exceeded a reasonable time".[174] Indeed in *Klamecki v. Poland*, the Court considered that the applicant's attitude in causing the adjournment of proceedings in a certain number of hearings, his failure to comply with the Court's summons, changing the lawyers representing him during the different stages of the proceedings, and challenging the judges of the Court by ill-founded applications to be "delaying tactics", prompting it to find no violation under the requirement of "a reasonable time" within the meaning of Article 6(1) of the Convention.[175]

168 *Ibid*; see also *Wemhoff v. Germany*, Application No. 2122/64, Eur. Ct. H.R., Judgment (Merits and Just Satisfaction) of 27/06/1968, para. 20 (opinion of the Commission shared by the Court).

169 *Krasuki v. Poland*, Application No. 61444/00, Eur. Ct. H.R., Judgment (Merits) of 14/06/2005, para. 56.

170 See e.g., but in a non-criminal context *Papachelas v. Greece*, Application No. 31423/96, Eur. Ct. H.R., Judgment (Merits and Just Satisfaction) of 25/03/1999, para. 38. Arguably, the idea of "technical difficulties", if accepted as a matter of principle, then could be applied in cases involving criminal issues as well.

171 *Rylski v. Poland*, Application No. 24706/02, Eur. Ct. H.R., Judgment (Merits) of 4/07/2006, para. 76. But see *Zappia v. Italy* (1), Application No. 24295/94, Eur. Ct. H.R., Judgment (Merits and Just satisfaction) of 26/09/1996, para. 25 (where the Court noted that although the applicants were responsible for three adjournments, "their conduct alone does not explain the length of the proceedings complained of", since the national authorities were responsible for no less than 13 adjournment).

172 *Corigliano v. Italy*, Application No. 8304/78, Eur. Ct. H.R., Judgment (Merits and Just Satisfaction) of 10/12/1982, paras. 40, 42.

173 *Calleja v. Malta*, Application No. 75274/01, Eur. Ct. H.R., Judgment (Merits and Just Satisfaction) of 7/04/2005, para. 129.

174 *Ibid.*, para. 132; *Eckle v. Germany*, Application No. (8130/78), Eur. Ct. H.R., Judgment (Merits) of 15/07/1982, para. 82.

175 *Klamecki v. Poland* , Application No. 25415/94, Eur. Ct. H.R., Judgment (Merits) of 28/03/2002, paras. 92 – 94.

1.2.4.3 The Conduct of the Relevant Authorities

In other situations, the ECHR found that the responsibility for the delay lay with the State, because certain acts or omissions that were committed were attributable to its relevant authorities. Arguably, this is to be regarded as the most relevant condition in the context of Article 17(2) (b) of the Statute, as it has a direct effect on its satisfaction. Article 17 in general distributes and organizes the rights and duties between the State concerned on the one hand and the ICC on the other. Thus, it establishes a direct relationship between the State in question and the Court. Article 17(2) (b) is part of this relationship. It follows that any deficiency on the part of the State's relevant organs that caused delays in the domestic criminal process has direct implications on the triggering of this provision.

In *Eckle v. Germany*, the ECHR pointed out that among the unacceptable periods of delay referable to the conduct of the domestic authorities was a period of 15 months required to open a formal preliminary investigation calculated from the date of lodging the complaint.[176] Also a period of almost 11 months to serve on the applicant the first judgment of the Regional Court, calculated from the date of its delivery, on the ground of the vast number of documents to be analysed for the purpose of drafting the decision, was considered unjustified.[177] Even the period of three years required to review a point of law in relation to the Regional Court's decision was also deemed lengthy.[178]

On this last point, the IACHR took a more stringent approach in *Genie Lacayo*, when considering the Nicaraguan Supreme Court of Justice's delay in ruling on an application for judicial review for a period of two years. Although the case was apparently more complex than *Eckle v. Germany*, as it involved a violation of the right to life and sophisticated factual circumstances, the IACHR still found a two-year delay unacceptable. The Court stated that having regard to the degree of complexity of the case under consideration, as well as "the excuses, impediments and substitution of judges of the Supreme Court of Justice, the two years that have elapsed since the application for judicial review was admitted is not reasonable; this Tribunal therefore deems it to violate Article 8(1) of the Convention".[179]

The IACHR treated the matter completely different in *Cantos v. Argentina*, where the Court found that a delay of 10 years since the applicant had filed his complaint with the Supreme Court was justified. The Court observed that this prolonged period, in principle, "violated the reasonable time" requirement. However, having given careful consideration to the behaviour of the applicant against that of the State, the Court found that it could not attribute the violation of the reasonable time requirement to the State. In considering, *inter alia*, the complexity of the case and the applicant's failure to take action to move the case forward, the Court concluded that "the

176 *Eckle v. Germany*, Application No. 8130/78, Eur. Ct. H.R., Judgment (Merits) of 15/07/1982, paras. 74, 83 – 84.

177 *Ibid.*, para. 27, 83 – 84.

178 *Ibid.*, paras. 29 – 33, 84.

179 *Genie- Lacayo v. Nicaragua*, Judgment of 29/01/1997, Inter-Am Ct. H.R. (Ser. C) No. 30 (1997), para. 80.

overall duration of the litigious proceedings would not be significant enough for a finding that the articles that protect access to the courts and judicial guarantees have been violated".[180]

In *Pélissier and Sassi v. France*, the ECHR believed that a 15-month period of inactivity between the transmission of the file of the investigation by the investigating judge to the public prosecutor and the committing of the applicants for trial before the Criminal Court was excessive and "unjustified".[181] The ECHR reacted in a similar manner in *Abdoella v. The Netherlands* in relation to more than 10 months' delay between the sending and receiving of documents of a case decided by The Hague Court of Appeal to the Supreme Court.[182]

Again, in *Pélissier and Sassi v. France*, 11 months of inactivity between the lodging of appeals by one of the applicants and the public prosecutor and the first hearing by the Court of Appeal was also deemed unsatisfactory.[183] The Court showed dissatisfaction when stated that it "considers in particular that the taking of procedural steps as basic and commonplace as serving summonses to appear, in proceedings in which the number of parties cannot be said to have been unusually high, cannot explain such a lengthy delay".[184]

In many instances the national authorities invoke the argument of "excessive case load" as an excuse for possible delays. But even such an argument failed as a legal justification for any sort of prolonged delay. As the ECHR stated in *Philis v. Greece*, the "Government excessive caseload…and organizational difficulties it had encountered" would not absolve the respondent State from its duty under the Convention. As the Court repeatedly held, "article 6(1) imposes on the Contracting States the duty to organise their national legal systems in a manner that permits them to meet each of its requirements including to hear cases within a reasonable time".[185]

It is clear that determining whether the length of proceedings in a specific case was justified depends on an evaluation of the three conditions explored above as-

180 *Cantos v. Argentina*, Judgment of 28/11/2002, Inter-Am Ct. H.R. (Ser. C) No. 97 (2002), para. 56.

181 *Pélissier and Sassi v. France*, Application No. 25444/94, Eur. Ct. H.R., Judgment (Merits and Just Satisfaction) of 25/03/1999, paras. 25 – 26, 73.

182 *Abdoella v. The Netherlands*, Application No. 12728/87, Eur. Ct. H.R., Judgment (Merits and Just Satisfaction) of 25/11/1992, para. 23.

183 *Pélissier and Sassi v. France*, Application No. 25444/94, Eur. Ct. H.R., Judgment (Merits and Just Satisfaction) of 25/03/1999, paras. 29 – 30, 73.

184 *Ibid.*, para. 73. It is not clear whether such delay would have been justified, as the Court has mentioned, if "the number of parties were high". Other scenarios of unacceptable delay attributable to the judicial authorities are found in *Di Pede v. Italy*, Application No. 15797/89, Eur. Ct. H.R., Judgment (Merits and Just Satisfaction) of 26/09/1996, paras. 30 – 31.

185 *Philis v. Greece* (no. 2) (1), Application No. 19773/92, Eur. Ct. H.R., Judgment (Merits and Just Satisfaction) of 27/06/1997, para. 40; *Abdoella v. The Netherlands*, Application No. 12728/87, Eur. Ct. H.R., Judgment (Merits and Just Satisfaction) of 25/11/1992, para. 24.

sessed in the light of the overall circumstances of each case.[186] The *Cantos* decision before the IACHR is a good example demonstrating that despite the excessive delay that took place before the Argentinean Supreme Court, which would normally violate the principle of reasonableness, the special circumstances of the case (including the criteria of complexity and conduct of the applicant and the relevant authority) weighed against a finding of excessive duration of the domestic proceedings. It follows that a determination of the reasonableness of time does not rely solely on the time spent, but rather on the duration examined in the light of all the circumstances of a given case.

But, one may also think of the extraordinary delays occurring in the context of the practice of the *ad hoc* tribunals. Slobodan Milošević was indicted for his role in a joint criminal enterprise aimed at the "forcible removal of the majority of the Croat and other non-Serb population from the approximately one-third of the territory of the Republic of Croatia that he planned to become part of a new-Serb-dominated state".[187] These events took place in late 1991 and early 1992. Yet, the indictment was not issued until the end of 2001.[188] In the *Butare* case before the ICTR, which began in 2001 and is expected to finish in 2007, its six defendants have been in custody since 1996 and 1997.[189] Also, in *Bagosora*, the defendant was detained in 1997 at the Detention Facility in Arusha, but his actual trial did not begin until April 2002.[190] One scholar noticed that it had not been "considered unreasonable that complex trials for the serious offences being prosecuted by the international tribunals can take many years to prepare and to complete".[191]

In any event, when applying the conditions obtained from the decisions explored above to the context of the ICC, the three conditions adopted by the ECHR may serve as guidelines for the Court that may be subject to even further elaboration by the Office of the Prosecutor (OTP), if necessary.[192] But, as mentioned earlier, these

186 Even the Human Rights Committee seems implicitly to adhere to these standards in its jurisprudence, yet in a non-systematic manner. See e.g., *Rajapakse et al. v. Sri Lanka*, HRC, Communication No. 1250/2004, UN Doc. CCPR/C/87/D/1250/2004, 5/09/2006, paras. 6.1, 9.4; *Ratiani v. Georgia*, HRC, Communication No.975/2001, 04/08/2005, UN Doc. CCPR/C/84/D/975/2001, 04/08/2005, para. 10.7; *Muñoz v. Spain*, HRC, Communication No. 1006/2001, UN Doc. CCPR/C/79/D/1006/2001, 4/02/2004, paras. 6.6, 7.1; *Pratt and Morgan v. Jamaica*, HRC, Communication Nos. 210/1986 and 225/1987, UN Doc. CCPR/C/35/D/210/1986, 7/04/1989, paras. 13.3,13.4.

187 *Prosecutor v. Slobodan Milošević*, Case No. (IT-01-50-I), *Indictment*, 8/10/2001.

188 William A. Schabas, *The UN International Criminal Tribunals: The Former Yugoslavia, Rwanda and Sierra Leone* (Cambridge: Cambridge University Press, 2006), p. 521 n. 100.

189 See e.g., *Prosecutor v. Joseph Kanyabashi*, Case No. (ICTR-96-15-T), *Decision on the Defence Motion on Jurisdiction*, 18/06/1997; *Minutes of Proceedings*, Case No. (ICTR-98-42-T), Commencement of Trial- Trial Day 1, 12 June 2001.

190 See *Minutes of Proceedings*, Case No. (ICTR-98-41-I), Trial Day 1, 2 April 2002.

191 Schabas, *supra* note 188, p. 521.

192 While the periods of delay examined in the cases cited above should provide the Court with some guidance in relation to similar scenarios, they are not often meant to be ap-

conditions have limited application to a certain period of the criminal proceedings, which run only from the moment the person is arrested until a decision becomes final.[193] An amnesty decision, for example, would also meet the finality requirement.[194] Furthermore, in the case of a dismissal, finality of the decision is still required.[195] This leaves the problem posed at the beginning of this section, namely that the assessment of domestic proceedings within the meaning of the ICC has a broader dimension that is triggered at an early stage, with the initiation of an investigation into a situation.

The complexity of the case (withn the context of a situation) and the acts of the relevant domestic authorities, perhaps with some necessary elaboration, may still be valid for testing a situation stage. Furthermore, actions of the relevant authorities, when examined in the light of the facts of a situation or case, would be useful in the determination of the last requirement of Article 17(2)(b), namely that, in the circumstances of the specific situation or case, the delay was "inconsistent with an intent to bring the person concerned to justice". To put it differently, the negative acts or omissions of the relevant authorities may or may not be for the purpose of shielding the accused from criminal responsibility. In order to determine such a purpose, this condition should be evaluated in the light of all the factual circumstances of the situation or case.

---

plied in the abstract as the assessment will also depend to a great extent on the overall factual circumstances of each case.

193 *Neumeister v. Austria*, Application No. 1936/63, Eur. Ct. H.R., Judgment (Merits) of 27/06/1968, para. 19; *König v. Germany*, Application No. 6232/73, Eur. Ct. H.R., Judgment (Merits) of 28/06/1978, para. 98; *Eckle v. Germany*, Application No. 8130/78, Eur. Ct. H.R., Judgment (Merits) of 15/07/1982, para. 76; For recent application see *Pélissier and Sassi v. France*, Application No. 25444/94, Eur. Ct. H.R., Judgment (Merits and Just Satisfaction) of 25/03/1999, para. 66; *La Palmeras v. Columbia*, Judgment of 6/12/2001, Inter-Am Ct. H.R. (Ser. C) No. 90 (2001), para. 64 ; *Suárez–Rosero v. Ecuador*, Judgment of 12/11/1997, Inter-Am Ct. H.R. (Ser. C) No. 35 (1997), para. 71. In this context, finality may also be reached through the expiry of the time-limit for appeal or cassation. See *Angelucci v. Italy*, Application No. 12666/87, Eur. Ct. H.R., Judgment (Merits and Just Satisfaction) of 19/02/1991, para. 13 (Merits). But the periods to be taken into consideration in the case of Articles 5(3) of the European Convention on Human Rights, 7(5) of the ACHR, and 9(3) of the ICCPR ends by "the day on which the charge is determined, even if only by a court of first instance". See, *inter alia*, *Wemhoff v. Germany*, Application No. 2122/64, Eur. Ct. H.R., Judgment (Merits and Just Satisfaction) of 27/06/1968, para. 9; *Matwiejczuk v. Poland*, Application No. 37641/97, Eur. Ct. H.R., Judgment (Merits and Just Satisfaction) of 2/12/2003, para. 70.

194 *Pugliese v. Italy* (No. 1), Application No. 11840/85, Eur. Ct. H.R., Judgment (Merits and Just Satisfaction) of 19/02/1991, paras. 23(facts), 14 (Merits) (noting that the period for determination of the length of proceedings ended when the Rieti Court pronounced an amnesty pursuant to Presidential Decree No. 865 of 16/12/1986).

195 *Angelucci v. Italy*, Application No. 12666/87, Eur. Ct. H.R., Judgment (Merits and Just Satisfaction) of 19/02/1991, para. 13 (Mertis); Manfred Nowak, *U.N. Covenant on Civil and Political Rights: CCPR Commentary*, 2nd revised edition (Kehl/Strasbourg/Arlington: N.P. Engel Publisher, 2005), p. 334.

Perhaps some of the scenarios examined under Article 17(1) (a) ("the concept of shielding") when attached to unjustified delays, such as those examined above, would be useful in proving the State's bad intentions. In other words, the Prosecutor may succeed in proving that the "unjustified delay" has taken place *deliberately* or *intentionally* by means of related factual circumstances such as those explored under the concept of shielding the person from criminal responsibility. While the scenarios explored under this concept may assist in proving that the "unjustified delay" was "inconsistent with an intent to bring the person concerned to justice", an "unjustified delay" may sometimes, on its own, help to verify the element of shielding a person in accordance with Article 17(2) (a), if the delay was found to be *deliberate.* It follows that these conditions are designed to function hand in hand, supporting one another to prove a common purpose – namely to check whether the State is evading justice.

Additional guidance on testing the duration of proceedings in the context of a situation may be also obtained by analogy from the recent *Report* submitted by the OTP,[196] pursuant to Pre-Trial Chamber's III request for information concerning the OTP's delay in determining whether to initiate an investigation into the Central African Republic.[197] The office relied on several factors that implicitly explain the delay which may be summarized as follows: 1) availability of the information; 2) nature and scale of the crimes; 3) the existence of national responses in respect of alleged crimes; and 4) the deteriorating security situation in northern areas making access to information increasingly difficult.[198] While these factors were confined to explaining the OTP's delay in initiating an investigation into the situation of the Central African Republic, they may equally apply in the assessment of the duration of domestic proceedings. All four summarized factors come under the umbrella of "complexity of the situation or case".[199] Although the OTP relied on further elements, such as admis-

196 *Prosecution's Report Pursuant to Pre-Trial Chamber III's 30 November 2006 Decision Requesting Information on the Status of the Preliminary Examination of the Situation in the Central African Republic,* No.: ICC-01/05-7, 15/12/2006 [hereinafter Prosecution's Report in CAR].

197 *Decision Requesting Information on the Status of the Preliminary Examination of the Situation in the Central African Republic,* No.: ICC-01/05-6, 30/11/2006.

198 *Prosecution's Report in CAR, supra* note 196, paras. 8 – 9.

199 Noticeably, in its 30 November decision, Pre-Trial Chamber III explicitly stated that the complexity of the situation at hand did not justify a delay in assessing whether to initiate an investigation within a reasonable time: "the preliminary examination of a situation pursuant to Article 53(1) of the Statute and rule 104 of the Rules must be completed within a reasonable time from the reception of a referral by a State Party under articles 13(a) and (14) of the Statute, regardless of its complexity". See *Decision Requesting Information on the Status of the Preliminary Examination of the Situation in the Central African Republic,* No.: ICC-01/05-6, 30/11/2006, p. 4. Still, the OTP relied on the factor of complexity of the situation in his submission. But what may constitute a reasonable delay is a question the Pre-Trial Chamber has failed to answer. The answer, however, may be deduced from the entire decision in the sense that a delay that concurs with the periods previously accepted in the other two situations, DRC and Uganda, and cited by the Pre-Trial Chamber (2 to 6 months assessment or perhaps a slightly longer period) may apply.

sibility assessment and gravity, to justify the delay, these factors are not relevant in this context.

One commentator argues that a valid method of making a finding on "unjustified delay", accompanied by an intention to evade justice, would invite a comparison of the case under consideration "with the usual procedures of the State" in similar serious cases.[200] This finding is consonant with the substance of Rule 51, which states that the Court "may consider, *inter alia,* information" that the State may choose to bring to the Court to demonstrate that its domestic courts meet "internationally recognized norms and standards" for conducting an "independent and impartial prosecution of similar conduct".[201] Rule 51, therefore, tends to show that in earlier similar cases, the domestic courts demonstrated the willingness and ability to prosecute similar conduct that the Court may want to take into account in its evaluation.[202] Apparently the Rule also leans toward the division of the burden of proof between the Prosecutor and the domestic authorities.[203]

In *Genie-Lacayo*, the Inter-American Commission drew a comparison between the period spent in this case and the "average time for judicial proceedings" regarding criminal cases in Nicaragua, and concluded that the period "far exceeded" the limits.[204] Although the Court found a violation of Article 8(1), the decision was not based solely on the Commission's comparison. Rather, the Court examined the three conditions set out by the ECHR as well as the delay throughout the entire process in the light of the circumstances of this case and concluded that a period of more than five years exceeds "the limits of reasonableness".[205] That is to say, a comparison of the case under consideration with the "usual procedures of the State" in similar cases is not a decisive criterion that leads *per se* to a final determination on Article 17(2) (b). On the contrary, it may be part of the overall evaluation under the factual circumstances of a given case. Still, not all States have had experience in prosecuting international crimes. Egypt is one example of such a State that has never prosecuted before its own courts crimes committed on a large scale, such as genocide or crimes

See *ibid* (citing the periods of 2 to 6 months as the periods of the preliminary examination in the DRC and Uganda cases).

200 Holmes, *Cassese Commentary, supra* note 22, p. 676.

201 ICC Rule 51.

202 John T. Holmes, "Jurisdiction and Admissibility", in Roy S. Lee et al. (eds.), *The International Criminal Court: Elements of Crimes and Rules of Procedure and Evidence* (Ardsley: Transnational Publishers, 2001), p. 336.

203 On this point, see e.g., *Hilaire, Constantine and Benjamin et al. v. Trinidad and Tobago,* Judgment of 21/06/2002, Inter-Am Ct. H.R. (Ser. C) No. 94 (2002), para. 122 (citing the Commission's opinion that in cases of "unacceptable delay, the burden of proof falls on the State to justify the delay...").

204 *Genie- Lacayo v. Nicaragua,* Judgment of 29/01/1997, Inter-Am Ct. H.R. (Ser. C) No. 30 (1997), paras. 38, 56.

205 *Ibid.*, paras. 76 – 81.

against humanity. Even domestic legislation defining and proscribing these crimes does not exist.[206]

Also, one cannot support the idea embodied in Rule 51, which apparently states that in "considering the matters" set out in Article 17(2) and "in the context of the circumstances of the case", the Court may take into account past similar cases prosecuted by the State in question to prove that its courts meet international due process standards. It is not clear how the Court can rule on admissibility, taking into account, *inter alia*, conduct that took place in another case with different circumstances. The fact that a State has investigated, prosecuted, tried and punished the perpetrators in a particular case with due diligence does not necessarily mean that that State is doing or will do so in another given case. Independence and impartiality as concepts are not automatically attached to every case begun. They appear and disappear from one case to another depending on the conduct pursued in a given set of proceedings. Accordingly each case must be scrutinized in the light of its own factual circumstances, in order to prove that the proceedings carried out were independent and impartial. Perhaps Rule 51 might be useful in the sense of providing the ICC with general information in relation to the capacity of the domestic system dealing with cases such as the one under consideration.

1.2.5 The Criterion of Independent or Impartial Proceedings

The third criterion in determining unwillingness is the independence and impartiality of the proceedings. If the ICC determines that the proceedings "were not or are not being conducted independently or impartially", but are in fact being conducted in a manner "which in the circumstances is inconsistent with an intent to bring the person to justice", the case will be admissible.[207] The idea of linking impartiality or independence to domestic proceedings was the outcome of negotiations that took place at the Preparatory Committee in 1996.

Article 35 of the 1994 International Law Commission draft should be "expanded to include cases which are being or have been prosecuted before national jurisdictions, subject to qualifications in respect of [*inter alia*] impartiality".[208] It was initially planned that this paragraph should be under the heading of inability. If the State was unable to provide impartial as well as independent proceedings, including the procedural guarantees for the accused person, the Court should step in.[209] This view was opposed by some delegations that argued that "procedural fairness" should not be a basis for "defining complementarity".[210] While this was the original intention of the drafters, the final language of Article 17(2) supports an interpretation, as argued

206 Mohamed M. El Zeidy, 'Egypt and Current Efforts to Criminalize International Crimes', 5 *International Criminal Law Review* 247 (2005); and generally Walid Abdelgawad, "Droit Égyptien", in Antonio Cassese (eds.), *Jurisdictions Nationales et Crimes Internationaux* (Paris: Puf, 2002), p. 367 *ff.*

207 Rome Statute, Art. 17(2) (c).

208 1996 *Preparatory Committee Report*, Vol. I, *supra* note 16, para. 164.

209 Williams, *supra* note 37, at 394.

210 Holmes, *supra* note 4, p. 50.

earlier, that "due process", which presumably includes the rights of the accused, might be an element of the assessment, yet it is insufficient on its own to make a case admissible. Furthermore, the practical determination of impartiality or independence will necessarily require a closer look at the jurisprudence of the human rights bodies which study the question in the context of the violations of the rights of the accused.

Other procedural problems encouraged the drafters to insert the concepts of independence and impartiality under the rubric of unwillingness. It has been said that there are a number of procedural problems that may occur in a State which, while they do not meet the test of shielding the accused, could be inconsistent with an intention to bring the accused to justice. A State may be genuinely endeavouring to prosecute someone, and therefore the intent to shield is not an issue, yet there may be individuals who are trying to cause a "mistrial", or "taint evidence" and ensure that the accused will not be found guilty.[211] Inserting sub-paragraph (2) (c) was therefore deemed necessary by the drafters although it may appear to duplicate the two other criteria of shielding or unjustified delay.[212]

Article 14(1) of the ICCPR states that "everyone shall be entitled" to a fair hearing by an independent and impartial tribunal.[213] Also Article 6(1) of the ERCHR,[214] as well as Article 8(1) of the ACHR,[215] uses similar language.[216] But these provisions talk about "independent and impartial tribunal", as opposed to Article 17(2)(c) of the Rome Statute which refers to proceedings "not being conducted independently or impartially".[217] Apparently these terms are different,[218] but actually they overlap when it comes to their practical application.

211 Williams, *supra* note 37, p. 394; Holmes, *supra* note 4, pp. 50 – 51. This suggests that Article 17(2)(a) is confined to acts attributed to the State organs, as the drafters seems to have been treating the concept of shielding as different from the intent not to bring the person to justice, as stated in sub-paragraphs (2)(b) and (c). It follows that if we apply this scenario, for example, to the context of delays in accordance with Article 17(2) (b) examined in the previous section, it would not fit neatly within the scope of conditions set out by the ECHR as it involves an element that attributes responsibility for delays to neither the relevant authorities nor the accused, but to a third party. However, arguably acts as such may still be determined as a part of the factual circumstances of the entire case.

212 Holmes, *supra* note 4, p. 51.

213 ICCPR, Art. 14 (1).

214 ERCHR, Art. 6 (1).

215 ACHR, Art. 8 (1).

216 But see the language of Article 7(1) of the African Charter, which only refers to the right to be tried by "an impartial court or tribunal". African [Banjul] Charter on Human and People's Rights, adopted June 27, 1981, OAU Doc. CAB/LEG/67/3 rev. 5, 21 I.L.M. 58 (1982), entered into force October 21, 1986, Art. 7 (1).

217 Rome Statute, Art. 17(2) (c).

218 Christoph J. M. Safferling, *Towards an International Criminal Procedure*, (Oxford: Oxford University Press, 2001), p. 90.

One way of looking at the question of independent or impartial proceedings would be to attempt to link these terms with the idea of an independent and impartial tribunal appearing in the human rights instruments referred to above. Domestic proceedings carried out by tribunals that are not impartial and independent will arguably have a *direct impact* on the domestic process in relation to independence and impartiality. In other words, the fact that a tribunal is short of the necessary prerequisites of independence or impartiality is in itself sufficient evidence to raise doubts about the independence and impartiality of the proceedings carried out by such body.[219] This view finds support in principle in a decision of the Appeals Chamber of the Special Court for Sierra Leone (SCSL) in the *Norman* case. The Chamber stated that:

> [A]n objection that the Court lacks judicial independence is basically, and in substance, an objection to the fairness of the trial and an allegation that the right of the accused to a fair hearing is likely to be infringed by the trial...[220]

Yet, the provisions of the human rights treaties seem to be stricter in terms of their dimensional reach. Because human rights treaties speak of an "independent and impartial tribunal", presumably the assessment is confined to the pre-trial and trial phases of the proceedings. As argued in the previous section, Article 17(2) (c) requires a broader examination of the entire set of proceedings that commences with an investigation into a situation.[221] This means that acts or omissions attributable to a party to the proceedings, including the relevant authorities, raise the question of independence or impartiality of any phase of the domestic process. Also, the mere proof that domestic proceedings were not conducted impartially or independently is insufficient for the purpose of determining admissibility. It has to be demonstrated that the lack of impartiality or independence accompanying the proceedings resulted, in the circumstances of the specific case, in the intent not to "bring the person concerned to justice". One way of proving this intent is to show that the "lack of independence or impartiality in fact worked in favour of the accused".[222] The human rights bodies have regularly been faced with cases involving these notions. Thus, an examination of the relevant decisions in this context seems necessary in order to understand in general terms what may be deemed partial or dependent proceedings for the purposes of Article 17(2) (c). The following examination will therefore build on the argument that a tribunal lacking the necessary independence and impartiality cannot by implication guarantee independent and impartial proceedings.

219 For further implications arising out of lack of independence or impartiality of judges see Theodor Meron, 'Judicial Independence and Impartiality in International Criminal Tribunals', 99 *American Journal of International Law* 359 (2005).

220 *Prosecutor v. Sam Hinga Norman*, (Case No. SCSL-2004-14-AR72 (E)), *Decision on Preliminary Motion Based on Lack of Jurisdiction (Judicial Independence)*, 13/03/2004, para. 4.

221 See e.g., Rome Statute, Arts. 13, 14.

222 Benzing, *supra* note 13, p. 613.

The term "independent" means "independent of the executive and also of the parties".[223] Independence of the Parliament has also been considered a feature of an independent tribunal.[224] Further characteristics of the concept of independence were set out in *Campbell and Fell*, where the ECHR stated that the Court should pay "regard to the manner of appointment of its members and the duration of their term of office, the existence of guarantees against outside pressures and the question whether the body presents an appearance of independence".[225] On this last point, the Court has said that "what is at stake is the confidence which such tribunals in a democratic society must inspire in the public and above all, as far as criminal proceedings are concerned, in the accused".[226]

As to the manner of appointment, a judge's independence may be challenged successfully if it is proved that the appointment procedure "as a whole is unsatisfactory", or at least that the establishment of the particular court deciding a case was influenced by improper "motives", tending to influence the outcome of the case.[227] Similarly, the substitution of a judge in a given case without a prior notice to the defence may sometimes raise the question of the independence of the tribunal.[228] But in order to prove such lack of independence it has to be shown, as the ECHR stated in *Barberà et al*, that in the light of the circumstances surrounding the impugned change in the membership of the tribunal, the change has "its possible consequences for the fairness of the trial" proceedings.[229] The judge does not have to be appointed for life. What is important is that there are safeguards against the executive discharging a judge at will.[230] If it has been proved that he or she is in "a subordinate position,

223 *Ringeisen v. Austria*, Application No. 2614/65, Eur. Ct. H.R., Judgment (Merits) of 16/07/1971, para. 95.

224 *Crociani, Palmiotti, Tanassi, Lefebvre D'ovidio v. Italy*, Application Nos. 8603/79; 8722/79; 8723/79, Eur. Comm. H.R., Decision of 18/12/1980 on the Admissibility of the Applications, pp. 212, 221.

225 *Campbell and Fell v. The United Kingdom*, Application No. 7819/77; 7878/77, Eur. Ct. H.R., Judgment (Merits and Just Satisfaction) of 28/06/1984, para. 78. The Court reiterated these conditions even in its recent jurisprudence on the subject. See, *inter alia*, *Baischer v. Austria*, Application No. 32381/96, Eur. Ct. H.R., Judgment (Merits and Just Satisfaction) of 20/12/2001, para. 23.

226 *G.W. v. The United Kingdom* Application No. 34155/96, Eur. Ct. H.R., Judgment (Merits and Just Satisfaction) of 15/06/2004, para. 42.

227 Harris, O'Boyle and Warbrick, *supra* note 145, p. 232.

228 *Barberà, Messegué and Jabardo v. Spain*, Application No. 10590/83, Eur. Ct. H.R., Judgment (Merits) of 06/12/1988, para. 53 – 59.

229 *Ibid.*, para. 57; see also the recent *Öcalan v. Turkey* Application No. 46221/99, Eur. Ct. H.R., Judgment (Merits and Just Satisfaction) of 12/03/2003, para. 119 (noting that "a change in the composition of a trial court in the course of the proceedings need not necessarily give rise to an issue under Article 6 § 1"). This means that only under certain circumstances such as those stated above in *Barberà et al.* may the issue of lack impartiality arise.

230 *Engel and Others v. The Netherlands*, Application Nos. 5100/71; 5101/71; 5102/71; 5354/72; 5370/72, Eur. Ct. H.R., Judgment (Merits) of 8/06/1976, paras. 30, 68;*Thomas Eccles and*

in terms of his duties and the organization of his service, vis-à-vis one of the parties", this raises a "legitimate doubt" in relation to the independence of the person concerned and, as a result, the tribunal.[231]

Impartiality "denotes absence of prejudice or bias".[232] Impartiality and independence are clearly connected.[233] As implicitly stated in the IACHR's famous Advisory Opinion on Judicial Guarantees, the "lack of necessary independence" clearly affects the possibility of "impartial decisions" being delivered.[234] A similar conclusion was come to by one scholar who argued that, although international human rights law distinguishes between "independence" and "impartiality", they are complementary in a way. "While independence is desirable in and of itself, its importance really lies in the fact that it creates the conditions for impartiality".[235] According to other scholars, a tribunal that falls short of independence of the executive will also fail to "comply with the requirement of impartiality in cases to which the executive is a party".[236]

In *Tadic*, the Trial Chamber stated that "whether a court is independent and impartial depends...upon its constitution, its judges and the way in which they function".[237] But it did not develop this point. The ECHR went further, as it has established some clear guidelines for testing independence and impartiality. In order to test the existence of impartiality, the ECHR adopted two main criteria in its early *Piersack* case, which is the first authority on the matter. First, there is a subjective test that relies "on the personal conviction of a given judge in a given case"[238] or, as stated in the recent *Warsicka* case, the "interest of a particular judge in a given case",[239] and, secondly, an objective test that determines whether the judge "offered guarantees suf-

others v. Ireland, Application No. 12839/87, Eur. Comm. H.R., Decision of 09/12/1988 on the Admissibility of the Application; van Dijk, van Hoof, *supra* note 158, 452.

231 *Sramek v. Austria*, Application No. 8790/79, Eur. Ct. H.R., Judgment (Merits and Just Satisfaction) of 22/10/1984, para. 42.

232 *Piersack v. Belgium*, Application No. 8692/79, Eur. Ct. H.R., Judgment (Merits) of 01/10/1982, para. 30.

233 See e.g., *Prosecutor v. Sam Hinga Norman* (Case No. SCSL-2004-14-AR72 (E)), *Decision on Preliminary Motion Based on Lack of Jurisdiction (Judicial Independence), Separate Opinion of Justice Geoffrey Robertson*, 13/03/2004 (pointing to such connection as well as the distinctions).

234 *Judicial Guarantees in States of Emergency* (Arts. 27(2), 25 and (8) American Convention on Human Rights), Advisory Opinion OC-9/87 of 6/10/1987, Inter-Am Ct. H.R. (Series A) No. 9, para. 24.

235 Schabas, *supra* note 188, p. 506.

236 Harris, O'Boyle and Warbrick, *supra* note 145, p. 234.

237 *Prosecutor v. Duško Tadić A/K/A* "Dule", Case No. (IT-94-1-T), *Decision on the Defence Motion on Jurisdiction*, 10/08/1995, para. 32.

238 *Piersack v. Belgium*, Application No. 8692/79, Eur. Ct. H.R., Judgment (Merits) of 01/10/1982, para. 30.

239 *Warsicka v. Poland*, Application No. 2065/03, Eur. Ct. H.R., Judgment (Merits) of 16/01/2007, para. 35; *Demicoli v. Malta*, Application No. 13057/87, Eur. Ct. H.R., Judgment (Merits and Just Satisfaction) of 27/08/1991, para. 40.

ficient to exclude any legitimate doubt in this respect".[240] The application of either test depends on the circumstances of each case.

According to the subjective test, a judge is to be presumed impartial until there is proof to the contrary.[241] Thus, it has to be shown, as stated in *De Cubber*, that the judge "had displayed any hostility or ill-will" towards the applicant;[242] or, as stated elsewhere in *Hauschildt*, the judge had acted "with personal bias".[243] Also if proven that the judge had arranged to have a case assigned to him for personal reasons, the subjective element would be satisfied.[244]

The application of the objective test is different in the sense that "quite apart from the personal conduct of any of the members of that body, there are ascertainable facts which may raise doubts as to its impartiality".[245] In proving this last point, "the standpoint" of the accused or applicant is important, yet not decisive.[246] Also appearances may be quite important.[247] What is decisive though is whether the fear of lack of impartiality "can be held to be objectively justified".[248] It follows that the mere fact that a judge has made previous decisions concerning the same offence or has previously taken part in the proceedings "cannot be held as in itself justifying fears as to his

240 *Piersack v. Belgium*, Application No. 8692/79, Eur. Ct. H.R., Judgment (Merits) of 01/10/1982, para. 30; *Langborger v. Sweden*, Application No. 11179/84, Eur. Ct. H.R., Judgment (Merits and Just Satisfaction) of 22/06/1989, para. 32.

241 *Steck –Risch and Others v. Liechtenstein*, Application No. 63151/00, Eur. Ct. H.R., Judgment (Merits and Just Satisfaction) of 19/05/2005, para. 40; *Thorgeir Thorgeirson v. Iceland*, Application No. 13778/88, Eur. Ct. H.R., Judgment (Merits and Just Satisfaction) of 25/06/1992, para. 50.

242 *De Cubber v. Belgium*, Application No. 9186/80, Eur. Ct. H.R., Judgment (Merits) of 26/10/1984, para. 25.

243 *Hauschildt v. Denmark*, Application No. 10486/83, Eur. Ct. H.R., Judgment (Merits and Just Satisfaction) of 24/05/1989, para. 47.

244 *Kyprianou v. Cyprus*, Application No. 73797/01, Eur. Ct. H.R., Judgment (Merits and Just Satisfaction) of 15/12/2005, para. 119. Other acts such as a judge publicly engaging in criticizing the defence and expressing surprise that the accused has pleaded not guilty also raise the issue of subjective impartiality. See *Lavents v. Latvia*, Application No. 58442/00, Eur. Ct. H.R., Judgment (Merits and Just Satisfaction) of 28/11/2002), paras. 118 – 119.

245 *Warsicka v. Poland*, Application No. 2065/03, Eur. Ct. H.R., Judgment (Merits) of 16/01/2007, para. 37;

246 *Ibid.*

247 *Castillo Algar v. Spain*, Application No. 28194/95, Eur. Ct. H.R., Judgment (Merits) of 28/10/1998, para. 45; *Morel v. France*, Application No. 34130/96, Eur. Ct.H.R., Judgment (Merits) of 06/06/2000, para. 42.

248 *Ferarantelli and Santangelo v. Italy*, Application No. 19874/92, Eur. Ct. H.R., Judgment (Merits and Just Satisfaction) of 07/08/1996, para. 58; *Wettstein v. Switzerland*, Application No. 33958/96, Eur. Ct. H.R., Judgment (Merits and Just Satisfaction) of 21/12/2000, para. 44.

impartiality",[249] as this will depend on the circumstances of each case.[250] What counts is "the extent and nature" of those decisions taken by the judge.[251] Further, acts such as the president of a court's public use of an expression which reflected the fact that he had already "formed unfavourable view" of the applicant's case before sitting on the court deciding it also trigger the objective test as to the lack of impartiality.[252]

Violations of the notions of independence and impartiality have also been carried out in a non-civilian context, that is, when either a court martial or military court deals with cases. In *Grieves*, the ECHR argued that since a naval Judge Advocate's court martial is subordinate to the CNJA (a naval officer who is responsible for the initial "ticketing" of a Judge Advocate), this position "cannot be considered to constitute strong guarantee of the independence of a naval court-martial".[253]

Similarly, in *Durand and Ugarte*, the IACHR, supporting the finding of the Commission, considered that military tribunals are neither independent nor impartial, because they belong to the Peruvian Ministry of Defence, which is an agency subordinate and belonging to the Executive Branch.[254] Where the "judicial post depends on the military rank or the status of active officer, decisions adopted by the judge or the tribunal shall be affected by an interest incompatible with justice".[255] A similar conclusion was reached in *Cantoral Benavides*, where the IACHR stated further that the independence and impartiality of a military judge "is affected by the fact that the armed forces have the dual function of combating insurgent groups with military force, and of judging and imposing sentence upon members of such groups".[256]

Following the *Tadic* decision, the ICTY seems to have elaborated its own set of conditions for the determination of impartiality, on the basis of those set out by the ECHR, reflected in its jurisprudence as well as the practice of domestic courts in civil and common law jurisdictions. In *Furundžija*, the ICTY Appeals Chamber, having reviewed some case law from common law and civil law jurisdictions, as well as deci-

249 *Schwarzenberger v. Germany* , Application No. 75737/01, Eur. Ct. H.R., Judgment (Merits) of 10/08/2006, para. 42; *Fehr v. Austria*, Application No. 19247/02, Eur. Ct. H.R., Judgment (Merits and just Satisfaction) of 3/02/2005, para. 30.

250 *Ibid.*

251 *Depiets v. France*, Application No. 53971/00, Eur. Ct. H.R., Judgment (Merits) of 10/02/2004, para. 35; *De Cubber v. Belgium*, Application No. 9186/80, Eur. Ct. H.R., Judgment (Merits) of 26/10/1984, paras. 29 – 30.

252 *Buscemi v. Italy*, Application No. 29569/95, Eur. Ct. H.R., Judgment (Merits and just Satisfaction) of 16/09/1999, para. 68.

253 *Grieves v. The United Kingdom*, Application No. 57067/00, Eur. Ct. H.R., Judgment (Merits and just Satisfaction) of 16/12/2003, paras. 85 – 87.

254 *Durand-Ugarte v. Perú*, Judgment of 16/08/2000, Inter-Am Ct. H.R. (Ser. C) No. 68 (2000), paras. 125 – 126.

255 *Ibid.*, para. 111. For an opinion on military courts in the context of the European Court on Human Rights, see *Sürek v. Turkey (No. 3)*, Application No. 24735/94, Eur. Ct. H.R., Judgment (Merits and Just Satisfaction) of 8/07/1999, para. 53.

256 *Cantoral- Benavides v. Perú*, Judgment of 18/08/2000, Inter-Am Ct. H.R. (Ser. C) No. 69 (2000), para. 114.

sions of the ECHR in relation to impartiality, concluded that "there is a general rule that a judge should not only be subjectively free from bias, but also that there should be nothing in the surrounding circumstances which objectively gives rise to an appearance of bias".[257] In applying the impartiality requirement, the ICTY adopted some principles on the basis of its review. The Appeals Chamber stated:

> A. A Judge is not impartial if it is shown that actual bias exits.
> B. There is an unacceptable appearance of bias if:
> i) a Judge is a party to the case, or has a financial or proprietary interest in the outcome of a case, or if the Judge's decision will lead to the promotion of a cause in which he or she is involved, together with one of the parties. Under these circumstances, a Judge's disqualification from the case is automatic; or
> ii) the circumstances would lead a reasonable observer, properly informed, to reasonably apprehend bias.[258]

On this last point, the Appeals Chamber went on to say:

> [T]he reasonable person must be an informed person, with knowledge of all the relevant circumstances, including the traditions of integrity and impartiality that form a part of the background and apprised also of the fact that impartiality is one of the duties that Judges swear to uphold.[259]

The Court may therefore, directly apply the ECHR or the ICTY standards or develop its own set of rules in the determination of elements of independence or impartiality, on the basis of the conditions explored above. It is evident that the criteria adopted by the ECHR and the ICTY are confined to testing the impartiality or independence of a tribunal, which is presumably limited to a certain phase of the domestic proceedings, that is the pre-trial or trial proceedings conducted by that tribunal including the outcome of the decision. As argued at the outset, Article 17(2) (c) requires a determination of independence or impartiality of the entire criminal process, including the investigative steps in a situation. Yet, nothing suggests that the main conditions examined above may not be valid to test the whole process.

For example, there are conditions that require the tribunal to be "independent of the executive and the parties" or that there have to exist "guarantees against outside pressure", which is reflected in the idea of the subordination of that body to a superior. Arguably these criteria may apply in principle to all phases of the proceedings, depending on the relevant organ conducting any set of proceedings. In other words, independence of the executive may also be a requirement that applies for example to any relevant authority that is in charge of a specific phase of the proceedings, such as the investigation stage. Similarly, the idea of guarantees from outside pressure, mir-

257 *Prosecutor v. Anto Furundžija*, Case No. (IT-95-17/1-A), Judgment 21/07/2000, para. 189.

258 *Ibid.*

259 *Ibid.*, para. 190.

rored in scenarios such as subordination to a superior, may also apply to the organ carrying out a certain set of proceedings. For instance, in the context of the right to life, the ECHR has consistantly stated that for an investigation to be deemed "independent" it has to be carried out independently of those who are implicated in the events.[260] As stated further in *Finucane*,[261] *Jordan*,[262] and *Ergi*,[263] "[t]his means not only a lack of hierarchical or institutional connection but also a practical independence".

The same rule applies to the determination of the impartiality of proceedings. Proceedings lack impartiality if it has been revealed that they are or were conducted with "bias". Bias exits, as explained earlier, if the person conducting the relevant part of the proceedings has some sort of interest in the case or its outcome. Thus, the fact that the conditions explored by the ECHR as well as the ICTY apply to the conduct of judges or tribunals does not mean that these guidelines would not qualify to test the conduct of other parties involved in conducting the various phases of the proceedings.

1.2.6 The Concept of Proceedings in Article 17(2) (a) – (c)

Although Article 17(2) (a)–(c) aims to evaluate the standards of domestic efforts, the provision fails to explain what the term "proceedings" entails. The term "proceedings" appeared for the first time in draft Article 35(3), during the work of the Working Group on Complementarity in the August 1997 session.[264] A footnote accompanying Article 35(3) stated that the term "covers both investigations and prosecutions".[265] An identical explanation later appeared in the *Report of the Inter-Sessional Meeting*

260 *Kismir v. Turkey*, Application No. 27306/95, Eur. Ct. H.R., Judgment (Merits and Just Satisfaction) of 31/05/2005, para.112 ; *Shanaghan v. The United Kingdom*, Application No. 37715/97, Eur. Ct. H.R., Judgment (Merits and Just Satisfaction) of 4/05/2001, para. 89; and also *Akkoc v. Turkey*, Application Nos. 22947/93, 22948/93, Eur. Ct. H.R., Judgment (Merits and Just Satisfaction) of 10/10/2000, para. 88 (noting that "where offences were committed by State officials in certain circumstances, the competence to investigate was removed from the public prosecutor in favour of administrative councils which took the decision whether to prosecute... These councils were made up of civil servants, under the orders of the Governor, who was himself responsible for the security forces whose conduct was in issue. The investigations which they instigated were often carried out by gendarmes linked hierarchically to the units concerned in the incident. The Court accordingly found in two cases that the administrative councils did not provide an independent or effective procedure for investigating deaths involving members of the security forces").

261 *Finucane v. The United Kingdom*, Application No. 29178/95, Eur. Ct. H.R., Judgment (Merits and Just Satisfaction) of 1/07/2003, para. 68.

262 *Hugh Jordan v. The United Kingdom*, Application No. 24746/94, Eur. Ct. H.R., Judgment (Merits and Just Satisfaction) of 4/05/2001, para. 106.

263 *Ergi v. Turkey* Application No. 23818/94, Eur. Ct. H.R., Judgment (Merits and just Satisfaction) of 28/07/1998, paras. 83 – 84.

264 1997 *Preparatory Committee Decisions, supra* note 39, Art. 35(3), p. 11, n. 24.

265 *Ibid.*

in Zutphen, [266]as well as in the *Report of the Preparatory Committee, Draft Statute and Draft Final Act* in 1998,[267] until it finally found its way into the current Article 17 of the Statute. In practice, the Office of the Prosecutor (OTP) seems to have adopted the same interpretation. In assessing two recent communications concerning the situations in Venezuela and Iraq, the OTP considered that the term "proceedings" mentioned in Articles 17(2) and 53(1)(b) "encompasses investigations and prosecutions".[268] But if this is so, does it mean that *trial* proceedings are excluded from the test of Article 17(2) (a) – (c)?

Article 17(2) (a) states that the "proceedings were or are being undertaken or the national decision was made for...". If the term "proceedings" excludes the *trial* stage, the reference to the "national decision" is broad enough to cover a decision delivered by a Court of law, as well as the proceedings leading to that decision. The problem still remains in the language used in sub-paragraphs (2) (b) and (c), as they refer only to the term "proceedings without any mention to "national decision", and accordingly, exclude the trial phase.

Strictly speaking the terms "prosecution" and "trial" are different. "Prosecution" stands for the criminal allegations instituted against a defendant, while "trial" means "test"[269] or "formal judicial examination",[270] i.e., "the prosecution allegations are put to the test"[271] or to the judicial examination in the course of the trial. Thus, the role of the prosecutor during trial is in itself a "prosecution". It follows that those irregularities of proceedings that take place during what is called the "prosecution" stage would continue into the "trial" phase.[272] Accordingly, the irregularities that take place during trial may also be covered. But, again looking at sub-paragraph (2)(c) and replacing the word "proceedings" with its alternatives "investigation" and "prosecution" suggests that the above interpretation does not fit neatly within the parameters of this provision. Sub-paragraph (c) reads: "[t]he investigation and prosecution were not or are not being conducted independently or impartially..." This means that a prosecution that is not independent or impartial may still take place during the trial stage; the is-

266 See *Report of the Inter-Sessional Meeting From 19 to 30 January 1998 in Zutphen, The Netherlands* (A/AC.249/1998/L.13,1998), Art. 11[35]2[3], p. 43, n. 60.

267 See *Report of the Preparatory Committee on the Establishment of an International Criminal Court, Draft Statute & Draft Final Act* (A/Conf.183/2/Add.1, 1998), Art. 15(2) (a), p. 49, n. 45.

268 Update on Communications received by the Prosecutor, Iraq response, 9 February 2006; Update on Communications received by the Prosecutor, Venezuela response, 9 February 2006, available at. http://www.icc-cpi.int/organs/otp/otp_com.html.

269 J. R. Spencer, "The English System", in Mireille Delmas-Marty et al. (eds.), *European Criminal Procedures* (Cambridge: Cambridge University Press, 2002), p. 181.

270 *Black's Law Dictionary, supra* note 42, p. 1510.

271 Spencer, *supra* note 269, p. 181.

272 This scenario excludes the prosecutor's other activities prior to the trial stage, which are considered as a "prosecution" only if they take place after the investigation stage has ended. For the different stages of proceedings of a case in England and Wales, see e.g., Spencer, *supra* note 269, pp. 165 – 185.

sue is confined to the prosecutor's actions, as opposed to the entire trial proceedings. This line of argument solves only part of the problem.

Nevertheless, Article 17(2)(c) and Article 20(3)(b) might be meant to complement one another, as the latter covers proceedings taking place during the trial phase, thus filling the gap found in Article 17(2)(b) and (c).[273] If "shielding the person concerned from criminal responsibility" is a catch phrase, this remedies the problem of drafting in sub-paragraphs (b) and (c), since sub-paragraph (a) would be broad enough to cover all sorts of irregularities set out in sub-paragraphs (b) and (c).

1.2.7 Crimes within the Jurisdiction of the Court *versus* Not Bringing the Person to Justice

A different problem flows from the language of sub-paragraph (2) (a) on the one hand and sub-paragraphs (b) – (c) on the other. Sub-paragraph (2) (a) talks about "shielding the person concerned from criminal responsibility for crimes within the jurisdiction of the Court referred to in article 5". By contrast, sub-paragraphs (b) – (c) refer to an intent not to "bring the person concerned to justice". The phrase "bring to justice" is broad and, when literally read in light of sub-paragraphs (b) – (c), may lead to a conclusion that if any State proceeded against a person on the basis of crimes or acts with different legal characterization, not included in the list of crimes set out in Article 5 or in the definition of acts under Articles 6 – 8, it may still challenge admissibility before the Court, on the basis that it has brought the person to "justice" within a reasonable time, in accordance with the letter of sub-paragraph (b) requesting the Court to defer jurisdiction. Although there is no possibility of success for a challenge of this kind, since this scenario clearly reflects the State's bad intentions, and thus Article 20(3) permits a second trial in this circumstances, the main problem is that a challenge of this kind would cause a delay in proceedings before the Court.

The Statute, as a multilateral treaty, is subject to the general rules of interpretation set out in Article 31 of the Vienna Convention on the Law of Treaties, which combines all schools of interpretation in a "single combined operation".[274] Accordingly Article 17(2)(b) – (c) should be interpreted "in good faith in accordance with the ordinary meaning to be given to the terms of the treaty in their context and in light of its object and purpose".

In one of its first major rulings, the Appeals Chamber indicated that in the interpretation of the Rome Statute it would be guided by the Vienna Convention, and especially by Articles 31 and 32.[275] According to the Appeals Chamber:

---

273 Article 20(3) and its application will be discussed in chapter IV *infra*.

274 Martin Dixon and Robert McCorquodale, *Cases and Materials on International Law*, 3rd. ed. (Oxford: Blackstone Press Limited, 2000), pp. 86 – 89. These schools of interpretation are "intentions of the parties" or the "founding fathers" school, the "textual" or "ordinary meaning of the words school", and the "teleological" or "aims and objects" school.

275 *Situation in the Democratic Republic of Congo, Judgment on the Prosecutor's Application for Extraordinary Review of Pre-Trial Chamber I's 31 March 2006 Decision Denying Leave to Appeal*, No.: ICC-01/04-168, para. 5. See also *Prosecutor v. Thomas Lubanga*

> The rule governing the interpretation of a section of the law is its wording read in context and in light of its object and purpose. The context of a given legislative provision is defined by the particular sub-section of the law read as a whole in conjunction with the section of an enactment in its entirety. Its objects may be gathered from the chapter of the law in which the particular section is included and its purposes from the wider aims of the law as may be gathered from its preamble and general tenor of the treaty. [...] The self-evident purpose of the Statute is to make internationally punishable the heinous crimes specified therein in accordance with the principles and the procedure institutionalised thereby.[276]

Thus, the object and purpose[277] of the Statute is to bring to justice those responsible for the most serious crimes of international concern, mentioned in Article 5 and defined in Articles 6 – 8.[278] The language of Article 17(2) (a) places this provision in its exact *context* by referring to "shielding" the person from "criminal responsibility" for *crimes within the jurisdiction of the Court.* This method of interpretation also finds support in academic writing. As one commentator puts it, the principle of interpretation in good faith "flows directly from the rule *pacta sunt servanda*",[279] which requires that the treaty is to be "read in some sense as a whole so that, one clause may be called in aid to explain an ambiguity in another".[280] In the same vein another com-

---

Dyilo, Decision on the Prosecutor's Application for a Warrant of Arrest, Art. 58, No.: ICC-01/04-01/06-8-US-Corr, 10/02/2006, para. 42, unsealed pursuant to Decision ICC-01/04-01/06-37 dated 17/03/2006; *Prosecutor v. Thomas Lubanga Dyil, Decision on the Practices of Witness Familiarisation and Witness Proofing*, No.: ICC-01/04-01/06-679, 8/11/2006, para. 8; *Decision the Prosecutor's Application that the Pre-Trial Chamber Disregard as Irrelevant the Submission Filed by the Registry on 5 December 2005*, No.: ICC 02/04-01/05-145, 9/03/2006, para. 25.

276 *Ibid.*, paras. 33, 37 (references omitted).

277 For further analysis of the notions of "object and purpose", see V. Crnic-Grotic, 'Object and Purpose of the Treaties in the Vienna Convention on the Law of Treaties', 7 *Asian Yearbook of International Law* 141 (1997).

278 See e.g., *Cayara v. Perú*, Preliminary Objections, Judgment of 3/02/1993, Inter-Am Ct. H.R. (Ser. C) No. 14 (1993), para. 37 ("[T]he Court must ratify its often stated opinion that the object and purpose of the treaty is the effective protection of human rights and that the interpretation of all its provisions must be subordinated to that object and purpose, as provided in Article 31 of the Vienna Convention on the Law of Treaties"). Thus, on a parallel line of argument the object and purpose of the Rome Statute as stated above and reflected in different parts of the preamble are "that the most serious crimes of concern to the international community as a whole must not go unpunished...[by] putting an end to impunity for the perpetrators of these crimes [listed under article 5]". It follows that any provision of the Rome Statute *must* be interpreted with such object and purpose in mind.

279 Vienna Convention on the Law of Treaties, Art. 26. On the principle of good faith see Anthony D'Amato, "Good Faith", in Rudolf Bernhardt (ed.), *Encyclopedia of Public International Law*, Vol. II (Amsterdam: North Holland, 1995), pp. 599 – 601.

280 P. K. Menon, *The Law of Treaties between States and International Organizations* (Cambridge: Cambridge University Press, 1992), p. 78.

mentator argued that "it would be a breach of [the obligation to perform treaties in good faith if] a party make use of an ambiguity in order to put forward an interpretation, which it was known to the negotiators of the treaty not to be the intention of the parties" (emphasis added).[281] A similar conclusion may be inferred from the Advisory Opinion on the Competence of the ILO to Regulate Agricultural Labour.[282]

2. The Impact of Human Rights Bodies' Decisions on Complementarity Determinations

Because Article 17(2) mirrors a human rights dimension embedded in concepts such as "unjustified delay" and "independent" or "impartial" proceedings, human rights related problems may impact on admissibility determinations. When tension has been created between the ICC and a particular State in relation to the question of complementarity, lawyers and legal advisers will try all possible means to interfere with the ICC process. Also when an accused is fighting the government's will, his or her lawyers will try different legal arguments for the sake of delaying domestic proceedings as well as influencing a decision that may be issued by the ICC. Sometimes delays occur in the domestic process and before the ICC rules on admissibility a person files a complaint before a human rights body challenging human rights issues arising out of Article 17(2). Several questions may arise in this context. 1) Should the ICC wait for the human rights body's ruling before deciding on admissibility? 2) Is the ICC bound by a human rights body's decision where a ruling has been made before the Court determines admissibility? To what extent should the ICC take into account the jurisprudence of different human rights bodies?

At least two complaints have been filed before the ECHR concerning people accused before the ICTY. Both complaints invoked fair trial issues under Article 6(1) of the European Convention on Human Rights. In *Milošević v. The Netherlands*, it was evident from the ECHR's case file that the ICTY had neither delayed proceedings against Milošević pursuant to the decision of the Constitutional Court of the Federal Republic of Yugoslavia to suspend his surrender until considering its legality,[283] nor had it adjourned proceedings pending a decision from the ECHR after he was trans-

281 A.D. McNair, *The Law of Treaties* (Oxford: Clarendon Press, 1961), p. 465.

282 "[I]n considering the question before the Court upon the language of the Treaty, it is obvious that the Treaty must be read as a whole, and that its meaning is not to be determined merely upon a particular phrases which, if detached from the context, may be interpreted in more than one sense". *Advisory Opinion, International labour Organization – Competence to Regulate Conditions of Agricultural Labor, Etc.*, 1922 P.C.I.J. (Ser. B) Nos. 2&3, p. 23; see also the early *Ionian Ships* case, where a British court stated that in interpretation it is significant to look "to the whole of the instrument and not to a part, [because] terms, however, strong and clear in themselves, whatever meaning may be attributed – necessarily attributed – to them standing alone, may be modified by other parts of the same instrument...". A.D. McNair, *The Law of Treaties: British Practice and Opinions*, (Oxford: Clarendon Press, 1938), p. 198.

283 *Slobodan Milošević v. The Netherlands*, App. No. 77631/01, Eur. Ct. H.R., Decision on the Admissibility of the Application No. 77631/01, 19/03/2002.

ferred to the Tribunal. Similarly, in *Naletilić v. Croatia*,[284] both the Zagreb County Court[285] and the ICTY proceeded against the accused by means of a decision for his surrender to the Tribunal, without waiting for a decision of the ECHR.

In both decisions, the ECHR seems to have taken into account cases that were under consideration by the ICTY in order to avoid a conflict between a State Party's obligations arising from the Convention and those arising from the ICTY Statute and the relevant Security Council resolutions. The ECHR relied on well-constructed arguments in the case enabling it to decide that both applications were inadmissible. Yet, it is not clear how the ECHR would react in the case of a well-founded application. These decisions suggest, to some extent, that the ICC should not adjourn a ruling on admissibility in accordance with Article 17(2) pending an ECHR decision. Also, neither the Statute nor the Rules or the Regulations directs the Court to postpone proceedings in such a situation.

The ICC is not bound by decisions of the different human rights bodies. This is because the Court is not a state party to any of the international human rights instruments.[286] Nor is there a hierarchy between the different international judicial bodies. In *Tadić* both the Trial and Appeals Chambers looked at the jurisprudence of the HRC and the ECHR, yet without clearly ruling on the extent to which these cases were binding on the ICTY.[287] Similarly, in the recent decision in *Milošević*, the ICTY rejected a motion regarding the illegal foundation of the Tribunal on the basis of the jurisprudence of the Human Rights Committee, without spelling out the extent of its binding effect on the Tribunal, if any. The Tribunal noted that "[h]uman rights bodies have on several occasions pronounced on the legitimacy of ad hoc tribunals. The

284 *Mladen Naletilić v. Croatia*, App. No. 51891/99, Eur. Ct. H.R., Decision on the Admissibility of the Application No. 51891/99, 4/05/2000.

285 The surrender decision was even supported in the appeal to both the Supreme and Constitutional Courts.

286 In this respect, only states are bound by the obligations arising from the decisions of the different human rights bodies. See Ian Brownlie, *Principles of Public International Law*, sixth ed. (Oxford: Oxford University Press, 2003), p. 654, who notes that international organizations (including the UN) do not enjoy the same rights and duties as states.

287 *Prosecutor v. Duško Tadić*, Case No. (IT-94-1-T), *Decision on the Defence Motion on Jurisdiction*, 10/08/1995, paras. 33 – 34; *Prosecutor v. Duško Tadić*, Case No. (IT-94-1-AR72), *Decision on the Defence Motion for Interlocutory Appeal on Jurisdiction*, 2/10/1995, paras. 42 – 47. In his separate opinion in the *Tadić*, Judge Sidhwa went a step further and questioned the extent to which the Tribunal may be bound by decisions of human rights bodies, in particular the ECHR. He said: "[W]e have not been shown any grounds that this Tribunal in the criminal jurisdiction is bound to follow such decisions. At best they have a persuasive value...I would treat the following view of both the European Court of Human Rights and of its Commission with respect and as being a source for guidance". See Separate Opinion of Judge Sidhwa on the *Defence Motion for Interlocutory Appeal on Jurisdiction*, 2/10/1995, para. 66.

decisions of these bodies establish that there is nothing inherently illegitimate in the creation of an ad hoc judicial body".[288]

It is clear that decisions of the different human rights bodies, although not binding on the *ad hoc* tribunals, may serve at least as guidelines.[289] The situation of the ICC is no different. Article 21 of the Rome Statute lists in terms of hierarchy the sources of law to be applied by the Court in making its decisions.[290] Although Article 21 does not state clearly whether decisions of the other international judicial bodies are considered an applicable source of law, arguably the phrase "principles and rules of international law" referred to in Article 21(1)(b) covers those decisions as a secondary source. Indeed, in the *Uganda* case before the ICC,[291] Pre-Trial Chamber II treated the jurisprudence of the *ad hoc* tribunals as being covered by the "principles and rules of international law", as long as they did not go "beyond the scope of article 21".[292] Accordingly, the ICC may also be guided by the legal principles that emanate from decisions of other international judicial and quasi-judicial bodies.[293]

In sum, if an admissibility ruling in relation to a certain situation or case before the ICC was still pending, the ICC might, if it found this appropriate, benefit from a decision delivered by the ECHR or any other international judicial body. A decision as such may assist the Court in making a determination on admissibility depending

288 *Prosecutor v. Milošević*, Case No. (IT-02-54), *Decision on Preliminary Motions*, 8/11/2001, paras. 8 – 9.

289 See in the same vein the situation in relation to the Special Court of Sierra Leone faced with the question whether it is bound by decisions of the *Ad hoc* Tribunals. In this context, the Trial Chamber stated that it "accepts that relevant jurisprudence such as decisions and judgments from the common Appeals Chamber of "the ICTY" and "ICTR" can provide important guidance, mutatis mutandis, to the implementation of the mandate of "the Special Court"." See *Prosecutor v. Samuel Hinga Norman*, (Case No. SCSL-2003-08-PT), *Decision on the Defence Preliminary Motion on Lack of Jurisdiction: Command Responsibility*, 15/10/2003, para. 20.

290 Rome Statute, Art. 21. The Statutes of the *Ad hoc* Tribunals lack any provision to that effect.

291 See *Decision on the Prosecutor's Position on the Decision of Pre-Trial Chamber II to Redact Factual Descriptions of Crimes from the Warrants of Arrest, Motion for Reconsideration, and Motion for Clarification*, No.: ICC-02/04-01/05-60, 28/10/2005, para. 19.

292 *Ibid.* This means that the ICC should be guided by decisions arising from other international judicial bodies as a secondary source and only "where appropriate": see the first sentence of Art. 21 (1) (b).

293 See *Decision on the Applications for Participation in the Proceedings of VPRS1, VPRS2, VPRS3, VPRS4, VPRS5, and VPRS6*, No.: ICC-01/04, 17/01/2006, (public redacted), No.: ICC-01/04-101-etEN-Corr., 17/02/2007, paras. 51 – 53 (Pre-Trial Chamber I referring to the jurisprudence of the ECHR and the IACHR); *Décision relative au système définitif de divulgation et à l'établissment d'un échéancier, Annexe I, Analyse de la décisions relative au système définitif de divulgation*, No. : ICC-01/04-01/06-102, 15/05/2006, para. 97; *Prosecutor's Further Submission*, No.: ICC-01/04-01/06 cited *in extenso* in *Prosecutor v. Thomas Lubanga Dyilo, Decision on the Prosecutor's Application for a Warrant of Arrest, Art. 58*, No.: ICC-01/04-01/06-8-US-Corr, 10/02/2006, paras. 9, 12, unsealed pursuant to Decision ICC-01/04-01/06-37 dated 17/03/2006.

on the outcome of that case. The ICC may therefore be guided by that decision, but not obliged to take it into account. These are the main legal parameters that govern the application of decisions of other international judicial bodies. However, the ICC might itself find the need in a particular case to wait for such a decision. The burden of proof of whether a State is unwilling as a result of excessive delays, for example, might be more difficult to achieve in a situation where the delay might be attributable to the conduct of the accused and his lawyers as opposed to the State. In order to make a reasonable finding, the ICC needs to scrutinize human rights issues and that may cost time and effort.

A more compelling scenario would emerge in a case where the Prosecutor determined delays in the domestic process, yet the State justified its position on the basis of the existence of *force majeure*[294] or a state of emergency. When a State declares a public emergency, it actually requests the suspension of some of the guarantees enshrined in the International Covenant on Civil and Political Rights, the European Convention on Human Rights or the American Convention on Human Rights.[295] The right to a speedy trial, explored earlier, is among those guarantees that are subject to derogation.

The determination of whether the State has acted within the parameters of the derogation clauses set out in these instruments is a matter that was generally addressed by the human rights bodies.[296] These bodies may decide that a State's deroga-

294 *Force majeure* is defined in Article 23(1) of the 2001 International Law Commission Draft on Responsibility of States for Internationally Wrongful Acts as: "[T]he occurrence of an irresistible force or of an unforeseen event, beyond the control of the State, making it materially impossible in the circumstances to perform the obligation". However, *force majeure* does not apply if "(a) the situation of *force majeure* is due, either alone or in combination with other factors, to the conduct of the State invoking it; or (b) the State has assumed the risk of that situation occurring", *ibid.*, para. 2. See *Official Records of the General Assembly, Fifty-sixth Session, Supplement No. 10* (A/56/10) and generally James Crawford, *The International Law Commission's Articles on State Responsibility: Introduction, Text and Commentaries* (Cambridge: Cambridge University Press, 2002), pp. 170 – 171.

295 Mohamed M. El Zeidy, 'The ECHR and States of Emergency: Article 15 – A Domestic Power of Derogation from Human Rights Obligations', 4 *San Diego International Law Journal* 277 (2003).

296 This does not deny the fact that other international judicial bodies such as the International Court of Justice may interpret human rights obligations. See *Case Concerning Armed Activities on the Territory of the Congo (Democratic Republic of the Congo v. Uganda)*, I.C.J.,19/12/2005.Yet, a human rights body such as the European Court of Human Rights was always faced with questions involving emergency situations. Although the ECHR provides national authorities with a wide margin of appreciation in determining whether the life of its nation is threatened by a public emergency, States do not enjoy unlimited freedom. As the ECHR stated in the *Brannigan* case, "Contracting Parties do not enjoy an unlimited power of appreciation. It is for the Court to rule on whether inter alia the States have gone beyond the "extent strictly required by the exigencies" of the crisis. The domestic margin of appreciation is thus accompanied by a European supervision... At the same time, in exercising its supervision the Court must give appropriate

tion was legitimate and, by implication, whether delays arising out of the situation were acceptable. Since the ICC was not meant to be a human rights court that deals in depth with human rights questions, it may be more plausible, in such cases, for the Prosecutor to await a decision issued by a human rights body that determines whether the emergency provision has been met; and, if so, whether the emergency justifies the delay. Certainly, being guided by such a decision will assist the ICC in making a sound ruling on complementarity.

3. The Practice of Self-referrals and Waivers of Complementarity

In a historical context, the basic idea of a self-referral and a State's waiver of the exercise of its jurisdiction may even be traced to the first international war crimes trial: that of Peter von Hagenbach or the *Breisach Trial* in 1474.[297] Archduke Sigismund of the Austrian Tyrol faced financial problems and mortgaged his domains of Alsace, the Austrian territory and the "forest towns" to Charles the Bold, Duke of Burgundy,[298] under the terms of the treaty of St Omer signed in 1469.[299] Charles the Bold handed over the administration of Alsace to his governor (Landvogt) Peter von Hagenbach. Complying with his master's orders, von Hagenbach enforced a regime of terror even towards the people of neighbouring territories.[300] His regime

weight to such relevant factors as the nature of the rights affected by the derogation, the circumstances leading to, and the duration of, the emergency situation". See *Brannigan and McBride v. The United Kingdom*, Application No. 14553/89;14554/89, Eur. Ct. H.R., Judgment (Merits) of 25/05/1993, para. 43; *Ireland v. The United Kingdom*, Application No. 5310/71, Eur. Ct. H.R., Judgment (Merits and Just Satisfaction) of 18/01/1978, para. 207.

297 In the *Ministries* case, it was said that "international penal law has long recognized the international character of certain types of atrocities and offenses shocking to the moral sense of all civilized nations...we are handing up to the Court a description of an international trial held in 1474 at Breisach on the Upper Rhine...": *Trials of War Criminals Before the Nürnberg Military Tribunals under Control Council Law No. 10 (Ministries case)*, Vol. XIII, p. 97; and *Trials of War Criminals Before the Nürnberg Military Tribunals under Control Council Law No. 10 (The High Command case)*, Vol. XI, p. 476. Some commentators, however, disagree that the tribunal was international on the ground that all cities involved in the trial were members of the Holy Roman Empire. McCormack described it as "supranational", while Woetzel saw it as more akin to a "confederate" tribunal. See Timothy L. H. McCormack, "From Sun Tzu to the Sixth Committee: The Evolution of an International Criminal Law Regime", in Timothy L. H. McCormack et al. (eds.), *The Law of War Crimes: National and International Approaches* (The Hague/London/Boston: Kluwer Law International, 1997), p. 39.

298 Jean Bérenger, *A History of the Habsburg Empire 1273-1700* (London, New York: Longman, 1994), p. 94; William Rospigliosi, *The Swiss for the Non-Swiss* (Maynooth: Aston Colour Press, 1995), p. 172.

299 Joseph Calmette, *The Golden Age of Burgundy: The Magnificent Dukes and their Courts* (Great Britain: Weidenfeld & Nicolson, 1962), p. 185.

300 Holger Kruse, "Ludwig XI (1461-1483)", in Joachim Ehlers et al., (eds.), *Die Französischen Könige des Mittelaters 888-1498* (München: Beck, 1996), pp. 354 – 355.

contributed to the acquisition of enemies from Berne, France, the towns and knights of the Upper Rhine, and even Austria, Burgundy's closest ally.[301] He was arrested in Breisach, where the Austrian Archduke, after resuming his sovereign rights over Alsace,[302] ordered his trial before an international tribunal consisting of 28 judges from the Allied States.[303]

One commentator correctly asserted that von Hagenbach could have been tried before a "local court, [but] the Allies agreed on an *ad hoc* tribunal".[304] At the time two local courts were considered for trying this case, a court in Ensisheim and another in Rottweil. Neither the Ensisheim court (Hofgericht), nor the Emperor's court ('Kaisars') in Rottweil was considered suitable to achieve "effective justice".[305] The Austrian Archduke's decision not to commit von Hagenbach for trial before a court local to where the crimes took place certainly mirrored the roots of the idea of *voluntary* deferment to an international mechanism.

In the contemporary practice of international criminal justice, the question of self-referrals and waivers of complementarity has become of great relevance to the discussion on complementarity before the International Criminal Court. A self-referral is distinct from a waiver of complementarity. The former goes to the triggering of the jurisdiction of the Court, while the latter is a question of admissibility. In the *Ad hoc* Committee in 1995, the issue of waiver of complementarity was raised in general terms for the first time during the negotiations of the Rome Statute. It has been suggested,

---

301 M. L. Bush, *Renaissance, Reformation and the Outer World*, 2nd ed. (London: Blandford Press, 1971), p. 37.

302 Kruse, *supra* note 300, p. 355.

303 Georg Schwarzenberger, 'The Inductive Approach to International Law', 60 *Harvard Law Review* 539, 548n. 23 (1946 – 1947). However, see Johannes Knebel, *Capellani Ecclesiae Basiliensis Diarium* (Basel,1880), p. 85 n. 4.(where it is debatable whether there were 27 or 29 judges); see also John Foster Kirk, *History of Charles the Bold, Duke of Burgundy*, Vol. II (London: William Clowes & Sons, 1863), p. 435 (arguing that there were 27 judges).

304 Georg Schwarzenberger, *International Law As Applied By International Courts and Tribunals: The Law of Armed Conflict*, Vol. II (London: Stevens & Sons Limited, 1968), p. 463.

305 Hildburg Brauer-Gramm, *Der Landvogt Peter von Hagenbach: Die Burgundische Herrschaft am Oberrhein 1469-1474* (Musterschmidt-Verlag: Göttingen. Berlin. Frankfurt, 1957), p. 310; M. De Barante, *Histoire Des Ducs De Bourgogne De La Maison De Valois, 1364-1477*, Vol. VIII (Bruxelles, 1839) pp. 157 – 158. Although the main target of the Allies was to reach "effective justice", and, according to the language of Sigismund and the Allies, an international court would appear more suitable to achieve this aim, this was not the sole reason for rejecting the idea of a local court, especially in relation to the "Kaiser's court" in Rottweil. The latter was known as the "imperial yard court" and was not competent at the time to hear criminal cases. On the contrary, it was considered to be the highest civil court in the late middle ages and, thus, only civil cases were considered. This could be, *inter alia*, a reason for rejecting this specific court. However, the general idea for rejecting a local court at the time appears to be based on the reason that proper and effective outcomes would not be achieved except through a joint effort.

by some, that the Statute should permit a situation where a State might "voluntarily decide to relinquish its jurisdiction in favour of the ICC".[306] Yet, others believed that such a proposal would be inconsistent with the principle of complementarity, since the ICC "should in no way undermine the effectiveness of national justice systems and should only be resorted to in exceptional cases".[307] In the Preparatory Committee in 1997, the drafters addressed the question of waiver of complementarity in a more precise manner. They inserted a footnote stating that "The present text of article [x] is without prejudice to the question whether complementarity-related admissibility requirements of this article may be waived by the State or States concerned".[308] This footnote remained unchanged through the entire drafting process until the Rome Conference.[309] It was not discussed in Rome, since many delegations believed that this question would be better dealt with in the Rules of Procedure and Evidence.[310] When the Rules were finalized, it was clear that the issue was left to the Court's interpretation.[311]

The term "waiver" or "waiver of complementarity" is neither found nor defined in the Rome Statute. Also, the expression "self-referral" does not appear in the Rome Statute either. A self-referral explains a factual situation where a State Party directly linked to the crimes refers its own situation to the Court. The term and its underlying meaning were endorsed by the Court.[312] Certainly, the fact that a self-referral generally fits within the regime of State Party referrals, made it less difficult for the Court to accept such a concept. Similarly, a waiver or a waiver of complementarity is also an idiom that describes a factual situation, which occurs when a State refrains from initiating domestic proceedings or explicitly conveys an intention to that effect.

306 1995 *Ad hoc Committee Report, supra* note 4, para. 47.

307 *Ibid.*

308 1997 *Preparatory Committee Decisions, supra* note 39, Art. 35, p. 11 n. 17.

309 *Report of the Inter-Sessional Meeting From 19 to 30 January 1998 in Zutphen, the Netherlands*, Art. 11, pp. 42 – 43, UN Doc. A/AC.249/1998/L.13 (1998), Art. 11, p. 42n.53 [hereinafter Zutphen Report]; *Report of the Preparatory Committee on the Establishment of an International Criminal Court, Draft Statute & Draft Final Act* (A/Conf.183/2/Add.1, 1998), Art. 15, p. 48 n. 38; A/CONF.183/2/Add.1, Art. 15, p. 40 n. 38.

310 Holmes, *supra* note 4, p. 78.

311 Canada was prepared to propose a provision in the Rules dealing with waiver. However, after "extensive informal consultations", it decided not to continue. The reasons were several. Some delegations believed that a provision regarding waiver would be "unwarranted" since it is implicit in the language of the Statute. If a State did nothing or decided not to take any action and informed the Court (as the case of Uganda) then the ICC could proceed. However, others thought that a provision was important since the Statute required a determination of unwillingness or inability before the Court could proceed: Conversation with John T. Holmes (Chair of the working group on the principle of complementarity during the preparatory work on the establishment of an International Criminal Court).

312 *Prosecutor v. Thomas Lubanga Dyilo, Decision on the Prosecutor's Application for a Warrant of Arrest, Art. 58*, Case No. ICC-01/04-01/06-8-US-Corr, 10/02/2006, para. 35, unsealed pursuant to Decision ICC-01/04-01/06-37 dated 17/03/2006.

Accordingly, the self-referring State would be actually waiving admissibility and its primacy to exercise jurisdiction over the situation at hands. This factual state would have further procedural implications as explored below. Thus, whether the Rome Statute explicitly refers to the expression "waiver of complementarity" or not, does not appear to be of great significance in this particular context.

A waiver of complementarity is generally understood that the referring State may have the possibility to waive admissibility. Based on this assumption, a waiver may take place without a self-referral and vice versa. Waiving admissiblity has two main implications. First, a State refrains from raising issues related to admissibility. Actually, it does not contest admissiblity. This suggests that the situation will be admissible with respect to the referring State, because Article 17 (1) (a) – (c) has not been satisfied (inaction) and generally admissible if no other State is investigating or prosecuting the situation or case and has made a challenge before the Court (uncontested admissibility).[313] Second, in response, the Court may or may not make an explicit determination on admissibility depending on the stage of the proceedings as explored further in section 3 of chapter IV.[314] A waiver may also be understood in a much broader manner. A State initially deciding to renounce its jurisdiction in favour of the ICC by referring its own situation is actually *waiving* its primacy over the situation (waiver to exercise jurisdiction as a direct consequence of a self-referral). In this context, it is not clear whether a waiver deprives the referring State as opposed to the accused from entering a future admissibility challenge.[315] The wide definition given to a waiver is actually in line with the idea introduced by the drafters during the work of the 1995 *Ad hoc* Committee. From this perspective, a waiver may be deemed as a corollary to a self referral. Nonetheless, both meanings of waiver lead to the same implications explained above. The following examination will proceed having in mind that a waiver may be understood from these two perspectives.

A self-referral carries with it some connotations. It also means that the territorial State is relinquishing its jurisdiction to the Court, despite its theoretical willingness and ability to carry out the proceedings. When the territorial State makes a formal declaration stating its intentions not to initiate domestic proceedings in relation to a situation and actually refers the situation to the Court, this will result in what is called a waiver of complementarity as explained in the preceding paragraph.

313 Mohamed M. El Zeidy, 'Critical Thoughts on Article 59(2) of the ICC Statute', 4 *Journal of International Criminal Justice* 448, 463(2006) [hereinafter Critical Thoughts]; Mohamed M. El Zeidy, 'The Ugandan Government Triggers the First Test of the Complementarity Principle: An Assessment of the First State's Party Referral to the ICC', 5 *International Criminal Law Review* 83, 104 (2005) [hereinafter Uganda]. Yet, sometimes a challenge could be made by an accused or a person for whom an arrest warrant or summons had been issued. Rome Statute, Art., 19(2) (a). For similar views see Héctor Olásolo, *The Triggering Procedure of the International Criminal Court* (Leiden. Boston: Martinus Nijhoff Publishers, 2005), p. 169.

314 Actually, bypassing the admissibility ruling may only take place during Article 19 stage: See Chapter IV, section 3 *infra*.

315 See on this question chapter IV, section 3.3 *infra*.

In September 2003, the OTP issued its first document concerning the future policy of the Office in executing its mandate. The application of the complementarity principle was a significant topic to be covered in this document. The document stated that:

> National investigations and prosecutions, where they can properly be undertaken, will normally be the most effective and efficient means of bringing offenders to justice; States themselves will normally have the best access to evidence and witnesses. To the extent possible the Prosecutor will encourage States to initiate their own proceedings. As a general rule, the policy of the Office of the Prosecutor will be to undertake investigations only where there is a clear case of failure to act by the State or States concerned.[316]

Elsewhere in the policy paper, the OTP stated that the ICC is not intended to replace "national courts, but to operate when national structures and courts are unwilling or unable to conduct investigations and prosecutions".[317] Where there is "concurrent jurisdiction" between domestic courts and the ICC, "the former have priority". Thus, in order to reach a decision whether to investigate or prosecute before the ICC, the Prosecutor "can proceed only where States fail to act, or are not "genuinely" investigating or prosecuting, as described in article 17 of the Rome Statute".[318]

Actually, in his first two referrals, the Prosecutor's practice seems to have run counter to the "prosecutorial priorities" set out in the policy paper when he invited as well as encouraged referrals of situations from States where the alleged crimes were committed – known as self-referrals. In an annex to the 2003 policy paper, it was made clear that among the main objectives in inviting self-referrals is that the Prosecutor enters into direct dialogue with State officials through "meetings in order to receive referrals of situations".[319] In his recent report on the activities of the Office during its first three years, it was pointed out that:

> [W]hile *proprio motu* power is a critical aspect of the Office's independence, the Prosecutor adopted the policy of inviting and welcoming voluntary referrals by territorial states as a first step in triggering the jurisdiction of the Court. This policy resulted in referrals for what would become the Court's first two situations; Northern Uganda and the DRC.[320]

Uganda and the DRC were the first two situations to be received by the Court by way of self-referral, followed by the Central African Republic, to bring to three the total number of self-referrals. In Uganda, for example, it was stated that the justice

316 *Paper on Some Policy Issues before the Office of the Prosecutor*, September 2003, p. 2 [hereinafter 2003 OTP Policy Paper]

317 *Ibid.*, p. 4.

318 *Ibid.*, pp. 2, 4.

319 Annex to the "Paper on Some Policy Issues before the Office of the Prosecutor": Referrals and Communications.

320 *Report on the Activities Performed during the First Three Years (June 2003 – June 2006)*, p. 7 [hereinafter (2003 – 2006) Activities Report].

system "seems capable enough of trying the rebels, to the extent that they can be apprehended".[321] The rebel group subject to prosecution before the ICC – known as the Lord Resistance Army (LRA)[322] – was the main cause for the Government to refer the situation to the Court on the assumption that it had failed to apprehend the leaders. But if this were the case, there was no need for the Prosecutor to intervene on such basis, since the ICC would by no means be in a better position to arrest these leaders. So far, practice has proved this point, as Pre-Trial Chamber II's activities in relation to the Uganda case have been slow since the issue of the arrest warrants against the five top LRA in September 2005. The Court also failed to secure the custody of the LRA leaders.

From a legal point of view, nothing in the Statute or in the Rules explicitly spells out the power of the Prosecutor either to invite States to refer situations or even to encourage them to do so. Article 13(a), in conjunction with Article 14(1) and Rule 45 governing referrals, speaks of a situation to be referred to the Prosecutor by a State Party "requesting the Prosecutor to investigate". Similarly, Article 15(1) and (2), together with Rule 46, triggers the *proprio motu* powers of the Prosecutor subject to his receipt of "information on crimes within the jurisdiction of the Court".

Article 42(1) covering the organization of the OTP states that the Office "shall be responsible for receiving referrals and any substantiated information on crimes within the jurisdiction of the Court, for examining them and for conducting investigations and prosecutions...". The language of these provisions suggests that the Prosecutor has a *passive* role until either a situation has been received by a State Party or a communication has been sent to the OTP requesting him to invoke his *proprio motu* powers.

While these provisions favour a presumption that the Prosecutor's role is submissive until a situation has been received, nothing in the language supports a conclusion that he is barred from encouraging referrals either. Again, reading the Chapeau of Article 13, which states that the "Court may exercise jurisdiction over the crimes listed under article 5...if: (a) A situation...is referred to the Prosecutor by a State Party...", also suggests that unless the Prosecutor acts under his *proprio motu* powers, his role is to wait until a situation has been referred to the Court by a State Party. This conclusion also finds support in the language of Article 14(1).

One commentator argues that a self-referral was never contemplated by the drafters as early as in the 1994 International Law Commission Draft Statute. Citing Article 25 of the Commission Draft as well as the *travaux préparatoires* to the Statute, he further argues that what was intended was a "complainant State...'lodg[ing] a complaint'

321 William A. Schabas, *An Introduction to the International Criminal Court*, 3 rd. ed. (Cambridge: Cambridge University Press, 2007), p. 51 [hereinafter Schabas Introduction 3rd ed.].

322 El Zeidy, *Uganda*, *supra* note 313, pp. 84 – 89; Kasaija Philip Apuuli, 'The International Criminal Court (ICC) and the Lord's Resistance Army (LRA) Insurgency in Northern Uganda', 15 *Criminal Law Forum* 391 (2004).

against *another* state".[323] The change in terminology from a "complaint" to "referring a situation" was due to the fact that "a complainant state was being prevented from submitting a specific case or crime to the Court. It could only refer a situation".[324]

While it is true that the drafting history of the ICC lacks a direct discussion concerning a State agreeing from the outset to refer its own situation to the Court, the issue was implicitly touched upon when the 1995 *Ad hoc* Committee suggested that the Statute should allow a situation where a State might voluntarily renounce jurisidiction to the ICC.[325] Because a self-referral results in the territorial State's inaction, leaving proceedings to be carried out by the ICC, which is a clear renouncement of jurisdiction, arguably the 1995 proposal was therefore meant to cover the situation of a self-referral. The fact that Article 25(1) – (3) of the 1994 International Law Commission Draft Statute speaks of "lodg[ing] a complaint"[326] does not necessarily mean that that complaint is targeting another State. Perhaps, it may not be logical to presume that a State would complain against itself, especially if it is directly involved in the commission of the crimes or tolerated their perpetration. But this does not rule out a possibility where the State was complaining against an organisation acting within the State to commit those crimes. Article 25(1) states that a State Party "which is also a Contracting Party to the Convention on the Prevention and Punishment of the Crime of Genocide...may lodge a complaint alleging that a crime of genocide appears to have been committed".[327]

Similarly, paragraph (2) permits a State Party which has accepted the Court's jurisdiction under Article 22 of the draft to "lodge a complaint with the Prosecutor" in relation to the crimes committed.[328] The only limitation may appear under paragraph 3 obliging the complainant State to "specify the circumstances of the alleged crime and the identity and whereabouts of any suspect",[329] which presumably suggests that a State, if directly involved, would never submit itself to the jurisdiction of the Court in order to avoid being in the position of having to declare the identity or places where any alleged perpetrator may be. Yet, in cases where the alleged perpetrators belong to an organisation acting within the State, as mentioned above, nothing would really prevent paragraph 3 from being applied to a State lodging a complaint against crimes committed by others in its own territory.

On a parallel line of argument, nothing in the language of Article 13(a) or 14(1) of the current ICC Statute prevents the territorial State from referring a situation of alleged crimes committed on its territory by groups not related to the government.

323 William A. Schabas, 'First Prosecutions at the International Criminal Court', 27 *Human Rights Law Journal* 25, 27 (2006); see also William A. Schabas, 'Complementarity in Practice: Some Uncomplementary Thoughts', 19 *Criminal Law Forum* (forthcoming 2008).

324 *Ibid.*

325 1995 *Ad hoc Committee Report, supra* note 4, para. 47.

326 1994 *ILC Draft Statute, supra* note 14, Art. 25(1) – (3).

327 *Ibid.*, para. (1).

328 *Ibid.*, para. (2).

329 *Ibid.*, para. (3).

This argument is not intended to prove that the idea of self-referrals was contemplated by the drafters. Rather, it aims to demonstrate that the language of Articles 13(a) and 14(1) does not seem to exclude the possibility of accommodating self-referrals. Otherwise, the outcome of the Uganda and DRC cases as well as the Central African Republic situation would be deemed void. Although the latter provisions cause no legal problem in relation to this type of referral, self-referrals may be seen as problematic when examined in the scope of the preamble to the Statute.

The first apparent obstacle that might raise doubts about accepting the theory of self-referrals, which results in a waiver, lies in the wording of the preamble to the Statute. Preambular paragraph 4 affirms that crimes within the subject matter jurisdiction of the Court "must not go unpunished" and that their "effective prosecution must be ensured by taking measures at the national level…".[330] Thus, it is "the duty of every State to exercise its criminal jurisdiction over those responsible for international crimes".[331] The use of the verb "must" in the second part of paragraph 4 in conjunction with the phrase "taking measures at the national level" makes it clear that the preamble imposes a positive obligation not only to ensure "effective prosecution", but also to ensure that it takes place "at the national level". In order to ensure effective prosecution at the national level, "measures" "must" be taken. The requirement that "measures" must be taken or "effective prosecution must be ensured by taking measures" implies that the State is obliged to take positive action. In other words, in the case of a self-referral, the State in question *initially* decides not to act followed by deciding to waive jurisdiction to the Court without even attempting to take positive action towards investigation.[332]

Furthermore, paragraph 6 comes into play to affirm this meaning by considering that the States' action at the national level is a "duty". Some commentators believe that this draft is "delightfully ambiguous", since it is not clear whether such a duty targets the territorial State or a "much broader jurisdiction of the universal kind, regardless of where the events occurred".[333] Arguably, preambular paragraph 6 addresses all States Parties that may exercise jurisdiction over these crimes.[334] It seems to have

330 Rome Statute, preamble, para. 4.

331 *Ibid.*, para. 6. A duty in general terms is defined as "A legal obligation that is owed or due to another and needs to be satisfied", and a legal duty is defined as "an obligation the breach of which would be a legal wrong": *Black's Law Dictionary*, *supra* note 42, pp. 521–522.

332 However, sometimes a State might start an investigation and then decide to refer the situation to the Court without even being deemed unwilling or unable to act (action followed by inaction).

333 Tuiloma Neroni Slade and Roger S. Clark, "Preamble and Final Clauses", in Roy S. Lee (ed.), *supra* note 4, p. 427; see also Otto Triffterer, "Preamble", *Triffterer Commentary*, *supra* note 37 , p. 13.

334 The idea behind preambular paragraph 6 is twofold. First, as stated above, it exhorts States Parties to the Statute to comply with their duty, since it could not impose an obligation on third States; secondly, it serves as a reminder even to third States which still have the right to exercise complementarity that they are under an existing duty to investigate those heinous crimes; see also Kristina Miskowiak, *The International Criminal Court:*

been inserted to emphasise the principle of complementarity in the sense that, despite the existence of the ICC, States are still under an existing obligation to exercise primary jurisdiction over those crimes of international concern. Thus, the ICC is a court of last resort. This conclusion may be inferred from the original proposal tabled by the Dominican Republic as well as from statements made by some delegates during the plenary meetings of the Rome Conference. On 8 July 1998, the Dominican Republic for the first timed introduced draft preambular paragraph 3 (currently para. 6), which emphasises "that each State still has the duty to exercise its penal jurisdiction over individuals responsible for crimes of international significance".[335] The drafting of this paragraph, as opposed to the substance, was later modified after informal consultation with the current language of preambular paragraph 6.[336] When reading the original proposal one may get a sense that the intention was to make sure that national courts should "still" play their role, regardless of the existence of the ICC. This understanding may be further supported by a reading of the statement made by the delegate of Brunei Darussalam when he stated:

> Complementarity was crucial to the jurisdictional relationship between national justice systems and the Court, which should supplement and not supplant national jurisdiction. States had the primary duty to investigate and prosecute those suspected or accused of committing the crimes which fell within the Court's jurisdiction.[337]

In the same vein, the Swiss delegate made it clear that the establishment of the Court "should not relieve national courts of their duty to punish individual acts that contravened the law of nations".[338] Indeed, in the *Gaddafi* case, the Paris Court of Appeal invoked preambular paragraph 6 to the Rome Statute as a ground for exercising its criminal jurisdiction over Colonel Gaddafi, the Libyan leader, alleging that he was implicated in the killing of 170 aircraft passengers, including French citizens. The court stated:

Consent, Complementarity and Cooperation (Copenhagen: DJØF Publishing, 2000), p. 35 (noting that paragraph 6 "bears evidence to an emerging customary law principle of universal jurisdiction for all the crimes of the Statute").

335 Dominican Republic: Proposal Regarding the Preamble, UN Doc. A/CONF. 183/C.1/L.52, 8 July 1998, preamble, para. 3.

336 Coordinator's Rolling Text Regarding the Preamble and Part 13, 10 July 1998, UN Doc. A/CONF.183/C.1/L.54/REV.2, preamble para. 5; Recommendations of the Coordinator Regarding the Preamble and Part 13, 11 July 1998, UN Doc. A/CONF.183/C.1/L.61, preamble para. 5; Recommendations of the Coordinator Regarding the Preamble, 14 July 1998, UN Doc. A/CONF.183/C.1/L.73, preamble para. 5; and Report of the Committee of the Whole, 17 July 1998, UN Doc. A/CONF.183/8, preamble para. 6.

337 *Summary Record of the 5 th Plenary Meeting*, 17 June 1998, UN Doc. A/CONF.183/SR.5, para. 15.

338 *Summary Record of the 7 th Plenary Meeting*, 18 June 1998, UN Doc. A/CONF.183/SR.7, para. 39.

> The Convention containing the Statute of the International Criminal Court,...recalls in its Preamble "that it is the duty of every State to exercise its criminal jurisdiction"...It is thereby recognized by this Convention that it is the duty of the States which have ratified it to exercise their jurisdiction over international crimes.[339]

How can a State waive its duty through a decision not to act coupled with a referral to the Court? It is hardly persuasive that a positive duty is subject to waiver. Moreover, in light of the preambular obligation, it is extremely doubtful whether the Prosecutor should cooperate with or even encourage such a practice. The Inter-American Court of Human Rights affirmed the view that a "duty" cannot be waived in the recent *Hilaire* and *Benjamin* cases. The Court noted that it "cannot abdicate [the issue under consideration], as it is a duty that the American Convention imposes upon it..."[340] It follows that accepting a self-referral resulting from deliberate State inaction might be seen as impermissible under the ICC Statute, since duties should not be relinquished or waived.

A different way of looking at the problem requires an understanding of the duty imposed by preambular paragraphs 4 and 6 in light of the essence of complementarity reiterated in preambular paragraph 10 and Articles 1 and 17. Although preambular paragraph 6 refers to the duty of every State to exercise its criminal jurisdiction, as a matter of fact not every state would be able to comply with such a duty *at all times*. The Statute *itself*, drafted on this theory, therefore, left room for such possibility through the system of complementarity, which permits the ICC to take over responsibility in the event of a State's failure genuinely to carry out its proceedings. The Swiss delegate who made the statement referred to above affirmed this view when he stated that the "goal of the Conference was to establish a permanent international court to punish..., whenever national courts could not or would not perform their duty".[341] Thus, the duty imposed under preambular paragraph 6 should be interpreted from this angle.

A corollary of the principle of complementarity seems to be the well-established principle of *aut dedere aut judicare* (prosecute or extradite), which grants the state

339 *Gaddafi, France, Court of Appeal of Paris (Chambre d'accusation)*, 20/10/2000, 125 I.L.R., 490, 497 (2004) [hereinafter Gaddafi case]; and for the French original version see Florence Poirat, 'Immunité de Jurisdiction pénale du chef d'Eatat étranger en exercise et régle coutumiére devant le Juge Judiciare', 105 *Revue Générale de Droit International Public* 473, 476 (2001). This decision was overturned by the Court of Cassation in relation to the question of the immunity of a Head of State: see *France, Court of Cassation*, 13/03/2001, 125 I.L.R., 508 (2004).

340 *Hilaire, Preliminary Objections*, Judgment of 1/09/2001, Inter-Am Ct. H.R. (Ser. C) No. 80 (2001), para. 80; *Benjamin et al., Preliminary Objections*, Judgment of 1/09/ 2001, Inter-Am Ct. H.R. (Ser. C) No. 81 (2001) para. 71.

341 *Summary Record of the 7 th Plenary Meeting*, 18 June 1998, UN Doc. A/CONF.183/SR.7, para. 35.

the choice of either action and does not prefer one over the other.[342] In the case of the ICC, the choice would be that the State prosecute, extradite to another State that is willing to prosecute or surrender to the Court. This, in essence, renders a self-referral and a waiver of complementarity, compatible with the spirit of the Statute.

One commentator reaches a similar conclusion, yet on the basis of a different legal argument, when he stated that preambular paragraph 6 should not be interpreted strictly. The "territorial State's duty to exercise criminal jurisdiction" should not be confined to "investigation", "prosecution" or "punishment";[343] rather the duty should be widely construed as the obligation "to ensure that a genuine investigation be undertaken, be it by the State itself, be it by way of extradition to another State, or even by way of surrender to an international criminal jurisdiction".[344]

Also, a self-referral resulting from a State's inaction fits neatly within the parameters of the admissibility provision (Article 17). Article 17(1) (a) states that the Court "shall determine that a case is inadmissible where... [t]he case is being investigated... by a State".[345] Thus, if a State fails to initiate an investigation or acknowledges that it is not intending to do so, the case should be *de facto* admissible, since none of the criteria set out in Article 17(1) (a)–(c) would be satisfied.[346] As explained earlier, the admissibility analysis involves two stages. The first stage applies in situations of States' inaction including those resulting from self-referrals, while the second phase comes into play once proceedings have been initiated. On this last point, the determination of the genuineness of domestic proceedings is tested by the "unwilling" or "unable" criterion.

Sometimes the decision of a State to relinquish its jurisdiction to the ICC may be based on a legitimate reason (as opposed to politically motivated decisions), for example, in such cases the ICC would better guarantee due process rights or because a

342 A principle that dates back to Grotius and was originally known as *aut dedre aut punire*, later developed to *aut dedre aut judicare* in the sense that a person should not technically be punished before being prosecuted and afforded all the judicial guarantees. For the origins see Hugo Grotius, *De Jure Belli Ac Pacis Libri Tres*, Vol. II (Oxford: Clarendon Press, 1925), pp. 527–529; M. Cherif Bassiouni and Edward M. Wise, *Aut Dedere Aut Judicare: The Duty to Extradite or Prosecute in International Law* (Dordrecht/Boston/London: Martinus Nijhoff, 1995), pp. 3–5, 56–57; Colleen Enache-Brown and Ari Fried, 'Universal Crime, Jurisdiction and Duty: The Obligation of Aut Dedere Aut Judicare in International Law', 43 *McGill Law Journal* 613, 626 (1998).

343 Claus Kress, "Self-Referrals' and 'Waivers of Complementarity': Some Considerations in Law and Policy', 2 *Journal of International Criminal Justice* 944, 946(2004). But see the *Gaddafi* case cited above, where the Paris Court of Appeal did not restrict the application of preambular paragraph 6 to the territorial State; rather it invoked the preamble to exercise domestic jurisdiction on the basis of the *passive personality principle: Gaddafi, France, Court of Appeal of Paris (Chambre d'accusation)*, 20/10/2000, 125 I.L.R., 490, 491 (2004).

344 Kress, *supra* note 343, p. 946.

345 Rome Statute, Art. 17(1)(a).

346 El Zeidy, *Critical Thoughts, supra* note 313, p. 463; El Zeidy, *Uganda, supra* note 313, p. 104; Kress, *supra* note 342, p. 946.

successful conviction could not be achieved in a specific case due to the state's unique judicial system or due to the circumstances surrounding that specific case. Thus, in such situations, there is no logic in rejecting a State's attempt initially to relinquish its jurisdiction in favour of the Court, especially if the situation or case passes the gravity test.

If the Court, as a matter of principle, rejected self-referrals and waivers, there is a great possibility that the situation would not be dealt with before both fora, leading to denial of justice. Self-referrals may be seen as useful from the point of view that the referring State should have the political will – to a certain extent – to offer the Court the necessary cooperation.[347] Perhaps, a self-referral, which results in a waiver of complementarity, might also be seen as a dangerous easy tool to be invoked by states, in order to avoid complying with their duties. Certainly, this would result in burdening the Court with case load and financial problems. Thus, it should be considered on a *case-by-*case basis.

4. The Criterion of Inability

Inability is a separate criterion, distinct in terms of application from that of unwillingness. Unlike "unwillingness", which relies to a certain extent on subjective assessment, "inability" concerns a case inspired by elements of objectivity.[348] A State might be anxious to proceed with a genuine investigation, prosecution and trial, but as a matter of fact be unable to do so for lack of capacity. This might be caused by public disorder, natural disasters and chaos resulting from a civil war or the unavailability of an effective judicial system, that is, one capable of guaranteeing a full, effective domestic criminal process in relation to a certain situation or case.[349]

The situation of Somalia, where there was no central government, was cited as one example.[350] Rwanda is another example that showed a State's inability in the mid-1990s.[351] Columbia was also provided as an example reflecting the incapacity of the judiciary as well as the government to put drug dealers on trial. As one member of the International Law Commission stated during the Commission's discussion on

---

347 Paola Gaeta, 'Is the Practice of 'Self-Referrals' a Sound Start for the ICC?', 2 *Journal of International Criminal Justice* 949, 950 (2004).

348 But see e.g., the statement made by Mr. El Masry, the Egyptian delegate, at the Rome Conference, considering that all the criteria for inability lacked objectivity with the exception of the criterion of "total collapse". *Summary Record of the 35th Meeting*, 13 July 1998, UN Doc. A/CONF.183/C.1/SR.35, para. 6.

349 In the same vein see *2003 OTP Policy Paper*, *supra* note 316, p. 4.

350 Mahnoush H. Arsanjani, "Reflections on the Jurisdiction and Trigger Mechanism of the International Criminal Court", in Herman A. M. von Hebel et al. (eds.), *supra* note 62, p. 70.

351 Support may be found in William A. Schabas, 'Genocide Trials and *Gacaca* Courts', 3 *Journal of International Criminal Justice* 879, 883 (2005); William A. Schabas, 'Justice, Democracy, and Impunity in Post-genocide Rwanda: Searching for Solutions to Impossible Problems', 7 *Criminal Law Forum* 523, 525 – 534 (1996).

establishing an international criminal court in 1990, "Colombian judges were unable to try [drug dealers] in their own country as...the national courts were incapable of bringing them to justice. That was what had prompted the idea of punishing them at the international level".[352]

Article 17(3) states:

> In order to determine inability in a particular case, the Court shall consider whether, due to a total or substantial collapse or unavailability of its national judicial system, the State is unable to obtain the accused or the necessary evidence and testimony or otherwise unable to carry out its proceedings.[353]

The provision entails different situations in which the ICC may rule a case admissible: 1) where the State fails to secure the custody of the accused; 2) where the State could not gather the necessary evidence and testimony; or 3) where the State is otherwise not able to conduct the proceedings. These situations must be resulting from either a total or substantial collapse or the unavailability of the State's national judicial system. Accordingly, the ICC may assert its jurisdiction only when it identifies a deficiency in State organs resulting from a breakdown of State judicial institutions, or "widespread anarchy".[354] The State must be unable to obtain an accused or key evidence, and its inability must relate to the total, or substantial, collapse or unavailability of its judicial system.[355]

But limiting the situations of inability to a set of specific conditions such as failure to capture the accused or obtain evidence seemed to some delegations to be insufficient.[356] It could in certain cases block the Court from ruling a situation or case admissible on the basis of different defects, not necessarily covered by these situations. The phrase "or otherwise unable to carry out its proceedings" was added during the

352 *Summary Records of the Meetings of the Forty – Second Session* (1 May – 20 July 1990), 1990 *YILC*, Vol. I, p. 16 (statement by Mr. Bennouna) [hereinafter 1990 *YILC*, Vol. I].

353 Rome Statute, Art. 17(3).

354 Paolo Benvenuti, "Complementarity of the International Criminal Court to National Criminal Jurisdictions" in Flavia Lattanzi et al., (eds.), *Essays on the Rome Statute of the International Criminal Court*, Vol. I (Il Sirente, 1999), p. 44.

355 See also Schabas, *supra* note 6, p. 86; Williams, *supra* note 37, p. 394; Holmes, *supra* note 4, p. 49. This poses a question in relation to *force majeure*, which is beyond the scope of this study but worth mentioning. Noticeably, while Article 17(3) renders a case admissible as a result of the failure of a State to carry out domestic proceedings as a result of total or substantial collapse or unavailability of the national judicial system, which actually represents a sort of *force majeure*, the occurrence of *force majeure* in itself is considered a justification releasing the State from responsibility for failing to fulfill its obligation. For a definition of *force majeur* see *supra* note 294; also Antonio Cassese, *International Law*, 2nd ed. (Oxford: Oxford University Press, 2005), pp. 254 – 255 (referring to some jurisprudence on the subject).

356 Some delegates believed that adding this criterion seemed superfluous. See Holmes, *supra* note 4, p. 49.

work of the Preparatory Committee to serve as a catch-all clause for all sorts of situations that might arise in the course of the domestic process.[357]

Further, subjecting States' inability to secure an offender to the conditions of total or substantial collapse or unavailability of the national judicial system has been criticized by some academics. According to one scholar, a "developed and functional justice system" that fails to secure the custody of an offender due to a lack of "extradition treaties" would still be able to defy ICC prosecution on the ground of complementarity.[358] Similarly, replacing the term "partial collapse", which initially appeared during the Preparatory Committee discussions, with "substantial collapse", at the Rome Conference,[359] will result in blocking the ICC's exercise of jurisdiction in relation to certain crisis situations. There are two main reasons for this change in language.

The first reason has been overlooked in the literature on the ICC. At the Rome Conference several delegations rejected the jurisdiction of the Court over internal armed conflicts unless "certain criteria, such as the total collapse of a country's central regime, were included".[360] The Qatari representative made it clear that his delegation "could not accept the jurisdiction of the Court over internal conflicts, except in cases of total collapse of a State's judicial system…".[361] The Omani representative shared this view, stating, "[i]nternal conflicts should not fall within the jurisdiction of the Court except in the event of total collapse of the judicial system".[362] Similar views were expressed by the Yemeni[363] and Pakistani representatives.[364] A term such as "partial collapse" would not have satisfied these delegations. Instead, "total collapse" was retained. Reaching a compromise by replacing the term "partial" with "substan-

357 See 1997 *Preparatory Committee Decisions*, *supra* note 39, Art. 35(4), p. 12 (where the phrase emerged for the first time); also Holmes, *Cassese Commentary*, *supra* note 22, p. 678, and Holmes, *supra* note 4 , p. 49. In this respect, some delegations reflected their concern by providing an example, i.e., if the accused and some evidence were obtained but other aspects of the national proceedings were affected by the collapse.

358 Schabas, *supra* note 6, p. 86.

359 At the Rome Conference, Mr. González Gálvez of Mexico argued that the word "partially" should be replaced by "substantial". See *Summary Record of the 31 st Meeting*, 9 July 1998, UN Doc. A/CONF.183/C.1/SR.31, para. 37; also Mexico Proposal, *supra* note 133, UN Doc. A/CONF.183/C.1/L.14/REV.1; also Mahnoush H. Arsanjani, W. Michael Reisman, 'The Law-in-Action of the International Criminal Court', 99 *American Journal of International Law* 385, 388 (2005) (noting that deleting the term "partial collapse" increased the "threshold" and the "magnitude" of admissibility).

360 *Summary Record of the 25th Meeting*, 8 July 1998, UN Doc. A/CONF.183/C.1/SR.25, para. 49 (statement made by the Syrian Arab Representative).

361 *Summary Record of the 35th Meeting*, 13 July 1998, UN Doc. A/CONF.183/C.1/SR.35, para. 57.

362 *Summary Record of the 36th Meeting*, 13 July 1998, UN Doc. A/CONF.183/C.1/SR.36, para. 20.

363 *Summary Record of the 27th Meeting*, 8 July 1998, UN Doc. A/CONF.183/C.1/SR.27, para. 62.

364 *Summary Record of the 35th Meeting*, 13 July 1998, UN Doc. A/CONF.183/C.1/SR.35, para. 54.

tial" collapse to stand alongside a "total collapse", was a Mexican proposal that finally found its way into the text on admissibility.

As to the second reason, according to some delegations the deletion of the term "partial collapse" was necessary, because there could be a situation where a breakdown caused in one region would not necessarily impact upon the efficiency of courts in other regions.[365] In a State where an armed conflict exists, the judiciary may be only "partially affected" and therefore there would be no need for the ICC to exercise jurisdiction.[366] The State might, instead, transfer the trial of a case to other courts, thus ensuring "genuine" results.[367] Apparently, the drafters were referring to situations that could result in a state of emergency, and that might impact on only parts of the territory as opposed to the entire nation.

Declarations of emergency which affect one part of a country have been accepted in the jurisprudence of the ECHR[368] as well as in legal doctrine. According to Nicole Questiaux, the former Special Rapporteur of the United Nations Sub-commission on the Prevention of Discrimination and Protection of Minorities, a valid emergency "must affect…, either the whole of the territory or certain parts thereof". It must also affect "the functioning of the organs of the State".[369] In the same vein, Thomas Buergenthal wrote that a "public emergency which threatens the life of the nation" could presumably exist even if the emergency appeared to be confined to one part of the country – for example, one of its provinces, states or cantons – and did not threaten to spill over to other parts.[370]

But the fact that the drafters deleted the term "partial collapse" leads to the conclusion that a situation of emergency similar to the one referred to by Buergenthal would fail to meet the threshold of Article 17(3) of the Statute. The collapse resulting from the emergency must have a "substantial" or "total" effect on the national judicial system. Again, when looking at the term "total or substantial collapse" set out in Article 17(3) together with the original term "partial collapse", one could observe the difficulty in drawing a demarcation line. A "substantial collapse" would presumably be a degree of intensity that was lower than a "total collapse", yet higher than a "partial collapse". Otherwise the word "substantial" would be redundant.

But, if the drafters' intentions were to strike out the term "partial", on the basis that a trial may take place in the context of an armed conflict before any functioning

365 Holmes, *supra* note 4, p. 55.

366 Holmes, *Cassese Commentary*, *supra* note 22, p. 677.

367 *Ibid.*

368 *Aksoy v. Turkey (1)*, Application No. 21987/93, Eur. Ct. H.R., Judgment (Merits and Just Satisfaction) of 18/12/1996, para. 70.

369 Nicole Questiaux, *Question of the Human Rights of Persons Subjected to any Form of Detention or Imprisonment: Study of the Implications for Human Rights of Recent Developments Concerning Situations Known as States of Siege or Emergency*, UN Doc. E/CN.4/Sub.2/1982/15, pp. 15 – 16.

370 Thomas Buergenthal, "To Respect and to Ensure: State Obligations and Permissible Derogations", in Louis Henkin (ed.), *The International Bill of Human Rights: The Covenant on Civil and Political Rights* (New York: Columbia University Press, 1981), pp. 72, 80.

court, this would mean that any collapse that was less than "total" was not acceptable. Assuming that as a result of an armed conflict a collapse occurred in all regions of a country with one exception. Would this be considered a "substantial or partial collapse"? If we consider this scenario as representing a "substantial collapse", this interpretation may run counter to the intentions of the drafters, who argued that as long as there was an alternative venue for the trial of a case, then the ICC should not step in, which is the same reason for deleting the term "partial".

Similarly, if, according to this scenario, the collapse would be deemed "partial", there is no room for applying the term "substantial", as the following acceptable step would reflect a "total collapse" – namely, one which affects all regions of a State.[371] Thus the problem in defining the term "substantial collapse" lies in the difficulty in drawing the line between it and a "total collapse". Nonetheless a literal interpretation of the term in its context, as set out in Article 17(3), would support a definition that a collapse will be considered "substantial" if it is of such intensity that it affects a significant or considerable part of the domestic justice system. A degree of intensity that is sufficient to paralyze the system in fulfilling its functions in relation to investigation, prosecution, trial and execution of sentences is required. In any event, collapse in general carries with it connotations such as the lack of judicial infrastructure as well as trained and equipped personnel responsible for carrying out the different phases of the domestic proceedings.[372]

An admissibility decision in relation to inability can be based on the "unavailability" of the State's national judicial system rather than its collapse. But would not a "total collapse" result in a situation of "unavailability" of the domestic justice system? If one interprets the latter phrase strictly, it may be argued that the "unavailability" of a judicial system means that it is "non-existent", which may also be caused by a total collapse. This finding is supported by one scholar who argued that the only possible interpretation, according to the authentic Spanish text of the Statute, would be that the "judicial system is unavailable when it is non-existent".[373] But if this is the "only interpretation", as argued by that scholar, then the phrase "unavailability of its national judicial system" would appear redundant, since it is a situation that might easily be covered by the term "total" or even "substantial" collapse. Accordingly, this provision should be given an "effective" and "practical" interpretation that "ensures its full

371 That is when the collapse affects the entire regions.

372 See e.g., *Informal Expert Paper*, *supra* note 49, pp. 15, 31.

373 Arvena, *supra* note 58, p. 124. Mention has been made of the idea of non-existence of the national judicial system by the Portuguese delegate, Mr. Matos Fernandes, during a plenary meeting at Rome. He said that the jurisdiction of the ICC "was not a matter of transferring jurisdiction from national courts, but of enabling the Court to intervene wherever national judicial systems were non-existent or unable or unwilling to take action. The Court alone should decide on the verification of such situations". See *Summary Record of the 4th Plenary Meeting*, 16 June 1998, UN Doc. A.CONF.183/SR.4, para. 27. Yet, there is nothing in this statement to suggest that the intention was to limit the term "unavailability" of a national judicial system to the non-existence of that system.

meaning and attaints its appropriate effects".[374] It is also very significant to avoid any restrictions in interpretation that render the system of the ICC "inoperative".[375]

Arguably, the scope of the phrase "unavailability of its national judicial system" goes beyond the idea of a "non-existent" judicial system. It may refer to situations such as, lack of substantive as well as procedural legislation. This element has two dimensions. First, where the State lacks the entire gamut of necessary implementing legislation in relation to arrest, surrender and all sorts of cooperation with the Court, enabling it to act upon the investigation of crimes under the jurisdiction of the Court; and, secondly, where the deficiency in domestic law is confined to a lack of definitions proscribing crimes in a manner that corresponds to those defined under the Statute. The former situation may easily lead to the triggering of the complementarity principle before the Court, while the second is still debatable.[376]

The existence of laws that serve as a bar to domestic proceedings is also relevant. These may include amnesties, immunities or a statute of limitations.[377] Lack of access to courts may also render the domestic system unavailable.[378] On this last point, the ECHR in the *Multiplex* case argued as a matter of principle that Article 6 of the European Convention on Human Rights guarantees the "right of access", which is "the

374 *Fairen Garbi and Solis Corrales*, Preliminary Objections, Judgment of 26/06/1987, Inter-Am.Ct.H.R. (Ser.C) No. 2 (1987), para. 35.

375 *Benjamin et al v. Trinidad and Tobago*, Preliminary Objections, Judgment of 1/09/2001, Inter-Am.Ct.H.R. (Ser.C) No. 80 (2001), para. 82.

376 Mauro Politi – Federica Gioia, 'The Criminal Procedure Before the International Criminal Court: Main Features', 5 *The Law and Practice of International Courts and Tribunals* 103, 108 (2006); But see Robert Cryer and Olympia Bekou, 'International Crimes and ICC Cooperation in England and Wales', 5 *Journal of International Criminal Justice* 441, 444 (2007) (noting that s. 50(1) and (2) of the ICC Act ensures full compliance with the exact definitions of the crimes set out in the Rome Statute in order to avoid "an adverse complementarity decision by the ICC"); Julio Bacio Terracino, 'National Implementation of ICC Crimes: Impact on National Jurisdictions and the ICC', 5 *Journal of International Criminal Justice* 421, 435 (2007) (stating that "if a state has not incorporated or harmonized the definitions of the crimes into its national legislation and declares it cannot prosecute after conducting an investigation, that state's judicial system is clearly unavailable"); also in the same vein see Lijun Yang, 'On the Principle of Complementarity in the Rome Statute of the International Criminal Court', 4 *Chinese Journal of International Law* 121, 125 – 126 (2005); Hugo Relva, 'The Implementation of the Rome Statute in Latin American States', 16 *Leiden Journal of International Law* 331, 338 (2003); and generally Larry Charles Dembowski, "The International Criminal Court: Complementarity and Its Consequences", in Jane E. Stromseth (ed.), *Accountability for Atrocities: National and International Reponses* (Ardsley, New York: Transnational Publishers, 2003), pp. 144 – 146.

377 See also William W. Burke-White, 'Complementarity in Practice: The International Criminal Court as Part of a System of Multi-Level Global Governance in the Democratic Republic of Congo', 18 *Leiden Journal of International Law* 557, 582 (2005); Cassese, *ICL*, *supra* note 138, p. 352.

378 *Informal Expert Paper*, *supra* note 49, pp. 15, 31.

right to institute proceedings before courts".[379] Yet, the scope of access to a court is not confined to the right to institute proceedings; rather it secures a determination "by a final decision in the judicial proceedings".[380] Further, the degree of access afforded has to be sufficient under the national legislation in order to satisfy the requirement of access to a court.[381] If these principles are to be applied in the context of the ICC, it could be argued that the lack of access to judicial proceedings before domestic courts, in relation to the crimes under consideration, may raise the question of the State's inability. Also, the shortage of national legislation to secure the possibility of initiating judicial proceedings (access to a Court) in relation to a certain crime before domestic courts may also trigger the element of inability. Similarly and in the light of the principles established by the ECHR, the partial access to domestic courts that lies in the failure to guarantee a final decision in relation to a certain case or the execution of a judgment given by a court[382] may perhaps involve the issue of the State's ability to conduct domestic proceedings.

4.1 *Pre-Trial Chamber I's Approach to Self-referrals and Waivers of Complementarity Coupled with Inability in the DRC Case*

In *Lubanga*, Pre-Trial Chamber I seemed to have treated the ideas of inability and a self-referral together as if they were linked. The Chamber briefly touched on the question of a self-referral (without *explicitly* addressing the question of waiver) and seems to have endorsed the practice, yet without properly spelling out the legal reasoning for reaching such a conclusion. It stated that in its view:

> [W]hen the President of the DRC sent the letter of referral to the Office of the prosecutor on 3 March 2004, it appears that the DRC was indeed unable to undertake the investigation and prosecution of crimes falling within the jurisdiction of the Court committed in the territory of DRC since 1 July 2002. In the Chamber's view, this is why the self-referral of the DRC appears consistent with the ultimate purpose of the complementarity regime,

379 *Multiplex v. Croatia*, Application No. 58112/00, Eur. Ct. H.R., Judgment (Merits and Just Satisfaction) of 10/07/2003, para. 41.

380 *Ibid.*, para. 45. But access to courts in the context of the ICC Statute should not be interpreted narrowly; rather it should look at all available venues or mechanisms for reporting crimes in order to secure access to justice in the widest sense of the term.

381 *Ibid.*, para. 44; *Ashingdane v. The United Kingdom*, Eur. Ct. H.R., Judgment (Merits and Just Satisfaction) of 28/05/1985, para. 57.

382 As the ECHR stated in *Hornsby*, "[t]o construe Article 6 (art. 6) as being concerned exclusively with access to a court and the conduct of proceedings would be likely to lead to situations incompatible with the principle of the rule of law which the Contracting States undertook to respect when they ratified the Convention... Execution of a judgment given by any court must therefore be regarded as an integral part of the "trial" for the purposes of Article 6 (art. 6)". *Hornsby v. Greece* (1), Application No. 18357/91, Eur. Ct. H.R., Judgment (Merits) of 19/03/1997, para. 40.

according to which the Court by no means replaces national criminal jurisdictions, but it is complementary to them.[383]

This paragraph suggests that the Chamber accepted the self-referral for the sole purpose of being requested to do so, since the DRC, as the Chamber noted, was "unable to undertake" the proceedings in relation to the crimes falling within the jurisdiction of the Court. This is what made the DRC's self-referral in the Chamber's opinion "consistent" with the "purpose of the complementarity principle".[384]

Also, the sentence "this is why the self-referral of the DRC appears consistent with the ultimate purpose of the complementarity regime" in its context suggests that the Chamber intended to treat self-referrals, which results in a waiver, on a *case-by-case* basis. In the case of the DRC, it was the letter of referral outlining the inability of the State to carry out the proceedings in relation to the crimes under the ICC Statute which prompted the Chamber to accept the self-referral and by implication the waiver. It was as if the Chamber intended to say that *mere* self-referral or waiver is unacceptable unless accompanied by reasons, such as the clear inability of the State to proceed with a certain situation or case.

As to the question of waiver, the decision lacks any direct reference to this effect. As explained at the outset of this chapter, a waiver may be given a narrow as well as a wide interpretation. Also, it has two main implications: one lies within the State's domain, while the second is under the control of the Court. A State may decide to voluntarily waive its primacy by renouncing jurisdiction in favour of the Court and without enetering into a debate on admissibility. The Court, on the other hand, may decide either to rule on the question of admissibility, despite the State's initial waiver or leave out such assessment depending on the stage of the proceedings.[385] DRC was actually waiving its superiority to exercise jurisdiction and admissibility by deciding not to initiate proceedings (inaction), but the fact that the Chamber made an *ex-officio* determination on admissibility at this stage of the proceedings indicates that the theory of waiver of complementarity was not fully applied. The Chamber could have avoided examining admissibility in accordance with Article 19(1). Yet, the Chamber's endorsment of the self-referral seems to suggest an implicit approval of the State's waiver resulting from that referral for the exact same reasons.[386]

The question of inability raised by the Chamber causes some confusion in relation to the understanding and appropriate application of Article 17 of the Statute. It is a common understanding that the Article 17(1) test is twofold. The Court *shall* determine that a case is inadmissible where: 1) the case is being investigated or prosecuted

383 *Prosecutor v. Thomas Lubanga Dyilo, Decision on the Prosecutor's Application for a Warrant of Arrest, Art. 58,* No.: ICC-01/04-01/06-8-US-Corr, 10/02/2006, para. 35, unsealed pursuant to Decision ICC-01/04-01/06-37 dated 17/03/2006.

384 *Ibid.*

385 See chapter IV, section 3 *infra.*

386 But, the fact that Pre-Trial Chamber I preferred to rule on admissibility at this phase does not mean that the above conclusion is inaccurate. This only means that the concept of waiver was applied only in part.

by a State with jurisdiction over it,[387] unless the State is unwilling or unable genuinely to carry out the investigation or prosecution.[388] Thus, the first question is whether the State with jurisdiction over the case is investigating or prosecuting. If the answer is in the negative, then the case is admissible *a contrario*. In cases where the answer is in the affirmative and the case is in the course of investigation or prosecution, then it has to be shown that the State is conducting a genuine investigation or prosecution within the meaning of Article 17(2) and (3).[389]

It follows that the issue of inability does not come into play until national proceedings are underway or have been initiated. Absent any such proceedings, the case would be admissible as a result of the State's *inaction*, since none of the criteria of Article 17(1) (a) – (c) would be satisfied.[390] In the *Lubanga* decision, Pre-Trial Chamber I *mistakenly* invoked the term "unable" in the technical sense, as reflected in Article 17(1)(a) – (b) and (3), when it construed the text of the DRC's referral to this effect.[391] Although the letter of referral explicitly states that the competent authorities of the DRC "are not able" to carry out proceedings concerning the crimes under the ICC's jurisdiction without the Court's "participation",[392] this terminology should not be interpreted in the *technical* sense of the words according to the meaning given to it by Article 17(1)(a) – (b) and (3). Rather, it should be construed within the parameters of the first part of Article 17(1) – namely as State *inaction*, regardless of whether the State is *de facto* unable or not.[393]

---

387 See first part of Art. 17(1)(a). Rome Statute, Art. 17(1) (a).

388 *Ibid.* Second part of Art. 17(1) (a).

389 Surprisingly, the Chamber acknowledged this point in paragraph 32 of the decision before examining the issues at hand when it stated: "The Chamber also notes that when a State with jurisdiction over a case is investigating, prosecuting or trying [a case], or has done so, it is not sufficient to declare such a case inadmissible.The Chamber observes on the contrary that a declaration of inadmissibility is subject to a finding that the relevant State is not unwilling or unable to genuinely conduct its national proceedings in relation to that case within the meaning of article 17 (1) (a) to (c), (2) and (3) of the Statute". Despite its understanding of this point, it erred when confusing the idea of a State's inability with a State's inaction as explored above. See *Prosecutor v. Thomas Lubanga Dyilo, Decision on the Prosecutor's Application for a Warrant of Arrest, Art. 58*, No.: ICC-01/04-01/06-8-US-Corr, 10/02/2006, para. 32, unsealed pursuant to Decision ICC-01/04-01/06-37 dated 17/03/2006.

390 Rome Statute, Art 17(1) (a) – (c).

391 *Prosecutor v. Thomas Lubanga Dyilo, Decision on the Prosecutor's Application for a Warrant of Arrest, Art. 58*, No.: ICC-01/04-01/06-8-US-Corr, 10/02/2006, paras. 35 – 36, unsealed pursuant to Decision ICC-01/04-01/06-37 dated 17/03/2006.

392 *Ibid.*, para. 34.

393 Although a State's abstention from instituting proceedings may actually result from the incapacity of its judicial system, as argued above, Art. 17 was drafted in a manner that did not seem to accommodate the application of the theories of *inaction* and *inability* concurrently. But see Schabas's entire different opinion noting that in respect to the DRC case amounting from the self-referral, "the issue is actually unwillingness, not [even] inability". Schabas, *supra* note 323.

In reaching its conclusion, Pre-Trial Chamber I proceeded on the same understanding that the DRC case was one of *inability* as opposed to *inaction*. It continued to assess the question of inability of the DRC from March 2004 – the date of receipt of the referral – until March 2005, when Lubanga was arrested by the DRC authorities. As to this period the Chamber observed that the:

> [N]ational judicial system has undergone certain changes, particularly in the region of Ituri where a *Tribunal de Grande Instance* has been reopened in Bunia. This has resulted *inter alia* in the issuance of of two warrants of arrest by the competent DRC authorities for Mr Thomas Lubanga Dyilo in March 2005 for several crimes, some possibly within the jurisdiction of the Court, committed in connection with military attacks from May 2003 onwards and during the so-called Ndoki incident in February 2005. Moreover, as a result of the DRC proceedings against Mr Thomas Lubanga Dyilo, he has been held in the *Centre Pénitentiaire et de Rééducation de Kinshasa* since 19 March 2005. Therefore, in the Chamber's view, the Prosecution's general statement that the DRC national judicial system continues to be unable in the sense of article 17(1) (a) to (c) and (3), of the Statute does not wholly correspond to the reality any longer.[394]

Based on this finding, it is clear that the Chamber changed its view from considering that the case represented a situation of *inability* (which was *de facto* one of *inaction*) to one of *action*, where national proceedings had been instituted against Lubanga. Based on the Prosecution's submissions, it was clear that the DRC authorities arrested Lubanga on 19 March 2005 "on charges of genocide pursuant to Article 164 of the DRC Military Criminal Code and crimes against humanity pursuant to Articles 166 to 169 of the same code", which "possibly" fall "within the jurisdiction of the Court", as the Chamber observed.[395]

Yet the Chamber observed that, because the arrest warrants issued by the DRC authorities fell short of any reference to Lubanga's alleged criminal responsibility "for the alleged UPC/FPLC's policy/practice of enlisting into the FPLC, conscripting into the FPLC and using to participate actively in hostilities children under the age of fifteen between July 2002 and December 2003", it cannot be said that the DRC "is acting in relation to the specific case before the Court", despite domestic proceedings having been initiated against Lubanga.[396] Having selected this line of reasoning, the Chamber finally reached the correct conclusion that the DRC case represented a scenario of State *inaction*. The Chamber, after initially confusing the ideas of *inaction* and *inability*, correctly stated:

> Concerning the first part of the admissibility test, the Chamber therefore holds that, on the basis of evidence and information provided by the Prosecution in the Prosecution's Ap-

394 *Prosecutor v. Thomas Lubanga Dyilo, Decision on the Prosecutor's Application for a Warrant of Arrest, Art. 58*, No.: ICC-01/04-01/06-8-US-Corr, 10/02/2006, para. 36, unsealed pursuant to Decision ICC-01/04-01/06-37 dated 17/03/2006.

395 *Ibid.*, para. 33.

396 *Ibid.*, paras. 37 – 40.

> plication, in the Prosecution's Submission, in the Prosecution's Further Submission and at the hearing of 2 February 2006, no State with jurisdiction over the case against Mr Thomas Lubanga Dyilo is acting, or has acted, in relation to such case. Accordingly, in the absence of any acting State, the Chamber need not make any analysis of unwillingness or inability.[397]

Thus, if the Chamber deems it true that in the "absence of any acting State [it] need not make any analysis of inability" as asserted, why did the Chamber speak of inability at the outset? Moreover, what if the DRC's judicial system remained unchanged during the period from March 2004 to March 2005? Would the Chamber still find the case admissible on the basis of the State's *inaction*?

Arguably, if this had been the case, the Chamber would have been prompted to examine the ability of the DRC's judicial system in relation to investigating the specific case of Lubanga in accordance with Article 17(1)(a) – (c) and (3) of the Statute, notwithstanding the proceedings instituted against him. This was not the case in fact, and the Chamber later acknowledged that the DRC judicial system was currently "able" to deal with cases falling "within the jurisdiction of the Court". This poses the question, why did it continue to accept the self-referral and waiver, making the case before the Court admissible, given the fact that the DRC's judicial system was able?

Based on the Court's initial argument, the acceptance of the self-referral seems to have mainly resulted from the DRC's letter stating that it was not capable of investigating the crimes within the jurisdiction of the Court requesting the latter's intervention. Thus, according to the Chamber's line of argument and in the absence of the main reason that prompted it to accept the DRC's self-referral and by implication the waiver of complementarity, the Chamber should have deemed the case *inadmissible*. It should have left the case against Lubanga to the DRC authorities to investigate, if it was true that "the ultimate purpose of the complementarity regime", as the Chamber asserted, was to ensure that the "Court by no means replaces national criminal jurisdictions".[398] Nonetheless, since it is evident that the *Lubanga* case is a clear example of a State's *inaction* in relation to the *crimes* or *conduct* subject to the Court's investigation, Pre-Trial Chamber I could not have been able to reach a decision of *inadmissibility* if the DRC's justice system had been deemed able to deal with the case as the Chamber asserted.

Actually, the decision does not suggest any straight answer to the reasons for the Chamber's attitude toward the question of self-referrals and admissibility. By referring the situation concerning crimes committed on its own territory the DRC had its own political "objectives", while the Court's attitude in accepting the DRC's self-referral and waiver shows how desperate it was to try a case within its jurisdiction.

397 *Ibid.*, para. 40.

398 *Ibid.*, para. 35.

4.2 *Pre-Trial Chamber II's Approach to Self-referrals and Waivers of Complementarity in Light of Inability in the Uganda Case*

In its "letter on Jurisdiction" dated 28 May 2004, which followed the letter of referral received on 16 December 2003, the Ugandan Government stated that:

> [I]t has been unable to arrest…persons who may bear the greatest responsibility" for the crimes within the referred situation; that "the ICC is the most appropriate and effective forum for the investigation and prosecution of those bearing the greatest responsibility" for those crimes; and that the Government of Uganda "has not conducted and does not intend to conduct national proceedings in relation to the persons most responsible".[399]

In contrast to Pre-Trial Chamber's I treatment of the issue, Pre-Trial Chamber II treated the Ugandan self-referral in an entirely different manner. Without getting involved in a detailed examination of the question of the admissibility of the case on the basis of inability or inaction, Pre-Trial Chamber II found it sufficient to make a *prima facie* finding that the case against the five LRA leaders "appears to be admissible".[400] However, in both decisions the Court could have benefited from the theory of waiver and avoided making an initial determination on admissibility in accordance with Article 19(1) of the Statute.

The core idea behind the *prima facie* finding does not seem to be entirely an innovation of the ICC. The International Court of Justice (ICJ) initially introduced a parallel standard to be applied for a *prima facie* determination that there was a basis upon which jurisdiction might be founded at the provisional measures stage.[401] Still, whether a *prima facie* determination of admissibility can meet the threshold of Ar-

---

399 *Warrant of Arrest for Joseph Kony Issued on 8 July 2005 as Amended on 27 September 2005*, No.: ICC-02/04-01/05-53, 27/09/2005, para. 37.

400 *Ibid.*, para. 38. But see, *Prosecutor v. Mathieu Ngudjolo Chui, Warrant of Arrest for Mathieu Ngudjolo Chui*, No.: ICC-01/04-02/07-1-tENG, unsealed pursuant to Decision ICC-01/04-02/07-10 dated 7/02/2008 (where Pre-Trial Chamber I considered that on the basis of the evidence submitted, the "case against Mathieu Ngudjolo Chui…is admissible". In this context, although Pre-Trial Chamber I did not make a detailed ruling on admissibility as in the Lubanga decision, it adopted a different approach than that followed by Pre-Trial Chamber II. The reason for this divergence is not mentioned in the decision. Yet, it is clear that in all the arrest warrant decisions issued by Pre-Trial Chamber I no waiver of admissibility took place on the part of the Court.

401 See *Case Concerning Avena and Other Mexican Nationals (Mexico v. United States of America), Request for the Indication of Provisional Measures*, 2003 I.C.J., 5/02/2003, paras. 38–39; *Case Concerning Armed Activities on the Territory of the Congo (Democratic Republic of Congo v. Rwanda), Request for the Indication of Provisional Measures*, 2002 I.C.J., 10/07/2002, paras. 58–59 ; and generally P. H. F. Bekker, 'Provisional Measures in the Recent Practice of the International Court of Justice', 7 *International Law Forum du Droit International* 24 (2005). Nevertheless, the *Uganda* decision lacks any indication of whether the approach of making a *prima facie* determination regarding the admissibility of the case may have been influenced by the standard applied by the ICJ.

ticle 17 of the Statute is an open question. The language of the Chapeau of Article 17, "the Court shall determine that a case is inadmissible…", suggests that once the Court engages in an examination of admissibility, it will be required to make a clear finding whether the situation or case is inadmissible not merely a presumption to that effect.

Although Pre-Trial Chamber II may have entirely bypassed the admissibility test in accordance with Article 17(1) together with Article 19(1), it found it more plausible to make a passing reference to admissibility by a *prima facie* finding. The grounds for proceeding in this manner were not explained in the decision. Perhaps the reason for so doing lies in the fact that the uncertainties surrounding the legality of self-referrals and waivers meant that it was crucial for the Chamber to make at least the smallest possible finding on admissibility at the earliest possible stage, in order to quash any doubt regarding the legality of the practice.[402]

On the other hand, although Pre-Trial Chamber I ruled on admissibility mainly because it was of the view that the admissibility test was a "prerequisite" for the issue of an arrest warrant, this does not deny the fact that the novelty of the question of a self-referral might had been an additional reason. Also, perhaps the Chamber considered that an admissibility determination prior to the issue of an arrest warrant was usefull in this particular case, since Thomas Lubanga was already in the custody of the DRC awaiting release. Had the Court determined that the case against him was inadmissible, the question of his surrender to the Court would have been moot.

Yet, Pre-Trial Chamber II, like Pre-Trial Chamber I, failed to sufficiently explain the legal or policy reasons for accepting the Ugandan self-referral. A reading of the "Letter on Jurisdiction" submitted to the Court by the Solicitor-General of the Republic of Uganda supports the conclusion that Uganda decided not to initiate proceedings against the five top LRA leaders, not due to a lack of capacity to do so, but due to its failure to "arrest" the alleged perpetrators.[403]

The latter scenario may fall within the definition of inability if it is proven that the failure to arrest the alleged perpetrator was linked to a total or substantial collapse or the unavailability of Uganda's national judicial system. It also has to be demonstrated that Uganda had instituted proceedings, yet failed genuinely to carry them out. But this was not the case with the *Ugandan* situation. The latter, like the *Lubanga* case, suggests that no proceedings had been undertaken. Thus, the case is also one of self-referral and waiver coupled with a State's inaction. Also, the Chamber seems to have relied to a great extent on the "Letter" sent by the Ugandan government to the ICC stating its incapability to capture the LRA leaders. This raises some doubt whether the ICC would be in a better position to help capture the alleged perpetrators. The Court merely relied on cooperation from States who themselves had failed to arrest those leaders.

402 Mohamed M. El Zeidy, 'Some Remarks on the Question of Admissibility of a Case During Arrest Warrant Proceedings before the International Criminal Court', 19 *Leiden Journal of International Law* 741, 750 (2006).

403 *Warrant of Arrest for Joseph Kony Issued on 8 July 2005 as Amended on 27 September 2005*, No.: ICC-02/04-01/05-53, 27/09/2005, para. 37.

When Pre-Trial Chamber II accepted the Ugandan self-referral on this ground, it made the same mistake as Pre-Trial Chamber I in the *Lubanga* case. If the Court continues accepting self-referrals on the basis of States' political motivations, there is a great danger that it will lose its credibility and effectiveness in the future.[404] Both the Uganda and DRC situations, as well as that of the Central African Republic, share a common striking feature – namely that the referring States requested the Prosecutor to "investigate crimes allegedly committed by *rebels* fighting against the central authorities".[405] As one commentator correctly puts it, Uganda and DRC "had their own strategic objectives...these appear to have been to use the Court in order to prosecute rebel bands within their territory".[406] Also, Cherif Bassiouni has argued that the clear tension, which arose out of the Ugandan referral in relation to the need to reconcile peace efforts with the duty to end impunity, shows the limitations of "the principle of complementarity within the context of an ongoing effort to halt hostilities".[407]

The Uganda and DRC self-referrals, therefore, "exemplify many of the limitations of the ICC".[408] But behind these self-referrals lie the Prosecutor's actual intentions. The Prosecutor may have clearly invoked his *proprio motu* powers in all three situations. In the DRC, it was clear that at some stage he threatened to use his powers under Article 15(1) if the circumstances so required. Yet, the fact that he encouraged the self-referrals exempted him from the responsibility to justify his actions for using such a threat to States' sovereignty.[409] Such a policy also proves to those States initially opposed to granting an ICC Prosecutor with *ex officio* powers that their fears have not been borne out by experience.[410] Self-referrals leading to waivers, therefore, ought to be accepted only in clear exceptional circumstances where it has been shown that the Court would *certainly* be in a better position to take up proceedings instead of a domestic court.

404 But see Payam Akhavan, 'The *Lord's Resistance Army* Case: Uganda's Submission of the First State Referral to the International Criminal Court', 99 *American Journal of International Law* 403, 411 (2005) (noting that "Uganda's objectives were fully compatible with the purposes of the ICC" and the latter was in a "much better position to conduct the prosecution").

405 Antonio Cassese, 'Is the ICC Sill Having Teething Problems?', 4 *Journal of International Criminal Justice* 434, 436 (2006).

406 Schabas, *Introduction 3rd ed., supra* note. 321, p. 36.

407 M. Cherif Bassiouni, 'Where is the ICC Heading? ; The ICC – *Quo Vadis?*', 4 *Journal of International Criminal Justice* 421, 424 – 425 (2006).

408 *Ibid.*, p. 424.

409 The fact that the State in which the alleged crimes were committed agreed voluntarily to refer the situation to the Court would clearly call for no justification from the Prosecutor.

410 For a similar observation see Gaeta, *supra* note 347, p. 950.

Concluding Observations

Chapter III has examined in detail the theoretical as well as the practical implications of the Rome Statute complementarity model. The Rome Statute complementarity principle is an idea that regulates and organizes the relationship between the jurisdictions of domestic courts and that of the International Criminal Court. Complementarity also provides national courts with the primary jurisdiction to investigate, prosecute and try the core crimes falling within the jurisdiction of the Rome Statute. This primacy is not absolute because a State loses its primacy when it manifests "unwillingness" or "inability" to exercise its jurisdiction over a specific situation or case. In practice, labelling a State as unwilling or unable to exercise its sovereign rights is not a simple accusation. The drafters of the Rome Statute defined these terms under Article 17 of the Statute to assist the Court in making a determination on whether a State was seriously investigating a given situation or case.

The notions underlying the terms "unwillingness" and "inability" remain extremely difficult to ascertain. Unwillingness has been defined under Article 17(2) as: a) shielding a person from criminal responsibility; b) causing a deliberate delay in carrying out the national proceedings; and c) conducting the domestic proceedings in a non-independent or impartial manner. Meeting the standard of proof for these criteria certainly requires a determination that goes beyond a State's apparent actions. What is required though is a determination that tests the State's acts or omissions in the context of its actual intention. The drafting history of the Rome Statute reveals enormous efforts to reduce the elements of subjectivity when defining these criteria. The final wording makes it evident that for the purpose of interpreting these criteria objectivity will often be accompanied by some sort of subjectivity of assessment. This is evident in Article 17(2) (a), which speaks of shielding the person from criminal responsibility. What may constitute a "shield" from criminal responsibility could not be determined under fixed rules. The evidential proof varies from one case to another depending on the circumstances of each case. On the basis of an analysis of the jurisprudence of the ECHR as well as the IACHR, this chapter has demonstrated that there are minimum standards in any criminal investigation that have to be met, the absence of which creates an assumption in favour a State's *bad faith*. Moreover, although the criteria of "unjustified delay" or the lack of "independent" and "impartial" proceedings are less subjective, the Court would still need some guidelines to assist in their interpretation. Similarly, the HRC, IACHR and the ECHR were constantly faced with cases involving these human rights questions. Arguably, the standards of proof applied by these bodies may apply *mutatis mutandis*, perhaps coupled with additional factors to be elaborated by the OTP in light of the nature of situations received by the Court.

Unlike that for "unwillingness", the test for "inability" as defined under Article 17(3) of the Statute is generally objective. Yet, there remain some problems of interpretation that may arise in the future when applying the test, as argued earlier. The striking part of the inability test lies in the criteria of "total" or "substantial" collapse. The term "substantial" replaced the originally proposed term "partial". This change may cause some confusion in practice, since it will be hard to find the demarcation line between "substantial" and "partial" collapse in light of the existing term "total collapse".

A question which is closely relevant to the application of Article 17 is that of self-referrals and waivers of complementarity. The question was not seriously discussed by the drafters and was left open to be considered when drafting the Court's Rules of Procedure and Evidence. Canada was prepared to propose a rule covering this question, but the proposal was seen by some as confusing. The question was finally left to the Court's interpretation. At first glance, self-referrals and waivers of complementarity might appear as legaly problematic. However, a study of the procedural regime of the Statute suggests that the idea whereby the territorial State with the direct link with the crimes allegedly committed decides to waive its primacy to the Court might be reconciled with the existing complementarity procedural regime. So far the practice of the Court seems to have welcomed the idea of self-referrals. The idea of waivers of complementarity was not explicitly referred to in the decisions. But accepting the self-referals suggests that, to a certain extent, the concept of waiver might have been accepted by implication. The DRC and Uganda decisions concerning the issue of warrants of arrest against the alleged perpetrators suggest that Pre-Trial Chambers I and II endorsed the practice. The problem remains that the Court agreed to contribute in executing the political agendas of the governments referring the situations. Thus, accepting self-referrals should be subject to a case-by-case assessment.

Also, the lack of clarity lies in the fact that Pre-Trial Chamber I confused the application of a self-referral resulting in a *priori inaction* with that of the criterion of inability under Article 17(3) of the Statute. By so doing, the Chamber suggested that a self-referral should always be linked to the inability of the State. This conclusion is not problematic *per se*. The lacuna lies in the fact that, at one part of the decision, the Chamber overlooked the appropriate interpretation of Article 17 and mixed the ideas of a self-referral resulting from a State's *inaction* with the test of inability, which requires *a priori action* before the Court puts this test into effect.

Chapter IV: Complementarity – Related Provisions (Articles 18 – 20)

The principle of complementarity reconciles two competing features and jurisdictions. The first is the sovereignty of the State, which claims national jurisdiction over its citizens and crimes committed on its territory, even though these crimes are of an international character and may fall within international jurisdiction. The second feature functions only in exceptional circumstances and gives an international tribunal the ability to exercise jurisdiction over these heinous crimes. The ICC Statute's procedural aspects either protect national sovereignty and domestic jurisdiction or strengthen the ICC's jurisdiction.[1] The complementarity regime under the Rome Statute is not confined to the application of Article 17.[2] The procedural regime is governed by other related provisions under the Statute defined in Articles 18 – 20.[3] Chapter IV of this book, like chapter III, studies these provisions in detail, highlights the gaps and offers some solutions. This chapter also engages in an in-depth examination of issues that have a direct effect on the procedural regime of Articles 18 and 19 of the Statute. This entails an examination of the impact of waivers of complementarity on the application of those Articles. The chapter concludes by challenging the classical idea of complementarity studied throughout Chapters III and IV, and instead shows that complementarity has a positive dimension that was not really contemplated by the drafters of the Statute.

1. Preliminary Rulings Regarding Admissibility in the Rome Statute Complementarity Model

Article 18 of the Rome Statute elaborates on the complementarity principle, as set out in Article 17, by providing a mechanism for preliminary rulings on admissibility. The provision was inserted by the Preparatory Committee and examined in depth

1 Rome Statute of the International Criminal Court, Adopted by the United Nations Diplomatic Conference of Plenipotentiaries on the Establishment of an International Criminal Court, 17 July 1998, UN Doc., A/CONF.183/9 [hereinafter ICC/Rome Statute].

2 Rome Statute, Art. 17.

3 *Ibid.*, Arts. 18 – 20.

at the Rome Conference.[4] It serves as a further procedural filter for the benefit of States' sovereignty.[5] The creation of a specific control aimed at evaluating the issue of admissibility when the Prosecutor decides to commence an investigation, at a very early stage, strengthens the first feature of complementarity. Such control precedes the procedure described by Article 19 relating to "challenges of the jurisdiction of the Court or the admissibility of a case".

According to Article 18(1), when a State Party refers a situation to the Court[6] and the Prosecutor identifies a reasonable basis for commencing an investigation into a situation or initiates an investigation *proprio motu*, the Prosecutor (The Jurisdiction, Complementarity and Cooperation Division (JCCD)) *shall*[7] notify "all States Parties

4 John T. Holmes, "Complementarity: National Courts *Versus* the ICC", in Antonio Cassese et al., (eds.), *The Rome Statute of the International Criminal Court*, Vol. I (Oxford: Oxford University Press, 2002), p. 681 [hereinafter Cassese Commentary].

5 David J. Scheffer, 'The United States and the International Criminal Court', 93 *American Journal of International Law* 12, 13 (1999) (noting that in early 1998 the United States successfully broadened the scope of the complementarity regime by allowing deferral to domestic efforts at a situation stage).

6 Rome Statute, Arts. 13(a), 14.

7 *Ibid.*, Arts. 13(c), 15(3), 53(1). Article 53(1) reads: "The Prosecutor shall, having evaluated the information made available to him or her, initiate an investigation unless he or she determines that there is no reasonable basis to proceed under this Statute. In deciding whether to initiate an investigation, the Prosecutor shall consider whether: a) The information available to the Prosecutor provides a reasonable basis to believe that a crime within the jurisdiction of the Court has been or is being committed; b) The case is or would be admissible under article 17; and c) Taking into account the gravity of the crime and the interests of victims, there are nonetheless substantial reasons to believe that an investigation would not serve the interests of justice". If the Prosecutor determines that there is no reasonable basis for proceeding and his or her determination is based solely on subparagraph (c) above, he or she shall inform the Pre-Trial Chamber. It should be noted, however, that where the Prosecutor acts *proprio motu* Article 15 applies, while in the case of referral by a State Party in accordance with Articles 13(a) and 14, Article 53 applies, and Article 15 does not. Thus, the question of a Pre-Trial Chamber authorization of the commencement of the full investigation becomes moot. In those situations, the Prosecutor proceeds directly to the consideration under Article 53(1). However, one might suggest that this does not preclude the Prosecutor from relying on the criteria set out in Article 53. This sounds logical, since Rule 48 clarifies the interplay between Articles 15 and 53 as follows: "in determining whether there is a reasonable basis to proceed with an investigation under Article 15, paragraph 3, the Prosecutor shall consider the factors set out in Article 53, paragraph 1(a) to (c)". *Report of the Preparatory Commission for the International Criminal Court*, UN Doc. PCNICC/2000/1/Add. 1 (2000), Rule 48 [hereinafter ICC Rule]; see also ICC Rule 51. The criteria set out in Article 53 are the appropriate ones, and those which, *inter alia*, the Pre-Trial Chamber or the Trial Chamber will later rely upon at the jurisdiction and admissibility stages. Moreover, Article 53 provides a further opening for prosecutorial discretion, by incorporating a consideration of interests of justice into the Prosecutor's final determination of whether actually to proceed with an investigation following authorization by the Pre-Trial Chamber under Article 15(4). In addition, Article 53 ensures an equal Prosecutorial burden in all triggering

and those States which, taking into account the information available, would normally exercise jurisdiction over the crimes concerned", of the investigation's commencement or that it is about to be commenced.[8]) Does the Prosecutor have an obligation to notify States that are not party to the Statute?[9]

In its decision on the issue of an arrest warrant for Jospeh Kony arising from the *Uganda* situation, Pre-Trial Chamber II acknowledged that the Prosecutor had distributed letters of notification to "all States parties under Article 18, paragraph 1, of the Statute, as well as to other States that would normally exercise jurisdiction".[10] The Chamber did not elaborate any further on the meaning of "other States that would normally exercise jurisdiction". In the *Central African Republic* situation, Pre-Trial Chamber III made no reference to the clause "other States that would normally exercise jurisdiction". The Chamber stated, "[c]considering that, pursuant to Article 18 (1) of the Statute, the Prosecutor shall notify all States Parties..."[11]

---

modes outlined in Article 13. New circumstances may arise after the Pre-Trial Chamber has given its authorization under Article 15(4), which further justifies the applicability of Article 53(2) to situations arising under Articles 13(c) and 15. The latter is not mentioned in the Rules, but can be inferred from the entire context of the Statute. For a discussion of Article 15 see generally Morten Bergsmo and Jelena Pejic, "Prosecutor", in Otto Triffterer (ed.), *Commentary on the Rome Statute: Observers' Notes, Article by Article* (Nomos Verlagsgesellschaft: Baden-Baden, 1999), pp. 367 – 370 [hereinafter Triffterer Commentary]; and also Jurg Lindenmann, "The Rules of Procedure and Evidence on Jurisdiction and Admissibility", in Horst Fischer et al. (eds.), International and National Prosecution of Crimes under International Law: Current Developments (Berlin Verlag: Arno Spitz Gmbh, 2001), pp. 182 – 184.

8 Rome Statute, Art. 18(1); ICC Rule 52(1) ("Subject to the limitations provided for in Article 18, paragraph 1, the notification shall contain information about the acts that may constitute crimes referred to in article 5, relevant for the purposes of article 18, paragraph 2"). In the case of a referral by the Security Council in accordance with Article 13(b), no pre-trial procedure or notification is necessary. In this regard, Benvenuti observed that this distinction may be considered reasonable, because there is no need for a specific filter aimed at protecting State sovereignty when the Prosecutor proceeds as a result of the referral of a situation by the Security Council acting under Chapter 7 of the UN Charter. See Paolo Benvenuti, "Complementarity of the International Criminal Court to National Criminal Jurisdictions" in Flavia Lattanzi et al. (eds.), *Essays on the Rome Statute of the International Criminal Court*, Vol. I (Il Sirente, 1999), p. 47.

9 When the general idea of notification was raised during the work of the 1996 Preparatory Committee, the drafters suggested "that the Prosecutor should notify all...States parties to the Statute, allowing them the opportunity to express their views on whether to proceed with the case before the Court decided". In this context, no reference was made to third States. See *Report of the Preparatory Committee on the Establishment of an International Criminal Court*, UN GAOR, 51st Sess., Vol. I, Supp. No. 22, UN Doc. A/51/22 (1996), para. 148 [hereinafter 1996 Preparatory Committee Report, Vol. I].

10 See *Warrant of Arrest for Joseph Kony Issued on 8 July 2005 as Amended on 27 September 2005*, No.: ICC-02/04-01/05-53, 27/09/2005, para. 36.

11 *Decision Requesting Information on the Status of the Preliminary Examination of the Situation in the Central African Republic*, No.: ICC-01/05-6, 30/11/2006, p. 3.

One possible construction of the clause is to limit it to States Parties, and particularly "those States [parties] that would normally exercise jurisdiction over the crimes concerned". States that would normally exercise jurisdiction are those with a direct link to the crime or the accused, such as the State where the crime was committed or whose nationals the alleged perpetrators or the victims were, or the custodial State.[12]

A different interpretation suggests that the clause also refers to States that are not parties to the Statute. This view finds support in the *deliberate* use of the conjunction "and" followed by "those States", which evidently refers to third States.[13] Otherwise the clause "and those States…would normally exercise jurisdiction" would be redundant. Indeed, if the drafters had demanded the limiting of notification to State Parties, they could have drafted the provision to state that, "the Prosecutor shall notify all States Parties, in particular, those States that would normally exercise jurisdiction over the crimes concerned". Thus, the additional clause that appears in Article 18(1) is not superfluous. But if this is true, why does paragraph 5 say, "States Parties shall respond to such requests without undue delay"?[14] Would this not mean that notification is confined to States Parties? The drafters' intention may have been to limit the application of Article 18 to States Parties only. A more plausible answer is that the drafters could not apply the strong language of paragraph 5 to non-party States. But this does not change the overall application of Article 18 to such States. The term "undue delay" provides the key to the appropriate interpretation of paragraph 5. The drafters used the word "undue" instead of the word "unjustified", which appears in Article 17(2) (b).

According to the drafting history, the term "unjustified" is more lenient and leaves room for justification in the event of any delay, while the term "undue" apparently removes this opportunity.[15] In addition, the strict language of paragraph 5 suggests that it is imposing an obligation on those States to respond to the Prosecutor's requests without any delay, even if justified. Since "a treaty does not create either obligations or rights for a third State without its consent",[16] according to the maxim *pacta tertiis nec nocent nec prosunt*, the drafters could not have explicitly mentioned third States

12 William A. Schabas, *An Introduction to the International Criminal Court*, 2nd ed. (Cambridge: Cambridge University Press, 2004), pp. 124 – 125.

13 See also Daniel D. Nsereko, "Preliminary Rulings Regarding Admissibility", *Triffterer Commentary, supra* note 7, p. 399.

14 However, according to Cassese, Article 18 applies also to "third States, i.e. States that are not parties to the Statute": Antonio Cassese, 'The Statute of the International Criminal Court: Some Preliminary Reflections', 10 *European Journal of International Law* 144, 159 (1999).

15 John T. Holmes, "The Principle of Complementarity", in Roy S. Lee (ed.), *The International Criminal Court: The Making of the Rome Statute, Issues. Negotiations. Results* (The Hague. London. Boston: Kluwer Law International, 1999), p. 54.

16 Vienna Convention on the Law of Treaties, Art. 34; the leading authority on this rule is the Permanent Court of International Justice in *Free Zones of Upper Savoy and The District of Gex*, Judgment of 7/06/1932, P.C.I.J. , Series A./B., No. 46 , p. 141.

in this context. Accordingly, one can infer that the Prosecutor is also obliged to notify non-party States. Yet, the 2003 OTP policy paper stated:

> The exercise of the Prosecutor's functions under article 18 of notifying States of future investigations will alert States with jurisdiction to the possibility of taking acting themselves. In a case where multiple States have jurisdiction over the crime in question the Prosecutor should consult with those States best able to exercise jurisdiction (eg. primarily the State where the alleged crime was committed, the State of nationality of the suspects, the State which has custody of the accused, and the State which has evidence of the alleged crime) with a view to ensuring that jurisdiction is taken by the State best able to do so.[17]

This statement poses the question whether the OTP intended to say that where several States have concurrent jurisdiction, notification will be limited to the four types of States mentioned above. This limits the scope of Article 18(1), which speaks of notifying "all States parties".[18] A practical interpretation of the OTP's statement would, therefore, be that once States have been notified the Prosecutor ought to confine *further consultation* to those States, whether parties or non-parties, with a direct connection to the crimes or the evidence "best able to exercise jurisdiction".

The purpose of the notification is twofold: first, to give general information to the "general assemblage" of States Parties and, secondly, as stated in the OTP policy paper, to put on notice those States that might otherwise have jurisdiction, which the Prosecutor intends should investigate the situation.[19] The State concerned is thus given an opportunity either to assert jurisdiction or to let the Prosecutor proceed with an investigation into the situation.[20] The notification may be made on a confidential basis, according to the prosecutorial assessment.[21] The Prosecutor may decide to limit the scope of information provided to the States in order to ensure that it does not fall into the wrong hands. Revealing the information to the wrong people may hurt innocent individuals, particularly potential witnesses and other providers of information, or may destroy evidence, or assist suspects and witnesses to abscond. Confidentiality was not an issue in the practice of the *ad hoc* tribunals, since information of the same sort was common knowledge, yet the tribunals succeeded in obtaining the custody of suspects, selecting evidence and protecting witnesses.[22]

Apparently, these privileges entrust the Prosecutor with a broad discretionary assessment. Article 18(1) leaves it to the Prosecutor to determine how much informa-

17 *Paper on Some Policy Issues before the Office of the Prosecutor*, September 2003, p. 5 [hereinafter 2003 OTP Policy Paper].

18 Rome Statute, Art. 18 (1).

19 2003 *OTP Policy Paper*, *supra* note 17, p. 5.

20 See e.g., Nsereko, *supra* note 13, p. 399.

21 Rome Statute, Art. 18(1); ICC Rule 52(1).

22 Schabas, *supra* note 12, p. 125.

tion is given to States. Nevertheless, Rule 52(2)[23] seems to weaken this discretionary assessment, since it grants States the right to request additional information from the Prosecutor. Thus, it may hinder the main purpose of Article 18(1), that is, to preserve valuable or other significant evidence. According to this Rule the State may request information and, based on such information, attempt to destroy the relevant evidence relating to the investigation.

This analysis of Article 18 suggests that the idea of notification is dangerous and has a double impact on the principle of complementarity. Although it apparently strengthens the first feature of it, because it encourages States to act and exercise their primary jurisdiction, it impacts negatively on the second feature, that of effective international prosecution. A State acting in bad faith, once it has received the information from the Prosecutor, could destroy the relevant evidence or act in a manner that would allow the accused to escape justice on the basis of the received information, while pretending that it was investigating or prosecuting in good faith. This to some extent affects the proper application of the second feature of complementarity reflected in the ICC's primacy to act in those exceptional situations as a result of the State's false assertions.[24]

Bergsmo suggests that such a problem may be partly ameliorated by the application of Article 18(6), which states that the Prosecutor may exceptionally request authorization from the Pre-Trial Chamber to "pursue necessary investigative steps for the purpose of preserving evidence where there is a unique opportunity to obtain important evidence or there is a significant risk that such evidence may not be subsequently available".[25] Yet, Cassese still found that paragraph 6 is an insufficient guarantee against State abuses, when he correctly said that "one is faced with a State bent on shunning international jurisdiction and therefore unwilling to cooperate in the search for and collection of evidence, or even willing to destroy such evidence to evade justice".[26]

Article 18(2), on the other hand, obliges the Prosecutor to defer to a State's investigation, if informed of the existence of domestic proceedings within one month of the

23 Rule 52(2) reads, "[a] State may request additional information from the Prosecutor to assist it in the application of article 18, paragraph 2. Such a request shall not affect the one-month time limit provided for in Article 18, paragraph 2, and shall be responded to by the Prosecutor on an expedited basis".

24 Notifying and providing the State concerned with further information will strengthen this assertion. See Cassese, *supra* note 14, 159. Cassese argued in similar terms: "Complementarity might lend itself to abuse. It might amount to a shield used by States to thwart international justice. This might happen with regard to those crimes (genocide, crimes against humanity) which are normally perpetrated with the help and assistance, or the connivance or acquiescence, of national authorities. In these cases, State authorities may pretend to investigate and try crimes, and may even conduct proceedings, but only for the purpose of actually protecting the allegedly responsible persons".

25 Rome Statute, Art.18(6); ICC Rule 57; Morten Bergsmo, 'The Jurisdictional Regime of the International Criminal Court (Part II, Articles 11-19)', 6 *European Journal of Crime, Criminal Law and Criminal Justice* 29, 45 (1998).

26 Cassese, *supra* note 14, p. 159.

notification sent to all States Parties and other States which would normally exercise jurisdiction. The Statute as well as the Rules and the Regulations does not solve the question of what happens where the State concerned does not respond at all to the Prosecutor's notification or, if it does, does not *explicitly* "request" the Prosecutor to defer to its investigations. As to the first part of the question, the absence of a reply from one or more States would implicitly mean that the State/States waived the right provided under Article 18(2), and thus the Prosecutor could go ahead with the investigation provided that no other State with jurisdiction had complied with the notification time limit and opposed the Court's investigation. Moreover, States which fail to oppose the ICC's investigations within the required time frame "will be definitely excluded from…the right of being opposing parties in the activation proceedings".[27] The only problem with the idea of the Prosecutor proceeding in the event of a State's failure to notify at all or within the requested time limit is that one or more States may have started an investigation leading to a situation of concurrent investigations of the same situation. As to the second part where a State informs the Prosecutor that it is investigating or has investigated, yet does not explicitly request deferral as a result of an error or mistake in the State's notification, the Prosecutor should certainly take such information as an implicit request for deferral to domestic investigations. Any other interpretation would result in unnecessary delays in the proceedings. This is consistent with the broader purpose of the complementarity regime, that the provisions on complementarity, including Article 17, are designed to work only where a State fails to administer justice properly. The fact that the State shows that it is conducting genuine investigations renders the ICC's intervention unsound.

The Prosecutor may also oppose the State's request for deferral if it applies in writing to the Pre-Trial Chamber and the latter decides to authorize the Prosecutor to investigate.[28] In this case, the Prosecutor bears the evidentiary and legal burden of showing by a preponderance of evidence that valid grounds exist to justify the

27 Héctor Olásolo, *The Triggering Procedure of the International Criminal Court* (Leiden. Boston: Martinus Nijhoff Publishers, 2005), p. 76.

28 Rome Statute, Arts.18(2), 15(4); also ICC Rule 53 ("When a State requests a deferral pursuant to article 18, paragraph 2, that State shall make this request in writing and provide information concerning its investigation, taking into account article 18, paragraph 2. The Prosecutor may request additional information from that State"); *ibid.* Rules 54 and 55. Rule 54 reads: "1. An application submitted by the Prosecutor to the Pre-Trial Chamber in accordance with article 18, paragraph 2, shall be in writing and shall contain the basis for the application. The information provided by the State under rule 53 shall be communicated by the Prosecutor to the Pre-Trial Chamber; 2. The Prosecutor shall inform that State in writing when he or she makes an application to the Pre-Trial Chamber under article 18, paragraph 2, and shall include in the notice a summary of the basis of the application…" Rule 55(2) reads: "the Pre-Trial Chamber shall examine the Prosecutor's application and any observations submitted by a State that requested a deferral in accordance with article 18, paragraph 2, and shall consider the factors in article 17 in deciding whether to authorize an investigation". *Ibid* ; also Bergsmo, *supra* note 25, p. 44; Leila Nadya Sadat and S. Richard Carden, 'The New International Criminal Court: An Uneasy Revolution', 88 *Georgetown Law Journal* 381, 420 (2000).

Prosecutor's investigation.[29] Additionally, the Prosecutor in submitting the application to the Pre-Trial Chamber can also rely on the criteria listed in Article 17 for holding a case admissible. The Pre-Trial Chamber's decision is subject to appeal,[30] but if the State avails itself of this right it cannot "attack" the investigation or prosecution on the basis of admissibility unless there is a subsequent change of circumstances or additional significant facts are raised.[31]

If the Prosecutor defers to a State's investigation,[32] he may review the deferral after six months or whenever there has been a "significant change of circumstances based on the State's unwillingness or inability genuinely to carry out the investigation".[33] Article 18(3) therefore allows the Prosecutor to monitor and reassess the State's ability and willingness to pursue justice.[34] In this context, one might suggest that this provision should be read in conjunction with Article 18(5). After six months the Prosecutor may review the deferral, and may request to be kept periodically apprised of the progress of the investigations and any subsequent prosecutions without "undue delay". In this regard, the inclusion of this strict language suggests that the idea of delaying the response is entirely unacceptable. Failure on the part of the State to respond at all or in a timely manner would be grounds for the Prosecutor to review the deferral and seek the Pre-Trial Chamber's authorization to initiate an investigation.[35] This seems logical, since paragraph 5 appears to forestall any attempt to escape justice. The monitoring authority provided to the Prosecutor could frighten States and encourage them to act in good faith.

If the Prosecutor observes any change of circumstances based on the State's unwillingness or inability prior to or following the six month period, he will investigate

29 Nsereko, *supra* note 13, p. 401.

30 Rome Statute, Arts. 18(4), 82(1) (a) and (d).

31 *Ibid.*, Art. 18(7). In this regard, a State which has challenged a ruling by the Pre-Trial Chamber under Article 18 is not prevented from challenging admissibility under Article 19 on the grounds of "additional significant facts or significant change of circumstances". For a discussion of this issue see Bergsmo, *supra* note 25, p. 45; Nsereko, *supra* note 13, p. 404; Sadat, Carden, *supra* note 28, p. 420.

32 It should be noted, however, that the Prosecutor's deferral applies not only to States Parties, but also to third States. Further on this point see Gerhard Hafner, "The Status of Third States before the International Criminal Court", in Mauro Politi et al. (eds.), *The Rome Statute of the International Criminal Court* (Aldershot. Burlington. USA. Singapore. Sydney: Ashgate Dartmouth, 2001), pp. 248 – 249.

33 Rome Statute, Art. 18(3). A similar idea was raised during the work of the International Law Commission in 1994. Mr. Bowet, a member of the Commission, argued that if it "was agreed that the court could waive its own jurisdiction in a case in favour of a national court that would be ready and willing to rule on it, there would have to be a mechanism enabling the court to monitor the proceedings in the national court, either by having the right to appoint an observer to that court, or by requiring that it should report on the results of the trial". See 1994 *YILC* Vol. I, para. 27.

34 Ruth B. Philips, 'The International Criminal Court Statute: Jurisdiction and Admissibility', 10 *Criminal Law Forum* 61, 80 (1999).

35 Rome Statute, Art. 18(2); ICC Rules 54, 55.

the matter subject to the Pre-Trial Chamber's authorization.[36] However, the Prosecutor must show by a preponderance of the evidence that such change has occurred.[37] The State concerned is also given the opportunity to present "further information" to the Pre-Trial Chamber and oppose the Prosecutor's application for authorization to investigate a matter of which it is already supposedly in charge.[38]

Paragraph 3 buttresses the two features of the complementarity principle. On the one hand, the provision on monitoring a State's investigation ensures that States are acting *bona fide* in their exercise of national jurisdiction. The provision fulfils the main purpose of the complementarity regime: not encroaching on national sovereignty and jurisdiction unless necessary. On the other hand, authorizing the Prosecutor to intervene when the State concerned is acting in bad faith ensures that the second feature of complementarity is functioning, that is, that the Court can assert primacy in the event of a State's unwillingness or inability. In any event, Article 18 was inserted in general as a result of the insistence of the American delegation in order to strengthen the first feature of complementarity by serving as an additional "safeguard" against the Court's intervention in accordance with complementarity's second feature.[39] As one commentator correctly puts it, "[s]trengthened complementarity" sounds positive – in reality it means a considerable weakening of the Court... especially if [the] State is not acting *bona fide*".[40]

2. Challenges to the Jurisdiction of the Court or the Admissibility of a Case

Article 19 seems to supplement the provisions of Article 18, but at a latter stage and in a broader sense. Unlike Article 18, which is applicable only in response to the referral of a situation by a State Party and in the event of an investigation by the Prosecutor *proprio motu*,[41] Article 19 applies to "Security Council referrals and cases in which States do not open investigations" in response to the Prosecutor's notifica-

36 *Ibid.*

37 ICC Rule 56(1); see also the statement made by the Pakistani delegate during the meetings of the Committee of the Whole: "the Prosecutor should be able to undertake investigations after a State party had referred a matter to him or her and if there had been a fundamental change in the circumstances, resulting in a total breakdown of State authority": *Summary Record of the 31 st Meeting*, 9 July 1998, UN Doc. A/CONF.183/C.1/SR.31, para. 19.

38 ICC Rule 56(2).

39 See *Summary Record of the 11th Meeting*, 22 June 1998, UN Doc. A/CONF.183/C.1/SR.11, para. 20.

40 Hans-Peter Kaul, "The International Criminal Court: Jurisdiction, Trigger Mechanism and Relationship to National Jurisdictions", in Mauro Politi et al. (eds.), *supra* note 32, p. 60.

41 Rome Statute, Art. 18(1).

tion.[42] Moreover, it increases the categories of parties that can challenge jurisdiction and admissibility before the Court.[43] This does not preclude the possibility of the Court[44] and the Prosecutor[45] also availing themselves of this right. Indeed, the Court may on its own motion determine the admissibility of a case brought before it,[46] but in doing so it must always satisfy itself that it has jurisdiction.[47] A parallel provision is found in Article 53(2) of the Statute of the International Court of Justice, which states that the "Court must ... satisfy itself, not only that it has jurisdiction in accordance with Articles 36 and 37, but also that the claim is well founded in fact and law".[48] In the *Military and Paramilitary Activities in and against Nicaragua* Judgment, the ICJ said:

> [T]he use of the term "satisfy itself" in the English text of the Statute (and in the French text the term "s'assurer") implies that the Court must attain the same degree of certainty as in any other case that the claim of the party appearing is sound in law, and, so far as the

42 Sadat and Carden, *supra* note 28, p. 420. But see George P. Fletcher and Jens David Ohlin, 'The ICC – Two Courts in One?', 4 *Journal of International Criminal Justice* 428, 431 – 432 (noting that because Article 19 makes no reference to Security Council referrals the Court "is not constrained by the usual rules on complementarity when a situation is referred to the Court from [the Council]". *Ibid.*, p. 431.

43 Article 19(2) states that "challenges to the admissibility of a case on the grounds referred to in article 17 or challenges to the jurisdiction of the Court may be made by: a) An accused or a person for whom a warrant of arrest or a summons to appear has been issued under article 58; b) A State which has jurisdiction over a case, on the ground that it is investigating or prosecuting the case or has investigated or prosecuted; or c) A State from which acceptance of jurisdiction is required under article 12". Rome Statute, Art. 19(2); ICC Rule 133. However, there is a clear distinction between Articles 18 and 19. Article 19 seems to widen the categories that can challenge the admissibility of a case, unlike Article 18, which limits a challenge to the admissibility of an investigation to a State Party or the Prosecutor acting *proprio motu;* still there is a technical distinction between them. Article 18 refers to situations referred to the Court, while Article 19 refers to individual cases, a further procedural step which is discussed in more detail below.

44 Rome Statute, Art. 19(1).

45 *Ibid.*, Art. 19(3).

46 M. Cherif Bassiouni, 'Explanatory Note on the ICC Statute', 71 *Revue Internationale de Droit Penal* 1, 20 (2000).

47 Rome Statute, Art. 19(1); ICC Rule 58(4) (stating that "the Court shall rule on any challenge or question of jurisdiction first and then on any challenge or question of admissibility"). The Court defined its jurisdictional parameters in a recent decision of the Appeals Chamber: see *Prosecutor v. Thomas Lubanga Dyilo, Judgment on the Appeal of Mr. Thomas Lubanga Dyilo against the Decision on the Defence Challenge to the Jurisdiction of the Court pursuant to article 19 (2) (a) of the Statute of 3 October 2006*, No.: ICC-01/04-01/06-772, 14/12/2006, paras. 21 – 22.

48 Statute of the International Court of Justice, Arts. 36, 37.

nature of the case permits, that the facts on which it is based are supported by convincing evidence.[49]

Applying this rule analogously to the situation of the ICC suggests that the term "satisfy itself" that it has jurisdiction" also "implies" that the Court must "attain the degree of certainty" that the jurisdictional parameters, defined under the provisions of the Statute, have been met. It is certainly evident that an international court has the power to determine its own jurisdiction.[50] The requirement in paragraph 1, that the Court "shall satisfy itself that it has jurisdiction in any case brought before it", seems redundant.[51]

This duty is limited to "any case" which is "brought before it". A "case" is narrower than the term "situation" within the meaning of Articles 13, 14 and 18.[52] These terms were discussed in the 1996 Preparatory Committee in relation to the *ex officio* powers to be granted to the Prosecutor. In the 1996 Preparatory Committee, those who opposed granting the Prosecutor *ex officio* powers asserted that referring "situations" rather than "individual cases" as subjects of a complaint would be sufficient to broaden the powers of the Prosecutor.[53] Also it has been pointed out that some delegations "were uneasy" with a system which allows a State party to select "individual suspects"

49 *Military and Paramilitary Activities in and Against Nicaragua (Nicaragua v. United States of America)*, 1986 I.C.J., Judgment (Merits) of 27/06/1986, paras. 28 – 29.

50 Indeed, in its latest *Case concerning the Application of the Convention on the Prevention and Punishment of the Crime of Genocide*, the ICJ recalled its earlier decisions where it had stated that it "must however always be satisfied that it has jurisdiction and must if necessary go into that matter *proprio motu*": see *Case concerning the Application of the Convention on the Prevention and Punishment of the Crime of Genocide (Bosnia and Herzegovina v. Serbia and Montenegro)*, 2007 I.C.J., Judgment (Merits), 26/02/2007, para. 118 and see also para. 138. Also, in its decision on jurisdiction and the admissibility of the application in the *Case concerning Military and Paramilitary Activities in and against Nicaragua*, the ICJ explicitly said that the "Court must always be satisfied that it has jurisdiction before proceeding to examine the merits of a case": see *Military and Paramilitary Activities in and Against Nicaragua (Nicaragua v. United States of America)*, 1984 I.C.J., Jurisdiction of the Court and Admissibility of the Application, 26/11/1984, para. 80. Similarly, in the *Fisheries Jurisdiction Case*, the ICJ said that "the establishment or otherwise of jurisdiction is not a matter for the parties but for the Court itself. Although a party seeking to assert a fact must bear the burden of proving it, this has no relevance for the establishment of the Court's jurisdiction" *Fisheries Jurisdiction Case (Spain v. Canada)*, 1998 I.C.J., Jurisdiction of the Court, 4/12/1998, para. 37; and also *Border and Transborder Armed Actions (Nicaragua* v. *Honduras), Jurisdiction and Admissibility, Judgment, I.C.J. Reports 1988*, para. 16.

51 See also Christopher K. Hall, "Challenges to the Jurisdiction of the Court or the Admissibility of a Case", *Triffterer Commentary*, *supra* note 7, pp. 405, 407.

52 Rome Statute, Arts. 13, 14, 18.

53 Silvia A. Fernandez, "The Role of the International Prosecutor, in The International Criminal Court: The Making of the Rome Statute", in Roy S. Lee (ed.), *supra* note 15, p. 180.

for the purpose of a complaint.[54] In their view, this "could encourage politicization of the complaint procedure".[55] Instead, States parties "should be empowered to refer 'situations' whereby the Prosecutor could later 'initiate a case against an individual'".[56] The United States delegation tabled a proposal to this effect, which gained the support of many States.[57]

At the Rome Conference, this problem emerged once more, but in a different context, namely, in regard to the Security Council's referrals. There was a division of opinions as to whether the Security Council should refer "situations", "cases" or "matters". The majority of delegates rejected the possibility of referring "cases" by the end of the preparatory negotiations, finding "cases" to be too narrow and not mindful enough of the Court's independence in the exercise of its jurisdiction. Consequently, only "matters" and "situations" were submitted to the Diplomatic Conference. Those who favoured the narrow concept of a "matter" believed that there ought to be "some degree of specificity in the referral before the Court could assert jurisdiction".[58] Others who were inclined towards the term "situation" thought that the Council referring a "matter" would interfere with the Court's independent functioning, especially because the term is "still too specific".[59] Despite the diversity of opinions, the term "situation" was finally adopted.[60]

---

54 1996 *Preparatory Committee Report*, Vol. I, *supra* note 9, para. 146.

55 *Ibid.*

56 *Ibid.*

57 *Report of the Preparatory Committee on the Establishment of an International Criminal Court*, Vol. II, (Compilation of Proposals) (G.A., 51 st Sess., Supp. No. 22, A/51/22, 1996), p. 109, Art. 25(2). The proposal reads: "A State Party…may lodge a complaint [in writing] with the Prosecutor…[that refers a situation to the Prosecutor as to which such crime appears to have been committed and requesting that the Prosecutor investigate the situation for the purpose of determining whether one or more specific persons should be charged with commission of such crime]"; also Fernandez, *supra* note 53, p. 180.

58 Lionel Yee, "The International Criminal Court and the Security Council: Articles 13(b) and 16", in Roy S. Lee (ed.), *supra* note 15, p.148. The same question was also discussed briefly during the meetings of the 1996 Preparatory Committee in relation to the functions of the Security Council. See 1996 *Preparatory Committee Report*, Vol. I, *supra* note 9, para. 136.

59 Yee, *supra* note 58 pp. 147 – 148.

60 The full debates on the question of "situations" and "matters" were far too long to be summarized in this book. Further accounts of the useful debates may be found in the following. *Summary Records of the 2nd to 5th Plenary Meetings*, UN Doc. A.CONF.183/SR. 2 – 5; and *Summary Records of the 7th to 36th Meetings*, UN Doc. A/CONF.183/C.1/SR. 7 – 36. Specific focus should be on statements made by the delegates of Sweden, UN Doc. A/CONF.183/SR. 7, para. 68; Malawi, UN Doc. A/CONF.183/SR. 8, para. 1; Spain, *ibid.* para. 11; Slovakia, *ibid*, para. 26; United Republic of Tanzania, *ibid.*, para. 28; Norway, *ibid.* , para. 35; Pakistan, *ibid.* para. 43; Mexico, *ibid.*, para. 63; Canada, UN Doc. A/CONF.183/SR. 9, para. 12; Italy, *ibid.*, para. 19; United States, *ibid.*, para. 21; and Turkey, *ibid.*, para. 42.

The entire process before the ICC starts with the referral of a "situation" to the Prosecutor. Then the Prosecutor conducts the investigation, which is monitored by the Pre-Trial Chamber through the different stages. In the end, the Prosecutor decides whether to file a case (within the narrow meaning in the above paragraph). Article 19 comes into play, therefore, once a "case" has emerged from the investigation of an entire situation leading to the identification of suspects who have committed one of the crimes listed in Article 5 of the Statute. As Hall argued, a "case" stage implies "formal proceedings" that exceed the investigation of a situation, which "might include an application" for an arrest warrant under Article 58 or the "questioning of a suspect who was at liberty" per Article 55.[61] In *Lubanga*, Pre-Trial Chamber I, quoting and relying on the latter passage in the Decision, reached the conclusion that:

> [C]ases, which comprise specific incidents during which one or more crimes within the jurisdiction of the Court seem to have been committed by one or more identified suspects, *entail proceedings that take place after the issuance of a warrant of arrest or summons to appear* (emphasis added).[62]

A comparison of Hall's passage referred to above with the conclusion reached by Pre-Trial Chamber I suggests that the Chamber misinterpreted the work quoted in its Decision. The author merely stated that "cases" imply formal proceedings, which "might include an application for a warrant under article 58", which is *clearly* different in meaning from "proceedings that take place after the issuance of a warrant of arrest or a summons to appear" as asserted by the Chamber. By so doing, Pre-Trial Chamber I delayed the start of a "case stage" from prior to the issue of a warrant when suspects have been identified, until an arrest warrant has already been issued. This conclusion may not be problematic *per se*. It gets problematic when applied within the context of examining admissibility during the arrest warrant phase. When reading Rule 58(2) and (3), one may reach the conclusion that Article 19 governing admis-

61 In this respect, the Pre-Trial Chamber's decision pursuant to Article 15(4) to authorize the Prosecutor to commence an investigation *proprio motu* would not bring a case "before" the Court within the meaning of Article 19(1), even though it mentions the word "case". The history and structure of Articles 13(c) and 15 demonstrate that their purpose is to permit the Prosecutor to investigate an entire "situation", not to make a definitive decision whether an individual case is admissible. Under Article 15(4), the Pre-Trial Chamber does not formally determine that a case "brought before it" is admissible, but simply makes a determination "that there is a reasonable basis to proceed with an investigation", and that "the case appears to fall within the jurisdiction of the Court, without prejudice to subsequent determinations by the Court with regard to the jurisdiction and admissibility of a case". See Hall, *supra* note 51, p. 408 n.8 (emphasis added) (text mistakenly refers to Article 5(3) instead of 15(4)). However, this does not mean that the Pre-Trial Chamber is precluded from determining "that there is a reasonable basis to proceed with an investigation" in light of Articles 17 and 53(3) (a).

62 *Decision on the Applications for Participation in the Proceedings of VPRS1, VPRS2, VPRS3, VPRS4, VPRS5, and VPRS6*, No.: ICC-01/04, 17/01/2006, (public redacted), No.:ICC-01/04-101-etEN-Corr., 17/02/2007, para. 65.

sibility questions during a "case" stage, may be meant to apply *following* the issue of an arrest warrant and not *prior to* or *during* its proceedings.[63]

Further, Article 19(2) (a), which states that "challenges to the admissibility of the case on the grounds referred to in Article 17...may be made by: An accused or a person for whom a warrant of arrest or a summons to appear has been issued under Article 58",[64] leads to the same conclusion, namely that Article 19 does not seem to cover arrest warrant proceedings under Article 58. Thus, if Chamber I's finding that a case "stage" does not begin until an arrest warrant has been issued was correct, on what legal basis did it examine the question of admissibility during the arrest warrant proceedings in the *Congo* situation as referred to below? Based on this particular reasoning, Pre-Trial Chamber I appeared to be inaccurate in its ruling that a "case" stage starts only after the issue of an arrest warrant. The reason is that suspects will already have been identified even before the issue of the warrant, which presupposes that the "case" phase may begin from that moment. Nonetheless, the problem may be solved by following a different legal reasoning based on the language of Article 19 (6) in conjunction with Article 19 (2) (a). Article 19(6) foresees the possibility of raising an admissibility challenge prior to "the confirmation of charges" under Article 61. It is clear that proceedings under Article 58 precede those under the confirmation of charges hearing. This suggests that Article 19 may be meant to cover arrest warrant proceedings under Article 58. Although Article 19(2) (a) limits a challenge to the admissibility of a case to a person after an arrest warrant was issued against him/her, this does not mean that examining admissibility in general cannot take place during arrest warrant proceedings. Rather, this means that only a person referred to in Article 19 (2) (a) is not permitted to raise an admissibility challenge before the Court unless he/she meets the status of an accused or in the event that an arrest warrant has been issued against him/her. Furthermore, examining the language of Article 58 together with that of Article 19 (2) (a) supports a conclusion that during arrest warrant proceedings questions of admissibility may only be raised by the prosecution, or examined *proprio motu* by the Pre-Trial Chamber.[65]

Moreover, Pre-Trial Chamber I stated:

> [T]he Chamber recalls the practice of Pre-Trial Chamber II in its decisions on the Prosecution's requests for warrants of arrest for Joseph Kony...which grants the Prosecution's requests only after finding that the cases fall within the jurisdiction of the Court and appear

63 ICC Rule 58 (2) and (3). These sub-rules read together as follows: "The Court shall transmit a request or application received [raising a challenge or question concerning its jurisdiction or the admissibility of a case in accordance with Article 19 paragraph 2 or 3, or is acting on its own motion] (ICC Rule 58 (2))...to the Prosecutor and the person referred to in article 19, paragraph 2, who has been surrendered to the Court or who has appeared voluntarily or pursuant to summons...". See ICC Rule 58 (3).

64 Rome Statute, Art. 19(2) (a).

65 See Mohamed M. El Zeidy, 'Some Remarks on the Question of the Admissibility of a Case During Arrest warrant Proceedings before the International Criminal Court', 19 *Leiden Journal of International Law* 741 (2006).

> admissible. In this regard, it is the Chamber's view that an *initial determination* on whether the case against Mr Thomas Lubanga Dyilo falls within the jurisdiction of the Court and *is admissible* is *a prerequisite* to the issuance of a warrant of arrest for him.[66]

Although the Chamber "recalls" the practice of Pre-Trial Chamber II in the arrest warrant decisions, nothing in these decisions supports a finding that Pre-Trial Chamber II intended to subject the issue of a warrant of arrest to a determination that the case against the five LRA leaders "is admissible".[67] By contrast, Pre-Trial Chamber II's decision lacks any reference to the fact that it was under an obligation to question the admissibility of the case at this stage, as in the case of Pre-Trial Chamber I. The latter's treatment of the question of admissibility raises some legal concerns.

If one admits that arrest warrant proceedings in accordance with Article 58 fit within the parameters of Article 19 stage as argued earlier, it is incorrect to decide that an admissibility finding is mandatory at this phase. Certainly, the wording of Article 19(1) shows that the admissibility examination is discretionary at this stage of the proceedings. This suggests that Pre-Trial Chamber I built its conclusions on a misinterpretation of the Statute, the Rules of Procedure and Evidence and Pre-Trial Chamber II's decision. Such conclusion is in line with the findings reached in a subsequent decision concerning the *Harun* and *Kushayb* case arising from the *Darfur* situation. Pre-Trial Chamber I seem to have recognized this error when it stated that "article 19(1) of the Statute gives the Chamber discretion to make an initial determination of the admissibility of the case before the issuance of a warrant of arrest or a summons to appear. Such discretion should be exercised only if warranted by the circumstances of the case, bearing in mind the interest of the person concerned".[68] However, the clause "[s]uch discretion should be exercised only if warranted by the circumstances of the case,…", which appeared for the first time in a Chamber's decision, is unclear. It seems to limit the Chamber's discretion to act in accordance with Article 19(1). Such restriction is neither supported by the language of Article 19(1) nor by that of Rule 58. The Chamber has also failed to offer examples of what, in her opinion, might be "warranted by the circumstances of the case" that would take into account the "interest of the person concerned".

66 *Prosecutor v. Thomas Lubanga Dyilo, Decision on the Prosecutor's Application for a Warrant of Arrest, Art. 58*, No.: ICC-01/04-01/06-8-US-Corr, 10/02/2006, para. 18, unsealed pursuant to Decision ICC-01/04-01/06-37 dated 17/03/2006; See also *Warrant of Arrest for Joseph Kony Issued on 8 July 2005 as Amended on 27 September 2005*, No.: ICC-02/04-01/05-53, 27/09/2005, para. 38.

67 Rome Statute, Art. 19(1), which states: "The Court may, on its own motion, determine the admissibility of a case in accordance with article 17". This makes the test discretionary during the Article 19 stage when the Court is acting *ex officio*, as in the *Lubanga* and *Uganda* decisions.

68 *Prosecutor v. Ahmad Muhammad Harun ("AHMAD HARUN") and Ali Muhammad Ali-Abd-Al-Rahman ("ALI KUSHAYB"), Decision on the Prosecution Application under Article 58(7) of the Statute*, No.: ICC-02/05-01/07-1-Corr, 27/04/2007, para. 18.

In the recent *Ngudjolo* case arising from the DRC situation, Pre-Trial Chamber I adopted the same approach outlined in the *Harun* and *Kushayb* case in relation to organising the exercise of its discretion when examining the question of admissibility in accordance with article 19(1).[69] Yet, the factual and legal reasoning outlined in the decision and explored below, revealed, to some extent, the justification for the Chamber to make an initial determination of admissibility during this stage. The Chamber argued that the "circumstances of the present case warrant an initial determination of the admissibility of the case prior to the issuance of a warrant of arrest".[70] It reached its conclusion after having examined the Prosecution submissions, which showed that DRC initiated domestic proceedings against Mathieu Ngudjolo Chui for, *inter alia*, "murders allegedly committed within an attack brought on the village Tchomia" as well as in relation to "his role within the Mouvement Revolutionaire Congolaise (MRC)".[71] This suggests that, on the basis of the facts presented, there was a clear possibility of rendering the case inadmissible, which encouraged the Chamber to rule on admissibility prior to the issue of the arrest warrants. Thus, it is clear that the existence of evidence supporting "a possible finding of inadmissibility" may be considered as one factor that meets the requirements of exceptional circumstances as well as the "interest of the person concerned".

Nevertheless, in order to maintain a balance that ensures the fairness of the proceedings, an examination of the question of admissibility of the case during the arrest warrant stage may not be feasible. At this stage of the proceedings, the Chamber generally lacks sufficient factual and perhaps legal basis on which to decide properly.[72] The right to submit evidence and information related to the case lies primarily with the Prosecutor, therefore prompting the Chamber to reach its verdict relying merely on a single source. Indeed, in reaching its decision on admissibility in the

69 *Prosecutor v. Mathieu Ngudjolo Chui, Decision on the Evidence and Information provided by the Prosecution for the Issuance of a Warrant of Arrest for Mathieu Ngudjolo Chui*, No.: ICC-01/04-02/07-3, para. 17, reclassified as public pursuant to Oral Decision dated 12/02/2008.

70 *Ibid.*, para. 20.

71 *Ibid.*, paras. 18 – 19, 21 – 22.

72 There is little doubt that may arise in relation to the legality of addressing admissibility during the arrest warrant proceedings. Such doubt is based on the fact that Article 58 does not include or refer to the examination of admissibility at this phase, as a constituent requirement or component of Article 58. Arguably, the Court may go beyond the plain language of Article 58 and treat the question as an additonal procedural step in view of the discretion provided to it under Article 19(1) of the Statute. More on the treatment of this question , see El Zeidy, *supra* note 65, p. 743 *ff*.

Lubanga,[73] *Harun* and *Kushayb,*[74]and *Chui*[75] cases arising from the DRC situation, Pre-Trial Chamber I relied exclusively on the evidence and information provided by the prosecution.

This would not have been be the case if admissibility had been examined, for example, during the confirmation hearing, where the "person charged, as well as his or her counsel",[76] should have been present in order to submit their views. The possibility of taking into consideration submissions and views of the defence is generally limited at the arrest warrant stage. Regulation 77 entrusts the Office of Public Council for the Defence (OPCD) with a limited mandate to represent and protect the rights of the defence. The role of the OPCD is focused on the "initial stages of the investigation, in particular...the application of Article 56, paragraph 2 (d), and rule 47, sub-rule 2".[77] To hear the defence fully at the stage of the confirmation hearing would allow a more balanced decision that takes into account the views of the two parties (instead of one).[78] The situation might also be exacerbated if proceedings were held *ex parte,* limited to the prosecution, as in the *Lubanga* case[79] In this respect, neither the suspect or his defence nor any other interested party[80] might participate or submit their views creating a situation of injustice. This conclusion makes it more plausible to examine admissibility during the confirmation hearing or there after rather in the course of issuing an arrest warrant. It is evident that according to Article 19 the Court will not have a duty to make a determination, *proprio motu,* of whether it has jurisdiction in relation to an investigation into a situation *vis-à-vis* a case being conducted

73 *Prosecutor v. Thomas Lubanga Dyilo, Decision on the Prosecutor's Application for a Warrant of Arrest, Art. 58,* No.: ICC-01/04-01/06-8-US-Corr, 10/02/2006, para. 40, unsealed pursuant to Decision ICC-01/04-01/06-37 dated 17/03/2006.

74 *Prosecutor v. Ahmad Muhammad Harun ("AHMAD HARUN") and Ali Muhammad Ali-Abd-Al-Rahman ("ALI KUSHAYB"), Decision on the Prosecution Application under Article 58(7) of the Statute,* No.: ICC-02/05-01/07-1-Corr, 27/04/2007, paras. 20 – 25.

75 *Prosecutor v. Mathieu Ngudjolo Chui, Warrant of Arrest for Mathieu Ngudjolo Chui,* No.: ICC-01/04-02/07-1-tENG, unsealed pursuant to Decision ICC-01/04-02/07-10 dated 7/02/2008, pp. 2 – 3.

76 Rome Statute, Art. 61; ICC Rule 121.

77 ICC Regulation 77 (1), (4).

78 It is not surprising that the Duty Counsel for the Defence challenged Pre-Trial Chamber's I findings on admissibility in the *Lubanga* case. See *Prosecutor v. Thomas Lubanga Dyilo, Appeal by the duty Counsel for the Defence against Pre-Trial Chamber I's Decision of 10 February 2006 on the Prosecutor's Application for a Warrant of Arrest, Article 58,* No.: ICC-01/04-01/06-57-Corr-tEN, 24/03/2006; See also *Prosecution Response to Thomas Lubanga Dyilo's Brief in Support of the Appeal,* No.: ICC-01/04-01/06-89, 1/05/2006.

79 *Prosecutor v. Thomas Lubanga Dyilo, Decision on the Prosecutor's Application for a Warrant of Arrest, Art. 58,* No.: ICC-01/04-01/06-8-US-Corr, 10/02/2006, para. 20, unsealed pursuant to Decision ICC-01/04-01/06-37 dated 17/03/2006.

80 Other interested parties are the referring State and victims who have communicated with the Court concerning the case or their legal representatives. See Rome Statute, Art. 19(3); ICC Rule 59.

by the Prosecutor.[81] This sounds logical, since this is a question that has to be dealt with the Prosecutor in the course of deciding whether to initiate an investigation into a situation.[82] Article 19(1) also provides, as mentioned earlier, that the Court (the Pre-Trial Chamber or Trial Chamber) has the discretion, on its own motion, to determine the "admissibility of a case in accordance with article 17". Indeed, in *Lubanga*, Pre-Trial Chamber I acknowledged that it has invoked its *ex officio* powers to review the jurisdiction of the Court as well as the admissibility of the case when it stated:

> As the Prosecution rightly points out, the Chamber notes that, in the present case, its review of jurisdiction and admissibility of the case against Mr Thomas Lubanga Dyilo is *ex officio* insofar as the Prosecution raised no issue of jurisdiction or admissibility in the Prosecution's Application. The Chamber also notes that rule 58(2) of the Rules establishes that, when the Chamber is acting in its own motion as provided for in article 19 (1) of the Statute, it shall decide on the procedure to be followed, may take appropriate measures for the proper conduct of the proceedings and may hold a hearing.[83]

By contrast to the duty of the Court to determine whether it has jurisdiction in a case brought before it, the Court may decide questions of admissibility at an earlier stage than that of Article 19, namely admissibility in the context of a situation. The Prosecutor has a duty under Article 53(1) (b) to consider the question of admissibility in the early stages of an investigation into a situation.[84] The Pre-Trial Chamber may review the Prosecutor's conclusions in the light of Article 53(3) (a).[85] However, according to Hall, the Court would review the Prosecutor's admissibility conclusions only if an admissibility challenge was brought pursuant to Article 19(2), unless clear circumstances required an admissibility determination in the interests of justice.[86]

While complementarity is a right accruing to States, a specified class of individuals may invoke complementarity on behalf of a State with jurisdiction. Article 19(2) (a) permits an accused[87] or a person "for whom a warrant of arrest or a summons to

81 Hall, *supra* note 51, pp. 407 – 408.

82 Rome Statute, Art. 53.

83 *Prosecutor v. Thomas Lubanga Dyilo, Decision on the Prosecutor's Application for a Warrant of Arrest, Art. 58*, No.: ICC-01/04-01/06-8-US-Corr, 10/02/2006, para. 19, unsealed pursuant to Decision ICC-01/04-01/06-37 dated 17/03/2006.

84 Rome Statute, Art. 53(1)(b).

85 *Ibid.*, Art. 53(3) (a).

86 Hall, *supra* note 51, p. 408.

87 Although the Rome Statute does not provide a definition for "accused", it would be consistent with the structure of the Statute and the Rules of Procedure and Evidence of the ICTY and ICTR to define an accused for the purposes of Article 19 as a person identified in the "the document containing the charges" referred to in Article 61(3)(a), as of the moment the document is provided to the Pre-Trial Chamber, whether "in camera" pursuant to a sealed indictment or publicly, rather than at the stage when the charges are confirmed in accordance with Article 61(7)(a), and to consider the person as an accused under the Statute until the charges fail to be confirmed or the person is acquitted or

appear has been issued" to challenge the jurisdiction or the admissibility of a case before the ICC.[88] This is in contradistinction to Article 18 and Rule 55(2), which limit the raising of the question of admissibility to the relevant State and the Prosecutor. Indeed, in its decision of 22 November 2006 concerning the *Darfur* situation, Pre-Trial Chamber I rejected the request filed by the ad hoc counsel on 13 October 2006 raising the question of the admissibility of the situation.[89] The Court noted that the applicant "had no procedural *locus standi* under Article 19 (2) of the Rome Statute to challenge the jurisdiction of the Court and the admissibility of the situation in Darfur at this stage of the investigation".[90] This finding is consistent with the purpose of Article 19(2) (a) and suggests that there is a distinction between the admissibility of a situation and that of a case depending on the stage of the proceedings.

Article 19(2)(b) specifies that challenges to the admissibility of a case or the jurisdiction of the Court on the grounds referred to in Article 17 "may be made by" a "State which has jurisdiction over a case, on the ground that it is investigating or prosecuting the case or has investigated or prosecuted" it.[91] In *Lubanga*, Pre-Trial Chamber I ruled on a defence challenge to the jurisdiction of the Court in accordance with Article 19(2)(a) in conjunction with Article 21(3) of the Statute. The Defence argued that since Article 21(3) requires consistency with "internationally recognized human rights", the Chamber's exercise of its jurisdiction *ratione personae* over the accused would be an "abuse of process", as his arrest and detention were illegal and

convicted. *Ibid.*, p. 409 ; also ICTY Rules Procedure and Evidence, UN Doc. IT/32/REV. 24 (2002), Rule 2(a) (defining an accused as "a person against whom an indictment has been submitted in accordance with Rule 47"). Rule 47 specifies the different stages for confirmation of the indictment by a Judge.

88 ICC Rule 58.

89 *Situation in Darfur, Conclusions aux fins d'exception d'incompétence et d'irrecevabilité,* No.: ICC-01/05-20-Corr., 13/10/2006.

90 *Situation in Darfur, Décision relative aux conclusions aux fins d'exception d'incompétence et d' irrecevabilité,* No.: ICC-02/05-34, 22/11/2006; and also in the context of the DRC situation, *Decision Following the Consultation held on 11 October 2005 and the Prosecution's Submission on Jurisdiction and Admissibility filed on 31 October 2005*, No.: ICC-01/04-93, 09/11/2005.

91 Holmes, *supra* note 15, p. 67. In this context, it is not sufficient for a State to have initiated national proceedings. The State must demonstrate to the Court that it has jurisdiction in the case. This addition was intended to forestall situations where a State could challenge (and delay) the Court from proceeding with a case on the ground that it was investigating, when in fact the investigation or prosecution was sure to fail because the State lacked jurisdiction even as far as its own courts were concerned. At the Rome Conference, one of the problems that emerged was whether third States could make a challenge. Although many delegations from the "like-minded" States believed that this right was limited to States Parties, many others insisted that the principle of complementarity "should apply to the Court regardless of whether the national proceedings were being conducted by a State Party or a non-party State". Those delegations feared the real possibility that "concurrent investigations or prosecutions" could occur, which could jeopardize the efficacy of both". *Ibid.*, pp. 66 – 67.

arbitrary.[92] The Chamber concluded that although Article 21(3) empowers the Court to examine "any violations of Thomas Lubanga Dyilo's rights in relation to his arrest and detention prior to 14 March 2006 [the date of his arrest] only once it has been established that there has been concerted action between the Court and the DRC's authorities"[93] would the application of the doctrine of "abuse of process" that would require the Court to decline jurisdiction "has been confined to instances of torture or serious mistreatment by national authorities…in some way related to the process of arrest and transfer of the person to the relevant tribunal".[94] Since no evidence of any such assertion exists, having regard to the observations submitted by the DRC[95] the Chamber decided that the challenge to jurisdiction was unfounded.[96]

On appeal pursuant to Article 82(1) (a),[97] the Appeals Chamber overturned Pre-Trial Chamber's I understanding of jurisdiction, as it considered that the Chamber erred in characterizing the defence application as one that went to the jurisdiction of the Court under Article 19 of the Statute. Instead the Appeals Chamber stated:

> Save for the prayer itemizing the relief sought – challenge to the jurisdiction of the Court – nothing was produced, said or done to contest the jurisdiction of the Court to take cognisance of the crimes involved in the accusations levelled against Mr. Lubanga Dyilo, nor was the decision of the Pre-Trial Chamber of 10 February 2006 to the effect that the Court is vested with jurisdiction to deal with the case against him doubted or disputed in any way. On the contrary, the application is founded on the premise that the Court has jurisdiction to address the case but should desist from assuming jurisdiction in the matter for the reason that so to do would be an abuse of the proceedings before the Court owing to the grave violations of the rights of the appellant entrenched in the Statute. The Pre-Trial Chamber treated the application of Mr. Lubanga Dyilo as going to jurisdiction without specifically saying so and without heeding the observations of the DRC and the victims to the contrary. In essence, what the Pre-Trial Chamber did was to treat the submission of the appellant

92 *Prosecutor v. Thomas Lubanga Dyilo, Decision on the Defence Challenge to the Jurisdiction of the Court pursuant to article 19 (2) (a) of the Statute,* No.: ICC-01/04-01/06-512, 3/10/2006, pp. 5, 9.

93 *Ibid.*, p. 9.

94 *Ibid.*, p. 10.

95 *Prosecutor v. Thomas Lubanga Dyilo, <<Observations de la République Démocratiqué du Congo>>, registered on 24 August 2006,* No.: ICC-01/04-01/06-348-Conf ; and see also *Prosecutor v. Thomas Lubanga Dyilo, <<Observations des victimes a/0001/06, a/0002/06 et a/0003/06 quant à l'exception d'incompétence soulevée par la defense dans la requêt du 23 mai 2006>>*, No.: ICC-01/04-01/06-349, 24/08/2006.

96 *Prosecutor v. Thomas Lubanga Dyilo, Decision on the Defence Challenge to the Jurisdiction of the Court pursuant to article 19 (2) (a) of the Statute,* No.: ICC-01/04-01/06-512, 3/10/2006, pp. 10 – 11.

97 *Prosecutor v. Thomas Lubanga Dyilo, Defence Appeal against the Decision on the Defence Challenge to Jurisdiction of 3 October 2006,* No.: ICC-01/04-01/06-620, 26/10/2006. On appeals and the ICC see, *inter alia*, Hans-Jörg Behrens, 'Investigation, Trial and Appeal in the International Criminal Court Statute (Parts V,VI,VIII)', 6 *European Journal of Crime, Criminal Law and Criminal Justice* 113, 121 – 122 (1998).

> that the Court should refrain from addressing his case as a challenge to the jurisdiction of the Court under article 19(2) of the Statute.[98]

It follows that the Appeals Chamber considered that invoking the doctrine of abuse of process goes to the power of the Court to exercise its jurisdiction, which already exists, and therefore the accused's challenge did not fall within the parameters of Article 19(2) as understood by the Pre-Trial Chamber.

The question of exercise of jurisdiction over a case, within the meaning of Article 19(2) (b), is trickier than the situation of Article 19(2)(a) as explored above, since all States may invoke their competence to exercise universal jurisdiction over the crimes within the jurisdiction of the Court, resulting in a large number of frivolous admissibility challenges. Paragraph (2) (b) should, therefore, be given a sort of strict interpretation. This means that a State with "jurisdiction over the case" should be one that meets the definition of jurisdiction within its wide sense, having regard to *ratione materiae, ratione personae, ratione loci, ratione temporis* requirements, ensuring that only a State which has met these requirements may be considered as having jurisdiction within the meaning of the Statute. In the recent *Bagaragaza* case before the ICTR, Trial Chamber III rejected the request to transfer the case to be tried in Norway in accordance with Rule 11 *bis* of the ICTR Statute, on the basis that one of these jurisdictional requirements had not been met. The Chamber said in this case:

> [T]he universal jurisdiction referred to in the submissions of the Kingdom of Norway will permit the prosecution of the Accused (*ratione personae*) for his acts allegedly committed in Rwanda (*ratione loci*) in 1994 (*ratione temporis*). The only aspect of jurisdiction which would not be covered by Norwegian law is the *ratione materiae*. The submission that Norwegian criminal law does not provide for the crime of genocide directly affects the finding of jurisdiction *ratione materiae*, where the legal qualification of the facts alleged in the confirmed Indictment is made.[99]

The ICTR Appeals Chamber confirmed this conclusion:

> Considering the submissions of the parties, the Appeals Chamber is not satisfied that the Prosecution has demonstrated that the Trial Chamber erred in denying its request to refer Mr. Bagaragaza's case to Norway for trial. As the *Amicus Curiae* Brief makes clear, Norway's jurisdiction over Mr. Bagaragaza's crimes would be exercised pursuant to legislative provisions dealing with the prosecution of ordinary crimes. The Appeals Chamber recalls that the basis of the Tribunal's authority to refer its cases to national jurisdictions flows

98 *Prosecutor v. Thomas Lubanga Dyilo, Judgment on the Appeal of Mr. Thomas Lubanga Dyilo against the Decision on the Defence Challenge to the Jurisdiction of the Court pursuant to article 19 (2) (a) of the Statute of 3 October 2006,* No.: ICC-01/04-01/06-772, 14/12/2006, paras. 20, 24.

99 *Prosecutor v. Michel Bagaragaza,* Case No. ICTR-2005-86-*R11*bis, *Decision on the Prosecution Motion for Referral to the Kingdom of Norway, Rule 11 bis of the Rules of Procedure and Evidence,* 19/05/2006, para. 13.

> from Article 8 of the Statute, as affirmed in Security Council resolutions. Article 8 specifies that the Tribunal has concurrent jurisdiction with national authorities to prosecute "serious violations of international humanitarian law". In other words, this provision delimits the Tribunal's authority, allowing it only to refer cases where the state will charge and convict for those international crimes listed in its Statute.[100]

One commentator argued that because States under international law may exercise universal jurisdiction over the crimes within the jurisdiction of the Court,[101] "it is likely that paragraph 2(b) meant only those States which had provided their own courts with jurisdiction over the case under national law. Jurisdiction could be based on territory, the protective principle, the nationality of the suspect or the victim, or universality".[102]

Another commentator took a different view, arguing that if the principle of complementarity were to be applicable to every State on the basis of any possible jurisdictional link, this could easily block effective prosecution in a large number of cases. Indeed, as argued above, any State could invoke the principle of universal jurisdiction and thus initiate a prosecution before its domestic courts, thereby impeding the work of the ICC.[103] Thus, it is more plausible to limit the principle of complementarity to those national jurisdictions with a direct link to the criminal conduct or the accused.[104]

Although the chapeau of Article 19(2) refers to "challenges to the admissibility of a case on the grounds referred to in article 17", an examination of the language of Article 19(2)(b) suggests that it limits these grounds to those listed in Article 17(1)(a) and (b). Therefore, it does not mention the circumstance where a person has already been *tried* as well as the gravity test as viable admissibility challenges. Nonetheless, once the State has investigated or prosecuted a case, then it has the opportunity to raise an admissibility challenge before the Court. If that State has gone further and tried the case, it is certain by implication that it has standing before the Court under

100 *Prosecutor v. Michel Bagaragaza*, Case No. ICTR-05-86-*AR11* bis, *Decision on Rule 11 bis Appeal*, 30/08/2006, para. 16.

101 Hall, *supra* note 51, p. 410. Recently on the crime of genocide see *Case concerning the Application of the Convention on the Prevention and Punishment of the Crime of Genocide (Bosnia and Herzegovina v. Serbia and Montenegro)*, 2007 I.C.J., Judgment (Merits), 26/02/2007.

102 Hall, *supra* note 51, p. 410.

103 Benvenuti, *supra* note 8, p. 48. In this context, if one follows the wider interpretation, namely that any State could assert jurisdiction based on universality, absent any direct connection to the conduct, this could have a negative effect on the second feature of complementarity. In other words, although the wide construction appears to strengthen the first feature of complementarity, that national jurisdiction is superior, it weakens the second feature if, for example, the State concerned was able and willing but the case meets the gravity requirements and should be tried before the ICC.

104 *Ibid.* (observing "these national jurisdictions may reasonably be presumed to be the ones in a position to collect evidence and testimony of the crime and/or implement a judgment, but are unwilling or unable to act").

Article 19(2)(b), since reaching the trial phase certainly means that the case has been prosecuted within the meaning of paragraph (2)(b).

Another notable omission is the lack of any reference to the criterion of gravity under Article 19. The discussion of gravity is beyond the scope of this study, although "gravity" is significant to the determination of the admissibility of a case during Article 19 proceedings, but arguably it is a test confined to the Court's application. When the element of gravity was first introduced by the International Law Commission in 1994, it was clear that it was a tool and a ground for the Court to declare a case "inadmissible". This idea remained unchanged and found its way in the 1998 Statute. It follows that the drafters could not have mentioned gravity in Article 19(2)(b) as it is not concerned with States' admissibility challenges. Perhaps the only scenario that may involve the application of the criterion of gravity on the part of the State is when a State that has investigated or prosecuted a case challenges its admissibility under Article 19(2) (b), and in order to enhance its argument states that the case is not even of sufficient gravity to "justify" the Court's intervention. Thus, although Article 19 appears to exclude "gravity" as a ground for challenging the admissibility of a case, the latter example shows that the absence of "gravity" does not necessarily prevent a State from using it to bolster its argument.

Another problem of drafting which might impede the Court's determination of admissibility challenges emerges from a reading of Article 19(2) in conjunction with Article 17(1). First, Article 19(2) (b) refers to a State that has prosecuted a case. This situation is not defined or mentioned in Article 17(1). Article 17(1) (a) refers to a case which is "being investigated" or being "prosecuted". Article 17(1) (b) refers to a case which has been investigated and in which the State decided not to try the person concerned. Thus, in this context, the text of Article 17(1) (b) should have included the following language: "The case has been investigated or prosecuted by a State which has jurisdiction over it and the State has decided not to prosecute or try the person concerned, unless the decision resulted from the unwillingness or inability of the State genuinely to prosecute or try such a person".

One wonders how the Court would rule on a challenge made in accordance with Article 19(2) (a) or (b), claiming that the State has prosecuted the case, since the latter criterion is not mentioned in Article 17(1). In other words, when the Court is ruling on an admissibility challenge, in order to decide that a case is inadmissible, it should apply the criteria set out in Article 17. Because Article 17 does not explicitly refer to a case that has been "prosecuted",, the defence may argue, for example, that the Court may be legally paralyzed to rule on an admissibility challenge based on this particular ground. Although reading these provisions strictly may appear problematic, certainly the Court will never react in a manner that hampers its judicial functions. These provisions were drafted in a way that ensures that there are always checks and balances. Even according to the scenario mentioned above, the Court may rely on the language of Article 17(1) (c), which refers to a person who has "already been tried". It is evident that that person has already been subject to a prosecution before reaching the trial stage. This reading certainly remedies the gap pointed out in Article 17(1) and serves as an example for similar problems.

Article 19(2)(c), on the other hand, allows a State from "which acceptance of jurisdiction is required under Article 12" to challenge the jurisdiction of the Court and the admissibility of a case. Acceptance of a State's jurisdiction is not required if the Security Council, pursuant to Article 13(b), refers a situation to the Prosecutor.[105] However, it is required when a situation is referred to the Prosecutor by a State in accordance with Articles 13(a) and 14, or when the Prosecutor has initiated an investigation *proprio motu* in accordance with Articles 13(c) and 15(1). In those circumstances, Article 12(2) requires the acceptance of jurisdiction by the State on whose territory, vessel or aircraft the crime occurred – known as the territoriality principle[106] – or the State of the accused's nationality, according to the principle of active personality.[107] In reading Article 19(2) (c) in conjunction with Article 12, one could conclude that a State that is not a party to the Statute but whose national is suspected of a crime cannot challenge jurisdiction or admissibility until the suspect is defined as an "accused" within the meaning of Article 12(2)(b).[108]

Furthermore, Article 19(2) (b) and (c) also covers challenges to the jurisdiction or admissibility of a case by a State which has challenged a ruling of the Pre-Trial Chamber under Article 18(7).[109] States that have had their Article 18 preliminary challenges rejected by the Pre-Trial Chamber may make a further challenge pursuant to Article 18(7) to the admissibility of the case under Article 19(2) and (4).[110] This addition-

105 Rome Statute, Art. 13(b).

106 Certainly, this might give rise to practical conflicts between States asserting jurisdiction on the basis of the two related types of the "territoriality principle", namely, "subjective territoriality" and "objective territoriality". "While subjective territoriality requires an element of the offense to occur within the asserting State, objective territoriality obtains when the effect or result of criminal conduct impacts on the asserting State, but the other elements of the offense take place wholly beyond its territorial boundaries". See Christopher L. Blakesley, "Extraterritorial Jurisdiction", in M. Cherif Bassiouni (ed.), *International Criminal Law: Procedural and Enforcement Mechanisms*, 2nd ed. (Ardsley: Transnational Publishers, 1999), p. 33. For a thorough discussion of the basis of jurisdiction see *ibid.*, pp. 33 – 70.

107 *Ibid*; also M. Cherif Bassiouni, *International Extradition: United States Law and Practice* (Dobbs Ferry, New York: Oceana Publications, 1996), pp. 295 – 312 [hereinafter International Extradition]; Michael P. Scharf, 'The ICC's Jurisdiction over the Nationals of Non-Party States: A Critique of the U.S. Position', 63 *Law and Contemporary Problems* 1, 44-45 (2000); Sharon A. Williams, The Rome Statute on the International Criminal Court: From 1947-2000 and Beyond, 38 *Osgoode Hall Law Journal* 298, 322 – 324 (2000).

108 Rome Statute, Art. 12(2)(b). This provision refers to "The State of which the *person accused* of the crime is a national" (emphasis added).

109 Rome Statute, Art. 18(7).

110 *Ibid.*, Art. 19(2) and (4); and generally ICC Rule 60.

al challenge is subject to the existence of "additional significant facts or significant changes of circumstances",[111] which should limit frivolous challenges.

Because of this additional challenge one can imagine a situation where the Pre-Trial Chamber rejected the State's initial challenge under Article 18(2) and Rule 55(2) on the basis of Article 17, and the State decides to challenge admissibility again under Articles 18(7) and 19(2)(b).[112] Should a State that the Court found was unwilling to carry out an investigation or prosecution be given a second chance and another opportunity to impede justice? What about a State whose proceedings "were undertaken, or the decision was made to shield the person concerned from criminal responsibility?",[113] or one whose proceedings "were not being conducted independently or impartially?"[114] Is it possible that "additional significant facts or changes of circumstances" would indicate a State's willingness to act, even though the State had already revealed its bad intentions earlier?

A State that was unable to carry out its duties due to the collapse or unavailability of its judicial system might become able at a later time due to changed circumstances. The only plausible possibility that a State involved or tolerated the commission of the crimes, which demonstrated its unwillingness to act, can later conduct a *bona fide* investigation or prosecution is that it experienced a change in government. This seems the only sensible reason for Article 18(7). This provision reflects the drafters' intention to create a strong complementarity regime and emphasize the favouring of national rather than ICC jurisdiction.

Article 19(3) entitles the Prosecutor to seek a ruling from the Court on a question of jurisdiction or admissibility. In such proceedings victims and those who have referred the situation under Article 13[115] may submit observations to the Court.[116] Rule

---

111 *Ibid.*, Art. 18(7).

112 Although Article 17 is not referred to in Article 18 as a ground for determination whether or not to authorize an investigation, Rule 55(2) makes it clear that the Pre-Trial Chamber "shall consider the factors in article 17 in deciding whether to authorize an investigation".

113 Rome Statute., Art. 17(2) (a).

114 *Ibid.*, Art. 17(2) (c).

115 Hall argues: although the "impetus" for this provision was the intent to guarantee that the right of victims to be heard at all stages of the proceedings was effectively secured, the language was broad and clear enough to include the Security Council or a State which referred the situation to the Court. The term "proceedings with respect to admissibility" seems sufficiently broad to cover proceedings regarding preliminary challenges to admissibility under Article 18. Hall, *supra* note 51, p. 412; also support for this conclusion is found in *Decision on the Applications for Participation in the Proceedings of VPRS1, VPRS2, VPRS3, VPRS4, VPRS5, and VPRS6*, No.: ICC-01/04, 17/01/2006, (public redacted), No:.ICC-01/04-101-etEN-Corr., 17/02/2007. For a discussion of the distinction between victims of a situation and victims of a case see Carsten Stahn, Héctor Olásolo and Kate Gibson, 'Participation of Victims in Pre-Trial Proceedings of the ICC', 4 *Journal of International Criminal Justice* 219 (2006).

116 See ICC Rules 59 and 133(3) (regulating the proceedings under Article 19(3)). According to Hall, those who have the right to submit observations are not limited to written

59 extends this right of victims and of the referring party to challenges submitted by a State or by the accused under Article 19(2).[117] Thus, there is clear interplay between Article 19(2) and (3) and Rule 59, since the rights derived from Article 19(3) in conjunction with Rule 59 apply *mutatis mutandis* to those parties challenging jurisdiction or admissibility under Article 19(2).

Indeed, in its decision of 24 July 2006, Pre-Trial Chamber I, acting upon the defence challenge to the jurisdiction of the Court pursuant to Article 19(2)(a), ordered the registrar to notify the DRC as well as the victims, and "invited" them to "make their submissions" on such challenge[118] in accordance with Article 19(3) and Rule 59.[119] In its judgment on the appeal against the decision of Pre-Trial Chamber I, filed by the defence on behalf of Lubanga, the Appeals Chamber, although it overturned the Pre-Trial Chamber's finding by saying that the defence challenge was no more than asking the Court to refrain from exercising jurisdiction which already existed over the case,[120] it seems to have *acknowledged and relied upon* the observations submitted by the DRC as well as the victims concerning the challenge to the jurisdiction of the Court.[121] The Appeals Chamber stated that the "Pre-Trial Chamber treated the application of Mr. Lubanga Dyilo as going to jurisdiction without specifically saying

submissions, "so the Court would be free to permit oral interventions". Hall, *supra* note 51, p. 411. However, Rule 59(3) states, "those receiving the information, as provided for in sub-rule 1, may make representation in writing to the competent Chamber within such time as it considers appropriate". Thus, it is not clear whether the Court limits such representation to written submissions or may extend this by also allowing oral observations. Nevertheless, one may suggest that oral observations may be possible also, since Rule 58(2) allows the Court to "hold a hearing" separately or "it may join the challenge or question to a confirmation or a trial proceeding ... and in this circumstance shall hear and decide on the challenge or question first".

117 ICC Rule 59(3); see also Lindenmann, *supra* note 7, p. 188.

118 *Prosecutor v. Thomas Lubanga, Decision Inviting the Democratic Republic of the Congo and the Victims in the Case to Comment on the Proceedings Pursuant to Article 19 of the Statute*, No.: ICC-01/04-01/06-206-tEN, 24/07/2006.

119 Article 19(3) and Rule 59 refer to the right of the referring State and the victims of the case to be informed "with a summary of the grounds on which the jurisdiction...has been challenged". ICC Rule 59. Also Article 19(3) provides these parties with the right to submit observations concerning jurisdiction or admissibility. Thus, there is clear interplay between Article 19(2) and (3).

120 *Prosecutor v. Thomas Lubanga Dyilo, Judgment on the Appeal of Mr. Thomas Lubanga Dyilo against the Decision on the Defence Challenge to the Jurisdiction of the Court pursuant to article 19 (2) (a) of the Statute of 3 October 2006*, No.: ICC-01/04-01/06-772, 14/12/2006, paras. 20, 24. Actually, the Appeals Chamber seems to have treated the question of abuse of process as one going to the admissibility of the case, yet concluded that even it falls outside the scope of Article 17. *Ibid.*, para. 23.

121 *Prosecutor v. Thomas Lubanga Dyilo, "Observations de la République Démocratiqué du Congo", registered on 24 August 2006*, No.: ICC-01/04-01/06-348-Conf ; and see also *Prosecutor v. Thomas Lubanga Dyilo, "Observations des vicitmes a/0001/06, a/0002/06 et a/0003/06 quant à l'exception d'incompétence soulevée par la defense dans la requêt du 23 mai 2006"*, No.: ICC-01/04-01/06-349, 24/08/2006.

so and *without heeding the observations of the DRC and the victims to the contrary*" (emphasis added).[122]

The statement suggests that the Appeals Chamber gave some weight to the DRC as well as to the victims' submissions, as if acknowledging that they had a right of submission under Article 19(3) and Rule 59. Since the right of submissions of this kind is confined to Article 19 proceedings, one fails to understand how the Appeals Chamber can *rely* on and *invoke* the DRC and the victims' submissions, which are limited in scope to Article 19 proceedings, while concluding that the defence challenge falls outside the parameters of Article 19? It seems that the Appeals Chamber was inaccurate in reaching this conclusion.

It has been argued that the Prosecutor may obtain a ruling from the Court on the questions of admissibility and jurisdiction "at any stage", whether the question involves an "entire situation" or an "individual case", since Article 19(3) does not confine this process to the case stage. In addition, he could seek a prompt determination on a State's unwillingness or inability to investigate or prosecute, thus "conserving the Court's resources" by not having each individual case litigated in a piecemeal fashion.[123] This argument is questionable on several grounds. If Article 19(3) were to be understood as covering the situation phase in addition to the case stage, then why was it not included in Article 18 or the Rules thereto?

One fails to see a solid reason for the Prosecutor to request a ruling on the admissibility of a situation in accordance with Article 19(3), given the fact that the Prosecutor has the power to look at the question of admissibility at the situation phase in accordance with Article 53(1) (b).[124] Moreover, in deciding whether to authorize an investigation into a situation pursuant to the Prosecutor's application under Article 18(2) and Rule 55(2), the Pre-Trial Chamber "shall consider the factors in Article 17",[125] thus providing the Prosecutor with a ruling on admissibility.

A look at Rule 59, which regulates the application of Article 19(3), suggests that sub-rule 1 directs the Registrar to inform those who referred the situation as well as the victims "of any question or challenge of jurisdiction or admissibility which has arisen pursuant to Article 19, paragraph 1, 2 and 3".[126] Arguably, the reference to Article 19(1) and (2) in this Rule suggests that the meaning targets proceedings that cover the "case stage" as opposed to the "situation stage". Similarly, Rule 59(2) explicitly states that the Registrar "shall provide those referred to in sub-rule 1,..., with a summary of the grounds on which the jurisdiction of the Court or the admissibility of the

---

122 *Prosecutor v. Thomas Lubanga Dyilo, Judgment on the Appeal of Mr. Thomas Lubanga Dyilo against the Decision on the Defence Challenge to the Jurisdiction of the Court pursuant to article 19 (2) (a) of the Statute of 3 October 2006*, No.: ICC-01/04-01/06-772, 14/12/2006, para. 20.

123 Hall, *supra* note 51, p. 411.

124 Rome Statute, Art. 53(1) (b).

125 ICC Rule 55(2).

126 *Ibid.*, Rule 59(1).

case has been challenged".[127] Again, reference is confined to the term "case". Any other interpretation of the sort of ruling required under Article 19(3) would mean that the provisions that regulate a situation stage which are already operative are redundant.

As a general rule, in accordance with Article 19(4) a State or a person referred to in paragraph (2) is permitted only one challenge to a determination of jurisdiction or admissibility. This challenge must be brought prior to or "at the commencement of the trial".[128] This provision was introduced to ensure a degree of finality. However, some exceptions still exist. While challenges to the jurisdiction of the Court must be made prior to or at the commencement of trial, in "exceptional circumstances" they may be made at a time subsequent to the commencement of the trial. Challenges to the admissibility of a case are limited to the period prior to the start of a trial. They may be brought at the commencement of a trial or subsequently, on grounds of *ne bis in idem*.[129] It seems that the drafters' intention was to narrow the possibility of challenges to admissibility at later stages, to avoid unnecessary delays during the trial proceedings. Prior to the confirmation of charges, challenges will be directed to the Pre-Trial Chamber and afterwards to the Trial Chamber.[130] The rulings of either Chamber are subject to appeal in accordance with Article 82.

Paragraph (1) (a) provides that "either party may appeal ... a) A decision with respect to jurisdiction or admissibility". The term "either party" is not defined and even the Rules of Procedure and Evidence are silent on this issue. It presumably would include a State making a jurisdictional or admissibility challenge. Yet, an examination of the text of Articles 19, 56(3) and 82(1) (c) implies that this right is not limited to

127 *Ibid.*, Rule 59(2); and also John T. Holmes, "Jurisdiction and Admissibility", in Roy S. Lee et al. (eds.), *The International Criminal Court: Elements of Crimes and Rules of Procedure and Evidence* (Ardsley: Transnational Publishers, 2001), p. 345 [hereinafter Elements].

128 In this respect, Article 19(5) ensures that the general rule is that challenges shall be made at the earliest opportunity. According to Bassiouni, the phrase "at the earliest opportunity" implies that this challenge should generally be made prior to or at the commencement of trial: Bassiouni, *supra* note 46, p. 20. Yet, this interpretation does seem to cover the exceptional circumstances mentioned in Article 19(4).

129 Rome Statute, Art. 19(4) in conjunction with Art. 17(1) (c).

130 Schabas, *supra* note 12, pp. 125 – 126; Rome Statute, Art. 19(6); ICC Rule 60 (regulating the procedures to be followed subsequent to the confirmation of the charges but before the constitution or designation of the Trial Chamber). Rule 60 reads: "if a challenge to the jurisdiction of the Court or to the admissibility of a case is made after a confirmation of the charges but before the constitution or designation of the Trial Chamber, it shall be addressed to the Presidency, which shall refer it to the Trial Chamber as soon as the latter is constituted or designated in accordance with rule 130". Rule 60 was introduced, as argued by one scholar, to "clarify a gap in Article 19, paragraph 6, where a challenge is made after the confirmation of proceedings but before a Trial Chamber is constituted or designated". See Holmes, *Elements, supra* note 127, p. 347. Rule 130 reads, "when the Presidency constitutes a Trial Chamber and refers the case to it, the Presidency shall transmit the decision of the Pre-Trial Chamber and the record of the proceedings to the Trial Chamber. The Presidency may also refer the case to a previously constituted Trial Chamber".

a State making a jurisdictional or admissibility challenge. It might extend to cover a person under Article 19(2) (a) or his defence[131] as well as the Prosecutor.[132] One may also assume that whoever is granted the right to challenge admissibility should be granted the right to appeal the outcome of that decision.

Paragraph (4) also permits the Court "in exceptional circumstances" to grant leave for a challenge to be brought more than once. Neither Article 19(4) nor the Rules spell out what those exceptional circumstances may be. Hall argues that for the sake of judicial economy and respect for due process there is a need to confine "exceptional circumstances", in admissibility challenges, to standards similar to those found under Article 84(1) (a) concerning revision of conviction or sentence.[133] The standards applicable under this provision require the discovery of new evidence which was not available earlier and the failure to obtain such evidence is not attributed to the State. Further, the new information might have influenced the outcome of the verdict.

When applying these standards by analogy to admissibility challenges, the Court ought similarly to accept such challenge when there are newly discovered facts or information which would have impacted on the outcome of the admissibility ruling if it had been known at the time. The Court should also make sure that the lack of such information at the time was not the responsibility of the State.[134] Consequently, the closer a case is to trial, the more exceptional the circumstances will have to be to permit a second challenge to admissibility. It is possible to imagine a situation in which records of a previous trial in a State where the judicial system had broken down were not available, through no fault of the accused or the State, at the time of the first challenge based on Article 17(1) (c).[135]

Although Article 19(4) appears to strengthen the first feature of the complementarity regime favouring States' primacy by granting any person or a State referred to in Article 19(2) multiple challenges, a close reading of paragraph (4) does not seem to suggest so. The last part of paragraph (4) restricts challenges to the admissibility of

131 One of the main concerns which emerged during the drafting process was to give an accused the right to appeal a ruling on admissibility in accordance with Article 82. Those who opposed the right to appeal, on an interlocutory basis, a ruling on admissibility, "pointed out that an accused can preserve his or her objection at the trial and maintain it for a later appeal against any final judgment, pursuant to article 81". Helen Brady and Mark Jennings, "Appeal and Revision", in Roy S. Lee (ed.), *supra* note 15, pp. 299 – 300.

132 ICC Statute, Art. 56(3) (b) (stipulates that "[a] decision of the Pre-Trial Chamber to act on its own initiative under this paragraph may be appealed by the Prosecutor"); also Rome Statute, Art. 82(1)(a) and (c) (stipulating that, "either party may appeal any of the following decisions ... a) A decision with respect to jurisdiction or admissibility; ... c) A decision of the Pre-Trial Chamber to act on its own initiative under article 56, paragraph 3"). Thus, a literal reading of the two articles together suggests that the Prosecutor also is authorized to appeal "[a] decision with respect to jurisdiction or admissibility".

133 *Ibid.*, Art. 84(1) (a).

134 Hall, *supra* note 51, pp. 412 – 413.

135 ICC Statute, Art. 17(1)(c) (providing that cases are inadmissible when a second trial was prohibited under Article 20(3), except when the first was designed to shield the person or was not independent or impartial).

a case to a situation based on *ne bis in idem*. The *ne bis in idem* provision deals only with the grounds and timing for challenging the admissibility of a case, and not with the number of challenges. However, a closer reading of Article 19(4) reveals that in practice it will limit even the number of challenges. For example, if one challenge is brought prior to trial, the second challenge will probably not be brought during the same period, but at a later stage – at the commencement of trial or subsequently "with the leave of the Court". These late challenges must be based on Article 17(1) (c) or *ne bis in idem* challenges. As a result, a State or a person concerned will not arbitrarily bring multiple challenges to admissibility in this context. This outcome makes sense, because allowing several challenges based on other grounds set out in Article 17 might result in a delay in carrying out an effective judicial process.

The Statute is unclear about the meaning of the phrase "may be challenged only once" in the first sentence of Article 19(4).[136] Should challenges to admissibility and jurisdiction be brought at once, meaning together at the same stage of the proceedings? Or must admissibility and jurisdiction be challenged in separate proceedings, but only one time?[137] Carden and Sadat argue that, except on the ground of *ne bis in idem*, it is possible to combine challenges to admissibility and jurisdiction. But, because jurisdiction goes to the Court's competence over the case, it might be necessary to allow an admissibility challenge first.[138]

However, the Rules seem to give the competent Chamber flexibility in organising the procedure. Rule 58(2) provides that the Chamber "shall decide on the procedure to be followed" and "may take appropriate measures for the proper conduct of the proceedings. [It] may join the challenge or question to a confirmation or a trial proceedings as long as this does not cause undue delay".[139] Although Rule 58(2) is not very clear on the procedure, it is clear that it leaves the question of a joinder of challenges to the discretion of the Court.[140]

If a State made a challenge,[141] the Prosecutor "shall suspend the investigation until" the Court makes its determination in accordance with Article 17.[142] But should the Prosecutor suspend the investigation if either type of challenge is brought? Since the last sentence of Article 19(7), "in accordance with article 17", addresses admissibility

136 Rome Statute, Art. 19(4).

137 See e.g., Michael A. Newton, Comparative Complementarity: Domestic Jurisdiction Consistent with the Rome Statute of the International Criminal Court, 167 *Military Law Review* 20, 57 (2001) (noting that "the text is vague as to whether this means one appeal as to jurisdiction with an additional appeal regarding admissibility, or whether both grounds for removing the case from the ICC authority should be combined in one appeal"). The author's reference to the word "appeal" in this context means challenge.

138 Sadat and Carden, *supra* note 28, p. 420.

139 ICC Rule 58(2).

140 On the question of joinder see Lindenmann, *supra* note 7, p. 177.

141 This refers to a State covered by paragraphs (2)(b) and (c). Rome Statute, Art. 19(2) (b) and (c).

142 *Ibid.* Art. 19(7). On this point see Bergsmo, Pejic, *Triffterer Commentary*, *supra* note 7, pp. 361 – 362; Bergsmo, *supra* note 25, p. 46; Bassiouni, *supra* note 46, p. 20.

vis-à-vis jurisdiction, it could be argued that the meaning is confined to admissibility challenges. It follows that the Prosecutor is not asked to suspend an investigation in the event of a challenge to the jurisdiction of the Court. Yet, if paragraph (7) is read as also covering challenges to the jurisdiction of the Court, which requires the Prosecutor to suspend his investigation "until such time as the Court makes a determination [on admissibility] in accordance with article 17", this may be problematic. One commentator sees the problem as leading to an indefinite suspension of investigation, as admissibility would not be examined until the Court acted under its *proprio motu* powers.[143]

Pending the ruling on admissibility, the Prosecutor "may seek authority" to proceed with investigatory steps if he deems significant to preserve important evidence and the risk of destruction is high;[144] to continue the gathering of evidence, which was initiated prior to the challenge and take witness statements as well as to prevent the "absconding of persons" in respect of whom the Prosecutor has already requested an arrest warrant.[145] On this last point, the authority granted to the Prosecutor is limited to persons for whom an "arrest warrant" has been requested under Article 58(1) and does not extend to people for whom the Prosecutor requests only a "summons" to appear, in accordance with Article 58(7).[146] This suggests that the Prosecutor will, as a precautionary measure, often request arrest warrants, ensuring that he can take effective measures during the suspension of an investigation if that person absconds.

Although Article 19(8) may authorize the Prosecutor to seek the specified measures set out in sub-paragraph (b) mentioned above,[147] sub-paragraph (a)[148] also allows the Prosecutor to take additional measures corresponding to those found in Article 18(6).[149] The language of Article 18(6) referred to in Article 19(8)(a) limits the Prosecutor's discretion to "seek authority" to "pursue necessary investigative steps for the purpose of preserving evidence" to an "exceptional basis". This poses the question whether the reference to Article 18(6) means that the Pre-Trial Chamber needs to raise the threshold of assessment by subjecting the grant of authority to the Prosecutor to "an exceptional basis" as mentioned in Article 18(6). While it seems evident that the Prosecutor's application to the competent Chamber would mean that he was facing either a certain risk or opportunity in relation to the investigation, which

143 Hall, *supra* note 51, p. 414.

144 Rome Statute, Arts. 18(6) and 19(8)(a). Paragraph (a) of Article 19(8) should be read in the light of Article 18(6), since the latter identifies those "necessary investigative steps" to be taken as mentioned above.

145 *Ibid.*, Art. 19(8); ICC Rule 61; also M. Cherif Bassiouni, *Introduction to International Criminal Law* (Ardsley, New York: Transnational Publishers, 2003), pp. 518 – 519 [hereinafter ICL].

146 Rome Statute, Art. 58(1) and (7). For a recent application of summons under Article 58(7) see *Situation in Darfur, Prosecutor's Application under Article 58 (7)*, No.: ICC-02/05-56, 27/02/2007.

147 *Ibid.*, Art. 19(8) (b).

148 *Ibid.* Art. 19(8) (a).

149 *Ibid.*, Art. 18(6); also ICC Rules 57 and 61.

reflects "an exceptional basis", Article 19(8) (a) *only* refers to the "kind" of "investigative steps" set out in Article 18(6) *vis-à-vis* the requirements established under this provision. It follows that even if the proper interpretation would suggest such an understanding, the plain reading of Article 19(8) (a) does not explicitly require the existence of "an exceptional basis".

On the other hand, one may note a degree of overlap between Articles 18(6), 19(8) (a) and (b) and 56(1). Neither the Statute nor the Rules expressly outline the relationship between these provisions. Article 56(1) even imposes an obligation on the Prosecutor to inform the Pre-Trial Chamber when he considers that there is "a unique opportunity to take testimony or to examine, collect or test evidence, which may not be available subsequently for the purposes of a trial".[150] Again, a reading of the Chapeau of Article 19(8) suggests that the provision serves a *certain specified period* of the proceedings – namely when there is a ruling pending by the Court and the Prosecutor deems it significant during this period to carry out some investigative steps. On the contrary, nothing in the language of Article 56 suggests that it is designed to serve a specific phase of the investigation; rather, that the provision is general in scope accompanying the different stages of the proceedings up to trial.[151] It follows that these provisions should function in a complementary manner.

Since Article 19(8)(a) speaks of "investigative steps of the kind referred to in Article 18, paragraph 6" rather than being confined to "the investigative steps" referred to in Article 19(8)(b) and (c), the steps identified in Article 19(8) should be seen as broader than those in Article 18(6), since it covers those found under Article 19(b) and (c) in addition to the "necessary investigative steps" under Article 18(6). This broad language, together with the powers identified in Article 19(8)(b) and (c), suggests that the Prosecutor could be authorized to use most of the powers he would have under Article 54 and other provisions to continue the investigation. This makes sense, because at this very critical stage the possibility that a State will act in bad faith in order to evade justice by destroying the evidence increases. Although as a result the Court may rule that a case is admissible, the Prosecutor will face some difficulty in the search for new evidence in support of the continuation of the investigation. If the Court deems a case inadmissible, the Prosecutor may appeal [152] or seek review

150 Rome Statute, Art. 56(1); ICC Rule 114.

151 *Ibid.*

152 Rome Statute, Art. 19(6). The decision of the Trial Chamber or the Pre-Trial Chamber may be appealed in accordance with Article 82(1) (a). See ICC Rule 150(3) and (4), 154(1) and (3). Rule 150 states: "1) Subject to sub-rule 2, an appeal against a decision of conviction or acquittal under article 74, a sentence under article 76 or a reparation order under article 75 may be filed not later than 30 days from the date on which the party filing the appeal is notified of the decision, the sentence or the reparation order; 2) The Appeals Chamber may extend the time limit set out in sub-rule 1, for good cause, upon the application of the party seeking to file the appeal; 3) The appeal shall be filed with the registrar; 4) If an appeal is not filed as set out in sub-rules 1 to 3, the decision, the sentence or the reparation order of the Trial Chamber shall become final". Rule 154 states: "1) An appeal may be filed under article 81, paragraph 3(c) (ii), or article 82, paragraph 1 (a) or (b), not later than five days from the date upon which the party filing the appeal is notified of the

by the Court if new facts or evidence arise.[153] Neither the challenge of the State concerned nor the appeal nor the Prosecutor's new request for a review of the decision will affect the validity of any "act performed by the Prosecutor or any order or warrant issued by the Court prior to the making of the challenge", but not prior to the request for review.[154]

Article 19 (10) imposes three requirements on the Prosecutor before he may ask the Court to review its decision. It first requires that "new facts have arisen". This phrase includes new facts that have occurred since the decision.[155] However, it also includes facts in existence at the time of the decision, but not discovered by the Prosecutor until after the decision was reached. Another requirement is that these facts must "negate the basis on which the case had been previously found inadmissible". This appears to be a highly objective criterion left to the Court's assessment. Finally, the Prosecutor must be "fully satisfied" that the other two requirements have been met. This requirement is a very subjective test, which the Prosecutor can apply with wide discretion.

In the absence of paragraph (10), the Prosecutor would have been able to seek a new ruling on the question of admissibility pursuant to paragraph (3). Paragraph (10) lacks any explicit reference permitting the Prosecutor to seek review of a determination that there was "no *jurisdiction* in a case". It follows that, once new information is discovered following such a determination, the Prosecutor "should be able to seek a new ruling on the question of jurisdiction or admissibility" in accordance with paragraph (3).[156] Without this provision, States which "concealed" the "evidence" could easily "frustrate the Court's exercise of jurisdiction".[157]

Finally, Article 19(10) is not clear on whether such a request for review is an extra right granted to the Prosecutor, in addition to the right to an appeal under paragraph (6). If the answer is in the affirmative, when can the Prosecutor exercise this right: prior to or following the appeal? Moreover, the first sentence of paragraph (10) reads: "If the Court has decided that a case is inadmissible under Article 17, the Prosecutor may submit a request for a review of the decision". The text is silent as to whether this decision is the outcome of proceedings before the Pre-Trial Chamber or Trial

decision.... 3) Rule 150, sub-rules 3 and 4, shall apply to appeals filed under sub-rules 1 and 2 of this rule".

153 Rome Statute, Art. 19(10); also ICC Rules, Rule 62 (providing that the Prosecutor should make his or her request before the Chamber which made the latest ruling on admissibility). Moreover, sub-rule 2 provides the States which challenged admissibility under Article 19(2) with the right to make representations and to be notified of the request of the Prosecutor.

154 Certainly, a request submitted by the Prosecutor for a review should not affect any act taken by him prior to the challenge of the State concerned.

155 This interpretation would be consistent with the approach taken with respect to reviews of convictions and sentences under Article 84(1).

156 Rome Statute, Art. 19(3). Notably, paragraph (3) restricts neither the time for making the request nor the number of times such request may be made.

157 See generally Hall, *supra* note 51, p. 417.

Chamber or the Appeals Chamber. These questions are not answered in the Statute or even in the Rules.

If the decision subject to review under Article 19(10) was the outcome of proceedings of the Appeals Chamber, the conclusion would be different from that if it was the outcome of proceedings of the Pre-Trial Chamber or the Trial Chamber. One way of looking at the question suggests that the right to a review should not be mixed with the right to appeal, since the Appeals Chamber is not authorised to rule on situations where "new facts have arisen". Thus, if the Pre-Trial Chamber or the Trial Chamber decided that "a case is inadmissible under article 17", the Prosecutor could appeal this decision. If, pending a ruling by the Appeals Chamber, "new facts ... arise which negate the basis on which the case had previously been found inadmissible under article 17", the Prosecutor may submit a request for a review of the decision "to the Chamber that made the latest ruling on admissibility". It follows that the Prosecutor can submit a request for review, even while the appeal is pending, since the appeal and the request for review are two separate and independent procedures.[158] In this context, the Prosecutor could also submit a request for review after a decision by the Appeals Chamber if new facts have arisen. Yet, this view seems to contradict the wording of Rule 62(1), which states that "if the Prosecutor makes a request under Article 19, paragraph 10, he or she shall make the request to the Chamber that made the latest ruling on admissibility".[159] This suggests that Rule 62(1) leaves room for the Appeals Chamber to rule on a request based on the emergence of new facts.[160]

In examining the exceptional situations for reviewing the Court's decisions under the Statute and Rules in the *Uganda* case before the ICC, Pre-Trial Chamber II referred to Article 19(10) of the Statute, yet without spelling out the sort of Chamber or Chambers expected to be responsible for making the "review" at this stage of the proceedings.[161] It follows that until such time as the Court makes a ruling on this

158 Arguably, if the Court has decided that a case is inadmissible in accordance with Article 19(10), the Prosecutor can file an appeal, and if the next day new facts arise in accordance with paragraph (10), he or she can request a review. According to Rule 62, a request for a review of the decision should be submitted "to the Chamber that made the latest ruling on admissibility". Thus, the request can be made to the Trial Chamber which ruled on the first decision or the Appeals Chamber if at the time the request is submitted it has decided the appeal.

159 Even the authority on the subject fell short of any explanation. See Holmes, *Elements*, *supra* note 127, pp. 346 – 347.

160 That the Appeals Chamber will not adopt residual or implied jurisdiction, in a general sense, but will follow strictly the terms of the Statute and the Rules in exercising its authority is most certainly confirmed by the Appeals Chamber decision of 13 July 2006, rejecting the Prosecutor's application for leave to appeal. See *Situation in the Democratic Republic of the Congo, Judgment on the Prosecutor's Application for Extraordinary Review of Pre-Trial Chamber I's 31 March 2006 Decision Denying Leave to Appeal*, No.: ICC-01/04-168, 13/07/2006.

161 See *Decision on the Prosecutor's Position on the Decision of Pre-Trial Chamber II to Redact Factual Descriptions of Crimes from the Warrants of Arrest, Motion for Reconsideration, and Motion for Clarification*, No.: ICC-02/04-01/05-60, 28/10/2005, para. 18.

question it could be suggested that the appropriate interpretation of these provisions will depend – to some extent – on the trend to be followed by the judges in adopting either the common or continental law approaches.

If the Prosecutor, having considered the criteria set out in Article 17, decides that the case is inadmissible and thus defers investigation to the State with jurisdiction, he may request "information on the proceedings" from the relevant State pursuant to Article 19(11). One commentator argues that the scope of information that can be requested under paragraph (11) appears to be broader than the information which can be requested under Article 18(5). Under Article 18(5), the Prosecutor can request information concerning "the progress of the State's investigations and any subsequent prosecutions". Yet, under Article 19(11), the Prosecutor would be requesting information in relation to an individual case *versus* a situation.[162]

The fact that the required information is related to a case stage does not necessarily mean that the scope of information required under Article 19(11) is broader than that under Article 18(5), as this will depend on the circumstances of each situation and case. Furthermore, a literal reading of the wording of both paragraphs suggests that the core of Article 18(5) is even wider than that of Article 19(11). Article 18(5) permits the Prosecutor who has deferred an investigation to request the State concerned "periodically [to] inform" him on "the progress of its investigations and any subsequent prosecutions". Under Article 19(11), the Prosecutor may ask the State concerned to "make available ... information on the proceedings". Thus, the strict requirement of regular information under paragraph 5 suggests that the amount of information required under Article 18(5) may even exceed that under Article 19(11). In addition, paragraph (5) imposes a duty upon States parties to respond to such "requests without undue delay", while paragraph (11) lacks such a requirement.

Those arguing that Article 19(11) is broader than Article 18(5) do not believe that the lack of a requirement to act "without undue delay" is decisive to this interpretation. They point out that the requirement that States Parties respond to the Prosecutor's request "without undue delay" under Article 18(5) is implicitly covered under the general obligation to cooperate fully in accordance with Article 86.[163] Article 86 of the ICC Statute places this duty upon all States Parties.[164] While it may be true that the obligations arising out of Article 86 are wide enough to cover all sorts of cooperation, it does not follow from the text of Article 86 that the State has to provide information "without undue delay" in a *systematic manner*, comparable to the strict requirements of Article 18(5).

The Prosecutor, at the request of the investigating State, has a duty to keep the information collected confidential. This is done so that the State's investigation is not undermined by the release of sensitive information, such as sealed indictments.

162 Hall, *supra* note 51, p. 418.

163 *Ibid.*

164 Rome Statute, Art. 86 reads: "States Parties shall, in accordance with the provisions of this Statute, co-operate fully with the Court in its investigation and prosecution of crimes within the jurisdiction of the Court"). See Claus Kress, 'General Obligation to Cooperate', *Triffterer Commentary*, *supra* note 7, p. 1051.

Moreover, the Prosecutor has a duty to inform the investigating State if he resumes the investigation. Paragraph (11), unlike Article 18(3), lacks the requirements or guidelines that the Prosecutor must follow when proceeding with an investigation after he has deferred to a State in accordance with paragraph (11). On this last point, paragraph (11) is broad enough to cover all possible situations, including that of Article 18(3), in order to assist the Prosecutor in pursuing the investigation if the situation thereafter so requires. The language of Article 19(11), "if the Prosecutor thereafter decides to proceed with an investigation", reflects a wide discretionary power to intervene at any time, according to his assessment.[165]

Articles 18 and 19 reflect the severe tension between the powers of the Prosecutor and the priority of States in the complementarity regime. The reason should not necessarily be considered to the gaps found under the procedural regime of the Statute *per se*, rather that the system of complementarity was drafted in a manner that envisaged conflicts of jurisdiction. The text of Article 19(4) fortifies States' primacy in carrying out domestic proceedings, while the text of paragraphs (8), (9), (10) and (11) reinforces the Court's ability to intervene when necessary. Once the Court engages with these types of questions, the conflicting provisions that reflect the tension between the two features of complementarity will be resolved either in favour of the Court or in favour of States. If the latter prevail, one could emphasize that the idea behind creating a Court based on the notion of complementarity has succeeded. In the event of the former, it could be emphasised that the ICC has succeeded in becoming a supranational institution, provided with implied primacy which, although not reflected in its Statute, is reflected in its practices. A more plausible approach favours a delicate balance in interpreting these provisions that compromise neither the primacy of States nor the effectiveness of the Court.

3. Consequences of Self-referrals and Waivers of Complementarity in Light of Articles 18 – 19 and 53

In chapter III, the discussion defined a self-referral and a waiver of complementarity and examined the legality of the practice in the context of Article 17. Also chapter III looked at how the Court treated these questions in the context of the criterion of inability. This section will examine the implications of a self-referral and its corollary, a waiver of complementarity, in the context of applying Articles 18 and 19 explored above. In so doing, one should look first at Article 53 as being an essential part that serves the main argument.

165 It may be argued that paragraph (11) appears to address a voluntary deferral by the Prosecutor of an investigation based on an assessment that the factors set out in Article 17 exist, rather than a deferral pursuant to Article 18(2) or suspension of an investigation pursuant to Article 19(7) after an admissibility challenge.

3.1 *Consequences of a Self-referral or Waiver in Light of Article 53*

As mentioned earlier in Chapter III, a waiver of complementarity has two major implications. One is related to the referring State, while the other involves the Court as a result of the State's waiver. The first implication is straight forward as explored in the previous chapter. Yet, the second, which deals with the Court's subsequent determinations as a direct result of a State's self-referral and waiver requires further elaboration as discussed below.

In this context, the relevant question that arises is what consequences a State's waiver amounting from a self referral has on admissibility determinations by the Court? It appears that a waiver does not deprive the Court of the obligation to examine admissibility in the context of certain provisions. Since a self-referral is in fact a State Party referral, Article 18 applies. The application of Article 18 is subject to a prior determination based on Article 53(1).[166] At this stage Article 53(1) serves as a filter to avoid any conflict of jurisdiction that may later arise between the Court and the State concerned even before Article 18 is triggered. Moreover, it guides the Prosecutor in determining whether to proceed with a situation and thus initiate an investigation. In reaching such a decision, the Prosecutor *shall* consider whether:

> (a) The information available to [him] provides a reasonable basis to believe that a crime within the jurisdiction of the Court has been or is being committed; (b) The case is or would be admissible under article 17; and (c) Taking into account the gravity of the crime and the interests of victims, there are nonetheless substantial reasons to believe that an investigation would not serve the interests of justice.[167]

However, an examination of the mandatory language of Article 53 reflected in the chapeau leads to the conclusion that Article 17's test is a requirement that must be satisfied before any investigation can be initiated.[168] Admissibility requirements, however, may be waived by the Court and the State concerned during the application of Article 19, as explained below.

In satisfying the Article 17 test, the Prosecutor may need to examine whether one or more of the criteria listed in Article 17 exist. Thus, in the context of a self-refer-

166 Rome Statute. Art. 18.

167 *Ibid.*, Art. 53(1). See generally Avril McDonald and Roelof Haveman, "Prosecutorial Discretion – Some Thoughts on 'Objectifying' the Exercise of Prosecutorial Discretion by the Prosecutor of the ICC", [Expert Consultation Process on general Issues relevant to the Office of the Prosecutor:], 15 April 2003, available at <http://www.icc-cpi.int/library/organs/otp/mcdonald_haveman.pdf>; see also Chris Gallavin, 'Article 53 of the Rome Statute of the International Criminal Court: In The Interests of Justice', 14 *King's College Law Journal* 179 (2003).

168 The chapeau of Article 53 used the word *shall* which makes the full examination set out in Article 53(1) mandatory. Moreover, from the prosecutor's side it is logical to say that Article 17 should always apply, since its application would help him in attaining his role of blocking unnecessary situations that do not warrant being tried before the Court.

ral, since no action is intended to be taken, as is implicitly acknowledged from this type of referral, the Prosecutor may conclude at this stage that none of the criteria of Article 17(1) (a)–(c) have been met (in the case that no other state is investigating or prosecuting and raised a challenge known as *uncontested admissibility*)[169] and therefore Article 53(1) (b) is satisfied. Nonetheless, in order for the Prosecutor to proceed, he needs more than the *notitia criminis* and the complementarity test. He must weigh the interests of victims and check whether the gravity of the alleged crimes as mentioned in Articles 53(1)(c) and 17(1)(d) reached the threshold of the Statute as mentioned in preambular paragraphs 3 and 9 and similarly expressed in Article 1. Above all, the most important criterion so far is to ensure that investigating the situation in question would "serve the interests of justice".

3.2 Consequences of a Self-referral or Waiver in the Light of Article 18

After satisfying the examination of Article 53(1), the Prosecutor has two choices: either to decide not to pursue an investigation or to proceed by initiating an investigation. If his decision inclines towards the former, then he should *promptly* inform the referring government in writing of his finding or decision.[170] Moreover, the Pre-Trial Chamber should also be informed in writing, but only if the Prosecutor's decision is based merely on Article 53(1) (c).[171]

The Prosecutorial discretion is reflected in his freedom to decide, and may be reviewed by the Pre-Trial Chamber at the referring government's request[172] or *proprio motu* if his decision is based merely on the view that an investigation would not "serve the interests of justice".[173] If the Pre-trial Chamber chooses not to review that decision or if it reviews it and its decision agrees with that of the Prosecutor that is the end of the matter. However, if he chooses the other avenue – that is, to proceed and initiate an investigation – the situation will be different and some interesting questions may arise.

A self-referral is governed by the regime organizing a State party referral and, since Article 53(1) is satisfied, Article 18 applies. Article 18(1) requires the Prosecutor to inform all States Parties and others that would generally exercise jurisdiction over the alleged crimes.[174] As argued earlier, those States are the territorial State, the State of nationality of the accused or the victim, or the custodial State, since normally they have direct links with the case. A more liberal interpretation suggests that all countries in the world which could exercise universal jurisdiction should be informed.[175]

169 Rome Statute, Art. 17(1)(a).

170 ICC Rule 105(1).

171 Rome Statute, Art. 53(1); ICC Rule 105(4).

172 Rome Statute, Art. 53(3) (a); ICC Rule 107(1) (the request should be in writing and within 90 days following the Prosecutor's notification under Rules 105 and 106).

173 Rome Statute, Art. 53(3)(b); ICC Rule 109(1).

174 Rome Statute, Art. 18(1); ICC Rule 52(1).

175 Schabas, *supra* note 12, pp. 124 – 125.

The question that remains to be resolved is whether, in the context of self-referral and waiver of complementarity, the Prosecutor should inform this government or any other State at all. To put it differently, since a self-referral is different from a referral by a State with no direct connection to or interest in the crime, one may assume that it has a bearing on other provisions of the Statute including the application of Article 18(1). The situation where a State waives its primacy to investigate, prosecute and try a case suggests that any proceedings relevant to the situation or case in question might not be carried out, since it is covered by its initial waiver. In other words, is the State's waiver or self referral sufficient to exempt the Prosecutor from notifying it or all other States under Article 18(1)? In fact both the Statute and the Rules of Procedure and of Evidence are silent regarding this question, and thus analysis is required to resolve this issue.

A waiver should not be read or understood in a way that hampers the essence of the procedural mechanism of the Statute. If a State has initially chosen not to investigate, this does not mean *de facto* that a prosecution or investigation will be authorised before the ICC. By virtue of the principle of complementarity, all States Parties and non-Parties have the right to challenge admissibility[176] and the ICC should be retained as a *forum* of last resort. Thus, it appears mandatory for the Prosecutor to notify all States that would normally exercise jurisdiction in order to preserve their right to challenge. With regard to the referring State, the question is trickier, since it could be argued that there is no need to inform the State that has already confirmed that it is not interested in investigating the situation. Nevertheless, the language of Article 18(1) suggests that the requirement of notification of all States is mandatory, and even includes notification of the referring State in this context. Indeed, this conclusion finds support in the recent *Decision Requesting Information on the Status of the Preliminary Examination of the Situation in the Central African Republic*. Pre-Trial Chamber III considered that "pursuant to article 18(1) of the Statute, the Prosecutor shall notify all State Parties, including the State Party *which referred the situation*" (emphasis added).

Once the Prosecutor notifies those States, there is the one month time limit for any interested State to request the Prosecutor's deferral based on that State's investigation.[177] But if no State objects then the investigation continues. However, what if the referring State decides at this stage to investigate the situation requesting the ICC's deferral? Should it be it allowed to step in once more, given the fact that it has unequivocally waived its primacy over the situation from the outset?

Given the fact that there is no clear answer to this question in either the Statute or the Rules, the jurisprudence of other human rights bodies may be instructive. The ECHR was constantly faced with the question of waiver, but in a different context – namely the possibility of waiving some of the elements to a fair trial (substantive rights). The general rule may, however, still apply to the situation of the ICC, as the ECHR has also considered the question in the context of waiving procedural rights. Indeed, in the *Pailot* and *Richard* cases the ECHR implicitly reached the conclusion

176 Rome Statute, Arts. 18(2), 19(2) (b) and (c), ICC Rules 55(2) and 58(2).

177 Rome Statute, Art. 18(2); ICC Rule 53.

that it is impermissible to regain a right that has already been waived, provided that the requirements of the initial waiver has been fulfilled.[178]

Furthermore, according to the established rules of international law, a declaration made by a State "by way of unilateral acts, concerning legal or factual situations, may have the effect of creating legal obligations".[179] Thus, once the self-referring State declares that it is not intending to open an investigation in relation to the situation under consideration and prefers that the ICC takes up the proceedings, such intention, "confers on the declaration the character of a legal undertaking", which should lead to estoppel.[180] Such legal undertaking, "if given publicly, and with an intent to be bound,...is binding...the intention is to be ascertained by interpretation of the act".[181] Also whether the State makes its statement or declaration orally or in writing does not make a substantial difference. As the International Court of Justice has rightly pointed out in the *Temple of Preah Vihear Case*, "Where...as is generally the case in international law, which places the principle emphasis on the intentions of the parties, the law prescribes no particular form, parties are free to choose what form they please provided their intention clearly results from it".[182] Elsewhere in the same decision the Court proceeded by saying, "...the sole relevant question is whether the language employed in any given declaration does reveal a clear intention...".[183]

It follows that, the Court should not yield to the referring State's request, since it initially waived primacy over the investigation of the situation and showed intention to be bound by this decision. The fact that the State formally declared in writing either through its letter of referral or separately that it was not intending to institute

178 *Pailot* v. *France*, App. No. 00032217/96, Judgment (Merits and just satisfaction) of 22/04/1998, paras. 49–53; *Richard* v. *France*, App. No. 00033441/96, Judgment (Merits and just satisfaction) of 22/04/1998, paras. 46–50. In this respect, the State in question waived the right to take any further action. Similarly see the New York Supreme Court in *Preiss/Breismeister Architects, Respondent,* v. *Westin Hotel Company-Plaza Hotel Division*, Supreme Court of New York, Appellate Division, First Department, 86 A.D.2d 844; 448 N.Y.S.2d 651, 25/02/1982, (Dissenting Opinion of Judge JJ. Silverman), pp. 653–654 (noting that "a waiver does not constitute a bar [to retain the right] unless it is intentional, that is, unless the party advisedly gives up the right; *Bernard Zuber, Respondent* v. *Commodore Pharmacy, Inc.*, Supreme Court of New York, Appellate Division, Second Department, 24 A.D.2d 649; 262 N.Y.S.2d 155, 19/07/1965, (Judges Beldock et al. Dissenting Opinion), p. 650 (noting that "[C]onduct inconsistent with the maintenance of a right may demonstrate an abandonment of that right despite the desire to retain it").

179 *Nuclear Tests Case (Australia v. France)*, 1974 I.C.J., 20/12/1974, para. 43; *Nuclear Tests Case (New Zealand v. France)*, 1974 I.C.J., 20/12/1974, para. 46.

180 *Ibid.;* George Schwarzenberger, *International Law*, Vol. I, 3rd ed., (London: Stevens & Sons ltd., 1957), p. 553.

181 *Nuclear Tests Case (Australia v. France)*, 1974 I.C.J., 20/12/1974, para. 44; *Nuclear Tests Case (New Zealand v. France)*, 1974 I.C.J., 20/12/1974, para. 47. The "binding character of an international obligation assumed by a unilateral declaration" is based on the principle of good faith. *Ibid.*, para. 46.

182 *Case Concerning the Temple of Preah Vihear Case (Cambodia v. Thailand), Preliminary Objections*, 1961 I.C.J., 26/05/1961, p. 31.

183 *Ibid.*, p. 32.

an investigation into the situation might be considered sufficient to deprive that State of the right to re-obtain control over the situation, even if it has initiated domestic investigation into the situation at this stage. The Court may reject the referring State's request for deferral on these grounds without even getting into the merits of the request. But, even if the relevant Chamber decided to examine the request on the merits, the relevant Chamber may determine that the situation is still admissible subject to the factual circumstances of each case.

In so doing, the Prosecutor has to apply in writing to the Pre-Trial Chamber, asking it to authorize the investigation.[184] The Pre-Trial Chamber may merely deny or reject the referring State's request on the grounds explored above. In case the Chamber decides to proceed on the merits, it may arrange for a hearing of both sides.[185] In reaching a decision on the substance or the merits of the request, the Chamber *shall* consider the grounds for the Prosecutor's application, the State's observations and the criteria set out in Article 17.[186] This decision is subject to appeal by either the challenging State or the Prosecutor if either is not satisfied with the Pre-Trial Chamber's decision.[187]

Nonetheless, another way of looking at the problem suggests that the referring State may be allowed to regain the opportunity to exercise its jurisdiction. The Statute is based on the notion of complementarity, which favours States' investigations and limits the ICC's intervention to exceptional cases where there is no prospect of initiating genuine domestic proceedings. It follows that, if there is a slight chance that the referring State in question may be willing and able to genuinely proceed, the Pre-Trial Chamber may prefer to yield to that State's challenge depending on the seriousness, circumstances and stage of domestic investigations. Instead, if not convinced, it may authorize an investigation and the Prosecutor may proceed if that State does not appeal or where it appeals and the Appeals Chamber confirms this decision authorizing an investigation before the Court.[188]

3.3 *Consequences of a Self-referral or Waiver in Light of Article 19*

If the referring State has been permitted to raise the question of admissibility under Article 18, then it loses the chance to challenge under Article 19 unless there are "additional significant facts", which have to be presented or there is a "significant change of circumstances" that warrants the Court to accept this kind of duplicative chal-

184 Rome Statute, Art. 18(2); ICC Rule 54; See also in respect to the State requesting the deferral, ICC Rule 53.

185 ICC Rule 55(1).

186 *Ibid.*, sub-rule (2). Sub-rule 2 states: "The Pre-Trial Chamber shall examine the Prosecutor's application and any observations submitted by a State that requested a deferral in accordance with article 18, paragraph 2, and shall consider the factors in article 17 in deciding whether to authorize an investigation".

187 Rome Statute, Arts. 18(4), 82(1) (a); ICC Rule, 154(1).

188 ICC Rule 158(1).

lenge.[189] However, in order to observe how the situation of waiver could arise at the Article 19 stage, we have to presume a different scenario.

If *arguendo* no steps have been taken by the referring State to request deferral by virtue of Article 18(2) and it is confirmed to the Prosecutor that the State will not open an investigation in accordance with its initial waiver during the Article 53(1) and (2) stages, Article 19 applies. Unlike Article 18, which is applicable at an early stage in situations, Article 19 applies at a later stage and in a broader sense to cases within the technical sense.[190] If the State in question attempts to challenge the admissibility of the case on the basis that it is or has taken action (that is suspending its initial waiver) under Article 19(2) (b), the question will arise again as to how would the Court receive a challenge as such in view of the self-referral and its explicit waiver to exercise jurisdiction over the situation.

Treating this question in the context of Article 19 is not as straight forward as it appears under Article 18. In relation to Article 19, there are three lines of argument that deserve consideration. One possibility might be that the Court considers a self-referral or a waiver of complementarity has no bearing effect on the general procedural regime governing complementarity. If the Court follows this trend then there is no problem in accepting the self-referring State's challenge.

Another possible argument suggests that since a State's self-referral and waiver to exercise jurisdiction takes place within the sphere and in relation to a situation, any possible repercussion resulting from that referral would be limited to that phase. Consequently, any potential effect would not necessarily extend to a case stage. According to this view, accepting an admissibility challenge under Article 19(2) (b) also would not be problematic.

A third line of argument suggests that although in a self-referral, the referring State waives its primacy in the context of a situation, this might be also meant to cover the entire process, namely, any possible cases arising from or in relation to that situation. Therefore, the admissibility challenge of the referring State under Article 19(2) (b) might not be successful. The relevant Chamber may deny or reject the challenge without getting into the merits on the basis that the referring State unequivocally waived its superiority in favour of the Court through the letter of referral. As explained earlier, the State's written declaration outlining its express intention to refrain from initiating domestic proceedings in relation to the situation at hands should have a binding effect in the sense of attaining the force of a legal obligation, according to the recognized principles of international law. Further, the complementarity provisions should not be understood or interpreted in a manner that serve State's political agendas, exhaust or devastate the Court's resources and as a result undermine its credibility. Yet, in case the Court decided to proceed on the merits of the challenge raised by the referring State, it may still decide that the case is admissible subject to the factual circumstances of each case. Perhaps, a preventive remedy, the self-referring State should explicitly reserve the right under its initial declaration or letter of

189 Rome Statute, Art. 18(7).

190 Bassiouni, *ICL*, *supra* note 145, pp. 518–519; Hall, *supra* note 51, pp. 403–418; Schabas, *supra* note 12, pp. 125–126.

referral to bring a future admissibility challenge pursuant to Article 19(2) (b). By doing so, it makes clear that its waiver was intended to be confined to a limited period and stage of the proceedings. If the Court endorsed such a practice, this will result in what may be called a *conditional waiver*. Whether the Court would accept this sort of reservation remains to be determined.

Although the possibility of permitting or denying a challenge to the admissibility of a case entered by the self-referring State is still contentious, the right of an accused or a person for whom an arrest warrant or a summons to appear has been issued under Article 58 to raise an admissibility challenge, is certainly retained and undisputable, as being recognised by the Statute, as a distinct procedural right from that of the State.[191] Thus, a State's self-referral or a waiver of complementarity should by no means interfere with this procedural right. The same holds true in relation to any other State (whether a party or a third State), which intends to challenge the admissibility of the case.

In the *Lubanga* and *Ngudjolo* cases, Pre-Trial Chamber I seems to have adopted the first view according to which the DRC's self-referral and its waiver to exercise jurisdiction over the situation has no bearing effect on any possible admissibility challenges made pursuant to Article 19(2) (a), (b) and in relation to these cases.

In *Lubanga*, the Chamber stated:

> [F]or the purpose of the admissibility analysis of the case against Mr Thomas Lubanga Dyilo, the Chamber observes that since March 2004 the DRC national judicial system has undergone certain changes...This has resulted *inter alia* in the issuance of two warrants of arrest by the competent DRC authorities for Mr Thomas Lubanga Dyilo in March 2005 for several crimes, some possibly within the jurisdiction of the Court,...Therefore, in the Chamber's view, the Prosecution's general statement that the DRC national judicial system continues to be unable in the sense of article 17 (1) (a) to (c) and (3), of the Statute does not wholly correspond to the reality any longer. However, the Chamber recalls that for a case arising from the investigation of a situation to be inadmissible, national proceedings must encompass both the person and the conduct which is the subject of the case before the Court...The Chamber observes that the warrants of arrest issued by the competent DRC authorities...contain no reference to his alleged criminal responsibility for the alleged UPC/FPLC's policy practice of enlisting into the FPLC, conscripting into the FPLC and using to participate actively in hostilities children under the age of fifteen.[192]

This paragraph reflects the implicit trend adopted by Pre-Trial Chamber I towards the question of a State suspending its waiver. The Chamber believed that the DRC's judicial system was able to deal with the "case arising from the investigation of a situation" after going through some reforms. Its legal reasoning denotes that it was theoretically willing to make the case inadmissible if the warrants of arrest issued by the

191 Rome Statute, Art. 19(2) (a), (b).

192 *Prosecutor v. Thomas Lubanga Dyilo, Decision on the Prosecutor's Application for a Warrant of Arrest, Art. 58*, Case No. ICC-01/04-01/06-8-US-Corr, 10/02/2006, paras. 36 – 39, unsealed pursuant to Decision ICC-01/04-01/06-37 dated 17/03/2006.

national authorities made out Lubanga's alleged criminal responsibility for the acts stated above. Although the DRC initially waived its primacy when it sent the letter of referral, the Court's statement suggests that it would have been permitted to suspend its initial waiver, if it was demonstrated that domestic proceedings encompassing both the person and the conduct subject of the case before the Court were initiated.

In a more recent decision concerning the issue of an arrest warrant against Mathieu Ngudjolo Chui, Pre-Trial Chamber I showed an explicit reaction towards this question. The Chamber stated that on the basis of the evidence and information submitted by the Prosecution "and without prejudice to the filing of any challenge to the admissibility of the case under articles 19(2) (a) and (b) of the Statute and without prejudice to any subsequent decision in this regard, the case…is admissible".[193] The Chamber failed to show the legal reasoning for reaching this conclusion. However, this shows an initial indication that despite DRC's self-referral and its initial waiver over the situation, the Chamber did not anticipate any obstacle in the face of accepting a future admissibility challenge raised either by the self-referring State or by a person mentioned under Article 19 (2) (a) during the case stage. Whether Pre-Trial Chamber I had in mind the possible implications of a self-referral, when it decided that a future admissibility challenge under Article 19 (2) (a) and (b) was possible, is unclear.

In practice, the question might get complicated in case a State waives investigation and prosecution in favour of the Court, then the accused challenges the admissibility of the case under Article 19(2)(a) requesting to be tried before his own domestic courts, leaving the Court stuck to decide. It is clear that the sole factor in determining admissibility is whether the State has initiated genuine domestic proceedings, and in case of a waiver, the State refrains from doing so. Yet, if the Court determined that the case is admissible on the sole basis that the State has not initiated domestic proceedings, this will result in a decision, which clearly compromised the desire of the accused for that of the State without even giving any weight to his challenge. This poses a question, what is the significance of providing an accused person with a right that has no effect in the Court's determination? The situation as it stands indicates that a challenge by an accused or any person referred to in Article 19(2) (a) will not be successful unless the self-referring State makes a challenge under Article 19(2)(b) requesting the same outcome, that is, a decision of inadmissibility. Possibly, when faced with a problem as such, the Court needs to draw a balance between these conflicting interests.

On the other hand, assuming that the referring State or any other State did not attempt to contest admissibility in accordance with Article 19(2) (b), the question of admissibility may be waived on the part of the Court. Article 17(1) states that the Court shall determine "that a case is inadmissible" if certain conditions have been met.[194] Article 19(1), on the other hand, states that the Court may "on its own mo-

193 *Prosecutor v. Mathieu Ngudjolo Chui, Warrant of Arrest for Mathieu Ngudjolo Chui*, No.: ICC-01/04-02/07-1-tENG, unsealed pursuant to Decision ICC-01/04-02/07-10 dated 7/02/2008, p. 3.

194 Rome Statute, Art. 17(1).

tion, determine the admissibility of a case in accordance with article 17".[195] Reading the two provisions together makes it clear that the admissibility test is discretionary from the Court's perspective when acting *proprio motu*, and is mandatory only when challenged by any of the categories listed in Article 19(2).[196] Thus, the general rule suggests that, if the State did not object even at this stage, the Court may easily bypass the complementarity test (unlike in the case of Articles 53(1) and (2) and Rule 55(2)), and proceed with the case.[197] Nonetheless, if the Court adopted the view that the self-referring State should not have a *locus standi* to challenge the admissibility of the case as a direct result of its initial waiver or estoppel, it could be argued that the admissibility determination would be no more mandatory and might also be waived in this particular context.

4. The Relationship between Complementarity and *Ne Bis In Idem*

The principle that a person should not be tried twice for the same offence is found in the majority of legal systems of the world[198] – known as the principle of *nemo debet*

195 *Ibid.*, Art. 19(1).

196 See also Leila Nadya Sadat, *The International Criminal Court and the Transformation of International Law: Justice for the New Millennium* (Ardsley, New York: Transnational Publishers, 2002), p. 126 n. 96; Mahnoush H. Arsanjani, "Reflections on the Jurisdiction and Trigger Mechanism of the International Criminal Court" in Herman A. M. von Hebel et al. (eds.), *Reflections on the International Criminal Court* (The Hague: T.M.C. Asser Press, 1999), p. 74.

197 One commentator argues that *ne bis in idem* and the gravity test should not be waived since they are fundamental for any trial before the Court: see Rome Statute, Art. 17(1) (c) and 19(4). For a similar conclusion see Sadat, *supra* note 196, p. 125.

198 But few countries' constitutions include an express provision protecting against double jeopardy. These may include, *inter alia*, India (Art. 20(2): "No person shall be prosecuted and punished for the same offence more than once"), South Africa (Art. 35(3) provides that : "a person not to be tried for an offence in respect of an act or omission for which that person has previously been either acquitted or convicted"), Canada (Section 11(h) of the Charter of Rights stipulates that any person charged with an offence has the right "if acquitted of the offence, not to be tried for it again and, if finally found guilty and punished for the offence, not to be tried or punished for it again"). Also the Fifth Amendment to the United States Constitution covers the prohibition against double jeopardy. See on these matters Jay A. Sigler, *Double Jeopardy: The Development of a Legal and Social Policy* (Ithaca: Cornell University Press, 1969); Paul A. Mc Dermott, *Res Judicata and Double Jeopardy* (Ireland: Butterworths, 1999), p. 201; Richard Clayton, Hugh Tomlinson, *The Law of Human Rights* (Oxford: Oxford University Press, 2000), p. 757 – 758; William A. Schabas, *International Human Rights Law and the Canadian Charter: A Manual for the Practitioner* (Toronto. Calgary. Vancouver: Carswell, 1991), pp. 111 – 112; Peter Hogg, *Constitutional Law of Canada*, 3rd. ed. (Scarborough: 1992), pp. 1111 – 1114.

bis vexari pro una et eadem causa,[199] *nemo bis in idipsum,*[200] *non bis in idem, ne bis in idem*, or double jeopardy.[201] Some countries use the terms *chose jugée, autrefois acquit/convict de même felonie*[202] or *autorité de la chose jugée,*[203] as targeting the same meaning and effects. Major human rights instruments include a provision on the principle of *ne bis in idem*.[204] Yet the scope of protection is confined to the same sovereign State, at least according to the case law of international human rights courts and treaty bodies.[205] Within the context of international criminal tribunals, the prin-

199 Gerard Conway, '*Ne Bis In Idem* in International Law', 3 *International Criminal Law Review* 217, 221 (2003); Chrisitne Van den Wyngaert and Guy Stessens, 'The International Non Bis In Idem Principle: Resolving Some of the Unanswered Questions', 48 *International & Comparative Law Quarterly* 779, 780 (1999).

200 Martin Friedland, *Double Jeopardy* (Oxford: Clarendon Press, 1969), p. 5.

201 Olaoluwa Olusanya, *Double Jeopardy Without Parameters: Re-Characterisation in International Criminal Law* (Antwerp – Oxford: Instersentia, 2004), p. 26; see also the human rights instruments cited below.

202 Akhil Reed Amar, 'Double Jeopardy Law Made Simple', 106 *Yale Law Journal* 1807, 1810 (1997).

203 Christian T. Campbell, *International Civil Procedures* (New York, London, Hamburg: Lloyd's of London Press, 1995), p. 270.

204 International Covenant on Civil and Political Rights (ICCPR), adopted 16 Dec. 1966, entered into force 23 March 1976, G.A. Res. 2200A (XXI), UN Doc. A/6316 (1966), 999UNTS 171, Art. 14(7); American Convention on Human Rights (Pact of San José) (ACHR), signed 22 Nov. 1969, entered into force 18 July 1978, OASTS 36, O.A.S. Off. Rec. OEA/Ser.L/V/11.23, doc.21, rev. 6 (1979), Art. 8 (4); and European Convention for the Protection of Human Rights and Fundamental Freedoms (ERCHR), signed 4 Nov. 1950, entered into force 3 Sept. 1953, 213 UNTS 221, ETS 5, Art. 6(1). As to the ERCHR, prior to the adoption of Protocol No. 7 to the Convention, the prohibition against *ne bis in idem* was implicitly covered under the right to a fair hearing in accordance with Article 6(1) of the Convention. On this last point see *X v. The Netherlands*, Application No. 9433/81, Eur. Comm. H.R., Decision of 11/12/1981 on the Admissibility of the Application, p. 235. The principle appears in various regional instruments. For a survey see Mohamed El Zeidy, 'The Doctrine of Double Jeopardy in International Criminal & Human Rights Law', 6 *Mediterranean Journal of Human Rights* 183 (2002).

205 *A.P. v. Italy*, HRC, Communication No. 204/1986, 2/11/1987, UN. Doc. CCPR/C/OP/1, p. 67; *United States v. Benitez*, 28 F. Supp. 2d 1361 (S.D. Fla. 1988), pp. 1363 – 1364; *Summary Record of the 1401 st Meeting on the Consideration of Reports submitted by States to the Human Rights Committee on the Work of its 53 rd Session*, 17 April 1995, UN Doc. CCPR/C/SR.1401; *Summary Record of the 1405 th Meeting on the Consideration of Reports submitted by States to the Human Rights Committee on the Work of its 53rd Session*, 24 April 1995, UN Doc. CCPR/C/SR.1405; *Explanatory Report to Protocol No. 7 to the Convention for the Protection of Human Rights and Fundamental Freedoms*, para. 27; and also El Zeidy, *supra* note 204, pp. 204 – 205, 212, 216.

ciple of *ne bis in idem* appeared for the first time[206] in the ICTY Statute,[207] followed by a corresponding provision appearing in the ICTR Statute.[208] When drafting the statute of the international criminal court, the International Law Commission also included a provision dealing with the issue of *non bis in idem* (art. 42).[209] Article 42 of the International Law Commission Draft was taken as the basis for further discussion, which led to the adoption of Article 20 of the 1998 Rome Statute.

The principle of *ne bis in idem* is a "corollary" of the principle of complementarity, mirrored in Article 17, which likewise prevents the Court from asserting jurisdiction when a competent national legal system has already tried the person concerned.[210] While Article 17 covers investigations and prosecutions, Article 20 covers cases that have already been tried. Article 20(3) sets the standards for assessing whether a domestic adjudication of a case makes it inadmissible before the ICC.

Discussions on the principle of *ne bis in idem* in Rome arose during the "hard fought compromises on the complementarity provisions", related to national investigations or current prosecutions. Unlike standards of "unwillingness" or "inability" which covers current State proceedings, the *ne bis in idem* provision relating to completed trials only "amplify" the "unwilling" criterion. The *ne bis in idem* standards applicable to domestic trials focus on domestic systems that have used "the facade of legal proceedings to frustrate the ends of justice".[211]

When a domestic court has already tried a case, the complementarity mechanism, reflected in the *ne bis in idem* article, points to a test whether the national trial proceedings were *bona fide*. Thus, the national judgment bars a prosecution by the Court except in the case of *sham* or *show* proceedings.[212] These are defined as trials held for:

---

206 With the exception of a few references appearing in a couple of trials under Control Council Law No. 10 following the Nuremberg Judgment: see *Trials of War Criminals Before the Nuernberg Military Tribunals Under Control Council Law No. 10 (Flick Case)*, Vol. VI (1952), p. 1213; and *ibid., (Justice Case)*, Vol. III (1951), pp. 1147 – 1149. On the question whether the principle was recognized under the IMT Charter see El Zeidy, *supra* note 204, pp. 225 – 226; Christine Van den Wyngaert and Tom Ongena, "*Ne bis in idem* Principle, Including the Issues of Amnesty", *Cassese Commentary, supra* note 4, p. 718.

207 ICTY Statute, Art. 10.

208 ICTR Statute, Art. 9.

209 *Report of the International Law Commission on the Work of its Forty – Sixth Session* (2 May – 22 July 1994), with Annex Draft Statute for an International Criminal Court, UN Doc. A/49/10, 1994 *YILC* Vol. II, Part Two, Art. 42, p. 57.

210 Bassiouni, *supra* note 46, p. 20.

211 Newton, *supra* note 137, pp. 58 – 59.

212 Rome Statute, Art. 20(3); also Michael J. Struett, 'The Transformation of State Sovereign Rights and Responsibilities under the Rome Statute of the International Criminal Court', 8 *Chapman Law Review* 179, 191 (2005); Schabas, *supra* note 12, p. 88. Show trials tend to have two sides: one reflects vengeance through the need to punish, while the other reflects the opposite, that is trials that "fail to redress wrongs". Article 20(3) certainly speaks of the latter. On the distinction see Jeremy Peterson, 'Unpacking Show Trials:

a) … the purpose of shielding the person concerned from criminal responsibility for crimes within the jurisdiction of the Court; or
b) Otherwise were not conducted independently or impartially … and were conducted in a manner which, in the circumstances, was inconsistent with an intent to bring the person concerned to justice.[213]

Paragraph (3), which is the most complicated and controversial part of Article 20, reflects the entire array of procedural and substantive provisions relevant for implementing complementarity. Thus, an individual who has been tried by a national court for conduct "also proscribed under article 6, 7, or 8" shall not "be tried by the Court with respect to the same conduct". The inclusion of this language was the outcome of compromises among different proposals submitted during the drafting process.[214]

At the 1998 Preparatory Committee, a proposal was submitted which substituted the following language: "A person who has been tried by another court for conduct constituting a crime referred to in article 5".[215] This proposal was rejected on the ground that conduct could constitute a crime only if a court has determined that the conduct was a crime. This would not be logical in the case of an acquittal. The Chairman proposed reintroducing the language of the International Law Commission Draft Statute, "acts constituting a crime of the kind referred to in Article 42(2)". This was also rejected.[216] Even the reference to the word "offence" did not find sup-

Situating the Trial of Saddam Hussein', 48 *Harvard International Law Journal* 257, 261 – 263 (2007).

213 ICC Statute, Art. 20(3). Two examples may cover paragraph (3). The first occurs when a State charges a perpetrator of genocide with assault. Such a trial, although respecting all the safeguards relating impartiality, would be aimed at shielding the person from responsibility for an extremely serious crime. A second scenario occurs in a broader spectrum of situations. The ICC will not intervene in every case where it judges that a procedural safeguard was violated in a trial conducted by a national court. In order for the ICC to start a new trial, the violation of procedural safeguards must have been committed with the aim of preventing the person concerned from being brought to justice.

214 Although various proposals were made to change the Article on *ne bis in idem* at the Rome Conference, "only two amendments were eventually included in the final package following bilateral consultations conducted by the coordinator". The first change was made to the Chapeau of paragraph (3) by inserting the phrase "with respect to the same conduct". The addition clarified that the Court could try someone even if that person had already been tried in a national court, as long as different conduct was the subject of the second prosecution. The second change added the same phrase as appears in the Article regarding admissibility to make the criteria more objective - namely, the phrase "in accordance with the norms of due process recognized by international law". Since this phrase had been accepted for the purposes of admissibility, it was believed that it should be made applicable in a case of *ne bis in idem*. Holmes, *supra* note 15, p. 59.

215 Immi Tallgren, "Article 20: Ne bis in idem", *Triffterer Commentary, supra* note 7, pp. 419, 430.

216 *Ibid*; Holmes, *supra* note 15, pp. 56 – 57. For a thorough discussion on the negotiating history see generally, *ibid*., pp. 56 – 60.

port. Consequently, the compromise proposal, "conduct also proscribed", was adopted. This term seems to be unclear and in practice may lead to more than one interpretation.

According to Immi Tallgren, this phrase should be understood broadly. Thus, if a national trial took place based on conduct falling under the jurisdiction of the ICC, the latter should be barred from trying the accused for that same conduct. This means that the State's categorization of the crime, whether ordinary or international, does not really matter.[217] Similarly, Ward Ferdinandusse argues, not without good reason, that, contrary to the provisions concerning *ne bis in idem* set out in the ICTY and ICTR Statutes, the ICC Statute "blocks a second prosecution if the accused has effectively been prosecuted by another court "for conduct also proscribed under" the Statute, thus leaving the characterization of the crime open to national courts".[218] A modest understanding of the problem was displayed by William Schabas who argued that there is:

> [S]ome doubt about the application of complementarity and the *ne bis in idem* rule to situations where an individual has already been tried by a national justice system, but for a crime under ordinary criminal law such as murder, rather than for the truly international offences of genocide, crimes against humanity and war crimes. It will be argued that trial for an underlying offence tends to trivialize the crime and contribute to revisionism or negationism. Many who violate human rights may be willing to accept the fact that they have committed murder or assault, but will refuse to admit the more grievous crimes of genocide or crimes against humanity. Yet murder is a very serious crime in all justice systems and is generally sanctioned by the most severe penalties. Article 20(3) seems to suggest this, when it declares that such subsequent proceedings before the International Criminal Court when there has already been a trial 'for conduct also proscribed under Articles 6, 7 and 8' is prohibited. In the alternative, the Statute ought to have said, 'for a crime referred to in Article 5', as it does in Article 20(2).[219]

---

217 Tallgren, *supra* note 215, p. 431.

218 Ward N. Ferdinandusse, *Direct Application of International Criminal Law in National Courts* (The Hague: T.M.C. Asser Press, 2006), p. 205. This view has also been supported by Jann K. Kleffner, 'The Impact of Complementarity on National Implementation of Substantive International Criminal Law', 1 *Journal of International Criminal Justice* 86, 96 (2003). But see Kriangsak Kittichaisaree, *International Criminal Law* (Oxford: Oxford University Press, 2001), p. 290 (noting that the "ICC may try a person who has been tried by another court for conduct also proscribed as a war crime, an act of genocide, or a crimes against humanity"); Philips, *supra* note 34, p. 82 (stating that "a person shall not be tried before any *other* court for an article 5 crime…, nor shall a person be tried by the ICC for such offenses unless, the trial was not conducted impartially or violated norms of due process, or was inconsistent with an intent to bring the person to justice". Thus, it is clear according to these references that the intention refers to acts constituting the international crime as opposed to the ordinary crime or offences listed under Article 5, which leads to the same meaning.

219 Schabas, *supra* note 12, p. 88.

In the recent *Hadžihasanović* case before the ICTY, Trial Chamber II briefly touched on the question of the applicability of *ne bis in idem* under Article 20(3) of the ICC Statute. The Chamber, citing Ferdinandusse's work,[220] stated:

> Unlike the prevailing practice at the Tribunal and at the ICTR, the Rome Statute of the International Criminal Court provides that, in its relations with national jurisdictions, the principle of *ne bis in idem* will block a second prosecution if an Accused has already been tried in a national court for conduct also proscribed under the Statute. In so doing, the Statute of the International Criminal Court leaves the characterisation of the crimes open to national courts.[221]

Indeed, the "ordinary crime" exception found in Article 10 of the ICTY Statute and Article 9 of the ICTR Statute is missing from the text of Article 20(3), which presumably means that even if national courts prosecuted for the crime of murder relating to a certain set of facts, the ICC should not interfere with such an attempt unless these proceedings were *sham* in accordance with sub-paragraphs (a) and (b).

If Article 7 of the Statute is taken as an example, it is clear that the chapeau of Article 20(3) targets any of the acts listed under this provision. Murder, for instance, is listed under Article 7(1)(a), and assuming that a national court tried the person for the "conduct also proscribed under article 7", such as murder, the ICC is barred from trying him for the same conduct,[222] even though the murder was to be considered as an *ordinary crime.*

According to a second interpretation, based on the same example, the phrase "conduct also proscribed under article 6, 7 or 8" is the key to the problem. Arguably for "conduct" to be "proscribed" under Article 6, 7 or 8, for the purpose of the Statute, such conduct or act should meet the *threshold requirements specified* in those provisions. Looking again at Article 7(1) (a), the murder must be "part of a wide spread or systematic attack directed against any civilian population, with knowledge of the attack".[223] It may be inferred that the drafters intended to refer to *crimes against*

220 Ferdinandusse, *supra* note 218, p. 205.

221 *Prosecutor v. Enver Hadžihasanović Amir Kubura*, Case No. IT-01-47-T, Judgment, 15/03/2006, para. 257.

222 According to Professor Clark "conduct" amounts to "an act or omission and a 'consequence' as the result of an act or omission". See Roger S. Clark, 'The Mental Element in International Criminal Law: The Rome Statute of the International Criminal Court and the Elements of Offences', 12 *Criminal Law Forum* 291, 306 (2001); see also Bassiouni, *International Extradition, supra* note 107, p. 602 (noting that the term "same conduct" means: "a) identical acts; b) a series of acts related to each other by the scheme or intent of the actor; or c) multiple acts committed at more than one place and at different times, but related by the actor's criminal design").

223 Rome Statute, Art. 7(1); also Clark, *supra* note 222, pp. 327 – 328; generally on crimes against humanity and the ICC see Roger S. Clark, "Crimes against Humanity and the Rome Statute of the International Criminal Court", in Mauro Politi et al. (eds.), *supra* note 32, p. 75*ff*; Darryl Robinson, "Crimes Against Humanity: Reflections on State Sovereignty, Legal Precision and The Dictates of the Public Conscience", in Flavia Lattanzi

humanity as opposed to an *ordinary crime* of murder. It follows that the ICC is only barred from trying the person who has previously been tried by a competent national court for a crime against humanity. But, if this is true, why did the drafters not refer to the term used in Article 20(2): "for a crime referred to in article 5"?[224]

The difference in formulation between paragraphs (2) and (3) suggests that the drafters could not have referred to "a crime referred to in article 5", since the crime of aggression under Article 5(1)(d) is not yet defined. It is possible that the drafters intended to give paragraph (3) the same meaning as paragraph (2), but they demanded that the scope of paragraph (3) be widened to cover those acts listed in Articles 6, 7 and 8 by using the term "conduct". It was not therefore possible to identify acts of aggression, as they are yet to be defined. Moreover, another possibility for such a distinction may lie in the fact that the drafters may have intended to refer to the acts listed under Article 6, 7 and 8 in order to reduce the degree of the Prosecutor's subjective assessment as to whether the crime in question, subject to the previous trial by a national court, falls within the Court's jurisdiction.[225]

Moreover, reading Article 20(3) (a) in conjunction with Article 22(1) further supports the conclusion that Article 20(3) rejects the idea of a trial on the basis of an ordinary crime. Article 20(3) (a) speaks of "shielding the person...for crimes within the jurisdiction of the Court". The Statute grants the Court jurisdiction *only* over the four crimes listed in Article 5 as opposed to ordinary crimes. Thus, what may be intended for the purpose of triggering the exceptions to the *ne bis in idem* principle is to prove *sham* proceedings in relation to one of the core crimes defined under the Statute. Further, Article 22(1) states: "A person shall not be criminally responsible under this Statute unless the conduct in question constitutes, at the time it takes place, a crime within the jurisdiction of the Court". Since Articles 5 and 7 of the Statute do not cover murder as an ordinary crime, the Court would not be empowered to exercise its jurisdiction over such a crime.

Further, the fact that Article 20(3) lacks explicit reference to the "ordinary crime exception", as in the ICTY and ICTR Statutes, does not necessarily mean that the principle of complementarity should not be triggered when a national court tries

et al. (eds.), *Essays on the Rome Statute of the International Criminal Court*, Vol. I (Italy: Il Sirente, 1999), p. 139 *ff.* In this context, one has to realize the difference between the chapeau element of crimes against humanity and that of war crimes. In the former it is one of the constituent elements, while in the latter it is only a jurisdictional threshold that ensures that the Court does not exercise jurisdiction except when war crimes are committed "as part of a plan or policy...".

224 Even the Rules are silent with regard to Article 20. The only Rule that exists is Rule 168, which deals with *ne bis in idem* within the context of offences against the administration of justice (Art. 70), albeit in the different context of Article 70.

225 For example, under Article 5 the Prosecutor could argue that the crime which was the subject of a previous trial before the national court is not a crime against humanity and, as a result, the person should be tried before the ICC. In a case using the term "conduct proscribed under Article 6, 7 or 8", however, the situation would be different, because every act that might establish or constitute a crime against humanity would be identified. Thus, the Prosecutor would not enjoy the broad subjective criterion in his assessment.

an accused person on the basis of an ordinary crime. At the Preparatory Committee, some delegations "felt that the term 'ordinary crime' in paragraph 2 of Article 42 needed further clarification", while some others "considered that it could be left out altogether since it might create a certain confusion".[226] Two commentators have rightly observed that "the 'ordinary crime exception' was omitted, not for reasons of substance, but because the drafters considered it to be too vague. Accordingly the omission of the exception does not mean that the idea was abandoned altogether".[227] It follows that the silence of the text of Article 20(3) should not be interpreted narrowly, as rejecting the "ordinary crime exception", as asserted by some scholars.[228]

One cannot disregard the idea of legal characterization of crimes, since there is a clear difference between treating an offence as an ordinary crime and as an international crime. This distinction was always acknowledged by the International Law Commission during its work on the draft codes, as well as in the jurisprudence of the *ad hoc* tribunals. In his fourth report submitted to the International Law Commission in 1986, the Special Rapporteur correctly argued that the "fact that an act may or may not be punishable under internal law does not concern international law, which has its own criteria, concepts, definitions and characterizations".[229]

Again, in his fifth report submitted in 1987, the Special Rapporteur attributed the idea "an act characterized as a crime under international criminal law is not so characterized under internal criminal law" to the leading scholar, V.V. Pella, who stated:

> It would be too easy for a State to cause its nationals who are guilty of international offences to be tried by its own courts, so that they could then plead such judicial decisions in order to escape international justice..., these [international] crimes are often committed in an abusive exercise of sovereignty. To try to punish them by applying municipal law would, in many cases, be tantamount to asking the offender to punish himself.[230]

In the same vein, a member of the Commission said the "question of characterization, which was dealt with..., involved the very basis of international criminal law. If the idea was not accepted that international law could itself characterize a particular act as a crime independently of internal law, the draft code lost its raison d'être".[231] Moreover, the practical implications of accepting the idea of prosecuting an ordinary crime

226 1996 *Preparatory Committee*, Vol. I, *supra* note 9, para. 171.

227 Van den Wyngaert and Ongena, *supra* note 206, pp. 725 – 726.

228 Tallgren, *supra* note 215, p. 431; Ferdinandusse, *supra* note 218, p. 205; Kleffner, *supra* note 218, p. 96.

229 *Fourth Report on the Draft Code of Offences against the Peace and Security of Man Kind, by Mr. Doudou Thiam, Special Rapporteur*, UN Doc. A/CN.4/398, 1986 *YILC*, Vol. II, Part One, para. 147.

230 See *Memorandum prepared by V.V. Pella*, UN Doc. A/CN.4/39, 24 November 1950, in 1950 *YILC* Vol. II, pp. 310 – 311; *Fifth Report on the Draft Code of Offences against the Peace and Security of Man Kind, by Mr. Doudou Thiam, Special Rapporteur*, UN Doc. A/CN.4/404, 1987 *YILC*, Vol. II, Part One, p. 3

231 1987 *YILC* Vol. I, para. 8.

in lieu of an international crime may emerge in relation to the difference between the elements of international crimes and those of ordinary crimes, including the modes of participation (such as public and direct incitement to commit genocide etc.).[232] Even the protected values under both categories are entirely different.[233] Otherwise there would be no reason to establish an international criminal court with jurisdiction over the four core crimes, based on the idea of complementary jurisdiction, to ensure that domestic courts pass the necessary implementing legislation allowing them effectively to prosecute those egregious crimes that threaten the international community.

In the recent *Bagaragaza* case before the ICTR, the Trial Chamber rejected the Prosecution's application to refer the case to the Kingdom of Norway pursuant to Rule 11 *bis* on the ground that Norwegian domestic law fell short of a definition of genocide. Rejecting the idea of trying the accused on the basis of the crime of homicide instead of genocide shows the distinction and implications resulting from the legal characterization. The Chamber correctly stated:

> [T]he Chamber recalls that the crimes alleged – genocide, conspiracy to commit genocide and complicity in genocide – are significantly different in term of their elements and their gravity from the crime of homicide, the basis upon which the Kingdom of Norway states that charges may be laid against the Accused under its domestic law. The Chamber notes that the crime of genocide is distinct in that it requires the "intent to destroy, in whole or in part, a national, ethnical, racial or religious group, as such". This specific intent is not required for the crime of homicide under Norwegian criminal law. Therefore, in the Chamber's view, the *ratione materiae* jurisdiction, or subject matter jurisdiction, for the acts alleged in the confirmed Indictment does not exist under Norwegian law. Consequently, Michel Bagaragaza's alleged criminal acts cannot be given their full legal qualification under Norwegian criminal law, and the request for the referral to the Kingdom of Norway falls to be dismissed.[234]

It is evident that the legal characterization of crimes, even in the context of the ICC, seems necessary for the purpose of interpreting the principle of complementarity. A national court that tries a person on the basis of ordinary murder should not be equated, for the purposes of complementarity, with one proceeded against on the basis of crimes against humanity. By so arguing, it is not the intention to confuse the

---

232 See, *inter alia*, *Prosecutor v. Radislav Krstic*, Case No. IT-98-33-T, Judgment, 02/08/2001, para. 682.

233 *Prosecutor v. Mucic et al. "Celebici"* Case No. (IT-96-21-T), Judgment, 16/11/1998, para. 1154; also Gerhard Werle, *Principles of International Criminal Law* (The Hague: T.M.C. Asser Press, 2005), pp. 27 – 30.

234 *Prosecutor v. Michel Bagaragaza*, Case No. ICTR-2005-86-*R11*bis, *Decision on the Prosecution Motion for Referral to the Kingdom of Norway, Rule 11 bis of the Rules of Procedure and Evidence*, 19/05/ 2006, para. 16; and also *Prosecutor v. Michel Bagaragaza*, Case No. ICTR-05-86-*AR11*bis, *Decision on Rule 11 bis Appeal*, 30/08/2006 (upholding the Trial Chamber's decision).

concepts of *lex lata* with *de lege ferenda*. Rather the argument suggests that if Article 20(3) leaves room for a more plausible interpretation, consistent with the purposes of the Statute, this interpretation should be adopted in accordance with the *lex lata*. This finding is also consistent with the language of the first part of Article 93(10) (a) of the Statute.[235] Paragraph (10) (a) states that the Court may provide assistance "to a State Party conducting an investigation into or trial in respect of *conduct which constitutes a crime within the jurisdiction of the Court*" (emphasis added). The provision speaks of "conduct" in similar terms to the language of Article 20(3), which constitutes "a crime" within the jurisdiction of the Court. This may suggest that what is meant by "conduct also proscribed" under Article 20(3) is one of the crimes defined under Articles 6, 7 and 8. Yet, the second part of paragraph (10) (a) adds the clause "or [conduct] which constitutes a serious crime under the national law of the requesting State". While this part seems to refer to investigation of ordinary crimes as a basis for cooperation, this does not make it a decisive factor that weighs one interpretation against another. Rather it suggests that Article 20(3) must be interpreted with caution taking into account the two different interpretations provided above.

Article 20(3) gives rise to yet other related problems of interpretation. The Court is barred from trying any person who has been tried by a national court with respect to the same conduct "unless the proceedings in the other court" were *sham* and met the requirements of subparagraphs (a) and/or (b).[236] What is meant by the term "proceedings" in this context?[237] Is it the proceedings at only the trial stage? Or does the term reflect the early intention of the drafters in preparing what eventually became Article 17 that the term "proceedings" should mean the process of investigation and prosecution.[238] The text is vague and the Rules of Procedure and Evidence are silent in this respect.[239]

If the term "proceedings" is to be construed as confined to the trial stage, then any procedural aspect of the trial which negatively affects its outcome may allow the ICC to intervene and try the accused after his trial in a national court. The practical application of this Article presents a serious problem. For example, the trial stage proceedings may have been perfect but the investigation or prosecution was not conducted independently or impartially, or was carried out for the purpose of shielding the person concerned. What would be the situation if this were not discovered until the trial before the domestic court was completed? In other words, there could be a

235 Generally on Article 93 see Kimberly Prost and Angelika Schlunck, "Other Forms of Cooperation", *Triffterer Commentary*, *supra* note 7, p. 1101*ff.*

236 Rome Statute, Art. 20(3) (a) and (b). In this context, the guidelines suggested for interpreting Article 17(2) should apply *mutatis mutandis*. See chapter III *supra*.

237 A similar question was discussed earlier in the context of proceedings governed by Article 17. See Chapter III *supra*.

238 *Ibid.*

239 The problem is that no specific rules were proposed, and none were adopted for a number of Articles in part 2, including the crimes within the jurisdiction of the Court as they were considered extensively in the context of the elaboration of the "Elements of Crimes". See e.g., Rome Statute Arts. 5 – 10, 16, 20, 21.

situation where the investigation or prosecution stage was not conducted properly, the trial proceedings were conducted in a *bona fide* manner, but the outcome of the trial would not be just, since it would be based on false evidence. According to the above construction of the term "proceedings", the Court would be barred from trying that person, since "proceedings" does not cover the investigation or the entire prosecution, but only the trial stage.

However, the Prosecutor may have other options available at this point. Under Article 19(10), if the Court has earlier found the case to be inadmissible, the Prosecutor may seek a review based on the new facts which "negate the basis on which the case had previously been found inadmissible".[240] The new facts may be facts not previously discovered or facts exposing the investigation and prosecution as *sham*. Hence the Court may conduct another trial. The State concerned also has a chance to defend itself and "shall be given a time limit within which to make representation".[241] In its defence the State could argue on the basis of Article 20(3) that the person has already been tried before its courts and the trial proceedings were conducted genuinely, in accordance with due process of law, and accordingly the Court should not request a second trial. It follows that the ICC would be barred from retrying that person, despite the *sham* investigation or prosecution.[242]

This outcome is far from hypothetical. Still, this situation may not always convince the Court. The Court may rely on the general rule which says that what is based on falsehood must be null and void,[243] or invoke the doctrine of "fruit-of-the poisonous-tree", known as the *"fruits doctrine"*,[244] and extend the term "proceeding" to cover *sham* investigations or prosecutions. Thus, since the evidence submitted to

240 *Ibid.*, Art. 19(10).

241 ICC Rule 62(2).

242 *Ibid.*, Rule 181. Although Article 19 seems to limit to the accused the right of bringing a challenge based on *ne bis in idem*, Rule 181 appears to leave room for the State concerned to act in favour of the accused in this respect. Rule 181 states: "When a situation described in article 89, paragraph 2, arises, and without prejudice to the provisions of article 19 and of rules 58 to 62 on procedures applicable to challenges to the jurisdiction of the Court or the admissibility of a case, the Chamber dealing with the case, if the admissibility ruling is still pending, shall take steps to obtain from the requested State all the relevant information about the *ne bis in idem* challenge brought by the person". However, since Rule 181 is concerned with pending admissibility challenges, one may wonder whether the rule covers situations where the Court decides that a case is inadmissible, and the Prosecutor requests a review based on new facts.

243 See e.g., *Egyptian Court of Cassation*, Criminal Appeal No. 61, Judicial Year 9, 12/12/1938, para. 1 (holding that the decision against the accused was null and void, since evidence relied upon was derived from void proceedings); *Egyptian Court of Cassation*, Criminal Appeal No 4117, Judicial Year 56, 11/12/1986, para. 6 (rejecting reliance on evidence directly obtained from illegal or void proceedings).

244 *Blacks Law Dictionary*, Seventh Edition (St.Paul, Minn.: West Publishing, 1999), p.679 (defining the doctrine as: "The rule that evidence derived from an illegal [proceedings are] inadmissible because the evidence (the 'fruit') was tainted by the illegality (the 'poisonous tree')".

the national court was the outcome of improper investigation and prosecution, the trial might therefore be deemed void or evidence submitted might be excluded. This might result in an unjust acquittal. This would be grounds deserving a re-trial before the ICC.

If the term "proceedings" were to be construed within the same frame and meaning of Article 17, covering investigation and prosecution, the conclusion would be different. A literal reading of the chapeau of Article 20(3) suggests that the term "proceedings" would not fit neatly into the rest of this paragraph because of the phrase "in the other court". It is, therefore, doubtful whether paragraph (3) refers only to investigation or prosecution, as the phrase "in the other court" seems to emphasize that what is in fact meant by "proceedings" is the procedures adopted during the trial. Nonetheless, a practical construction of the term "proceedings" would take into account the entire set of proceedings covering a certain case. Thus, the Court might examine the genuineness of the investigation, of the prosecution and of the trial. Any other construction might lead to a complete blocking of the Court's jurisdiction. It seems that the drafters of paragraph (3) intended there to be a very strong first feature of the complementarity regime, favouring national sovereignty. Its formulation and the different scopes of its interpretation suggest this conclusion. The gaps resulting from the different interpretations empower States to build strong arguments that may lead the Court to determine that a case is inadmissible.

Article 20(3) does not refer to the type of decision required for the satisfaction of paragraph (3). The provision is silent with respect to whether the national court should reach a decision. If so, what kind of decision is required? Is a verdict needed, or does the paragraph refer to a decision to dismiss or stay proceedings? Is the decision of the court of first instance sufficient? Or should the decision be final – that is, *res judicata*? These questions are not clearly answered in the Statute or in the Rules of Procedure and Evidence.

According to Tallgren, a decision rendered for not proceeding due to lack of sufficient evidence or "because prosecution would not serve the interest of justice would suffice". A national decision resulting in neither an acquittal nor a conviction, "must be subject to the same criteria, the negligence of which lead to the application of the exception".[245] In certain common law jurisdictions, the decision not to proceed with an indictable offence could be made during the trial stage by either the judge or the prosecutor (with the judge's consent). This is the case in England and Wales, for example, where the prosecutor, a member of the Crown Prosecution Service, invites the court to grant him permission not to proceed with the case.[246]

In certain continental law jurisdictions such as Egypt this decision could not happen during a trial for indictable offences, because neither the prosecutor nor the judge is authorized to take such action during the trial stage. The prosecutor can dismiss or decide not to proceed with a case only after the preliminary investigation has been completed and a decision is required whether to commit the case to trial.

245 Tallgren, *supra* note 215, p. 431.

246 J. R. Spencer, "The English System", in Mireille Delmas-Marty et al. (eds.), *European Criminal Procedures* (Cambridge: Cambridge University Press, 2002), pp. 170 – 171.

This takes place prior to the trial stage. Once the case is committed for trial, the only possibility for the judge is to deliver a decision – an acquittal or a conviction – on the merits, ruling out any possibility of other ways of not proceeding.[247] It is uncertain, when monitoring domestic proceedings, whether the ICC will follow the continental or the common law approach, since the Statute is a combination of both. Perhaps the Court ought to take both systems into consideration, depending on which jurisdiction the case comes from. This requires the Court to study the domestic justice systems of many countries.

If the Court follows the example of certain common law practices, then the above interpretation would seem to run counter to the wording of the chapeau of paragraph (3), since the latter speaks of completed trials: "[n]o person who has been tried by another court…". Yet, if what is meant is a decision amounting to an acquittal or conviction, why is paragraph (3) formulated differently from paragraph (2), which requires that the person "has already been convicted or acquitted by the Court"? Could a completed trial be so called without a court reaching a verdict or decision to acquit or convict?

Professor Bassiouni seems to suggest an answer to this question. He argues that "an individual, who has been either previously acquitted or convicted by a national court for conduct that formed the basis of crimes under the Statute, may not be prosecuted by the Court", unless the proceedings meet the requirements of Article 20(3)(a) and/or (b).[248] It seems that he ignored the previously mentioned possibility that might arise from applying certain practices under the common law approach.[249]

Moreover, should a national court's decision on whether to acquit or convict be final?[250] Although this seems vague according to Bassiouni's construction, one may draw at least two conclusions on the basis of two different arguments. A first observation looks at Article 20(1) and (2), which anticipates final decisions. Accordingly, it could be argued that the outcome of the national court's proceedings should be final. This argument presumes that the drafters had the same intention, evidenced in

247 This is the general rule, but does not apply if the court, for example, has determined that the accused is dead. In this context, the court will have to declare this through a decision to stay proceedings. For different possibilities under common law jurisdictions such as the United States see Frank Meyer, 'Complementing Complementarity', 6 *International Criminal Law Review* 549, 555n.23 (2006).

248 Bassiouni, *supra* note 46, p. 21. According to Bassiouni's argument, a decision must be either an acquittal or a conviction.

249 However, Bassiouni's argument could work when applying the common law approach if a dismissal is considered to be the equivalent of an acquittal.

250 See e.g., *Report of the Inter-Sessional Meeting From 19 to 30 January 1998 in Zutphen, The Netherlands* (A/AC.249/1998/L.13,1998), p. 47. In the proposal, the drafters referred to final decisions of national courts as follows: any person(s) mentioned in the submission to the Court had already been acquitted or convicted by a final decision in a State for the acts in question unless the decision failed to take account of all facts contained in the submission or the proceedings were conducted in the State concerned by evading the rule of international law for the manifest purpose of relieving the persons concerned of criminal responsibility. *Ibid.*

earlier proposals,[251] in relation to the entire provision, although the finality required under paragraphs (1) and (2) is confined to decisions of the ICC. A second argument suggests that finality is not required in a domestic decision, because in situations where the Court requires prompt intervention awaiting a final decision would block the Court's jurisdiction for a certain time, resulting in unnecessary delay.[252]

A final related problem is the question of pardons. The Statute's omission of the issue of pardons is considered the greatest weakness of the second feature of the complementarity regime – namely the competence of the ICC to exercise its jurisdiction at a given stage. The question of pardons was raised during the work of the Preparatory Committee in 1997. The United States tabled a working paper on State practice in 13 countries. The paper was not seriously discussed and the question was omitted.[253] At the Rome Conference, bilateral consultations proceeded on a proposal concerning pardons, but failed to find its way due to the severe resistance of some

251 "As regards article 42, the remark was made that the principle of *non bis in idem* ... should apply only to *res judicata* and not to proceedings discontinued for technical reasons". See 1996 *Preparatory Committee Report*, Vol. I, *supra* note 9, para. 170.

252 In this situation, the Prosecutor would act in accordance with either Article 19(3) or (10), and in both situations the Court would hold a hearing to determine the admissibility of the case concerned. However, the problem lies within the aforementioned constructions concerning finality. If the requirement is that the national decision should be final, then the Court may face the problem of ruling on the admissibility of the case, since the person concerned may argue that he or she has not been tried except before the court of first instance. Article 89(2) permits the person arrested to bring a challenge before the national court on the basis of *ne bis in idem*. The national court does not, however, have the power to rule upon this. In fact, the Statute requires the requested State immediately to consult the Court in order to determine whether or not it has already ruled thereon. If the Court has decided that the case is admissible, the State must proceed with the execution of the request or, in other words, surrender of the person in question. If, however, an admissibility ruling is pending before the Court, the requested State may postpone surrender. Accordingly, the ICC would be coerced to postpone its ruling until the judgment of the national court was final, and the State might postpone his or her surrender of the person until that time (this is very risky, since the person could flee). Thus, the whole situation is very dangerous, despite the authority of the Prosecutor to act in accordance with Article 19(8) to preserve evidence. It should be noted, however, that Article 89(2) does not grant the requested State the right to raise the *ne bis in idem* plea before the Court. Although this seems strange, Article 19(2) (b) suggests the same conclusion, as it limits the challenge to the admissibility of a case to pending investigations and prosecutions or completed investigations and prosecutions. Thus, trials are excluded. On the other hand, if a first instance decision is sufficient, this may solve the former problem, but may run counter to an accused's rights regarding the judicial guarantees or norms of due process. For a detailed discussion concerning *ne bis in idem* and surrender see Dino Rinoldi and Nicoletta Parisi, "International Co-operation and Judicial Assistance between the International Criminal Court and States Parties", in Flavia Lattanzi et al. (eds.), *supra* note 8, pp. 348 – 351.

253 Adriaan Bos, "From the International Law Commission to the Rome Conference (1994 – 1998)", *Cassese Commentary, supra* note 4, p. 57.

States. They believed that the question was one which interfered with the "national decision-making process".[254]

The regime as it currently stands allows a State to investigate, prosecute, convict and sentence a person, and yet shortly pardon that person.[255] In the early 1970s, a U.S. court convicted William Calley of war crimes for massacring hundreds of civilians in My Lai village in Vietnam. For this he was sentenced to life imprisonment. "Then the United States President, Richard Nixon, however, intervened and granted him a pardon after only a brief term of detention had been served".[256]

According to one reading of Article 20(3), in a situation such as this there is no prospect that the ICC may invoke its competence to re-try someone, on the basis of the complementarity principle. This view finds support in the opinion of William Schabas, who believes that in an event of this type "the Court would seem to be permanently barred from intervening".[257] Yet, according to John Holmes, the fact that a pardon or parole was given shortly after a conviction creates a presumption in favour of the conclusion that the "entire proceedings" were not "genuine" – a fact that "may not have been evident during the proceedings themselves".[258]

While this argument has merit, it does not accommodate all possible situations. The example offered by William Schabas shows that there could be a case where a State genuinely investigates, prosecutes, tries and sentences an individual. However, that person was pardoned shortly afterwards due to a change of administration. In this context, those proceedings could not be deemed "for the purpose of shielding the person concerned from criminal responsibility", or not "conducted independently or impartially and in a manner which, in the circumstances, was inconsistent with

254 Holmes, *supra* note 15, pp. 59 – 60. See e.g., *Summary Record of the 11th Meeting*, 22 June 1998, UN Doc. A/CONF.183/C.1/SR.11, para. 33 (where the Afghan delegation "believed that it was the sovereign right of States to decide on the commutation of sentence or on a pardon according to its national interests and crime policy").

255 Holmes, *supra* note 15, at 76.

256 Schabas, *supra* note 12, p. 88. But Nixon granted Calley only a partial pardon, freeing him from the stockade and allowing him to stay under house arrest while his lawyers appealed his sentence. A series of appeals reduced Calley's life sentence to 20 years and then to 10. He was eventually paroled after serving only three and a half years under house arrest: William George Eckhardt, 'My Lai: An American Tragedy', 68 *University of Missouri Kansas-City Law Review* 671, 683 n.48 (2000); Court TV Online, The Greatest Trials of All Time: The Court Martial of Lt. Calley, available at, <http://www.courttv.com/greatesttrials/mylai/aftermath.html>.

257 Schabas, *supra* note 12, p. 88. During the meetings of the Committee of the Whole at the Rome Conference the Belgian delegate reopened the discussion on a provision originally proposed by Belgium, which dealt with a situation where a person was convicted, but "the sentence was subsequently rendered ineffective through a manifestly unfounded decision on the suspension of its enforcement, or through a pardon, parole or commutation of sentence". See *Summary Record of the 11th Meeting* , 22 June 1998, UN Doc. A/CONF.183/C.1/SR.11, para. 28.

258 Holmes, *supra* note 15, p. 77.

an intent to bring the person concerned to justice" (emphasis added).[259] Thus, even if the new administration's intention was *de facto* suspect, following a *bona fide* trial the Court seems to be barred from asserting jurisdiction on the basis of Article 20(3). The conjunction "and", used in Article 20(3) (b), seems to suggest that the Court must look not only to the manner in which the proceedings were conducted, but also to a factor such as the administration's intentions at the time the proceedings took place. It follows that Holmes's interpretation may be valid in a situation where the administration that oversaw the trial proceeding is the same one granting the pardon.[260] That being said, it is evident that the drafters intended a very strong complementarity regime favouring domestic jurisdiction. The Prosecutor would face a difficult task in distinguishing good faith from bad faith pardons.

5. Final Thought on Complementarity: Positive – Dynamic versus Traditional Complementarity

The previous sections under chapters III and IV mainly focused on how traditional complementarity should be understood and applied when it comes to interpreting the provisions governing its application (Articles 17 – 20). In this final section, the book shows that the principle of complementarity under the Rome Statute has a different dimension that exceeds the classical understanding of complementarity examined in the previous sections. This is known as the practice of *positive* or *dynamic* complementarity. This innovative policy is considered one of the three essential principles underlying the Prosecutorial Strategy[261] and will most likely shape the Court's treatment of the principle of complementarity for years to come. Being aware that the Court would not be able to deal with all situations referred to it, including the lower-level perpetrators, which might leave an "impunity gap", the Prosecutor, as a matter

259 Rome Statute, Art. 20(3).

260 The idea behind the new administration argument is that a person could be tried perfectly, yet following his trial and prior to the grant of any pardon, a new president is inaugurated. Presumably, the latter does not have any ties to the trial. She or he wants to pardon all the accused persons in the country. In this situation, it is unimaginable to say that this pardon reflects the fact that the entire previous proceedings were not conducted independently or impartially, or were conducted for the purpose of shielding the person from criminal responsibility. In addition, even if this new president intended to shield that person, a close reading of paragraph (3) suggests that it does not cover such a situation.

261 *Report on Prosecutorial Strategy*, 14 September 2006, p. 4 [hereinafter 2006 Strategy Report]. Also, Carsten Stahn has developed the concept of positive complementarity from a theoretical perspective. He argues that positive complementarity is based on three key assumptions: (i) "The ICC and domestic jurisdiction share a common burden"; (ii) "The desirability of Court action is not only exclusively determined by state failure, but influenced by comparative advantages"; (iii) "Complementarity is not only built on threat-based compliance by states, but leaves room for cooperation and assistance from the Court to domestic jurisdictions". See Carsten Stahn, *Complementarity: A Tale of Two Notions*, 19 *Criminal Law Forum* (forthcoming 2008).

of policy, decided to assist and encourage States to undertake their own national proceedings. In 2003, the Prosecutor made it clear that:

> National investigations and prosecutions, where they can properly be undertaken, will normally be the most effective and efficient means of bringing offenders to justice; States themselves will normally have the best access to evidence and witnesses. To the extent possible the Prosecutor will encourage States to initiate their own proceedings.[262]

Moreover, since the Court is an "institution with limited resources", his Office will function "with a two tiered approach to combat impunity".[263] While the Court will focus its investigations on those who bear the greatest responsibility, it will not leave lower-ranking perpetrators to go unpunished. Instead, the Court will "encourage national prosecutions, where possible", ensuring that offenders are brought to justice.[264] Thus, when the Court does not prosecute a particular person, "it does not mean that impunity is thereby granted – the Court is complementary to national efforts, and national measures against other offenders should still be encouraged".[265]

National efforts may be encouraged through the provision to a State genuinely willing to assume its responsibility with the necessary non-confidential information in the OTP's possession.[266] National efforts may also take the form of establishing national and international networks as well as participating in a system of international cooperation.[267] In so doing, the OTP has so far developed legal tools which provide legal information covering national as well as international legislation, case law, commentaries and documents related to the drafting history of the Rome Statute.[268] These tools are clearly intended to "facilitate deep and sustained cooperation and empower domestic criminal jurisdictions" as well as assisting in "harmonizing" the development and application of international criminal law at the domestic level.[269] It follows that the *positive* side of complementarity targets an increase in the number of genuine investigations, prosecutions and trials "at the national level", which by its role mirrors the degree of success of the Court as well as the Rome Statute.[270]

The general idea of encouraging domestic prosecutions through reinforcing the national criminal justice systems is not in itself new. The innovation lies, however, in

262 2003 *OTP Policy Paper*, *supra* note 17, p. 2.

263 *Ibid.*, p. 3.

264 *Ibid.*

265 2006 *Strategy Report*, *supra* note 261, p. 5.

266 2003 *OTP Policy Paper*, *supra* note 17, p. 5. If this information would prejudice current investigations by the OTP, then it should not be subject to disclosure. See Rome Statute, Art. 54(3) (e) and (f).

267 *Report on the Activities Performed during the First Three Years (June 2003 – June 2006)*, pp. 22 – 23 [hereinafter (2003 – 2006) Activities Report].

268 *Ibid.*, p. 32.

269 *Ibid.*, pp. 32 – 33.

270 *Ibid.*, p. 23.

doing so through the channel of an international judicial body whose initial role is confined to the prosecution of certain international crimes that States fail to address before their own courts. In its 1992 report of the Working Group on the Question of an international criminal jurisdiction, the idea of strengthening domestic criminal justice systems for the purpose of trying crimes of an international character was briefly addressed.[271] Yet, it was not the intention that the future international criminal court directly contribute to reinforcing national judicial systems. Rather the aim was to study whether strengthening national courts through the various forms of assistance may suffice in avoiding egregious cases involving "international crimes to go unpunished for lack of an available [effective] forum";[272] therefore, excluding the possibility of establishing an international criminal court.

According to this proposal, the Working Group suggested that there was "a need to strengthen national courts, to enable them to deal more effectively with crimes of an international character".[273] International judicial assistance may take the form of, *inter alia,* "judicial education and training", the "secondment of experienced judges" from other legal systems.[274] Flexible forms of international judicial assistance might, therefore, assist "some countries, especially smaller countries with limited legal and judicial resources".[275] These few proposals show that one of the main elements underlying the idea of *positive* complementarity is not novel – that is, reinforcing the national judicial systems for the sole purpose of reducing the impunity gap. It was grounded in the minds of legal authorities, such as members of the Commission. This conclusion may contribute to some extent to justifying the ICC Prosecutor's policy for invoking *positive* complementarity.

At a first glance, the traditional or passive side of complementarity does not seem concurrently to accommodate the positive side. Article 17 of the Statute,[276] which mainly regulates the application of the traditional system of complementarity, provides for a situation where the State is unwilling or unable before the Court may exercise its jurisdiction.[277] Thus, the provision expects the Prosecutor to wait passively for a situation to be referred by a State Party or the Security Council, before the Court may express its intention whether or not to exercise its jurisdiction in relation to a certain situation. Once the situation reaches the stage of admissibility analysis

271 *Report of the International Law Commission on the Work of its Forty – Fourth Session* (4 May – 24 July 1992), Annex *Report of the Working group on the Question of an International Criminal Jurisdiction*, UN.Doc. A/47/10, 1992 *YILC*, Vol. II, Part Two.

272 *Ibid.*, p. 70.

273 *Ibid.*, p. 63.

274 *Ibid.*, p. 70.

275 *Ibid.*

276 Rome Statute, Art. 17(1).

277 For a quite similar observation see Christopher Keith Hall, 'The Powers and Role of the Prosecutor of the International Criminal Court in the Global Fight against Impunity', 17 *Leiden Journal of International Law* 121, 135 – 136 (2004).

under Article 53(1) (b) (which is the first test of admissibility),[278] Article 17(1) comes into play, requiring only for a case to be rendered *inadmissible* that it is at least being genuinely investigated by a State with jurisdiction and that its gravity is not sufficient to warrant the Court's intervention.[279]

This literally means that once the Prosecutor initially determines that the case "is" not, or "would" not be "admissible" under Article 53(1) (b), it does not matter whether that case, which has been rejected, will be dealt with before domestic courts. In other words, Article 17 in conjunction with Article 53(1) does not explicitly impose any sort of obligations upon States to investigate a case which has been deemed inadmissible. Nor is the Statute drafted on the basis of taking into account the idea of *transfer of proceedings* to a specific State resulting from the positive conflict of jurisdiction between the State's courts and the ICC. It follows that the literal language of these provisions does not seem to visualize the Court taking *positive* action in relation to a certain situation.

The same conclusion may be reached when one understands the philosophy underpinning the insertion of the initial admissibility provision introduced by James Crawford in 1994. Article 35 of the International Law Commission's Draft was inserted for the main purpose of acting as an additional filter that ensured that the Court might be able to get rid of unnecessary cases at an early stage of the proceedings, thus avoiding the Court being flooded with complaints involving lower-level perpetrators.[280] The same philosophy was transferred to Article 17 of the current ICC Statute. It follows that Article 17 may only contribute to blocking cases involving lower-level alleged perpetrators, but does not ensure their prosecution at the national level, as the idea of *positive* complementarity suggests.

The fact that the literal language of Articles 53(1) and 17 does not seem explicitly to foresee the *positive* side of complementarity does not lead to the conclusion that doubts overshadow the legality of the strategy or practice. One should not overlook the language of preambular paragraphs 4 – 6, which clearly reflects the purposes underlying the Statute.[281] Preambular paragraph 4 *affirms* that the crimes falling within the jurisdiction of the Court, which are considered the most serious crimes, "must not go unpunished".[282] Their prosecution must be "effective" through measures to be taken at the national level as well as by "enhancing international cooperation".[283] Paragraph 6 comes into play to confirm this meaning and to strengthen the wording by reminding States that the exercise of their domestic criminal jurisdictions is also an existing "duty".[284]

278 Rome Statute, Art. 53(1) (b); ICC Rule 104. A similar test applies after an investigation before the Court. See Rome Statute, Art. 53(2) (b); ICC Rule 106.

279 Rome Statute, Art. 17(1) (a) and (d).

280 1994 *YILC* Vol. I, p. 9.

281 Rome Statute, preamble, paras. 4 – 6.

282 *Ibid.*, para. 4.

283 *Ibid.*

284 *Ibid.*, para. 6. For further discussion on preambular paragraph 6 see chapter III *supra*.

Paragraph (5) mirrors the broader idea behind the entire Statute – this is to "put an end to impunity"..."and thus to contribute to the prevention of such crimes".[285] It follows that in order to "contribute" to the "prevention" of such crimes for the sake of putting an "end to impunity", *positive* action is required, be it at the international or the national level. Thus, the fact that the ICC Prosecutor has chosen to go beyond the scope of prevention of crimes at the international level by directing some of his efforts to the national level does not really raise any problem from a legal perspective, and is clearly consistent with the purposes of the Statute reflected in the preamble.

Some commentators stated that the originally intended interpretation of the fifth preambular paragraph "reflects both a determination to end impunity and the belief that the punishment of those guilty of international crimes will lead to the deterrence of others".[286] This interpretation suggests that the reference to the phrase "contribute to the prevention of such crimes" was not meant to refer to a duty of prevention rather than to express the expected consequences in terms of deterrence resulting from punishing "those guilty of international crimes".[287] While this might have been the underlying intention behind inserting this paragraph at the time, interpretation of multilateral treaties of the same kind as the Rome Statute should not remain unaffected by the rapid development of the law.

As the ICJ stated in its *Advisory Opinion on Namibia*, "interpretation cannot remain unaffected by the subsequent development of law,...an international instrument has to be interpreted and applied within the framework of the entire legal sys-

285 Rome Statute., preamble, para. 5.

286 Tuiloma Neroni Slade and Roger S. Clark, in Roy S. Lee (ed.), *supra* note 15, p. 427. But see Otto Triffterer, "Preamble", in *Triffterer Commentary, supra* note 7, p. 12 (noting that "An effective enforcement at the same time contributes to the *prevention* of such crimes..."). On the drafting history see Coordinator's Rolling Text Regarding the Preamble and Part 13, 10 July 1998, UN Doc. A/CONF.183/C.1/L.54/REV.2, preamble para. 6; Reccomendations of the Coordinator Regaridng the Preamble and Part 13, 11 July 1998, UN Doc. A/CONF.183/C.1/L.61, preamble para. 6; Recommendation of the Coordinator Regarding the Preamble, 14 July 1998, UN Doc. A/CONF.183/C.1/L.73, preamble para. 6; Report of the Committee of the Whole, 17 July 1998, UN Doc. A/CONF.183/8, preamble para. 5.

287 But see e.g., some of the statements made during the plenary meetings of the Rome Conference that may suggest that the overall purpose of establishing an international criminal court is *also* to contribute in *preventing* those crimes defined under the Statute. See statements made by the delegates of Austria, *Summary Record of the 4th Plenary Meeting*, 16 June 1998, UN Doc. A/CONF.183/SR4, para. 40 ("A truly effective, independent and permanent court would play a major role in upholding the principles of justice and the rule of law. A particular advantage would be its preventive role, through its deterrent effect on potential criminals..."; Democratic Republic of Congo, *Summary Record of the 7 th Plenary Meeting*, 18 June 1998, UN Doc. A/CONF.183/SR7, para. 91 ("The international community had proved powerless to prevent atrocities or even punish the perpetrators...the creation of an international criminal court was an imperative"; and Bosina and Herzegovina, *Summary Record of the 8th Plenary Meeting*, 18 June 1998, UN Doc. A/CONF.183/SR8, para. 16 ("the establishment of the International Criminal Court would create a strong instrument for preventing and punishing the perpetrators of serious crimes").

tem prevailing at the time of the interpretation".[288] Similarly, in his earlier concurring opinion in the *Advisory Opinion* on the *Membership in the United Nations,* Judge Alvarez correctly observed that "an institution, once established, acquires a life of its own, independent of the elements which have given birth to it, and it must develop, not in accordance with the views of those who created it, but in accordance with the requirements of international life".[289] Accordingly, preambular paragraph 5 should be interpreted in a manner that ties in with the current trend adopted at the ICC. These rules may also support a finding that applying complementarity in a *positive* manner is a necessary development required by the needs of international criminal law.

One scholar arguing in favour of the legality of positive complementarity even invokes Articles 15, 18 and 54 as further grounds justifying its application.[290] While these provisions clearly establish a dialogue between the Prosecutor and States, one has to be cautious when giving too wide an interpretation to these provisions. Article 15 deals with the Prosecutor's *proprio motu* powers to investigate a situation in response to a communication received by his office.[291] Although Article 15(2) sets up the link between the two parties, as it permits the Prosecutor to "seek additional information from States",[292] such a relationship is not intended to serve the interests of the State, rather than those of the Prosecutor. The provision is clearly intended to assist the Prosecutor in obtaining access to information that he himself is interested in for his own investigations. Thus, it might seem awkward if one interprets the provision as serving the State's investigations or, in general, a policy of positive complementarity.

The same holds true for Article 54, which spells out the duties and powers of the Prosecutor in relation to an investigation.[293] Article 54(3)(c) speaks of the Prosecutor's powers to "seek the cooperation of any State…"[294] Sub-paragraph (d) further permits the Prosecutor to enter into "arrangements or agreements, not inconsistent with this Statute, as may be necessary to facilitate the cooperation of a State…".[295] Again, this provision lends support to the Prosecutor in carrying out his own investigations. Thus, concluding "agreements" or entering into "arrangements" would be for the sole purpose of serving his investigations. This is understood from the last part of sub-

288 *Legal Consequences for States of the Continued Presence of South Africa in Namibia (South-West Africa), Advisory Opinion of 21/06/ 1971,* I.C.J. Reports 1971, p. 31.

289 *Conditions of Admission of a State to Membership in the United Nations (Article 4 of Charter), Advisory Opinion of 28/05/ 1948,* I.C.J. Reports 1947 – 1948, pp. 67 – 68.

290 William W. Burke-White, 'Implementing a Policy of Positive Complementarity in the Rome Statute of Justice', 19 *Criminal Law Forum* (forthcoming 2008).

291 Rome Statute, Art. 15(1); ICC Rule 46.

292 Rome Statute, Art. 15(2), ICC Rule 47.

293 Rome Statute, Art. 54.

294 *Ibid.*, sub-paragraph (3)(c).

295 *Ibid.*, sub-paragraph (3)(d).

paragraph (d), which talks of "cooperation of a State".[296] Certainly, the State would cooperate to assist the Prosecutor's investigations, and not *vice versa*.

The situation may be different in relation to Article 18.[297] Article 18(2) and (5) also opens a different channel of communication between the Prosecutor and the State.[298] The Prosecutor, who has deferred investigation to the requesting State under Article 18(2),[299] may "periodically" enquire into the "progress" of the State's investigations or any subsequent prosecution".[300] Apparently, this provision, as argued earlier in Chapter III, seems to reflect an unfriendly relationship between the State in question on one hand and the Court on the other, each demanding control over a situation or case. If one construes this provision in the light of this understanding, then there is no room to argue that the Prosecutor will offer any sort of assistance to the State in carrying out its investigations. Yet, Article 18(5) may be interpreted effectively[301] to accommodate a scenario where the Prosecutor's role does not end with just requesting the information, rather than *positively* providing assistance to the State to continue its investigations effectively. This interpretation would, to a certain extent, change the traditional understanding of complementarity as representing a conflict between the two parties. Such an interpretation would also provide for another legal foundation vital to positive complementarity.

Again, a look at the overall goal of the principle of complementarity in the light of the purposes of the Statute suggests that the aim is to encourage States to pass national implementing legislation enabling them to deal effectively with the crimes that fall under the jurisdiction of the Court in the domestic arena. Thus, complementarity serves as a "catalyst for compliance" with the duty to investigate, prosecute and try the core crimes falling within the jurisdiction of the Court.[302] A State failing to comply runs the risk of being deprived of the ability to exercise its primacy over a certain situation or case. That said, it could be argued that one of the main objectives of complementarity is to *encourage* States to investigate these heinous crimes *at the national level*. This also ensures that the *positive* side of complementarity fits neatly within the parameters of the overall objectives of the principle.

---

296 *Ibid.*

297 Rome Statute, Art. 18.

298 *Ibid.* paragraphs (2) and (5); ICC Rule 53.

299 Rome Statute, Art. 18(2); ICC Rule 53.

300 See the interplay between Article 18(3) and (5). Rome Statute, Art. 18(3) and (5); ICC Rule 56.

301 *Mamatkulov and Abdurasulovic v. Turkey*, Application No. 00046827/99, Judgment (Merits) of 6/02/ 2003, para. 93; *Öcalan v. Turkey*, Application No. 00046221/99, Judgment (Merits) of 12/03/2003, paras. 153, 155; *Loizidou v. Turkey*, Application No. 00015131/89, (Preliminary Objections) of 23/03/ 1995, para. 72.

302 Jann K. Kleffner, "Complementarity as a Catalyst for Compliance", in Jann K. Kleffner et al. (eds.), *Complementary Views on Complementarity: Proceedings of the International Roundtable on the Complementary Nature of the International Criminal Court*, Amsterdam, 25/26 June 2004 (The Hague: T.M.C. Asser Press, 2006), p. 79 *ff.*

In practice, *positive* complementarity may initially prevent unnecessary communications and situations being referred to the Court, since the policy targets strengthen national justice systems, which reduces the need for an ICC. This does not deny the fact that in other instances minor situations or communications may still be referred to the Court. The Prosecutor will have to apply the *passive* complementarity provided under Articles 53 and 17 of the Statute[303] before being able to invoke the *positive* aspect of the principle by rendering assistance (such as sharing of information or giving legal advice in relation to the investigation) to the State or States in question in exercising their own jurisdiction. There may also be a case where the Prosecutor initiates an investigation into a situation and finally selects specific incidents for prosecution – implicitly leaving the others involving lower-level alleged perpetrators to be dealt with before the national courts of the State in question.[304] In this context, the Prosecutor may offer support to national efforts in relation to the other cases.

In the case of Northern Uganda, the OTP selected six incidents out of hundreds that occurred in the region[305] – presumably leaving some of the remaining incidents to the responsibility of the State. Indeed, in a recent report issued by the OTP it was reported that the Office "has offered… technical assistance to the DRC judicial authorities in relation to certain criminal investigations".[306] Similarly, in his first report to the Security Council concerning the situation in Darfur, the Prosecutor made it clear that his Office "will conduct focused investigations and prosecutions of those individuals who bear the greatest responsibility", while national efforts would be required for other offenders through "traditional and other mechanisms".[307] The ICC would, therefore, "cooperate with and support such efforts, the combination of which will mark a comprehensive response to the need for peace, justice and reconciliation".[308] These statements provide good examples of how a policy of *positive* complementarity may apply hand in hand and without any interference with the Court's primary duties to investigate high-level perpetrators.

The practice of positive complementarity seems useful as it clearly helps in reducing the impunity gap as well as the Court's case load. Yet some caution is required. For example, assisting national efforts by sharing information or giving legal advice in relation to domestic proceedings relating or linked to an investigation currently before the Court is problematic. In situations like this, the efficiency of the Court's investigations is at risk. Moreover, working too closely with States' national authorities might prejudice the OTP's independence – as in the case of self-referrals. In sum, *positive* complementarity is a useful innovation that may certainly help reduce the

303 Rome Statute, Arts. 53(1) (b) and 17.

304 *Ibid.*, Art. 53(2)(b).

305 (2003 – 2006) *Activities Report, supra* note 267, p. 8.

306 *Ibid.*, p. 14.

307 *First Report of the Prosecutor of the International Criminal Court, Mr. Luis Moreno Ocampo, To the Security Council Pursuant to UNSCR 1593(2005)*, 29 June 2005, p. 10.

308 *Ibid.*

sort of tension mirrored in some of the complementarity-related provisions under the Statute, yet should not be invoked at all times.

Concluding Observations

While Article 17 is central to the interpretation of complementarity, Articles 18, 19 and 20 regulate the procedural regime of its application. As mentioned earlier in this chapter, the Rome Statute complementarity model reconciles two competing features and jurisdictions. The first is State sovereignty, which claims national jurisdiction over its citizens or those crimes committed on its territory, even though these crimes are of an international character and may fall within the international jurisdiction. The second feature functions only in exceptional circumstances and gives an international tribunal the ability to exercise jurisdiction over these heinous crimes. The ICC Statute's procedural aspects either protect national sovereignty and domestic jurisdiction or strengthen the ICC's jurisdiction. Articles 17, 18, 19 and 20 clearly reflect the tension between these two competing features. Under these provisions, certain paragraphs work in favour of States, while others serve the interests of the Court. What functions in favour of States targets a strong complementarity regime that preserves State sovereignty. Since the Court has not so far issued more than a handful of decisions that touch briefly on Articles 18 and 19, some questions of interpretation explored earlier in this chapter are likely to arise in the future.

The practice of self-referral and waiver of complementarity examined in Chapter III as a constituent element of the application of Article 17 may involve some implications on the procedural regime governing Articles 18 and 19. While the procedural regime under the Statute does not exempt the Court from examining admissibility during the Article 18 phase, it does permit bypassing this test during the Article 19 stage, if the Court was acting *ex officio* or admissibility had not been challenged by any of the parties covered by Article 19(2) and (3).[309] It also poses the question whether a State which initially waived its primacy in favour of the Court may regain the right to exercise jurisdiction over the case

Article 20(3), on the other hand, is part of the complementarity procedural regime that governs domestic proceedings in relation to trials. Paragraphs (3)(a) and (b) copy the criteria set out in Article 17(2) for determining a State's "unwillingness". Also, Article 20(3) is relevant to the *inadmissibility determination* in accordance with Article 17(1). Thus, there is a clear interplay between these provisions. Three significant observations ought to be made in this context. First, since the criteria found under Article 17(2) correspond to those of Article 20(3), the admissibility assessment in relation to these provision overlaps to a certain extent. The difference lies, however, in the stage of proceedings where these criteria apply. Secondly, when comparing the language of Article 20(2) with that of paragraph (3), one may observe that there is a technical difference that may lead to confusion as well as different interpretations.

309 If admissibility has been challenged by the self-referring State and the Court denies that State the right to challenge, then the admissibility examination would not be examined, and thus, waived by the Court.

Unlike Article 20(2), which makes clear that a second trial is barred "for a crime referred to in article 5" of the Statute, the language of Article 20(3) speaks of "conduct also proscribed under articles 6, 7 or 8".

This inconsistency has led to a division of scholarly opinion as to whether the ICC may re-try a person who has already been tried before a domestic court for an "ordinary crime". It is likely that the Court would also face some difficulty in deciding which route to follow. Finally, Article 20(3) causes another problem in relation to the question of pardons. The provision is drafted in a manner whereby a State acting in *bad faith* may take advantage of its language. According to one reading, the State may investigate, prosecute, convict and sentence a person, and shortly pardon that person, without the ICC being able to request another trial. This interpretation takes into account the criteria set out in paragraph (3)(a) – (b), which literally suggest that what is actually required to block a second trial before the ICC is *bona fide* proceedings until a sentence is imposed. A different view supports the conclusion that Article 20(3) is a key solution to the problem of pardons. The fact that a pardon or a parole has taken place shortly after a conviction creates a presumption in favour of the view that the "entire proceedings" were not "genuine". Although according to a literal interpretation of Article 20(3) the Court would have to adopt the first reading, the fact that the latter interpretation fills in a gap under the Statute makes it difficult to predict which line of reasoning the Court may follow.

The examination of Articles 17 – 20 referred to above and explored in detail under the different sections of chapters III and IV shows how the traditional type of complementarity, initially intended by the drafters, should function when the Court is called to apply the relevant provisions governing the system. So far, practice has revealed that the principle of complementarity embodies a different side – known as positive complementarity. This notion, which was adopted by the Prosecutor as a constituent part of his Office's strategy, will re-shape to some extent the traditional understanding of the principle of complementarity. The Rome Statute's traditional complementarity model suggests that the Court would exercise its jurisdiction only when the State was "unwilling" or "unable" to proceed with a genuine investigation, prosecution or trial. The Prosecutor would, therefore, have to wait until a situation has been referred by a State Party or the Security Council before showing any position as to initiating an investigation into a situation. This shows that the Prosecutor's role is almost passive until a referral is received.

Acknowledging that the Prosecutor could not investigate all situations referred to the Court, the Prosecutor adopted a policy of encouraging as well as assisting States in carrying out their investigations at the national level in accordance with the principle of complementarity. By so proposing, he invoked a *positive* feature of the principle of complementarity. Positive complementarity does not seem to pose problems from a legal point of view. The idea is grounded in law under several provisions of the Statute, as explored in section 5. It may even prove useful in practice in reducing the tension arising out of some of the complementarity-related provisions such as Article 18(5) of the Statute. Also, it helps in reducing the number of unnecessary referrals, thus narrowing the impunity gap. Nonetheless, applying a policy of positive complementarity necessitates some vigilance. The Prosecutor needs to retain the Court's independence as well as balance the equation involving the Court's interests in certain investigations on the one hand, and that of the States, on the other hand.

Conclusions

This work has attempted to correct the misconceptions surrounding the idea of complementarity. Part A provided a new dimension to the understanding of the notion of complementarity in international criminal law by engaging in an exhaustive historical and statutory analysis of it. This is unprecedented in the currently available literature and important to provide the context for a better understanding of the Rome Statute and its shortcomings. Part A identifies misconceptions regarding the origin of the idea of complementarity by demonstrating that is neither new nor the sole product of the work of the International Law Commission. Some academic commentators claim that the concept of complementarity was first referred to in 1992 when the Working Group of the International Law Commission was studying the question of establishing an international criminal court. Many other scholars believe that the concept appeared for the first time in the 1994 International Law Commission's Draft Statute. These are inaccurate observations. This book traces the first precedent in modern history concerning the application of complementarity to the drafting of the Peace Treaties following World War I. The relationship established between the inter-Allied tribunals and the German Supreme Court sitting in Leipzig mirrored a complementarity mechanism very similar to the Rome Statute model. Without repeating what was said in Chapters I and II, suffice it to say that the 79-year period between the end of World War I and the conclusion of the Rome Statute of the International Criminal Court witnessed the crystallisation of the concept of complementarity in various forms. The idea behind highlighting and examining the different proposals over this period is to show that the notion of complementarity may emerge in different forms or models. The reasons or philosophy underlying the adoption of each model often overlapped. When we compare them, we may see differences. This is important because it opens broader avenues for interpreting complementarity under the Rome Statute and it puts the Rome Statute into perspective. The following few pages will highlight and categorise only the major complementarity models and compare them with the current 1998 model. Part B of the book offered a further contribution to the field of international criminal law by conducting a systematic analysis of the complementarity-related provisions of the Rome Statute (specifically Articles 17 to 20) and examining how they interrelate. This Part shed light on a number of issues with respect to these provisions by undertaking both a textual statutory and a case-law analysis. It then offered some interpretive guidelines that could alleviate the problems that have been identified. This analysis is the first of its kind and it comes at a crucial time in the Court's history, as the ICC is now taking on a growing number of investigations and the prospect of the Court handing down becoming a reality.

I will first summarize the findings regarding the various models of complementarity.

Aside from the system of complementarity created under the Treaty of Versailles, the first apparent complementarity model is that appearing under the 1937 League of Nations Convention. The draft provisions of the London International Assembly, the International Commission for Penal Reconstruction and Development, the United Nations War Crimes Commission, and the 1951 and 1953 Committee on International Criminal Jurisdiction rely on a common idea of State consent and the voluntary relinquishment of jurisdiction to the proposed international criminal court. As noted earlier, the 1953 model was taken as the main basis for the future work of the International Law Commission. The 1990, 1992 and 1993 Working Groups, as well as the Special Rapporteur's ninth and eleventh reports, also proposed an optional, concurrent and complementary regime inspired by the 1953 model. The system of complementarity established by these draft statutes and proposals fits under the umbrella of one major model that may be defined as *optional complementarity.* The common problem with these models lay in the fact that, in practice, if the unwilling State decided neither to prosecute nor to refer the case to the international criminal court the latter had no power to request deferment to its jurisdiction, and this rendered these models toothless.

The second major model is that applied during the Nuremberg experience. This model was introduced after the Allies agreed that the establishment of an Allied court under the auspices of the United Nations War Crimes Commission, which was based on a system of optional complementarity, was not feasible at the time. The Nuremberg complementarity model was not based on the idea of a State's *unwillingness* or *inability* or on a system of *voluntary* relinquishment of jurisdiction. Rather the system was merely based on the idea of division of labour or responsibilities between national and international jurisdictions. The complementary relationship was exercised in a friendly manner between the two levels of jurisdiction. In 1988 and 1989, the International Law Commission proposed a mechanism of complementary jurisdiction that seemed to have been inspired by the Nuremberg experience. National courts were to deal with minor crimes, such as war crimes, while the international criminal court was to focus on other types of crimes such as aggression. This proposal was also based on the idea of division of labour and symmetry in exercising the two-tier jurisdiction. The only difference was that the Nuremberg model distributed the powers between national and international jurisdictions on the basis of the level or degree of responsibility of the perpetrators. By contrast, the model proposed by the International Law Commission relied on the nature of the crimes. Both ideas, however, represent one major model that may be defined as *friendly* or *amicable* complementarity.

The third major model was a modified scheme of complementarity adopted by the 1994 Working Group of the International Law Commission. This model was based on a combination of the consensual system introduced in the first major model and an admissibility mechanism that acted as a safety valve to frame a new version of complementarity. Although the system contemplated by the drafters shared with the first major model the mechanism of optional, concurrent and complementary jurisdiction that provided States with the freedom to choose the *forum conveniens*, this modified version had a higher threshold that was not triggered by just meeting the regular jurisdictional requirements that were set out in Articles 21, 22 and 25 of the 1994 International Law Commission's Draft Statute, as in the case of the previously mentioned drafts. Thus, if, for example, the custodial State, a party to the Statute which accepted the jurisdiction of the proposed court, chose to lodge a complaint with the Prosecutor and refer a particular case to the international criminal court due to its unwillingness to try a case before its national courts, that case had to pass an admissibility test for the court. This last requirement was missing in all of the preceding draft statutes proposed by the Commission. Yet, this model shared with the first the lack of enforcement powers on the part of the court in the event of a State's inaction, resulting from the latter's unwillingness or inability.

The fourth major model is the henceforth classical complementarity concept enshrined in the 1998 Rome Statute. This model is based on a reverse approach, yet it was still inspired by the theories underpinning the first and third models with technical modifications with respect to its application.

Under the current regime, the jurisdiction of the ICC is compulsory and, thus, once a State has ratified the Statute, it is automatically subject to its jurisdiction, provided that certain requirements have been met. In order for this jurisdiction to be activated – as in the 1994 International Law Commission's Draft – preconditions to the exercise of jurisdiction (accompanied by a referral by a State Party or the Security Council) as well as admissibility conditions have to be satisfied. The technical difference, however, lies in the fact that the Rome Statute complementarity model created a dual regime of *mandatory* and *optional* complementarity that function alongside each other. According to the *mandatory* structure, the question of the determination of *inadmissibility* seems obligatory according to a literal reading of the chapeau of Article 17, which states that the "Court *shall* determine that a case is *inadmissible* where." Such determination is *mandatory*, at least during the situation phase.[1] The 1994 model lacked any reference to the distinction between situations and cases, and thus there was no question of determining the admissibility of a situation *versus* a case. According to the Rome Statute complementarity model, if the State was unwilling or unable to deal with a situation or case before its own domestic courts, the Court could proceed with it without the further consent of any State. This was not the case under the terms of the 1994 Draft, which left the State free to decide whether it would defer jurisdiction to the Court if it was unwilling to act domestically. According to the jurisdictional mechanism vested in the 1994 Draft, a State's failure to investigate, prosecute or try a case before its domestic courts did not automatically trigger the jurisdiction of the ICC by requesting the situation or case to be trans-

1 See Arts. 18, 53(1)(b), ICC Rule 55(2) (emphasis added). Such a determination is optional during the case stage when the Court is acting *proprio motu*, as in the 1994 ILC Draft. See Rome Statute, Art. 19(1).

ferred to its jurisdiction. If the custodial State Party which accepted the jurisdiction of the Court under Article 22 lodged a complaint under Article 25(2) against another State in which the crimes were alleged to have been committed, and the territorial State refused to accept the jurisdiction of the Court in accordance with Article 21(1)(b) (ii), the ICC had no power to exercise jurisdiction over the case and, by implication, the question of admissibility would not arise.

Arguably, the 1994 model pointed in the direction of the 1998 model when discussions in the 1995 *Ad hoc* Committee on an independent prosecutor began. The Rome Statute complementarity model empowers the Prosecutor to "initiate" an investigation *proprio motu*, and, if satisfied that there was a "reasonable basis to proceed", to request the Pre-Trial Chamber to authorize the commencement of the investigation after having evaluated the supporting materials including, *inter alia*, the question of admissibility of the situation. It follows that the Rome Statute complementarity model enables the ICC to pursue a situation or case and request deferment to its jurisdiction in the event of a State's failure to act upon a certain situation – a system that is in a sense the reverse of what is in the 1994 Draft, which leaves the decision to refer a case to the court to the discretion of the State.

Moreover, having a Pre-Trial Chamber that plays a role during the stages of admissibility of the situation or case in order to balance the powers of the independent Prosecutor was an innovation in the 1998 model.

When compared to earlier draft proposals, the Rome Statute model *in essence* seemed to have roots in the mechanisms established by the penalty provisions found in the peace treaties of World War I, as well as in a United States proposal tabled in the *Ad hoc* and reiterated in the Sixth Committees during the drafting of the 1948 Genocide Convention. According to the interpretation given to the penalty provisions in the treaty of Versailles, if the German trials were unsatisfactory the Inter-Allied Tribunals would have stepped in to adopt the proceedings, which deprived national courts of the supremacy to decide. The United States proposal during the drafting of the Genocide Convention similarly provided the proposed international criminal court with the competence to find to the effect that a State had either failed to take appropriate measures to bring the accused to justice or failed to impose appropriate punishment. Based on this finding, the court would have exercised jurisdiction in lieu of the national court. Despite these similarities, there was no documented evidence that these early ideas inspired the International Law Commission or members of the Committees that followed that path until the Rome Conference. Instead, during the work of the International Law Commission reference was often made to the 1953 revised Draft Statute.

As to *optional complementarity*, it clearly applied to a situation of self-referral. The admissibility system seemed to accept a situation whereby a State Party, from the outset, decided to waive its primary jurisdiction to the ICC (State inaction) without even being deemed unwilling or unable by the Court. A self-referral was always followed by a waiver of complementarity. This was the reversed regime of *mandatory complementarity*; it was not because the Court determined that the State was unwilling or unable that the situation came before the Court, but rather because the State itself consented to relinquish jurisdiction in favour of the Court. This feature was not clear-cut or obvious in the 1994 model. Article 25 talked about a State "lodging a complaint" as opposed to "referring a situation", which perhaps meant that a State was not expected to lodge "a complaint" against itself.[2] Yet, there was no evidence in the *travaux préparatoires* to support either assumption. But, the fact that the 1994 jurisdictional model established a system of *optional* concurrent jurisdiction made it strange to assume that the State with a direct link to the crimes might not think of choosing the international criminal court as an alternative venue for trial. This holds true in relation to the earlier complementarity proposals tabled during the work of the 1922 International Law Association, the draft statutes of the 1937 League of Nations Convention, the London International Assembly, the United Nations War Crimes Commission and the 1951 and 1953 Committees on International Criminal Jurisdiction. The system of complementarity established under these instruments certainly accommodated the ideas of self-referrals and waivers of complementarity.[3]

This does not deny the fact that the drafters of these instruments did not regard the same method and implications of self-referral and waiver of complementarity as understood nowadays. Self-referrals and waivers of complementarity were not seriously contemplated by the drafters of the 1998 Statute. But recent practice shows their acceptance in implicit form embedded in the text of Article 17.

Finally, there is another set of models resulting from the practice of the *ad hoc* tribunals. Originally, the tribunals exercised primacy over the jurisdiction of national courts. Primacy as traditionally known seeks to entrust the international tribunal with the upper hand over any case that is under its jurisdiction. But practice has proved that, in some instances, although the tribunal could have invoked its primacy *proper* to solve a conflict of jurisdiction over a specific case, it has sometimes chosen a different practice, namely to defer to the jurisdiction of national courts on the basis of a division of labour. This has been exercised within the framework of the prosecutorial discretionary powers. While such practice is not strictly the exercise of primacy, it may create a relationship between national courts and the tribunal that is closer to complementarity. This complementary relationship stands alongside the existing mechanism of primacy. Although the complementarity scheme established under the umbrella of prosecutorial discretionary powers shares with the Rome Statute complementarity model the idea of the division of tasks, the technicalities underlying the application of both systems are different – making each a distinct model of complementarity.

The existence of a plan for a "completion strategy" and the amendment of Rule 11 *bis* of the Rules of Procedure and Evidence reflect a new angle in the understanding of primacy and complementarity. Rule 11 *bis* as it currently stands permits the tribunals to refer mid- and lower-level cases that are already before them to national courts, thereby entrusting them with the primary responsibility to investigate, prosecute and try a referred case. This decision to refer may be revoked by the Referral Bench if the State fails to conduct proper proceedings. While the initial decision to bring the

2 See chapters III and IV *supra*.

3 Also the notions underlying the idea were rooted in the first international war crimes trial. See chapter III, section 3 *supra*.

case before the tribunal is clearly one of primacy, the subsequent decision to send the case back to the national authorities providing them with the primary jurisdiction to proceed is closer to a practice of complementarity based on co-operation and the distribution of tasks – similar in idea to the model created under the exercise of prosecutorial discretion, but different in terms of application as well as the philosophical foundations – thus forming another model of its own. This model seems to be inspired to some extent by an earlier one created by the Nuremberg International Military Tribunal. A fourth model appears in the decision to revoke an order for referral of a case to a State due to its failure "diligently [to] prosecute" or provide a "fair trial". Like the Rome Statute complementarity model, the fourth model provides national courts as opposed to the tribunals with primary jurisdiction over referred cases. Such primacy of domestic courts is subject to a test of genuine proceedings. Failing this test would still trigger the jurisdiction of the tribunal to take up the proceedings. This model, although different, is the closest to the current Rome Statute mandatory complementarity model, as it seems to apply "diligent prosecution" and "fair trial" as criteria acting to restricts the exercise of the tribunal's jurisdiction over a case that has already been referred to a national court. As the philosophical foundations underlying all of these models and the technicalities of their application differ, as explored earlier in the book, complementarity may emerge also in different forms creating various overlapping models. Yet all of these models are based on a common idea – the distribution of powers between national and international jurisdictions.

The above conclusions suggest that complementarity is not an *absolute* principle, but rather a notion that is subject to variations depending on the mode of its conclusion. Despite the similarities and distinctions between the various models, they all share one common denominator – that is *doing what the others could not do.* All of this suggests that the Rome Statute complementarity model does not represent a final form or understanding of complementarity. Rather, there may be other future efforts that build on the current system, creating a further modified model.

3. We turn now to the assessment of the Rome Statute complementarity model. It is clear that the success in Rome was due in no small measure to the delicate balance developed for the complementarity regime. States that were concerned primarily with ensuring respect for national sovereignty and the primacy of national proceedings were able to accept the provisions governing the principle of complementarity because they dealt, to some extent, with these concerns. Where the Court was given authority to intervene, the criteria on which such interventions would be based were clearly defined as objectively as possible. One of the fundamental features of the Statute's complementarity regime is that the interpretation and application of the provisions is left to the Court itself.[4] The Court may develop the understanding of these provisions to balance the powers granted to States and those provided to the Court. This ensures that the application of complementarity serves its main goal – namely

4 See e.g., *Summary Record of the 2 nd Plenary Meeting*, 15 June 1998, UN Doc. A/CONF.183/SR.2, para. 70; *Summary Record of the 3 rd Plenary Meeting*, 16 June 1998, UN Doc. A/CONF.183/SR.3, para. 88; *Summary Record of the 4 th Plenary Meeting*, 16 June 1998, UN Doc. A/CONF.183/SR.4, para. 27.

to encourage domestic exercise of jurisdiction as a primary duty, while preserving the powers of the Court to intervene when required. However there is some risk in leaving the interpretation of the complementarity-related provisions to the discretionary assessment of the Court in the absence of clear guidance in the Statute and the Rules. Chapters III and IV provide the analysis and offer some suggestions in that respect.

Article 17(1) (a) and (b) speaks of the inadmissibility of a case where a domestic investigation or prosecution is being carried out. Without delving into the question of Truth Commissions and amnesties, which are beyond the scope of this study, suffice it briefly to highlight that the provision fails to clarify what type of investigation is required. It is not clear whether an investigation carried out by a Truth Commission would suffice to satisfy this provision, especially if such investigation did not lead to an amnesty.[5] Paragraph (a) of Article 17(1) refers to investigation or prosecution. The problem is that generally an investigation carried out by a non-judicial body is not judicial in nature and would not necessarily lead to a prosecution. When paragraph (a) refers to a "prosecution", which is always a judicial activity, carried out by a purely judicial body, one gets the sense that Article 17(1) is concerned with "judicial proceedings" as opposed to alternative mechanisms of justice. Leaving the Court to fill this gap is problematic, as it involves opposing legal views.

The hardest part of the complementarity regime appears in the exceptions to the criteria for inadmissibility under Article 17(1) (a) – (c) and (2) – (3), defined by the terms "unwilling" and "unable" "genuinely". A second difficult part of the admissibility test lies in assessing the gravity of the situation or case, which is beyond the scope of this study.

The first noticeable gap arises out of Article 17(2), which governs the test of "unwillingness". The Statute proposes some criteria to assist the Court in making a determination on a State's unwillingness. Still, paragraph (2) leaves open some questions that require the Court's attention. The language of paragraph (2) left it undecided

5 On the types of Truth Commissions and their mandates *see* Thomas Buergenthal, "Truth Commissions Functions and Due Pocess", in Christian Tomuschat et al. (eds.), *Völkerrecht als Wertordnung. Common Values in International Law* (Kehl, Germany: N.P. Engel Verlag, 2006), p. 103; Priscilla B. Hayner, *Unspeakable Truths: Facing the Challenge of Truth Commissions* (New York: Rutledge, 2002). More specifically on the relationship between TRCs and international courts see William A. Schabas, 'The Relationship between Truth Commissions and International Courts: The Case of Sierra Leone', 25 *Human Rights Quarterly* 1035 (2003). For a discussion in the context of the ICC see Carsten Stahn, 'Complementarity, Amnesties and Alternatives forms of Justice: Some Interpretative Guidelines for the International Criminal Court', 3 *Journal of International Criminal Justice* 695 (2005); Darryl Robinson, 'Serving the Interests of Justice: Amnesties, Truth Commissions and the International Criminal Court', 14 *European Journal of International Law* 481(2003); Anja Seibert-Fohr, 'The Relevance of the Rome Statute of the International Criminal Court for Amnesties and Truth Commissions', 7 *Max Planck Yearbook of United Nations Law* 553, 567 – 569 (2003); Karlijn Van Der Voort and Marten Zwanenburg, 'From 'Raison d' État' to 'état de droit international' – Amnesties and the French Implementation of the Rome Statute 1 *International Criminal Law Review* 315 (2001).

whether the list of conditions for making a finding on unwillingness is open-ended or exhaustive. Certainly, going beyond the criteria expressed in paragraph (2) widens the Court's monitoring powers to assess unwillingness. There is a danger in supporting this interpretation, since this would provide the Court with unlimited powers of assessment that might act as a double-edged sword. In some instances, this may work in favour of States, when the situation actually requires a decision supporting the Court's interference. On other occasions, this may solve the question of admissibility in support of the Court, when a finding of inadmissibility is desired by the State.

Article 17(2) (a) speaks of shielding a person from criminal responsibility for the purpose of making a case admissible before the Court. The test is clearly subjective in nature. Although the chapeau of Article 17(2) reduces such subjectivity by requiring the Court to take into account "the principles of due process recognized by international law", this does not deny the fact that such an examination requires exceeding States' apparent actions. It requires one to enquire into the States' hidden intentions, which makes part of the test complex and certainly subjective. Also, the language of Article 17(2)(a) does not seem to embody the terms necessary to assist the Court in making any straightforward determination of whether the domestic proceedings are intended to "shield the person concerned" from criminal responsibility. Nor does it spell out what may render domestic proceedings inadequate for the purpose of reflecting a State's evil intentions. Although it was impossible for the drafters to provide specified conditions for making a determination on the notion of shielding a person from criminal responsibility, they should at least have offered some interpretive guidelines. Chapter III attempts to fill this gap and provide a strategy to assist the Court in interpreting this provision.

Article 17(2) (a) refers to the term "proceedings", without giving it an exact meaning for the purpose of interpreting paragraph (a). The drafting history reveals that the word "proceedings" was intended to cover investigations and prosecutions. In recent practice, the Office of the Prosecutor has construed the term to the same effect. This raises the question whether the provision excludes "trial proceedings" from the complementarity test. If the term were to be read strictly according to the interpretation given to it earlier, there is a risk that some cases that reached the trial stage before domestic courts would bypass the admissibility barrier, even if trial proceedings were *sham*. The same problem emerges in paragraphs (2) (b) and (c). Article 17(2) (b) refers to "unjustified delay" in the proceedings. Domestic proceedings may move forward in adequate intervals, yet a delay may occur at the trial stage accompanying or reflecting the State's intention not proceed against the accused. Similarly, domestic investigations and prosecutions may be perfect, while, during the trial, intentional miscarriage of justice occurs, leading to partial or non-independent trial proceedings. Thus, the Court ought to provide a liberal interpretation for this provision so that the complementarity test covers all stages of the proceedings, as argued earlier in the book.

Article 17(2) (b) – (c) is intended to ease the difficulty of making a determination on complementarity as reflected in paragraph (2)(a) by providing an element of objectivity. The reference to the key words "unjustified" justice, "delay" and the lack of "independence or impartiality" in carrying out the domestic proceedings draws, to a certain extent, some *objective boundaries* for the assessment. The objectivity of the test is further supported by reference to the "principles of due process" in the chapeau of paragraph (2). Yet the Statute fails to guide the Court on how to meet these requirements.

Although the drafters demanded a strong complementarity regime that ensured the primacy of States over cases at all stages by increasing the degree of objectivity of the test, this provision may have a negative implication in practice. The test adds to the burden of proof on the Prosecutor, leaving room for a State acting in bad faith to raise different sorts of excuses, making the complementarity assessment more difficult to meet. The difficulty intensifies because the test requires the Court to determine further whether the delay in the circumstances of the specific case "is inconsistent with an intent to bring the person concerned to justice". The Statute and its Rules of Procedure and Evidence also lack any guidance on what may constitute a delay or an unjustified delay for the purposes of meeting the complementarity test. Chapter III provides some guidelines in making any such determination, bearing in mind that assessing delays always depends on the factual circumstances of each case. Yet the Report on the Court Capacity Model stated that the length of the proceedings from the moment of arrest until final judgment should not exceed three years. The report laid down three months for the confirmation of charges, six months for disclosure and preparation for trial, fifteen months for the trial itself, and finally nine months for the appeal. The main problem is that the Court itself failed to meet these deadlines in the *Lubanga* case. This raises some doubts about how the Court would apply the same test to national proceedings. The Court also needs to take into account delays that have taken place in relation to the trial of similar crimes by the *ad hoc* tribunals. The *Melosovic* and *Butar* cases are good examples of extraordinary delays. A significant reference concerning the idea of "unjustified delay" emerged in relation to the *Central African Republic* situation. Pre-Trial Chamber III complained of the Prosecutor's delay in deciding under Article 53(1) whether he intended to initiate an investigation into the situation. The Prosecutor invoked several reasons justifying the delay, some of which tied in with the conditions adopted by the different human rights bodies. Perhaps these reasons provide some indication of how the Prosecutor will in the future approach the question of delays in national proceedings.

In testing delays for the purpose of complementarity, the Court needs also to be aware of the fact that not every "unjustified delay" qualifies for a complementarity determination. The delay has to be one that *directly* affects the domestic proceedings leading to the punishment of the alleged perpetrators. Further, if the Court has chosen to be guided by the jurisprudence of the different human rights bodies, it has to be cognizant of the distinction between the application of the test of delay before these bodies and that before the International Criminal Court. These considerations are not addressed in paragraph (2) (a).

A similar problem of interpretation will arise in relation to Article 17(2) (c), because neither the Statute nor the Rules of Procedure and Evidence or the Regulations of the Court defines situations involving "independent or impartial" proceedings. Nor do they spell out how the Court may assess the validity of domestic proceedings for the purpose of Article 17(2) (c). Because these terms appear in different human rights instruments, the Court ought to be aware that there are some distinctions regarding their application, as explored in Chapter III. For the purposes of meeting the complementarity test under the Statute, it should be noted that the test is broader than that applied by human rights bodies.

A final observation concerning Article 17(2) shows that the drafters of the Statute distinguished the language of paragraph (2) (a) from that of paragraphs (2) (b) and (c). Paragraph (2) (a) refers to shielding from criminal responsibility "for crimes within the jurisdiction of the Court referred to in article 5", while paragraphs (2) (b) and (c) speak of not bringing the "person concerned to justice". The phrase "bring to justice" is wide, and suggests that if any State proceeded against a person on the basis of crimes or acts with different legal characterisations, lacking under the list of crimes in Article 5 or in the definition of acts set out in Articles 6 – 8, it may still challenge admissibility before the Court. This challenge may be based on the fact that the State has brought the accused to "justice" within a reasonable time, in accordance with the letter of paragraph (b) requesting the Court to defer jurisdiction. Although it is unlikely that the Court will defer jurisdiction on the basis of such grounds as the scenario mirrors the State's bad intentions, the main problem lies in the fact that these sorts of challenges would cause a delay in proceedings. Thus, the Court should not construe paragraphs (2)(b) and (c) as having a different purpose from paragraph (a). Rather, the Court should ensure that there is harmony in interpreting this Article for the sake of ensuring effective results.

The admissibility of the case is not always determined by testing a State's unwillingness; rather, there is another test of the "ability" of the State which is defined in Article 17(3). Although, as argued in Chapter III, the inability test is less complex than the one concerning "unwillingness", paragraph (3) of Article 17 regulating inability raises some problems of interpretation. One such problem is similar to the one encountered with respect to Article 17(2), i.e., determining the meaning of the terms used in Article 17(3). The Statute and its Rules altogether fail to define the words "total or substantial collapse" or "unavailability" of a national judicial system for the purpose of applying the provision. The difficulty in drawing a demarcation line between the words "total" and "substantial" will certainly emerge in the future once the Court puts the provision into practice. The deletion of the term "partial collapse" originally proposed by the drafters is one main reason for the confusion.

A study of the regime of Article 17 demonstrates that the complementarity test is not confined to a determination by the Court of a State's unwillingness or inability; rather the regime implicitly contains another element that triggers the Court's exercise of jurisdiction. Article 17(1) allows the Court to determine that a case is admissible where no State has acted (State inaction) or explicitly stated that it is not willing to act. This scenario could be clearly observed in the situation of a self-referral where a State waives its primacy in favour of the Court by declaring that it is not going to institute proceedings. This is what the book called *optional* complementarity. In fact, the first two situations received by the International Criminal Court came by way of self-referrals. These came from the Democratic Republic of Congo (DRC) and Uganda, as the States with a direct link to the alleged crimes. A third self-referral later came to the Court from the Central African Republic.

It is known that the Prosecutor has invited and even encouraged this type of referral. This policy was mentioned as one of the Office of the Prosecutor's strategies. However, self-referrals which result in waivers of complementarity were not seriously contemplated by the drafters of the Statute, and thus the issue raised some concerns in legal doctrine. Studying the question proves that while self-referrals and waivers of complementarity may not cause legal problems *per se*, the Court should not accept the practice as a matter of general policy. The practice may be useful when the territorial State, best suited with evidence and closest to the scene of the crime, shows political will to cooperate with the Court in carrying out its investigations. However, caution is required when dealing with such practice, since the Court may turn into a forum for all States that wish to refrain from carrying out their duties. Unless, there are clear, reasonable and exceptional circumstances, the Court should not really accept a self-referral.

In practice, the Court has briefly dealt with the question of self-referral, in two of its decisions concerning the DRC and Uganda. It failed however to explicitly address the question of waiver of complementarity. The Court endorsed the practice of self-referral, which actually led in the two situations to a partial waiver of complementarity.[6] This conclusion indicates that the Court, to a certain extent, accepted the general idea of waiver of complementarity. Yet, both Chambers could have fully benefited from the theory of waiver if they entirely avoided to make a ruling on admissibility pursuant to Article 19(1) of the Statute. The Court surprisingly confused the questions of self-referrals with the criterion of inability under Article 17(3). In *Lubanga*, the line of reasoning followed by Pre-Trial Chamber I suggested that a self-referral may be accepted on a *case-by-case* basis. Yet, in this decision it accepted the DRC's self-referral, because the State was "unable" to initiate proceedings regarding crimes falling under the jurisdiction of the Court. This suggests that a self-referral should always be accompanied by a State's "inability". This observation is not problematic *per se*, as it deters unwarranted self-referrals from reaching the Court. What is certainly remarkable is the legal treatment of the concepts of *inaction* (resulting in a self-referral and a waiver of complementarity) and *inability* under Article 17.

According to the latter provision, if the State failed to institute proceedings for whatever reason, such as a blanket amnesty or the State's incapability of doing so, this would represent a clear scenario of *inaction* in accordance with the first part of Article 17(1) as opposed to *inability* under Article 17(1) (a) – (b) and (3). This suggests that the Chamber confused the idea of a self-referral arising out of a State's *priori inaction* with the notion of *inability* as set out in Article 17(1) (a) – (b) and (3) of the Statute. Moreover, when a self-referral is followed by a waiver of complementarity, this means that the situation is admissible in relation to the *passive* State and generally admissible if no other State has challenged the admissibility of the situation or case (uncontested admissibility). When the Chamber was requested to issue an arrest warrant against Thomas Lubanga, no State challenged admissibility.

6 In this context, a partial waiver means that although the State waived admissibility and its primacy to exercise jurisdiction, the Court did not avoid the admissibility examination under Article 19(1).

Since the Court was acting *ex officio* during the issue of the arrest warrant against Lubanga under Article 58, it could have bypassed the admissibility examination.[7] Pre-Trial Chamber II treated the question differently. To a limited extent it implicitly relied on the waiver of complementarity in light of the permissible language of Article 19(1) of the Statute. Instead of getting involved in an actual detailed examination of the question of admissibility like Pre-Trial Chamber I, Pre-Trial Chamber II deemed it sufficient at this stage of the proceedings to confine itself to a *prima facie* determination, without ruling out the subsequent possibility of determinations, deciding that the cases against the five LRA leaders "appear to be admissible". The approach of a *prima facie* determination was later adopted by Pre-Trial I in the *Decision on the Prosecutor Application under Article 58(7) of the Statute*, in the *Darfur* situation. The Chamber revisited its initial approach and decided that "[o]n the basis of the evidence and information provided...in relation to both Ahmad Harun and Ali Kushayb,...the Chamber finds that the case against Ahmad Harun and Ali Kushayb falls within the jurisdiction of the Court and appears to be admissible".[8] The endorsement of the *prima facie* method for testing admissibility might place both Chambers in a questionable position. It is not certain whether the admissibility mechanism under the Statute can accommodate this practice.

Although Pre-Trial Chamber II acknowledged the Ugandan self-referral on the basis of the State's letter declaring its inability to arrest the LRA leaders, it did not confuse the question of *priori inaction* with that of *inability*. Nonetheless, in both decisions the Court remarkably accepted the self-referrals that served these States' political agenda. Continuing to accept self-referrals on this basis raises the risk of the Court losing its credibility and effectiveness.

Assessing the complementarity regime under the Statute does not end with Article 17. Article 17 is only central to other provisions that were drafted to serve the whole procedural regime (Articles 18 – 20). Certainly, as argued in Chapter IV, there are strengths and weakness in the complementarity regime. Some provisions seem to work in favour of States, which inevitably strengthens the first feature of the complementarity regime, while others seem to work in favour of the Court and reinforce the second feature. This reflects a clear tension between States and the Court when applying the procedural provisions. As the Court has not been faced with questions involving the interpretation of these provisions, one may only speculate as to the

7 See Rome Statute, Art. 19(1), which makes admissibility consideration discretionary at this stage. Arguably, *ne bis in idem* as well as the gravity test should not be waived.

8 *Prosecutor v. Ahmad Muhammad Harun ("Ahmad Harun") and Ali Muhammad Ali Abd-Al-Rahman ("Ali Kushayb")*, Decision on the Prosecution Application under Article 58(7) of the Statute, No.:ICC-02/05-01/07-1-Corr, 27/04/2007, para. 25. But see the most recent decision, *Prosecutor v. Mathieu Ngudjolo Chui, Warrant of Arrest for Mathieu Ngudjolo Chui*, No.: ICC-01/04-02/07-1-tENG, unsealed pursuant to Decision ICC-01/04-02/07-10 dated 7/02/2008(where Pre-Trial Chamber I avoided the idea of *prima facie* determination and decided that the case against Mathieu Ngudjolo Chui "is admissible".

effectiveness of the complementarity regime in light of these provisions. There are some apparent gaps, however, that merit attention.

Through Article 18 States are given early notice of the Court's interest in a situation, permitting them to inform it of their own investigations and prosecutions. This provision clearly reflects an effective complementarity practice that works in favour of States. Yet the provision reduces the chance for the ICC to assert jurisdiction when it is supposed to step in. If the State receiving the information is not acting *bona fide*, the notification procedure could be very dangerous to the preservation of evidence. Moreover, the Rules of Procedure and Evidence render the situation more critical, since Rule 52(2) allows the State concerned to seek additional information. Accordingly, this weakens the second feature of complementarity. Although, the main goal of introducing a regime of complementarity is to provide States with primary responsibility, the regime should not be understood and applied in such a manner as to defeat the main purpose of creating an ICC by rendering the Court useless. Article 18(3) and (5) seems to balance the equation by permitting the ICC Prosecutor to supervise the proceedings undertaken by the national courts. Thus, this provision strengthens the role of the ICC.

Another observation regarding Article 18 is that it grants States a second chance to challenge the admissibility of a case under Article 19. This provision is unclear as it fails to spell out what sort of significant new facts or change of circumstances may be required to trigger this provision. It does not clarify whether the change of circumstance is relevant to a State's intention or attitude. A State which was deemed unable or unwilling for reasons regarding the collection of evidence and taking action may become able to carry out the proceedings. But if this was the intended meaning, it would appear problematic, because it is hardly doubtful for the Court to trust a State which has previously shown bad faith to continue carrying out domestic proceedings. This demonstrates that the drafters' desire was to build a strong complementarity regime that served the interests of States' rather than the Court.

Article 19, which appears to be broader than Article 18, poses other critical questions which could affect the appropriate application of complementarity. It covers only "cases" as opposed to "situations" under Articles 15, 18 and 53 of the Statute. So far, the Court's practice has demonstrated that the distinction between "situations" and "cases" requires delicate treatment. The deviation of approach caused by the jurisprudence of Pre-Trial Chambers I and II in relation to the time where a case stage begins[9] is self-evident.

The formulation of Articles 19(2)(b) and 17 may cause problems of interpretation. Article 17(1) lacks any reference to a situation where the accused was prosecuted but the State decided not to try him or her. Article 17(1) read together with Article 19(2)(b) may cause some confusion. A similar problem emerges from a reading of the chapeau of Article 19(2) together with Article 19(2)(b). The chapeau refers to challenges to admissibility on the grounds referred to in Article 17. Article 19(2)(b), on the con-

9 While Pre-Trial Chamber I considered that a "case" stage begins only after the issue of an arrest warrant, nothing in the corresponding decision of Pre-Trial Chamber II supports this conclusion.

trary, limits those challenges to situations found under Article 17(1)(a) – (b), thereby omitting the other possibilities set out in Article 17(1)(c) – (d).

By contrast, provisions such as Article 19(4) would certainly assist in reducing delays and the number of unnecessary admissibility challenges. The provisions of Article 19(8) in conjunction with Article 18(6) are also significant, and hopefully will help the Prosecutor in preserving the effectiveness of the Court's investigations. Also, Article 19(10) draws the balance between the two complementarity features explained above. While the provision ensures the primacy of national investigations, it does not interfere with the Court's powers to obtain primacy over the case if new facts have arisen that prove the Court's initial decision on deferment to have been unfounded. In making such assessment, Article 19(11) seems to impose an obligation on the relevant State to make available to the Prosecutor information concerning the domestic proceedings allegedly being carried out by the State. This reduces the fear of unwarranted domestic investigations that are aimed at evading justice. The main problem, however, is that the provision does not seem to impose an obligation on the State to provide information "without undue delay" in a sort of *systematic manner* comparable to the strict requirements of Article 18(5).

A final observation relevant to the application of complementarity in the light of the procedural regime of Articles 18 and 19 is the implications of self-referrals and waivers of complementarity within the scope of these provisions. As stated earlier, self-referrals and waivers of complementarity do not seem to raise major legal concerns *per se*. Chapter III proved this claim in the light of the provisions of the Statute as well as the jurisprudence of the Court. Yet, a waiver may seem to some as having a bearing on admissibility determinations by the Court through the procedural regime of Articles 18 and 19 of the Statute. While the procedural regime under the Statute does not exempt the Court from testing admissibility during Article 18 proceedings, it does permit bypassing the admissibility examination during the Article 19 stage, if the Court was acting *ex officio* or if admissibility has not been challenged by any of the parties covered by Article 19(2) (uncontested admissibility). Also the question whether a State, which initially waived its primacy to the Court may regain the right to exercise jurisdiction over the case deserves closer consideration.

The last requirement regarding the complementarity test that merits some attention is Article 20(3), which monitors domestic proceedings during the trial stage. Notably, Article 20(3) (a)–(b) copies the criteria set out in Article 17(2) for determining a State's "unwillingness". Moreover, Article 20(3) is relevant to the finding of *inadmissibility* in accordance with Article 17(1). Hence, there is clear interplay between these provisions. The Court ought to take into consideration several observations concerning the application of Article 20(3).

First, the interpretation given to admissibility criteria listed under Article 17(2)(a) – (c) may apply *mutatis mutandis* to those set out in Article 20(3)(a) – (b). Secondly, there is a diversity of opinion whether the Court should interfere on the basis of complementarity in cases where domestic courts have tried a person on the basis of an ordinary crime. Thirdly, the reference to the term "proceedings" in the chapeau of Article 20(3) may lead to confusion and different findings depending on the scope to be given to the term. Whether the term applies only to the proceedings conducted during the trial stage or those covering the entire process remains unclear. Paragraph (3) is also silent with respect to whether the trial of the national court should reach a decision and what sort of decision is required. These questions require further attention to avoid any difficulty of interpretation that may arise in the future.

The provisions implementing complementarity are complex and often call for difficult subjective assessments by the Court and its Prosecutor. Certainly, one of the biggest weaknesses of the complementarity regime lies in the failure of the Statute to include provisions relating to pardons. The lacuna may allow a State to investigate, prosecute, convict and sentence a person, and then pardon him soon thereafter. The possibility exists and there is a clear example in the present study concerning this issue. The *travaux préparatoires* indicate that the question was raised on several occasions but was not included in the final package.

Complementarity is an intellectually simple concept that masks the deep philosophical and political difficulties that the ICC must overcome if it is ever to become an effectively functioning institution. The drafters of the ICC Statute and the delegates who negotiated the Rules of Procedure and Evidence clearly understood that the ICC should not be the Court of first resort. However, the political will which prevailed during the whole drafting process led to some being ignorant of the significant legal issues. These issues will inevitably cause problems for the Prosecutor and the Court when dealing with future cases. The provisions addressed in this book make this fact self-evident and are formulated in a manner which reflects the continuous tension between national jurisdictions and the ICC. The Court can overcome these obstacles if it deals with each situation on a *case-by-case* basis. Some cases will require a broad construction of the Statute, while others will require the restriction of the reading of some provisions. The current policy of the Office of the Prosecutor will hopefully contribute to reducing the tension reflected in the complementarity procedural mechanism explored above. The Office introduced a new dimension to the understanding and application of the principle of complementarity, known as "positive" complementarity. This is considered to be one of the three main elements shaping the policy of the Office of the Prosecutor that far exceeds the classical understanding and application of the principle. The positive side of complementarity encourages States to carry out their own investigations with the support and assistance of the International Criminal Court. This guarantees the reduction of the impunity gap and, to some extent, of the conflict created by the already established complementarity procedural regime, by avoiding unnecessary admissibility challenges. As argued in Chapter IV, positive complementarity does not pose problems from a legal point of view. The idea certainly finds support from different provisions of the Statute, yet it should be exercised with some caution in order to ensure the independence and effectiveness of the Court.

It is clear that the Statute lacks any direct form of enforcement. Thus, the effectiveness of the Court will rely solely on States' cooperation. States themselves could make the ICC effective, and could render it useless. Yet, it is not certain whether the State that has been deemed "unwilling" will effectively cooperate with the Court. The *Darfur* situation is a case in point. The Prosecutor's reports to the Security Council show that Sudan attempted to meet the admissibility threshold of the Statute. The

Prosecutor still found that some cases falling within the jurisdiction of the Court and within the scope of his Office were not dealt with before the Sudanese courts.[10] The recent decision by the Prosecutor to summon Harun and Kushayb as bearing the greatest responsibility for crimes against humanity and war crimes committed in Darfur in 2003 and 2004[11] led Sudan to decide to refrain from further cooperation with the Court. "It is not even a question of cooperation any more, it's a question that [the ICC] want to try Sudanese citizens, which is absolutely nonsensical", said the Sudanese Minister for Justice.[12] The Sudanese government even decided to refrain from contesting admissibility in accordance with Article 19(2)(b) of the Statute.[13] This was not the case in the Uganda and DRC proceedings, which, as explored earlier, found their way to the Court by way of self-referrals. This shows one positive aspect of the theories of self-referral and waiver, since they merely rely on the idea of voluntary relinquishment of jurisdiction.

In the case of DRC, the Prosecutor at a certain stage threatened to use his *proprio motu* powers. When the DRC agreed to the Court dealing with the situation, the Prosecutor encouraged the self-referral. Perhaps, this explains why the Prosecutor preferred self-referral to his *proprio motu* powers.

A final word concerning the complementarity regime was addressed by former ICTY Prosecutor Louise Arbour when she mentioned that the regime would work in favour of rich and against poor countries.[14] The Court and its Prosecutor can reasonably be expected to develop some guidelines and standards for evaluating domestic systems. These standards, if assessed in the light of the systems of the richer countries, would probably not be met by the poor countries. So far, the Court has failed to prove the opposite, since it has confined its focus to poor African countries, leaving the crimes committed by British soldiers against Iraqis untouched.

10 See e.g., *Fifth Report of the Prosecutor of the International Criminal Court to the UN Security Council Pursuant to UNSCR 1593 (2005)*, 7 June 2007, p. 8.

11 See *Situation in Darfur*, Prosecutor's Application under Article 58(7), No.: ICC-02/05-56, 27 February 2007; Rome Statute, Art. 58 (7).

12 Associated Press, 'Sudan Announces It Will Suspend Cooperation with International Criminal Court', March 18, 2007, available at <http://www.iht.com/articles/ap/2007/03/18/africa/AF-GEN-Sudan-ICC.php>, last visited March 31, 2007; See also other statements made by Sudanese Foreign Affairs and Justice Ministers, *Sixth Report of the Prosecutor of the International Criminal Court to the UN Security Council Pursuant to UNSCR 1593(2005)*, 5 December 2007, p. 3.

13 Wasil Ali, 'Sudan Rules Out Plans to Challenge ICC Jurisdiction over Darfur', Sudan Tribune, March 18, 2007, available at, <http://www.sudantribune.com/spip.php?article20845>, last visited March 31, 2007.

14 William A. Schabas, *An Introduction to the International Criminal Court*, 2nd ed., (Cambridge: Cambridge University Press, 2004), p. 86.

Bibliography

Books

Almond, Nina, and Lutz, Ralph, Haswell, (eds.), *The Treaty of St. Germain: A Documentary History of Its Territorial and Political Clauses: With A Survey of the Documents of the Supreme Council of the Paris Peace Conference,* (California: Stanford University Press, 1935)

Arnold, Roberta, *The ICC as a New Instrument for Repressing Terrorism,* (Ardsley, New York: Transnational Publishers, 2004)

Bass, Gary, Jonathan, *Stay the Hand of Vengeance: The Politics of War Crimes Tribunals,* (Princeton and Oxford: Princeton University Press, 2000)

Bassiouni, M., Cherif, *The Legislative History of the International Criminal Court: Introduction, Analysis,* and Integrated Text of the Statute, Elements of Crimes and Rules of Procedure and Evidence, Vol. I, (Ardsley, New York, Transnational Publishers, 2005)

Bassiouni, M., Cherif, *The Legislative History of the International Criminal Court: An Article by Article Evolution of the Statute from 1994 – 1998,* Vol. II, (Ardsley, New York, Transnational Publishers, 2005)

Bassiouni, M., Cherif, *The Legislative History of the International Criminal Court: Introduction, Analysis,* and Integrated Text, Vol.I, (Ardsley, New York, Transnational Publishers, 2005)

Bassiouni, M., Cherif, *A Draft International Criminal Code and Draft Statute for an International Criminal Tribunal,* (Dordrecht /Boston / Lancaster: Martinus Nijhoff Publishers, 1987)

Bassiouni, M., Cherif, *Al Mahkama Al Genaia Al Dewaliah: Nashatoha Wa Nezameha Al Asasy Maa Derasah Ltarikh Legan Al Tahkik Al Dewaliah Wa Al Mahakem Al Genaia Al Dewaliah Al Sabekah* (The International Criminal Court: Its Establishment and Its Statute with a Study of the History of the International Investigative Commissions & The Former International Criminal Tribunals), (Cairo: Nadi Al Koudah, 2001)

Bassiouni, M., Cherif, *Al Mahkama Al Genaia Al Dowaliah: Madkhal Lederaset Ahkam wa Aliate Al Infaz Alwatani Lelnizam Al Asassy* (The International Criminal Court: Studying the Rome Statute's mechanisms for National Implementing Legislation), (Cairo: Dar-Al Sherouk, 2004)

Bassiouni, M., Cherif, and Paust, Jordan, et al., *International Criminal Law Cases and Materials,* 2nd ed., (Durham, North Carolina: Carolina Academic Press, 2000)

Bassiouni, M., Cherif, and Wise, Edward, M., *Aut Dedere Aut Judicare: The Duty to Extradite or Prosecute in International Law*, (Dordrecht/Boston/London: Martinus Nijhoff, 1995)

Bassiouni, M., Cherif, *Crimes Against Humanity in International Criminal Law*, 2nd rev. ed., (The Hague/London/Boston: Kluwer Law International, 1999)

Bassiouni, M., Cherif, *Crimes Against Humanity in International Criminal Law* (Dordrecht/Boston/London: Martinus Nijhoff Publishers, 1992)

Bassiouni, M., Cherif, *International Extradition: United States Law and Practice*, 3 rd ed., (Dobbs Ferry, New York: Ocean Publications, 1996)

Bassiouni, M., Cherif, *International Terrorism: Multilateral Conventions (1937-2001)*, (Ardsley, New York: Transnational Publishers, 2001)

Bassiouni, M., Cherif, *Introduction to International Criminal Law*, (Ardsley, New York: Transnational Publishers, 2003)

Bassiouni, M., Cherif, *The Law of the International Criminal Tribunal for the Former Yugoslavia* (Irvington-on-Hudson, New York: Transnational Publishers, 1996)

Bérenger, Jean, *A History of the Habsburg Empire 1273-1700*, (London, New York: Longman, 1994)

Bodin, Jean, *Les Six Livres de la République*, (A Paris: chez Jacques du Puys, 1577) [VIII]

Brierly, J.L., *The Law of Nations: An Introduction to the International Law of Peace*, 6 th ed., (Oxford: Clarendon Press, 1963)

Broomhall, Bruce, *International Justice and The International Criminal Court*, (Oxford: Oxford University Press, 2003)

Brownlie, Ian, *Principles of Public International Law*, 6 th ed., (Oxford: Oxford University Press, 2003)

Bush, M., L., *Renaissance, Reformation and the Outer World*, 2nd ed., (London: Blandford Press, 1971)

Calmette, Joseph, *The Golden Age of Burgundy: The Magnificent Dukes and their Courts*, (Great Britain: Weidenfeld & Nicolson, 1962)

Caloyanni, Mégalos, A., *La Justice Pénale Internationale*, (Pologne: Varsovie, (1929)

Campbell, Christian, T., *International Civil Procedures*, (New York, London, Hamburg: Lloyd's of London Press, 1995)

Capra, Fritjof, *The Tao of Physics: An Explanation of the Parallels Between Modern Physics and Eastern Mysticism*, 3 rd ed, (Great Britain: Flamingo, 1992)

Carnegie Endowment for International Peace (Division of International Law), *Reports of Majority and Dissenting Reports of American and Japanese Members of the Commission of Responsibilities: Conference of Paris 1919*, (Oxford: Clarendon Press, 1919)

Cassese, Antonio, *International Law*, 2 nd ed., (Oxford: Oxford University Press, 2005)

Cassese, Antonio, *International Criminal Law*, (Oxford: Oxford University Press, 2003)

Cassese, Antonio, "From Nuremberg to Rome: International Military Tribunals to the International Criminal Court", in Cassese, Antonio, et al., (eds.), *The Rome Statute of the International Criminal Court*, Vol. I, (Oxford: Oxford University Press, 2002)

Cassese, Antonio, *International Law*, (Oxford: Oxford University Press, 2001)

Chalk, Frank and Jonassohn, Kurt, *The History And Sociology of Genocide: Analysis and Case Studies*, (New Haven &London: Yale University Press, 1999)

Clayton, Richard, and Tomlinson, Hugh, *The Law of Human Rights*, (Oxford: Oxford University Press, 2000)

Collins English Dictionary: 21st Century Edition, 5 th ed., (Collins: Harper Collins Publishers, 2001)

Crawford, James, *The Creation of States in International Law*, 2 nd ed., (Oxford: Oxford University Press, 2006)

Crawford, James, *The International Law Commission's Articles on State Responsibility: Introduction, Text and Commentaries*, (Cambridge: Cambridge University Press, 2002)

Cryer, Robert, *Prosecuting International Crimes: Selectivity and the International Criminal Law Regime*, (Cambridge: Cambridge University Press, 2005)

Deák, Francis, *Hungary at the Paris Peace Conference: The Diplomatic History of the Treaty of Trianon*, (New York: Morningside Heights: Columbia University Press, 1942)

De Barante, M., *Histoire Des Ducs De Bourgogne De La Maison De Valois, 1364-1477*, Vol. VIII, (Bruxelles, 1839)

Dixon, Martin and McCorquodale, Robert, *Cases and Materials on International Law*, 3 rd ed., (Great Britain: Blackstone Press Limited, 2000)

Dubin, Martin, David, *International Terrorism: Two League of Nations Conventions, 1934-1937*, (Millwood, New York: Kraus Microform, 1991)

Eisberg, Robert and Resnick, Robert, *Quantum Physics of Atoms, Molecules, Solids, Nuclei, and Particles*, (New York. London: John Wiley and Sons, 1974).

Ferdinandusse, Ward, N., *Direct Application of International Criminal Law in National Courts*, (The Hague: T.M.C. Asser Press, 2006)

Ferencz, Benjamin, B., *An International Criminal Court: A Step Toward World Peace: A Documentary History*, (London. Rome. New York: Oceana Publications, 1980), 2 Volumes

Friedland, Martin, *Double Jeopardy*, (Oxford: Clarendon Press, 1969)

Garner, Bryan, A., (ed.), *Black's Law Dictionary*, Seventh Edition, (St. Paul, Minn.: West Group, 1999)

German War Trials: Report of the Proceedings before the Supreme Court in Leipzig, (London, 1921)

Goller-Calvo, Karin, N., *The Trial Proceedings of the International Criminal Court ICTY and ICTR Precedents*, (Leiden/Boston: Martinus Nijhoff Publishers, 2006)

Gove, Philip, Babcock et al., (eds.), *Webster's Third New International Dictionary of the English Language Unabridged*, (Germany: Ursula Schumer, 1993)

Gramm- Brauer, Hildburg, *Der Landvogt Peter von Hagenbach: Die Burgundische Herrschaft am Oberrhein 1469*-1474, (Musterschmidt-Verlag: Göttingen. Berlin. Frankfurt, 1957)

Grewe, Wilhelm, G., (ed.), *Fontes Historiae Iuris Gentium: Sources Relating to the History of the Law of Nations*, Vol. 2, Bd. 2 (1493 – 1815), (Berlin. New York: Walter de Gruyter, 1988)

Grotius, Hugo, *De Jure Belli Ac Pacis Libri Tres*, in Francis W. Kelsey et al., (eds.), (Oxford: Clarendon Press, 1925)

Hanks, Patrick (ed.), *The New Oxford Thesaurus of English*, (Oxford: Oxford University Press, 2000)

Hassan, Said, Abd-El Latif, *Al Mahkama Al Genaia Al Dowaliah (Inshaa Al Mahkamah-Nezameha Alassasy- Ikhtisasoha Al Tashriay wa Al Kadaiy)wa Tatbikat Al Kadaa Al Genaiy Al Dowaly Alhadith wa Al Moaaser (The International Criminal Court: The Establishment of the Court-Its Statute-Its Legislative and Judicial Competence) and the Application of the Contemporary International Criminal Justice)*, (Cairo: Dar Al-Nahda Al-Arabia, 2004)

Harris D., J., and O'Boyle, M., Warbrick, C., *Law of the European Convention on Human Rights*, (London, Dublin, Edinburgh: Butterworths, 1995)

Priscilla B. Hayner, *Unspeakable Truths: Facing the Challenge of Truth Commissions*, (New York: Rutledge, 2002)

Henig, Ruth, *Versailles and After1919-1933*, 2 nd ed., (London, New York: Routledge, 1995)

Hinsley, F. H., *Sovereignty*, 2 nd ed., (Cambridge: Cambridge University Press, 1986)

Hogg, Peter, *Constitutional Law of Canada*, 3 rd ed., (Scarborough: 1992)

Holton, Gerald, *Thematic Origins of Scientific Thought: Kepler to Einstein*, rev ed., (Cambridge, Massachusetts: Harvard University Press, 1988)

Hosney, Mahmoud, Nagib, *Deroose Fee Al Kanoon Al Genaie Al Dowaly* (Lessons in International Criminal Law), (Cairo: Dar Al-Nahda Al-Arabia, 1959 – 1960)

Jennings, Robert, and Watts, Arthur (eds.), *Oppenheim's International Law: Peace*, 9 th ed., Vol. I., (UK: Longman, 1992).

Kim, Young Sok, *The International Criminal Court: A Commentary of the Rome Statute*, (England. India. USA: Wisdom House, 2003)

Kirk, Foster, *History of Charles the Bold, Duke of Burgundy*, Vol. II (London: William Clowes & Sons, 1863)

Kittichaisaree, Kriangsak, *International Criminal Law* (Oxford: Oxford University Press, 2001)

Knebel, Johannes, *Capellani Ecclesiae Basiliensis Diarium*, (Basel,1880)

Lachs, Manfred, *War Crimes: An Attempt to Define the* Issues, (London: Stevens &Sons, 1945)

LeBlanc, Lawrence, J., *The United States and the Genocide Convention*, (Durham, London: Duke University Press, 1991)

Lemkin, Raphael, *Axis Rule in Occupied Europe*, (Carnegie Endowment for International Peace, (1944)

Levie, Howard, S., *Terrorism in War: The Law of War Crimes*, (Oceana Publications, 1993)

Luckau, Alma, Maria, *The German Delegation At the Paris Peace Conference: A Documentary Study of Germany's Acceptance of the Treaty of Versailles*, (New York: Columbia University Press, 1941)

Maogoto, Jackson, Nyamuya, *War Crimes and RealPolitik: International Justice from World War I to the 21st Century*, (Boulder, London: Lynne Rienner Publishers, 2004)

Mc Dermott, Paul, A., *Res Judicata and Double Jeopardy*, (Ireland: Butterworths, 1999)

McNair, A., D., *The Law of Treaties: British Practice and Opinions*, (Oxford: Clarendon Press, 1938)

McNair, A., D., *The Law of Treaties*, (Oxford: Clarendon Press, 1961)

Menon, P., K., *The Law of Treaties between States and International Organizations*, (Cambridge: Cambridge University Press, 1992)

Meron, Theodor, *The Humanization of International Law*, (Leiden. Boston: Martinus Nijhoff Publishers, 2006)

Miskowiak Kristina, *The International Criminal Court: Consent, Complementarity and Cooperation*, (Copenhagen: DJØF Publishing, 2000)

Morris, Virginia, and Scharf, Michael, P., *An Insider's Guide to the International Criminal Tribunal for the Former Yugoslavia*, Vol. I (Irvington-on-Hudson, New York: Transnational Publishers, 1995)

Mott, Rodney, L., *Due Process of Law: A Historical and Analytical Treaties of the Principles and Methods Followed by the Courts in the Application of the Concept of the "Law of the Land"*, (Indianapolis, 1926)

Mullins, Claud, *The Leipzig Trials: An Account of the War Criminals Trials and a Study of German Mentality*, (London: H. F. & G. Witherby, 1921)

Nowak, Manfred, *U.N. Covenant on Civil and Political Rights: CCPR Commentary*, 2 nd revised edition (Kehl/Strasbourg/Arlington: N.P. Engel Publisher, 2005)

Olásolo, Héctor, *The Triggering Procedure of the International Criminal Court*, (Leiden. Boston: Martinus Nijhoff Publishers, 2005)

Olusanya, Olaoluwa, *Double Jeopardy Without Parameters: Re-Characterisation in International Criminal Law*, (Antwerp – Oxford: Instersentia, 2004)

Oppenheim, L., *International Law: A Treatise, Disputes, War and Neutrality*, Vol. II., Sixth Impression, (London: Longmans, Green and Co Ltd., 1965)

Oppenheim, L., *International Law: A Treatise, Peace*, Vol. I., Eighth Impression, (London: Longmans, Green and Co Ltd., 1967)

Oppenheim, L., *International Law: A Treatise*, Vol. I. – Peace, 6 th ed., (London. New York. Toronto: Longmans &Co., 1947)

Papers Relating to the Foreign Relations of the United States: The Paris Peace Conference 1919, Vol. VIII, (Washington: Government Printing Office, 1946)

Papers Relating to the Foreign Relations of the United States: The Paris Peace Conference 1919, Vol. VII, (Washington: Government Printing Office, 1946)

Papers Relating to the Foreign Relations of the United States: The Paris Peace Conference 1919, Vol. V, (Washington: Government Printing Office, 1946)

Pearsall, Judy and Trumble, Bill (eds.), *The Oxford English Reference Dictionary*, 2 nd ed., (Oxford, New York: Oxford University Press, 1996).

Pella, Vespasien, V., *La Guerre – Crime et Les Criminels De Guerre*, (Genéve: ?, 1946)

Pella, Vespasien, V., *La Guerre-Crime et les Criminels de Guerre*, (Geneva: ?, 1964)

Power, Samantha, *A Problem From Hell: America and the Age of Genocide*, (New York: Basic Books, 2002)

Prefontaine, Daniel, International Criminal Court: Manual for the Ratification and Implementation of the Rome Statute (Vancouver, 2000)

Reeder, René, Marius, *The Establishment of an International Criminal Court: Some General Problems,* (Amsterdam: Uitgeverij en Drukkerij A. J. Nuss, 1962)

Rospigliosi, William, *The Swiss for the Non-Swiss,* (Maynooth: Aston Colour Press, 1995)

Sadat, Leila, Nadya, *The International Criminal Court and the Transformation of International Law: Justice for the New Millennium,* (Ardsley, New York: Transnational Publishers, 2002)

Safferling, Christoph, J., M., *Towards an International Criminal Procedure,* (Oxford: Oxford University Press, 2001)

Schabas, William, A., *Genocide in International Law: The Crimes of Crimes,* (Cambridge: Cambridge University Press, 2000)

Schabas, William, A., *International Human Rights Law and the Canadian Charter: A Manual for the Practitioner,* (Toronto. Calgary. Vancouver: Carswell, 1991)

Schabas, William, A., *An Introduction to the International Criminal Court,* 2nd ed., (Cambridge: Cambridge University Press, 2004)

Schabas, William, A., *An Introduction to the International Criminal Court,* 3 rd ed., (Cambridge: Cambridge University Press, forthcoming 2007)

Schabas, William, A., *The UN International Criminal Tribunals: The Former Yugoslavia, Rwanda and Sierra Leone,* (Cambridge: Cambridge University Press, 2006)

Scharf, Michael, and Schabas, William, A., *Slobodan Milosevic on Trial: A Companion,* (New York, London: Continum, 2002)

Schonfield, Hugh, J., *The Treaty of Versailles: The Essential Text and* Amendments, (London: Peace Book Company, 1940)

Schwarzenberger, George, *International Law,* Vol. I, 3rd ed., (London: Stevens & Sons Limited, 1957)

Schwarzenberger, Georg, *International Law As Applied By International Courts and Tribunals: The Law of Armed Conflict,* Vol. II, (London: Stevens & Sons Limited, 1968)

Sharp, Alan, *The Versailles Settlement: Peace Making in Paris,* (Hampshire: Palgrave, 1991)

Sigler, Jay, A., *Double Jeopardy: The Development of a Legal and Social Policy,* (Ithaca: Cornell University Press, 1969)

Sorour, Ahmed, Fathi, *Al Sharaiah Al Dostoriah wa Hokook Al Insan fee Al Igraat Al Genaiah* (Constitutional Legality and Human Rights in Criminal Procedures), rev ed., (Cairo: Dar Al-Nahda Al-Arabia, 1995)

Sottile, Antoine, *The Problem of the Creation of a Permanent International Criminal Court,* (Nendeln.Liechtenstein: Kraus Reprint Ltd., 1966)

Taylor, Telford, *The Anatomy of the Nuremberg Trials* (New York, 1992)

The International Law Association: Its Object, Origin, and Work, (London: Temple, 1910)

The Reichstag Trial Defence Committee, *Is Leipzig Fair?: A Note on the Methods of the Leipzig Trial During the First Period, September 21 to October 7,* (London: The Reichstag Trial Defence Committee, no publication date available)

The Treaties of Peace 1919-1923, Vol. I, (New York: Carnegie Endowment for International Peace, 1924)

Tomuschat, Christian, *Human Rights between Idealism and Realism*, (Oxford: Oxford University Press, 2003)

Trainin, Aron, Naumovich, *Hitlerite Responsibility under Criminal Law*, (London: New University Press, 2000). York, Hutchinson & Co., 1945)

Van Dijk, P., and Van Hoof, G., J., H., *Theory and Practice of the European Convention on Human Rights*, Third Edition, (The Hague-London-Boston: Kluwer Law International, 1998)

Watts, Arthur, *The International Law Commission 1949-1998: Volume Two: The Treaties, Part* II, (Oxford: Oxford University Press, 1999)

Werle, Gerhard, *Principles of International Criminal Law*, (The Hague: T.M.C. Asser Press, 2005)

Wheeler-Bennett J., W., and Nicholls A., *The Semblance of Peace, The Political Settlement after the Second World War*, (New York: St. Martin's Press, 1972)

William James, *The Principles of Psychology*, (United States: Harvard College, 1983)

Willis, James, F., *Prologue To Nuremberg: The Politics and Diplomacy of Punishing War Criminals of the First World War*, (Westport. Connecticut: Greenwood Press, 1982)

Williams, John, Fischer, *Chapters on Current International Law and the League of Nations*, (London. New York. Toronto: Longmans, Green and Co., 1929)

Woetzel, Robert, K., *The Nuremberg Trials in International Law*, (London: Stevens & Sons, 1960)

Yussef, Mohamed, Safy, *Al- Itar Alaam Lelkanoon Al Dowaly AlGenaiy fe Doa Ahkam AlNezam Alassay Lelmahkamah Al Genaia Al Dowaliah* (The General Frame of Criminal International Law in light of the Statute of the International Criminal Court), (Cairo: Dar Al-Nahda Al-Arabia, 2002)

Zappala, Salvatore, *Human Rights in International Criminal Proceedings*, (Oxford: Oxford University Press, 2003)

Articles

Abdelgawad, Walid, "Droit Égyptien", in Cassese, Antonio, et al., (eds.), *Jurisdictions Nationales et Crimes Internationaux*, (Paris: Puf, 2002)

Akhavan, Payam, 'The International Criminal Tribunal for Rwanda: The Politics and Pragmatic of Punishment', 90 *American Journal of International Law* 501(1996)

Akhavan, Payam, 'The *Lord's Resistance Army* Case: Uganda's Submission of the First State Referral to the International Criminal Court', 99 *American Journal of International Law* 403 (2005)

Amar, Akhil, Reed, 'Double Jeopardy Law Made Simple', 106 *Yale Law Journal* 1807 (1997)

Ambos, Kai, 'The International Criminal Court and the Traditional Principles of International Cooperation in Criminal Matters', 9 *Finnish Yearbook of International Law* 413 (1998)

Ambos, Kai, 'Establishing an International Criminal Court and an International Criminal Code – Observations from an International Criminal Law Viewpoint', 7 *European Journal of International Law* 519 (1996)

Apuuli, Kasaija, Philipp, 'The ICC Arrest Warrants for the Lord's Resistance Army Leaders and Peace Prospects for Northern Uganda', 4 *Journal of International Criminal Justice* 179 (2006)

Aravena, Claudia, Cárdenas, "The Admissibility Test Before the International Criminal Court under Special Consideration of Amnesties and Truth Commissions", in Kleffner, Jann, K., et al., (eds.), *Complementary Views on Complementarity: Proceedings of the International Roundtable on the Complementary Nature of the International Criminal Court*, Amsterdam, 25/26 June 2004, (The Hague: T.M.C. Asser Press, 2006)

Apuuli, Kasaija, Philip, 'The International Criminal Court (ICC) and the Lord's Resistence Army (LRA) Insurgency in Northern Uganda', 15 *Criminal Law Forum* 391 (2004)

Arbour, Louise and Bergsmo, Morten, "Conspicuous Absence of Jurisdictional Overreach", in von Hebel, Herman, A., M., et al., (eds.), *Reflections on the International Criminal Court*, (The Hague: T.M.C. Asser Press, 1999)

Arsanjani, Mahnoush, H., "Reflections on the Jurisdiction and Trigger Mechanism of the International Criminal Court", in von Hebel, Herman, A., M., et al., (eds.), *Reflections on the International Criminal Court*, (The Hague: T.M.C. Asser Press, 1999)

Arsanjani, Mahnoush, H., and Reisman, W., Michael, 'The Law-in Action of the International Criminal Court', 99 *American Journal of International Law* 385 (2005)

Baeza, Paz, Rojas, 'Impunity: An Impossible Reparation', 69 *Nordic Journal of International Law* 27 (2000)

Bassiouni, M., Cherif, 'Explanatory Note on the ICC Statute', 71 *Revue Internationale de Droit Penal* 1 (2000)

Bassiouni M., Cherif, 'From Versailles to Rwanda in Seventy-Five Years: The Need to Establish a Permanent International Criminal Court', 10 *Harvard Human Rights Journal* 11 (1997)

Bassiouni, M. Cherif, and Derby, Daniel, H., 'Final Report on the Establishment of an International Criminal Court for the Implementation of the Apartheid Convention and other Relevant International Instruments: Symposium on the Future of Human Rights in the World Legal Order', 9 *Hofstra Law Review* 523 (1980 – 1981)

Bassiouni, M., Cherif, 'Negotiating the Treaty of Rome on the Establishment of an International Criminal Court', 32 *Cornell International Law Journal*443 (1999)

Bassiouni, M., Cherif, 'The Time Has Come for an International Criminal Court', 1 *Indiana International & Comparative Law Review* 1 (1991)

Bassiouni, M., Cherif, 'Combating Impunity for International Crimes', 71 *University of Colorado Law Review* 409 (2000)

Bassiouni, M., Cherif, 'International Law and the Holocaust', 9 *California Western International Law Journal* 202 (1979)

Bassiouni, M., Cherif, 'Where is the ICC Heading? ; The ICC – *Quo Vadis?*', 4 *Journal of International Criminal Justice* 421 (2006)

Bassiouni, M., Cherif, "International Criminal Investigations and Prosecutions: From Versailles to Rwanda", in Bassiouni, M., Cherif (ed.), *International Criminal Law: Enforcement*, 2 nd ed., Vol. II (Ardsley, New York: Transnational Publishers, Inc, 1999)

Bassiouni, M., Cherif, World War I: "The War To End All Wars" and the Birth of a Handicapped International Criminal Justice System, 30 *Denver Journal of International Law and Policy* 244 (2002)

Behrens, Hans-Jörg, 'Investigation, Trial and Appeal in the International Criminal Court Statute (Parts V, VI, VIII)', 6 *European Journal of Crime, Criminal Law and Criminal Justice* 113 (1998)

Bekker, P., H., F., 'Provisional Measures in the Recent Practice of the International Court of Justice', 7 *International Law Forum du Droit International* 24 (2005)

Bekou, Olympia, Cryer, Robert, 'The International Criminal Court and Universal Jurisdiction: A Close Encounter?', 56 *International and Comparative Law Quarterly* 49 (2007)

Bellot, Hugh, H-L., 'La Cour Permanente Internationale Criminelle', 3 *Revue Internationale de Droit Pénal* 333 (1926)

Benzing, Markus, 'The Complementarity Regime of the International Criminal Court: International Criminal Justice Between State Sovereignty and the Fight Against Impunity', 7 *Max Planck Yearbook of United Nations Law* 591 (2003)

Benvenuti, Paolo, "Complementarity of the International Criminal Court to National Criminal Jurisdictions", in Lattanzi, Flavia, et al., (eds.), *Essays on the Rome Statute of the International Criminal Court,* Vol. I (Italy: Il Sirente, 1999)

Berg, Bradley E., 'The 1994 I.L.C. Draft Statute for an International Criminal Court: A Principled Appraisal of Jurisdictional Structure', 28 *Case Western Reserve Journal of International Law* 221(1996)

Bergsmo, Morten, 'Occasional Remarks on Certain State Concerns about the Jurisdictional Reach of the International Criminal Court, and Their Possible Implications for the Relationship Between the Court and the Security Council', 69 *Nordic Journal of International Law* 87 (2000)

Bergsmo, Morten, 'The Jurisdictional Régime of the International Criminal Court (Part II, Articles 11 – 19)', 6 *European Journal of Crime, Criminal Law and Criminal Justice* 29 (1998)

Bergsmo, Morten, Pejic, Jelena, "Prosecutor", in Triffterer, Otto, (ed.), *Commentary on the Rome Statute of the International Criminal Court: Observers' Notes, Article by Article,* (Baden – Baden: Nomos Verlagsgesellschaft, 1999)

Billings, Warren, M., 'Pleading, Procedure, and Practice: The Meaning of Due Process of Law in Seventeenth-Century Virginia', 47 *The Journal of Southern History* 569 (1981) Brennan, William, J., 'International Due Process and the Law', 48 *Virginia Law Review* 1258 (1962)

Blackburn, Thomas, R., 'Sensuous- Intellectual Complementarity in Science', 172 *Science* 1003 (1971)

Blakesley, Christopher, L., "Extraterritorial Jurisdiction", in Bassiouni, M., Cherif, (ed.), *International Criminal Law: Procedural and Enforcement Mechanisms,* 2 nd ed., (Ardsley: Transnational Publishers, 1999)

Bleich, L., Jeffrey, 'The International Criminal Court: Report of the ILA Working Group on Complementarity', 25 *Denver Journal of International Law and Policy* 281 (1997)

Bleichrodt, Edwin, "*Ne Bis In Idem* (Article 4 of Protocol No. 7)", in Van Dijk, Pieter et al., (eds.), *Theory and Practice of the European Convention on Human Rights,* 4 th ed., (Antwerpen – Oxford: Intersentia, 2006)

Bleich, L., Jeffrey, 'Complementarity', 13 *Nouvelles études pénales* 245(1997)

Bohlander, Michael, 'Referring an Indictment from the ICTY and ICTR to another Court – Rule 11 *Bis* and the Consequences for the Law of Extradition', 55 *International and Comparative Law Quarterly* 219 (2006)

Bohr, Niels, 'On the Notions of Causality and Complementarity', 111 *Science* 51 (1950)

Bohr, Niels, 'Mathematics and Natural Philosophy', 82 *The Scientific Monthly* 85(1956)

Born, M., 'Physics and Metaphysics', 82 *The Scientific Monthly* 229(1956)

Born, Max, 'Statistical Interpretation of Quantum Mechanics', 122 *Science* 675 (1955)

Bos, Adriaan, "From the International Law Commission to the Rome Conference (1994 – 1998)" in Cassese, Antonio, et al., (eds.), *The Rome Statute of the International Criminal Court*, Vol. I, (Oxford: Oxford University Press, 2002)

Boven, Theo, Van, "The Principle of Complementarity: The International Criminal Court and National Laws", in Wouters, Jan et al., (eds.), *De Genocidewet in Internationaal perspectief*, (Brussel: Larcier, 2002)

Brady, Helen, Jennings, Mark, "Appeal and Revision", in Lee, Roy, S., (ed.), *The International Criminal Court: The Making of the Rome Statute, Issues. Negotiations. Results*, (The Hague. London. Boston: Kluwer Law International, 1999)

Branch, Adam, 'Uganda's Civil War and the Politics of ICC Intervention', 21 *Ethics and International Affairs* 179 (2007)

Bridge, John, W., 'The Case for an International Criminal Court of Criminal Justice and the Formulation of International Criminal Law', 13 *International & Comparative Law Quarterly* 1255 (1964)

Brierly, J., L., 'Do We Need An International Criminal Court?',8 *British Yearbook of International Law* 81(1927)

Brown, Bartram, S., 'Primacy or Complementarity: Reconciling the Jurisdiction of National Courts and International Criminal Tribunals', 23 *Yale Journal of International Law* 383 (1998)

Brown, Philip, Marshal, 'From Sévres to Lausanne', 18 *American Journal of International Law* 113 (1924)

Brown, Philip, Marshal, 'International Criminal Justice', 35 *American Journal of International Law* 118 (1941)

Brubacher, Mathew, R., 'Prosecutorial Discretion within the International Criminal Court', 2 *Journal of International Criminal Justice* 71(2004)

Bub, Jeffrey, "Complementarity", in Lerner, Rita, G., et al., (eds.), *Encyclopedia of Physics*, (London. Amsterdam: Addison-Wesley Publishing, 1981)

Buergenthal, Thomas, "Truth Commissions Functions and Due Pocess", in Tomuschat, Christian, et al., (eds.), *Völkerrecht als Wertordnung. Common Values in International Law*, (Kehl, Germany: N.P. Engel Verlag , 2006)

Buergenthal, Thomas, "To Respect and to Ensure: State Obligations and Permissible Derogations", in Henkin, Louis, (ed.), *The International Bill of Human Rights: The Covenant on Civil and Political Rights*, (New York: Columbia University Press, 1981)

Burke-White, William, 'A Community of Courts: Toward a System of International Criminal law Enforcement', 24 *Michigan Journal of International Law* 1 (2003)

Burke-White, William, W., 'Complementarity in Practice: The International Criminal Court as Part of a System of Multi-level Global Governance in the Democratic Republic of Congo', 18 *Leiden Journal of International Law* 557 (2005)

Burke-White, William, W., 'Implementing a Policy of Positive Complementarity in the Rome Statute of Justice', 18 *Criminal Law Forum* (forthcoming 2007)

Bush, Jonathan, A., '"The Supreme...Crime" and its Origins: The Lost Legislative History of the Crime of Aggressive War', 102 *Columbia Law Review* 2324 (2002)

Caloyanni, M., A., 'Memorandum on International Criminal Legislation and Peace', 17 *Revue Internationale de Droit Penal* 305 (1946)

Caloyanni, Mégalos A., 'La Guerre-Crime et Les Criminels de Guerre', 17 *Revue Internationale de Droit Penal* 6 (1946)

Caloyanni, M., Mégalos A., 'The Permanent International Court of Criminal Justice', 2 *Revue Internationale de Droit Pénal* 326 (1925)

Cameron, Iain, "Jurisdiction and Admissibility Issues under the ICC Statute", in McGoldrick, Dominic, et al., (eds.), *The Permanent International Criminal Court: Legal and Policy Issues*, (Oxford and Portland Oregon: Hart Publishing, 2004)

Cassese, Antonio, 'Is the ICC Still Having Teething Problems?', 4 *Journal of International Criminal Justice* 434 (2006)

Cassese, Antonio, 'The Statute of the International Criminal Court: Some Preliminary Reflections', 10 *European Journal of International Law*144 (1999)

Chadwick, Elizabeth, 'A Tale of Two Courts: The 'Creation' of a Jurisdiction?', 9 *Journal of Conflict & Security Law* 71 (2004)

Ciampi, Annalisa, 'The International Criminal Court', 4 *The Law and Practice of International Courts and Tribunals* 165 (2005)

Clapham, Andrew, "Issues of Complexity, Complicity and Complementarity: From the Nuremberg trials to the Dawn of the New International Criminal Court", in Sands, Philippe, (ed.), *From Nuremberg to the Hague: The Future of International Criminal Justice*, (Cambridge: Cambridge University Press, 2003)

Clark, Roger, S. and Madelein Sann, 'Coping with Ultimate Evil through the Criminal Law', 7 *Criminal Law Forum* 1 (1996)

Clark, Roger, S., 'Creating a Statute for the International Criminal Court: A Jurisdictional Quandary', 22 *Suffolk Transnational Law Review* 461 (1999)

Clark, Roger, S., 'The Mental Element in International Criminal Law: The Rome Statute of the International Criminal Court and the Elements of Offences', 12 *Criminal Law Forum* 291 (2001)

Clark, Roger, S., "Crimes against Humanity and the Rome Statute of the International Criminal Court", in Politi, Mauro, et al., (eds.), *The Rome Statute of the International Criminal Court*, Aldershot. Burlington. USA. Singapore. Sydney: Ashgate Dartmouth, 2001)

Clark, Roger, S., "Nuremberg and Tokyo in Contemporary Perspective", in McCormack , Timothy, L.H., et al., (eds.), *The Law of War Crimes: National and International Approaches*, (The Hague/London/Boston: Kluwer Law International, 1997)

Concannon, Brian, 'Beyond Complementarity: The International Criminal Court and National Prosecutions, A View from Haiti', 32 *Columbia Human Rights Law Review* 201 (2000)

Conway, Gerard, '*Ne Bis In Idem* in International Law', 3 *International Criminal Law Review* 217 (2003)

Crawford, James, 'Prospects for an International Criminal Court', 48 *Current Legal Problems* 303 (1995)

Crawford, James, "The Drafting of the Rome Statute", in Sands, Philippe (ed.), *From Nuremberg to the Hague: The Future of International Criminal Justice*, (Cambridge: Cambridge University Press, 2003).

Crawford, James, "The Work of the International Law Commission", in Cassese, Antonio, et al., (eds.), *The Rome Statute of the International Criminal Court*, Vol. I, (Oxford: Oxford University Press, 2002)

Crnic-Grotic, V., 'Object and Purpose of Treaties in the Vienna Convention on the Law of Treaties', 7 *Asian Yearbook of International Law* 141 (1997)

Cryer, Robert and Bekou, Olympia, 'International Crimes and ICC Cooperation in England and Wales', doi:10.1093/jicj/mq1083, 22 February 2007

D'Amato, Anthony, "Good Faith", in Bernhardt, Rudolf, (ed.), *Encyclopedia of Public International Law*, Vol. II (Amsterdam: North Holland, 1995)

Dadrian, Vahakn, N., 'Genocide as a Problem of National and International Law: The World War I Armenian Case and Its Contemporary Legal Ramifications', 14 *Yale Journal of International Law* 221 (1989)

Dadrian, Vahakn, N., 'The Armenian Genocide and the Legal and Political Issues in the Failure to Prevent or To Punish the Crime', 29 *The University of West Los Angeles Law Review* 43 (1998)

Dadrian, Vahakn, N., 'The Historical and Legal Interconnections Between the Armenian Genocide and the Jewish Holocaust: From Impunity to Retributive Justice', 23 *Yale Journal of International Law* 503 (1998)

Dadrian, Vahakn, N., "Armenian Genocide, Court-Martial of Perpetrators", in Charny, Israel, W., (ed.), *Encyclopedia of* Genocide, Vol. I, (Denver, Colorado, Oxford, England: ABC-CLIO, 1999)

Dautricourt, J., Y., "The International Criminal Court: The Concept of International Criminal Jurisdiction – Definition and Limitation of the Subject", in Bassiouni, M., Cherif, et al., (eds.), *A Treatise on International Criminal Law: Crimes and Punishment*, Vol. I, (Springfield. Illinois. U.S.A.: Charles C Thomas Publisher, 1973)

Delmas-Marty, Mireille, 'Integrations between National and International Criminal Law in the Preliminary Phase of Trial at the ICC', 4 *Journal of International Criminal Justice* 2 (2006)

Dembowski, Larry, Charles, "The International Criminal Court: Complementarity and Its Consequences", in Stromseth, Jane, E. (ed.), *Accountability for Atrocities: National and International Responses*, (Ardsley, New York: Transnational Publishers, 2003)

De Vabres, H., Donnedieu, 'La Cour Permanente De Justice Internationale et Sa Vocation en Matière Criminelle', 1 *Revue Internationale de Droit Pénal* 175 (1924)

De Vabres, H., Donnedieu, 'Les Problems De La Justice Penale Internationale', 30 *Revue de Droit International de Sciences Diplomatiques et Politiques* 156 (1952)

De Vabres, H., Donnedieu, 'Some Observations on the Scheme for the Establishment of a Permanent International Criminal Court', 30 *Revue de Droit International de Sciences Diplomatiques et Politiques* 227(1952)

De Vabres, Henri, Donnedieu, 'De L'Organisation d'une Jurisdiction Penale Internationale', 20 *Revue Internationale de Droit Penal* 1(1949)

Dickerson, Allen, J., 'Who's in Charge Here?--International Criminal Court Complementarity and the Commander's Role in Courts-Martial', 54 *Naval Law Review* 141 (2007)

Doherty, Katherine L. and McCormack, Timothy, L., H., '"Complementarity" as a Catalyst for Comprehensive Domestic Penal Legislation', 5 *University of California Davis Journal of International Law & Policy* 147 (1999)

Domb, Fania, 'Treatment of War Crimes in Peace Settlements – Prosecution or Amnesty?', 24 *Israel Yearbook on Human Rights* 253 (1994)

Doty, Patricia J., 'Complementarity and its Analogies', 55 *The Journal of Philosophy* 1089 (1958)

Dugard, John, 'Obstacles in the Way of an International Criminal Court', 56 *Cambridge Law Journal* 329 (1997)

Dugard, John, 'Towards the Definition of International Terrorism', 67 *American Society of International Law Proceedings* 94 (1973)

Dumas, Jacques, 'Y A-T-IL Des Crimes Internationaux', 59 *Revue de Droit International et de Législation Comparée* 721(1932)

Eckhardt, William George, 'My Lai: An American Tragedy', 68 *University of Missouri Kansas-City Law Review* 671 (2000)

El Zeidy, Mohamed, M., 'The Gravity Threshold Under the Statute of the International Criminal Court', 19 *Criminal Law Forum* (forthcoming 2008)

El Zeidy, Mohamed, M., 'Critical Thoughts on Article 59(2) of the ICC Statute', 4 *Journal of International Criminal Justice* 448 (2006)

El Zeidy, Mohamed, M., 'Some Remarks on the Question of the Admissibility of a Case During Arrest Warrant Proceedings before the International Criminal Court', 19 *Leiden Journal of International Law* 741(2006)

El Zeidy, Mohamed, M., 'Egypt and Current Efforts to Criminalize International Crimes', 5 *International Criminal Law Review* 247 (2005)

El Zeidy, Mohamed, M., 'The Ugandan Government Triggers the First Test of the Complementarity Principle: An Assessment of the First State's Party Referral to the ICC', 5 *International Criminal Law Review* 83 (2005)

El Zeidy, Mohamed, M., 'The ECHR and States of Emergency: Article 15 – A Domestic Power of Derogation from Human Rights Obligations', 4 *San Diego International Law Journal* 277 (2003)

El Zeidy, Mohamed, 'The Doctrine of Double Jeopardy in International Criminal and Human Rights Law', 6 *Mediterranean Journal of Human Rights* 183 (2002)

El Zeidy, Mohamed, M., 'The Principle of Complementarity: A New Machinery To Implement International Criminal Law', 23 *Michigan Journal of International Law* 869 (2002)

El Zeidy, Mohamed, M., Stahn, Carsten and Olásolo, Héctor, 'The International Criminal Court's Ad Hoc Jurisdiction Revisited', 99 *American Journal of International Law* 421 (2005)

Enache-Brown, Colleen and Fried, Ari, 'Universal Crime, Jurisdiction and Duty: The Obligation of Aut Dedere Aut Judicare in International Law', 43 *McGill Law Journal* 613 (1998)

Englard, Izhak, "The Idea of Complementarity as a Philosophical Basis for Pluralism in Tort Law," in David G. Owen (ed.), *Philosophical Foundations of Tort Law*, (New York. Oxford: Clarendon Press, 1995)

Feller, S., Z., 'Concurrent Criminal Jurisdiction in the International Sphere', 16 *Israel Law Review* 40 (1981)

Ferencz, Benjamin, B., 'An International Criminal Code and Court: Where they Stand and Where they're Going', 30 *Columbia Journal of Transnational Law* 375 (1992)

Ferencz, Benjamine, B., 'The Draft Code of Offences Against the Peace and Security of Mankind', 75 *American Journal of International Law* 647 (1981)

Ferencz, Benjamine, B., 'Nuremberg Trial Procedure and the Rights of the Accused', 39 *Journal of Criminal Law & Criminology* 144 (1948 – 1949)

Ferri, M., Enrico, 'The Italian Criminology at the International Congresses of Brussels and Vienna', 4 *Revue Internationale de Droit Pénal* 156 (1927)

Fife, Rolf, Einar, 'The International Criminal Court: *Whence It Came, Where it Goes*', 69 *Nordic Journal of International Law* 63 (2000)

Finch, George, A., 'Draft Statute for an International Criminal Court', 46, *American Journal of International Law* 89 (1952)

Finch, George, A., 'The Peace conference of Paris, 1919: Its Organization and Method of Work', 13 *American Journal of International Law* 159 (1919)

Fletcher, George, P. and Ohlin, Jens, David, 'The ICC – Two Courts in One?', 4 *Journal of International Criminal Justice* 428 (2006)

Fohr-Anja, Seibert, 'The Relevance of the Rome Statute of the International Criminal Court for Amnesties and Truth Commissions', 7 *Max Planck Yearbook of United Nations Law* 553, 567 – 569 (2003)

Folse, Henry, J., and Bohr, Niels, 'Complementarity, and Realism', 1*PSA: Proceedings of the Biennial Meeting of the Philosophy of Science Association* 96 (1986)

Franck, Thomas, M., and Bert B. Lockwood, 'Preliminary Thoughts Towards an International Convention on Terrorism', 68 *American Journal of International Law* 69 (1974)

Fernandez, Silvia, A., "The Role of the International Prosecutor", in Lee, Roy, S., (ed.), *The International Criminal Court: The Making of the Rome Statute, Issues. Negotiations. Results"*, (The Hague. London. Boston: Kluwer Law International, 1999)

Gaeta, Paola, "Is the Practice of 'Self-Referrals' a Sound Start for the ICC?', 2 *Journal of International Criminal Justice* 949 (2004)

Gallant, Kenneth S., 'The International Criminal Court in the System of States and International Organizations', 16 *Leiden Journal of International Law* 553 (2003)

Gallavin, Chris, 'Article 53 of the Rome Statute of the International Criminal Court: In The Interests of Justice', 14 *King's College Law Journal* 179 (2003)

Garner, W., 'Punishment of Offenders Against the Laws and Customs of War', 14 *American Journal of International Law* 70 (1920)

Gianaris, William, N., 'The New World Order and the Need for an International Criminal Court', 16 *Fordham International Law Journal* 88 (1992 – 1993)

Gioia, Federica, 'State Sovereignty, Jurisdiction, and 'Modern' International Law: The Principle of Complementarity in the International Criminal Court', 19 *Leiden Journal of International Law* 1095 (2006)

Gitti, Angelo, 'Impunity Under National Law and Accountability Under International Human Rights Law: Has the Time of a Duty to Prosecute Come?', 9 *Italian Yearbook of International Law* 64 (1999)

Gillett, Matthew, 'Fighting Impunity: Assisted Arrests at the ICC', 3 *Yale Journal of International Affairs* 16 (2008)

Graefrath, Bernhard, 'Universal Jurisdiction and an International Criminal Court', 1 *European Journal of International Law* 67 (1990)

Graven, Jean, "Les Decisions Fondamentales De L'Assemblee Generale Des Nations Unies Et Leur Suit: La Resolution Sur Le Genocide Et Sa Repression", in Stone, Julius, et al., (eds.), *Toward A Feasible International Criminal Court*, (Geneva: World Peace Through law Center, 1970)

Green, L., C., 'International Crimes and the Legal Process', 29 *International and Comparative Law Quarterly* 567 (1980)

Green, L., C., 'Is There an International Criminal Law', 21 *Alberta Law Review* 251 (1983)

Grigorian, Meher, "The Role of Impunity in Genocide: An Analysis of War Crimes Trials Within the Context of International Criminal Law", in Tatz, Colin, et al., (eds.), *Genocide Perspectives II: Essays on Holocaust and Genocide*, (Sydny: Brandl & Schlesinger, 2003)

Gross, Leo, 'International Terrorism and International Criminal Jurisdiction', 67 *American Journal of International Law* 508 (1973)

Hafner, Gerhard, "The Status of Third States before the International Criminal Court", in Politi, Mauro, et al., (eds.), *The Rome Statute of the International Criminal Court*, Aldershot. Burlington. USA. Singapore. Sydney: Ashgate Dartmouth, 2001)

Hagan, John, Scott Greer, 'Making War Criminal', 40 *Criminology* 231 (2002)

Hall, Christopher, K., "Challenges to the Jurisdiction of the Court or the Admissibility of a Case", in Triffterer, Otto, (ed.), *Commentary on the Rome Statute of the International Criminal Court: Observers' Notes, Article by Article*, (Baden – Baden: Nomos Verlagsgesellschaft, 1999)

Hall, Christopher, Keith, 'The Powers and Role of the Prosecutor of the International Criminal Court in the Global Fight against Impunity', 17 *Leiden Journal of International Law* 121 (2004)

Hall, Christopher, Keith, 'The Third and Fourth Sessions of the UN Preparatory Committee on the establishment of an International Criminal Court', 92 *American Journal of International Law* 124 (1998)

Harhoff, Frederik, 'Legal and Practical Problems in the International Prosecution of Individuals', 69 *Nordic Journal of International Law* 53 (2000)

Heller, Kevin, Jon, 'The Shadow Side of Complementarity: The Effect of Article 17 of the Rome Statute on National Due Process', 17 *Criminal Law Forum* 255 (2006)

Holmes, John, T., "The Principle of Complementarity", in Lee, Roy, S., (ed.), *The International Criminal Court: The Making of the Rome Statute, Issues.Negotiations. Results*, (The Hague.London.Boston: Kluwer Law International, 1999)

Holmes, John, T., "Complementarity: National Courts *Versus* the ICC", in Cassese, Antonio, et al., (eds.), *The Rome Statute of the International Criminal Court*, Vol. I, (Oxford: Oxford University Press, 2002)

Holmes, John, T., "Jurisdiction and Admissibility", in Lee, Roy, S. et al., (eds.), *The International Criminal Court: Elements of Crimes and Rules of Procedure and Evidence* (Ardsley: Transnational Publishers, 2001)

Hudson, Manley O., 'The Proposed International Criminal Court', 32 *American Journal of International Law* 549 (1938)

Hunt, David, 'The International Criminal Court: High Hopes, 'Creative Ambiguity' and an Unfortunate Mistrust in International Judges', 2 *Journal of International Criminal Justice* 56 (2004)

Jensen, Rod, "Complementarity, 'Genuinely' and Article 17: Assessing the Boundaries of an Effective ICC", in Kleffner, Jann, K., et al., (eds.), *Complementary Views on Complementarity: Proceedings of the International Roundtable on the Complementary Nature of the International Criminal Court*, Amsterdam, 25/26 June 2004, (The Hague: T.M.C. Asser Press, 2006)

Johnson, D., H., N., 'The Draft Code of Offences against the Peace and Security of Mankind', 4 *International and Comparative Law Quarterly* 445 (1955)

Karibi-White, Adolphus, G., 'The Twin Ad hoc Tribunals and Primacy Over National Courts', 9 *Criminal Law Forum* 55 (1999)

Kaul, Hans-Peter, 'Construction Site for More Justice: The International Criminal Court After Two Years', 99 *American Journal of International Law* 370 (2005)

Kaul, Hans-Peter, "The International Criminal Court: Jurisdiction, Trigger Mechanism and Relationship to National Jurisdictions", in Politi, Mauro, et al., (eds.), *The Rome Statute of the International Criminal Court*, Aldershot.Burlington USA. Singapose. Sydney: Ashgate Dartmouth, 2001)

Kaul, Hans-Peter, 'Special Note: The Struggle for the International Criminal Court's Jurisdiction', 6 *European Journal of Crime, Criminal Law and Criminal Justice* 48 (1998)

Kerno Ivan, 'Le Projet De Statut De La Cour Criminelle Internationale', 29 *Revue de Droit International de Sciences Diplomatiques et Politiques* 363 (1951)

Kirsch, Philippe and Holmes John, T., 'The Rome Conference on an International Criminal Court: The Negotiating Process', 93 *American Journal of International Law* 2 (1999)

Kirsch, Philippe, and Robinson Darryl, "Reaching Agreement at the Rome Conference", in Cassese, Antonio et al., (eds.), *The Rome Statute of the International Criminal Court*, Vol. I, (Oxford: Oxford University Press, 2002)

Kleffner, Jann, K., 'The Impact of Complementarity on National Implementation of Substantive International Criminal Law', 1 *Journal of International Criminal Justice* 86 (2003)

Kleffner, Jann, K., "Complementarity as a Catalyst for Compliance", in Kleffner, Jann, K., et al., (eds.), *Complementary Views on Complementarity: Proceedings of the International Roundtable on the Complementary Nature of the International Criminal Court*, Amsterdam, 25/26 June 2004, (The Hague: T.M.C. Asser Press, 2006)

Klip, André, 'Complementarity and Concurrent Jurisdiction', 19 *Nouvelles Études Pénales* 173 (2004)

Kor, Gerben, "Sovereignty in the Dock", in Kleffner, Jann, K., and Kor, Gerben (eds.), *Complementary Views on Complementarity: Proceedings of the International Roundtable on the Complementary Nature of the International Criminal Court*, Amsterdam, 25/26 June 2004, (The Hague: T.M.C. Asser Press, 2006)

Kovác, Péter, 'La Société des Nations et son Action Aprés L'attentat Contre Alexandre, roi de Yugoslavie', 6 *Revue d'Histoire du Droit International* 65 (2004)

Kress, Claus, "Self-Referrals' and 'Waivers of Complementarity", 2 *Journal of International Criminal Justice* 944 (2004)

Kress, Claus, 'General Obligation to Cooperate', in Triffterer, O., (ed.), *Commentary on the Rome Statute of the International Criminal Court: Observers' Notes, Article by Article* (Baden Baden: Nomos Verlagsgesellschaft, 1999)

Kruse, Holger, "Ludwig XI (1461-1483)", in Joachim Ehlers et al., (eds.), *Die Französischen Könige des Mittelaters 888-1498*, (München: Beck, 1996)

Kuhn, Arthur, K., 'The Complaint of Yugoslavia against Hungary with Reference to the Assassination of King Alexander', 29 *American Journal of International Law* 87 (1935)

Lansing, Robert, 'Some Legal Questions of the Peace Conference', 13 *American Journal of International Law*, 631 (1919)

Lattanzi, Flavia, "The Complementarity Character of the Jurisdiction of the Court with Respect to National Jurisdictions", in Lattanzi, Flavia, (ed.), *The International Criminal Court: Comments on the Draft Statute*, (Napoli: Editoriale Scientifica, 1998)

Lauterpacht, H., 'The Law of Nations and the Punishment of War Crimes', 21 *British Yearbook of International Law* 58 (1944)

Lemkin, Raphael, 'Genocide a New International Crime Punishment and Prevention', 17 *Revue Internationale de Droit Penal* 360 (1946)

Levin, Avner, 'Discussion: Quantum Physics in Private Law', 14 *Canadian Journal of Law & Jurisprudence* 249 (2001)

Liang, Yuen-Li, 'Notes on Legal Questions Concerning the United Nations: The Establishment of an International Criminal Court – the Second Phase', 47 *American Journal of International Law* 638 (1953)

Liang, Yuen-Li, 'The Establishment of an International Criminal Jurisdiction: The First Phase', 46 *American Journal of International Law* 73 (1952)

Liang, Yuen-Li, 'The General Assembly and the Progressive Development and Codification of International Law', 42 *American Journal of International Law* 66 (1948)

Lindenmann, Jurg, "The Rules of Procedure and Evidence on Jurisdiction and Admissibility", in Fischer, Horst, et al., (eds.), International and National Prosecution of Crimes under International Law: Current Developments, (Berlin Verlag: Arno Spitz Gmbh, 2001)

Lindsay, R., B., 'Where is Physics Going?' 38 *The Scientific Monthly* 240 (1934)

Lippman, Matthew, 'The Convention on the Prevention and Punishment of the Crime of Genocide: Fifty Years Later', 15 *Arizona Journal of International & Comparative Law* 415 (1998)

Llewelyn, Jennifer, J., 'A Comment on the Complementary Jurisdiction of the International Criminal Court: Adding Insult to Injury in Transnational Contexts?', 24 *Dalhousie Law Journal* 190 (2001)

M, Leeladhara, Bhandary, 'International Criminal Court: Developments in Prosecution', 45 *Indian Journal of International Law* 256 (2005)

Marquardt, Paul, D., 'Law without Borders: The Constitutionality of an International Criminal Court', 33 *Columbia Journal of Transnational Law* 73 (1995)

Manner, George, 'The Legal Nature and Punishment of Criminal Acts of Violence Contrary to the Laws of War', 37 *American Journal of International Law* 407 (1943)

Marcin, Raymond, B., 'Schopenhauer's Theory of Justice', 43*Catholic University Law Review* 813(1994)

Marcovitch, Lazare, 'Quelques Remarques Sur Le Projet D'un Code Penal International', 30 *Revue de Droit International De Sciences Diplomatiques et Politiques* 359 (1952)

McCormack, Timothy L. H., "From Sun Tzu to the Sixth Committee: The Evolution of an International Criminal Law Regime, in McCormack, Timothy, H.L., and Gerry Simpson J., (eds.), *The Law of War Crimes: National and International Approaches*, (The Hague/London/Boston: Kluwer Law International, 1997)

McNeal, Gregory, S., 'ICC Inability Determinations in light of the Dujail Case', 39 *Case Western Reserve journal of International Law* 325 (2006-2007)

Murphy, Ray, 'Gravity Issues and the International Criminal Court', 17 *Criminal Law Forum* 281 (2006)

Murphy, Ray, 'International Criminal Accountability and the International Criminal Court', *Columbia International Affairs Online* (2005)

Murphy, Ray, 'The International Criminal Court - A Victory for the Rule of Law over the Might is Right Principle?', 12 *Irish Criminal Law Journal* 8 (2002)

Murphy, Ray, 'The Permanent International Criminal Court – solving the missing link in the international legal system?' 18 *Irish Law Times* 319 (2000)

Møse, Erik, 'Main Achievements of the ICTR', 3 *Journal of International Criminal Justice* 920 (2005)

Morris, Madeline, H., 'The Trials of Concurrent Jurisdiction: The Case of Rwanda', 7 *Duke Journal of Comparative and International Law* 349 (1997)

Morris, Madeline, H., "Complementarity and Its Discontents: States, Victims, and the International Criminal Court", in Shelton, Dinah, (ed.), *International Crimes*, Peace, and Human Rights: The Role of the International Criminal Court, Ardsley, New York: Transnational Publishers, 2000)

MacKinnon, Edward, 'Niels Bohrs on the Unity of Science: PSA: Proceedings of the Biennial Meeting of the Philosophy of Science Association', 2 *PSA* 224, (1980)

McCormack, Timothy L.H. and Simpson, Gerry, J., 'The International Law Commission's Draft Code of Crimes against the Peace and Security of Mankind: An Appraisal of the Substantive Provisions', 5 *Criminal Law Forum* 1 (1994)

McCormack, Timothy L.H. and Simpson, Gerry, J., "Achieving the Promise of Nuremberg: A New International Criminal Law Regime?" in McCormack, Timothy, H.L., and Gerry Simpson J., (eds.), *The Law of War Crimes: National and International Approaches*, (The Hague/London/Boston: Kluwer Law International, 1997)

Mégret, Frédéric, "The International Criminal Court and State Sovereignty: The 'Problem of an International Criminal Law' Re-examined", in Pritchard, R., John, and Dunlap, William, V., (eds.), *International Humanitarian Law* (New York: Transnational Publishers, 2003)

Mégret, Frédéric, "Why Would States want to Join the ICC? A theoretical Exploration Based on the Legal Nature of Complmentarity", in Kleffner, Jann, K., and Kor, Gerben (eds.), *Complementary Views on Complementarity: Proceedings of the International Roundtable on the Complementary Nature of the International Criminal Court*, Amsterdam, 25/26 June 2004, (The Hague: T.M.C. Asser Press, 2006)

Meron, Theodor, 'Judicial Independence and Impartiality in International Criminal Tribunal', 99 *American Journal of International Law* 359 (2005)

Meron, Theodor, 'Reflection on the Prosecution of War Crimes by International Tribunals', 100 *American Journal of International Law* 551 (2006)

Meyer, Frank, 'Complementing Complementarity', 6 *International Criminal Law Review* 549 (2006)

Mundis, Daryl, A., 'Completing the Mandates of the Ad hoc International Criminal Tribunals: Lessons from the Nuremberg Process? 28 *Fordham International Law Journal* 591(2004)

Mundis, Daryl, A., 'The Judicial Effects of the "Completion Strategies" on the Ad hoc International Criminal Tribunals', 99 *American Journal of International Law* 142 (2005)

Munson, Valerie J., Note, 'The Case Concerning United States Diplomatic and Consular Staff in Tehran', 11 *California Western International Law Journal* 543 (1981)

Murphy, John, F., 'Defining International Terrorism: A Way Out of the Quagmire', 19 *Israel Yearbook on Human Rights* 13 (1989)

Murphy, Sean D., 'Progress and Jurisprudence of the International Criminal Tribunal for the Former Yugoslavia', 93 *American Journal of International Law* 57 (1999)

Nsereko, Daniel, D., "Preliminary Rulings Regarding Admissibility", in Triffterer, Otto, (ed.), *Commentary on the Rome Statute of the International Criminal Court: Observers' Notes, Article by Article*, (Baden – Baden: Nomos Verlagsgesellschaft, 1999)

Nsereko, Daniel, 'The International Criminal Court: Jurisdiction and Related Issues', 10 *Criminal Law Forum* 87 (1999)

Newton, Michael, A., Comparative Complementarity: Domestic Jurisdiction Consistent with the Rome Statute of the International Criminal Court, 167 *Military Law Review* 20 (2001)

Olásolo, Héctor, 'The Lack of Attention to the Distinction between Situations and Cases in National Laws on Co-operation with the International Criminal Court with Particular Reference to the Spanish Case', 20 *Leiden Journal of International Law* 193 (2007)

Olásolo, Héctor, 'Reflections on the International Criminal Court's Jurisdictional Reach', 16 *Criminal Law Forum* 279 (2005)

Olásolo, Héctor, 'The Prosecutor of the International Criminal Court Before the Initiation of Investigations: A Quasi-Judicial or a Political Body?',3 *International Criminal Law Review* 87 (2003)

Olásolo, Héctor, 'The Triggering Procedure of the International Criminal Court, Procedural Treatment of the Principle of Complementarity, and the Role of the Office of the Prosecutor', 5 *International Criminal Law Review* 121 (2005)

Pella, V., V., 'Draft for a Statute Establishing a Criminal Chamber in the Permanent Court of International Justice', 17 *Revue Internationale de Droit Penal* 230 (1946)

Pella, V., V., 'L'Association Internationale de Droit Pénal et La Protection de La Paix', 17 *Revue Internationale de Droit Penal* 185 (1946)

Pella, V., Vespasien, 'Le Code Des Crimes Contre La Paix et La Securite De L'Humanite', 30 *Revue De Droit International De Sciences Diplomatiques et Politiques* 337 (1952)

Pella, Vespasien, V., 'Towards an International Criminal Court', 44 *American Journal of International Law* 37 (1950)

Peter, Matthew, D., 'The Proposed International Criminal Court: A Commentary on the Legal and Political Debates Regarding Jurisdiction that Threaten the Establishment of an Effective Court', 24 *Syracuse Journal of International Law and Commerce* 177 (1997)

Peterson, Jeremy, 'Unpacking Show Trials: Situating the Trial of Saddam Hussein', 48 *Harvard International Law Journal* 257 (2007)

Philips, Ruth, B., 'The International Criminal Court Statute: Jurisdiction and Admissibility', 10 *Criminal Law Forum* 61(1999)

Phillmore, Lord, 'An International Criminal Court and the Resolutions of the Jurists', 3 *British Yearbook of International Law* 79 (1922 – 1923)

Poirat, Florence, 'Immunité de Jurisdiction pénale du chef d'Eatat étranger en exercise et régle coutumiére devant le Juge Judiciare', 105 *Revue Générale de Droit International Public* 473 (2001)

Politi, Mauro, "The Rome Statute of the ICC: Rays of Light and Some Shadows", in Politi,Mauro, and Nesi Giuseppe (eds.), *The Rome Statute of the International Criminal Court: A Challenge to Impunity*, (Aldershot: Ashgate, 2001)

Politi, Mauro and Gioia Federica, 'The Criminal Procedure before the International Criminal Court: Main Features', 5 *The Law and Practice of International Courts and Tribunals* 103 (2006)

Prost, Kimberly and Schlunck, Angelika, "Other Forms of Cooperation" in Triffterer, Otto, (ed.), *Commentary on the Rome Statute of the International Criminal Court: Observers' Notes, Article by Article*, (Baden – Baden: Nomos Verlagsgesellschaft, 1999)

Raab, Dominic, 'Evaluating the ICTY and its Completion Strategy: Efforts to Achieve Accountability for War Crimes and their Tribunal', 3 *Journal of International Criminal Justice* 82 (2005)

Rao, P., Sreenivasa, 'Trends in International Criminal Jurisdiction', 35 *Indian Journal of International Law* 17 (1995)

Rayfuse, Rosemary, 'The Draft Code of Crimes against the Peace and Security of Mankind: Eating Disorders at the International Law Commission', 8 *Criminal Law Forum* 43 (1997)

Relva, Hugo, 'The Implementation of the Rome Statute in Latin American States', 16 *Leiden Journal of International Law* 331 (2003)

Rinoldi, Dino and Parisi, Nicoletta, "International Co-operation and Judicial Assistance between the International Criminal Court and States Parties", in Lattanzi, Flavia, Schabas, William, A., (eds.), *Essays on the Rome Statute of the International Criminal Court*, Vol. I, (Italy: Il Sirente, 1999)

Robinson, Darryl, 'Serving the Interests of Justice: Amnesties, Truth Commissions and the International Criminal Court', 14 *European Journal of International Law* 481(2003)

Robinson Darryl, "Crimes Against Humanity: Reflections on State Sovereignty, Legal Precision and The Dictates of the Public Conscience", in Lattanzi, Flavia et al., (eds.), *Essays on the Rome Statute of the International Criminal Court*, Vol. I (Italy: Il Sirente, 1999)

Rodley, Nigel, S., 'Breaking the Cycle of Impunity for Gross Violations of Human Rights: The Pinochet Case in Perspective', 69 *Nordic Journal of International Law* 11 (2000)

Rojo, Enrique, Carnero, 'The Role of Fair Trial Considerations in the Complementarity Regime of the International Criminal Court: From 'No Peace Without Justice' to 'No Peace with Victor's Justice", 18 *Leiden Journal of International Law* 829 (2005)

Sadat, Leila, Nadya, Carden, S., Richard, 'The New International Criminal Court: An Uneasy Revolution', 88 *George Town Law Journal* 381 (2000)

Sarooshi, Dan, 'The ICC Takes Off Prosecutorial Policy and the ICC: Prosecutor's *Proprio Motu* Action or Self-Denial?' 2 *Journal of International Criminal Justice* 940 (2004)

Scharf, Michael, P., 'The ICC's Jurisdiction over the Nationals of Non-Party States: A Critique of the U.S. Position', 63 *Law and Contemporary Problems* 1 (2000)

Scharf, Michael, P., 'The Jury Is Still Out on the Need for an International Criminal Court', 1 *Duke Journal of International and Comparative Law* 135 (1991)

Scheffer, David, J., 'The United States and the International Criminal Court', 93 *American Journal of International Law* 12 (1999)

Schaak, Beth, Van, 'The Establishment of the Permanent International Criminal Court: An International Symposium', 17 *Chinese Yearbook of International Law and Affairs* 1 (1998-1999)

Schabas, William, A., 'Complementarity in Practice: Some Uncomplimentary Thoughts', 19 *Criminal Law Forum* (forthcoming 2008)

Schabas, William, A., 'First Prosecutions at the International Criminal Court', 27 *Human Rights Law Journal* 25 (2006)

Schabas, William, A., 'The Relationship between Truth Commissions and International Courts: The Case of Sierra Leone', 25 *Human Rights Quarterly* 1035 (2003)

Schabas, William, A., 'Genocide Trials and *Gacaca* Courts', 3 *Journal of International Criminal Justice* 879 (2005)

Schabas, William, A., 'International Criminal Court: The Secret of Its Success', 12 *Criminal Law Forum* 415 (2001)

Schabas, William, A., 'The follow up to Rome: Preparing for the Entry into Force of the International Criminal Court Statute', 20 *Human Rights Law Journal* 157(1999)

Schabas, William, A., 'Justice, Democracy, and Impunity in Post-genocide Rwanda: Searching for Solutions to Impossible Problems', 7 *Criminal Law Forum* 523 (1996)

Schabas, William, A., "International Sentencing: From Leipzig (1923) to Arusha (1996)", in Bassiouni, M., Cherif, (ed.), *International Criminal Law: Enforcement* 2 nd ed., Vol. II (Ardsley, New York: Transnational Publishers, Inc, 1999)

Schermers, Henry, "Different Aspects of Sovereignty", in Kreijen, Gerard, et al., (eds.), *State, Sovereignty, and international Governance*, (Oxford: Oxford University Press, 2002)

Schick, F., B., 'International Criminal Law – Facts and Illusions', 11 *The Modern Law Review* 290 (1948)

Schwarzenberger, Georg, 'The Inductive Approach to International Law', 60 *Harvard Law Review* 539 (1946 – 1947)

Schwarzenberger, George, 'The Judgment of Nuremberg', 21 *Tulane Law Review* 329 (1946 – 1947)

Schwarzenberger, Georg, 'The Problem of an International Criminal Law', 3 *Current Legal Problems* 263(1950)

Sharp, Walter Gary, S., R., 'International Obligations to Search for and Arrest War Criminals: Government Failure in the Former Yugoslavia?', 7 *Duke Journal of Comparative & International Law* 411(1996 – 1967)

Shdanov, I., Blishchenko, N., 'The Problem of International Criminal Jurisdiction', 14 *The Canadian Yearbook of International Law* 283 (1976)

Shraga, Daphna and Zacklin, Ralph, 'The International Criminal Tribunal for the Former Yugoslavia', 5 *European Journal of International Law* 360 (1994)

Šimonović, Ivan, 'The Role of the ICTY in the Development of International Criminal Adjudication', 23 *Fordham International Law Journal* 440 (1999 – 2000)

Slade, Tuiloma, Neroni and Clark, Roger, S., "Preamble and Final Clauses", in Lee, Roy, S., (ed.), *The International Criminal Court: The Making of the Rome Statute, Issues. Negotiations. Results*, (The Hague. London. Boston: Kluwer Law International, 1999)

Solera, Oscar, 'Complementary Jurisdiction and International Criminal Justice', 84 *International Review of the Red Cross* 145 (2002)

Sottile, Antoine, 'Le Probleme De La Creation D'une Cour Penale Internationale Permanente', 29 *Revue de Droit International de Sciences Diplomatiques et Politiques* 117 (1951)

Sottile, Antoine, 'The Creation of a Permanent International Criminal Court', 29 *Revue de Droit International de Sciences Diplomatiques et Politiques* 267 (1951)

Spencer, J., R., "The English System", in Delmas-Marty, Mireille and Spencer, J., R., (eds.), *European Criminal Procedures*, (Cambridge: Cambridge University Press, 2002)

Spiermann, Ole, "'Who Attempts Too Much Does Nothing well': The 1920 Advisory Committee of Jurists and The Statute of the Permanent Court of International Justice", 73 *British Yearbook of International Law* 187 (2002)

Ssenyonjo, Manisuli, 'The International Criminal Court and the Lord's Resistance Army Leaders: Prosecution or Amnesty?', 54 *Netherlands International Law Review* 51(2007)

Stahn, Carsten, 'Complementarity: A Tale of Two Notions', 19 *Criminal Law Forum* (forthcoming 2008)

Stahn, Carsten, 'Complementarity, Amnesties and Alternatives forms of Justice: Some Interpretative Guidelines for the International Criminal Court', 3 *Journal of International Criminal Justice* 695 (2005)

Stahn, Carsten,'The Geometry of Transitional Justice; Choices of Institutional Design', 18 *Leiden Journal of International Law* 425, 449 (2005)

Stahn, Carsten, Olásolo, Héctor and Gibson, Kate, 'Participation of Victims in Pre-Trial Proceedings of the ICC', 4 *Journal of International Criminal Justice* 219 (2006)

Starke, J., G., 'The Convention for the Creation of an International Criminal Court', 19 *British Yearbook of International Law* 216 (1938)

Starita, Massimo, 'Amnesty for Crimes Against Humanity: Coordinating the State and Individual Responsibility for Gross Violations of Human Rights', 9 *Italian Yearbook of International Law* 86 (1999)

Steven, Lyn, L., 'Towards A Permanent International Criminal Court', 6 *European Journal of Crime, Criminal Law and Criminal Justice* 236 (1998)

Struett, Michael, J., 'The Transformation of State Sovereign Rights and Responsibilities under the Rome Statute of the International Criminal Court', 8 *Chapman Law Review* 179 (2005)

Strydom, Hennie, 'South Africa and the International Criminal Court', 6 *Max Planck Yearbook of United Nations Law* 345 (2002)

Schwelb, Egon, 'Crimes Against Humanity', 23 *British Yearbook of International Law* 178 (1946)

Turns, David, "Aspects of National Implementation of the Rome Statute: The United Kingdom and Selected Other States", in McGoldrick, Dominic, et al., (eds.), *The Permanent International Criminal Court: Legal and Policy Issues*, (Oxford and Portland Oregon: Hart Publishing, 2004)

Tallgren, Immi, "Article 20: Ne bis in idem", in Triffterer, Otto, (ed.), *Commentary on the Rome Statute of the International Criminal Court: Observers' Notes, Article by Article*, (Baden – Baden: Nomos Verlagsgesellschaft, 1999)

Tallgren, Immi, 'Completing the "International Criminal Order": The Rhetoric of International Repression and the Notion of Complementarity in the Draft Statute for an International Criminal Court 67 *Nordic Journal of International Law* 107 (1998)

Terracino, Bacio, Julio, 'National Implementation of ICC Crimes: Impact on National Jurisdictions and the ICC', 5 *Journal of International Criminal Justice* 421 (2007)

Tidmarsh, Jay, 'A Process Theory of Torts', 51 *Washington & Lee Law Review* 1313 (1994)

Turlington, Edgar, 'The Settlement of Lausanne', 18 *American Journal of International Law* 696 (1924)

Vadasz, M., Emeric, 'Jurisdiction Criminelle Internationale', 5 *Revue De Droit International De Sciences Diplomatiques et Politiques* 274 (1927)

Van Den Wyngaert, Christine, and Ongena, Tom, "*Ne bis in idem* Principle, Including the Issues of Amnesty" in Cassese, Antonio, Gaeta, Paola, and Jones, John, R.W.D., (eds.), *The Rome Statute of the International Criminal Court*, Vol. I, (Oxford: Oxford University Press, 2002)

Van den Wyngaert, Chrisitne, and Stessens, Guy, "The International *Non Bis In Idem* Principle: Resolving Some of the Unanswered Questions," 48 *International & Comparative Law Quarterly* 779 (1999)

Van Der Voort, Karlijn and Zwanenburg, Marten, 'From 'Raison d' État' to 'état de droit international' – Amnesties and the French Implementation of the Rome Statute 1 *International Criminal Law Review* 315(2001)

Verhoeven, J., 'Article 21 of the Rome Statute and the Ambiguities of Applicable Law', 33 *Netherlands Yearbook of International Law* 3(2002)

Vicuña, Fransisco, Orrego, 'The International Criminal Court and the In and Out Club', 2 *Journal of International Criminal Justice*, 35 (2004)

Wiener, Imre, A., 'Criminal Jurisdiction and International Crimes', 35 *Acta Juridica Hungarica* 33 (1993)

Williams, Sharon, A., 'The Rome Statute on the International Criminal Court: From 1947-2000 and Beyond', 38 *Osgoode Hall Law Journal* 298 (2000)

Williams, Sharon, "Issues of Admissibility", in Triffterer, Otto, (ed.), *Commentary on the Rome Statute:Observers' Notes, Article by Article*, (Nomos Verlagsgesellschaft: Baden- Baden, 1999)

Wexler Sadat, Leila, 'Panel Discussion: Association of American Law Schools Panel on the International Criminal Court, 36 *American Criminal Law Review* 223 (1999)

Wright, Quincy, 'Proposal for an International Criminal Court', 46 *American Journal of International Law* 60 (1952)

Wright, Quincy, 'The Legal Liability of the Kaiser', 13 *The American Political Science Review* 120 (1919)

Wright, Quincy, 'The Law of the Nuremberg Trial', 41 *American Journal of International Law* 38 (1947)

Yee, Lionel, "The International Criminal Court and the Security Council: Articles 13(b) and 16" in Lee, R., S., (ed.), *The International Criminal Court: The Making of the Rome Statute, Issues. Negotiations. Results*,(The Hague. London. Boston: Kluwer Law International, 1999)

Yang, Lijun, 'On the Principle of Complementarity in the Rome Statute of the International Criminal Court', 4 *Chinese Journal of International Law* 121 (2005)

Index

M

N

Y

www.ingramcontent.com/pod-product-compliance
Lightning Source LLC
LaVergne TN
LVHW080631011026
849160LV00014B/1177
* 9 7 8 9 0 0 4 1 6 6 9 3 6 *